Pearson Education

We work with leading authors to develop the strongest
educational materials in business and management,
bringing cutting-edge thinking and best learning practice
to a global market.

Under a range of well-known imprints, including
Financial Times Prentice Hall, we craft high quality print
and electronic publications which help readers to
understand and apply their content, whether studying
or at work.

To find out more about the complete range of our
publishing, please visit us on the World Wide Web at:
www.pearsoneduc.com

Second Edition

INTERNET MARKETING

Strategy, Implementation and Practice

Dave Chaffey

Richard Mayer

Kevin Johnston

Fiona Ellis-Chadwick

FT Prentice Hall
FINANCIAL TIMES

An imprint of **Pearson Education**
Harlow, England • London • New York • Boston • San Francisco • Toronto • Sydney • Singapore • Hong Kong
Tokyo • Seoul • Taipei • New Delhi • Cape Town • Madrid • Mexico City • Amsterdam • Munich • Paris • Milan

Pearson Education Limited

Edinburgh Gate
Harlow
Essex CM20 2JE
England

and Associated Companies throughout the world

Visit us on the World Wide Web at:
www.pearsoneduc.com

First published 2000
Second edition published 2003

© Pearson Education Limited 2000, 2003

ISBN 0 273 65883 2

British Library Cataloguing-in-Publication Data
A catalogue record for this book is available from the British Library

Library of Congress Cataloging-in-Publication Data
Internet marketing : strategy, implementation, and practice / Dave Chaffey . . . [et al.]. –
2nd ed.
       p.   cm.
    Includes bibliographical references and index.
    ISBN 0-273-65883-2 (pbk.)
       1. Internet marketing.   2. Internet.   I. Chaffey, Dave, 1963–

    HF5415.1265 .I57 2002
    658.8′4–dc21   2002066303

10 9 8 7 6 5 4 3 2 1
06 05 04 03

Typeset in 9.5/12.5pt Stone Serif by 35
Printed and bound by Rotolito Lombarda, Italy

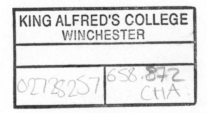

Brief contents

Contents

8 Interactive marketing communications   309

9 Maintaining and monitoring the online presence   374

● Introduction

The Internet – opportunity and threat

The Internet represents a tremendous opportunity. For customers, it gives a much wider choice of products, services and prices from different suppliers and the means to select and purchase items more readily. For organisations marketing these products and services it gives the opportunity to expand into new markets, offer new services and compete on a more equal footing with larger businesses. For those working within these organisations it gives the opportunity to develop new skills and to use the Internet to improve the competitiveness of the company.

At the same time, the Internet gives rise to many threats to organisations. For example, start-up companies such as Amazon (books) (www.amazon.com), Expedia (travel) (www.expedia.com), AutoByTel (cars) (www.autobytel.com) and CDNow! (CDs) (www.cdnow.com) have captured a significant part of their market and struck fear into the existing players. Indeed the phrase 'amazoning a market sector' has become an often-used expression among marketers.

The Internet – how to react?

With the success stories of companies capturing market share together with the rapidly increasing adoption of the Internet by consumers and business buyers has come a fast-growing realisation that all organisations must have an effective Internet presence to prosper, or possibly even survive! Michael Porter has said:

> *The key question is not whether to deploy Internet technology – companies have no choice if they want to stay competitive – but how to deploy it.*

But, how is an effective Internet presence achieved in a medium that is alien to most companies? Are existing marketing concepts, theories and models still valid? What is the effect on channel and market structures? How should the Internet be used to support existing business and marketing strategies? How should the web site be structured and designed? How should the site be promoted online and offline? How can the Internet be used to communicate with customers and build loyalty? How can we assess whether we are achieving these objectives? The aim of this book is to answer this type of question so that graduates entering employment and practitioners can help the companies for which they work to compete successfully using this new, digital medium in conjunction with existing media.

The Internet – skills required?

This book has been written to help marketers develop the knowledge and skills they need in order to be able to use the Internet effectively. Specifically, this book addresses the following needs:

- There is a need to know to what extent the Internet changes existing marketing models and whether new models and strategies can be applied to exploit the medium effectively.
- Marketing practitioners will need practical Internet marketing skills to market their products effectively. Knowledge of the new jargon – terms such as 'portal',

'clickthrough', 'cookie', 'hits', 'page impressions', 'digital certificate' – and of effective methods of site design and promotion will be necessary, either for direct 'hands-on' development of a site or to enable communication with other staff or suppliers who are implementing and maintaining the site.

● Given the rapidly changing market characteristics and best practices of Internet marketing, Web-based information sources are needed to update knowledge regularly. This text and the supporting companion web site contain extensive links to web sites to achieve this.

The content of this book assumes some existing knowledge of marketing in the reader, perhaps developed through experience or by students studying introductory modules in marketing fundamentals, marketing communications or buyer behaviour. However, the text outlines basic concepts of marketing such as the modern marketing concept, communications theory, buyer behaviour and the marketing mix, and there is, at the end of each chapter, a comprehensive list of further reading materials. This includes widely used marketing texts as well as electronic media sources.

Changes for second edition

The structure has been revised to provide a clear sequence to the stages of strategy development and implementation. The main changes are:

● new chapter on how the Internet can be used to vary the marketing mix;
● new chapters on micro- and macro-environment for the Internet to provide a foundation for strategy development;
● chapter on strategy updated to reflect latest thinking;
● chapter on relationship marketing now has a CRM-oriented approach;
● greater detail on Internet marketing communications, including the latest techniques such as pay-per-click search engines and viral marketing;
● new case studies have been added.

● The structure and contents of this book

The book is divided into three parts, each covering a different aspect of how organisations use the Internet for marketing to help them achieve competitive advantage. Table P.1 indicates how the book is related to existing marketing topics.

Part 1 Internet marketing fundamentals (Chapters 1–3)

Part 1 relates the use of the Internet to traditional marketing theories and concepts, and questions the validity of existing models given the differences between the Internet and other media.

● *Chapter 1 An introduction to Internet marketing* reviews the relationship between the Internet and the modern marketing concept, the relationship between Internet marketing, e-marketing, e-commerce and e-business, and the benefits the Internet can bring to adopters, and outlines differences from other media.
● *Chapter 2 The Internet micro-environment* reviews how the Internet changes the immediate environment of an organisation, including marketplace and channel structure. It describes the type of environment analysis need to support Internet strategy by examining how customers, competitors and intermediaries and the interplay between them can be evaluated.
● *Chapter 3 The Internet macro-environment* reviews the impact of social, technological, economic, political and legal environmental influences on Internet strategy and its implementation.

Structure of the book

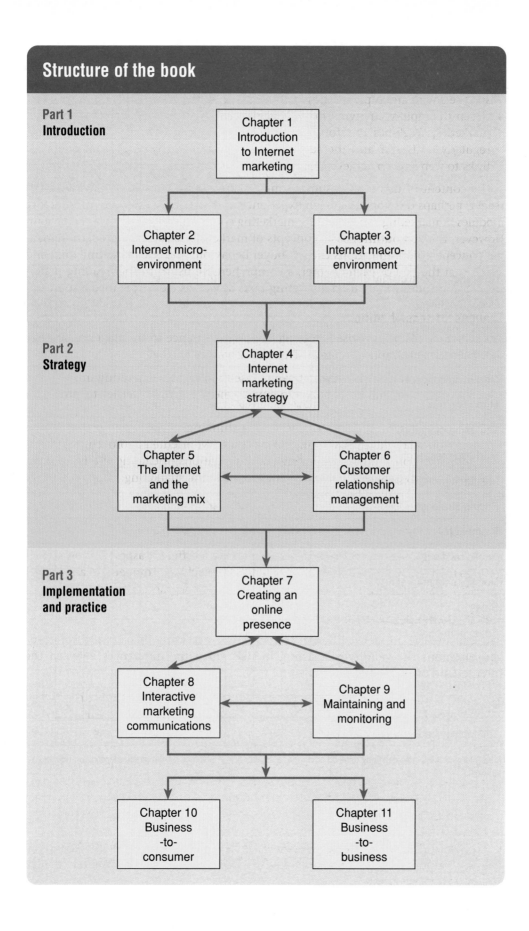

Part 1
Introduction

Chapter 1
Introduction
to Internet
marketing

Chapter 2
Internet micro-
environment

Chapter 3
Internet macro-
environment

Part 2
Strategy

Chapter 4
Internet
marketing
strategy

Chapter 5
The Internet
and the
marketing mix

Chapter 6
Customer
relationship
management

Part 3
**Implementation
and practice**

Chapter 7
Creating an
online
presence

Chapter 8
Interactive
marketing
communications

Chapter 9
Maintaining and
monitoring

Chapter 10
Business
-to-
consumer

Chapter 11
Business
-to-
business

Table P.1 Coverage of marketing topics in different chapters

Topic	Chapter										
	1	2	3	4	5	6	7	8	9	10	11
Advertising	✓						✓	✔			
Branding					✔		✓	✓			
Buyer behaviour		✓	✓	✓	✓	✓	✔	✓	✓	✓	✓
Channel and market structure		✔		✔	✔					✓	✓
Communications mix						✓	✓	✔			
Communications theory							✓	✔			
Customer service quality				✓	✓		✔		✔	✓	
Direct marketing						✔	✓	✔			
Ethical marketing			✔								
International marketing	✓	✓	✔	✓	✓		✓				
Marketing concept	✔	✓		✓	✓				✓		
Marketing mix	✓	✓		✓	✔		✓	✓			
Marketing planning				✔			✔	✓	✓		
Marketing research		✔							✔		
Monitoring/measurement				✓					✓	✔	
Pricing strategy				✓	✔					✓	✓
Promotion					✓	✓	✓	✔		✓	
Public relations								✔			
Relationship marketing						✔	✓				
Sales					✓		✓				
Sales promotions						✓		✔			
Segmentation		✔		✔	✓	✓	✔	✓			
Services marketing			✓	✓	✓	✔					
Strategy	✓	✓	✓	✔	✔	✔		✓	✓	✓	✓
Technology background	✔						✓		✓		

Note: A large tick ✔ indicates fairly detailed coverage; a smaller tick ✓ indicates a brief direct reference or indirect coverage.

Part 2 Internet strategy development (Chapters 4–6)

Part 2 describes the emerging models for developing strategy and provides examples of the approaches companies have used to integrate the Internet into their marketing strategy.

- *Chapter 4 Internet marketing strategy* considers how the Internet strategy can be aligned with business and marketing strategies and describes a generic strategic approach with phases of situation review, goal setting, strategy formulation and resource allocation and monitoring.
- *Chapter 5 The Internet and the marketing mix* assesses how the different elements of the marketing mix can be varied in the online environment as part of strategy formulation.
- *Chapter 6 Relationship marketing using the Internet* details the strategies and tactics for using the Internet to build and sustain 'one-to-one' relationships with customers.

Part 3 Internet marketing: implementation and practice (Chapters 7–11)

Part 3 of the book explains practical approaches to implementing an Internet marketing strategy. Techniques for communicating with customers, building relationships and facilitating electronic commerce are all reviewed in some detail. Knowledge of these practical techniques is essential for undergraduates on work placements involving a web site and for marketing managers who are dealing with suppliers such as design agencies.

- *Chapter 7 Achieving online service quality* explains the work involved in the different stages of building a web site in order to achieve the goal of service quality. The stages include analysis of customer needs, design of the site structure and layout, and creating the site.
- *Chapter 8 Interactive marketing communications* describes the novel characteristics of new media, and then goes on to review different online and offline promotion techniques necessary to build traffic to a web site and for other promotion objectives. Among the techniques covered are banner advertising, affiliate networks, promotion in search engines and directories, co-branding and sponsorship, e-mail, loyalty techniques and PR.
- *Chapter 9 Maintaining and monitoring the online presence* defines a process for successful updating of a site and online and offline methods for assessing the effectiveness of the site in delivering business and marketing benefits.
- *Chapter 10 Business-to-consumer Internet marketing* examines models of marketing to consumers, and provides case studies of how retail businesses are tackling such marketing.
- *Chapter 11 Business-to-business Internet marketing* examines the different area of marketing to other businesses, and provides many examples of how companies are achieving this to support international marketing. It also discusses the different stages of the buying decision such as supplier search, product evaluation and selection, purchase, post-purchase customer service, and evaluation and feedback.

● Who should use this book?

Students

This book has been created primarily as the main student text for undergraduate and postgraduate students taking specialist marketing courses or modules which cover e-marketing, Internet and digital marketing, electronic commerce and e-business. The book is relevant to students who are:

- *undergraduates on business programmes* which include modules on the use of the Internet and e-commerce. This includes specialist degrees such as Internet marketing, electronic commerce, marketing, tourism and accounting or general business degrees such as business studies, business administration and business management;
- *undergraduate project students* who select this topic for final-year projects/ dissertations – this book is an excellent supporting text for these students;
- *undergraduates completing a work placement* in a company using the Internet to promote its products;
- *students at college aiming for vocational qualifications* such as the HNC/HND in Business Management or Computer Studies;
- *postgraduate students* taking specialist masters degrees in electronic commerce or Internet marketing, generic MBAs and courses leading to qualifications such as Certificate in Management or Diploma in Management Studies which involve modules on electronic commerce and digital marketing.

Practitioners

There is also much of relevance in this book for marketing practitioners, including:

- *marketing managers or specialists such as e-commerce managers or e-marketing managers* responsible for defining an Internet marketing strategy and implementing and maintaining the company web site;
- *senior managers and directors* wishing to understand the potential of Internet marketing for a company and who need practical guidelines on how to exploit this potential;
- *technical project managers or webmasters* who may understand the technical details of building a site, but have a limited knowledge of marketing fundamentals and how to develop an Internet marketing strategy.

What does the book offer to lecturers teaching these courses?

The book is intended to be a comprehensive guide to all aspects of using the Internet and other digital media to support marketing. The book builds on existing marketing theories and concepts, and questions the validity of models in the light of the differences between the Internet and other media. The book references the emerging body of literature specific to Internet marketing. It can therefore be used across several modules. Lecturers will find the book has a good range of case studies, activities and exercises to support their teaching. Web site references are given in the text and at the end of each chapter to important information sources for particular topics.

● Student learning features

A range of features have been incorporated into this book to help the reader get the most out of it. They have been designed to assist understanding, reinforce learning and help readers find information easily. The features are described in the order in which you will encounter them.

At the start of each chapter

The 'chapter at a glance' page provides easy navigation for each chapter. It contains:

- *main topics:* the main topics and their page numbers;
- *case studies:* the main cases;
- *learning objectives:* a list describing what readers can learn through reading the chapter and completing the exercises;
- *key questions for marketers:* explains the relevance of the chapter for practitioners;
- *links to other chapters:* a summary of related information in other chapters.

In each chapter

- *Definitions:* when significant terms are first introduced the main text contains succinct definitions in boxes for easy reference.
- *Web references:* where appropriate, web addresses are given to enable readers to obtain further information. They are provided in the main text where they are directly relevant as well as at the end of the chapter.
- *Case studies:* real-world examples of how companies are using the Internet for marketing. Questions at the end of the case study are intended to highlight the main learning points from the example.
- *Mini case studies:* short features which give a more detailed example, or explanation, than is practical in the main text. They do not contain supplementary questions.
- *Activities:* exercises in the main text which give readers the opportunity to practise and apply the techniques described in the text.
- *Chapter summaries:* intended as revision aids to summarise the main learning points from the chapter.

At the end of each chapter

- *Self-assessment exercises:* short questions which will test understanding of terms and concepts described in the chapter.
- *Discussion questions:* these require longer essay-style answers discussing themes from the chapter. They can be used either as topics for individual essays or as the basis for seminar discussion.
- *Essay questions:* conventional essay questions.
- *Examination questions:* typical short-answer questions of the type that are encountered in exams. These can also be used for revision.
- *References:* these are references to books, articles or papers referred to within the chapter.
- *Further reading:* supplementary texts or papers on the main themes of the chapter. Where appropriate a brief commentary is provided on recommended supplementary reading on the main themes of the chapters.
- *Web links:* these are significant sites that provide further information on the concepts and topics of the chapter. This list does not repeat all the web site references given within the chapter, for example company sites. For clarity, the web site address prefix 'http://' is omitted.

At the end of the book

- *Glossary:* definitions of all key terms and phrases used within the main text, cross-referenced for ease of use.
- *Index:* all key words and abbreviations referred to in the main text.

● Support material

Free supplementary materials are available via the Pearson Education companion books web site at www.booksites.net/chaffey to support all users of the book. This regularly updated web site contains advice, comment, support materials and hyperlinks to reference sites relevant to the text. There is a password-protected area for lecturers only to discuss issues arising from using the text; additional examination-type questions and answers; a multiple-choice question bank with answers; additional cases with suggestions for discussion; and a downloadable version of the Lecturer's Guide and OHP Masters.

A Companion Website accompanies
INTERNET MARKETING, 2ed

by Dave Chaffey, Richard Meyer, Kevin Johnston and Fiona Ellis-Chadwick

Visit the *Internet Marketing* Companion Website at
www.booksites.net/chaffey to find valuable teaching and learning material
including:

For Students:

● Study material designed to help you improve your understanding

● Extensive links to useful websites, including:
  – academic and practitioner-oriented articles
  – case study materials
  – examples of best practice
  – guidance on tools and techniques for effective websites

● An online glossary

For Lecturers:

● A secure, password protected site with teaching material

● Downloadable Instructor's Manual and Overhead Masters to assist in lecturing

● Links to articles, company sites, and internet marketing resources on the web

● A syllabus manager that will build and host your very own course web page

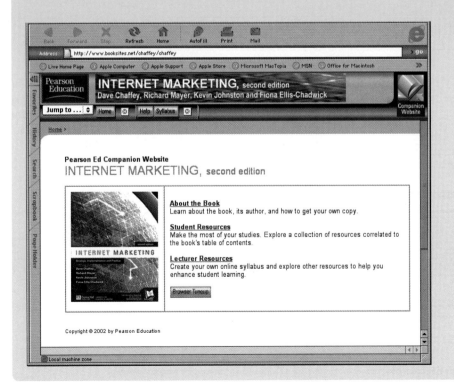

Guided tour

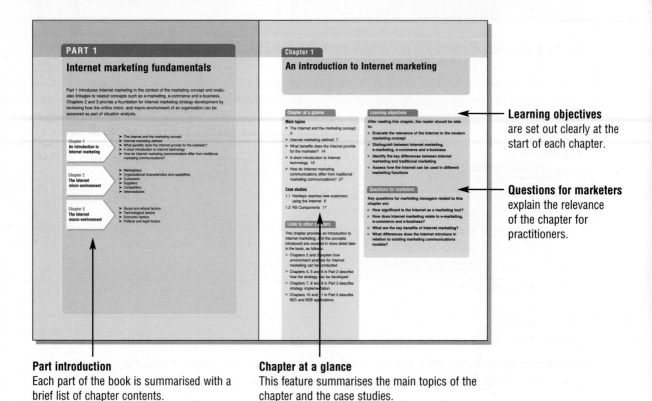

Learning objectives
are set out clearly at the start of each chapter.

Questions for marketers
explain the relevance of the chapter for practitioners.

Part introduction
Each part of the book is summarised with a brief list of chapter contents.

Chapter at a glance
This feature summarises the main topics of the chapter and the case studies.

Activities
Exercises which give readers the opportunity to practice and apply the techniques described in the text.

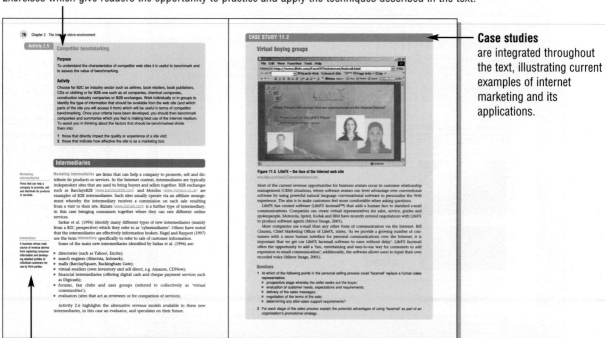

Case studies
are integrated throughout the text, illustrating current examples of internet marketing and its applications.

Key terms
are explained through the text in a margin glossary.

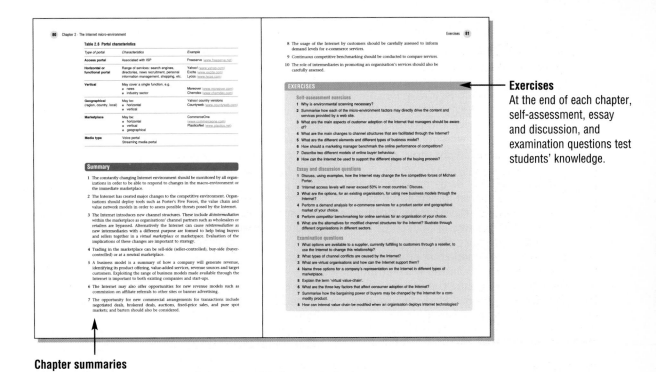

Exercises
At the end of each chapter, self-assessment, essay and discussion, and examination questions test students' knowledge.

Chapter summaries
Revision aids to summarise the main learning points from each chapter.

References
An extensive set of references is included in every chapter.

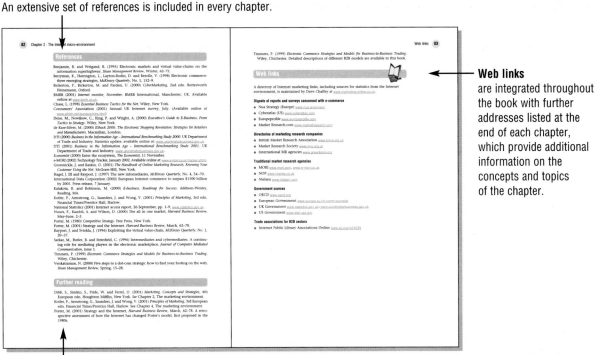

Web links
are integrated throughout the book with further addresses listed at the end of each chapter, which provide additional information on the concepts and topics of the chapter.

Further reading
directs the reader to alternative sources.

Dave Chaffey BSc, PhD, MCIM

Dave is director of Marketing Insights Limited, a consultancy specialising in e-marketing consultancy and training. He continues to lecture in e-marketing on a part-time basis at postgraduate level at the universities of Derby, Warwick and Leeds. He has extensive experience of working in industry on corporate information systems projects for companies such as Ford Europe, WH Smith, North West Water and the Halifax Bank in roles varying from business/systems analyst, programmer and trainer to project manager. Dave has been course director for Chartered Institute of Marketing seminars in e-marketing since 1997 and is a senior examiner for the e-marketing professional development award. Dave is author or co-author of six business books including *Groupware, Workflow and Intranets, Internet Marketing: Strategy, Implementation and Practice, E-business and E-commerce Management, eMarketing eXcellence* and *Total E-mail Marketing*. Dave has compiled a regularly updated website of resources at www.marketing-online.co.uk to support students and delegates attending courses and using these books.

Richard Mayer MA, DipM, MCIM

Richard is a Senior Lecturer in marketing, at the University of Derby, specialising in strategic marketing and marketing communications. Previously product manager for Delta Crompton Cables, Richard was director of his own packaging business for four years. In addition, he is an examiner for the Chartered Institute of Marketing and has contributed to two published study revision kits on marketing communications strategy, and marketing fundamentals. Richard has considerable experience in conducting marketing seminar/training programmes; in particular he is course director for the Chartered Institute of Marketing seminars in the *Fundamentals of Marketing* and *Marketing a Service* and he has conducted many in-company training courses throughout Europe.

Kevin Johnston BSc, MBA

Kevin is currently a Consultant with Esprit Soutron Partnership Limited where he trains clients in the UK and abroad to use information management tools and the bespoke enterprise portals created by the company. Before that he was a senior lecturer in marketing, strategy and e-commerce at the University of Derby where he created one of the UK's first e-commerce degree programmes. He has been published in a number of marketing journals and several times in the *International Journal of Internet Research*. He obtained his MBA from the Bradford University School of Management and first degree in Computer Science from the University of Kent.

Fiona Ellis-Chadwick PhD, BSc, Dip Sys Prac, PGCCE

Fiona has wide experience of working in the retail industry. Her previous industrial career in retail management involved new product development, project management, and design and development of retail operations. She has worked on projects with a number of major UK retailers. Fiona's career took a significant change in direction when she became interested in the Internet in the early 1990s. She gave up her retail career to pursue her research interests in Internet commerce, which initially led to completion of her PhD thesis titled *An Empirical Study of Internet Adoption Among Leading United Kingdom Retailers* in 2000. Currently, Fiona is a lecturer in retailing and e-commerce at Loughborough University Business School. Her research interests focus on the impact of e-commerce in consumer and industrial markets, online customer relationship management and strategic implications of adoption of the Internet to business management. She has published in a range of marketing and retailing journals and attended a number of National and European Conferences. Fiona is a member of WiC (Women into Computing) and is Chair of the Board of a Nottingham arts-based charity.

Acknowledgements

We are grateful to the following for permission to reproduce copyright material:

Figure 1.6 from www.guinness-webstore.com, used with permission from Guinness UDV; Figures 1.7 and 3.6 from www.rswww.com, reproduced with the kind permission of RS Components Ltd. RS and the RS logo are trademarks of RS Components Ltd. An Electrocomponents Company; Figure 2.3 from Deise et al. (2000) *Executive's Guide to E-business. From Tactics to Strategy*. Copyright © John Wiley & Sons, Inc. 2000. This material is used by permission of John Wiley & Sons. Inc.; Figure 2.5 from www.vauxhall.co.uk site with permission from Vauxhall Motors Ltd; Figure 2.9 from www.priceline.com, used with permission from Priceline Europe; Figure 2.11 from www.mondus.de, used with permission from Mondus Ltd; Figures 2.14, 2.15 and 2.16 from www.e-mori.co.uk/tracker/shtml, used with permission from Market & Opinion Research International (MORI) Ltd; Figures 2.17 and 2.19 from 'The Internet Monitor', used with permission from BMRB International; Figure 2.18 from www.netpoll.net, used with permission from Netpoll Ltd; Figure 2.22 from www.hitwise.co.uk, used with permission from Hitwise UK; Figure 2.23 from www.kelkoo.com, used with permission from Kelkoo.com; Figure 3.2 from www.truste.org, used with permission from TRUSTe; Figure 3.16 adapted from www.eiu.com, Economist Intelligence Unit and Pyramid Research e-readiness ranking, used with permission from Pyramid Research; Figure 4.3 from McDonald, M. (1999) 'Strategic marketing planning: theory and practice' in M. Baker (ed.) *The CIM Marketing Book* (4th edn.). Reprinted by permission of Elsevier Science; Figure 4.11 from www.dabs.com, used with permission from dabs.com; Figure 4.13 from www.blackstar.co.uk, used with permission from BlackStar; Figure 5.4 from www.citroen.co.uk, used with permission from Citroën UK Ltd. Citroën's website is being regularly updated, and any information captured in a screenshot is likely to be revised. As such, Citroën UK cannot be held responsible for the accuracy of any information displayed within the screenshot; Figure 5.6 from www.guinness.com, used with permission from Guinness UDV; Table 7.2 from www.keynote.com, used with permission from Keynote Europe Ltd; Table 7.4 from Chaffey, D. and Edgar, M. (2000) 'Measuring online service quality' in *Journal of Targeting, Analysis and Measurement for Marketing*, 8(4) (May), © Henry Stewart Publications, used with permission from Henry Stewart Publications; Figure 7.6 from www.durex.com, used with permission from SSL International plc; Figure 7.7 from Bickerton et al. (1998) *Cyberstrategy* and Figure 7.8 from Friedman, L. and Furey, T. (1999) *The Channel Advantage*. Reprinted by permission of Elsevier Science; FigureTables 7.10 and 7.11 from www.netratings.com, used with permission from Nielsen//Netratings; Figures 7.11 and 7.12 from www.commontime.com with thanks to Ollie Omotosho, Internet Marketer and Vice President Marketing, Commontime Mobile Computing, Inc.; Figure 7.13 from www.egg.com, used with permission from Egg.plc; Figure 7.15 from www.sainsburys.co.uk, used with permission from J. Sainsbury plc; Table 8.1 from Janal, D. (1998) *Online Marketing Handbook. How to Promote, Advertise and Sell your Products and Services on the Internet*. Copyright © John Wiley & Sons, Inc. 1998. This material is used by permission of John Wiley & Sons, Inc.; Figure 8.4 used with permission from Millward Brown UK Ltd; Figure 8.11 from www.freeserve.com. This screenshot has been reproduced with the express permission of Freeserve.com plc. Its content is for illustrating purposes only and does not reflect what may currently be displayed on the freeserve.com homepage. This image, or any images contained therein, may not be reproduced or used for any purpose whatsoever without the express permission of Freeserve.com plc; Figure 8.12 used with permission from Lakeland Limited; Figure 8.15 from www.senior.co.uk, used with permission from Senior Internet Ltd; Figure 8.18 from www.crackermatic.com, used with permission from Dial Media Group; Figure 8.21 from www.investis.com, used with permission from Egg plc; Figure 10.1 from www.telegeography.com, © TeleGeography, Inc. 2001, used with permission from TeleGeography, Inc.; Figure 10.3 from www.respond.com, used with permission from Respond.com, Inc.; Figure 10.5 from www.john-lewis-partnership.co.uk, used with permission from Mantra PR; Figure 10.6 from www.thorntons.co.uk, used with permission from Thorntons plc; Figure 10.7 from www.richersounds.com, used with permission from Richer Sounds plc; Figure 11.4 from www.vendorvillage.com, used with permission from Vendor Village.com.

BlackStar for the example of their automatic e-mail response from their website www.blackstar.co.uk; BMRB International for an extract from their e-mail newsletter 'The Internet Monitor' on banner advertisements; A. Branthwaite for an extract from his article 'The medium is part of the message' published in the proceedings of the ARF/ESOMAR Conference, Rio de Janiero, 12–14 November 2000, published in the *ESOMAR Publications Series*, Vol. 241 (Mini Case Study 8.1); and Commerce One (UK) Ltd for an extract on XCBL 3.0 standards for publishing catalogue data from their website www.commerceone.net (Mini Case Study 1.1).

We are grateful to the Financial Times Limited for permission to reprint the following material: Figure 4.15 'Internet distribution strategies' from FT Mastering Information Management, No 7, www.ftmastering.com, © *Financial Times*; Case Study 1.1 from 'Hamley's: where to buy a gold-plated model of James Bond's Aston Martin' from FT.com, © *Financial Times*, 2 August, 2000; Case Study 2.1 from 'Survey – FT Information Technology Review: Bold strategy for the internet dimension', © *Financial Times*, 5 April, 2000; Case Study 3.1 from 'What went wrong with WAP?' from FT Connectis, © *Financial Times*, 29 May, 2001; Case Study 4.1 from 'Sandvik – setting the Internet revenue contribution', © *Financial Times*, 4 June, 2001; Case Study 5.1 from 'Survey – FTIT: Premium payments may boost web revenues', © *Financial Times*, 6 February, 2002; Case Study 8.1 from 'Survey – Creative Business: Affiliate Marketing', © *Financial Times*, 31 July, 2001; Case Study 8.2 from 'Companies & Finance International: Google's hunt for a winning formula', © *Financial Times*, 9 June, 2001; Case Study 9.1 from 'Survey – FTIT: Useful aid for internet marketing campaigns', © *Financial Times*, 4 April, 2001.

In some instances we have been unable to trace the owners of copyright material, and we would appreciate any information that would enable us to do so.

PART 1

Internet marketing fundamentals

Part 1 introduces Internet marketing in the context of the marketing concept and evaluates linkages to related concepts such as e-marketing, e-commerce and e-business. Chapters 2 and 3 provide a foundation for Internet marketing strategy development by reviewing how the online micro- and macro-environment of an organisation can be assessed as part of situation analysis.

Chapter 1
An introduction to Internet marketing

➤ The Internet and the marketing concept
➤ Internet marketing defined
➤ What benefits does the Internet provide for the marketer?
➤ A short introduction to Internet technology
➤ How do Internet marketing communications differ from traditional marketing communications?

Chapter 2
The Internet micro-environment

➤ Marketplace
➤ Organisational characteristics and capabilities
➤ Customers
➤ Suppliers
➤ Competitors
➤ Intermediaries

Chapter 3
The Internet macro-environment

➤ Social and ethical factors
➤ Technological factors
➤ Economic factors
➤ Political and legal factors

An introduction to Internet marketing

Chapter at a glance

Main topics

Case studies

Links to other chapters

This chapter provides an introduction to Internet marketing, and the concepts introduced are covered in more detail later in the book, as follows:

- ➤ Chapters 2 and 3 explain how environment analysis for Internet marketing can be conducted
- ➤ Chapters 4, 5 and 6 in Part 2 describe how the strategy can be developed
- ➤ Chapters 7, 8 and 9 in Part 3 describe strategy implementation
- ➤ Chapters 10 and 11 in Part 3 describe B2C and B2B applications

Learning objectives

After reading this chapter, the reader should be able to:

- Evaluate the relevance of the Internet to the modern marketing concept
- Distinguish between Internet marketing, e-marketing, e-commerce and e-business
- Identify the key differences between Internet marketing and traditional marketing
- Assess how the Internet can be used in different marketing functions

Questions for marketers

Key questions for marketing managers related to this chapter are:

- How significant is the Internet as a marketing tool?
- How does Internet marketing relate to e-marketing, e-commerce and e-business?
- What are the key benefits of Internet marketing?
- What differences does the Internet introduce in relation to existing marketing communications models?

Introduction

How significant is Internet marketing to businesses? Today, the answer to this question varies dramatically for different products and markets. For companies such as electronics equipment manufacturer Cisco (www.cisco.com), the answer is 'very significant' – Cisco now gains over 90% of its multi-billion-dollar global revenue online. It also conducts many of its other business processes such as new product development and customer service online. Similarly, easyJet (www.easyjet.com), the low-cost European airline, gains 90% of its ticket sales online and aims to fulfil the majority of its customer service requests via the Internet. However, the picture is quite different for the manufacturers of high-involvement purchases such as cars or fast-moving consumer goods (FMCG) brands. Here the impact is less significant – the majority of their consumer sales still occur through traditional retail channels. However, the influence cannot be described as insignificant any longer since the Internet is becoming increasingly important in *influencing* purchase decisions – many new car purchasers will research their purchase online, so manufacturers need to invest in Internet marketing to persuade customers of the features and benefits of their brands. The FMCG manufacturer finds that consumers are spending an increasing proportion of their time on the Internet and less time using other media so the Internet has become an effective way of reaching its target markets. The Internet can be used to increase the frequency and depth of interactions with the brand, particularly for brand loyalists who are the advocates of these brands. For example, drinks brand Tango (www.tango.com) uses competitions and games on its web site to encourage interactions of the consumer with the brand (Figure 1.1).

Figure 1.1 The Tango web site (www.tango.tv) is used to increase the frequency and depth of brand interactions with consumers

The media portrayal of the Internet often suggests that it is merely an alternative for traditional advertising or only of relevance for online purchases of books or CDs. In fact, the Internet can be readily applied to all aspects of marketing communications and can and will need to support the entire marketing process. The e-marketing imperative is also indicated by recent research in financial services, media and entertainment, consumer goods and retail organisations with a turnover of £25 million conducted for E-marketing (www.e-marketing.com). This showed that online marketing has become a significant part of the marketing mix in many organisations. The organisations in the study were increasing their online marketing spending to an average of around 8% of total marketing budget. Eighty per cent of respondents had increased the amount they spend on online marketing during the last year and 75% expect to increase their spend again over the next year.

This book covers all the different ways in which the Internet can be used to support the marketing process. In this introductory chapter we review how Internet marketing relates to the traditional concept of marketing. We also introduce basic concepts of Internet marketing, placing it in the context of e-commerce and e-business.

The Internet and the marketing concept

In this section, we introduce the marketing concept, and then consider its relationship to more recent concepts such as Internet marketing, e-commerce and e-business.

The word 'marketing' has two distinct meanings in modern management practice. It describes:

1 *The range of specialist marketing functions* carried out within many organisations. Such functions include market research, brand and product management, public relations and customer service.

2 *An approach or concept that can be used as the guiding philosophy* for all functions and activities of an organisation. Such a philosophy encompasses all aspects of a business. Business strategy is guided by an organisation's market and competitor focus and everyone in an organisation should be required to have a customer focus in their job.

The modern marketing concept (Houston, 1986) unites these two meanings and stresses that marketing encompasses the range of organisational functions and processes that seek to determine the needs of target markets and deliver products and services to customers and other key stakeholders such as employees and financial institutions. Increasingly the importance of marketing is being recognised both as a vital function and as a guiding management philosophy within organisations. Marketing has to be seen as the essential focus of all activities within an organisation (Valentin, 1996). The marketing concept should lie at the heart of the organisation, and the actions of directors, managers and employees should be guided by its philosophy.

Modern marketing requires organisations to be committed to a market/customer orientation (Jaworski and Kohli, 1993). All parts of the organisation should co-ordinate activities to ensure that customer needs are met efficiently, effectively and profitably. Marketing encompasses activities traditionally seen as the sole domain of accountants, production, human resources management (HRM) and information technology (IT). Many of these functions had little regard for customer considerations. Increasingly such functions are being reorientated, evidenced by the importance of initiatives such as Total Quality Management (TQM), Business Process

Reengineering, Just-in-Time (JIT) and supply chain management. Individuals' functional roles are undergoing change, from being solely functional to having a greater emphasis on process. Individuals are therefore being encouraged to become part-time marketers. Processes have a significant impact on an organisation's ability to service its customers' needs.

The Internet can be applied by companies as an integral part of the modern marketing concept since:

- it can be used to support the full range of organisational functions and processes that deliver products and services to customers and other key stakeholders;
- it is a powerful communications medium that can act as a 'corporate glue' that integrates the different functional parts of the organisation;
- it facilitates information management, which is now increasingly recognised as a critical marketing support tool to strategy formulation and implementation;
- the future role of the Internet should form part of the vision of a company since its future impact will be significant to most businesses.

Without adequate information, organisations are at a disadvantage with respect to competitors and the external environment. Up-to-date, timely and accessible information about the industry, markets, new technology, competitors and customers is a critical factor in an organisation's ability to plan and compete in an increasingly competitive marketplace.

● Avoiding Internet marketing myopia

Theodore Levitt, writing in the *Harvard Business Review* (Levitt, 1960), outlined the factors that underlie the demise of many organisations and at best seriously weaken their longer-term competitiveness. These factors still provide a timely reminder of traps that should be avoided when embarking on Internet marketing.

1 Wrongly defining which business they are in.
2 Focusing on:
   - products (many web sites are still product-centric rather than customer-centric);
   - production;
   - technology (technology is only an enabler, not an objective);
   - selling (the culture on the Internet is based on customers seeking information to make informed buying decisions rather than strong exhortations to buy);
   rather than:
   - customer needs (the need for market orientation is a critical aspect of web site design and Internet marketing strategy); and
   - market opportunities (the Internet should not just be used as another channel, but new opportunities for adding value should be explored).
3 Unwillingness to innovate and 'creatively destruct' existing product or service lines.
4 Shortsightedness in terms of strategic thinking.
5 The lack of a strong and visionary CEO (Baker (1998) found that this was important to companies' effective use of the Internet).
6 Giving marketing only 'stepchild status', behind finance, production and technology.

Any organisation that sees and hence defines its business in anything other than customer-benefit terms has not taken the first step in achieving a *market orientation*. Any organisation that defines its business by what it produces is said to be suffering from 'marketing myopia'. Such myopia results from a company having a shortsighted and narrow view of the business that it is in.

If Internet marketing is to become integrated and fully established as a strategic marketing management tool, then the focus of attention needs to move towards understanding its broader applications within the total marketing process rather than just using it as a communication and selling tool. This is not to detract from the capability of the Internet to communicate and sell, but recognises that this is only one important aspect of the marketing process to which the Internet can contribute. The danger for those currently considering developing Internet technology is that the focus of such involvement will be too narrow and the true power of the Internet and its potential contribution to the marketing process will be missed.

One of the elements of developing an Internet marketing strategy is deciding which marketing functions can be assisted by the Internet. There is a tendency amongst companies first using the Internet to restrict applications to promotion and selling rather than a relationship-building and service delivery tool. In later chapters in this book, we explore the full range of marketing applications of the Internet.

Internet marketing defined

What, then, is Internet marketing? Internet marketing or Internet-based marketing can be defined as the use of the Internet and related digital technologies to achieve marketing objectives and support the modern marketing concept. These technologies include the Internet media and other digital media such as wireless mobile, cable and satellite media.

In practice, Internet marketing will include the use of a company web site in conjunction with online promotional techniques such as search engines, banner advertising, direct e-mail and links or services from other web sites to acquire new customers and provide services to existing customers that help develop the customer relationship. However, for Internet marketing to be successful there is a necessity for integration with traditional media such as print and TV, and this will be a consistent theme in this book.

Internet marketing
The application of the Internet and related digital technologies in conjunction with traditional communications to achieve marketing objectives.

● E-marketing defined

The term 'Internet marketing' tends to refer to an external perspective of how the Internet can be used in conjunction with traditional media to acquire and deliver services to customers. An alternative term is e-marketing or electronic marketing (see for example McDonald and Wilson, 1999 and Smith and Chaffey, 2001) which can be considered to have a broader scope since it refers to the Internet, interactive digital TV and mobile marketing together with other technology approaches such as database marketing and electronic customer relationship management (CRM) to achieve marketing objectives. It has both internal and external perspectives considering how internal and external marketing processes and communications can be improved through information and communications technology.

E-marketing
Achieving marketing objectives through use of electronic communications technology.

As with many terms with the 'e' prefix, we need to return to an original definition of the topic to more fully understand what e-marketing involves. The definition of marketing by the Chartered Institute of Marketing (www.cim.co.uk) is:

Marketing is the management process responsible for identifying, anticipating and satisfying customer requirements profitably

This definition emphasises the focus of marketing on the customer, while at the same time implying a need to link to other business operations to achieve this profitability. Smith and Chaffey (2001) note that Internet technology can be used to support these aims as follows:

- *Identifying* – the Internet can be used for marketing research to find out customers' needs and wants (Chapters 7 and 9).
- *Anticipating* – the Internet provides an additional channel by which customers can access information and make purchases – understanding this demand is key to governing resource allocation to e-marketing as explained in Chapters 2 and 4.
- *Satisfying* – a key success factor in e-marketing is achieving customer satisfaction through the electronic channel, which raises issues such as: is the site easy to use, does it perform adequately, what is the standard of associated customer service and how are physical products dispatched? These issues of customer relationship management are discussed further in Chapters 6 and 7.

A broader definition of marketing has been developed by Dibb, Simkin, Pride and Ferrell (Dibb et al., 2000):

Marketing consists of individual and organizational activities that facilitate and expedite satisfying exchange relationships in a dynamic environment through the creation, distribution, promotion and pricing of goods, services and ideas.

This definition is useful since it highlights different marketing activities necessary to achieve the 'exchange relationship', namely product development, pricing, promotion and distribution. We will review the way in which the Internet affects these elements of the marketing mix in Chapter 5.

Many organisations began the process of Internet marketing with the development of web sites in the form of brochureware or electronic brochures introducing their products and services, but are now enhancing them to add value to the full range of marketing functions. In Chapters 2 and 4 we look at stage models of development of Internet marketing services, which start with brochureware sites that can be used to assess and inform an organisation's current and future application of Internet marketing. Another key aspect of Internet marketing planning is using the Internet for what it is best suited – reaching particular types of customers using innovative selling techniques. Case Study 1.1 gives one example of such applications of the Internet.

Brochureware

A simple web site with limited interaction with the user that replicates offline marketing literature.

Stage models

Models for the development of different levels of Internet marketing services.

CASE STUDY 1.1

Hamleys reaches new customers using the Internet

Hamleys toy shop in London's Regent Street seems quintessentially British, so it may come as a surprise to learn that the majority of the sales from its website are to the US.

This is not an accident, however. The content and appearance of the shop's e-commerce site have been carefully designed to attract a very particular kind of customer: those who have the money to spend on expensive toys, but little time to visit toy shops.

While its London store stocks approximately 40 000 toys, the site offers only a small fraction of that number. There are already numerous toy shops online offering cheap, plentiful toys aimed at the mass market.

Hamleys wanted to differentiate itself, so it called in Equire, an e-commerce company specialising in designing and hosting websites for retailers of luxury items, including Links of London and jewellers Van Peterson.

Hamleys and Equire decided to use the website to sell goods it was difficult to obtain any-where else: Steiff bears, die-cast figures and other collectors' items. Apart from collectors, says Pete Matthews, Equire founder and chairman, customers tend to be parents and grandparents looking for unusual gifts.

An article in the *New York Times* before Father's Day, for example, resulted in the site selling a large number of gold-plated models of the James Bond Aston Martin.

Because the brand name is crucial to the kind of customers Hamleys wants to attract, the look of the site (www.hamleys.com) is also distinctive, with numerous graphics and animations, a prominent Hamleys logo on each page and menu options with names such as Collectables, Exclusive and Executive.

As well as designing and hosting the website, Equire manages all other aspects of the e-commerce operation, including holding the stock in its warehouse, taking care of orders and delivery, and running the customer care centre.

Its financial arrangement with Hamleys is unusual: instead of charging a large fee for hosting the site, it charges a smaller fee and takes a cut of the revenue. The idea is that it has a stake in making sure the site works, giving the customer confidence that it will do the job well.

It also means a smaller investment for the customer. 'The typical cost of implementing an infrastructure like ours would be in the many millions of dollars. Typically, Equire's customers don't contribute anything like that', says Mr Matthews.

Because of the site's target customers, speed of delivery is important. Some e-commerce sites have become notorious for not being able to fulfil orders quickly or efficiently. But Mr Matthews says most of the US orders are delivered within three days – and many in fewer than that.

The Hamleys site uses the Broadvision e-commerce platform, which is integrated with the call centre, the fulfilment centre and Equire's despatch partners, who allow online tracking of every parcel. 'When an order comes in, it automatically informs the customer-care centre. At the same time, it tells the fulfilment centre an order has come in and needs to go out today. It gets picked, packed, gift-wrapped and despatched and is then tracked throughout its life via our despatch partners, UPS and Parcelforce', says Mr Matthews. Returns are low – less than two per cent.

Recently, Hamleys has announced a drop in profits. Part of its plan for drawing in more revenue is to expand the website to include a wider range of toys: 50 per cent of calls and e-mails to the customer care centre are enquiries about toys not stocked on the site.

Instead of simply increasing sales to existing customers, the site has given Hamleys the opportunity to attract many new customers who, according to Mr Matthews, spend more on an average visit to the site than visitors to the London shop. Other planned improve-ments include greater emphasis on 'personalisation', so that customers will be guided to their particular interests.

Mr Matthews believes his company has a model that works. 'Over a period of five years, we're able to deliver a very healthy net margin, their revenues flow to the bottom line, they have no depreciation or amortisation to consider, while we deliver them net incremental revenue, and we help to build brand franchise outside their immediate geography.'

Source: Kim Thomas, 'Hamleys: Where to buy a gold-plated model of James Bond's Aston Martin', *Financial Times*, 2 August 2000, www.ft.com/ftsurveys/spbf9a.htm

Questions

1 What best-practice principles of marketing and e-marketing does this case indicate?

2 Visit the web site (www.hamleys.com) and assess changes in strategy since the article was written.

● E-commerce and e-business defined

The terms 'e-commerce' and 'e-business' are often used in a similar context to 'Internet marketing', but what are the differences between these terms and do the finer distinctions between them matter to the practitioner? In fact, the differences are significant and do matter, since managers within an organisation require a consistent understanding of the opportunities to enable their organisation to have a cohesive strategy to best utilise new technology.

Electronic commerce (e-commerce) is often thought to simply refer to buying and selling using the Internet; people immediately think of consumer retail purchases from companies such as Amazon. However, e-commerce involves much more than electronically mediated *financial* transactions between organisations and customers. Many commentators now refer to e-commerce as *both financial and informational* electronically mediated transactions between an organisation and any third party it deals with (Chaffey, 2002). By this definition, non-financial transactions such as customer enquiries and support are also considered to be part of e-commerce. Kalakota and Whinston (1997) refer to a range of different perspectives for e-commerce:

Electronic commerce (e-commerce)

All financial and informational electronically mediated exchanges between an organisation and its external stakeholders.

1 *A communications perspective* – the delivery of information, products/services or payment by electronic means.
2 *A business process perspective* – the application of technology towards the automation of business transactions and workflows.
3 *A service perspective* – enabling cost cutting at the same time as increasing the speed and quality of service delivery.
4 *An online perspective* – the buying and selling of products and information online.

Zwass (1998) uses a broad definition of e-commerce noting the significance of information transfer. He refers to it as:

> *the sharing of business information, maintaining business relationships, and conducting business transactions by means of telecommunications networks.*

The UK government also uses a broad definition:

> *E-commerce is the exchange of information across electronic networks, at any stage in the supply chain, whether within an organisation, between businesses, between businesses and consumers, or between the public and private sector, whether paid or unpaid.*
>
> E-commerce@its.best.uk, 1999

All these definitions imply that electronic commerce is not solely restricted to the actual buying and selling of products, but also includes pre-sale and post-sales activities across the supply chain.

When evaluating the impact of e-commerce on an organisation's marketing, it is instructive to identify the role of buy-side and sell-side e-commerce transactions as depicted in Figure 1.2. **Sell-side e-commerce** refers to transactions involved with selling products to an organisation's customers. Internet marketing is used directly to support sell-side e-commerce. **Buy-side e-commerce** refers to business-to-business transactions to procure resources needed by an organisation from its suppliers. This is typically the responsibility of those in the operational and procurement functions of an organisation. Remember, though, that each e-commerce transaction can be considered from two perspectives: sell-side from the perspective of the selling organisation and buy-side from the perspective of the buying organisation. So for organisational marketing we need to understand the drivers and barriers to buy-side e-commerce in order to accommodate the needs of organisational buyers. For

Sell-side e-commerce

E-commerce transactions between a supplier organisation and its customers.

Buy-side e-commerce

E-commerce transactions between a purchasing organisation and its suppliers.

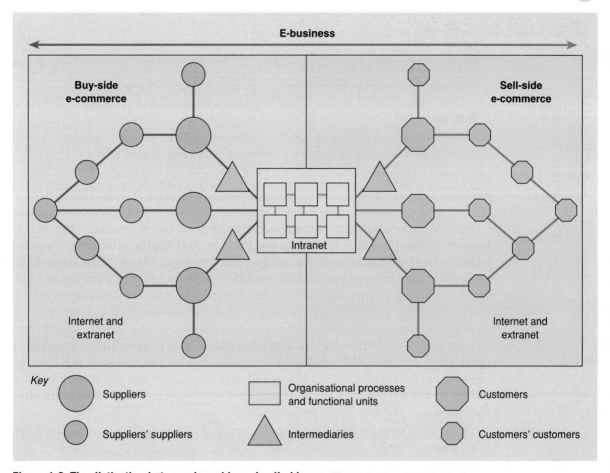

Figure 1.2 The distinction between buy-side and sell-side e-commerce

example, marketers from RS Components (www.rswww.com) promote its sell-side e-commerce service by hosting seminars for buyers within the purchasing department of its customers that explain the cost savings available through e-commerce.

● E-business defined

Given that Figure 1.2 depicts different types of e-commerce, what then is e-business? Let us start from the definition by IBM (www.ibm.com/e-business), which was one of the first suppliers to coin the term:

> ***e-business (e' biz' nis)**: The transformation of key business processes through the use of Internet technologies.*

Referring back to Figure 1.2, the key business processes in the IBM definition are the organisational processes or units in the centre of the figure. They include research and development, marketing, manufacturing and inbound and outbound logistics. Complete activity 1.1 to gain an appreciation of the type of processes involved. The buy-side e-commerce processes with suppliers and the sell-side e-commerce processes involving exchanges with distributors and customers can also be considered to be key business processes.

Electronic business (e-business)

All electronically mediated information exchanges, both within an organisation and with external stakeholders, supporting the range of business processes.

Activity 1.1

Marketing processes in the e-business

Purpose

To highlight how Internet technologies can be used to support marketing.

Question

A comprehensive analysis of all business processes requiring support in a typical organisation is available as part of the Andersen 'Global Best Practices' site (www.globalbestpractices.com). Identify those processes that directly and indirectly relate to marketing and explain how technology can be used to enhance these processes.

Figure 1.3 presents some alternative viewpoints of the relationship between e-business and e-commerce. Which do you think is most appropriate? In (a) there is a relatively small overlap between e-commerce and e-business. We can reject Figure 1.3(a) since the overlap between buy-side and sell-side e-commerce is significant. Figure 1.3(b) seems to be more realistic, and indeed many commentators seem to consider e-business and e-commerce to be synonymous. It can be argued, however, that Figure 1.3(c) is most realistic since e-commerce does not include reference to many of the transactions that are part of e-business but are *within* a business such as processing a purchasing order. In an international benchmarking study assessing the adoption of e-business in SMEs the Department of Trade and Industry emphasises the application of technology in the full range of business processes, but also emphasises how it involves innovation. It describes e-business as follows:

> *when a business has fully integrated information and communications technologies (ICTs) into its operations, potentially redesigning its business processes around ICT or completely reinventing its business model . . . e-business, is understood to be the integration of all these activities with the internal processes of a business through ICT.*

DTI (2000)

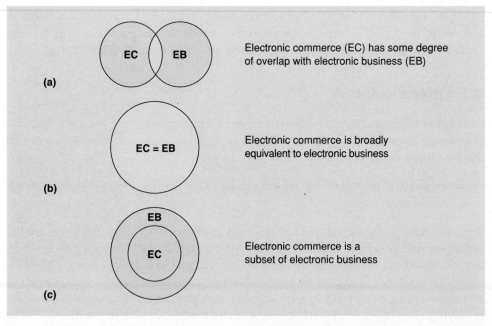

Figure 1.3 Three alternative definitions of the relationship between e-commerce and e-business

So e-commerce can best be conceived of as a subset of e-business, and this is the perspective we will use in this book. Since the interpretation in Figure 1.3(b) is equally valid, what is important within any given company, is that managers involved with the implementation of e-commerce/e-business are agreed on the scope of what they are trying to achieve!

● Business or consumer model

It is now commonplace to describe Internet marketing opportunities in terms of whether an organisation is transacting with consumers (business-to-consumer – B2C) or other businesses (business-to-business – B2B).

Figure 1.4 gives examples of different companies operating in the business-to-consumer (B2C) and business-to-business (B2B) spheres. It also presents two additional types of transaction, those where consumers transact directly with other consumers (C2C) and where they initiate trading with companies (C2B). Note that the C2C and C2B monikers are less widely used (e.g. *Economist*, 2000), but they do highlight significant differences between Internet-based commerce and earlier forms of commerce. Consumer-to-consumer interactions were relatively rare, but are now very common in the form of customer support and feedback – the community components of sites and online auctions. Indeed, Hoffman and Novak (1996) suggest that C2C interactions are a key characteristic of the Internet that is important for companies to take into account as is shown by Activity 1.2. It should be noted before we leave C2C and C2B interactions that although it is useful to identify these separately, both types of site are set up by intermediary *businesses*, so they can be considered to be part of B2C.

Business-to-consumer (B2C)

Commercial transactions between an organisation and consumers.

Business-to-business (B2B)

Commercial transactions between an organisation and other organisations (interorganisational marketing).

Consumer-to-consumer (C2C)

Informational or financial transactions between consumers, but usually mediated through a business site.

Consumer-to-business (C2B)

Consumers approach the business with an offer.

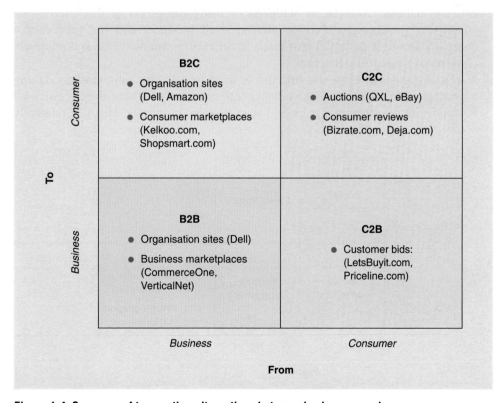

Figure 1.4 Summary of transaction alternatives between businesses and consumers

As well as the models shown in Figure 1.4, it has also been suggested that employees should be considered as a separate type of consumer through the use of intranets, which is referred to as employee-to-employee or E2E.

Why are C2C interactions important?

Purpose

To highlight the relevance of C2C transactions to B2C companies.

Activity

Consult with fellow students and share experience of C2C interactions online. Think of C2C on both independent sites and organisational sites. How can C2C communications assist these organisations?

What benefits does the Internet provide for the marketer?

Case Study 1.1 highlights the key reason why many companies are seeking to harness the Internet. This reason is an additional source of revenue made possible by an alternative marketing and distribution channel. The marketing opportunities of using the Internet can be appreciated by applying the strategic marketing grid (Ansoff, 1957) for exploring opportunities for new markets and products (Figure 1.5). The Internet can potentially be used to achieve each of the four strategic directions as follows:

1 *Market penetration.* The Internet can be used to sell more existing products into existing markets. This can be achieved by using the power of the Internet for advertising products to increase awareness of products and the profile of a company amongst potential customers in an existing market. This is a relatively conservative use of the Internet.

2 *Market development.* Here the Internet is used to sell into new markets, taking advantage of the low cost of advertising internationally without the necessity for a supporting sales infrastructure in the customers' countries. This is a relatively

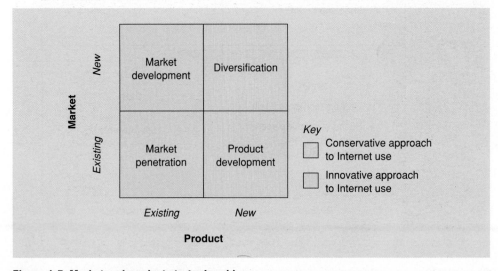

Figure 1.5 Market and product strategic grid

conservative use of the Internet, but it does require the overcoming of the barriers to becoming an exporter or operating in a greater number of countries. Case Study 1.1 is an example of an organisation using the Internet in this way.

3 *Product development.* New products or services are developed which can be delivered by the Internet. These are typically information products such as market reports which can be purchased using electronic commerce. This is innovative use of the Internet.

4 *Diversification.* In this sector, new products are developed which are sold into new markets.

Companies can use the Internet to adopt new approaches to selling products which involve positioning in one part of the grid presented in Figure 1.5, or in multiple quadrants. Examples of these applications are considered in Activity 1.3.

DTI (2000) has identified different types of drivers or benefits why companies adopt e-commerce. The main drivers for sell-side e-commerce are:

● *Cost/efficiency drivers*
   1. increasing speed with which goods can be dispatched;
   2. reduced sales costs;
   3. reduced operating costs.

● *Competitiveness drivers*
   1. customer demand;
   2. improving the range and quality of services offered;
   3. avoiding losing market share to businesses already using e-commerce.

As an example, consider Figure 1.6. The Internet provides Guinness with the opportunity to provide non-core merchandising activity at a relatively low cost.

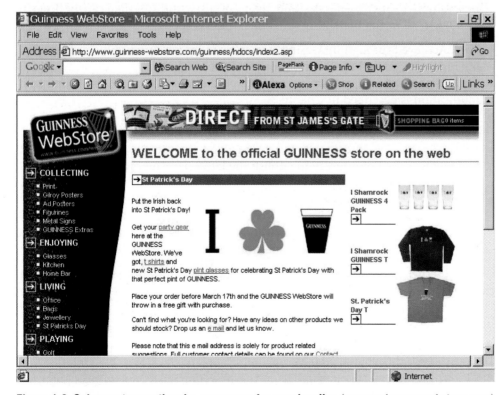

Figure 1.6 Guinness transactional e-commerce for merchandise (www.guinness-webstore.com)

The lure of new sales and the threat of market share erosion has driven many companies on to the Internet, but there are many other benefits of establishing an Internet presence. Consider the example of the parcel courier companies. These companies now provide a range of customer services over the Internet which were traditionally delivered by telephone operators, thus reducing operating costs. In such situations, the online services may give better 24-hour, 7-days-a-week, 365-days-of-the-year customer service if measured by convenience, but some customers will want the option of the personal touch, and phone services must be provided for this type of customer. Many companies will also reduce the costs of the printing and distribution of promotional material, price lists and other marketing communications.

Activity 1.3

Using the Internet for new markets and products

For each of the following companies identify which strategy the company has adopted relative to Figure 1.5, the market and product strategic grid. Explain how the new markets or products are exploited.

1 The purchase by the book retailer WH Smith of the Internet bookshop (www.bookshop.co.uk) in 1998 for £9 million.
2 The PC seller Dell Computer (www.dell.com), which now gains over 50% of its revenue from the web site.
3 The software company Microsoft launched a range of new sites to help consumers purchase cars, holidays, shares and other items.
4 A UK company such as HR Johnson (www.johnson-tiles.com), which is selling tiles to international distributors and has created an extranet to obtain orders over the Internet.

In addition to increased sales and reduced costs, the Internet can be used to advantage in all of the marketing functions, for example:

- *Sales*. Achieved through increasing awareness of brands and products, supporting buying decisions and enabling online purchase (Chapter 7).
- *Marketing communications*. The use of the web site for the range of marketing communication is described in Chapter 8.
- *Customer service*. Supplementing phone operators with information available online and other techniques described in Chapters 7 and 8.
- *Public relations*. The Internet can be used as a new channel for public relations (PR) and provides the opportunity to publish the latest news on products, markets and people (Chapter 8).
- *Marketing research*. Through search engines and e-mail alert services, the Internet enables more efficient techniques to be used for finding a range of market information. It also enables new methods for collecting primary research online through focus groups and online questionnaires (Chapters 7 and 9).

The Internet also changes the way in which companies do business with their trading partners as seen in the section on 'industry restructuring' later in this chapter.

To conclude this section, the benefits of an Internet presence can be summarised using the '6 Cs' of, for example, Bocij et al. (2003):

1 *Cost reduction*. Achieved through reducing the need for sales and marketing enquiries to be handled by telephone operators and the reduced need for printing and distributing marketing communications material, which is instead published on the web site.

2 *Capability*. The Internet provides new opportunities for new products and services and for exploiting new markets.

3 *Competitive advantage*. If a company introduces new capabilities before its competitors, then it will achieve an advantage until its competitors have the same capability. For example, customers who transferred to Federal Express because of its new Internet services are likely to be less disposed to revert to an existing courier since they are 'locked in' to using the particular tools provided by Federal Express.

4 *Communications improvement*. These include improved communications with customers, staff, suppliers and distributors. This is a major topic within this book and is covered in more depth in Chapter 2.

5 *Control*. The Internet and intranets may provide better marketing research through tracking of customer behaviour and the way in which staff deliver services.

6 *Customer service improvement*. Provided by interactive queries of databases containing, for example, stock availability or customer service questions.

The benefits that are possible through use of the Internet are also illustrated by Case Study 1.2. A key phrase in this article articulated by the head of Internet trading is that the project *'isn't just about a site, it's about the whole integrated way of doing business on a very substantial scale'*. Developing a structured plan to achieve these potential benefits is considered in Part 2 of this book.

CASE STUDY 1.2

RS Components

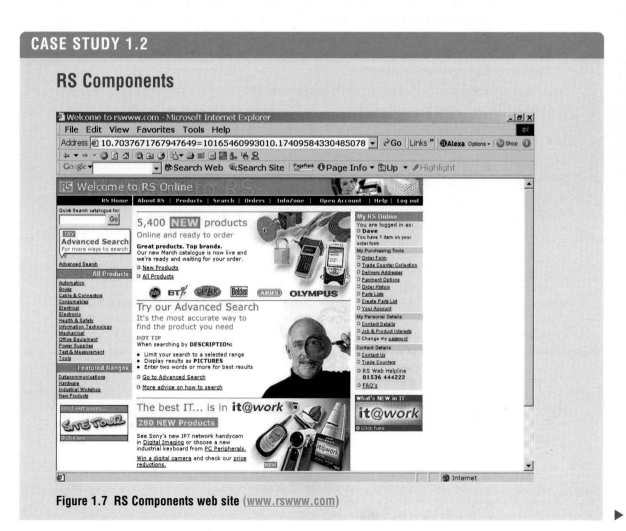

Figure 1.7 RS Components web site (www.rswww.com)

RS Components (www.rswww.com), which is part of Electrocomponents plc, is a distributor of electronic components, for example in the motor trade. In the mid 1990s it launched a CD-ROM of its catalogue, which featured tens of thousands of products. The CD had a 25 000 print-run, but the company was surprised that its stocks of the CD were soon depleted. This was an early indication of demand from consumers for interactive services. At the same time, Internet adoption was increasing, so the organisation decided to develop a transactional web site. It launched a transactional site for the 107 000 products in its catalogue in February 1998. In its first six months 44 000 customers registered as users of the site and there have been 84 000 repeat visits. The average order value is £81 and the average site visit across all 280 000 site visits is 23 minutes.

Traditionally RS Components operated in the business-to-business sector by selling direct to garages or through distributors. A benefit of the new site has been that a tenth of all registrations were from private individuals who represent a new customer sector.

The web site uses personalisation software from Broadvision to tailor over 50 different versions of the home page to different types of visitors. Further capabilities that are unavailable via other channels are:

- the facility for online users to check on stock availability
- return to unfinished orders which are interrupted part-way through
- different parcels can be sent to different fulfilment addresses from a single order

The company has made a substantial investment and commitment to new media, spending £2.5 million on the new system to 1998. Bernard Hewitt, head of Internet trading at RS Components, justified this expenditure, saying:

We're this committed to new media because we believe in the future. No one like us is doing anything close to what we're doing. It isn't just about a site, it's about the whole integrated way of doing business on a very substantial scale.

In the first eight months from when the site was introduced RS Components (rswww.com) recorded:

- 280 000 sessions (visits);
- 44 000 registered customers;
- 84 000 repeat visits;
- 23 minutes average time on site;
- £81 average order value;
- 10 per cent private rather than trade.

In 2001, the results from the web site are as follows:

- 350 000 site registrations.
- 80 000 visits per month.
- 53 000 repeat visits each month.
- 8000 new registrations each month.
- 8% of sales in the UK are Internet-based amounting to £30 per year.
- Each of Electrocomponents' operating companies in 26 countries has an internet trading site with on-line catalogue, in all major languages including Chinese and Japanese. In Japan, online sales are 20% of total sales.
- Europe (Austria, Belgium, Denmark, France, Germany, Ireland, Italy, the Netherlands, Spain and the UK) is served by one central hub, the European Internet Trading Channel (Euro ITC), which manages 10 different catalogues, offers 7 different languages and 11 currencies (including the euro). Support, fulfilment and content, however, remain local.

Source: *Revolution*, November 1998 and Keith Laroche, E-commerce sales manager, RS Components speaking at eMarketplaceWorld, 6 February 2002. Electrocomponents plc corporate web site (www.electrocomponents.com/about_us/ecommerce.htm)

Questions

1 Explain how the company has used the Internet to achieve each of the '6 Cs' of cost reduction, new capability, competitive advantage, communications improvement, improved control and customer service.

2 Compare the facility the Internet provides to measure the way the site is used with a traditional phone- or fax-based ordering system.

3 What does the extent of the investment made by the company suggest about the directors' commitment to the Internet?

A short introduction to Internet technology

Marketers require a basic understanding of Internet technology in order to discuss the implementation of e-marketing with partners. Knowing some of the pitfalls is useful also. The Internet has existed since the late 1960s when a limited number of computers were connected in the United States to form the ARPAnet. This was mainly used to enable academics and military personnel to exchange defence information.

Why then has the Internet only recently been widely adopted for business purposes? The recent dramatic growth in the use of the Internet has occurred because of the development of the World Wide Web. This became a commercial proposition in 1993 after development of the original concept by Tim Berners-Lee, a British scientist working at CERN in Switzerland in 1989. The World Wide Web changed the Internet from a difficult-to-use tool for academics and technicians to an easy-to-use tool for finding information for businesses and consumers. The World Wide Web is an interlinked publishing medium for displaying graphic and text information. This information is stored on web server computers and then accessed by users who run web browser programs, which display the information and allow users to select links to access other web sites (the process known as 'surfing').

Figure 1.8 gives an example of a web site accessed through the Internet Explorer web browser. This site has the web address or location 'www.marketing-online.co.uk'. The technical name for web addresses is uniform or universal resource locators (URLs). URLs can be thought of as a standard method of addressing similar to postal or ZIP codes that make it straightforward to find the name of a site.

The Internet

The Internet refers to the physical network that links computers across the globe. It consists of the infrastructure of network servers and wide-area communication links between them that are used to hold and transport the vast amount of information on the Internet.

World Wide Web

The World Wide Web is a medium for publishing information on the Internet. It is accessed through *web browsers*, which display web pages and can now be used to run business applications. Company information is stored on *web servers*, which are usually referred to as *web sites*.

Web servers

Web servers are used to store the web pages accessed by web browsers. They may also contain databases of customer or product information which can be queried and retrieved using a browser.

Web browsers

Browsers such as Netscape Navigator or Microsoft Internet Explorer provide an easy method of accessing and viewing information stored as web documents on different servers.

Uniform (universal) resource locator (URL)

A web address used to locate a web page on a web server.

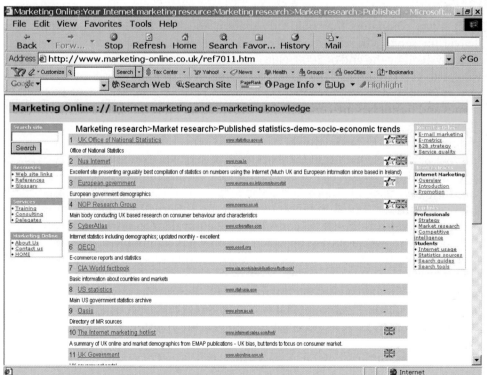

Figure 1.8 A web site providing links to different Internet marketing information sources viewed using Microsoft Internet Explorer browser

Web addresses are structured in a standard way as follows:

http://www.domain-name.extension/filename.html

The domain name refers to the name of the web server and is usually selected to be the same as the name of the company, and the extension will indicate its type. The extension is also commonly known as the global top-level domain (gTLD). Note that gTLDs are currently under discussion and there are proposals for adding new types such as .store and .firm.

Common gTLDs are:

- **.com** represents an international or American company such as http://www.travelagency.com
- **.co.uk** represents a company based in the UK such as http://www.thomascook.co.uk.
- **.ac.uk** is a UK-based university (e.g. http://www.derby.ac.uk)
- **.org.uk** and **.org** are not-for-profit organisations (e.g. www.greenpeace.org)
- **.net** is a network provider such as www.freeserve.net.

The 'filename.html' part of the web address refers to an individual web page, for example 'products.html' for a web page summarising companies' products. When a web address is typed in without a filename, for example www.bt.com, the browser automatically assumes the user is looking for the home page, which by convention is referred to as index.html. When creating sites, it is therefore vital to name the home page index.html.

● How does the Internet work?

The Internet enables communication between millions of connected computers worldwide. Information is transmitted from client PCs whose users request services from server computers that hold information and host business applications that deliver the services in response to requests. Thus, the Internet is a large-scale client–server system. By the end of 2000, Nua compilations estimated that worldwide, there were over 450 million users or clients accessing over 30 million web sites hosted on servers (Web update, www.nua.ie/surveys, www.cyberatlas.com). The client PCs within homes and businesses are connected to the Internet via local internet service providers (ISPs) which, in turn, are linked to larger ISPs with connection to the major national and international infrastructure or backbones (Figure 1.9). In the UK, at the London Internet Exchange which is in the Docklands area of east London, a facility exists to connect multiple backbones of the major ISPs within the UK onto a single high-speed link out of the UK into Europe and the rest of the world. These high-speed links can be thought of as the motorways on the 'information superhighway' while the links provided from ISPs to consumers are equivalent to slow country roads.

Figure 1.10 shows the process by which web browsers communicate with web servers. A request from the client PC is executed when the user types in a web address, clicks on a hyperlink or fills in an online form such as a search. This request is then sent to the ISP and routed across the Internet to the destination server. The server then returns the requested web page if it is a static (fixed) web page, or if it requires reference to a database, such as a request for product information, it will pass the query on to a database server and will then return this to the customer as a dynamically created web page. Information on all page requests is stored in a transaction log file which records the page requested, the time it was made and the source of the enquiry. This information can be analysed using a log file analyser along with different browser-based techniques to assess the success of the web site as explained in Chapter 9.

Client–server

The client–server architecture consists of client computers such as PCs sharing resources such as a database stored on more powerful server computers.

Internet service provider (ISP)

A provider enabling home or business users a connection to access the Internet. They can also host web-based applications.

Backbones

High-speed communications links used to enable Internet communications across a country and internationally.

Static web page

A page on the web server that is invariant.

Dynamic web page

A page that is created in real time, often with reference to a database query, in response to a user request.

Transaction log file

A web server file that records all page requests.

Log file analyser

Software to summarise and report the information in the transaction log file.

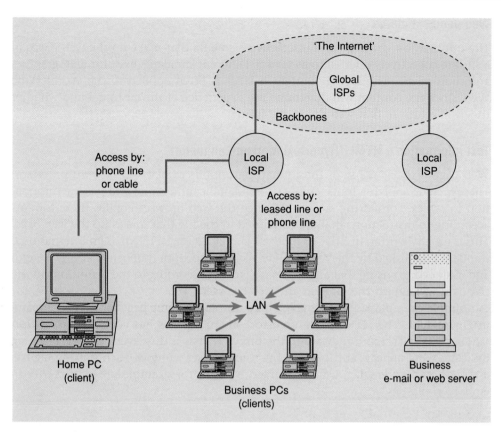

Figure 1.9 Infrastructure components of the Internet

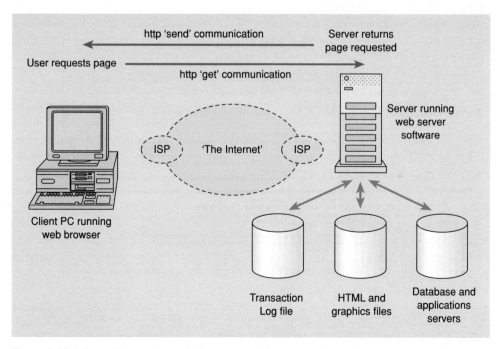

Figure 1.10 Information exchange between a web browser and a web server

Web page standards

The information, graphics and interactive elements that make up the web pages of a site are collectively referred to as content. Different standards exist for text, graphics and multimedia. The saying 'content is king' is often applied to the World Wide Web, since the content will determine the experience of the customer and whether they will return to that web site in the future.

Content

Content is the design, text and graphical information which forms a web page. Good content is the key to attracting customers to a web site and retaining their interest or achieving repeat visits.

Text information – HTML (Hypertext Markup Language)

Web page text has many of the formatting options available in a word processor. These include applying fonts, emphasis (bold, italic, underline) and placing information in tables. Formatting is possible since the web browser applies these formats according to instructions that are contained in the file that makes up the web page. This is usually written in HTML or Hypertext Markup Language. HTML is an international standard established by the World Wide Web Consortium (published at www.w3.org) and intended to ensure that any web page written according to the definitions in the standard will appear the same in any web browser.

A simple example of HTML is given for a simplified home page for a B2B company in Figure 1.11. The HTML code used to construct pages has codes or instruction tags such as <TITLE> to indicate to the browser what is displayed. The <TITLE> tag indicates what appears at the top of the web browser window. Each starting tag has a corresponding end tag, usually marked by a '/', for example <B>plastics</B> to embolden plastics.

HTML (Hypertext Markup Language)

HTML is a standard format used to define the text and layout of web pages. HTML files usually have the extension .HTML or .HTM.

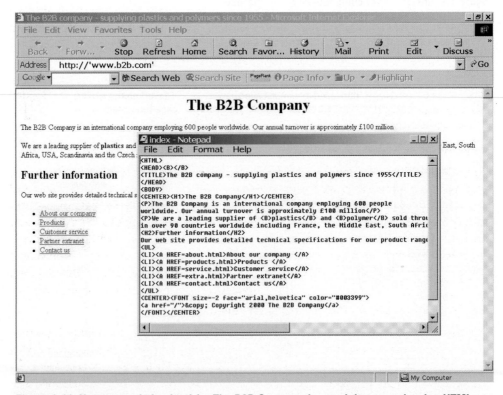

Figure 1.11 Home page index.html for The B2B Company in a web browser showing HTML source in text editor

The simplicity of HTML compared to traditional programming languages makes it possible for simple web pages to be developed by non-specialists such as marketing assistants, particularly if templates for more complex parts of the page are provided. Interactive forms and brochures and online sales are more complex and usually require some programming expertise, although tools are available to simplify these. See detailed information on creating HTML pages (Chapter 7).

Text information and data – XML (Extensible Markup Language)

When the early version of HTML was designed by Tim Berners-Lee at CERN, he based it on the existing standard for representation of documents. This standard was SGML, the Standard Generalised Markup Language which was ratified by the ISO in 1986. SGML uses tags to identify the different elements of a document such as title and chapters. HTML used a similar approach, for example the tag for title is <TITLE>. While HTML proved powerful in providing a standard method of displaying information that was easy to learn, it was purely presentational. It lacked the ability to describe the data on web pages. A metadata language providing data about data contained within pages would be much more powerful. These weaknesses have been acknowledged, and in an effort coordinated by the World Wide Web consortium, the first XML or eXtensible Markup Language was produced in February 1998. This is also based on SGML. The key word describing XML is 'extensible'. This means that new markup tags can be created that facilitate the searching and exchange of information. For example, product information on a web page could use the XML tags <NAME>, <DESCRIPTION>, <COLOUR> and <PRICE>. The tags can effectively act as a standard set of database field descriptions so that data can be exchanged through B2B exchanges.

The importance of XML is indicated by its incorporation by Microsoft into its BizTalk server for B2B integration and the creation of ebXML (electronic business XML) standard by their rival Sun Microsystems. It is also the main standard for data exchange for CommerceOne B2B Marketplace (see 'Example XML for Online Marketplace catalogue' case study) and industry standards, for example transferring data between companies in the chemical process industry. In future, XML may become increasingly important for search engines.

Graphical images (GIF and JPEG files)

Graphics produced by graphic designers or captured using digital cameras can be readily incorporated into web pages as images. GIF (Graphics Interchange Format) and JPEG (Joint Photographics Experts Group) refer to two standard file formats most commonly used to present images on web pages. GIF files are limited to 256 colours and are best used for small simple graphics, such as banner adverts, while JPEG is best used for larger images where image quality is important, such as photographs. Both formats use image compression technology to minimise the size of downloaded files.

Animated graphical information (GIFs and plug-ins)

GIF files can also be used for interactive banner adverts. Plug-ins are additional programs, sometimes referred to as 'helper applications', and work in association with the web browser to provide features not present in the basic web browser. The best-known plug-ins are probably that for Adobe Acrobat which is used to display documents in .pdf format (www.adobe.com) and the Macromedia Flash and Shockwave products for producing interactive graphics (www.macromedia.com).

Metadata

Literally, data about data – a format describing the structure and content of data.

XML or eXtensible Markup Language

A standard for transferring structured data, unlike HTML which is purely presentational.

GIF (Graphics Interchange Format)

A graphics format and compression algorithm best used for simple graphics.

JPEG (Joint Photographics Experts Group)

A graphics format and compression algorithm best used for photographs.

Plug-in

An add-on program to a web browser providing extra functionality such as animation.

Example XML for Online Marketplace catalogue

This example is taken from the Commerce One (www.commerceone.net) xCBL 3.0 standard for publishing catalogue data. It can be seen that specific tags are used to identify:

- product ID
- manufacturer
- long and short description
- attributes of product and associated picture.

There is no pricing information in this example.

```
<CatalogData>
<Product>
<Action Value="Delete"/>
<ProductID>118003-008</ProductID>
</Product>
<Product Type="Good" SchemaCategoryRef="C43171801">
<ProductID>140141-002</ProductID>
<UOM><UOMCoded>EA</UOMCoded></UOM>
<Manufacturer>Compaq</Manufacturer>
<LeadTime>2</LeadTime>
<CountryOfOrigin>
<Country><CountryCoded>US</CountryCoded></Country>
</CountryOfOrigin>
<ShortDescription xml:lang="en">Armada M700 PIII 500
12GB</ShortDescription>
<LongDescription xml:lang="en">
This light, thin powerhouse delivers no-compromise performance in a sub-five pound form
factor. Size and Weight(HxWxD): 12.4 X 9.8 X 1.1 in 4.3 - 4.9 lbs (depending on
configuration) Processor: 500-MHZ Intel Pentium III Processor with 256K integrated
cache Memory: 128MB of RAM, expandable to 576MB Hard Drive: 12.0GB Removable
SMART Hard Drive Display Graphics: 14.1-inch color TFT with 1024 x 768 resolution
(up to 16M colors internal) Communication: Mini-PCI V.90 Modem/Nic Combo Operating
System: Dual Installation of Microsoft Windows 95 &amp; Microsoft Windows 98
</LongDescription>
<ProductAttachment>
<AttachmentURL>file:\5931.jpg</AttachmentURL>
<AttachmentPurpose>PicName</AttachmentPurpose>
<AttachmentMIMEType>jpg</AttachmentMIMEType>
</ProductAttachment>
<ObjectAttribute>
<AttributeID> Processor Speed</AttributeID>
<AttributeValue>500MHZ</AttributeValue>
</ObjectAttribute>
<ObjectAttribute>
<AttributeID>Battery Life</AttributeID>
<AttributeValue>6 hours</AttributeValue>
</ObjectAttribute>
</Product>
```

Source: www.commerceone.com/download/xCBL3ForContent.pdf

Audio and video standards

Traditionally sound and video or 'rich media' have been stored as the Microsoft standards .WAV and .AVI. A newer sound format for music is MP3. These formats are used on some web sites, but they are not appropriate for sites such as that of the BBC (www.bbc.co.uk), since the user would have to wait for the whole clip to download before hearing or viewing it. Streaming media are now used for many multimedia sites since they enable video or audio to start playing within a few seconds – it is not necessary for the whole file to be downloaded before it can be played. Formats for streaming media have been established by Real Networks (www.realnetworks.com).

Streaming media
Sound and video that can be experienced within a web browser before the whole clip is downloaded.

Internet-access software applications

Over its lifetime, many tools have been developed to help find, send and receive information across the Internet. Web browsers used to access the World Wide Web are the latest of these applications. These tools are summarised in Table 1.1. In this section we will briefly discuss the relevance of some of the more commonly used tools to the modern organisation. The other tools have either been superseded by the use of the World Wide Web or are of less relevance from a business perspective.

Table 1.1 Applications of different Internet tools

Internet tool	Summary
Electronic mail or e-mail	Sending messages or documents, such as news about a new product or sales promotion between individuals. A primitive form of 'push' channel.
Internet Relay Chat (IRC)	This is a synchronous communications tool which allows a text-based 'chat' between different users who are logged on at the same time. Of limited use for marketing purposes.
Usenet newsgroups	A widely used electronic bulletin board used to discuss a particular topic such as a sport, hobby or business area. Traditionally accessed by special newsreader software, but can now be accessed via a web browser from www.deja.com (now part of Google – www.google.com).
FTP file transfer	The File Transfer Protocol is used as a standard for moving files across the Internet. FTP is used for marketing applications such as downloading files such as product price lists or specifications. Also used to update HTML files on web pages.
Gophers, Archie and WAIS	These tools were important before the advent of the web for storing and searching documents on the Internet. They have largely been superseded by the web which provides better searching and more sophisticated document publishing.
Telnet	This allows remote access to computer systems. For example a retailer could check to see whether an item was in stock in a warehouse using a telnet application.
Push channel	Information is broadcast over the Internet or an intranet and received using a web browser or special program for which a subscription to this channel has been set up. This technique is still used for automated software distribution, but has not proved popular as a method for accessing web content by users.
World Wide Web	Widely used for publishing information and running business applications over the Internet.

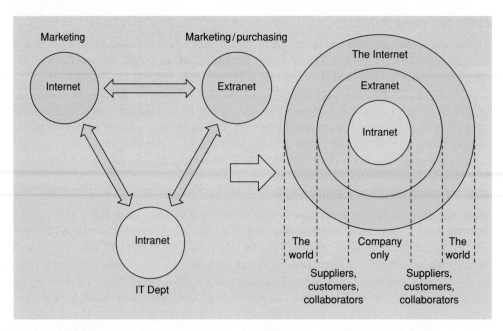

Figure 1.12 The relationship between access to intranets, extranets and the Internet

The application of the Internet for marketing in this book concentrates on the use of e-mail and the World Wide Web since these tools are now most commonly used by businesses for digital marketing. Many of the other tools such as IRC and newsgroups, which formerly needed special software to access them, are now available from the WWW.

● From the Internet to intranets and extranets

Intranet

A network within a single company which enables access to company information using the familiar tools of the Internet such as web browsers. Only staff within the company can access the intranet, which will be password-protected.

Extranet

Formed by extending the intranet beyond a company to customers, suppliers, collaborators or even competitors. This is again password-protected to prevent access by all Internet users.

'Intranet' and 'extranet' are two terms that arose in the 1990s to describe applications of Internet technology with specific audiences rather than anyone with access to the Internet. Access to an **intranet** is limited by username and password to company staff, while an **extranet** can only be accessed by authorised third parties such as registered customers, suppliers and distributors. This relationship between the Internet, intranets and extranets is indicated by Figure 1.12. It can be seen that an intranet is effectively a private-company Internet with access available to staff only. An extranet permits access to trusted third parties, and the Internet provides global access.

Extranets provide exciting opportunities to communicate with major customers since tailored information such as special promotions, electronic catalogues and order histories can be provided on a web page personalised for each customer.

Opportunities for using intranets and extranets to support the marketing process can be considered in two different ways. First, we must consider that the Internet can be used for marketing communications both within and beyond the company. As well as using the Internet to communicate with customers, companies find that internal use of an intranet or use of an extranet facilitates communication and control between staff, suppliers and distributors. Second, the Internet, intranet and extranet can be applied at different levels of management within a company. Table 1.2 illustrates potential marketing applications of both Internet and intranet for supporting marketing at different levels of managerial decision making. Vlosky et al. (2000) examine in more detail how extranets impact business practices and relationships.

Table 1.2 Opportunities for using the Internet, extranets and intranets to support marketing functions

Level of management	Internet	Intranet and extranet
Strategic	Environmental scanning Competitor analysis Market analysis Customer analysis Strategic decision making Supply chain management	Internal data analysis Management information Marketing information Database Operations efficiency Business planning Monitoring and control Simulations Business intelligence (data warehouses)
Tactical and operational	Advertising/promotions Direct marketing Public relations Distribution/logistics Workgroups Marketing research Publishing	Electronic mail Data warehousing Relationship marketing Conferencing Training Technology information Product/service information Customer service Internet trading Sponsorship

How do Internet marketing communications differ from traditional marketing communications?

Internet marketing differs from conventional marketing communications because of the digital medium used for communications. The Internet and other digital media such as digital television, satellite and mobile phones create new forms and models for information exchange. A useful summary of the differences between these new media and traditional media has been developed by McDonald and Wilson (1999) – they describe the '6 Is of the e-marketing mix'. Note that these can be used as a strategic analysis tool, but they are not used in this context here. The six Is are useful since they highlight factors that apply to practical aspects of Internet marketing such as personalisation, direct response and marketing research, but also strategic issues of industry restructuring and integrated channel communications. By considering each of these facets of the new media, marketing managers can develop marketing plans that accommodate the characteristics of the new media. This presentation of the '6 Is' is an interpretation of these factors using new examples and diagrams to illustrate these concepts.

1 Interactivity

John Deighton was one of the first authors to summarise the key characteristics of the Internet. He identifies the following characteristics inherent in a digital medium (Deighton, 1996):

- the customer initiates contact;
- the customer is seeking information (pull);
- it is a high-intensity medium – the marketer will have 100 per cent of the individual's attention when he or she is viewing a web site;

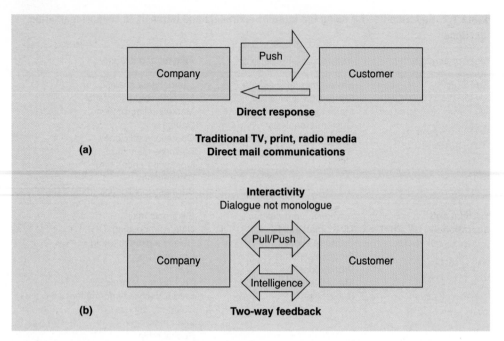

Figure 1.13 Summary of communication models for: (a) traditional media, (b) new media

- a company can gather and store the response of the individual;
- individual needs of the customer can be addressed and taken into account in future dialogues.

Figure 1.13(a) shows how traditional media are predominantly *push media* where the marketing message is broadcast from company *to* customer and other stakeholders. During this process, there is limited interaction with the customer, although interaction is encouraged in some cases such as the direct-response advert or mail-order campaign. On the Internet, it is usually a customer who initiates contact and is *seeking* information on a web site. In other words it is a *'pull'* mechanism unless e-mail is used (this can be considered as a push technique). Figure 1.13(b) shows how the Internet should be used to encourage two-way communications, which may be extensions of the direct-response approach. For example, FMCG suppliers such as Nestlé (www.nescafe.co.uk) use their web site as a method of generating interaction by providing incentives such as competitions and sales promotions to encourage the customer to respond with their names, addresses and profile information such as age and sex.

Hoffman and Novak (1997) believe that this change is significant enough to represent a new model for marketing or a new marketing paradigm. They suggest that the facilities of the Internet including the web represent a computer-mediated environment in which the interactions are not between the sender and receiver of information, but with the medium itself. They say:

consumers can interact with the medium, firms can provide content to the medium, and in the most radical departure from traditional marketing environments, consumers can provide commercially-oriented content to the media.

The content customers can provide may be directly commercial such as auctioning of their possessions such as via eBay (www.ebay.com) or could include comments on companies and products submitted via a newsgroup.

2 Intelligence

The Internet can be used as a relatively low-cost method of collecting marketing research, particularly about customer perceptions of products and services. In the competitions referred to above, Nestlé are able to profile their customers on the basis of the information received in questionnaires. The Internet can be used to create two-way feedback which does not usually occur in other media. Financial services provider Egg (www.egg.com) collects information about their online service levels through a questionnaire that is continuously available in the customer service part of their site. What is significant is that the company responds via the web site to the main concerns from the customer; if the length of time it takes to reply to customer service e-mails is seen as a problem it will explain what the organisation is trying to do to resolve this problem.

A wealth of marketing research information is also available from the web site itself, since every time a user clicks on a link this is recorded in a transaction log file summarising what information on the site the customer is interested in. Since these log files quickly grow to be many thousands of lines long, analysis software tools are needed to summarise the information contained within them. Log file analysers, of which Webtrends (www.webtrends.com) is the most widely used, will highlight which type of products or promotions customers are responding to and how patterns vary through time. This enables companies to respond in real time to buyer behaviour. UK e-tailer (short for e-retailer) Jungle.com uses this technique to change the offers on its home page if customers are not responding to a special offer.

3 Individualisation

Another important feature of the interactive marketing communications referred to above is that they can be tailored to the individual (Figure 1.14(b)) unlike in traditional media where the same message tends to be broadcast to everyone (Figure 1.14(a)). The process of tailoring is also referred to as **personalisation** and is an important aspect of achieving customer relationship management online. Personalisation is often achieved through extranets which are set up with key accounts to manage the buying and after-sales processes. Dell (www.dell.com/premierpages) has set up 'Premier Pages' for key accounts such as the Abbey National where special offers and bespoke customer support are delivered. Another example of personalisation is that achieved by business-to-business e-tailer RS Components (www.rswww.com). Every customer who accesses their system is profiled according to their area of product interest and information describing their role in the buying unit. When they next visit the site information will be displayed relevant to their product interest, for example office products and promotions if this is what was selected. This is an example of what is known as **mass customisation** where generic customer information is supplied for particular segments, i.e. the information is not unique to individuals, but is relevant to those with a common interest. The online booksellers such as Amazon (www.amazon.co.uk) use this approach to communicate details of new books to groups of customers. Gardeners, for instance, who have previously purchased a gardening book, will receive a standard e-mail advertising the latest gardening tome. This is again mass customisation. These concepts are explored further in Chapter 6.

Personalisation

Delivering individualised content through web pages or e-mail.

Mass customisation

Delivering customised content to groups of users through web pages or e-mail.

4 Integration

The Internet provides further scope for integrated marketing communications. Figure 1.15 shows how it is just one of many different media channels (these channels are also offered by intermediaries). When assessing the success of a web site, the

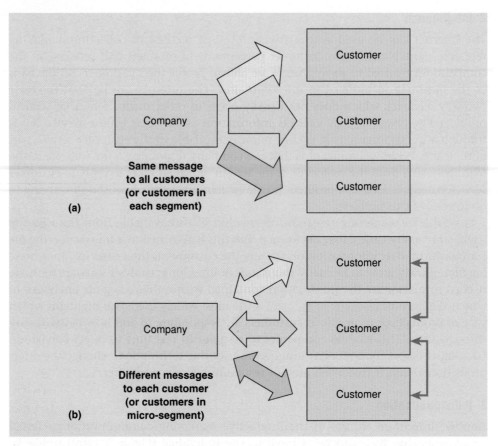

Figure 1.14 Summary of degree of individualisation for: (a) traditional media (same message), (b) new media (unique messages and more information exchange between customers)

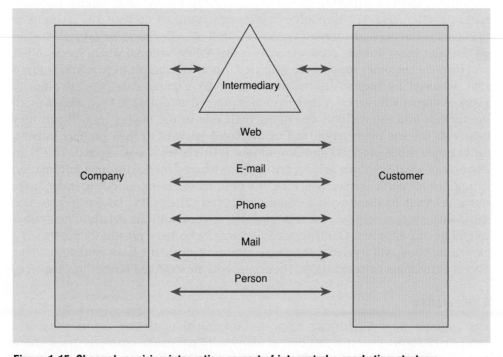

Figure 1.15 Channel requiring integration as part of integrated e-marketing strategy

role of the Internet in communicating with customers and other partners can best be considered from two perspectives. First, organisation-to-customer direction: how does the Internet complement other channels in communication of proposition for the company's products and services to new and existing customers with a view to generating new leads and retaining existing customers? Second, customer-to-organisation: how can the Internet complement other channels to deliver customer service to these customers? Many companies are now considering how they integrate e-mail response and web-site callback into their existing call-centre or customer service operation. This may require a substantial investment in training and new software.

Some practical examples of how the Internet can be used as an integrated communications tool are as follows:

- The Internet can be used as a direct-response tool, enabling customers to respond to offers and promotions publicised in other media.
- The web site can have a direct response or callback facility built into it. The Automobile Association has a feature where a customer service representative will contact a customer by phone when the customer fills in their name, phone number and a suitable time to ring.
- The Internet can be used to support the buying decision even if the purchase does not occur via the web site. For example, Dell has a prominent web-specific phone number on their web site that encourages customers to ring a representative in the call centre to place their order. This has the benefits that Dell is less likely to lose the business of customers who are anxious about the security of online ordering and Dell can track sales that result partly from the web site according to the number of callers on this line. Considering how a customer changes from one channel to another during the buying process is referred to as mixed-mode buying. It is a key aspect of devising online marketing communications since the customer should be supported in changing from one channel to another.

Mixed-mode buying
The process by which a customer changes between online and offline channels during the buying process.

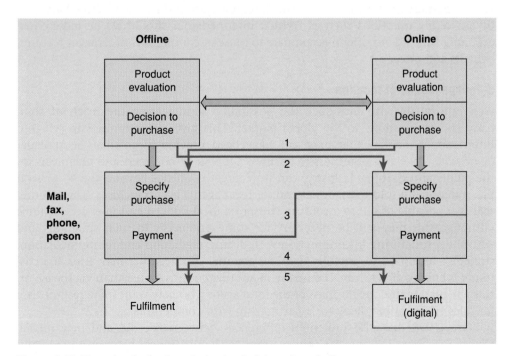

Figure 1.16 The role of mixed-mode buying in Internet marketing

- Customer information delivered on the web site must be integrated with other databases of customer and order information such as those accessed via staff in the call centre to provide what Seybold (1999) calls a '360 degree view of the customer'.
- The Internet can be used to support customer service. For example easyJet (www.easyjet.com), which receives over half its orders electronically, encourages users to check a list of frequently asked questions (FAQ) compiled from previous customer enquiries before contacting customer support by phone.

Activity 1.4

Integrating online and offline communications

Purpose

To highlight differences in marketing communications introduced through the use of the Internet as a channel and the need to integrate these communications with existing channels.

Activity

List communications between a PC vendor and a home customer over the lifetime of a product such as a PC. Include communications using both the Internet and traditional media. Refer to channel-swapping alternatives in the buying decision in Figure 1.16 to develop your answer.

5 Industry restructuring

Disintermediation

The removal of intermediaries such as distributors or brokers that formerly linked a company to its customers.

Reintermediation

The creation of new intermediaries between customers and suppliers providing services such as supplier search and product evaluation.

Disintermediation and reintermediation are key concepts of industry restructuring that should be considered by any company developing an e-marketing strategy and are explored in more detail in Chapters 2, 4 and 5.

For the marketer defining their company's communications strategy it becomes very important to consider a company's representation on these intermediary sites by answering questions such as 'Which intermediaries should we be represented on?' and 'How do our offerings compare to those of competitors in terms of features, benefits and price?'.

6 Independence of location

Electronic media also introduce the possibility of increasing the reach of company communications to the global market. This gives opportunities to sell into international markets that may not have been previously possible. Scott Bader (www.scottbader.com), a business-to-business supplier of polymers and chemicals for the paints and coatings industry, can now target countries beyond the 40 or so it has traditionally sold to via a network of local agents and franchises. The Internet makes it possible to sell to a country without a local sales or customer service force (although this may still be necessary for some products). In such situations and with the restructuring in conjunction with disintermediation and reintermediation, strategists also need to carefully consider channel conflicts that may arise. If a customer is buying direct from a company in another country rather than via the agent, this will marginalise the business of the local agent who may want some recompense for sales efforts or may look for a partnership with competitors.

Kiani (1998) has also presented differences between the old and new media, which are shown in Table 1.3. Annotations to the differences between the old and new media have been added to the table.

Table 1.3 An interpretation of the differences between the old and new media

Old media	New media	Comment
One-to-many communication model	One-to-one or many-to-many communication model	Hoffman and Novak (1996) state that theoretically the Internet is a many-to-many medium, but for company-to-customer-organisation(s) communications it is best considered as one-to-one
Mass marketing push model	Individualised marketing or mass customisation. Pull model for web marketing	Personalisation possible because of technology to monitor preferences and tailor content (Deighton, 1996)
Monologue	Dialogue	Indicates the interactive nature of the World Wide Web, with the facility for feedback
Branding	Communication	Increased involvement of customer in defining brand characteristics. Opportunities for adding value to brand
Supply-side thinking	Demand-side thinking	Customer pull becomes more important
Customer as a target	Customer as a partner	Customer has more input into products and services required
Segmentation	Communities	Aggregations of like-minded consumers rather than arbitrarily defined target segments

Source: After Kiani (1998)

● Conversion marketing

One of the key features of Internet marketing using the web is that the customer has to consciously decide to visit a particular site according to the particular information or experience they are seeking (Hoffman and Novak, 1996). As we have said, it is a pull medium, which contrasts with the push media used for mass marketing.

The problem of encouraging site visitors is compounded since it is difficult for potential customers to find a company web site. It is estimated that there are over one billion web pages amongst which a company is competing for the attention of customers. It follows that promoting the location of the web site is critical for companies.

The implication for marketers is that Internet marketing communications strategies for most companies should focus on the acquisition of site visitors, converting them to a required action on the site and then retaining these visitors. Internet marketers seek to use **conversion marketing** to convert as many *potential* site visitors into *actual* visitors and then convert these into customers and repeat visitors. A widely quoted conceptual measurement framework based on the industrial marketing concepts of purchasing decision processes and hierarchy of effects models, which can be applied for conversion marketing, was proposed by Berthon et al. (1998). The model assesses efficiency of offline and online communications in drawing the prospect through different stages of the buying decision. The main measures defined in the model were the following ratios:

Conversion marketing

Using marketing communications to maximise conversion of potential customers to actual customers.

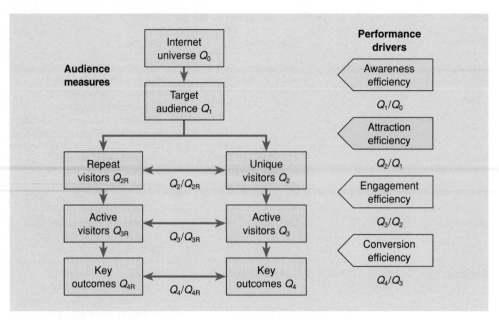

Figure 1.17 A model of the Internet marketing conversion process

- *Awareness efficiency*: target web-users/all web-users.
- *Locatability or attractability efficiency*: number of individual visits/number of seekers.
- *Contact efficiency*: number of active visitors/number of visits.
- *Conversion efficiency*: number of purchases/number of active visits.
- *Retention efficiency*: number of repurchases/number of purchases.

This model is instructive for improving Internet marketing within an organisation since these different types of conversion efficiency are key to understanding how effective online and offline marketing communications are in achieving marketing outcomes. Figure 1.17 is an adaptation of the original model of Berthon et al. (1998) from Chaffey (2001), which highlights the key conversion metrics of attraction efficiency and conversion efficiency. It shows key traffic or audience measures (Q_0 to Q_4) and key conversion efficiency ratios. The model has been revised to reflect current nomenclature. Also the original work was focused on conversion to purchase – the model is more widely applicable since it applies to any marketing outcome achieved on site, whether this be a new lead from a potential customer, a competition entrant or a sale. Additionally, it has been modified to distinguish between first-time visitors (Q_2) and repeat visitors (Q_{2R}). E-marketers need to know how conversion effectiveness differs between first-time users and repeat users. An additional important aspect of online buyer behaviour not shown in the figure is the site path or **clickstream** for different audience types or segments.

Clickstream

The sequence of clicks made by a visitor to the site to make a purchase.

Figure 1.18 shows an example of how measuring conversion rates can be used to improve web marketing. Numbers are across a fixed time period of one month. If for a particular market there is a potential audience (market) of 250 000 (Q_1), then if online and offline promotion techniques (Chapter 8) achieve 100 000 visitors to the site (Q_2), marketers have achieved an impressive conversion rate of 50%. The online marketers are then looking to convert these visitors to action. Before this is achieved, the visitors must be engaged. Data from log files shows that many visitors leave when they first visit the home page of a site if they do not find the site acceptable

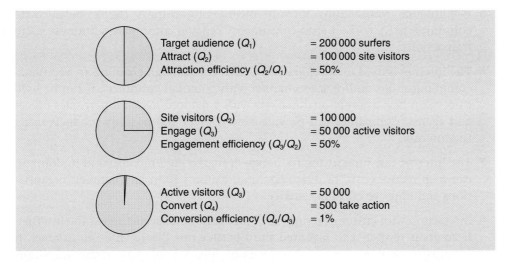

Figure 1.18 An example of the conversion process

or they are not happy with the experience. The number of visitors engaged (Q_3) is 50 000, which is half of all visitors. For the visitors that are engaged, the next step is to convert them to action. This is achieved for 500 visitors (Q_4), giving a conversion rate (Q_4/Q_3) of 1%. If what is calculated (as is most common) is (Q_4/Q_2), this gives a conversion rate of 0.5%.

In this example, the organisation seems highly efficient in attracting visitors to the site, but less efficient at converting them to action – future marketing improvements could be directed at improving this. Some organisations will measure different conversion rates for different segments and for different goals such as generating new leads, responding to a sales promotion or signing up for a seminar. Analysis by Agrawal et al. (2001) suggests that the strongest sites may have conversion rates as high as 12%, as against 2.5% for average sites and 0.4% for poorly performing ones. Clearly measurement of the conversion rate and taking actions to improve this rate are key e-marketing activities. The marketing communications techniques used to increase these conversion rates are considered further in Chapters 7 and 8.

Summary

1 Internet marketing refers to the use of Internet technologies, combined with traditional media, to achieve marketing objectives. E-marketing has a broader perspective and implies the use of other technologies such as databases and approaches such as customer relationship management.

2 Electronic commerce refers to both electronically mediated financial and informational transactions.

3 Sell-side e-commerce involves all electronic business transactions between an organisation and its customers, while buy-side e-commerce involves transactions between an organisation and its suppliers.

4 'Electronic business' is a broader term referring to how technology can benefit all internal business processes and interactions with third parties. This includes buy-side and sell-side e-commerce and the internal value chain.

5 E-commerce transactions include business-to-business (B2B), business-to-consumer (B2C), consumer-to-consumer (C2C) and consumer-to-business (C2B) transactions.

6 The Internet is used to develop existing markets through enabling an additional communications and/or sales channel with potential customers. It can be used to develop new international markets with a reduced need for new sales offices and agents. Companies can provide new services and possibly products using the Internet.

7 The Internet can support the full range of marketing functions and in doing so can help reduce costs, facilitate communication within and between organisations and improve customer service.

8 Interaction with customers, suppliers and distributors occurs across the Internet. If access is restricted to favoured third parties this is known as an *extranet*. If Internet technologies are used to facilitate internal company communications this is known as an *intranet* – a private company internet.

9 It is important for marketers to understand how visitors are likely to become aware of their web site and how efficient they are at converting this interest to visits and actions. Online and offline promotion techniques are used to capture new visitors and on-site communications are used to convert visitors to action.

10 The marketing benefits the Internet confers are advantageous both to the large corporation and to the small or medium-sized enterprise. These include:
● a new medium for advertising and PR;
● a new channel for distributing products;
● opportunities for expansion into new markets;
● new ways of enhancing customer service;
● new ways of reducing costs by reducing the number of staff in order fulfilment.

EXERCISES

Self-assessment exercises

1 Which measures can companies use to assess the significance of the Internet to their organisation?

2 Why did companies only start to use the Internet widely for marketing in the 1990s, given that it had been in existence for over thirty years?

3 Distinguish between Internet marketing and e-marketing.

4 Explain what is meant by electronic commerce and electronic business. How do they relate to the marketing function?

5 What are the main differences and similarities between the Internet, intranets and extranets?

6 Summarise the differences between the Internet and traditional media using the six Is.

7 How is the Internet used to develop new markets and penetrate existing markets? What types of new products can be delivered by the Internet?

Essay and discussion questions

1 The Internet is primarily thought of as a means of advertising and selling products. What are the opportunities for use of the Internet in other marketing functions?

2 'The World Wide Web represents a *pull* medium for marketing rather than a *push* medium.' Discuss.

3 You are a newly installed marketing manager in a company selling products in the business-to-business sector. Currently, the company has only a limited web site containing electronic versions of its brochures. You want to convince the directors of the benefits of investing in the web site to provide more benefits to the company. How would you present your case?

4 Explain the main benefits that a company selling fast-moving consumer goods could derive by creating a web site.

Examination questions

1 Contrast electronic commerce to electronic business.

2 Internet technology is used by companies in three main contexts. Distinguish between the following types and explain their significance to marketers.
(a) intranet
(b) extranet
(c) Internet.

3 An Internet marketing manager must seek to control and accommodate all the main methods by which consumers may visit a company web site. Describe these methods.

4 Imagine you are explaining the difference between the World Wide Web and the Internet to a marketing manager. How would you explain these two terms?

5 What is the relevance of 'conversion marketing' to the Internet?

6 Explain how the Internet can be used to increase market penetration in existing markets and develop new markets.

References

Agrawal, V., Arjona, V. and Lemmens, R. (2001) E-performance: the path to rational exuberance, *Mckinsey Quarterly*, No 1, 31–43.

Ansoff, H. (1957) Strategies for diversification, *Harvard Business Review*, September–October, 113–24.

Berthon, P., Lane, N., Pitt, L. and Watson, R. (1998) The World Wide Web as an industrial marketing communications tool: models for the identification and assessment of opportunities, *Journal of Marketing Management*, 14, 691–704.

Bocij, P., Chaffey, D., Greasley, A. and Hickie, S. (2003) *Business Information Systems. Technology, Development and Management in E-Business*, 2nd edn. Financial Times/Prentice Hall, Harlow.

Chaffey, D. (2001) Optimising e-marketing performance – a review of approaches and tools. In *Proceedings of IBM Workshoop on Business Intelligence and E-marketing*. Warwick, 6 December.

Chaffey, D. (2002) *E-Business and E-Commerce Management*. Financial Times/Prentice Hall, Harlow.

Deighton, J. (1996) The future of interactive marketing, *Harvard Business Review*, November–December, 151–62.

Dibb, S., Simkin, S., Pride, W. and Ferrel, O. (2001) *Marketing. Concepts and Strategies*, 4th European edn. Houghton Mifflin, New York. *See* Chapter 1, An overview of the marketing concept.

DTI (2000) *Business in the Information Age – International Benchmarking Study 2000*. UK Department of Trade and Industry. Available online at: www.ukonlineforbusiness.gov.uk.

Economist (2000) E-commerce survey. Define and sell, pages 6–12. *Economist supplement*, 26 February.

Hoffman, D.L. and Novak, T.P. (1996) Marketing in hypermedia computer-mediated environments: conceptual foundations, *Journal of Marketing*, 60 (July), 50–68.

Hoffman, D.L. and Novak, T.P. (1997) A new marketing paradigm for electronic commerce, *The Information Society*, special issue on electronic commerce, 13 (January–March), 43–54.

Houston, F. (1986) The marketing concept: what it is and what it is not, *Journal of Marketing*, 50 (April), 81–7.

Jaworski, B. and Kohli, A. (1993) Market orientation: antecedents and consequences, *Journal of Marketing*, July, 53–70.

Kalakota, R. and Whinston, A. (1997) *Electronic Commerce. A Manager's Guide*. Addison-Wesley, Reading, MA.

Kiani, G. (1998) Marketing opportunities in the digital world, *Internet Research: Electronic Networking Applications and Policy*, 8(2), 185–94.

Levitt, T. (1960) Marketing myopia, *Harvard Business Review*, July–August, 43–56.

McDonald, M. and Wilson, H. (1999) *E-Marketing: Improving Marketing Effectiveness in a Digital World*. Financial Times/Prentice Hall, Harlow.

Seybold, P. (1999) *Customers.com*. Century Business Books, Random House, London.

Smith, P.R. and Chaffey, D. (2001) *EMarketing Excellence – at the Heart of EBusiness*. Butterworth Heinemann, Oxford.

Valentin, E. (1996) The marketing concept and the conceptualisation of marketing strategy, *Journal of Marketing Theory and Practice*, Fall, 16–27.

Vlosky, R., Fontenot, R. and Blalock, L. (2000) Extranets: impacts on business relationships, *Journal of Business and Industrial Marketing*, 15(6), 438–57.

Zwass, V. (1998) Structure and macro-level impacts of electronic commerce: from technological infrastructure to electronic marketplaces, in Kendall, K. (ed.) *Emerging Information Technologies*. Sage, Thousand Oaks, CA.

Further reading

Baker, M. (ed.) (1999) *The Marketing Book*. Butterworth Heinemann, Oxford. Chapter 1, One more time – what is marketing, by Michael Baker, reviews the meaning of marketing and marketing myopia. Chapter 30, The Internet: the direct route to growth and development, by Jim Hammill and Sean Ennis, reviews the impact of the Internet on different sizes and types of company.

Brassington, F. and Petitt, S. (2000) *Principles of Marketing*, 2nd edn. Financial Times/Prentice Hall, Harlow. *See* companion Prentice Hall web site (www.booksites.net/brassington2). Chapter 1, Marketing dynamics, describes the marketing concept and the move from product orientation to marketing orientation.

Deighton, J. (1996) The future of Interactive marketing, *Harvard Business Review*, Nov.–Dec., 151–62. One of the earliest articles to elucidate the significance of the Internet for marketers. Readable.

Dibb, S., Simkin, S., Pride, W. and Ferrel, O. (2001) *Marketing. Concepts and Strategies*, 4th European edn. Houghton Mifflin, New York. *See* Chapter 1, An overview of the marketing concept.

DTI (2000) *Business in the Information Age – International Benchmarking Study 2000*. UK Department of Trade and Industry. Available online at www.ukonlineforbusiness.gov.uk.

Hoffman, D.L. and Novak, T.P. (1997) A new marketing paradigm for electronic commerce, *The Information Society*, Special issue on electronic commerce, 13 (Jan.–Mar.), 43–54. This was the seminal paper on Internet marketing when it was published, and is still essential reading for its discussion of concepts. Available online at Vanderbilt University (ecommerce.vanderbilt.edu/papers.html).

Kalakota, R. and Whinston, A. (1997) *Electronic Commerce. A Manager's Guide*. Addison-Wesley, Reading, MA.

Smith, P.R. and Chaffey, D. (2001) *EMarketing Excellence: at the Heart of EBusiness*. Butterworth Heinemann, Oxford.

Web links

General sources on marketing and Internet marketing

- Biz/ed Internet Catalogue (http://catalogue.bized.ac.uk/roads/market.html) has some online marketing resources, particularly in the sections on Marketing Channels and Marketing Resources.

- Marketing Online (www.marketing-online.co.uk) is a source for links to web sites concerned with Internet marketing strategy, implementation and practice. Updated by Dave Chaffey.

- eLab (http://ecommerce.vanderbilt.edu or www.eLabWeb.com) was founded in 1994 as Project 2000 by Tom Novak and Donna Hoffman at School of Management, Vanderbilt University, to study marketing implications of the Internet. Useful links/papers.

- University of Strathclyde, Department of Marketing, Marketing Resource Gateway (MRG) www.marketing.strath.ac.uk/dcd/. A comprehensive directory of marketing-related links.

Market reports on electronic commerce (*see also* further references in Chapter 2)

- CyberAtlas (www.cyberatlas.com) gives Internet statistics including demographics; updated monthly.

- E-consultancy (www.e-consultancy.co.uk) A good compilation of reports and white papers about new media.

- Nua Internet Surveys (www.nua.ie/surveys) is the definitive source of news on Internet developments, and reports on company and consumer adoption of Internet and characteristics in Europe and worldwide.

Print media

- *New Media Age* (www.newmediazero.com/nma). A weekly magazine reporting on the UK new media interest. Content now available online.

- *New Television Strategies* (www.newmediazero.com/ntvs). Sister publication to New Media Age.

- *Revolution* magazine (www.revolutionmagazine.com). A weekly magazine available for both UK and US on new media including Internet marketing.

Chapter 2

The Internet micro-environment

Links to other chapters

This chapter, together with the following one, provide a foundation for later chapters on Internet marketing strategy and implementation:

Learning objectives

After reading this chapter, the reader should be able to:

● Identify the different elements of the Internet environment that impact on an organisation's Internet marketing strategy

● Assess competitor, customer and intermediary use of the Internet

● Evaluate the relevance of changes in trading patterns and business models enabled by e-commerce

Questions for marketers

Key questions for marketing managers related to this chapter are:

● How are the competitive forces and value chain changed by the Internet?

● How do I assess the demand for Internet services from customers?

● How do I compare our online marketing with that of competitors?

● What is the relevance of the new intermediaries?

Introduction

All organisations operate within an environment that influences the way in which they conduct business. The Internet introduces many new facets of the environment that must be considered by marketers since strategy development is strongly influenced by considering the environment the business operates in. Figure 2.1 illustrates the key elements of a business's environment that will influence its organisation. Many authors such as Porter (1980) on corporate strategy or Kotler et al. (2001) on marketing strategy make the distinction between micro-environment and macro-environment. The micro-environment is the immediate marketplace of an organisation. For Internet marketing strategy, the most significant influences are arguably those of the micro-environment. This is shaped by the needs of customers and how services are provided to them through competitors, intermediaries and upstream suppliers. The Internet and electronic communications have major implications for organisations and these must inform their Internet marketing strategy. We consider the changes to the micro-environment and their implications in this chapter.

The macro-environment influences are broader, provided by local and international economic conditions and legislation together with what business practices are acceptable to society. These factors impact equally on all stakeholders within an organisation's micro-environment. Technological innovations are vital in providing opportunities for superior services to competitors and to changing the shape of the marketplace. The Internet and electronic communications have also introduced major changes to the macro-environment. Their impact will vary according to context. For example, laws about online taxation will have strategic implications for a company that trades online, but will not affect the strategy of a services company that does

Micro-environment

Specific forces on an organisation generated by its stakeholders.

Macro-environment

Broader forces affecting all organisations in the marketplace including social, technological, economic, political and legal aspects.

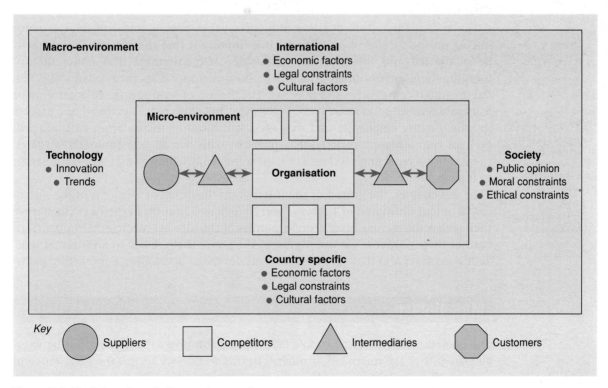

Figure 2.1 The Internet marketing environment

Table 2.1 Factors in the macro- and micro-environment of an organisation and Internet-marketing-related issues

Micro-environment	Macro-environment
The marketplace: ● Competitive forces ● From value chain to value network ● New channel structures ● Location of trading ● Commercial arrangements for transactions ● New business and revenue models	*Social*: ● Privacy ● Acceptable usage ● Internet culture
The organisation: ● Adaptability to change	*Technological*: ● Selecting new technologies ● Coping with technological change
Its customers: ● Access levels to the Internet ● Propensity to use and buy ● Buyer behaviour	*Economic*: ● The current and future economic situation
Its suppliers: ● Access levels to the Internet ● Propensity to use ● Integration with existing systems	*Political, legal, ethical and taxation*: ● Legal and tax constraints ● Government incentives ● Internet governance
Its competitors: ● Competitor capabilities	
Intermediaries: ● New capabilities ● New intermediaries	

not offer online fulfilment. We consider the changes to the micro-environment in Chapter 3.

Given that the nature of these influences varies rapidly and will have a major impact on the success of a company, it is important that the current environment be monitored and future trends anticipated. Organisations that either do not monitor these environmental factors or do not respond to them adequately will fail to remain competitive and may fail. The process of monitoring the environment is usually referred to as **environmental scanning**. This often occurs as an ad hoc process in which many employees and managers will monitor the environment and will perhaps respond appropriately. The problem with the ad hoc approach is that if there is not a reporting mechanism then some major changes may not be apparent to managers.

Environmental scanning and analysis
The process of continuously monitoring the environment and events and responding accordingly.

In this chapter, the impact of the Internet on the different elements of the micro-environment illustrated in Table 2.1 will be reviewed in turn. In the next chapter we then review the constraints and opportunities of the Internet macro-environment. For each of these elements we will highlight the issues that are key to an Internet marketing manager and that they need to consider when developing e-marketing plans.

Marketplace

The operation of an organisation's marketplace comprises the interactions between all elements of the micro-environment. In this section we review the great range of changes that the Internet has brought to the marketplace. The issues we will review include:

- *Competitive forces.* How are the major external forces on an organisation affected by the Internet?
- *From value chain to value network.* The value network concept describes a more dynamic version of the value chain with increased interaction between partners.
- *New channel structures.* What changes can occur to linkages to upstream and downstream partners in the supply chain?
- *Location of trading.* What are the options for location of trading online?
- *Commercial arrangements for transactions.* How are these changed?
- *New business and revenue models.* What business and revenue models can be adopted in the Internet marketplace?

● Competitive forces

Michael Porter's classic 1980 model of the five main competitive forces that impact a company still provides a pertinent framework for reviewing threats arising in the e-business era. We will use it here to introduce the different competitive forces arising from the interplay between the different stakeholders of the micro-environment, each of which will be explored in more depth later in the chapter. Table 2.2 summarises the main impacts of the Internet on the five competitive forces affecting an organisation. Note that, as seen later in this chapter and in Chapter 4, this form of analysis does not stress the importance of neutral intermediaries and strategic partnerships in affecting the marketplace.

Table 2.2 Impact of the Internet on the five competitive forces

Five forces				
Bargaining power of buyers	**Bargaining power of suppliers**	**Threat of substitute products and services**	**Barriers to entry**	**Rivalry between existing competitors**
• The power of online buyers is increased since they have a wider choice and prices are likely to be forced down through increased customer knowledge and price transparency (see Chapter 5). • For a B2B organisation, forming electronic links with customers may deepen a relationship and it may increase switching costs, leading to 'soft lock-in'.	• When an organisation purchases, the bargaining power of its suppliers is reduced since there is wider choice and increased commodisation due to e-procurement and e-marketplaces. • The reverse arguments regarding bargaining power of buyers.	• Substitution is a significant threat since new digital products or extended products can be readily introduced. • The introduction of new substitute products and services should be carefully monitored to avoid erosion of market share. • Internet technology enables faster introduction of products and services. • This threat is related to new business models which are covered in a later section in this chapter.	• Barriers to entry are reduced, enabling new competitors, particularly for retailers or service organisations that have traditionally required a high-street presence or a mobile sales force. • New entrants must be carefully monitored to avoid erosion of market share. • Internet services are easier to imitate than traditional services, making it easy for 'fast followers'.	• The Internet encourages commoditisation which makes it less easy to differentiate products. • Rivalry becomes more intense as product lifecycles decrease and lead times for new product development decrease. • The Internet facilitates the move to the global market, increasing the number of competitors.

Activity 2.1

Assessing the impact of the Internet on competitive forces in different industries

Purpose

To assess how some of the changes to the competitive forces caused by electronic communications impact particular industries.

Activity

Referring to Table 2.1, assess the impact of the Internet on a sector you select from the options below. State which you feel are the most significant impacts.

1 Banking (see Case Study 2.1).
2 Grocery retail.
3 Book retail.
4 B2B engineering component manufacturer.
5 B2B software services company selling customer relationship management software.
6 Not-for-profit organisation such as hospital, local government or charity.

Examples of changes to the five forces

In this section further examples are given of changes to the five competitive forces.

Bargaining power of buyers

The increase in customer power and knowledge is perhaps the single biggest threat posed by electronic trading. The bargaining power of customers is greatly increased when they are using the Internet to evaluate products and compare prices. This is particularly true for standardised products for which offers can be compared for different suppliers through price comparison engines provided by intermediaries such as easyShop (www.easyshop.com) or MySimon (www.mysimon.com). For commodities, auctions on business-to-business exchanges can also have a similar effect of driving down price. Purchase of some products that have not traditionally been thought of as commodities, may become more price-sensitive. This process is known as commoditisation. Examples of goods that are becoming commoditised include electrical goods and cars. The issue of online pricing is discussed in Chapter 5.

In the business-to-business arena, a further issue is that the ease of use of the Internet channel makes it easier for customers to swap between suppliers – switching costs are lower. With a specific EDI (electronic data interchange) link that has to be set up between one company and another, there may be reluctance to change this arrangement (soft lock-in due to switching costs). With the Internet, which offers a more standard method for purchase through web browsers, the barriers to swapping to another supplier will be lower. It should be noted, however, that there are still barriers and costs to switching since once a customer has invested time in understanding how to use a web site to select and purchase products, they may not want to learn another service. This is one reason why it is a competitive advantage for a company to offer a web-based service before its competitors.

A significant downstream channel threat is the potential loss of partners or distributors if there is a channel conflict resulting from disintermediation (see section on new channel structures below). For example, a car distributor could switch to an alternative manufacturer if its profitability were threatened by direct sales from the manufacturer. *The Economist* (2000) reported that to avoid this type of conflict, Ford US are now using dealerships as part of the e-commerce solution and are still paying

Commoditisation

The process whereby product selection becomes more dependent on price than on differentiating features, benefits and value-added services.

Soft lock-in

Electronic linkages between supplier and customer increase switching costs.

commission when sales are achieved online. This also helps protect their revenue from the lucrative parts and services market.

An additional downstream threat is the growth in number of intermediaries (another form of partners) to link buyers and sellers. These include consumer portals such as Which (www.which.net) and business-to-business exchanges such as CommerceOne (www.commerceone.net). This threat links to the rivalry between competitors. If a company's competitors are represented on a portal while the company is absent or, worse still, the portal is in an exclusive arrangement with a competitor, then this can potentially exclude a substantial proportion of the market.

Bargaining power of suppliers

This can be considered as an opportunity rather than a threat. Companies can insist, for reasons of reducing cost and increasing supply chain efficiency, that their suppliers use electronic links such as EDI or Internet EDI to process orders. Additionally, the Internet tends to reduce the power of suppliers since barriers to migrating to a different supplier are reduced, particularly with the advent of business-to-business exchanges. However, if suppliers insist on proprietary technology to link companies, then this creates soft lock-in due to the cost or complexity of changing supppliers.

Barriers to entry reduced

For traditional companies, new online entrants have been a significant threat for retailers selling products such as books and financial services. For example, in Europe, traditional banks have been threatened by the entry of completely new start-up competitors, such as First-e (www.first-e.com) (which later became financially unviable), or of traditional companies from one country that use the Internet to facilitate their entry into another country. Citibank (www.citibank.com) used the latter approach. These new entrants have been able to enter the market rapidly since they do not have the cost of developing and maintaining a distribution network to sell their products and these products do not require a manufacturing base. However, to succeed, new entrants need to be market leaders in executing marketing and customer service. These could perhaps be described as *barriers to success* rather than barriers to entry. The costs of achieving these will be high, for example, First-e has not survived as an independent business. This competitive threat is less common in vertical business-to-business markets involving manufacture and process industries such as the chemical or oil industry since the investment barriers to entry are much higher.

Threat of substitute products and services

This threat can occur from established or new companies. The Internet is particularly good as a means of providing information-based services at a lower cost. The greatest threats are likely to occur where product fulfilment can occur over the Internet as is the case with delivering banking, share dealing, industry-specific news or software. Indeed many new banks have been created by existing organisations as part of their Internet strategy. In photography, Kodak has responded to a major threat of reduced demand for traditional film by increasing its range of digital cameras to enhance this revenue stream and by providing online services for customers to print and share digital photographs.

From this review of the competitive forces, it should be apparent that the extent of the threats will be dependent on the particular market a company operates in. Generally, the threats are greatest for companies that currently sell through retail distributors and have products that can be readily delivered to customers across the Internet or by parcel. Case Study 2.1 highlights how one company has analysed its competitive threats and developed an appropriate strategy.

Internet EDI

Use of electronic data interchange standards delivered across non-proprietary Internet protocol networks.

Business-to-business exchanges or marketplaces

Virtual intermediaries with facilities to enable trading between buyers and sellers.

CASE STUDY 2.1

E-commerce strategy at Deutsche Bank

Online competition is forcing banks to rethink drastically how they can best serve their customers.

In a disused factory building at the edge of Frankfurt, executives and managers of Germany's biggest bank are hard at work learning about the immense changes that the internet will wreak on their business.

It is an incongruous setting for an induction into e-commerce, and all it implies for the traditional world of banking – especially in Germany, where change tends to be gradual and there are more banks per head of population than in most countries.

But Deutsche Bank is determined to ram the message home to managers and employees that the internet will change the banking world – and thus their bank – out of all recognition. It also chose the old factory hall as the venue to announce its e-commerce strategy, Global E, to the press.

The high-tech presentation included a dizzy array of internet partnerships, initiatives and projects aimed at transforming Deutsche Bank from an old economy institution to a financial concern more in tune with the new web-based economy.

It is an ambitious undertaking which goes beyond the plans of some rival banks in the internet age. But Hermann-Josef Lamberti, the director who heads the bank's IT operations and is masterminding the e-commerce thrust, says Global E had to be launched as an entire programme rather than as a series of piecemeal projects. Previously, the bank had about 200 separate e-commerce projects.

'We want to bring the capital markets of this world and the customers together', says Mr Lamberti, former head of IBM in Germany who joined the bank in December 1998. 'We believe that the possibilities of the internet will catapult us into a completely new form of business model.'

Mr Lamberti and his fellow directors – notably Rolf Breuer, the chairman – wanted to make this clear inside as well as outside the bank. 'The whole management team and employees have to be included in this transformation process', adds Mr Lamberti. 'It can't work if these new technologies are separated from the real world.'

Managing its own internal change will be just as hard, if not harder, than meeting the challenge of the internet, believes Mr Lamberti. 'We have analysed how the internet affects our individual business sectors – and we had to accept that none of them could be excluded.'

Hence the wide scope of the Global E programme. It covers all types of customers – institutional, corporate and individual – and includes a host of partnerships with internet and industry names such as SAP, America Online, Yahoo!, Nokia, Lycos and La Caixa.

'It would not have been enough to talk of individual projects, to say "let's do retail brokerage here and maybe business customers can do foreign exchange tomorrow over the internet and then we can discuss ECNs (electronic communications networks or quasi-securities exchange systems)".'

'Those are all product elements – they are important in themselves but do not lead to transformation.' The bank wanted to show how new technology could be used to bring customers and markets together online. Thus it was keen to announce the full range of its e-commerce strategy at once, under the branding of Global E 'as the unifying element'.

The news of the merger with Dresdner Bank followed shortly after the e-commerce presentation, putting Global E rather in the shade. Analysts were generally impressed with the scope and style of the e-commerce launch, but wonder whether Deutsche Bank has taken on too much. Also, they note that other banks are also rapidly moving into e-commerce, especially the business-to-business market.

Mr Lamberti insists that the merger will not distract Deutsche's attention from its internet strategy. He says the deal 'will increase the importance of the e-commerce strategy even further'.

While Dresdner has announced e-commerce plans, these are by no means as advanced as Deutsche Bank's. 'We will extend our strategy to Dresdner's operations and work together', he says. This could be especially important in the arena of electronic marketplaces, where companies carry out business transactions online. 'The merger should give us even more clout in the corporate market.'

With planned e-commerce investments of some €1bn a year – a figure unlikely to change much after the merger – Deutsche Bank is betting heavily on its internet strategy. Mr Lamberti is adamant that the surge of internet competition leaves it no choice. Globalisation will anyway lead to a further concentration on the investment banking scene, where the German bank intends to remain a leading operator in such areas as debt capital markets, derivatives and clearing.

'There will be fewer players in the top leagues in the US, Europe and Japan. We don't see anyone else in Germany, France or the UK as big rivals, but we see the Americans.' Among noteworthy US competitors, he names Citibank, Chase Manhattan, Merrill Lynch and Morgan Stanley Dean Witter.

But perhaps the most threatening source of competition comes from the rapidly evolving internet scene – from niche providers who can target the most promising markets.

'These are the retail brokers, the Charles Schwabs, the ConSors [the German online broker], the E*Trades, the E-Loans, the e-mortgage providers – the e-whatever you want.'

Such niche operators must not be under-estimated, believes Mr Lamberti. 'They will be in a position to act very quickly and play a role through alliances, unburdened by the legacy systems which a traditional bank carries.'

On the retail side, where Deutsche Bank will concentrate on more affluent clients, he foresees a further challenge as the internet makes it easier for banks to tackle foreign markets without having to open expensive branch networks. Similar retail banking models will develop in the US and Europe. 'Five or 10 years ago, we would have said this is absurd – there are completely different market conditions, consumer behaviour and regulatory conditions.'

But now, the banking market is set to change direction. For US banks, especially, freed from the restraints imposed by the Glass–Steagall Act – which separated commercial and investment banking and has just been repealed after 66 years – this opens up new horizons. 'For the first time, they see an opportunity to break through Fortress Europe, including the retail market.'

'Through the removal of the Glass–Steagall Act, the US has created for itself the regulatory conditions to reorder its banking structure. This newly structured banking sector will use the possibilities of the internet to include other continents in its strategy.'

Mr Lamberti expects this to happen on two levels. Firstly, US banks, brokerages or other financial providers will link up with portals, internet service providers (ISPs), application service providers (ASPs) or telephone companies. This will link their services with a large potential customer base.

Secondly, they could target specific customer segments with tailored products and services – such as access to online IPOs (initial public offerings) – using the ISP location as the base.

Thus Mr Lamberti foresees the rise of 'the global retail customer' as the internet breaks down regional barriers. Citibank has aimed its services at the worldwide market, but other banks have so far tended to shy away from such a strategy – 'the dimensions are just enormous'.

Source: Article by Andrew Fisher in the *Financial Times*, based on an interview with Hermann-Josef Lamberti of Deutsche Bank, 5 April 2000

Questions

1 Summarise the analysis of the bank's competitive environment in the second part of the article.

2 Referring to Porter's Five Forces analysis, summarise the typical competitive threats for a bank such as the Deutsche Bank and the strategy it can take to counter these threats.

● From value chain to value network

Value chain

A model that considers how supply chain activities can add value to products and services delivered to the customer.

Michael Porter's **value chain** (VC) is a well-established concept for considering key activities that an organisation can perform or manage with the intention of adding value for the customer. This value is added as products and services move from conception to delivery to the customer (Porter, 1980). The value chain is a model that describes different value-adding activities that connect a company's supply side with its demand side. We can identify an *internal* value chain within the boundaries of an organisation and an *external* value chain where activities are performed by partners. By analysing the different parts of the value chain managers can redesign internal and external process to improve their efficiency and effectiveness. Value can be added to the customer by reducing cost *and* adding value to customers:

- *within each* element of the value chain such as procurement, manufacture, sales and distribution;
- *at the interface between* elements of the value chain such as between sales and distribution.

In equation form:

$$\text{Value} = (\text{Benefit of each VC activity} - \text{its cost}) +$$
$$(\text{Benefit of each interface between VC activities} - \text{its cost})$$

Electronic communications can be used to enhance the value chain by making value chain activities such as procurement more efficient while also enabling data integration between activities. For, example if a retailer shares information electronically with a supplier about demand for its products, this can enhance the value chain of both parties since the cycle time for ordering can be reduced, resulting in lower inventory holding and hence lower costs for both.

Traditional value chain analysis (Figure 2.2(a)) distinguishes between *primary activities* which contribute directly to getting goods and services to the customer

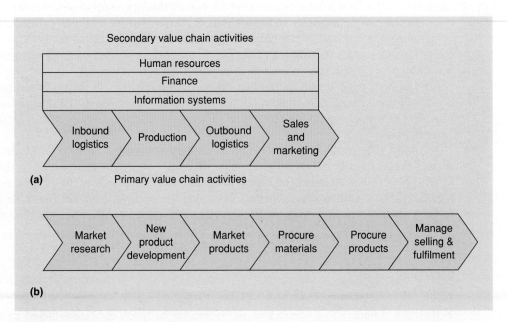

Figure 2.2 Two alternative models of the value chain: (a) traditional value chain model, (b) revised value chain model

(such as inbound logistics, including procurement, manufacturing, marketing and delivery to buyers, support and servicing after sale) and *support activities* which provide the inputs and infrastructure that allow the primary activities to take place. Support activities include finance, human resources and information systems. It can be argued that, with the advent of e-business, the support activities offer much more than support, indeed having effective information systems and management of human resources is critical in contributing to the primary activities.

Internet technologies can reduce production times and costs by increasing the flow of information as a way to *integrate* different value chain activities. Through doing this the value chain can be made more efficient and services delivered to customers more readily. Rayport and Sviokla (1996) contend that the Internet enables value to be created by gathering, organising, selecting, synthesising and distributing information. They refer to a separate parallel *virtual value chain* mirroring the physical value chain. The virtual value chain involves electronic commerce used to mediate traditional value chain activities such as market research, procurement, logistics, manufacture, marketing and distributing. The processing is machine-based or 'virtual' rather than paper-based. The situation is not truly virtual in that human intervention is still required in many value chain activities such as procurement. The 'virtuality' of the virtual value chain will increase as software agents increasingly perform these activities.

Restructuring the internal value chain

Traditional models of the value chain (such as Figure 2.2 (a)) have been re-evaluated with the advent of global electronic communications. It can be suggested that there are some key weaknesses in the traditional value chain model:

- It is most applicable to manufacturing of physical products as opposed to services.
- It is a one-way chain involving pushing products to the customer; it does not highlight the importance of understanding customer needs through market research and responsiveness through innovation and new product development.
- The internal value chain does not emphasise the importance of value networks (although Porter (1980) did produce a diagram that indicated network relationships).

A revised form of the value-chain has been suggested by Deise et al. (2000); an adaptation of this model is presented in Figure 2.2(b). This value chain starts with the market research process, emphasising the importance of real-time environment scanning made possible through electronic communications links with distributors and customers. For example, leading e-tailers now monitor, on an hourly basis, how customers are responding to promotional offers on their web site and review competitors' offers and then revise them accordingly. Similarly, manufacturers such as Cisco have feedback forms and forums on their sites to enable them to collect information from customers and channel partners that can feed through to new product development. As new product development occurs the marketing strategy will be refined and at the same time steps taken to obtain the resources and production processes necessary to create, store and distribute the new product. Through analysis of the value chain and looking at how electronic communications can be used to speed up the process, manufacturers have been able to significantly reduce time from conception of a new product idea through to launch on the market. For example, car manufacturers have reduced time to market from over 5 years to 18 months.

In addition to changes in the efficiency of value chain activities, electronic commerce also has implications for whether these activities are achieved under external control or internal control. These changes have been referred to as value-chain *disaggregation* (Kalakota and Robinson, 2000) or *deconstruction* (Timmers, 1999) and value-chain *reaggregation* (Kalakota and Robinson, 2000) or *reconstruction* (Timmers, 1999). Value-chain disaggregation can occur through deconstructing the primary activities of the value chain and then outsourcing as appropriate. Each of the elements can be approached in a new way, for instance by working differently with suppliers. In value-chain reaggregation the value chain is streamlined to increase efficiency between each of the value-chain stages. Indeed, Timmers (1999) notes that the conventional wisdom of the value chain as a separate of discrete steps may no longer be tenable as steps such as inbound logistics and operations become more tightly integrated through technology.

Value networks

Reduced time to market and increased customer responsiveness can be achieved through reviewing the efficiency of internal processes and how information systems are deployed. However, these goals are also achieved through consideration of how partners can be involved to outsource some processes that have traditionally been considered to be part of the internal value chain of a company. Porter's original

Value network

The links between an organisation and its strategic and non-strategic partners that form its external value chain.

work considered both the internal value chain and the external value chain or network. Since the 1980s there has been a tremendous increase in outsourcing of both core value-chain activities and support activities. As companies outsource more and more activities, management of the links between the company and its partners become more important. Deise et al. (2000) describe value network management as:

> the process of effectively deciding what to outsource in a constraint-based, real-time environment based on fluctuation.

Electronic communications have facilitated this shift to outsourcing, enabling the transfer of information necessary to create, manage and monitor partnerships. These links are not necessarily mediated directly through the company, but can take place through intermediaries known as value-chain integrators or directly between partners. As a result the concept of managing a value network of partners has become commonplace.

The value network offers a different perspective which is intended to emphasise:

- the electronic interconnections between partners and the organisation and directly between partners that potentially enables real-time information exchange between partners;
- the dynamic nature of the network. The network can be readily modified according to market conditions or in response to customer demands. New partners can readily be introduced into the network and others removed if they are not performing well;
- different types of links can be formed between different types of partners. For example, EDI links may be established with key suppliers, while e-mail links may suffice for less significant suppliers.

Figure 2.3, which is adapted from the model of Deise et al. (2000), shows some of the partners of a value network that characterises partners as:

1 supply-side partners (upstream supply chain) such as suppliers, business-to-business exchanges, wholesalers and distributors;

2 partners who fulfil primary or core value-chain activities. The number of core value-chain activities that will have been outsourced to third parties will vary with different companies and the degree of virtualisation of an organisation. In some companies the management of inbound logistics may be outsourced, in

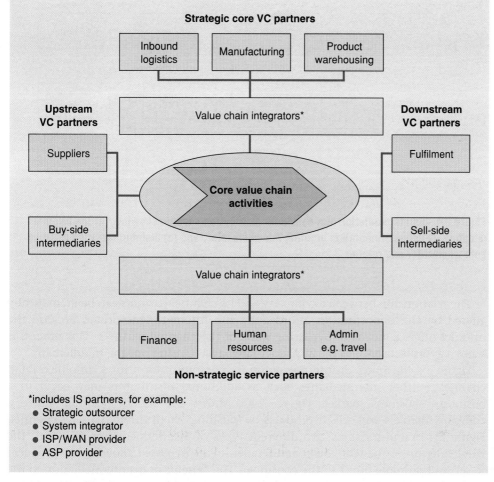

Figure 2.3 Members of the value network of an organisation
Source: Adapted from Deise et al. (2000)

others different aspects of the manufacturing process. In the virtual organisation all core activities may be outsourced;

3 sell-side partners (downstream supply chain) such as business-to-business exchanges, wholesalers, distributors and customers (not shown, since they are conceived as distinct from other partners);

4 value-chain integrators or partners who supply services that mediate the internal and external value chain. These companies typically provide the electronic infrastructure for a company and include strategic outsourcing partners, system integrators, ISP providers and application service providers (ASPs).

● New channel structures

Channel structures describe the way a manufacturer or selling organisation delivers products and services to its customers. The distribution channel will consist of one or more intermediaries such as wholesalers and retailers. For example, a music company is unlikely to distribute its CDs directly to retailers, but will use wholesalers who have a large warehouse of titles which are then distributed to individual branches according to demand. A company selling business products may have a longer distribution channel involving more intermediaries.

Channel structures

The configuration of partners in a distribution channel.

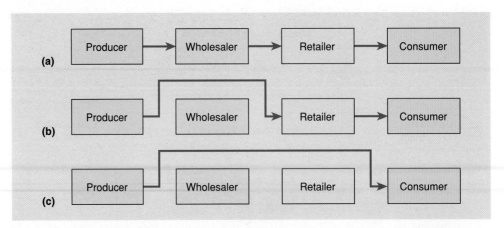

Figure 2.4 Disintermediation of a consumer distribution channel showing: (a) the original situation, (b) disintermediation omitting the wholesaler, and (c) disintermediation omitting both wholesaler and retailer

The relationship between a company and its channel partners can be dramatically altered by the opportunities afforded by the Internet. This occurs because the Internet offers a means of bypassing some of the channel partners. This process is known as **disintermediation** or, in plainer language, 'cutting out the middleman'.

Disintermediation

The removal of intermediaries such as distributors or brokers that formerly linked a company to its customers.

Figure 2.4 illustrates disintermediation in a graphical form for a simplified retail channel. Further intermediaries such as additional distributors may occur in a business-to-business market. Figure 2.4(a) shows the former position where a company markets and sells it products by 'pushing' them through a sales channel. Figure 2.4(b) and (c) show two different types of disintermediation in which the wholesaler (b) or the wholesaler and retailer (c) are bypassed allowing the producer to sell and promote direct to the consumer. The benefits of disintermediation to the producer are clear – it is able to remove the sales and infrastructure cost of selling through the channel. Benjamin and Weigand (1995) calculate that, using the sale of quality shirts as an example, it is possible to make cost savings of 28% in the case of (b) and 62% for case (c). Some of these cost savings can be passed on to the customer in the form of cost reductions.

At the start of business hype about the Internet in the mid-1990s there was much speculation that widespread disintermediation would see the failure of many intermediary companies as direct selling occurred. While many companies have taken advantage of distintermediation, the results have sometimes been less than spectacular. Vauxhall (www.vauxhall.co.uk, Figure 2.5), the UK part of General Motors, started selling its cars direct to customers in the mid-1990s, but despite a major advertising campaign, only several hundred cars were sold direct over the Internet in the first year.

Reintermediation

The creation of new intermediaries between customers and suppliers providing services such as supplier search and product evaluation.

Purchasers of products still require assistance in the selection of products and this led to the creation of new intermediaries, a process referred to as **reintermediation**. In the UK Screentrade (www.screentrade.co.uk) was established as a broker to enable different insurance companies to sell direct. While it was in business for several years, it eventually failed as online purchasers turned to established brands.

Figure 2.6 shows the operation of reintermediation in a graphical form. Following disintermediation, where the customer goes direct to different suppliers to select a product, this become inefficient for the consumer. Take, again, the example of someone buying insurance, to decide on the best price and offer, they would have

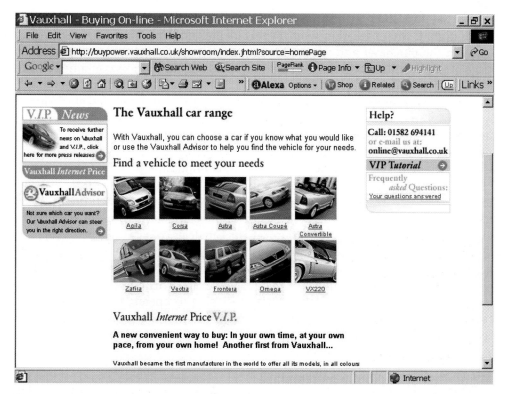

Figure 2.5 Vauxhall e-commerce site

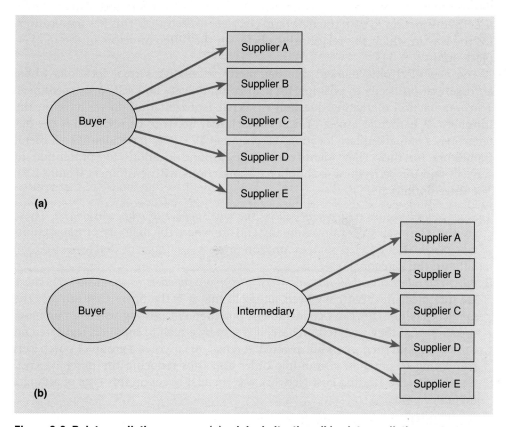

Figure 2.6 Reintermediation process: (a) original situation, (b) reintermediation contacts

to visit say five different insurers and then return to the one they decide to purchase from. Reintermediation removes this inefficiency by placing an intermediary between the purchaser and seller. This intermediary performs the price evaluation stage of fulfilment since its database has links updated from prices contained within the databases of different suppliers.

What are the implications of reintermediation for the Internet marketer? First, it is necessary to make sure that your company, as a supplier, is represented with the new intermediaries operating within your chosen market sector. This implies the need to integrate, using the Internet, databases containing price information with that of different intermediaries. Secondly, it is important to monitor the prices of other suppliers within this sector (possibly by using the intermediary web site for this purpose). Thirdly, it may be appropriate to create your own intermediary to compete with existing intermediaries or to pre-empt similar intermediaries. For example, the Thomson Travel Group set up Latedeals.com (www.latedeals.com) in direct competition with Lastminute.com (www.lastminute.com). A further example is that, in the UK, Boots the Chemist has set up its own intermediaries Handbag (www.handbag.com) and Wellbeing (www.wellbeing.com). This effectively created barriers for entry for other new intermediaries wishing to operate in this space. Such tactics to counter or take advantage of reintermediation are sometimes known as **countermediation**.

Countermediation

Creation of a new intermediary by an established company.

● Location of trading in marketplace

While traditional marketplaces have a physical location, Internet-based markets have no physical presence – it is a virtual marketplace. Rayport and Sviokla (1997) use this distinction to coin the new term **electronic marketspace**. This has implications for the way in which the relationships between the different actors in the marketplace occur.

Electronic marketspace

A virtual marketplace such as the Internet in which no direct contact occurs between buyers and sellers.

The new electronic marketspace has many alternative virtual locations where an organisation needs to position itself to communicate and sell to its customers. Thus one tactical marketing question is: 'What representation do we have on the Internet?'. A particular aspect of **representation** that needs to be reviewed is the different types of marketplace location. Berryman et al. (1998) have identified a useful framework for this. They identify three key online locations for promotion of services and for performing e-commerce transactions with customers (Figure 2.7). The three options are:

Representation

The locations on the Internet where an organisation is located for promoting or selling its services.

1 *Seller-controlled sites (sell-side at sellers' site, one supplier to many customers).* These are the main web site of the company and are where the majority of transactions take place. Most e-tailers such as Amazon (www.amazon.com) or Dell (www.dell.com) fall into this category.
2 *Buyer-controlled sites (buy-side at buyers' site, many suppliers to one customer).* These are intermediaries that have been set up so that it is the buyer that initiates the market-making. This can occur through procurement posting where a purchaser specifies what they wish to purchase, it is sent by e-mail to suppliers registered on the system and then offers are awaited. Aggregators involve a group of purchasers combining to purchase a multiple order and thus reducing the purchase cost. General Electric Trading Post Network was the first to set up this type of arrangement (tpn.geis.com).
3 *Neutral sites are intermediaries (neutral location – many suppliers to many customers).* For consumers these are often evaluator intermediaries that enable price and

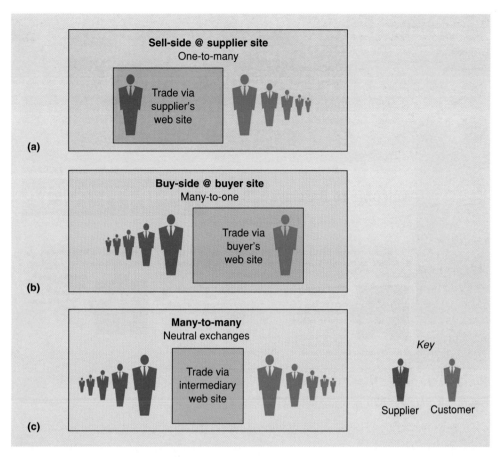

Figure 2.7 Different types of online trading location

product comparison. For B2B they are referred to as *trading exchanges*, *marketplaces* or *hubs*. These may be created by independent companies. Examples of independent exchanges are Vertical Net (www.vertical.net) which offers vertical or industry-specific marketplaces and CommerceOne Marketsite (www.commerceone.com) which is a horizontal exchange that operates across different types of marketplace. Increasingly, a consortium of companies in an industry will be involved, for example Ford and General Motors formed Covisint (www.covisint.net). An example of such a hub is shown in Figure 2.8.

● Commercial arrangement for transactions

Markets can also be considered from another perspective – that of the type of commercial arrangement that is used to agree a sale and price between the buyer and supplier. This can be considered a macro-economic factor, but it is pertinent to consideration of marketplace factors. The main alternative commercial arrangements are shown in Table 2.3.

It can be seen from Table 2.3 that each of these commercial arrangements is similar to a traditional arrangement. Although the mechanism cannot be considered to have changed, the relative importance of these different options has changed with the Internet. Owing to the ability to rapidly publish new offers and prices, auction has become an important means of selling on the Internet. A turnover of several billion dollars has been achieved by eBay from consumers offering items from cars

Figure 2.8 Barclays B2B (www.barclaysb2b.com)

Table 2.3 Commercial mechanisms and online transactions

Commercial (trading) mechanism	Online transaction mechanism of Nunes et al. (2000)
1 Negotiated deal Example: can use similar mechanism to auction as on Commerce One (www.commerceone.net)	● Negotiation – bargaining between single seller and buyer ● Continuous replenishment – ongoing fulfilment of orders under preset terms
2 Brokered deal Example: intermediaries such as Screentrade (www.screentrade.co.uk)	● Achieved through online intermediaries offering auction and pure markets online
3 Auction C2C: eBay (www.ebay.com) B2B: Industry to industry (www.itoi.com)	● Seller auction – buyers' bids determine final price of sellers' offerings ● Buyer auction – buyers request prices from multiple sellers ● Reverse – buyer posts desired price for seller acceptance
4 Fixed price sale Example: All e-tailers.	● Static call – online catalogue with fixed prices ● Dynamic call – online catalogue with continuously updated prices and features
5 Pure markets Example: Electronic share dealing	● Spot – buyers' and sellers' bids clear instantly
6 Barter Example: www.bartertrust.com	● Barter – buyer and seller exchange goods

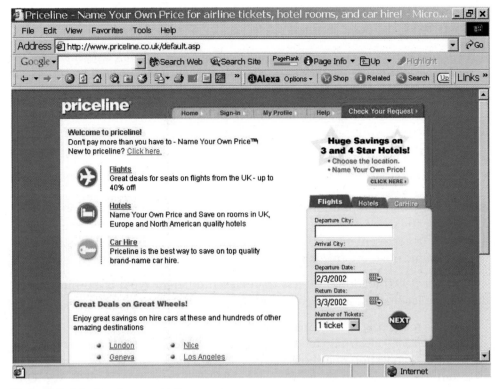

Figure 2.9 Priceline (www.priceline.com)

to antiques. Many airlines have successfully trialled auctions to sell seats remaining on an aircraft just before a flight, and this has led to the site www.lastminute.com which can broker or link to such offers.

An example of a completely new commercial mechanism that has been made possible through the web is provided by Priceline (Figure 2.9). This can be characterised as a 'name your price' site. Here, users enter the price they wish to pay together with their credit card details. If retailers can match the price, the deal will go ahead. This business model has been successful in the USA where the user base in 2000 numbered more than 5 million. Profitability was forecast for 2001. When it was launched in Europe, there would be four core services: travel, hotels, telecoms and car rentals, and Priceline faced a major challenge in that, not only was it a new method of purchasing for European consumers, but the Priceline brand was unknown. The difficulty is that consumers have to enter their credit card details, even if they don't know who they are purchasing from. This is a similar situation to LetsBuyit! (www.letsbuyit.com) which had to present the concept of aggregated buying to consumers.

● Business models in e-commerce

A consideration of the different business models made available through e-commerce is of particular importance to both existing and start-up companies. Venkatraman (2000) points out that existing businesses need to use the Internet to build on current business models while at the same time experimenting with new business models. New business models may be important to gain a competitive advantage over existing competitors and at the same time head off similar business models created by new entrants. For start-ups or dot-coms the viability of a business model

Business model

A summary of how a company will generate revenue identifying its product offering, value-added services, revenue sources and target customers.

will be crucial to funding from venture capitalists. But what is a business model? Timmers (1999) defines a 'business model' as:

> *An architecture for product, service and information flows, including a description of the various business actors and their roles; and a description of the potential benefits for the various business actors; and a description of the sources of revenue.*

It can be suggested that a business model for e-commerce requires consideration of the marketplace from several different perspectives:

- Does the company operate in the B2B or B2C arena, or a combination?
- How is the company positioned in the value chain between customers and suppliers?
- What is its value proposition and for which target customers?
- What are the specific revenue models that will generate different income streams?
- What is its representation in the physical and virtual world, i.e. high-street presence, online only, intermediary, mixture?

Timmers (1999) identifies no less than eleven different types of business model that can be facilitated by the web as follows:

1 *e-shop* – marketing of a company or shop via web;
2 *e-procurement* – electronic tendering and procurement of goods and services;
3 *e-malls* – a collection of e-shops such as BarclaySquare (www.barclays-square.com);
4 *e-auctions* – these can be for B2C, e.g. eBay (www.ebay.com) or B2B, e.g. QXL (www.qxl.com);
5 *virtual communities* – these can be B2C communities such as Xoom (www.xoom.com) or B2B communities such as Clearlybusiness (www.clearlybusiness.com/community) which are both important for their potential in e-marketing and are described in the virtual communities section in Chapter 6 (p. 244);
6 *collaboration platforms* – these enable collaboration between businesses or individuals, e.g. E-groups (www.egroups.com), now part of Yahoo! (www.yahoo.com) services;
7 *third-party marketplaces* – marketplaces are intermediaries that facilitate online trading by putting buyers and sellers in contact. They are sometimes also referred to as 'exchanges' or 'hubs';
8 *value-chain integrators* – offer a range of services across the value chain;
9 *value-chain service providers* – specialise in providing functions for a specific part of the value chain such as the logistics company UPS (www.ups.com);
10 *information brokerage* – providing information for consumers and businesses, often to assist in making the buying decision or for business operations or leisure;
11 *trust and other services* – examples of trust services include Which Web Trader (www.which.net/webtrader) or Truste (www.truste.org) which authenticate the quality of service provided by companies trading on the web.

Figure 2.10 suggests a different perspective for reviewing alternative business models. There are three different perspectives from which a business model can be viewed. Any individual organisation can operate in different categories, as the examples below show, but most will focus on a single category for each perspective. Such a categorisation of business models can be used as a tool for formulating e-business strategy. The three perspectives, with examples are:

1 *Marketplace position perspective*. The book publisher is the manufacturer, Amazon is a retailer and Yahoo! is both a retailer and a marketplace intermediary.

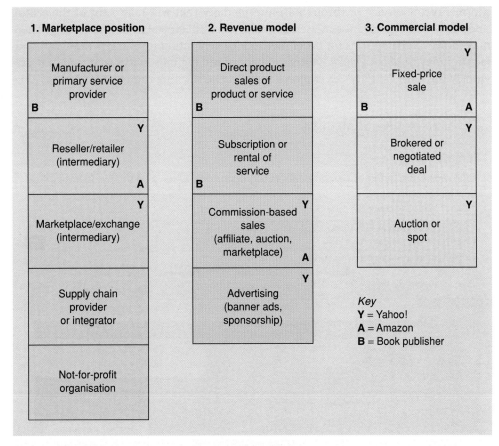

Figure 2.10 Alternative perspectives on business models

2 *Revenue model perspective.* The book publisher can use the web to sell direct and Yahoo! and Amazon can take commission-based sales. Yahoo! also has advertising as a revenue model.

3 *Commercial arrangement perspective.* All three companies offer fixed-price sales, but in its place as a marketplace intermediary, Yahoo! also offers other alternatives.

Michael Porter (2001) urges caution against overemphasis on new business or revenue models and attacks those who have suggested that the Internet invalidates his well-known strategy models. He says:

Many have assumed that the Internet changes everything, rendering all the old rules about companies and competition obsolete. That may be a natural reaction, but it is a dangerous one . . . decisions that have eroded the attractiveness of their industries and undermined their own competitive advantages.

He gives the example of some industries using the Internet to change the basis of competition away from quality, features and service and towards price, making it harder for anyone in their industries to turn a profit.

● Revenue models

Revenue models specifically describe different techniques for generation of income. For existing companies, revenue models have been based upon the income from sales of products or services. This may be either for selling direct from the manufacturer or

Revenue models
Describe methods of generating income for an organisation.

supplier of the service or through an intermediary that will take a cut of the selling price. Both of these revenue models are, of course, still crucial in online trading. There may, however, be options for other methods of generating revenue: perhaps a manufacturer may be able to sell advertising space or sell digital services that were not previously possible. Activity 2.2 explores some of the revenue models that are possible.

Activity 2.2

Revenue models at Mondus

Purpose

To illustrate the range of revenue generating opportunities for a company operating as an Internet pure-play.

Figure 2.11 Mondus (www.mondus.de)

Mondus (www.mondus.com) is a business-to-business intermediary that has operated in Europe since 1999. It has separate sites for each of the markets it serves: UK, Germany, France and Italy. It provides a service to meet the purchasing needs of small and medium-sized businesses ranging from desktop PCs and print services to office equipment and web site design.

Mondus was founded in April 1999 by Oxford University Rhodes Scholars Rouzbeh Pirouz, CEO, and Alexander Straub. The concept behind Mondus was realised after winning the *Sunday Times* and 3i 1999 Technology Catapult Competition, for which they received $1.7 million in funding. Since then the company has grown exponentially with over 170 000 registered businesses, with operations across Europe.

Activity

Visit one of the Mondus sites such as www.mondus.co.uk and explore the different facilities on the site for revenue generation.

Organisational characteristics and capabilities

A review of the characteristics and capabilities of an organisation to make increased use of electronic communications should occur as part of developing Internet marketing plans. Typical organisational factors and questions to be considered are highlighted by the 7S framework which was developed by consultants at McKinsey at the start of the 1980s:

- *Strategy* – approaches to achieve organisational objectives.
- *Structure* – How will the introduction of Internet marketing and other aspects of e-business change be managed? Is the current structure adequate or is a separate department or division required or can the change be matrix-managed?
- *Systems* – Do new operating procedures or business processes need to be introduced? Can existing information systems be used to implement change or will new systems be required?
- *Style* – Is the current style and culture of a company consistent with the way the company wants to project its image? Perhaps an organisation is traditionally conservative in its approach to change. Will decisions be made fast enough? Will risks be taken to trial new business models and new technology?
- *Staff* – Is the appropriate mix of staff available?
- *Skills* – Are the correct skills available internally? What training is required? Do they need to outsource some services?
- *Superordinate goals* – This refers to the higher goals of the company which may be encapsulated in its mission statement. In modern parlance, do the senior managers 'get' the significance of the Internet and will they act?

The role of internal audits to assess the organisation is discussed further in Chapter 4.

Customers

It is essential for Internet marketing and e-marketing managers to understand the different factors that affect how many people actively use the Internet. If these are understood for customers in a target market, action can be taken to overcome some of these barriers. For example, marketing communications can be used to explain the value proposition (see Chapter 5) and reduce fears of complexity and security. Surveys indicate that that the following factors are important in governing adoption:

1 *Cost of access*. This is certainly a barrier for those who do not already own a home computer – a major expenditure for many households. The other main costs are the cost of using an ISP to connect to the Internet and the cost of using the media to connect (telephone or cable charges). Free access will certainly increase adoption and usage.
2 *Value proposition*. Customers need to perceive a need to be online – what can the Internet offer that other media cannot? Examples of value proposition include access to more supplier information and possibly lower prices. In 2000, company advertisements started to refer to 'Internet prices'.
3 *Ease of use*. This includes the ease of first connecting to the Internet using the ISP and the ease of using the web once connected.
4 *Security*. While this is only, in reality, a problem for those who shop online, the perception generated by news stories may be that if you are connected to the Internet then your personal details and credit card details may not be secure. It

will probably take many years for this fear to diminish as using the Internet slowly becomes established as a standard way of purchasing goods.

5 *Fear of the unknown*. Many will simply have a general fear of the technology and the new media which is not surprising since much of the news about the Internet non-adopters will have heard will concern pornography, fraud and privacy infringements.

● Assessing demand for e-commerce services

To set realistic strategic objectives such as online revenue contributions for digital channels (as described in Chapter 4), e-marketing managers need to assess the level of customer access and activity for different markets. For each customer segment and for each digital channel such as Internet, interactive digital TV or mobile we need to know the proportion of customers who:

1 have access to the channel;
2 are influenced by using the channel;
3 purchase using the channel.

This can be simplified to the ratios: 'Access : Choose : Buy'. This information can be gathered as secondary research by the researcher by accessing the many online data sources. Primary research can be used to better understand these characteristics in the target market. We will now review each of these three factors that affect demand for e-commerce services, starting with consumers in the B2C marketplace.

1 Internet access

E-commerce provides a global marketplace, and this means we must review access and usage of the Internet channel at many different geographic levels: worldwide and between and within continents and countries.

On a worldwide basis, a relatively small proportion of the population has access to the Internet. Figure 2.12 shows that despite rapid growth from the mid-1990s to about 400 million users by the start of 2001 this only represents less than 10% of the population. This level of access will be determined by the five factors governing adoption listed above, but clearly the cost of arranging access will be the major factor explaining the overall proportion of access.

Analyst reports on Internet access and usage

At the global level, despite the rapid growth from the mid-1990s to about 445 million users by the end of 2001, this only represents less than 10% of the world population (http://cyberatlas.internet.com/big_picture/stats_toolbox/article), but current forecasts from the International Data Corporation (www.idc.com) suggest numbers will grow to one billion by 2005. But don't you think it's amazing that the Internet media have reached this many people so rapidly? No other media have grown this fast. Furthermore, no medium has ever replaced another – radio did not replace print, the TV did not replace the radio, and likewise the Internet will complement traditional media. But the Internet has reduced consumption of other media.

The two best places to find up-to-the minute analyst data about access and usage of the Internet are Nua (www.nua.ie/surveys) and Cyberatlas (www.cyberatlas.com), both of which provide searchable archives of research reports from different analysts.

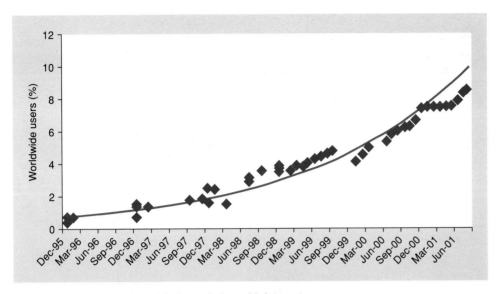

Figure 2.12 Percentage of global population with Internet access

(based on Nua and Cyberatlas compilations at www.nua.ie/surveys and www.cyberatlas.com)

If we look at individual countries, the proportion of consumers and businesses accessing the Internet is startling. If we take the United Kingdom, the quarterly government Internet reports (National Statistics, 2001) show that 51% of consumers have accessed the Internet, with 41% having accessed it in the last month, with twice as many accessing from home rather than work. For younger age groups such as 16–24-year-olds, the figure stands at 88%. As this cohort ages, clearly the overall numbers accessing the Internet will increase. There is evidence, however, that growth will plateau in most countries since there is a significant majority of the population who do not wish to or cannot afford to access the Internet.

To look at the scale of variation between different continents complete Activity 2.3.

Other digital access platforms

Although we focus on Internet usage in this book, technology offerings for consumers are in constant flux, so e-marketers need to assess how well new technologies fulfil their objectives. Already interactive digital TV and mobile Internet access are used by more people than the web (Figure 2.14). These technologies are studied in more detail in Chapter 3.

Demographic variations

Within each country, adoption of the Internet also varies significantly according to individual **demographic characteristics** such as sex, age and social class or income. This analysis is important as part of the segmentation of different groups within a target market. Since these factors will vary throughout each country there will also be regional differences. Access is usually much higher in capital cities.

From Activity 2.4 it can be seen that the stereotype of the typical Internet user as male, around 30 years of age and with high disposable income no longer holds true. Many females and more senior 'silver surfers' are also active.

Demographic characteristics

Variations in attributes of the populations such as age, sex and social class.

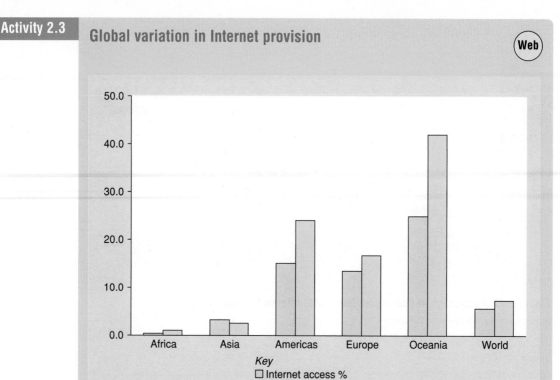

Activity 2.3

Global variation in Internet provision

Web

Key
☐ Internet access %
☐ PCs per 100 population

Figure 2.13 Global variation in number of PCs per hundred population and percent Internet access in 2000
Source: ITU (www.itu.int)

Visit the web site of the International Telecommunications Union (ITU) (www.itu.int/ti/industryoverview/index.htm). Choose Internet indicators. This presents data on Internet and PC penetration in over 200 countries. A summary of the indicators for different continents is presented in Figure 2.13.

Questions

1 Find your country and compare the number of PCs per hundred population and percentage Internet access compared with other countries in your region and on a global basis.
2 Now attempt to explain reasons for the disparity between your country and other countries.
3 Can you see your country equalling or exceeding the USA in terms of these indicators?

Note that PCs are recorded as PCs per hundred population. This figure may be skewed in developed countries by people with more than one PC (e.g. at home and at work).

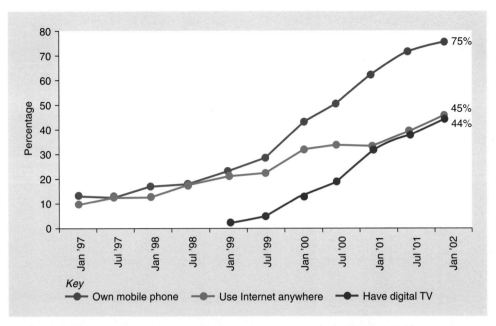

Figure 2.14 UK rate of adoption of different new media, base c. 4000 GB adults aged 15+, December 2001

Source: e MORI Technology Tracker, January 2002. See http://www.e-mori.co.uk/tracker.shtml for details

Activity 2.4

Adoption of the Internet and other new media according to demographic characteristics

(Web)

Purpose

To highlight variation in Internet access according to individual consumer characteristics.

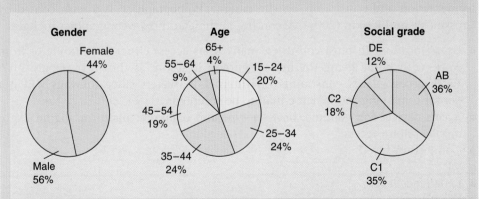

Figure 2.15 Summary of current demographic characteristics of Internet users, base 1673 GB Internet users aged 15+, January 2002

Source: e MORI Technology Tracker, January 2002. See http://www.e-mori.co.uk/tracker.shtml for details

See www.emori.co.uk/tracker.htm for up-to-date data on demographics in the UK.

Activity

1   Refer to Figure 2.15, which is typical for most countries with Internet use at more than 50% of the population. What differences are there in the demographics compared to those for the national population?

▶

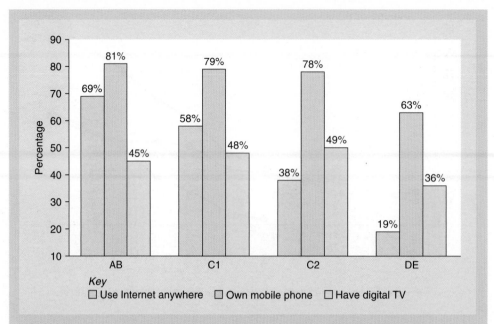

Figure 2.16 Summary of variation in different access to new media according to social group, base 4222 GB adults aged 15+, January 2002

Source: e MORI Technology Tracker, January 2002. See http://www.e-mori.co.uk/tracker.shtml for details

2 Now refer to Figure 2.16. Summarise the variation in different access platforms for digital media across different social groups. Attempt to explain this variation and suggest its implications for marketers.

To fully understand online customer access we also need to consider the user's access location, access device and 'webographics', all of which are significant for segmentation and constraints on site design. 'Webographics' is a term coined by Grossnickle and Raskin (2001). According to these authors webographics includes:

- Usage location. In most countries, many users access either from home or from work, with home being the more common location, as shown by Figure 2.17. Work access places constraints on Internet marketers since firewalls will not permit some plug-ins or rich e-mail to be accepted.
- Access device. For example, browser type and computer platform, digital TV or mobile phone access.
- Connection speed
- ISP
- Experience level
- Usage type
- Usage level

Finally, we must not forget the non-users who comprise more than half of the adult population in many countries. The Consumers' Association Annual Internet survey in July 2001 (Consumers' Association, 2001) states:

It is difficult to see how the Internet will ever be used universally when a substantial proportion of the population have absolutely no desire to gain access to it. 6 in 10 non-users say they will never get connected. This is actually an increase on the figure observed last year (52%) but as the total number of non-users has declined, the proportion of the entire

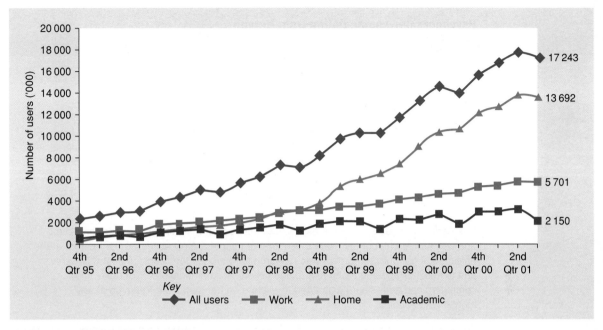

Figure 2.17 Different types of Internet access location
Source: The Internet Monitor, BMRB, www.bmrb.co.uk

GB population who never want access has remained steady at just over a third. It seems as if it will be a real challenge to convince this particularly resistant group of people to convert to Internet users.

Resistance to the Internet increases dramatically with age. 1 in 3 15–34 year olds don't think they will ever connect, compared with just under half of all 35–54s and 85% of over 55s.

What do you think about these non-users? Are you are concerned about the problem of social exclusion? Do you think their minds will change, perhaps in response to government campaigns such as those initiated by the UK government (www.ukonlineforbusiness.gov.uk) or will they gradually be replaced by a more computer-literate generation?

2 Consumers influenced by using the online channel

Next we must look at the extent to which consumers are influenced by online media – a key aspect of buyer behaviour. Although the proportion of e-commerce transactions for all purchases is low, the role of the Internet in influencing purchase is significant for high-involvement purchases such as financial services, holidays or cars. For example, it is now estimated that over half the purchasers of new cars in some Western countries will research the purchase online even though the proportion purchasing entirely online is only in single figures. Understanding the reach of a web site and its role in influencing purchase is clearly important in setting e-marketing budgets.

As we have seen in finding information about goods and services is a popular online activity, but each organisation needs to capture data about online influence in the buying process for their own market.

To help them better understand their customers, marketers develop **psychographic segmentations**. Specialised psychodemographic profiles have been developed for web users, for example see Bickerton et al. (2000). See the box 'Psychographic segmentation from Netpoll' for an example of this type of segmentation. Which profile do you fit?

Psychographic segmentation

A breakdown of customers according to different characteristics.

Psychographic segmentation from Netpoll

The GameBoy aged 15 – still at school and living at home – accesses the Internet mainly at home (or at his mates' homes) – or sometimes at school/college or at a cybercafé. Into playing online games and getting into role-playing (in MUDs – multiple user dungeons) – thinks he is pretty net savvy and pretty hip. Other interests include football (could have a 'chelsea.co.uk' email address).

The CyberLad aged 23 – basically 'loaded man' online – accesses at work and at home. Bit of a Jack the lad and thinks he knows it all as far as the Net is concerned. He certainly doesn't want anyone telling him how he should use it. Interests include sex and sport, and sport and sex – spends a lot of time online searching for smut and then emailing it to his mates. Probably not the sort of bloke you'd want to run into after closing time on a Friday night.

The CyberSec aged 31 – works as a p.a. to the boss of a small firm – super-competent and well turned out, but also very much 'one of the girls'. Only accesses the Internet at the office – first got online in order to do research for the boss (on clients, industry news etc.) and to make arrangements for him (plane tickets, accommodation). 'Not really into computers and that' – but has started to explore on her own a bit. Perks up at any mention of shopping.

The InfoJunky aged 40 (could be either male or female), married with two children – possibly a middle-rank civil servant or a partner at a small firm of solicitors. Probably inclined to wear tweed jackets and hush puppies. Likes the feeling of being in touch and in control that the Internet gives him. He is under the impression that the time he spends online is a big benefit to his job, but given that he gets side-tracked so much, this is very debatable. Reads too many newspapers and magazines.

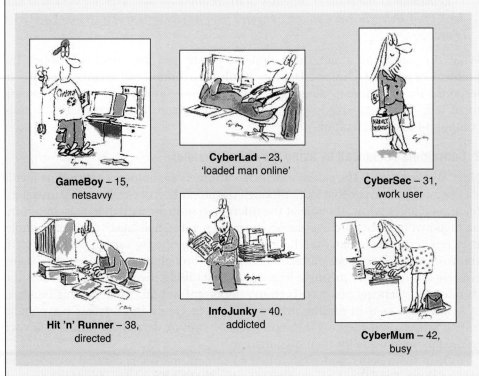

GameBoy – 15, netsavvy

CyberLad – 23, 'loaded man online'

CyberSec – 31, work user

Hit 'n' Runner – 38, directed

InfoJunky – 40, addicted

CyberMum – 42, busy

Figure 2.18 Psychographic segmentation for Web users

Source: Netpoll (www.netpoll.net)

The Hit 'n' Runner aged 38 (could be either male or female), successful professional or a high flying marketing exec. Both seriously career-minded, she and her partner aren't sure if they're going to get round to having kids. Accesses the Internet at work and certainly doesn't see the Net as any form of entertainment but as a way of accessing information. Very impatient if she can't find what she wants or if the site is slow to download. She banks online and manages her portfolio, and is also researching that holiday she never gets the time to take.

The CyberMum aged 42 – married with three kids, aged 17, 14 and 8, and works in a 'caring' profession. Slightly overweight and can't keep to her diet – but other things are more import-ant to her. Her husband thought it would be a good idea if they got online when he started spending one week in four at company HQ in Holland, so that they could exchange email messages. She really likes email and uses it to keep in touch with her sister in Australia. The kids seem to spend so much time on the Internet, but she can't see what all the fuss is about – she'd rather read a magazine, if she ever got the time. Having said that, she would like to be able to shop online – if only she knew how it worked.

3 Purchased online

Customers will only purchase products online that meet the criteria of the Electronic Shopping Test. The propensity to purchase online is dependent on different vari-ables over which the marketer has relatively little control. However, factors that affect the propensity to purchase can be estimated for different types of products. De Kare-Silver (2000) suggests factors that should be considered include product characteristics, familiarity and confidence, and consumer attributes. Typical results from the evaluation are: Groceries (27/50), Mortgages (15/50), Travel (31/50) and books (38/50). De Kare-Silver states that any product scoring over 20 has good poten-tial, since the score for consumer attributes is likely to increase through time. Given this, he suggests companies will regularly need to review the score for their products. The effectiveness of this test is now demonstrated by data for online purchases in different product categories (Figure 2.19).

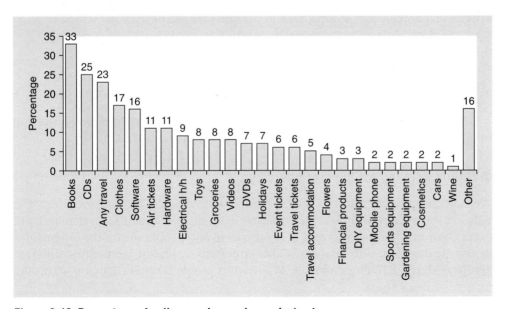

Figure 2.19 Percentage of online purchasers by product category

Note: There are 9.9 million online shoppers (54% of Internet users aged 15+)

Source: The Internet Monitor, BMRB, November 2001 (www.bmrb.co.uk)

The Electronic Shopping or ES test

The ES test was developed by de Kare-Silver (2000) to assess the extent to which consumers are likely to purchase a retail product using the Internet. De Kare-Silver suggests factors that should be considered in the ES test:

1 *Product characteristics.* Does the product need to be physically tried, or touched, before it is bought?
2 *Familiarity and confidence.* Considers the degree to which the consumer recognises and trusts the product and brand.
3 *Consumer attributes.* These shape the buyer's behaviour – is he or she amenable to online purchases (i.e. in terms of access to the technology and skills available) and does he or she no longer wish to shop for a product in a traditional retail environment? For example, a student familiar with technology may buy a CD online because they are comfortable with the technology. An elderly person looking for a classical CD would probably not have access to the technology and might prefer to purchase the item in person.

In his book, de Kare-Silver describes a method for ranking products. Product characteristics and familiarity and confidence are marked out of 10, and consumer attributes are marked out of 30. Using this method, he scores products as shown in Table 2.4.

Table 2.4 Product scores in de Kare-Silver's (2000) Electronic Shopping (ES) potential test

Product	Product characteristics (10)	Familiarity and confidence (10)	Consumer attributes (30)	Total
1. Groceries	4	8	15	27
2. Mortgages	10	1	4	15
3. Travel	10	6	15	31
4. Books	8	7	23	38

De Kare-Silver states that any product scoring over 20 has good potential, since the score for consumer attributes is likely to increase through time. Given this, he suggests companies will regularly need to review the score for their products.

Understanding of customer buyer behaviour is important to designing a site and other communications. Variations in behaviour are discussed in Chapter 7.

● Online demand for business services

We now turn our attention to how we profile online access for business users. The B2B market is more complex than that for B2C in that variation in demand will occur according to different types of organisation and people within the buying unit in the organisation. This analysis is also important as part of segmenting different groups within a B2B target market. We need to profile business demand according to:

Variation in organisation characteristics
- size of company (employees or turnover)
- industry sector and products

- organisation type (private, public, government, not-for-profit)
- division?
- country and region

Individual role
- role and responsibility from job title, function or number of staff managed
- role in buying decision (purchasing influence)
- department
- product interest
- demographics: age, sex and possibly social group

For generating demand estimates, we can also profile business users of the Internet in a similar way to consumers by assessing the following three factors.

1 The percentage of companies with access

In the business-to-business market, Internet access levels are higher than for business-to-consumer. The DTI International Benchmarking Study for 2001 (DTI, 2001) shows that with Sweden, the UK has the highest proportion of businesses (87%) that are connected. This is just ahead of Germany (86%), the USA (84%) and Canada (82%). However, this figure masks lower levels of access for SMEs (small and medium-sized enterprises). Understanding access for different members of the organisational buying unit amongst their customers is also important for marketers. In most developed countries, more than three-quarters of businesses, regardless of size, have Internet access, suggesting that the Internet is very effective in terms of reaching companies (see Figure 2.20).

Although the Internet seems to be used by many companies we also need to ask whether it reaches the right people in the buying unit. The answer is 'not necessarily' – access is not available to all employees. Although over three-quarters of businesses have access, DTI (2000) data show that access is usually available to less than 50% of employees. For example, restricting access to a single PC in a department is common practice.

2 Influenced online

For B2B, there appears to be less use of the Internet for identifying suppliers and gathering pre-purchase information (Figure 2.21). DTI (2001) reports that in Europe this figure lies between 24% and 39%, but with a higher proportion of businesses in the USA and Canada (53%).

Figure 2.21 indicates that for many companies the Internet is important in identifying online suppliers, with the majority identifying some suppliers online, especially in the larger companies.

3 Purchase online

In terms of access device and purchase method, e-mail and the Web are widely used for online purchases, with extranets and EDI less important since these are the preserve of larger companies.

The data suggest that business users are less active in purchasing online than are consumers. The DTI (2001) survey reveals that while there has been an increase in the proportion of businesses that enable their customers to order (from 27% to 29%) or pay (from 13% to 16%) online, this is offset by a drop in the proportion that use these facilities to order (from 45% to 31%) or pay for (from 28% to 15%) goods or

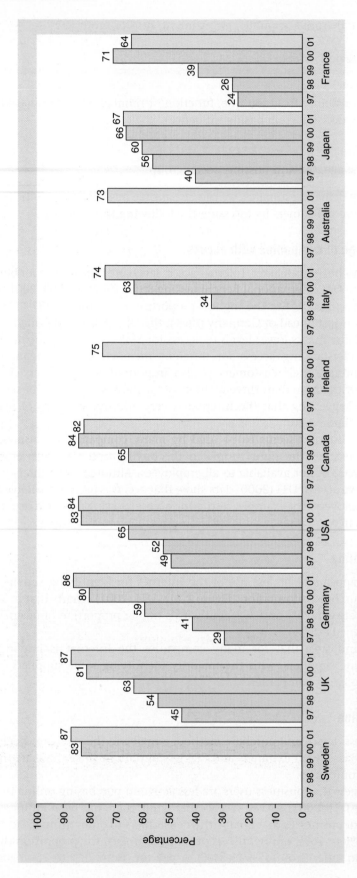

Figure 2.20 Percentage of businesses with Internet access

Note that results are weighted by business size and that some countries are included for different years

Source: DTI, 2001

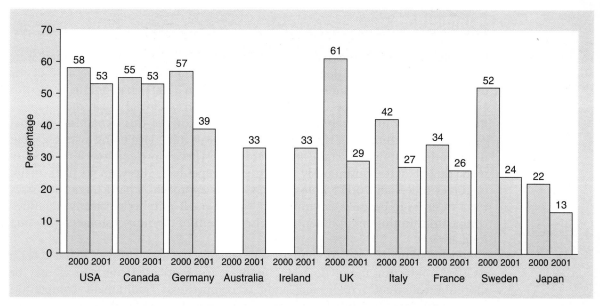

Figure 2.21 Percentage of businesses that identify suppliers online by business size
Source: DTI, 2001

services from their suppliers. Payment online tends to be lower still. A reduction in those using online marketplaces for purchase is also apparent. This suggests that many businesses have experimented with using the Internet for procurement, but seem not to have been convinced by the benefits or have not enjoyed a positive experience. However, those businesses that do seem convinced by the benefits and experience are ordering more online. The same survey showed that all countries have seen significant growth in the proportion of businesses that use online ordering to order more than 20% of the total value of their purchases. In the UK, Italy and France, the proportion tripled.

When the first edition of this book was written in 1999, it was forecast that B2B commerce would dwarf B2C commerce by ten times or more, which is consistent with commerce in the offline world. In 2001, B2B revenue is estimated to be about four to five times B2C (IDC, 2002). This suggests that organisational issues with implementing B2B e-commerce such as integration with legacy systems or human resistance to change may have restricted its adoption.

In summary, to estimate online revenue contribution to determine the amount of investment in e-business we need to research the number of connected customers, the percentage whose offline purchase is influenced online and the number who buy online.

Suppliers

The most significant aspect of monitoring suppliers is with respect to the effect suppliers have on the value of quality of product or service delivered to the end customer. Key issues include the effect of suppliers on product price, availability and features. This topic is not discussed further since it is less significant than other factors in an Internet marketing context.

Competitors

Competitor analysis

Review of Internet marketing services offered by existing and new competitors and adoption by their customers.

Competitor analysis or the monitoring of competitor use of Internet marketing for acquisition and retention of customers is especially important because of the dynamic nature of the Internet medium. As Porter (2001) has pointed out, this enables new services to be launched and promotions changed much more rapidly than through print communications. The implications of this dynamism are that competitor benchmarking is not a one-off activity while developing a strategy, but needs to be continuous. Train manufacturer ADTRanz now employs a member of marketing staff to continuously scan their competitors' sites and to track major customer orders and other industry news. This approach is particularly necessary for a business-to-business environment with a small number of clearly identified competitors. In this environment, it is also prudent to monitor customers' web sites frequently.

Benchmarking is used to compare e-commerce services within a market. For a retailer, conducting a benchmarking audit of Internet-based competitors may be more difficult than a traditional audit of competitors. Traditionally competitors will be well known. With the Internet and the global marketplace there may be new entrants that have the potential to achieve significant market share. This is particularly the case with retail sales. For example, successful new companies have developed on the Internet who sell books, music, CDs and electronic components. As a consequence, companies need to review the Internet-based performance of both existing and new players. Companies should review:

- well-known local competitors (for example, UK or European competitors for British companies);
- well-known international competitors;
- new Internet companies local and worldwide (within sector and out of sector).

Chase (1998) advocates that when benchmarking, companies should review competitors' sites, identifying best practices, worst practices and 'next practices'. Next practices are where a company looks beyond their industry sector at what leading Internet companies such as Amazon (www.amazon.com) and Cisco (www.cisco.com) are doing. For instance, a company in the financial services industry could look at what portal sites are providing and see if there are any lessons to be learnt on ways to make information provision easier. When undertaking scanning of competitor sites, the key differences that should be watched out for are:

- new approaches from existing companies;
- new companies starting on the Internet;
- new technologies, design techniques and customer support on the site which may give a competitive advantage.

Deise et al. (2000) suggest an equation that can be used in combination to assess competition when benchmarking:

$$\text{Competitive capability} = \frac{\text{Agility} \times \text{Reach}}{\text{Time-to-market}}$$

'Agility' refers to the speed at which a company is able to change strategic direction and respond to new customer demands. 'Reach' is the ability to connect to, or to promote products and generate new business in new markets. 'Time to market' is the

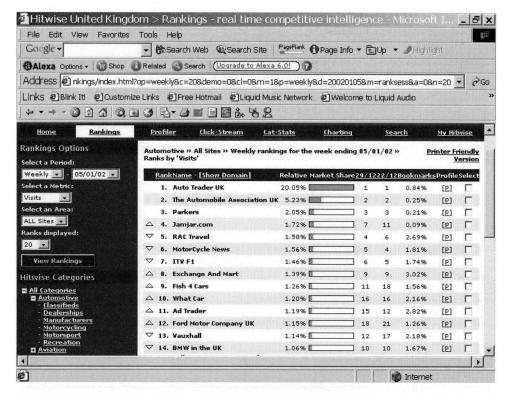

Figure 2.22 Hitwise rankings for the travel industry in the UK (www.hitwise.co.uk)

product lifecycle from concept through to revenue generation. Companies can also turn to benchmarking organisations such as Gomez (www.gomez.com) to review e-commerce scorecards.

Deise et al. (2000) also suggest a further equation that can be used to appraise competitors from their customer's viewpoint. This is

$$\text{Customer value (brand perception)} = \frac{\text{Product quality} \times \text{Service quality}}{\text{Price} \times \text{Fulfilment time}}$$

Some companies such as NSK bearings (www.nsk-rhp.co.uk) ask customers to complete a questionnaire on their site to rank their offering relative to competitors' in these areas of customer value.

To assess the success of competitors in building traffic to their web sites, a variety of data sources can be used; the methods of collection are explained further in Chapter 9.

- Panel data can be used to compare number of visitors to competitor sites through time.
- Summaries of ISP data such as Hitwise (www.hitwise.co.uk) can be used to assess visitor rankings for different competitors (Figure 2.22).
- Audits of web site traffic such as that produced by ABCelectronic (www.abce.org) can be used for basic comparison of visitors.

Now complete Activity 2.5 to gain an appreciation of how this can be approached.

Activity 2.5

Competitor benchmarking

Purpose

To understand the characteristics of competitor web sites it is useful to benchmark and to assess the value of benchmarking.

Activity

Choose for B2C an industry sector such as airlines, book retailers, book publishers, CDs or clothing or for B2B one such as oil companies, chemical companies, construction industry companies or B2B exchanges. Work individually or in groups to identify the type of information that should be available from the web site (and which parts of the site you will access it from) which will be useful in terms of competitor benchmarking. Once your criteria have been developed, you should then benchmark companies and summarise which you feel is making best use of the Internet medium. To assist you in thinking about the factors that should be benchmarked divide them into:

1 those that directly impact the quality or experience of a site visit;
2 those that indicate how effective the site is as a marketing tool.

Intermediaries

Marketing intermediaries

Firms that can help a company to promote, sell and distribute its products or services.

Marketing intermediaries are firms that can help a company to promote, sell and distribute its products or services. In the Internet context, intermediaries are typically independent sites that are used to bring buyers and sellers together. B2B exchanges such as BarclaysB2B (www.barclaysb2b.com) and Mondus (www.mondus.co.uk) are examples of B2B intermediaries. Such sites usually operate via an affiliate arrangement whereby the intermediary receives a commission on each sale resulting from a visit to their site. Bizrate (www.bizrate.com) is a further type of intermediary, in this case bringing consumers together where they can rate different online services.

Sarkar et al. (1996) identify many different types of new intermediaries (mainly from a B2C perspective) which they refer to as 'cybermediaries'. Others have noted that the intermediaries are effectively information brokers. Hagel and Rayport (1997) use the term infomediary specifically to refer to sale of customer information.

Some of the main new intermediaries identified by Sarkar et al. (1996) are:

Infomediary

A business whose main source of revenue derives from capturing consumer information and developing detailed profiles of individual customers for use by third parties.

- directories (such as Yahoo!, Excite);
- search engines (Altavista, Infoseek);
- malls (BarclaySquare, Buckingham Gate);
- virtual resellers (own inventory and sell direct, e.g. Amazon, CDNow);
- financial intermediaries (offering digital cash and cheque payment services such as Digicash);
- forums, fan clubs and user groups (referred to collectively as 'virtual communities');
- evaluators (sites that act as reviewers or for comparison of services).

Activity 2.6 highlights the alternative revenue models available to these new intermediaries, in this case an evaluator, and speculates on their future.

Kelkoo.com, an example of revenue models for new intermediaries

 Web

Purpose

To provide an example of the services provided by cybermediaries and explore their viability as businesses.

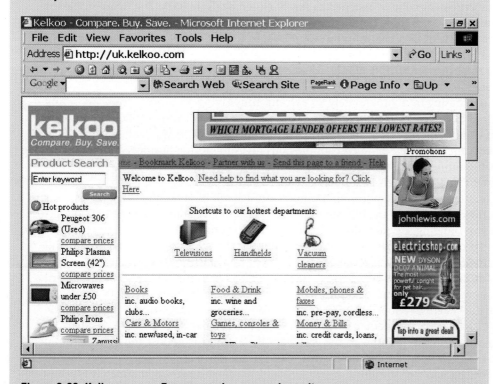

Figure 2.23 Kelkoo.com, a European price comparison site

Questions

1 Visit the Kelkoo web site (www.kelkoo.com) and search for this book, a CD or anything else you fancy. Explain the service that is being offered to customers.

2 Write down the different revenue opportunities for this site (some may be evident from the site, but others may not); write down your ideas also.

3 Given that there are other competing sites in this intermediary category such as Shopsmart (www.shopsmart.com), assess the future of this online business using press releases and comments from other sites such as Moreover (www.moreover.com).

A further type of intermediary is the *virtual marketplace* or virtual trading community. These are of vital importance in the B2B marketplace. From the supplier's or manufacturer's perspective they provide a new channel for selling their products. If the marketplace is set up by major players in an industry such as the Covisint marketplace created by Ford, GM and DaimlerChrysler (www.covisint.com) it will probably be essential to trade with key customers via this method, since this will be a prerequisite for trading with the customer. However, where suppliers are stronger they may collaborate and refuse to take part in such auctions. From the viewpoint of the B2B customer procuring supplies, the virtual marketplace offers the opportunity for lower prices as pricing becomes more transparent, giving rise to greater price competition.

DaimlerChrysler use Covisint intermediary

In the 512 online bidding events processed through Covisint in the last twelve months, DaimlerChrysler AG grossed a purchasing volume of approximately €10 billion. That is a third of the total procurement volume assigned in newly closed deals in 2001. The figure surpassed planned estimates. In May 2001, DaimlerChrysler staged the largest online bidding event ever, with an order volume of €3.5 billion in just four days. In total, 43 percent of the total value of the parts for a future Chrysler model series was negotiated online with over 50 online bidding events in the third quarter of 2001 alone.

Above savings in material purchasing prices, DaimlerChrysler succeeded in reducing throughput times in purchasing by approximately 80 percent, thus saving on process costs. According to Dr Rüdiger Grube, Deputy Member of the Board of Management responsible for corporate development, 'the economic effects achieved with e-Procurement in the first year of implementation have already covered the costs of previous investment in e-Business and hold great potential for the future, too. Therefore, we will continue to pursue our e-Business activities to the fullest extent in 2002 as well.'

With the online catalog system 'eShop' DaimlerChrysler will be able to reduce process costs by 50% after the completion of the blanket rollout, which will give approximately 15 000 users the possibility of ordering several millions of articles. By the end of 2002 about 1500 business partners will be connected to the electronic document exchange system 'eDocs', which will enable them to process approximately 500 000 document transmissions per year. Initital results using the 'FastCar' program for networking change management in automotive development at Chrysler show cuts in communication processes by 60–90%. In 2001, over 600 managers connected to the system developed over 300 product improvement suggestions online with the 'New Product Change Management' used in the development department of Mercedes-Benz. In the meantime the Internet website of the Mercedes-Benz brand is almost fully standardized (www.mercedes-benz.com) in 50 countries with over 20 million page impressions per month worldwide. The German web site alone (www.mercedes-benz.de) registers approximately 800 000 visitors and 40 000 new vehicles configurations per month. The number of monthly visitors of the Chrysler, Jeep and Dodge web sites rose from 1.5 million in December 2000 to 2.5 million. Chrysler, Jeep and Dodge dealers receive on average of 60 000 qualified online customer inquiries per month through the 'Get-a-quote' configurator.

'e-Business activities are already closely intertwined from development through procurement, logistics, sales and marketing. To a great extent, they are already a part of everyday business', says Olaf Koch, Vice President of Corporate e-Business. Dr Grube: 'We're a good deal closer to our goal of making DaimlerChrysler the first automotive company to be networked throughout the entire value chain'.

For the quality assurance of parts and components on vehicles, DaimlerChrysler is currently implementing a new web-enabled advanced quality planning tool that was created by the software vendor Powerway. This new quality management system offers real-time tracking of specific party quality measurements, making the information visible to both DaimlerChrysler and its suppliers. The solution accelerates the quality process right through to the release of parts and increases efficiency levels in quality assurance by 50%. Covisint is developing a worldwide industrial portal for DaimlerChrysler on the basis of industry standards to ensure an Internet-aided standard method of binding suppliers to all areas of the company – from development through logistics. External suppliers will profit just as well as DaimlerChrysler: the supplier portal will do away with the current time-consuming and costly parallel operation of different interfaces and applications.

Source: Covisint press release, 4 February 2002 (www.covisint.com)

Table 2.5 The most visited sites in the UK

Property	Unique audience	Reach %	Time per person
1. MSN	7 983 985	47.95	0: 35: 45
2. Yahoo!	6 561 773	39.41	0: 37: 28
3. AOL Time Warner	5 800 518	34.84	0: 18: 04
4. Microsoft	5 027 384	30.20	0: 09: 44
5. Google	4 524 311	27.17	0: 15: 23
6. Wanadoo	4 522 450	27.16	0: 15: 19
7. Ask Jeeves	3 961 822	23.80	0: 10: 49
8. British Telecom	3 905 792	23.46	0: 15: 20
9. Lycos Network	3 583 862	21.53	0: 10: 17
10. BBC	3 443 794	20.68	0: 17: 21

(Web update: www.nielsen-netratings.com)

At the time that Sarkar et al. (1996) listed the different types of cybermediaries listed above, there were many separate web sites offering these types of services. For example, Altavista (www.altavista.com) offered **search engine** facilities and Yahoo! (www.yahoo.com) offered a **directory** of different web sites. Since this time, such sites have diversified the services offered. Altavista now also offers a directory obtained from the Open Directory service (www.dmoz.org). Yahoo! now offers a search engine using the Google service (www.google.com). It is apparent that diversification has occurred through the introduction of new intermediaries that provide services to other intermediaries and also through acquisition and merger. How search engines are used for Internet marketing communications is described further in Chapter 8.

The concept of the **portal** has evolved to reflect the range of services offered by some cybermediaries. The term 'portal' originated with reference to sites that were the default home pages of users. In other words, when users started their web browser, the first page they saw was their personal home page. When users use a newly installed browser it will be set up so that the home page is that of the company that produces it. In the case of Microsoft this is usually www.msn.com (the Microsoft Network) or www.microsoft.com, and for Netscape it is home.netscape.com.

Portals are significant since they are the prime real estate of the Internet. Inspection of the most visited sites in the UK (Table 2.5) show that all of the top ten are portals acting as gateways to information elsewhere on the Internet. Portals are important to companies looking to use banner advertising or sponsorship to promote their products (Chapter 8). Owing to their importance, companies owning web sites have attracted significant investment that has increased or, some would say, over-inflated their stock prices.

Search engines, spiders and robots

Automatic tools known as 'spiders' or 'robots' index registered sites. Users search by typing key-words and are presented with a list of pages.

Directories or catalogues

Structured listings of registered sites in different categories.

Portal

A web site that acts as a gateway to information and services available on the Internet by providing search engines, directories and other services such as personalised news or free e-mail.

Types of portals

Portals vary in scope and in the services they offer, so naturally terms have evolved to describe the different types of portals. It is useful, in particular, for marketers to understand these terms since they act as a checklist that companies are represented on the different types of portals. Table 2.6 shows different types of portals. It is apparent that there is overlap between the different types of portal. Yahoo! for instance, is a horizontal portal since it offers a range of services, but it has also been developed as a geographical portal for different countries and, in the USA, even for different cities.

Table 2.6 Portal characteristics

Type of portal	Characteristics	Example
Access portal	Associated with ISP	Freeserve (www.freeserve.net)
Horizontal or functional portal	Range of services: search engines, directories, news recruitment, personal information management, shopping, etc.	Yahoo! (www.yahoo.com) Excite (www.excite.com) Lycos (www.lycos.com)
Vertical	May cover a single function, e.g. ● news ● industry sector	Moreover (www.moreover.com) Chemdex (www.chemdex.com)
Geographical (region, country, local)	May be: ● horizontal ● vertical	Yahoo! country versions Countyweb (www.countyweb.com)
Marketplace	May be: ● horizontal ● vertical ● geographical	CommerceOne (www.commerceone.com) PlasticsNet (www.plastics.net)
Media type	Voice portal Streaming media portal	

Summary

1 The constantly changing Internet environment should be monitored by all organizations in order to be able to respond to changes in the macro-environment or the immediate marketplace.

2 The Internet has created major changes to the competitive environment. Organisations should deploy tools such as Porter's Five Forces, the value chain and value network models in order to assess possible threats posed by the Internet.

3 The Internet introduces new channel structures. These include *disintermediation* within the marketplace as organisations' channel partners such as wholesalers or retailers are bypassed. Alternatively the Internet can cause *reintermediation* as new intermediaries with a different purpose are formed to help bring buyers and sellers together in a *virtual marketplace* or marketspace. Evaluation of the implications of these changes are important to strategy.

4 Trading in the marketplace can be sell-side (seller-controlled), buy-side (buyer-controlled) or at a neutral marketplace.

5 A business model is a summary of how a company will generate revenue, identifying its product offering, value-added services, revenue sources and target customers. Exploiting the range of business models made available through the Internet is important to both existing companies and start-ups.

6 The Internet may also offer opportunities for new revenue models such as commission on affiliate referrals to other sites or banner advertising.

7 The opportunity for new commercial arrangements for transactions include negotiated deals, brokered deals, auctions, fixed-price sales, and pure spot markets; and barters should also be considered.

8 The usage of the Internet by customers should be carefully assessed to inform demand levels for e-commerce services.

9 Continuous competitive benchmarking should be conducted to compare services.

10 The role of intermediaries in promoting an organisation's services should also be carefully assessed.

EXERCISES

Self-assessment exercises

1 Why is environmental scanning necessary?

2 Summarise how each of the micro-environment factors may directly drive the content and services provided by a web site.

3 What are the main aspects of customer adoption of the Internet that managers should be aware of?

4 What are the main changes to channel structures that are facilitated through the Internet?

5 What are the different elements and different types of business model?

6 How should a marketing manager benchmark the online performance of competitors?

7 Describe two different models of online buyer behaviour.

8 How can the Internet be used to support the different stages of the buying process?

Essay and discussion questions

1 Discuss, using examples, how the Internet may change the five competitive forces of Michael Porter.

2 'Internet access levels will never exceed 50% in most countries.' Discuss.

3 What are the options, for an existing organisation, for using new business models through the Internet?

4 Perform a demand analysis for e-commerce services for a product sector and geographical market of your choice.

5 Perform competitor benchmarking for online services for an organisation of your choice.

6 What are the alternatives for modified channel structures for the Internet? Illustrate through different organisations in different sectors.

Examination questions

1 What options are available to a supplier, currently fulfilling to customers through a reseller, to use the Internet to change this relationship?

2 What types of channel conflicts are caused by the Internet?

3 What are virtual organisations and how can the Internet support them?

4 Name three options for a company's representation on the Internet in different types of marketplace.

5 Explain the term 'virtual value-chain'.

6 What are the three key factors that affect consumer adoption of the Internet?

7 Summarise how the bargaining power of buyers may be changed by the Internet for a commodity product.

8 How can internal value chain be modified when an organisation deploys Internet technologies?

References

Benjamin, R. and Weigand, R. (1995) Electronic markets and virtual value-chains on the information superhighway, *Sloan Management Review*, Winter, 62–72.

Berryman, K., Harrington, L., Layton-Rodin, D. and Rerolle, V. (1998) Electronic commerce: three emerging strategies, *McKinsey Quarterly*, No. 1, 152–9.

Bickerton, P., Bickerton, M. and Pardesi, U. (2000) *CyberMarketing*, 2nd edn. Butterworth Heinemann, Oxford.

BMRB (2001) *Internet monitor, November.* BMRB International, Manchester, UK. Available online at www.bmrb.co.uk.

Chase, L. (1998) *Essential Business Tactics for the Net.* Wiley, New York.

Consumers' Association (2001) Annual UK Internet survey, July. (Available online at www.which.net/surveys/intro.htm)

Deise, M., Nowikow, C., King, P. and Wright, A. (2000) *Executive's Guide to E-Business. From Tactics to Strategy.* Wiley, New York.

de Kare-Silver, M. (2000) *EShock 2000. The Electronic Shopping Revolution: Strategies for Retailers and Manufacturers.* Macmillan, London.

DTI (2000) *Business in the Information Age – International Benchmarking Study 2000.* UK Department of Trade and Industry. Statistics update: available online at: www.ukonlineforbusiness.gov.uk.

DTI (2001) *Business in the Information Age – International Benchmarking Study 2001.* UK Department of Trade and Industry. www.ukonlineforbusiness.gov.uk.

Economist (2000) Enter the ecosystem, *The Economist*, 11 November.

e-MORI (2002) Technology Tracker, January 2002. Available online at: www.e-mori.co.uk/tracker.shtml.

Grossnickle, J. and Raskin, O. (2001) *The Handbook of Online Marketing Research, Knowing Your Customer Using the Net.* McGraw-Hill, New York.

Hagel, J. III and Rayport, J. (1997) The new infomediaries, *McKinsey Quarterly*, No. 4, 54–70.

International Data Corporation (2002) European Internet commerce to surpass $1500 billion by 2005. Press release, 7 January.

Kalakota, R. and Robinson, M. (2000) *E-business. Roadmap for Success.* Addison-Wesley, Reading, MA.

Kotler, P., Armstrong, G., Saunders, J. and Wong, V. (2001) *Principles of Marketing*, 3rd edn. Financial Times/Prentice Hall, Harlow.

National Statistics (2001) Internet access report, 26 September, pp. 1–9, www.statistics.gov.uk.

Nunes, P., Kambil, A. and Wilson, D. (2000) The all in one market, *Harvard Business Review*, May–June, 2–3.

Porter, M. (1980) *Competitive Strategy.* Free Press, New York.

Porter, M. (2001) Strategy and the Internet. *Harvard Business Review*, March, 62–78.

Rayport, J. and Sviokla, J. (1996) Exploiting the virtual value-chain, *McKinsey Quarterly*, No. 1, 20–37.

Sarkar, M., Butler, B. and Steinfield, C. (1996) Intermediaries and cybermediaries. A continuing role for mediating players in the electronic marketplace, *Journal of Computer Mediated Communication*, issue 1.

Timmers, P. (1999) *Electronic Commerce Strategies and Models for Business-to-Business Trading.* Wiley, Chichester.

Venkatraman, N. (2000) Five steps to a dot-com strategy: how to find your footing on the web, *Sloan Management Review*, Spring, 15–28.

Further reading

Dibb, S., Simkin, S., Pride, W. and Ferrel, O. (2001) *Marketing. Concepts and Strategies*, 4th European edn. Houghton Mifflin, New York. *See* Chapter 2, The marketing environment.

Kotler, P., Armstrong, G., Saunders, J. and Wong, V. (2001) *Principles of Marketing*, 3rd European edn. Financial Times/Prentice Hall, Harlow. See Chapter 4, The marketing environment.

Porter, M. (2001) Strategy and the Internet, *Harvard Business Review*, March, 62–78. A retrospective assessment of how the Internet has changed Porter's model, first proposed in the 1980s.

Timmers, P. (1999) *Electronic Commerce Strategies and Models for Business-to-Business Trading.* Wiley, Chichester. Detailed descriptions of different B2B models are available in this book.

Web links

A directory of Internet marketing links, including sources for statistics from the Internet environment, is maintained by Dave Chaffey at www.marketing-online.co.uk.

Digests of reports and surveys concerned with e-commerce

● Nua Strategy (Europe) www.nua.ie/surveys

● Cyberatlas (US) www.cyberatlas.com

● Europeprofile www.europeprofile.com

● Market Research.com www.marketresearch.com

Directories of marketing research companies

● British Market Research Association www.bmra.org.uk

● Market Research Society www.mra.org.uk

● International MR agencies www.greenbook.org

Traditional market research agencies

● MORI www.mori.com, www.e-mori.co.uk

● NOP www.nopres.co.uk

● Nielsen www.nielsen.com

Government sources

● OECD www.oecd.org

● European Government www.europa.eu.int/comm/eurostat

● UK Government www.statistics.gov.uk; www.ukonlineforbusiness.gov.uk

● US Government www.stat-usa.gov

Trade associations for B2B sectors

● Internet Public Library Associations Online www.ipl.org/ref/AON

Chapter 3

The Internet macro-environment

Chapter at a glance

Main topics

Case studies

Links to other chapters

Like the previous chapter, this one provides a foundation for later chapters on Internet marketing strategy and implementation:

Learning objectives

After reading this chapter, the reader should be able to:

● Identify the different elements of the Internet macro-environment that impact on an organisation's Internet marketing strategy and execution

● Assess the impact of legal, moral and ethical constraints and opportunities on an organisation and devise solutions to accommodate them

● Evaluate the significance of other macro factors such as economics, taxation and legal constraints

Questions for marketers

Key questions for marketing managers related to this chapter are:

● Which factors affect the environment for online trading in a country?

● How do I make sure my online marketing is consistent with evolving online culture and ethics?

● How do I assess new technological innovations?

● Which laws am I subject to when trading online?

Introduction

In the last chapter we reviewed the micro-economic factors an organisation must consider in order to assess the impact of the Internet. In this chapter we review the implications of the macro-economic factors. These macro-economic factors have a broad influence and affect all stakeholders in the micro-environment equally. We will review the role of the Internet in shaping these macro-economic factors:

- *Social and ethical factors* – how changes in opinion about the Internet affect Internet marketing. In this section we will review the ethics of Internet usage.
- *Technological factors* – how changes in technology affect Internet marketing. In this section we will discuss how marketing managers can review technological change and the actions that should be taken. We look at interactive digital TV and mobile or wireless access to the Internet as two examples of this challenge.
- *Economic factors* – those that affect spending patterns and international trade.
- *Political and legal factors* – the role of national governments and transnational organisations in determining the future of the Internet and the rules by which it is governed.

These macro-economic factors will determine the overall characteristics of the micro-environment described in the previous chapter. For example, the social, economic and political environment in any country will directly affect the demand for e-commerce services by both consumers and businesses. Governments may promote the use of e-commerce while social conventions may limit its popularity. For instance, some southern European countries do not have a culture suited to catalogue shopping since consumers tend to prefer personal contact. In these countries there will be a lower propensity to buy online.

Social and ethical factors

In the last chapter, in the sections on customer adoption, we looked at how Internet usage varies across different countries, and how it is used for different purposes. These variations are in part related to the social impact of the Internet.

Like other innovations such as mechanised transport, electricity or the phone, the Internet has been used to achieve social progress. Those with special needs and interests can now communicate on a global basis and empowering information sources are readily available to all. However, these same technologies, including the Internet, can have negative social impacts such as damaging the environment, changing traditional social ideals and being used to cause crime.

● Social exclusion

The social impact of the Internet has concerned many commentators because the Internet has the potential effect of accentuating differences in quality of life, both within a society in a single country, and between different nations, essentially creating 'information haves' and 'information have-nots'. This may accentuate social exclusion where one part of society is excluded from the facilities available to the remainder and so becomes isolated. The United Nations, in a 1999 report on human development, noted that parallel worlds are developing where

Social exclusion

Part of society is excluded from the facilities available to the remainder.

those with income, education and – literally – connections have cheap and instantaneous access to information. The rest are left with uncertain, slow and costly access . . . the advantage of being connected will overpower the marginal and impoverished, cutting off their voices and concerns from the global conversation.

While the problem is easy to identify, it is clearly difficult to rectify: McIntosh (1999) rightly questions the likelihood of income redistribution and the impact of anti-poverty programmes. Developed countries with the economies to support it are promoting the use of IT and the Internet through social programmes such as the UK government's UK online initiative (www.ukonlineforbusiness.gov.uk), which offers training to children and adults and provides access through public facilities such as libraries. While such government intervention can have benefits in the field of education, it can be hoped that the desire of companies to communicate with a larger market through new digital media will also help reduce the problem. Competition amongst ISPs in the UK has given rise to many 'free-access' services such as Freeserve, Virgin and BT ClickFree, and this decrease in cost will increase the use of the Internet further. Coupled with this, the growth in interactive digital television services will help fuel access to information. If Internet access becomes a standard feature of television sets, the gap between information 'haves and have-nots' will decline. In the longer term such facilities will become available worldwide in the same way that television is now widely used throughout the world.

Although this book concentrates on the new commercial opportunities offered by the Internet, the medium is also widely used for cause-related marketing. Many charities are advanced in their use of the Internet. For example, Oxfam use e-mail campaigns (Figure 3.1) to boost donations by running sales promotions and also

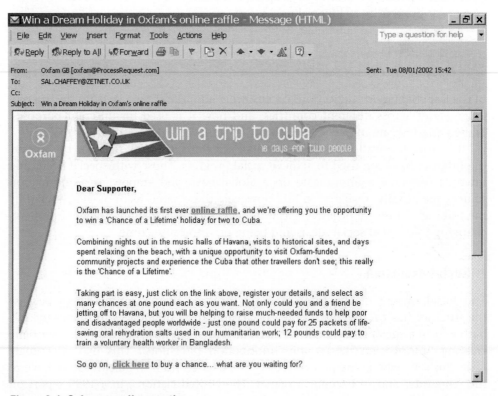

Figure 3.1 Oxfam e-mail promotion

alerting supporters of current crises. Other charities such as Christian Aid use transactional facilities on the web site as a means for collecting donations.

● Ethical issues of Internet usage

Ethical issues or the morality of approaches to Internet marketing is a key consideration of the Internet business environment for marketers. It will be shown in this section that a company that has a poor grasp of the ethics of e-commerce will be likely to damage its brand and haemorrhage online customers. Effective e-commerce requires a delicate balance to be struck between the benefits the individual customer will gain to their online experience through providing personal information and the amount and type of information that they are prepared for companies to hold about them. For business-to-business marketing the benefits to both parties of sharing information may be more readily apparent since this typically involves stronger relationships between buyers and sellers. For business-to-consumer marketing the synergy is less clear and the privacy issue is more of a barrier to the development of the Internet. It is on this aspect of privacy that we will concentrate. Ethical issues concerned with personal information ownership have been usefully summarised by Mason (1986) into four areas:

- *Privacy* – what information is held about the individual?
- *Accuracy* – is it correct?
- *Property* – who owns it and how can ownership be transferred?
- *Accessibility* – who is allowed to access this information, and under which conditions?

Fletcher (2001) provides an alternative perspective, raising these issues of concern for both the individual and the marketer:

- *Transparency* – who is collecting what information?
- *Security* – how is information protected once it has been collected by a company?
- *Liability* – who is responsible if data are abused?

All of these issues arise in the next section which reviews actions marketers should take to achieve privacy and trust.

Privacy and trust

Privacy refers to a moral right of individuals to avoid intrusion into their personal affairs by third parties. Privacy of personal data such as our identities, likes and dislikes is a major concern to consumers. Yet, for marketers to better understand their customers' needs, this type of information is required. Through collecting such information it will also be possible to use more targeted communications and develop products that are more consistent with users' needs. How should marketers respond to this dilemma?

Privacy
A moral right of individuals to avoid intrusion into their personal affairs.

First and foremost, marketing activities should be consistent with privacy law. The revised 1998 Data Protection Act in the UK, which includes local enactment of European legislation, is typical of what has been evolved in many countries to help protect personal information. Under the new Act, companies must:

1 Inform the user, before asking for information:
   - who the company is;
   - what personal data are collected, processed and stored;
   - what is the purpose of collection.

2 Ask for consent for collecting sensitive personal data and good practice to ask before collecting any type of data.

3 Provide a statement of privacy policy. 'A privacy statement helps individuals to decide whether or not to visit a site and, when they do visit, whether or not to provide any personal information to the data controller.'

4 Always let individuals know when 'cookies' or other covert software are used to collect information about them.

5 Never collect or retain personal data unless it is strictly necessary for the organisation's purposes. For example, a person's name and full address should not be required to provide an online quotation. If extra information is required for marketing purposes this should be made clear and the provision of such information should be optional.

6 Amend incorrect data when informed and tell others. Enable correction on-site.

7 Only use data for marketing (by the company, or third parties) when a user has been informed this is the case and has agreed to this. (This is opt-in.)

8 Provide the option for customers to stop receiving information. (This is opt-out.)

9 Use technology to protect the customer information on your site.

This summary of the implications of the Act is based on information at the UK Data Protection web site (www.dataprotection.gov.uk/dprhome.htm).

Secondly, the marketer has to act as an educator, explaining why the information is being collected and the benefits that will be received by the customer in exchange for divulging the personal information. Additionally, Fletcher (2001) suggests that the primary customer concern is not what information is collected – but rather whether the information will be passed on to a third party. Reassurance should also target this fear.

What are the main information needs of the Internet marketer and how do these relate to the technologies used to collect them? The information needs are:

1 *Contact information.* This is the name, postal address, e-mail address and, for B2B companies, web site address.

2 *Profile information.* This is information about a customer's characteristics that can be used for segmentation. The specific types of information were referred to in Chapter 2. They include age, gender and social group for consumers, and company characteristics and individual role for business customers. The use of this information as part of customer relationship management and direct marketing is described in Chapter 6.

3 *Behavioural information (on a single site).* This is purchase history, but also includes the whole buying process. Web logs (Chapter 9) can be used to assess the content accessed by individuals.

4 *Behavioural information (across multiple sites).* This shows how a user accesses multiple sites.

Table 3.1 shows how these different types of customer information are collected and used through technology.

There are three main aspects of managing personal customer data that are of concern to Internet marketers. We will deal with them in turn:

1 collecting and holding personal information;

2 disclosing personal information to third parties;

3 sending unsolicited e-mails to consumers.

Table 3.1 Types of information collected online and related technologies

Type of information	Approach and technology used to capture and use information
Contact information	Collected through online forms in response to an incentive for the customer. Stored in databases linking to web site. Cookies are used to remember a specific person on subsequent visits.
Profile information	Also collected through online forms. Cookies can be used to assign a person to a particular segment by linking the cookie to a customer database record and then offering content consistent with their segment.
Behavioural information on a single site	Purchase histories are stored in the sales order database. Web logs are used to store clickstreams of the sequence of web pages visited. A single pixel GIF is used to assess whether a reader had opened an e-mail. Cookies are also used in e-mails for monitoring.
Behavioural information across multiple sites	Web logs can tell the previous site visited by a customer. Banner advertising networks (Chapter 8) and ISPs can potentially assess all sites visited.

1 Collecting and holding personal information

One of the difficulties of using the Internet for one-to-one marketing (see Chapter 6), is that it is not easy to identify the end-user in order to target them with specific promotional information. To do this, it is necessary to invade the user's privacy by planting **cookies** or electronic tags on the end-user's computer. Alternatively, customers can be made to log-in to an extranet with a user name and password which is a less subversive method of personalisation. It is also necessary to ask customers about their personal details such as name, address, job and services required in order to match the cookie or log-in with the preferences of the person. By doing this it is possible to identify a user's preferences and behaviour since each time they visit a site, the cookie on the PC will be read to confirm the identity of the user (see the box 'What are cookies?' for more information).

It is possible to block cookies if the user finds out how to block them, but this is not straightforward and many customers do not know that their privacy is being infringed. Currently it is estimated that in the UK and Europe around 10–20% of users may have cookies disabled. Cookies have a bad reputation since it is believed that they could be used to capture credit-card information or other personal information. In reality, this is unlikely to occur since cookies usually only contain an identification number that does not give away any personal secrets. The information about individuals is stored in a database. Perhaps a more serious concern for the consumer is how secure the information in the database is from hackers.

Cookies

Small text files stored on an end-user's computer to enable web sites to identify them.

What are cookies?

A 'cookie' is a data file placed on your computer that identifies that individual computer. The cookie is placed on the computer via the web browser by the web site you visit. There are two main types of cookies. **Session cookies** are used *during* a visit to a web site to manage the interaction such as the different stages of purchasing a product. **Persistent cookies** remain on the computer *between* sessions and are a powerful marketing technique since they can be used to identify a particular customer on a repeat visit and tailor the web session accordingly – a key goal of personalisation.

Note that without the use of cookies it is not possible to uniquely identify an individual since the log files mentioned in Chapter 9 simply record an IP address (a unique number specific

Session cookie

A cookie that is used during a single visit to the web site to assist in interactions with the user.

Persistent cookie

A cookie that is used across multiple visits to a web site.

to a computer used to access the Internet) which may differ between different sessions if connecting using an ISP. 'Cookie' derives from the Unix term 'magic cookie' which meant something passed between routines or programs that enables the receiver to perform some operation.

Cookies are stored as individual text files in the directory \windows\cookies on a personal computer. There is usually one file per company, e.g. dave_chaffey@british-airways.txt. This file contains encoded information as follows: FLT_VIS|K:bapzRnGdxBYUU|D:Jul-25-2002|british-airways.com/ 0 425259904 29357426 1170747936 29284034 *

The information in the cookie file is essentially just an identification number and a date of the last visit, although other information can be stored.

Cookies are specific to a particular browser and computer, so if a user connects from a different computer or starts using a different browser the web site will not identify them as the same user.

Some examples of cookie use

- Cookies can be used to deliver personalised content when linked with preferences expressed using collaborative filtering. The cookie is used to identify the user and retrieve their preferences from a database.
- DoubleClick (www.doubleclick.net) uses cookies to track the number of times a particular computer has been shown a particular banner advertisement. When advertisers register with DoubleClick they create one or more target audience profiles. When a user visits a registered site a banner dynamically matches them to the target user profile. For any future visits by that user the DoubleClick server retrieves the ID number from the cookie and stores information about the visit.
- Cookies are increasingly used within HTML e-mails to monitor responses to e-mails.
- 'Shopping carts' in e-commerce sites use what are known as session cookies to store what the user wishes to order at the site prior to finalising a purchase. When the user is ready to check out the server reads the cookie file and initiates a transaction based on what is in the shopping trolley.
- Log-file analysis software such as WebTrends (www.webtrend.com) relies on cookies to find the proportion of repeat visitors to a web site.
- Amazon and other book e-tailers customise pages according to buying preferences of individuals visiting. This is based on identifying individual return visitors by cookies. For example, if a customer has previously bought a cookery book the e-tailer may change the web site to highlight the launch of a high-profile cookery book. Similarly, recommendations are made according to other purchasers' interests.

Privacy concerns about cookies

Antagonism exists towards the cookie due to a lack of disclosure – the cookies are passed surreptitiously and hence the feeling that the user's privacy has been invaded. Scare stories have been spread that cookies contain personal and credit card details, but this is not the case unless an error has been made by the webmaster. Normally they only contain an identification code that is used to retrieve these details from a database.

A study of almost 60 000 Internet users at the University of Michigan for the Hermes project (www-personal.umich.edu/~sgupta/hermes) indicated that over 81% felt that cookies were undesirable.

Despite these concerns, the cookie is becoming ubiquitous at major commercial sites as a means of tracking users.

In Europe there is continued concern about legislation over cookies, since a current proposal includes a proposal to end the usage of persistent cookies.

For additional information about cookies visit
www.netscape.com/newsref/std/cookie_spec.html
www.cookiecentral.com.

In the future, user awareness of cookies will increase, and an increasing number of users may block cookies which may reduce the effectiveness of one-to-one marketing. Complete Activity 3.1 to assess people's perceptions of them.

Privacy policies

Privacy policies typically contain three areas of ethics:

● *Privacy* – is information confidential, secure and used only for expressed purposes?
● *Ownership* – is information collection authorised and will the ownership be transferred to third parties?
● *Access* – is access to personal details restricted and can the consumer access and update their details?

Typical contents of privacy policies such as those referred to above contain these sorts of entries which aim to reassure the customer and explain their rights:

1 What information is collected about you?
2 What techniques are used for data collection, e.g. cookies, single-pixel .GIFs?
3 With whom will the information be shared?
4 How will your information be used?
5 How can you access, modify and delete the data?
6 Security in place to prevent the alteration, misuse or deletion of the data.

Further information on issues of privacy online are discussed at Br@ndlegal (www.marketinglaw.co.uk).

An indication of users' opinion about privacy is indicated by the Pew Internet and American Life Project (Pew, 2000). The report found that 86% of the 1017 Internet users surveyed favoured an 'opt-in' privacy policy. However, 27% of users said they would never submit personal information and 24% provided a false name or information.

With regard to cookies, 54% of users think tracking is harmful because it invades privacy, but 56% of Internet users are unaware that the 'cookie' is the primary online tracking tool. The number of users who set their browsers to reject cookies was 10% while 9% used encryption to scramble their e-mail and 5% used anonymising software, which hides the computer identity from web sites.

Another study (Cyber Dialogue, 2000) presents a different perspective, finding that consumers are not concerned about giving their personal details online, rather they are concerned with how this personal information is used by companies. In the study of 1500 Internet users, 80% said they were willing to give their name, details of education, age and hobbies in exchange for customised or personalised content, while 49% believed that a site that shares their personal information with another site is violating their privacy.

There are several initiatives that are being taken by industry groups to reassure web users about threats to their personal information. The first of these is TRUSTe (www.truste.org), sponsored by IBM and Netscape with sites validated by PricewaterhouseCoopers and KPMG (Figure 3.2). The validators will audit the site to check each site's privacy statement to see whether it is valid. For example, a privacy statement will describe:

● how a site collects information;
● how the information is used;

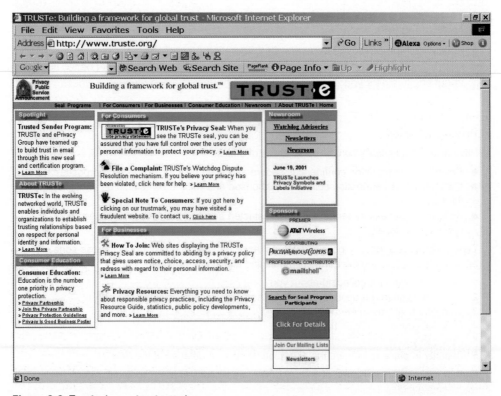

Figure 3.2 Truste (www.truste.org)

- who the information is shared with;
- how users can access and correct information;
- how users can decide to deactivate themselves from the site or withhold information from third parties.

A UK initiative is the Consumers' Association/Which? Web Trader (www.which.net/webtrader) which aims to 'ensure consumers get a fair deal and to provide them with protection if things go wrong'. E-tailers that have signed up to this include BarclaySquare, Blackwells, Carphone Warehouse and easyJet.

Government initiatives will also define best practice in this area and may introduce laws to ensure guidelines are followed. In the UK, the Data Protection Act covers some of these issues and the 1999 European Data Protection Act also has draft laws to help maintain personal privacy on the Internet.

2 Disclosing personal information to third parties

Customers may be quite happy to give personal information to a company they have formed a relationship with. They are likely to be less than happy if this company then sells this information on to another company and they are subsequently bombarded with promotional material either online or offline. For this reason the TRUSTe mentioned in the previous section also sets down best practice for disclosing information to third parties. The other risk in this category is that of hackers accessing information held about a customer on servers within a company. For example, the infamous hacker Kevin Mitnick was known for accessing over 20 000 credit card numbers on a company server.

3 Sending e-mail to customers

Despite its potential, use of e-mail for direct marketing has negative connotations due to **spam**. The best-known 'spam' is tinned meat (a contraction of 'spiced ham'), but a modern version of this acronym is 'Sending Persistent Annoying e-Mail'. The negative perception of e-mail derives from the many unsolicited e-mails we all receive from unscrupulous 'get-rich-quick merchants'. The spammers rely on sending out millions of e-mails in the hope that even if there is only a 0.01% response they may make some money, if not get rich.

> **Spam**
> Unsolicited e-mail (usually bulk-mailed and untargeted).

Many anti-spam activists have formed organisations such as CAUCE (the Coalition against Unsolicited Commercial E-mail, www.cauce.org). These organisations take a dim view of commercial organisations that send unsolicited mail and prepare a list of all spam perpetrators. They have also been successful in creating legislation to outlaw spam. It is now illegal within Europe, but it is often difficult to trace the originators of spam since they use hijacked e-mail addresses and postal boxes to collect their money.

Spam does not mean that e-mail cannot be used as a marketing tool. As explained below, opt-in is the key to successful e-mail marketing. Before starting an e-mail dialogue with customers, according to European law, companies must ask customers to provide their e-mail address and then give them the option of 'opting into' further communications. Ideally they should proactively opt in by checking a box. E-mail lists can also be purchased where customers have opted in to receive e-mail.

> **Opt-in**
> A customer proactively agrees to receive further information.

Privacy issues marketers should consider when conducting e-mail marketing are well covered by EMM@, the E-mail marketing association (www.emmacharter.org) which was created in June 2001 by e-mail marketing agencies to promote best practice. Perhaps the most important facilities on an e-commerce site to provide for legal and ethical reasons are the principles of 'opt-in' and 'opt-out'. The concept of opt-in is that communications are only sent to the customer if they have agreed to receive

> **Opt-out**
> A customer declines the offer to receive further information.

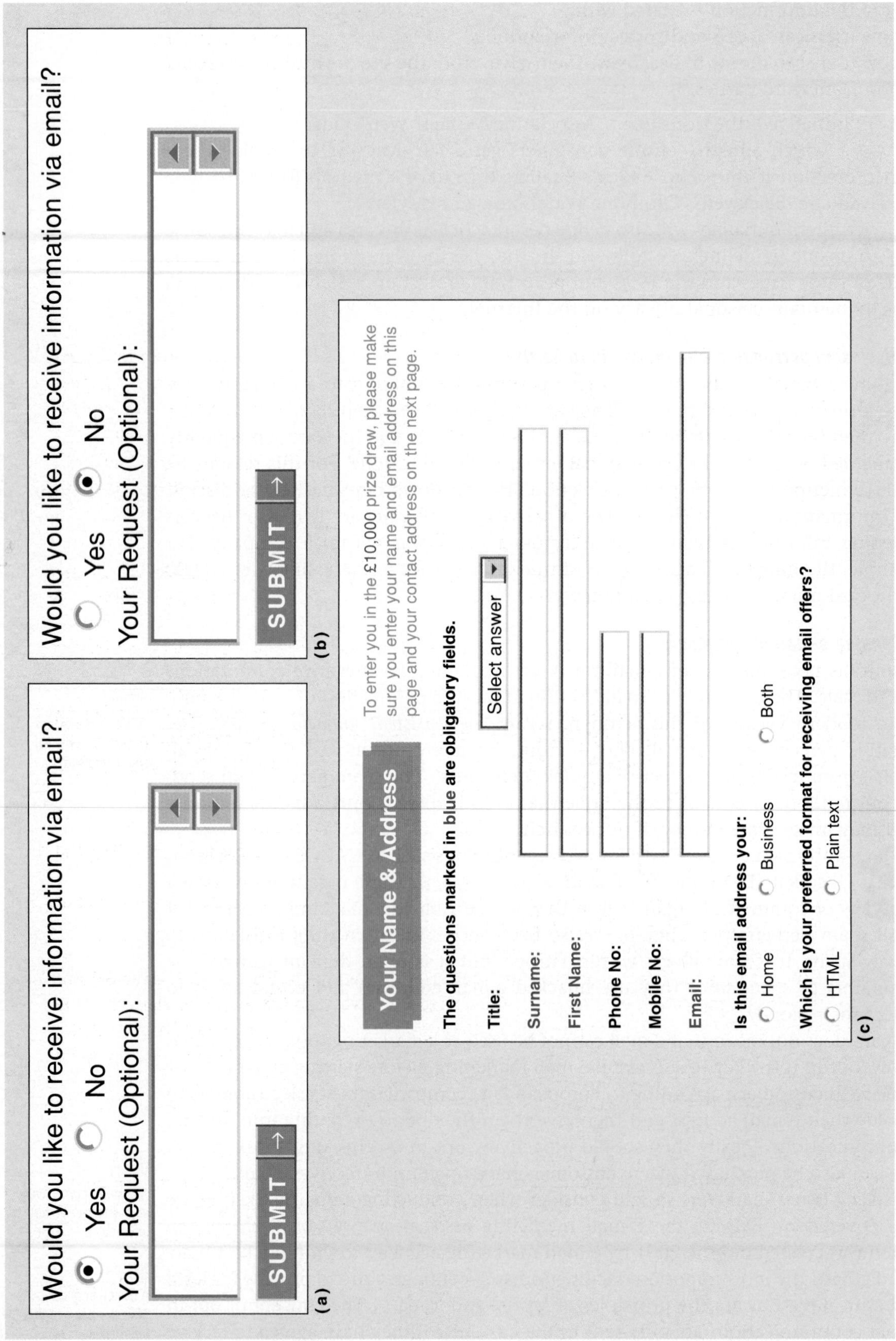

(a)

Would you like to receive information via email?

○ Yes ○ No

Your Request (Optional):

SUBMIT ↑

(b)

Would you like to receive information via email?

○ Yes ● No

Your Request (Optional):

SUBMIT ↑

(c)

Your Name & Address

To enter you in the £10,000 prize draw, please make sure you enter your name and email address on this page and your contact address on the next page.

The questions marked in blue are obligatory fields.

Title: [Select answer ▾]

Surname:

First Name:

Phone No:

Mobile No:

Email:

Is this email address your:

○ Home ○ Business ○ Both

Which is your preferred format for receiving email offers?

○ HTML ○ Plain text

Figure 3.3 Examples of opt-in and opt-out

information, for example, by filling in an online form and ticking a box to say they are happy to receive further communications. The principle of opt-out is that the customer will not be contacted in future if they have asked not to be. For example, if a customer is on an e-mail list, they will no longer be sent it, if they ask to be opted out or removed from the list.

What do opt-in and opt-out mean in practice? Consider Figure 3.3. Which are opt-in and opt-out? Here Figure 3.3(a) is opt-out since the user of the site has to take

Mini Case Study 3.1

E-mail marketing law

E-mail marketing is covered by law in the European Union directive 31/00/EC 'on certain legal aspects of information society services in particular electronic commerce in the Internal Market'. Such legislation is mainly targeted at reducing the threat of spam, but also at protecting consumers' privacy. Stephen Groom, of Osborne Clark (www.marketinglaw.co.uk), says that under proposed legislation all EU states permitting unsolicited commercial e-mail ('UCEM') must ensure that every e-mail sent 'shall be identifiable clearly and unambiguously as an advertising message as soon as it is received.

- UCEM users must be legally obliged to consult/respect opt-out registers.
- On-line promotional games, competitions, discounts, premiums, gifts must be clearly identifiable as such and participation conditions easily accessible and presented clearly and unambiguously.
- All price indications on-line must be clear/unambiguous and indicate whether inclusive of packaging/delivery costs.'

Further guidelines on e-mail marketing ethics are provided by EMM@ (the e-mail marketing association), a European body that has been set up to promote good ethical practice amongst its members. The EMM@ charter (www.emmacharter.org) recommends that the privacy policy should include but not be limited to the following:

- the identity and company address of the list owner (or data controller);
- the uses to which the personal data will be put and the choices the user has regarding the use of the personal data;
- the categories of third parties to whom the personal data may be disclosed, including, but not limited to, any list manager, service bureau or database manager;
- the nature of the personal data collected;
- the means by which data regarding the user are collected, including cookies, clear-GIFs or other similar indicators. It is recommended that the privacy policy should explain that the data collected by such techniques do not constitute personal data and are only used for the purposes of analysing the effectiveness of e-mail marketing material. There should also be links to the opt-out sections in relation to use of such techniques;
- the possibility that the list owner may acquire information about the user from other sources and add such information to its house files;
- whether the requested personal data are necessary to the transaction between user and list owner, or voluntary, and the consequences of failing to provide the requested information;
- the steps taken by the list owner to ensure the technical and organisational measures taken to protect the security of the personal data;
- how to opt out of the mailing list;
- the ability of the user to be provided with a copy of their personal data, and to contest and correct inaccuracies, or request that their personal data be deleted.

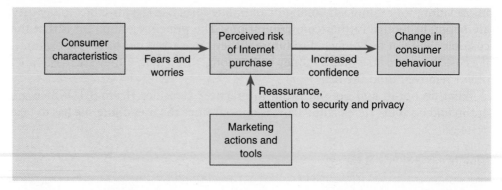

Figure 3.4 The relationship between consumer risk perception and behaviour and how it can be influenced by marketers

action to avoid receiving e-mails. Although this approach is currently legal and will lead to more e-mail addresses being captured, it is unethical. The problem with this approach is that some recipients of the e-mail who did not notice this option will receive unexpected e-mails which they may consider to be spam and this may damage the brand. Response rates will also be lower than to an opt-in list, although the actual number of respondents may be higher. Figure 3.3(b) is opt-in and this is considered best practice – the user has to proactively select that they want to receive e-mail. Figure 3.3(c) is also opt-in, but is a more subtle approach since the user is opting in by completing the form and agreeing to receive the e-mail in a particular format and to a particular location. This is best practice since the needs of the user in terms of access location and preferred format are requested.

To summarise this section, we can suggest it is important for Internet marketers to understand the issues that concern customers of different characteristics and act as a barrier to purchasing online. Marketing communications should then be used to reduce the perceived risk by reassuring customers and so resulting in a change to their behaviour (Figure 3.4).

We can suggest that e-commerce managers need to take the following marketing actions to overcome ethical issues such as privacy to achieve reassurance, gain trust and build loyalty.

1 Reassure customers by providing clear and effective privacy statements and explaining the purpose of data collection.
2 Follow privacy and consumer protection guidelines and laws in all local markets.
3 Make security of customer data a priority.
4 Use independent certification bodies.
5 Emphasise the excellence of service quality in all marketing communications.

Technological factors

Disruptive technologies

New technologies that prompt businesses to reappraise their strategic approaches.

Electronic communications are disruptive technologies that have, as we saw in Chapter 2, already caused major changes in industry structure, marketplace structure and business models. Consider a B2B organisation. Traditionally it has sold its products through a network of distributors. With the advent of e-commerce it now has the opportunity to bypass distributors and trade directly with customers via a web site; it also has the opportunity to reach customers through new B2B marketplaces.

Knowledge of the opportunities and threats presented by these changes is essential to those involved in defining marketing strategy.

One of the great challenges for Internet marketers is to be able to successfully assess which new technological innovations can be applied to give competitive advantage. For example, personalisation technology (Chapter 6) is intended to enhance the customer's online experience and increase their loyalty. However, a technique such as personalisation requires a large investment in proprietary software and hardware technology such as Broadvision, Bladerunner or Engage to be able to implement it effectively. How does the manager decide whether to proceed and which solution to adopt? In addition to technologies deployed on the web site, the suitability of new approaches for attracting visitors to the site must be evaluated – for example should registration at a paid-for search engine, or new forms of banner adverts or e-mail marketing be used? Deciding on the best mix of traffic building techniques is discussed further in Chapter 8.

The manager may have read articles in the trade and general press or spoken to colleagues which has highlighted the potential of a new technology-enabled marketing technique. They then face a difficult decision as to whether to

- ignore the use of the technique completely, perhaps because it is felt to be too expensive or untried, or because they simply don't believe the benefits will outweigh the costs;
- ignore the technique for now, but keep an eye on the results of other companies that are starting to use it;
- evaluate the technique in a structured manner and then take a decision whether to adopt it according to the evaluation;
- enthusiastically adopt the technique without a detailed evaluation since the hype alone convinces the manager that the technique should be adopted.

Depending on the attitude of the manager, this behaviour can be summarised as:

1 cautious, 'wait and see' approach;
2 intermediate approach, sometimes referred to as 'fast-follower'. Let others take the majority of the risk, but if they are proving successful, then rapidly adopt the technique, i.e. copy them;
3 risk-taking, early-adopter approach.

Different behaviours by different adopters will result in different numbers of adopters through time. This diffusion–adoption process (represented by the bell curve in Figure 3.5) was identified by Rogers (1983) who classified those trialling new products from innovators, *early adopters*, early majority, late majority, through to the laggards.

Figure 3.5 can be used in two main ways as an analytical tool to help managers. First, it can be used to understand the stage at which customers are in adoption of a technology, or any product. For example, the Internet is now a well-established tool and in many developed countries we are into the late majority phase of adoption with larger numbers of users of services. This suggests it is essential to use this medium for marketing purposes. But if we look at WAP technology (see below) it can be seen that we are in the innovator phase, so investment now may be wasted since it is not clear how many will adopt the product. Secondly, managers can look at adoption of a new technique by other businesses – from an organisational perspective. For example, an online supermarket could look at how many other e-tailers have adopted personalisation to evaluate whether it is worthwhile adopting the technique.

Early adopters

Companies or departments that invest in new technologies and techniques.

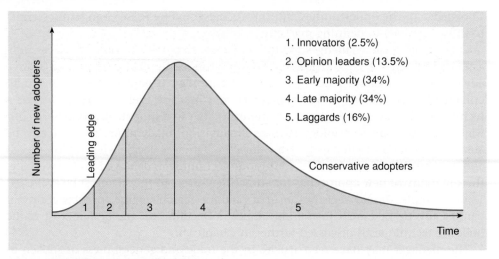

Figure 3.5 Diffusion–adoption curve

Trott (1998) looks at this organisational perspective to technology adoption. He identifies different requirements that are necessary within an organisation to be able to respond effectively to technological change or innovation. These are:

● growth orientation – a long- rather than short-term vision;
● vigilance – the capability of environment scanning;
● commitment to technology – willingness to invest in technology;
● acceptance of risk – willingness to take managed risks;
● cross-functional cooperation – capability for collaboration across functional areas;
● receptivity – the ability to respond to externally developed technology;
● slack – allowing time to investigate new technological opportunities;
● adaptability – a readiness to accept change;
● diverse range of skills – technical and business skills and experience.

The problem with being an early adopter (as an organisation) is that being at the leading edge of using new technologies is often also referred to as the 'bleeding edge' due to the risk of failure. New technologies will have bugs, may integrate poorly with the existing systems or the marketing benefits may simply not live up to their promise. Of course, the reason for risk taking is that the rewards are high – if you are using a technique that your competitors are not, then you will gain an edge on your rivals. For example, RS Components (www.rswww.com) was one of the first UK suppliers of industrial components to adopt personalisation as part of their e-commerce system (Figure 3.6). They have learnt the strengths and weaknesses of the product and now know how to position it to appeal to customers. It offers facilities such as customised pages, access to previous order history and the facility to place repeat orders or modified re-buys. This has enabled them to build up a base of customers who are familiar with using the RS Components online services and are then less likely to swap to rival services in the future.

It may also be useful to identify how rapidly a new concept is being adopted. When a product or service is adopted rapidly this is known as *rapid diffusion*. The access to the Internet is an example of this. In developed countries the use of the Internet has become widespread more rapidly than the use of TV, for example. It seems that interactive digital TV and Internet-enabled mobile phones are relatively slow-diffusion products! Activity 3.2, later in this chapter, considers this issue further.

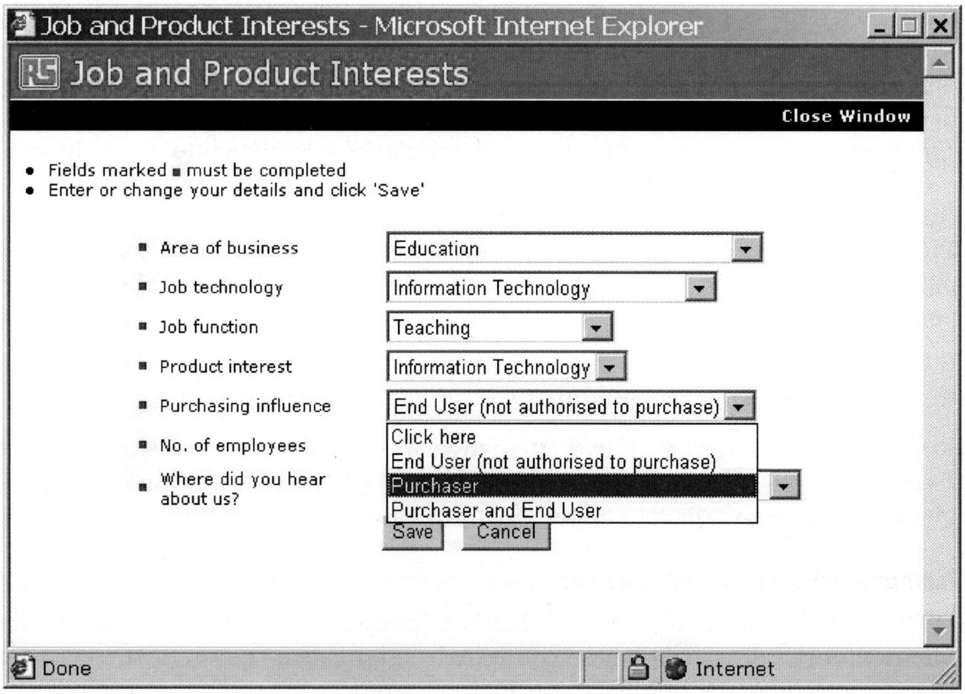

Figure 3.6 **Personalisation at RS Components** (www.rswww.com)

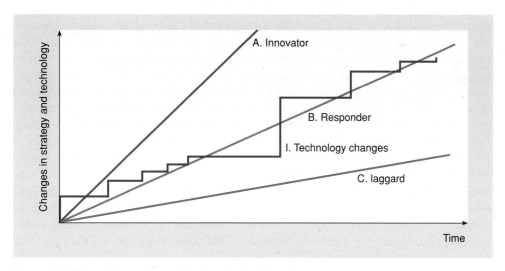

Figure 3.7 **Alternative responses to changes in technology**

So, what action should e-commerce managers take when confronted by new techniques and technologies? There is no straightforward rule of thumb, other than that a balanced approach must be taken. It would be easy to dismiss many new techniques as fads, or classify them as 'not relevant to my market'. However, competitors are likely to be reviewing new techniques and incorporating some, so a careful review of new techniques is required. This indicates that benchmarking of 'best of breed' sites within sector and in different sectors is essential as part of environmental scanning. However, by waiting for others to innovate and review the results on their web site, a company has probably already lost 6 to 12 months. Figure 3.7 summarises the choices. The stepped curve I shows the variations in technology through time. Some changes may be small incremental changes such as a new operating systems; others such as the introduction of personalisation technology are more significant in delivering value to customers and so improving business performance. Line A is a company that is using innovative business techniques, adopts technology early, or is even in advance of what the technology can currently deliver. Curve C shows the conservative adopter whose use of technology lags behind the available potential. Curve B, the middle ground, is probably the ideal situation where a company monitors new ideas as early adopters, trials them and then adopts those that will positively impact the business.

● Alternative digital technologies

Access platform

A method for customers to access digital media.

In this section we introduce two alternative access platforms to PC-based Internet access, which provide many similar advantages. Two other access platforms or environments are interactive digital TV and mobile or wireless access to the Internet.

Mobile or wireless access devices

Mobile technologies are not new – it has been possible for many years to access the Internet for e-mail using a laptop connected via a modem. However, the need for large devices directly connected to the Internet was overcome with the development of personal digital assistants (PDAs) such as the Palm Computing Palm VII or Psion, and then mobile phones. These access the Internet using a wireless connection.

The characteristics that mobile or wireless connections offer to their users can be summarised by the supposedly idyllic image used in many adverts of a user accessing the Internet via a laptop or phone from a field, river bank or mountain top. They provide ubiquity (can be accessed from anywhere), reachability (their users can be reached when not in their normal location) and convenience (it is not necessary to have access to a power supply or fixed-line connection). In addition to these obvious benefits, there are additional benefits that are less obvious: they provide security – each user can be authenticated since each wireless device has a unique identification code; their location can be used to tailor content; and they provide a degree of privacy compared with a desktop PC – looking for jobs on a wireless device might be better than under the gaze of a boss. An additional advantage that will shortly be available is that of instant access or 'always-on'; here there is no need to dial up a wireless connection. Table 3.2 provides a summary of the mobile or wireless Internet access proposition. There are considerable advantages in comparison to PC-based Internet access, but it is currently limited by the display limitations such as small screen size and limited graphics.

Short Message Service (SMS)

The formal name for text messaging.

In addition to offering voice calls, mobile phones have increasingly been used for e-mail and Short Message Service (SMS). SMS is effectively a simple form of e-mail that enables messages to be transferred between mobile phones. These consist of voice mail notifications, alerts about news or messages direct between phone users. According to MobileCommerceWorld (2002), 1.3 billion text messages were sent in December 2001, bringing the total number of messages sent in 2001 in the UK to 12.2 billion. This suggests an average of nearly 300 messages per person annually and a much higher figure for some users.

Wireless application protocol (WAP)

WAP is a technical standard for transferring information to wireless devices, such as mobile phones.

In 1999 the first of a new generation of mobile phones such as the Nokia 7110 were introduced – these offered the opportunity to access the Internet. These are known as wireless application protocol or WAP phones, or, in more common parlance, 'web-enabled or Internet phones'. What these phones offer is the facility to access information on web sites that has been specially tailored for display on the small screens of

Table 3.2 Summary of mobile or wireless Internet access consumer proposition

Element of proposition	Evaluation
Not fixed location	The user is freed from the need to access via the desktop, making access possible when commuting, for example
Location-based services	Mobiles can be used to give geographically based services, e.g. an offer in a particular shopping centre. Future mobiles will have global positioning services integrated
Instant access/convenience	The latest GPRS and 3G services are always on, avoiding the need for lengthy connection (see section on alternative digital technologies)
Privacy	Mobiles are more private than desktop access, making them more suitable for social use or for certain activities such as an alert service for looking for a new job
Personalisation	As with PC access, personal information and services can be requested by the user, although these often need to be set up via PC access
Security	In the future mobile may become a form of wallet, but thefts of mobiles make this a source of concern

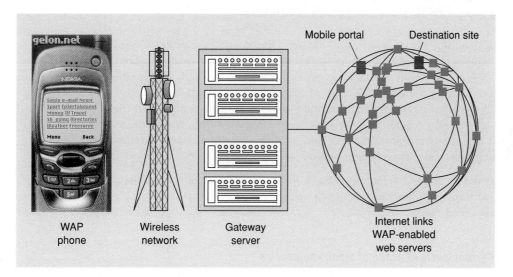

Figure 3.8 Hardware and software infrastructure for a WAP system

mobile phones. There was a tremendous amount of hype about these phones since they provide all the benefits that have been provided by the World Wide Web, but in a mobile form. However, usage has been much lower than for the Internet.

How does WAP work?

Figure 3.8 summarises the hardware requirements for a WAP system. A user needs a WAP-enabled handset that is used to type in WAP web addresses. WAP pages are then accessed using wireless techniques from a WAP gateway that is connected to a traditional web server where the WAP pages are hosted. Portals from the mobile phone companies or new phone portals will be used to configure the services on the phone such as setting up Short Message Service.

Technical standards for wireless access are consistent with those for the Internet. Pages are written in WML (Wireless Markup Language). This is similar to HTML in that it is a markup language, but introduces new concepts in accordance with the media.

Wireless Markup Language (WML)

Standard for displaying mobile pages such as those transferred by WAP.

To speed access, each WML file is referred to a 'deck' and consists of several 'cards' that can be displayed sequentially without reconnecting. For more information on the technology see www.anywhereyougo.com.

Mobile services

The services delivered for consumers, to date, have included transactional and informational. Consumer applications to date include retail (WH Smith Online books, the Carphone Warehouse), ticketing (lastminute.com), broking, banking (the Woolwich), gambling (Ladbrokes), bill payment and job searching. Some informational services based on personalisation such as those of Excite UK and Yahoo! have also been launched. These include information such as sports news, stock prices, news, cinemas, weather, horoscopes and reminders.

Services for businesses delivered by WAP are currently less developed, but are forecast to centre on supply-chain integration where there will be facilities to place orders, check stock availability, notify of dispatch and track orders.

Mini Case Study 3.2

Guinness uses SMS to reach a young audience

Revolution (2001a) described how brand owner Diageo used Nightfly 30 SMS channels described as 'your mobile nightlife guide' to reach 18–24-year-old users. On St Patrick's Day (17 March 2001), a promotion went out to the 3612 Nightfly users in Nottingham who had opted to receive drinks promotions; 92% were aged between 18 and 29 and 63% were male. Two alerts were involved in the promotion, one a week in advance and one on the day – each listing the bars and clubs where the promotions were available. Follow-up research suggested that sales had increased substantially, with 43.7% of those influenced to purchase Guinness! Ellie Calver, brand manager at Guinness, was quoted as saying:

> the results were very encouraging and it looks as if this might be an exciting addition to the marketing mix, particularly for informing customers about below-the-line activity.

Current levels of usage of mobile commerce

Mobile commerce (m-commerce)

The use of wireless devices such as mobile phones for informational or monetary transactions.

Mobile commerce (m-commerce) refers to the use of wireless devices such as mobile phones for informational or monetary transactions. Levels of product purchase by mobile phone have proved very low in comparison with the Internet, even for standardised products such as books and CDs. Many m-commerce providers such as Sweden's M-box went into receivership. However, analysts expect that with new access platforms, such as 3G (third-generation mobile devices which will have higher access speeds offering video transmissions), this will change. Consider the example of travel, which is the leading e-commerce category in Europe by revenue for the fixed Internet. Analysts IDC (2002) estimate that by 2005, 23 million Europeans will buy travel products and services using their mobile phones.

i-Mode

A mobile access platform that enables display of colour graphics and content subscription services.

The Japanese experience with i-Mode suggests that with suitable access devices that support colour images, the impact of 3G could be significant. MobileCommerceWorld (2001) reports that Japanese i-Mode users spend an average of ¥2614 (US$21.60) each month on wireless content and m-commerce. Mobile phone ringtones and other music downloads are the most popular i-Mode purchase, followed by other paid-for information services. The strength of the proposition is indicated by the fact that over 30 million Japanese were using this service despite a launch less than two years previously.

Strategies for mobile commerce

Different types of strategy can be identified for two main different types of organisations. For portal and media owners the options are to migrate their own portal to WAP/SMS (the option followed by Excite and the *Guardian*) or to partner with other WAP portals and provide content for these. Revenue models may include sponsorship or subscription for individual content items or on a subscription basis. Options for advertising are also being explored – www.247europe.com is one of the first companies to offer WAP-based advertisements. For destination sites such as banks and retailers, the options available include:

- marketing communications (to support purchase and support);
- e-commerce (sale of products on-site);
- brand building – improving brand image by being one of the first suppliers to offer an innovative service.

Future mobile services

In 2001 new services became available on GPRS (General Packet Radio Service). This is approximately five times faster than GSM (Global System for Mobile Communications) and is an 'always-on' service which is charged according to usage. Display is still largely text-based and based on the WAP protocol. Later, in 2002, a completely new generation (3G) of services would become available by UMTS (Universal Mobile Telecommunications System); with this delivery of sound and images should be possible, enabling continuous, instant access to the Internet ('always on'). In the UK auctions for the licence to operate on these frequencies have exceeded £20 billion – such is the perceived importance of these services to the telecommunications companies. Many commentators now believe it will be difficult for the telcos to recoup this money, and this has resulted in large falls in their share prices.

Figure 3.9 summarises these new standards for mobile access of the Internet. For each new technology there is a significant range between the lowest and highest possible transmission speeds. Very often the hype is based on the upper limit, but when implemented only the lower limit is achieved. Figure 3.10 shows the potential of 3G devices.

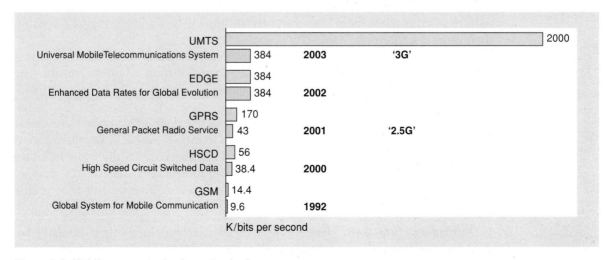

Figure 3.9 Mobile access technology standards

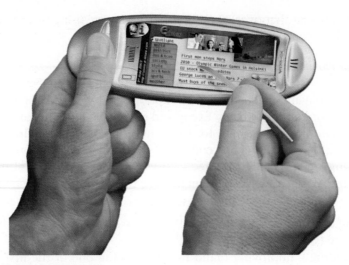

Figure 3.10 Prototype 3G device (www.nokia.com)

Interactive digital television

Interactive digital TV (iDTV)

Television displayed using a digital signal delivered by a range of media – cable, satellite, terrestrial (aerial). Interactions can be provided through phone line or cable service.

Interactive digital television (iDTV) has now been used in Europe for several years to deliver broadcasting to homes and offer new interactive services. In France, Canal Plus launched iDTV in 1996, Télévision par satellite launched in 1997 and Spain, Italy and Germany have had these facilities since 1996 or 1997.

In the UK, levels of access to interactive digital TV rival those of the Internet. All three main new media are tracked by the e-MORI Technology Tracker (www.e-mori.co.uk) (Figure 2.14). In January 2002, in the UK, the level of access in new media was reported as:

- own mobile phone (75%);
- use Internet anywhere (45%);
- have digital TV (44%).

The importance of digital TV is indicated by these figures. This medium has taken just two years to catch up with the Internet and is likely to surpass Internet access in future. Research by Jupiter MMXI (2002) suggests a similar picture in the rest of Europe to that in the UK, although access levels are currently lower. Total digital TV penetration is set to increase from 20% in 2002 up to 52% in 2006. The research indicates that by 2006 more European households will be watching digital television than using the Internet.

Interactive digital TV offers similar e-commerce facilities to the Internet, but is provided with a simpler interface that can be operated from a remote control. The amount of information available from providers is lower because of limited bandwith on site.

Table 3.3 summarises the proposition for interactive digital TV. It is evident that it is more similar to PC-based Internet access than to mobile access. A key difference is that TV viewing is more likely to involve several members of a family while PC usage is more individual. This may cause conflict in use of some individualised iDTV services.

Curry (2001) has proposed three alternative types of interactivity that online marketers can exploit:

1 *Distribution interactivity*. Here the user controls when the content is delivered. Video-on-demand is an example of this. Using personal video recorders such as TiVO is a further example, since users can choose to watch content at a later time and possibly omit adverts.

Table 3.3 Summary of interactive digital TV consumer proposition

Element of proposition	Evaluation
Instant access/convenience	Interactive services are available quite rapidly, but return path connections using phone lines for purchase are slower
Personalisation	This is less practical for PC and mobile since there are usually several viewers
Security	Credit card details can be held by the iDTV provider, making it theoretically unnecessary to repeatedly enter personal details

2 *Information interactivity.* Here the user can select different information. Curry gives the example of teletext and games which are, together, the most popular interactive TV activity. A further example is where a viewer of an advert can access a micro-site with further information on the advert (see Mini Case Study 3.3). Information can be exchanged via a **return path** such as entering a competition. This provides an improved option for direct response advertising in comparison to traditional TV.

3 *Participation activity.* This is where the user can select different options during a programme such as choosing a different camera angle in a football match or different news stories. There is no return path in this case.

Return path

An interaction where the customer sends information to the provider using a phone line or cable.

Taking the UK as an example, there are several providers. For example, Sky Digital is viewed by over 5 million subscribers and has content from banks such as HSBC and Woolwich, retailers such as Woolworths, Dixons and Carphone Warehouse. This is known as a '**walled garden** service' since it is not open-access like the Internet. The online shopping service was formerly branded as 'Open', but has been rebranded as Sky Active since 2001 (Figure 3.11). Although there are few reported

Walled garden

A limited range of e-commerce services (compared to the Internet).

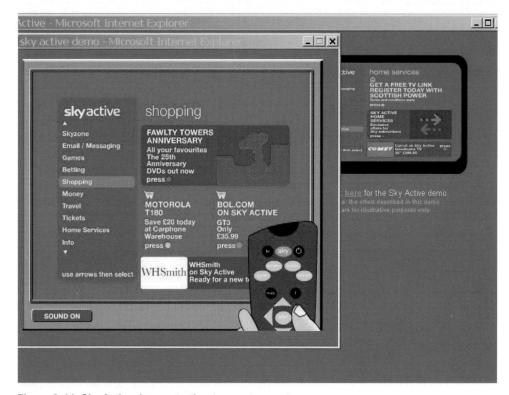

Figure 3.11 Sky Active demonstration (www.sky.com)

figures of the overall use of these services, individual examples indicate some early success: HSBC registered 80 000 customers within 3 weeks, of whom 20 000 were new. Domino's Pizza had 10 000 requests in the first 10 days; it expects 5% of sales to come from this source by 2001. Curry (2001) reviews the success of online shopping on the Open platform: he reports that while 80% have heard of the Open platform, only 50% have used Open and just 10% have bought through it. In contrast, he reports that 50% of Internet users have bought online and have spent more, more often.

Cable providers ntl and Telewest are the other main UK providers.

Mini Case Study 3.3

Sharwood's test interactive TV as marketing channel

This campaign ran for three months on the ntl: platform and offered Virgin Atlantic flights and Sharwood's coupons as prizes. Revolution (2001b) reported that Sharwoods were looking to use iDTV to reach a different demographic sector, test the medium and also promote the brand.

Creative in phase one of the campaign used 'Take your tastebuds on an adventure with Sharwood's' emblazoned across a colourful banner, but this was changed later on so that the banner read 'Korma Blimey!', which doubled click-through.

Users were asked three questions on the micro-site about Sharwood's products as part of the competition in order to promote registration and data capture. Further information about recipes was also available.

Results were reported as 2175 entries and 1.37 million page impressions after 12 959 click-throughs. Phase one of the banner campaign achieved an average click-through of 1.25 per cent and phase two saw 1.37 per cent.

How does interactive digital TV work?

Figure 3.12 shows that a set-top box is an important component of the interactive digital TV system. This is used to receive and decode the message from a satellite dish or cable that is then displayed on a conventional TV. The set-top box also includes a modem that is used to pass back selections made on the interactive shopping channel to the company across the Internet using standard phone lines for the connection. For digital cable connections, there is a continuous connection between the set-top box and the provider which means that more detailed information on customer behaviour is available. The image displayed is lower-resolution than a PC and each supplier uses a different display standard. This means that HTML web content cannot readily be transferred to iDTV and needs to be **repurposed**.

Repurposing

Developing for a new access platform content that was previously used for a different platform such as the Web.

When a company decides how to respond to iDTV several levels of commitment can be identified:

- *promotion* – using interactive ads;
- *content* – repurpose web site;
- *content* – new interactive services;
- *e-commerce* – perhaps for a limited range of products.

Other new digital access devices may affect the future infrastructure requirements. These include digital home storage. Its promoters are describing this as 'The biggest

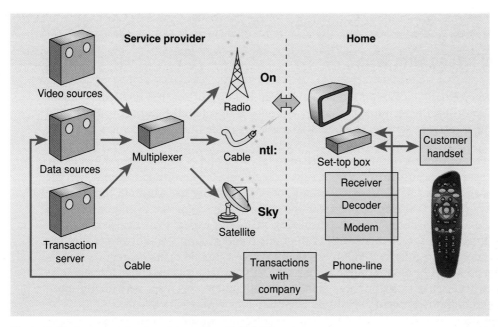

Figure 3.12 Components of an interactive digital TV system

change in conventional broadcasting since the industry began'. Variously referred to as 'personal video recorders', 'home media servers' or 'content refrigerators', they all involve recording a TV programme direct to a magnetic disk which gives 20 hours of recording time. Examples are TiVo and ReplayTV. These offer the opportunity to pause a programme while it is being transmitted, record it and return to it later. It may also be possible to filter out adverts.

As a conclusion to this section complete Activity 3.2, which illustrates the type of technology dilemma marketers face as new technologies are introduced. Case Study 3.1 can be used to support Activity 3.2.

Activity 3.2

Assessing new technology options

Purpose

To illustrate the process for reviewing the relevance of new technology options.

Activity

You work for a FMCG brand and are attending an industry trade show where you see a presentation about the next-generation (3G) mobile phones which are due to launch in your country in one year's time. You need to decide whether your organisation adopts the new phone and if so when. Complete the following:

1 How would you assess the significance of this new technology?
2 Summarise the proposition of the new access devices for both consumers and your organisation.
3 What recommendations would you make about when to adopt and which services to offer?

CASE STUDY 3.1

What went wrong with Wap?

Wireless commerce has a credibility problem and Wap is a big part of that problem. Wireless Application Protocol is the technology that once promised to catapult Europe into the digital age by bringing interactive services to a potential market of more than 250m owners of mobile phones.

But this vision of wireless commerce has failed to take root and Wap has taken much of the blame. Only 12m Europeans had Wap phones at the end of 2000, according to Durlacher, the London-based investment bank. Worse news still, once the novelty has worn off, these people rarely visit any of the 10 000 Wap-enabled websites or 7.8m Wap pages that exist today. 'Whilst most of these end-users will use their Wap browsers, we do not expect that their usage will be high', says Durlacher. A survey of Swedish Wap phone owners found that only 6 per cent use the Wap functionality regularly. T-Mobil, Germany's largest mobile operator, reports that its Wap users spend only 17 minutes online per month. This creates a vicious circle: if usage stays low, it makes little sense to spend large sums creating content for Wap, particularly given today's more cautious investment climate. So what has gone wrong with Wap?

Experts say the technology should not be held solely responsible. 'Wap is just a simple protocol and it's not fair to just blame the technology', says Tomas Franzén, chief executive of AU-System, a Swedish company that developed the Wap browser used by Ericsson and others. 'There were just too many expectations placed on technology.'

The Wap protocol is not the only way to handle data on mobile devices. In Japan, NTT DoCoMo has created a market of 20m with its rival i-mode technology. In the US, the popularity of wireless devices such as the Palm VII organiser has led many developers to use HDML, another rival standard. 'Wireless commerce should not be seen as Wap-centric', says Karl Andersson, vice-president of m-commerce for Scandinavia at Cap Gemini Ernst & Young, the IT services company.

Just one of many standards

The Nordic region has the highest wireless penetration in the world and many m-commerce services are available – Helsinki even allows its motorists to pay for their parking space using their mobile phone. However, most of these services were developed using SMS, the simple text-only messaging technology that is built into every mobile phone. 'There are many examples of text-based services that are generating revenues for operators', says Mr Andersson. Despite the success of SMS, i-mode and other alternatives to Wap, the future of Europe's fledgling wireless commerce market has become inextricably linked to Wap. So, when users complained that early Wap services failed to live up to expectations, the Wap standard got much of the blame. Most complaints centred on the achingly slow speeds when accessing Wap services over today's GSM networks.

This problem may be solved with new, higher-speed, cellular networks based on GPRS technology, and then on third-generation UMTS telephony. The first GPRS mobile phones will be available this year, but many operators and handset manufacturers have got cold feet over GPRS and it may not become widely available until 2002. UMTS will not appear until 2003–2004.

Other complaints have focused on difficulty in viewing content such as web pages on the diminutive screens of Wap phones. In a study carried out by the Nielsen Norman Group, a US research firm, people who had used Wap services for a week were asked whether they were likely to still be using a Wap phone one year later. A resounding 70 per cent answered no. 'Wap is not ready for prime time yet, nor do users expect it to be usable any time soon', concluded Marc Ramsay and Jakob Nielsen, authors of the report.

The drubbing given to Wap has poured cold water on the feverish expectations of Europe's m-commerce industry, which once had a vision of Wap opening a cornucopia of revenue-generating services such as stock alerts, ticketing or wireless banking. Wireless Commerce (WCL), a Finnish start-up, believes there is still a bright future for these types of service, particularly in Finland, where mobile phones already outnumber fixed lines. But Wap is unlikely to be part of that future. 'We are not often asked for Wap services by the operators as Wap is not used very much in Finland', says Hannu Vähäsaari, managing director of WCL. 'The thinking behind Wap is very good but it was just too early.' WCL has developed various m-commerce services, including a travel alert service for Railtrack, the UK train network operator, and mobile auctions for eTori, a Finnish website. These services were developed principally for SMS, which Mr Vähäsaari believes is sufficient to handle most if not all of the data services that operators want to offer today.

Compared with the sophisticated graphics capabilities of Wap – soon to be enhanced with colour – SMS may seem basic, but that is part of its attraction, according to Mr Vähäsaari. 'SMS is a very robust way to do wireless business today', he says. SMS works well, whereas developers of Wap applications have to contend with multiple versions of the Wap standard and idiosyncracies in how Wap is implemented by the handset manufacturers. Jinny Software, an Irish start-up, is another fan of SMS. It has created an SMS-based banking service for AIB, the big Irish bank, among other customers. 'SMS is blooming all over Europe and you can do some pretty clever things with SMS', says Ciazan Carey, head of m-commerce at Jinny. Earlier this year, Jinny was acquired by Acotel, an Italian company, for $14m (£9.7m) in cash. Acotel plans to use Jinny's SMS technology to develop and host SMS applications for Telecom Italia Mobile, which means a potential market of 35m GSM users in Italy and around the world.

Wireless commerce continues to generate great interest in Europe, as this deal demonstrates. However, the Wap backlash has had its effect and companies are turning to SMS, an established and trusted technology, to unlock the market's potential, at least for the next couple of years. 'In contrast to SMS, Wap has not built up goodwill because its benefits currently simply do not outweigh its inconvenience', says Durlacher. There could be 72m Wap-enabled phones in Europe by the end of 2003, predicts Durlacher, but it will be SMS, not Wap, that produces most of the data and content revenues that these users generate.

Source: Geoff Nairn, What went wrong with WAP?, Connectis, 29 May 2001, www.ft.com/connectis (now discontinued)

Questions

1 Describe the evidence for the failure of Wap and explain reasons for this according to the article.

2 What are the lessons of the relative failure of Wap for a manager? How you would advise a manager at a news magazine publisher to assess the relevance of the next generation wireless technology such as 3G?

● Security

We now focus on security, a key aspect of the Internet macro-environment. Security fears are a major barrier to e-commerce adoption, by both businesses and consumer. On 24 August 2000, the *Financial Times* reported how a criminal gang used bogus identities to obtain credit cards and loans from online bank Egg. The bank was defrauded of approximately £10 000 through multiple applications for online banking. Once the cards and loans were granted, with spending limits of up to £2000, the gang used them to make thousands of pounds of purchases, both online and in shops. Bank spokesmen said the crime represented no threat to the bank's customers, but fraud is still a risk to the banks. The spokesman was also keen to point out that fraudulent applications for credit existed long before the Internet. Although this example suggests that customer data is not at risk, this is not the case. When a customer of an e-commerce site enters their credit card details, these are typically stored on servers of the merchant (retailer) of the third party. Once here, they are vulnerable to downloading by hackers who can use the numbers for fraudulent purchase. Customers may lose the first £50, for which the credit card issuer does not cover them. For larger amounts the risk lies with the credit card issuer. As a result, Internet-related fraud is now the largest source of fraud affecting credit card companies such as Visa and Mastercard. To summarise we can identify the following security risks from the customer or merchant perspective:

A. transaction or credit card details stolen in transit;
B. customer's credit card details stolen from merchant's server;
C. merchant or customer are not who they claim to be.

In this section we assess the measures that can be taken to reduce the risk of these breaches of e-commerce security. We start by reviewing some of the theory of online security and then review the techniques used.

Principles of secure systems

Before we look at the principle of secure systems, it is worth reviewing the standard terminology for the different parties involved in the transaction:

- *Purchasers*. These are the consumers buying the goods.
- *Merchants*. These are the retailers.
- *Certification authority (CA)*. This is a body that issues digital certificates that confirm the identity of purchasers and merchants.
- *Bank*. These are traditional banks.
- *Electronic token issuer*. A virtual bank that issues digital currency.

The basic requirements for security systems from these different parties to the transaction are as follows:

1 *Authentication* – are parties to the transaction who they claim to be (risk C above)?
2 *Privacy and confidentiality* – is the transaction data-protected? The consumer may want to make an anonymous purchase. Are all non-essential traces of a transaction removed from the public network and all intermediary records eliminated (risks B and C above)?
3 *Integrity* – checks that the message sent is complete, i.e. that it isn't corrupted.
4 *Non-repudiability* – ensures sender cannot deny sending message.
5 *Availability* – how can threats to the continuity and performance of the system be eliminated?

Approaches to developing secure systems

Digital certificates

Digital certificates (keys)

Consist of keys made up of large numbers that are used to uniquely identify individuals.

Symmetric encryption

Both parties to a transaction use the same key to encode and decode messages.

There are two main methods of encryption using digital certificates:

1 **Secret-key (symmetric) encryption**. This involves both parties' having an identical (shared) key that is known only to them. Only this key can be used to encrypt and decrypt messages. The secret key has to be passed from one party to another before use in much the same way a copy of a secure attaché case key would have to be sent to a receiver of information. This approach has traditionally been used to achieve security between two separate parties, such as major companies conducting EDI. Here the private key is sent out electronically or by courier to ensure it is not copied.

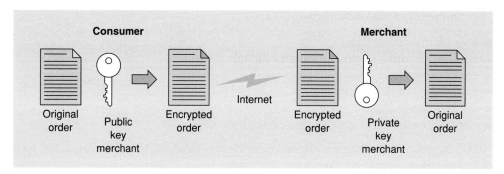

Figure 3.13 Public-key or asymmetric encryption

This method is not practical for general e-commerce since it would not be safe for a purchaser to give a secret key to a merchant since control of it would be lost and it could not then be used for other purposes. A merchant would also have to manage many customer keys.

2 **Public-key (asymmetric) encryption.** Asymmetric encryption is so called since the keys used by the sender and receiver of information are different. The two keys are related by a numerical code, so only the pair of keys can be used in combination to encrypt and decrypt information. Figure 3.13 shows how public-key encryption works in an e-commerce context. A customer can place an order with a merchant by automatically looking up the public key of the merchant and then using this key to encrypt the message containing their order. The scrambled message is then sent across the Internet and on receipt by the merchant is read using the merchant's private key. In this way only the merchant who has the only copy of the private key can read the order. In the reverse case the merchant could confirm the customer's identity by reading identity information such as a digital signature encrypted with the private key of the customer using their public key.

> **Asymmetric encryption**
> Both parties use a related but different key to encode and decode messages.

Digital signatures

Digital signatures can be used to create commercial systems by using public-key encryption to achieve authentication: the merchant and purchaser can prove they are genuine. The purchaser's digital signature is encrypted before sending a message using their private key and on receipt the public key of the purchaser is used to decrypt the digital signature. This proves the customer is genuine. Digital signatures are not widely used currently due to the difficulty of setting up transactions, but will become more widespread as the public-key infrastructure (PKI) stabilises and use of certificate authorities increases.

> **Digital signatures**
> A method of identifying individuals or companies using public key encryption.

The public-key infrastructure (PKI) and certificate authorities

In order for digital signatures and public-key encryption to be effective it is necessary to be sure that the public key intended for decryption of a document actually belongs to the person you believe is sending you the document. The developing solution to this problem is the issuance by a trusted third party (TTP) of a message containing owner identification information and a copy of the public key of that person. The TTPs are usually referred to as **certificate authorities (CAs)**, and various bodies such as banks and the Post Office are likely to fulfil this role. That message is called a **certificate**. In reality, as asymmetric encryption is rather slow, it is often only a sample of the message that is encrypted and used as the representative digital signature.

> **Certificate and certificate authorities (CAs)**
> A certificate is a valid copy of a public key of an individual or organisation together with identification information. It is issued by a trusted third party (TTP) or certificate authority (CA). CAs make public keys available and also issue private keys.

Examples of certificate information are:

- user identification data;
- issuing authority identification and digital signature;
- user's public key;
- expiry date of this certificate;
- class of certificate;
- digital identification code of this certificate.

It is proposed that different classes of certificates would exist according to the type of information contained. For example:

1 name, e-mail address;
2 driver's licence, national insurance number, date of birth;
3 credit check;
4 organisation-specific security clearance data.

Virtual private networks

Virtual private network

Private network created using the public network infrastructure of the Internet.

A **virtual private network** (VPN) is a private wide-area network (WAN) that runs over the public network, rather than a more expensive private network. The technique by which VPN operates is sometimes referred to as *tunnelling*, and involves encrypting both packet headers and content using a secure form of the Internet Protocol known as IPSec. As explained in Chapter 3, VPNs enable the global organisation to conduct its business securely, but using the public Internet rather than more expensive proprietary systems.

Current approaches to e-commerce security

In this section we review the approaches used by e-commerce sites to achieve security using the techniques described above.

Secure Sockets Layer protocol (SSL)

Secure Sockets Layer (SSL)

A commonly used encryption technique for scrambling data as it is passed across the Internet from a customer's web browser to a merchant's web server.

SSL is a security protocol, originally developed by Netscape, but now supported by all browsers such as Microsoft Internet Explorer. SSL is used in the majority of B2C e-commerce transactions since it is easy for the customer to use without the need to download additional software or a certificate.

When a customer enters a secure checkout area of an e-commerce site SSL is used and the customer is prompted that 'you are about to view information over a secure connection' and a key symbol is used to denote this security. When encryption is occurring they will see that the web address prefix in the browser changes from 'http://' to 'https://' and a padlock appears at the bottom of the browser window.

How does SSL relate to the different security concepts described above? The main facility it provides is security and confidentiality. SSL enables a private link to be set up between customer and merchant. Encryption is used to scramble the details of an e-commerce transaction as it is passed between the sender and receiver and also when the details are held on the computers at each end. It would require a determined attempt to intercept such a message and decrypt it. SSL is more widely used than the rival S-HTTP method.

The detailed stages of SSL are as follows:

1 Client browser sends request for a secure connection.
2 Server responds with a digital certificate which is sent for authentication.
3 Client and server negotiate *session keys*, which are symmetrical keys used only for the duration of the transaction.

Since, with enough computing power, time and motivation, it is possible to decrypt messages encrypted using SSL, much effort is being put into more secure methods of encryption such as SET. From a merchant's point of view there is also the problem that authentication of the customer is not possible without resorting to other methods such as credit checks.

Secure Electronic Transaction (SET)

Secure Electronic Transaction (SET) is a significant security protocol based on digital certificates; it was developed by a consortium led by Mastercard and Visa and allows parties to a transaction to confirm each other's identity. By employing digital certificates, SET allows a purchaser to confirm that the merchant is legitimate and conversely allows the merchant to verify that the credit card is being used by its owner. It also requires that each purchase request include a digital signature, further identifying the cardholder to the retailer. The digital signature and the merchant's digital certificate provide a certain level of trust.

Secure Electronic Transaction (SET)
A standard for public-key encryption intended to enable secure e-commerce transactions developed by Mastercard and Visa.

Despite being launched in the late 1990s, SET is not widely used currently due to the difficulty of exchanging keys. For a customer to have their own key, they need to install a secure 'software wallet' on their PC that contains their private key. The transaction verification process is also slower than SSL and the merchant must use special SET software on their server. SET may become more widespread as the public-key infrastructure (PKI) stabilises and use of certificate authorities increases. There is also likely to be a move to a single online wallet for customers, which means that their details will not be stored on multiple servers and entered separately for each site. The card issuers are also keen to introduce such a scheme since it will counter fraud. However, demand for this service has not been demonstrated by customers.

A key feature of SET is that the customer's credit card number is not stored on the server, so reducing the risk of credit card fraud. Storage is not necessary since SET also involves a bank. The SET process is described by Figure 3.14 and it operates as follows:

1 When a customer places an order, the merchant's SET software sends the order information and the merchant's digital certificate to the client's digital wallet.
2 The credit card and order information are encrypted using the merchant's *bank's* public key along with the customer's digital certificate.
3 The merchant then forwards the payment details to the bank.
4 The bank decrypts payment information since it was encrypted using the bank's public key, and if appropriate it sends authorisation to the merchant, who then confirms payment with the customer.

Certificate authorities (CAs)

For secure e-commerce, there is a requirement for the management of the vast number of public keys. This management involves procedures and protocols necesssary throughout the lifetime of a key – generation, dissemination, revocation and change – together with the administrative functions of time and date stamping and archiving. The successful establishment of a CA is an immense challenge involving trust building and complex management. There are two opposing views on how that challenge should be met.

● *Decentralised*: market-driven, creating brand-name-based 'islands of trust' such as the Consumers' Association. There is a practical need for a local physical office to present certificates of attestational value, e.g. passports, driver's licences. Banks and post offices have a huge advantage.

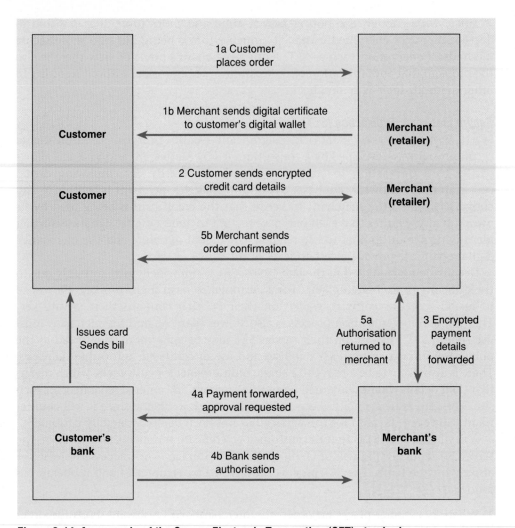

Figure 3.14 An example of the Secure Electronic Transaction (SET) standard

- *Centralised*: in the UK, the Department of Trade and Industry (DTI) has proposed a hierarchical tree, ultimately leading to the government.

The best-known commercial CA is Verisign (www.verisign.com) and this is commonly used for merchant verification. For example, the Avon site uses Verisign to prove to its customers that it is the genuine site. Post offices and telecommunications suppliers are also acting as CAs. Examples in the UK include the Post Office and British Telecom.

Hackers and viruses

Hackers can use techniques such as 'spoofing' to hack into a system and find credit card details. Spoofing, as its name suggests, involves someone masquerading as someone else – as either an individual or an organisation. Spoofing can be of two sorts:

- IP spoofing is used to gain access to confidential information by creating false identification data such as the originating network (IP) address. The objective of this access can be espionage, theft or simply to cause mischief, generate confusion and damage corporate public image or political campaigns. Firewalls can be used to reduce this threat.

● Site spoofing, i.e. fooling the organisation's customers: using a similar URL such as www.amazno.com can divert customers to a site which is not the bona fide retailer.

Firewalls can be used to minimise the risk of security breaches by hackers and viruses. Firewalls are usually created as software mounted on a separate server at the point the company is connected to the Internet. Firewall software can then be configured to only accept links from trusted domains representing other offices in the company or key account customers. A firewall has implication for marketers since staff accessing a web site from work may not be able to access some content such as graphics plug-ins.

Firewall

A specialised software application mounted on a server at the point where the company is connected to the Internet. Its purpose is to prevent unauthorised access into the company from outsiders.

Denial-of-service attacks

The risk to companies of these attacks was highlighted in the spring of 2000, when the top web sites were targeted. The performance of these sites such as Yahoo! (www.yahoo.com) and eBay (www.ebay.com) was severely degraded as millions of data packets flooded the site from a number of servers. This was a distributed attack where the sites were bombarded from rogue software installed on many servers, so it was difficult for the e-tailers to counter.

Alternative payment systems

The preceding discussion has focused on payment using credit card systems since this is the prevalent method for e-commerce purchases. Throughout the 1990s there were many attempts to develop alternative **payment systems** to credit cards. These focused on those for **micropayments** or electronic coinage such as downloading an online newspaper, for which the overhead and fee of using a credit card was too high.

Payment systems

Methods of transferring funds from a customer to a merchant.

Micropayments

Small-denomination payments.

Electronic payment systems can be divided into two basic types: those where no credit occurs and those where credit occurs.

Non-credit or pre-paid systems

Most of the non-credit systems operate using a pre-pay principle. In other words, before purchasing an item electronically, the purchaser must already have electronic funds available that can be immediately transferred to the merchant. These funds can exist in a variety of forms known as **electronic tokens**. Electronic tokens are usually purchased from various electronic token issuers using a traditional payment device such as a credit card or a transfer of cash into a personal account.

Electronic tokens

Units of digital currency that is in a standard electronic format.

Some examples of non-credit systems are:

1 *Digital, virtual or electronic cash (e-cash).* Several companies have attempted to establish payment systems which replicate cash in that they are anonymous systems (from the retailer's perspective). The names to describe these systems are confusing, particularly since some of the concepts have a limited life. DigiCash (www.digicash.com) was one of the 'early runners' in this area, but this company filed for bankruptcy in 1998 and the technology and concept are now owned by eCash (www.ecash.com). Digital cash usually follows what is known as a 'bearer certificate system' where blank tokens are issued by the user and certified by the bank. It is very secure as the merchant must make an online real-time connection to the bank to ensure credit is available – this can make it difficult to implement for small-to-medium retailers. Cybercoin from CyberCash (www.cybercash.com) is a notational system using pre-paid funds that does not require inter-bank clearing. CyberCoin was terminated in 1998 and users migrated to instabuy (www.instabuy.com), a credit-card-based system.

2 *Microtransactions or micropayments such as Millicent.* These are digital cash systems which allow very small sums of money (fractions of a penny) to be transferred, but with lower security. Such small sums do not warrant a credit card payment, because processing is too costly. The Digital Millicent scheme dating back to the mid-1990s is the best known of these, but has never been widely used in Europe. ECoin (www.ecoin.net) is a newer micropayment system that is becoming more popular. Such micropayment systems may become important for purchasing information or music to play on devices such as the Rio, a credit-card-sized personal stereo, which downloads CD-quality music direct from the Internet for a small charge.

3 *Debit cards.* Cards issued with standard bank accounts could theoretically be used for e-commerce purchase, but credit cards are preferred by merchants since the payment is secured by the bank. Debit cards have been used by Bank Austria to enable payments by teenagers who cannot have credit cards, but can use debit cards up to the limit of their accounts.

4 *Smartcards.* These are different from the other items in the list since they are physical cards rather than virtual, so must be inserted into a smartcard reader before items can be purchased. Since such readers aren't yet a standard feature of home PCs, the use of smartcards for purchase is limited to trials in areas such as Swindon (Mondex/Mastercard) and Leeds (Visa Cash) where purchase across the Internet occurs through public kiosks in shopping centres which have smartcard readers. The Visa Cash system is a bearer certificate system (chip-card), cleared through the conventional banking system, where the issuing institution earns float. This was trialled in Leeds with 60 000 cards in circulation and 1400 businesses accepting them. *Computing* (29 October 1998) reported that 'Ken Bignall, managing director of Visa UK said that the Leeds programme has shown that an electronic purse adds real convenience for cardholders'. For example, Visa Cash transactions have already replaced cash use by up to 10% in car parks and have also proved popular in fast-food restaurants, sandwich shops and newsagents. They are not commonly used for the Internet at present, because of a lack of card-reading devices, but they do offer this potential.

Post-paid or credit-based systems

1 *Digital/electronic cheques.* These are modelled on conventional cheques except that they are authorised using digital signatures rather than handwritten signatures. An example of a digital cheque payment system operating within the UK is the BankNet service at mkn.co.uk/bank which is an online banking service set up by MarketNet and Secure Trust Bank plc. It offers the facility to write digitally signed cheques using public-key/private-key cryptographic techniques (see earlier section for definitions).

2 *Credit cards such as Visa or Mastercard.* These are the predominant form of online payment. The reason for this is that they fulfil well the requirements for a payment system coupled with their being an existing standard.

Although credit card payment is usually made direct to the merchant, by filling in the card number and address on an online form, there may be some instances where it is more convenient for the customer to register their credit card details with a third party. In this case it is easier to make frequent purchases, and the credit card details do not have to be divulged to each retailer. Such a concept is provided by Pay2See (www.Pay2See.com) which enables downloadable products such as music and reports to be paid for.

Business payment systems

There is currently no standard business payment system. Most businesses use existing payment-by-account arrangements and there is no integrated transfer between merchant, bank and customer. The lack of a standard can perhaps be explained by the complexity of the transaction, which must fulfil these requirements:

● The system must provide facilities for different members of the buying organisation including the requisitioner, authoriser and purchasing department.
● The system must allow for repeat orders and complex orders with many items.
● The system must allow for specialised or bespoke orders.
● The system must have high levels of security for the potentially high value of the orders.
● The bank or payment authority must be fully integrated into the system.

There are currently three main standards under development:

1 The Open Buying on the Internet (OBI, www.openbuy.org) created by the Internet Purchasing Roundtable is intended to ensure that different e-commerce systems can talk to each other. It is managed by CommerceNet (www.commerce.net) and backed by, among others, 3M, Ford, Mastercard, Visa and Microsoft. Figure 3.15 shows the model proposed by the OBI.
2 The Open Trading Protocol (OTP, www.otp.org) is intended to standardise a variety of payment-related activities including purchase agreements, receipts for purchases and payments. It is backed by, among others, AT&T, Cybercash, Hitachi, IBM, Sun and BT. Despite this impressive line-up the web site has not featured any updated press releases since 1998 and seems set to be eclipsed by OBI.

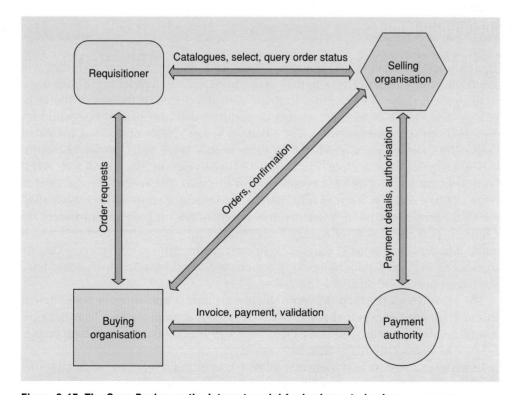

Figure 3.15 The Open Buying on the Internet model for business-to-business e-commerce

3 Internet-based EDI. Traditional EDI standards have also been extended for use on the Internet, but mainly through initiatives of individual suppliers rather than a cross-industry move.

Reassuring the customer

Once the security measures are in place, content on the merchant's site can be used to reassure the customer, for example Amazon (www.amazon.com) takes customer fears about security seriously judging by the prominence and amount of content it devotes to this issue. Some of the approaches used indicate good practice in allaying customers' fears. These include:

- use of customer guarantee to safeguard purchase;
- clear explanation of SSL security measures used;
- highlighting the rarity of fraud ('ten million customers have shopped safely without credit card fraud');
- the use of alternative ordering mechanisms such as phone or fax;
- the prominence of information to allay fears – the guarantee is one of the main menu options.

Companies can also use independent third parties that set guidelines for online privacy and security. The best-known international bodies are Truste (www.truste.org) and Verisign for payment authentication (www.verisign.com). Within particular companies there may be other bodies such as in the UK, Which Web Trader (www.which.net/webtrader), TrustUK (www.trustuk.org) and ChambersOnline (www.chambersonline.co.uk).

Economic factors

The economic prosperity and competitive environment in different countries will determine the e-commerce potential of each. Managers developing e-commerce strategies will target the countries that are most developed in the use of the technology. Knowledge of different economic conditions is also part of budgeting for revenue from different countries. For example, Fisher (2000) noted that the Asian market for e-commerce is predicted to triple within three years. However, within this marketplace there are large variations. Relative to income, the cost of a PC is still high in many parts of Asia for people on low incomes. Fisher (2000) suggests that there will be a division between information 'haves' and 'have-nots' and, as we shall see in the section on political factors, this is dependent on government factors. In China there is regulation on foreign ownership of Internet portals and ISPs which could hamper development. User access to certain content is also restricted. Despite this, access in China is doubling every 6 months and at this rate China could have the largest user base within 10 years!

The trend to globabilisation can arguably insulate a company to some extent from fluctuations in regional markets, but is of course no protection from a global recession. Managers can also study e-commerce in leading countries to help predict future e-commerce trends in their own country.

In Chapter 2 we saw that there is wide variation in the level of use of the Internet in different continents and countries, particularly for consumer use. According to Roussel (2000), economic, regulatory and cultural issues are among the factors

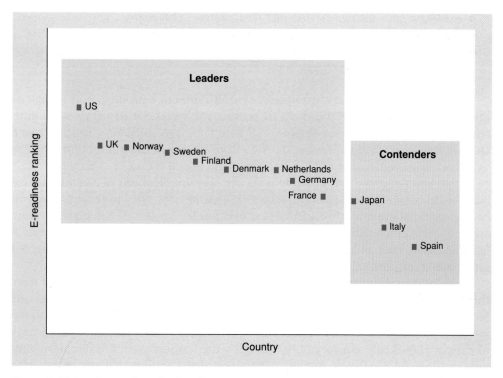

Figure 3.16 Leaders and contenders in e-commerce
Source: Adapted from the Economist Intelligence Unit/Pyramid Research e-readiness ranking (www.eiu.com)

affecting use of the Internet for commercial transactions. The relative importance of these means e-commerce will develop differently in every country. Roussel (2000) rated different countries according to their readiness to use the Internet for business (Figure 3.16). This was based on two factors – propensity for e-commerce and Internet penetration. To calculate the propensity of a country for e-commerce transactions, the business environment was evaluated using the Economic Intelligence Unit (www.eiu.com) rating of countries according to 70 different indicators, such as the strength of the economy, political stability, the regulatory climate, taxation policies and openness to trade and investment. Cultural factors were also considered, including language and the attitude to online purchasing as opposed to browsing. The two graphed factors do not correspond in all countries, for example Scandinavian users frequently use the Internet to gain information, helped by widespread English usage, but they are less keen to purchase online due to concerns about security. Internet penetration varies widely and is surprisingly low in some countries, for example in France, which was earlier a leader in e-commerce through its Minitel system, and in Japan.

● Globalisation

Globalisation refers to the move towards international trading in a single global marketplace and the blurring of social and cultural differences between countries. Some perceive it as 'Westernisation' or even 'Americanisation'.

Quelch and Klein (1996) point out some of the consequences for organisations that wish to compete in the global marketplace. They say a company must have:

Globalisation

The increase of international trading and shared social and cultural values.

- *a 24 hour order taking and customer service response capability;*
- *regulatory and customs-handling experience to ship internationally;*
- *in-depth understanding of foreign marketing environments to assess the advantages of its own products and services.*

Language and cultural understanding may also present a problem and a small or medium-sized company is unlikely to possess the resources to develop a multi-language version of its site or employ staff with language skills. On the other hand, Quelch and Klein (1996) note that the growth of the use of the Internet for business will accelerate the trend of English becoming the lingua franca of commerce.

Hamill and Gregory (1997) highlight the strategic implications of e-commerce for business-to-business exchanges conducted internationally. They note that there will be increasing standardisation of prices across borders as businesses become more aware of price differentials. Secondly, they predict that the importance of traditional intermediaries such as agents and distributors will be reduced by Internet-enabled direct marketing and sales.

Larger organisations typically already compete in the global marketplace, or have the financial resources to achieve this. But what about the smaller organisation? Most governments are looking to encourage SMEs to use electronic commerce to tap into the international market. Advice from governments must reassure SMEs wishing to export. Hamill and Gregory (1997) identify the barriers to SME internationalisation in Table 3.4. Complete Activity 3.3 to look at the actions that can be taken to overcome these barriers.

Activity 3.3 **Overcoming SME resistance to e-commerce**

Purpose

To highlight barriers to exporting amongst SMEs and suggest measures by which they may be overcome by governments.

Activity

For each of the four barriers to internationalisation given in Table 3.4 suggest the management reasons why the barriers may exist and actions governments can take to overcome these barriers. Evaluate how well the government in your country communicates the benefits of e-commerce through education and training.

Table 3.4 Issues in SME resistance to exporting (barriers from Hamill and Gregory (1997) and Poon and Jevons (1997))

Barrier	Management issues	How can barrier be overcome?
1. Psychological		
2. Operational		
3. Organisational		
4. Product/market		

Embracing difference in a globalised world

Globalisation, or maybe more specifically anti-globalisation, issues are never far from the head-lines, whether it's coverage of the latest anti-WTO demonstration or news that McDonald's has replaced Ronald McDonald in France with Asterix – in a move to 'appease anti-globalisation protesters' (BBC News, 22 January 2002).

But what does globalisation actually mean? Stemming from the application of free market principles it has manifested the belief that the world is small and that consumers are becoming more and more alike, thus allowing companies to use the same advertising and marketing across regions and countries. Such a doctrine has enabled companies to act global and think global, much to the distaste of the anti-globalisation lobbies. Indeed, in 1985 it was Friends of the Earth that coined the slogan 'think global, act local' in its desire to counter such global forces – particularly with regards to environmental issues.

However, such 'glocalisation' makes a lot of sense for multinational companies operating today and planning new market entry, for a number of reasons. Firstly, the term globalisation for many Europeans is virtually synonymous with that of 'Americanisation'. For some this has negative connotations of materialism, loss of native culture and the encroachment of the English language. At its extreme, it drives many of the anti-globalisation activists. Thus there is real risk that companies will damage their brand and reputation if they *don't* recognise the importance of localisation when considering market entry.

Secondly, consumers are as different as they are similar – local and regional cultures have a profound affect in shaping consumer demand. These differences are potentially more interesting than the similarities, in that they can allow product and service differentiation as well as new approaches to segmentation and marketing communications. To take advantage of such opportunities, businesses have to have a clear insight into how and why consumers in one market may differ from ones in another.

Americanisation – a strong undercurrent

Feelings of anti-Americanisation are a strong undercurrent in Europe. Businesses have to plan how to counter such a groundswell of feeling if planning on entering new markets – given that some 50% of Europeans believe that 'our society is too Americanised' and such an attitude has increased over the past 10 years. While the degree of agreement varies within Europe (e.g. 67% of Spaniards agreeing with the statement, as compared with 44% of Brits) it is a significant influence of customer behaviour. To compound matters, multinational companies are the least trusted of 27 entities when European consumers have been asked to state which they trust to be honest and fair.

As a result, not only have we seen an increase in consumer activism (such as anti-WTO protests, growth of the slow food movement in Europe etc.), but also we have seen global brands coming under threat from emergent local brands which are gaining in currency. We would expect this to continue. This is not to say that there is no room for global brands! Many global brands have successfully tapped into local culture and tastes and recognised the need to either modify the product/service completely or change different elements of the offer and how it is ultimately marketed. Thus companies expanding into new geographic markets have to ensure that their strategies are based on a real understanding of regional and local markets.

The need to understand differences between consumers

Globalisation is not making the world a smaller, homogeneous place. While this presents many opportunities for businesses, it also implies a need for a clear understanding of what shapes

▶

consumer needs and desires in the different nations. Not surprising perhaps that many businesses found the notion of a 'globalised' world compelling given the significant implications for researching a multitude of different markets in terms of time and money budgets. Similarly, it is easy to understand the temptation of taking well-established national stereotypes and assuming that they are representative of the truth.

Recent attitudinal studies in Europe and the US undertaken by The Henley Centre show the complexity of attempting to categorise consumers on a broad scale. Let's take an example. At one level, results show that all consumers take pride in their family, so a global advertising campaign using the 'family' as a theme may feel like safe territory. To some extent it is. Dig down a bit deeper however and you find that different people define 'family' in very different ways, so what people take pride in will be subtly different. At a country level, many more differences expose themselves.

Businesses wanting to broaden their geographic reach have to consider at a strategic level what level of understanding of consumer needs they require. Generalisations are important and are a good place to start, but it is critical to then delve further – national stereotypes are too simplistic. Differences, rather than similarities, have to be considered, and interrogated in terms of how these will impact customer needs.

Source: Based on information from www.henleycentre.com

Question

Based on this article and your experiences, debate the question: 'Site localisation is essential for each country for an e-commerce offering to be tenable'.

Political and legal factors

The political and regulatory environment is shaped by the interplay of government agencies, public opinion, consumer pressure groups such as CAUCE (the coalition against unsolicited e-mail), www.cauce.org, and industry-backed organisations such as TRUSTe (www.truste.org) that promote best practice amongst companies. The political environment is one of the drivers for establishing the laws to ensure privacy and to collect taxes as described in previous sections.

Political action enacted through government agencies to control the adoption of the Internet can include:

- promoting the benefits of adopting the Internet for consumers and business to improve a country's economic prosperity;
- sponsoring research leading to dissemination of best practice amongst companies, for example the DTI (2000) international benchmarking survey;
- enacting legislation to regulate the environment, for example to protect privacy or control taxation;
- setting up international bodies to coordinate the Internet such as ICANN (the Internet Corporation for Assigned Names and Numbers, www.icann.com) which will introduce new domains such as .biz and .info.

Some examples of the role of government organisations in promoting and regulating e-commerce is given by these examples from the European Commission:

- In 1998 new data protection guidelines were enacted, as is described in the section on privacy, to help protect consumers and increase the adoption of e-commerce by reducing security fears.

- In May 2000 the eEurope Action Plan was launched with objectives of 'a cheaper, faster, more secure Internet; investing in people's skills and access; and stimulating the use of the Internet'. The Commission intends to increase Internet access relative to the USA, in order to make Europe more competitive.
- Also in May 2000 the Commission announced that it wants the supply of local loops, the copper cables that link homes to telephone exchanges, to be unbundled so that newer companies can compete with traditional telecommunications suppliers. The objective here is the provision of widespread broadband services as a major aim of the EU.
- In June 2000 an e-commerce directive was adopted by the European Union. Pullen and Robinson (2000) note that the most fundamental provision of the Act is in Article 3 which defines the principles of country of origin and mutual recognition. This means that any company trading in an EU member state is subject in that country to the laws of that country and not those of the other member states. This prevents the need for companies to adhere to specific advertising or data protection laws in the countries in which they operate.

The type of initiative launched by governments is highlighted by the launch in the UK in September 1999 of a new 'UK online' campaign (www.ukonlineforbusiness.gov.uk), a raft of initiatives and investment aimed at moving people, business and government itself online (**e-government**). E-envoy posts and an e-minister have also been appointed. The prime minister said:

> *There is a revolution going on in our economy. A fundamental change, not a dot.com fad, but a real transformation towards a knowledge economy. So, today, I am announcing a new campaign. Its goal is to get the UK on-line. To meet the three stretching targets we have set: for Britain to be the best place in the world for e-commerce, with universal access to the Internet and all Government services on the net. In short, the UK on-line campaign aims to get business, people and government on-line.*

E-government
The use of Internet technologies to provide government services to citizens.

Specific targets have been set for the proportion of people and businesses that have access including public access points for those who cannot currently afford the technology. Managers who are aware of these initiatives can tap into sources of funding for development or free training to support their online initiatives.

● Internet governance

Internet governance describes the control put in place to manage the growth of the Internet and its usage. Governance is traditionally undertaken by government, but the global nature of the Internet makes it less practical for a government to control cyberspace. Dyson (1998) says:

Internet governance
Control of the operation and use of the Internet.

> *Now, with the advent of the Net, we are privatising government in a new way – not only in the traditional sense of selling things off to the private sector, but by allowing organisations independent of traditional governments to take on certain 'government' regulatory roles. These new international regulatory agencies will perform former government functions in counterpoint to increasingly global large companies and also to individuals and smaller private organisations who can operate globally over the Net.*

The US approach to governance, formalised in the Framework for Global Electronic Commerce in 1997 is to avoid any single country taking control.

Dyson (1998) describes different layers of jurisdiction. These are:

1 physical space comprising each individual country where their own laws such as those governing taxation, privacy and trading and advertising standards hold;
2 ISPs – the connection between the physical world and virtual world;
3 domain name control (www.icann.net) and communities;
4 agencies such as TRUSTe (www.truste.org).

Knowledge of legal issues is, of course, also vital to e-commerce managers since when they seek to exploit new marketplaces, they will be subject to local legal constraints. For example, Germany has specific laws that prohibit explicit comparisons between products, and Belgium has a law that discount sales may occur only in January and July. Governments looking to foster e-commerce develop guidelines to help companies adhere to laws in countries in which they are seeking to operate.

Some of the main e-commerce-related legal issues that companies need to seek specific legal advice on are:

1 *Domain name registrations and trademarking of new Internet brands*. There have been many disputes about ownership of company domains (URLs).
2 *Advertising standards*. Most countries have specific laws to avoid misrepresentation to the consumer and uncompetitive practices.
3 *Defamation and libel*. Information published on a site critical of another company's people or products could represent libel.
4 *Copyright and intellectual property rights (IPR)*. Permissions must be sought for information or images sourced elsewhere in the same way as for any other media.
5 *Data Protection Act and privacy law*. Sites must protect data held on consumers according to the local law as described in the Ethics section of this chapter.
6 *Taxation on electronic commerce*. For companies involved in e-commerce, sales tax must be collected from consumers.

Zugelder et al. (2000) give a fuller review of legal issues associated with Internet marketing, including consumer rights, defamation and disparagement, intellectual property protection, and jurisdiction.

● Taxation

How to change tax laws to reflect the globalisation through the Internet is a problem that many governments are grappling with. The fear is that the Internet may cause significant reductions in tax revenues to national or local governments if existing laws do not cover changes in purchasing patterns. In Europe, the use of online betting in lower-tax areas such as Gibraltar has resulted in lower revenues to governments in the countries where consumers would have formerly paid gaming tax to the government via a betting shop. Large UK bookmakers such as William Hill and Victor Chandler are offering Internet-based betting from 'offshore' locations such as Gibraltar. The lower duties in these countries offer the companies the opportunity to make betting significantly cheaper than if they were operating under a higher-tax regime. This trend has been dubbed LOCI or Location Optimised Commerce on the Internet by Mougayer (1998). Meanwhile the government of the country from which a person places the bet will face a drop in its tax revenues. In the UK the government has sought to reduce the revenue shortfall by reducing the differential between UK and overseas costs.

The extent of the taxation problem for governments is illustrated by the US ABC News (2000) reporting that between $300 million and $3.8 billion of potential tax revenue was lost by authorities in 2000 in the USA as more consumers purchased online. The revenue shortfall occurs because online retailers need to impose sales or use tax only when goods are being sent to a consumer who lives in a state (or country) where the retailer has a bricks-and-mortar store. Buyers are supposed to voluntarily pay the appropriate sales taxes when buying online but this rarely happens in practice. This makes the Internet a largely tax-free area in the USA.

Since the Internet supports the global marketplace it could be argued that it makes little sense to introduce tariffs on goods and services delivered over the Internet. Such instruments would, in any case, be impossible to apply over products delivered electronically. This position is currently that of the USA. In the document 'A Framework for Global Electronic Commerce', President Clinton stated that:

> The United States will advocate in the World Trade Organisation (WTO) and other appropriate international fora that the Internet be declared a tariff-free zone.

● Tax jurisdiction

Tax jurisdiction determines which country gets tax income from a transaction. Under the current system of international tax treaties, the right to tax is divided between the country where the enterprise that receives the income is resident ('residence' country) and that from which the enterprise derives that income ('source' country). Laws on taxation are rapidly evolving and vary dramatically between countries. A proposed EU directive intends to deal with these issues by defining the place of establishment of a merchant as where they pursue an economic activity from a fixed physical location. At the time of writing the general principle that is being applied is that tax rules are similar to those for a conventional mail-order sale; for the UK, the tax principles are as follows:

(a) if the supplier (residence) and the customer (source) are both in the UK, VAT will be chargeable;
(b) exports to private customers in the EU will attract either UK VAT or local VAT;
(c) exports outside the EU will be zero-rated (but tax may be levied on import);
(d) imports into the UK from the EU or beyond will attract local VAT, or UK import tax when received through customs;
(e) services attract VAT according to where the supplier is located. This is different from products and causes anomalies if online services are created. For example, a betting service located in Gibraltar enables UK customers to gamble at a lower tax rate than with the same company in the UK.

● Freedom-restrictive legislation

Although governments enact legislation in order to protect consumer privacy on the Internet as described earlier, it is also worth noting that some individuals and organisations believe that legislation may also be too restrictive. In the UK, a new Telecommunications Act and Regulation of Investigatory Powers Act (RIP) took several years to enact since companies were concerned to ensure security and to give security forces the ability to monitor all communications passing through ISPs. This was fiercely contested due to cost burdens placed on infrastructure providers and in particular the Internet service providers (ISPs), and of course many citizens and employees may not be happy about being monitored either!

The Freedom House (www.freedomhouse.org) is a human rights organisation created to reduce censorship since it believes government censorship laws may be too restrictive. It notes in a report (Freedom House, 2000) that governments in many countries, both developed and developing, are increasingly censoring online content. Only 69 of the countries studied have completely free media, while 51 have partly free media and 66 countries suffer heavy government censorship. Censorship methods include implementing licensing and regulation laws, applying existing print and broadcast restrictions to the Internet, filtering content and direct censoring after dissemination. In Asia and the Middle East, governments frequently cite protection of morality and local values as reasons for censorship. Countries where Internet access is mostly or totally controlled by the authorities include Azerbaijan, Belarus, Burma, China, Cuba, Iran, Iraq, Kazakhstan, Kyrgyzstan, Libya, North Korea, Saudi Arabia, Sierra Leone, Sudan, Syria, Tajikistan, Tunisia, Turkmenistan, Uzbekistan and Vietnam. Even the US government tried to control access to certain Internet sites with the Communications Decency Act in 1996, but this was unsuccessful.

Summary

1 Environmental scanning and analysis of the macro-environment are necessary in order that a company can respond to environmental changes and act on legal and ethical constraints on its activities.

2 Social factors include variation in usage of the Internet while ethical issues include the need to safeguard consumer privacy and security of details. Privacy issues include collection and dissemination of customer information, cookies and the use of direct e-mail. Marketers must act within current law, reassure customers about their privacy and explain the benefits of collection of personal information.

3 Rapid variation in technology requires constant monitoring of adoption of the technology by customers and competitors and appropriate responses.

4 Economic factors considered in the chapter are the regional differences in the use of the Internet for trade. Different economic conditions in different markets are considered in developing e-commerce budgets.

5 Political factors involve the role of governments in promoting e-commerce, but also in trying to restrict it.

6 Legal factors to be considered by e-commerce managers include taxation, domain name registration, copyright and data protection.

EXERCISES

Self-assessment exercises

1 Summarise the key elements of the macro-environment that should be scanned by an e-commerce manager.

2 Give an example of how each of the macro-environment factors may directly drive the content and services provided by a web site.

3 What actions should e-commerce managers take to safeguard consumer privacy and security?

4 Give three examples of techniques web sites can use to protect the user's privacy.

5 How do governments attempt to control the adoption of the Internet?

6 Suggest approaches to managing technological innovation.

Essay and discussion questions

1 You recently started a job as e-commerce manager for a bank. Produce a checklist of all the different legal and ethical issues that you need to check for compliance on the existing web site of the bank.

2 How should the e-commerce manager monitor and respond to technological innovation?

3 Benchmark different approaches to achieving and reassuring customers about their privacy and security using three or four examples for a retail sector such as travel, books, toys or clothing.

4 Select a new Internet-access technology (such as phone, kiosks or TV) that has been introduced in the last two years and assess whether it will become a significant method of access.

Examination questions

1 Explain the different layers of governance of the Internet.

2 Summarise the macro-environment variables a company needs to monitor when operating an e-commerce site.

3 Explain the purpose of environmental scanning in an e-commerce context.

4 Give three examples of how web sites can use techniques to protect the user's privacy.

5 Explain the significance of the diffusion–adoption concept to the adoption of new technologies to:
   (a) consumers purchasing using technological innovations;
   (b) businesses deploying technological innovations.

6 What action should an e-commerce manager take to ensure compliance with ethical and legal standards of their site?

References

ABC News (2000) *Ecommerce Causes Tax Shortfall in US*. News story on ABC.com. 27/07/00
http://abcnews.go.com/sections/business/DailyNews/internettaxes000725.html

Curry, A. (2001) What's next for interactive television, *Interactive Marketing*, 3(2), October/December, 114–28.

Cyber Dialogue (2000) Privacy report, 25 April, published online at: www.cyberdialogue.com/resource/press/releases/2000/04-19-cd-privacy.html

DTI (2000) *Business in the Information Age – International Benchmarking Study 2000*. UK Department of Trade and Industry. Available online at: www.ukonlineforbusiness.gov.uk.

Dyson, E. (1998) *Release 2.1. A Design for Living in the Digital Age*. Penguin, London.

Fisher, A. (2000) Gap widens between the 'haves' and 'have-nots', *Financial Times*, 5 December.

Fletcher, K. (2001) Privacy: the Achilles heel of the new marketing, *Interactive Marketing*, 3(2), October/December, 128–41.

Freedom House (2000) *Censoring Dot-gov Report*, 17 April, www.freedomhouse.org/news/pr041700.html, New York.

Hamill, J. and Gregory, K. (1997) Internet marketing in the internationalization of UK SMEs, *Journal of Marketing Management*, Special edition on internationalization, J. Hamill (ed.), 13 (1–3).

IDC (2002) Online travel services set to boost mobile commerce. IDC Research press release, 23 January, www.idc.com.

Jupiter MMXI (2002) Low cost set top boxes kick start Digital TV market in Europe. Press release, 7 March, uk.jupitermmxi.com/xp/uk/press/releases/pr_030702.xml.

McIntosh, N. (1999) The new poor, *Guardian*, 22 July, p. 19.

Mason, R. (1986) Four ethical issues of the information age, *MIS Quarterly*, March.

MobileCommerceWorld (2001) i-Mode users spending more on content. 26 November Press release based on data from Infocom, www.mobilecommerceworld.com.

MobileCommerceWorld (2002) British SMS records smashed in December. 24 January Press release based on data from the mobile data association, www.mobilecommerceworld.com.

Mougayer, W. (1998) *Opening Digital Markets – Battle Plans and Strategies for Internet Commerce*, 2nd edn. CommerceNet Press, McGraw-Hill, New York.

Pew (2000) Pew Internet and American Life Project. http://pewinternet.org/reports. Reported by Nua (www.nua.ie) 22 August.

Poon, S. and Jevons, C. (1997) Internet-enabled international marketing: a small business network perspective, *Journal of Marketing Management*, 13, 29–41.

Pullen, M. and Robinson, J. (2001) The e-commerce directive and its impact on pan-European interactive marketing, *Interactive Marketing*, 2(3), 272–5.

Quelch, J. and Klein, L. (1996) The Internet and international marketing, *Sloan Management Review*, Spring, 61–75.

Revolution (2001a) Campaign of the week, *Revolution*, 16 May, p. 38.

Revolution (2001b) The night belongs to text messages, *Revolution*, 16 May, pp. 30–2.

Rogers, E. (1983) *Diffusion of Innovations*, 3rd edn. Free Press, New York.

Roussel, A. (2000) Leaders and laggards in B2C commerce. Gartner Group report. 4 August. SPA-11-5334, www.gartner.com.

Trott, P. (1998) *Innovation Management and New Product Development*. Financial Times/Prentice Hall, Harlow.

Zugelder, M., Flaherty, T. and Johnson, J. (2000) Legal issues associated with international Internet Marketing, *International Marketing Review*, 17(3), 253–71.

Further reading

Dibb, S., Simkin, S., Pride, W. and Ferrel, O. (2001) *Marketing. Concepts and Strategies*, 4th European edn. Houghton Mifflin, New York. *See* Chapter 2, The marketing environment.

Dyson, E. (1998) *Release 2.1. A Design for Living in the Digital Age*. Penguin, London. Chapters 5 Governance, 8 Privacy, 9 Anonymity and 10 Security are of particular relevance.

Garfinkel, S. (2000) *Database Nation*. O'Reilly, Sebastopol, CA. This book is subtitled 'the death of privacy in the 21st century' and this is the issue on which it focuses (includes Internet- and non-Internet-related privacy).

Kotler, P., Armstrong, G., Saunders, J. and Wong, V. (2001) *Principles of Marketing*, 3rd European edn, Financial Times/Prentice Hall, Harlow. See Chapter 4, The marketing environment.

Laudon, K. and Traver, C. (2001) *E-commerce. Business. Technology. Society.* Addison-Wesley, Boston. Chapter 9, Ethical, social and political issues in e-commerce, is relevant.

Slevin, J. (2000) *The Internet and Society*. Polity Press, Cambridge. A book about the Internet that combines social theory, communications analysis and case studies from both academic and applied perspectives.

Zugelder, M., Flaherty, T. and Johnson, J. (2000) Legal issues associated with international Internet marketing, *International Marketing Review*, 17(3), 253–71. Gives a detailed review of legal issues associated with Internet marketing including consumer rights, defamation and disparagement, intellectual property protection, and jurisdiction.

Web links

- *E-MORI Technology Tracker* (www.e-mori.co.uk/tracker.shtml). Provides a summary of access to new media platforms.
- *Mobile Commerce World* (www.mobilecommerceworld.com). Source on usage of m-commerce.
- *New Media Age* (www.newmediazero.com/nma). A weekly magazine reporting on the UK new media interest. Content now available online.
- *New Television Strategies* (www.newmediazero.com/ntvs). Sister publication to *New Media Age*.
- *Revolution* magazine (www.revolutionmagazine.com). A weekly magazine available for the UK, covering a range of new media platforms.

PART 2

Internet strategy development

In Part 2 approaches for developing an Internet marketing strategy are explored. These combine traditional approaches to strategic marketing planning with specific Internet-related issues that need to be considered by Internet marketers. In Chapter 4 a strategy framework is described, Chapter 5 discusses the opportunities for varying the marketing mix online and Chapter 6 reviews strategies for online customer relationship management.

**Chapter 4
Internet marketing
strategy**

➤ An integrated Internet marketing strategy
➤ A generic strategic approach
➤ Situation review
➤ Strategic goal setting
➤ Strategy formulation
➤ Strategy implementation

**Chapter 5
The Internet and
the marketing mix**

➤ Product
➤ Price
➤ Place
➤ Promotion
➤ People, process and physical evidence

**Chapter 6
Relationship
marketing using
the Internet**

➤ Relationship marketing
➤ Key concepts of online customer relationship management
➤ Approaches to implementing e-CRM
➤ Techniques and technologies for implementing e-CRM
➤ Integrating the Internet with other forms of direct marketing

Chapter 4

Internet marketing strategy

Chapter at a glance

Main topics

Case studies

Links to other chapters

This chapter is related to other chapters as follows:

➤ It builds on the evaluation of the Internet environment from Chapters 2 and 3

➤ Chapter 5 describes the potential for varying different elements of the marketing mix as part of Internet marketing strategy

➤ Chapter 6 describes customer relationship management strategies

➤ Chapter 7 describes development of an Internet marketing plan to support the strategy

Learning objectives

After reading this chapter, the reader should be able to:

● Relate Internet marketing strategy to marketing and business strategy

● Identify opportunities and threats arising from the Internet

● Evaluate alternative strategic approaches to the Internet

Questions for marketers

Key questions for marketing managers related to this chapter are:

● What approaches can be used to develop Internet marketing strategy?

● How does Internet marketing strategy relate to other strategy development?

● What are the key strategic options for Internet marketing?

Introduction

The importance of the Internet to modern business strategy is indicated by Michael Porter (2001), who says:

The key question is not whether to deploy Internet technology – companies have no choice if they want to stay competitive – but how to deploy it.

An **Internet marketing strategy** is needed to provide consistent direction for an organisation's e-marketing activities that integrates with its other marketing activities and supports the overall objectives of the business.

For many companies, the first forays into Internet marketing are not the result of a well-defined, integrated Internet strategy; rather, they are a necessary response to a rapid market development. The decision to create the web site and use interactive communication tools is reactive: a response to the development of sites by new companies in their sector, or by existing competitors, or a response to customer demands. After a site has been in existence for a year or so, marketing staff and senior managers in a company will naturally question its effectiveness. This is often the point at which the need for a coherent Internet marketing strategy becomes apparent. As a consequence of this approach, our starting point in this chapter is not solely that of creating a strategy for a completely new site; rather, it involves assessing the current site and its effectiveness with a view to future improvements.

When discussing Internet marketing strategy it is useful to keep in mind that Internet strategy involves much more than the narrow focus of a strategy to develop a web site. Although this is part of Internet marketing strategy, we also examine broader issues of using the Internet strategically to redesign business processes and integrate with partners such as suppliers and distributors in new ways.

We can suggest that the Internet marketing strategy has many similarities to traditional marketing strategies, in that it will:

- provide a future direction to Internet marketing activities;
- involve analysis of the organisation's external environment and internal resources to inform strategy;
- articulate Internet marketing objectives that support marketing objectives;
- involve selection of strategic options to achieve Internet marketing objectives and create sustainable differential competitive advantage;
- include strategy formulation to include include typical marketing strategy options such as target markets, positioning and specification of the marketing mix;
- specify how resources will be deployed and the organisation will be structured to achieve the strategy.

This chapter examines each of these elements of strategy. We start by considering, in more detail, an appropriate process for developing an Internet marketing strategy, and then consider the following aspects of strategy:

1. situation review;
2. goal setting;
3. strategy formulation.

An integrated Internet marketing strategy

The integration of an Internet marketing strategy into business and marketing strategies represents a significant challenge for many organisations, in part because

---

Internet marketing strategy

Definition of the approach by which Internet marketing will support marketing and business objectives.

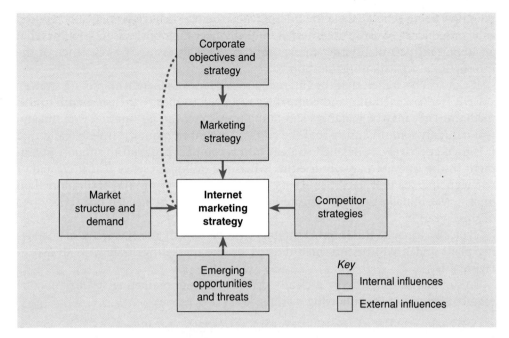

Figure 4.1 Internal and external influences on Internet marketing strategy

they have traditionally considered them separately and in part because of the profound implications for change at an industry level and within the organisation. The Internet is a recent and rapidly growing application and it is this recency and rapid growth that have created the need for its consideration as an important management agenda.

Figure 4.1 indicates the context for the Internet marketing strategy. The internal influences include corporate objectives and strategy, and these in turn influence marketing strategy that should directly influence the Internet marketing strategy. There have been few research surveys on how Internet strategies are developed, but anecdotal evidence suggests the approaches are ad hoc, with Internet marketing being influenced to some extent directly by corporate strategies.

Key external influences include the market structure and demand, competitor strategies and the current and evolving opportunities and threats. Methods for monitoring the external environment to anticipate external opportunities and threats and competitors' actions have been introduced in Chapters 2 and 3, as were methods of assessing the demand of the market for Internet-delivered services.

● Is a separate Internet marketing strategy needed?

It can be argued that companies do not require a separate Internet marketing strategy; rather, the Internet marketing plan should be an adjunct to a strategic marketing plan, in the same way as organisations have product, pricing and advertising strategies and plans. This argument is valid if the Internet is simply 'just another channel to market'. However, the potential significance of the Internet as a contributor to sales and reduced costs is such that it warrants separate attention. For example, for companies selling electronic components and hardware, such as Cisco and Dell, the Internet warranted a separate strategy in that it has radically changed the ways in which these companies operate, with a significant proportion of their sales now being generated via the Internet, and their costs have been greatly reduced as a consequence of using the Internet to re-engineer their businesses. It follows that an important part of Internet marketing strategy is assessing the relevance of the Internet to a particular organisation.

It can also be argued that the Internet also warrants a separate marketing strategy since it is a new medium, and companies will need to specify their response to this medium. They may be making a substantial investment in an Internet web site and will naturally want to ensure that the correct amount of money is invested and that it is used effectively. A detailed strategy and accompanying plan to support investment in the Internet may occur either when the online presence is first created or when an upgrade to its facilities occurs. Such upgrades may need to occur more than once a year initially or, as a web site matures, they may be needed once every two or three years.

Typically though, the Internet strategy will be part of the hierarchy of marketing plans and it will be informed directly by the marketing strategy as shown in Figure 4.1.

To summarise this section, a clearly defined Internet marketing strategy may be required for any of the following reasons:

1 as a detailed strategy that is part of the broader strategic marketing planning process;
2 as part of the investment proposal for a new web site;
3 as part of an investment proposal for upgrading a web site;
4 to inform a detailed e-marketing plan which is used to coordinate all Internet- and IT-related marketing activities over a period of time, typically a year;
5 as a distinct strategy for a company for which the Internet is a significant communications or sales channel.

A generic strategic approach

Strategy process model
A framework for approaching strategy development.

A **strategy process model** provides a framework that gives a logical sequence or 'roadmap' to follow to ensure inclusion of all key activities of strategy development and implementation.

Figure 4.2 shows an overall strategy process model for Internet marketing. The Internet marketing strategy is informed by environment or situation analysis together with the obectives and strategies of the marketing plan. The Internet marketing strategy should be developed with clearly defined strategic goals. Only through setting realistic goals and then assessing whether they are achieved can a company be sure of the contribution Internet-based marketing is making. The Internet marketing strategy informs the Internet marketing or e-marketing plan which details the plan for creating the online presence and executing the online presence. Figure 4.2 shows the relationship between goal setting and measurement. First, goals and objectives are defined in the Internet marketing strategy. These then form an input to the Internet marketing plan, which shows how these goals will be achieved. After the site has been designed and created or modified, it is necessary to monitor it in order to assess whether strategic objectives have been achieved and feed this information back to influence future strategy and its implementation.

A more detailed strategy process for marketing has been suggested by McDonald (1999), Figure 4.3. This approach can be readily applied to Internet marketing. The corporate objectives of phase 1 are replaced by marketing objectives. In this approach there are four main phases, which relate to Figure 4.2 as follows:

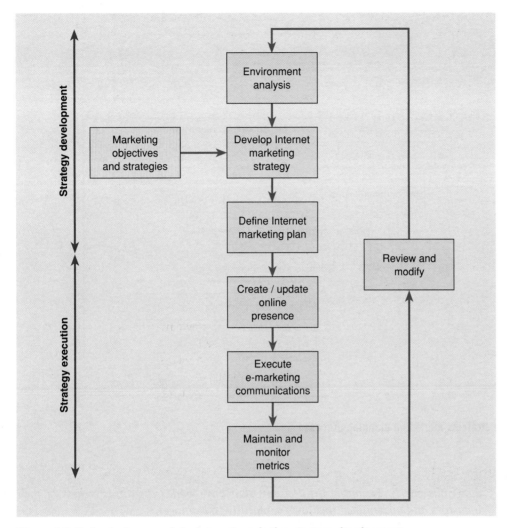

Figure 4.2 A simple framework for Internet marketing strategy development

1 goal setting (marketing objectives and strategies which feed into the Internet marketing strategy);
2 situation review (environment analysis);
3 strategy formulation (develop Internet marketing strategy). This stage includes detailed objective setting for Internet marketing which occurs after situation analysis. Note that the generation of marketing objectives and strategies, estimating expected results and identifying alternative plans and mixes are iterative processes;
4 resource allocation and monitoring (define Internet marketing plan and monitor).

In this chapter, we will use this framework as a basis to review each of the four main stages in turn.

Some have suggested that existing strategy process models such as those of Figures 4.2 and 4.3 are not relevant in the Internet era. Michael Porter (2001) attacks those who have suggested that the Internet invalidates well-known approaches to strategy. He says:

Many have assumed that the Internet changes everything, rendering all the old rules about companies and competition obsolete. That may be a natural reaction, but it is a

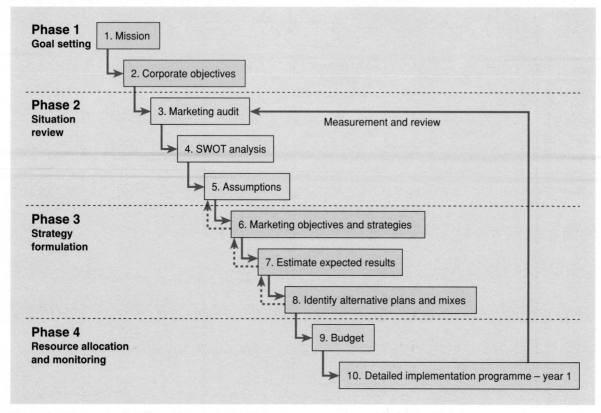

Figure 4.3 A ten-step strategic marketing planning process
Source: McDonald, 1999

dangerous one . . . [resulting in] decisions that have eroded the attractiveness of their industries and undermined their own competitive advantages.

He gives the example of some industries using the Internet to change the basis of competition away from quality, features and service and towards price, making it harder for anyone in their industries to turn a profit.

It can be argued, however, that there is a need for more responsive strategic process models where reaction can occur to events in the marketplace. Mintzberg and Quinn (1991) and other authors commenting on corporate strategy, such as Lynch (2000), distinguish between **prescriptive** and emergent strategy approaches. In the prescriptive strategy approach, similar to Figure 4.3, Lynch identifies three elements of strategy – strategic analysis, strategic development and strategy implementation, and these are linked together sequentially. Strategic analysis is used to develop a strategy, and it is then implemented. In other words, the strategy is prescribed in advance. Alternatively, the distinction between the three elements of strategy may be less clear. This is the **emergent strategy** approach where strategic analysis, strategic development and strategy implementation are interrelated. It can be suggested that the emergent strategy approach is an essential part of any e-business strategy to enable response in a highly dynamic environment. This approach is best able to respond to sudden environmental changes which can open **strategic windows**. Strategic windows may occur through changes such as introduction of new technology (the Internet is the obvious example here!), changes in regulation of an industry, changes to distribution channels in the industry (again the Internet

Prescriptive strategy

The three core areas of strategic analysis, strategic development and strategy implementation are linked together sequentially.

Emergent strategy

Strategic analysis, strategic development and strategy implementation are interrelated and are developed together.

Strategic windows

Opportunities arising through a significant change in environment.

has had this impact), development of a new segment or redefinitions of markets (an example is the growth in leisure and health clubs during the 1990s).

Based on preliminary findings by Brian Smith, Daniel et al. (2002) have suggested that planning styles adopted by organisations for e-commerce will be governed by a combination of market complexity and turbulence. Smith identifies three main modes of strategy development:

1 *Logical rational planning.* Uses analytical tools and frameworks to formulate and implement strategy.
2 *Pragmatic incremental.* Strategy develops in response to minor adjustments to the external environment.
3 *Subjective visionary.* Strategy is the result of a leader, typically dominant or charismatic.

Daniel et al. suggest that in low-complexity high-turbulence markets vision and incrementalism will be dominant, in high-complexity low-turbulence markets rational planning approaches are dominant, while in highly complex, turbulent markets all three styles may be required.

Kalakota and Robinson (2000) recommend a dynamic, emergent strategy process specific to e-business. The elements of this strategy approach are shown in Figure 4.4. It essentially shares similar features to Figure 4.3, but with an emphasis on responsiveness with continuous review and prioritisation of investment in new Internet applications. Clearly, the quality of environment scanning and information collection, dissemination and analysis and the speed of response will be key for organisations following such as responsive, emergent approach. One example of an approach to collecting this market event data is competitive intelligence or CI.

We will now start reviewing the four main stages of Internet marketing strategy development.

Competitive intelligence (CI)

A process that transforms disaggregated information into relevant, accurate and usable strategic knowledge about competitors, position, performance, capabilities and intentions.

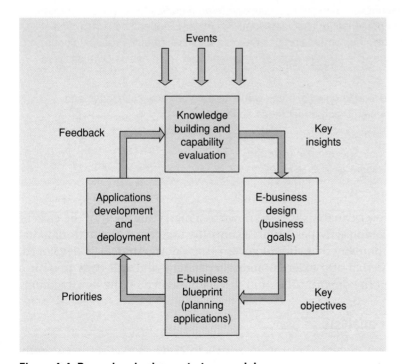

Figure 4.4 Dynamic e-business strategy model
Source: Adapted from description in Kalakota and Robinson (2000)

Situation review

Strategic analysis

Collection and review of information about an organisation's internal processes and resources and external marketplace factors in order to inform strategy definition.

Strategic analysis or situation analysis involves review of

- the internal resources and processes of the company and a review of its activity in the marketplace;
- the immediate competitive environment (micro-environment) including customer demand and behaviour, competitor activity, marketplace structure and relationships with suppliers and partners. These micro-environment factors were reviewed in Chapter 2 and are not considered in detail in this chapter;
- the wider environment (macro-environment) in which a company operates, which includes economic development and regulation by governments in the form of law and taxes together with social and ethical constraints such as the demand for privacy. These macro-environment factors including the social, legal, economic and political factors were reviewed in Chapter 3 and are not considered further in this chapter.

Now complete Activity 4.1, which illustrates the type of analysis that needs to be performed for an Internet marketing situation analysis.

Activity 4.1

Situation analysis for an e-commerce operation

Purpose

To introduce the different types of Internet marketing analysis required as part of situation review.

Activity

You are a newly incumbent e-commerce manager in an organisation that has operated a B2B e-commerce presence for two years in all the major European countries. The organisation sells office equipment and has been an established mail-order catalogue operation for 25 years. The UK, Germany, France and Italy each has its own localised content.

List the e-commerce-related questions you would ask of your new colleagues and research you would commission under these headings:

- internal analysis;
- external analysis (micro-economic factors);
- internal analysis (macro-economic factors).

The situation review or analysis is best known as a marketing audit of the current effectiveness of marketing activities within a company together with environmental factors outside the company that should govern the way the strategy is developed. We will consider internal and external audits separately, and will then present a structured analysis of the opportunities and threats presented by the new medium.

Resource analysis

Review of the technological, financial and human resources of an organisation and how they are utilised in business processes.

● Internal audit or analysis

The internal audit will review the way in which Internet marketing is currently conducted in relation to other media and will assess its effectiveness. The internal audit will also include a resource analysis. This involves assessing the capabilities of the organisation to deliver its online services. Aspects that should be reviewed include:

- *financial resources* – the cost components of running online presence including site development, promotion and maintenance;
- *technology infrastructure resources* – availability and performance (speed) of web site and service level agreements with the ISP;
- *human resources* and software assistance for answering customer queries and dispatching goods;
- *structure* – what are the responsibilities and control mechanisms used to coordinate Internet marketing across different departments and business units? We return to this topic later in the chapter;
- *strengths and weaknesses* – SWOT analysis is referred to in the next section where generic strengths and weaknesses are summarised in Figure 4.8. Companies will also assess their distinctive competencies. Chaston (2000) suggests a resource–advantage matrix should be produced which compares the costs of different online services against the value they provide to customers. These can then be evaluated to select strategic options. For example, a high-cost, low-value service might be terminated while a medium-cost, high-value service might be extended. This is a form of **portfolio analysis** where different e-commerce services are assessed for future potential. See also the strategy formulation section later in this chapter.

A key aspect of assessing current provision of e-commerce services is to assess the current level of Internet services and integration of Internet marketing with other marketing activities. Stage models of development of the online presence assist in this evaluation.

Portfolio analysis
Evaluation of value of current e-commerce services or applications.

Stage models of the online presence

As we have mentioned, due to the newness of the medium, few companies have a clearly defined strategy for their web site. This does not mean, however, that sites develop randomly. Rather, there is a logical way in which the facilities offered by a web site can be gradually developed.

Many companies have followed a natural progression in developing their web site to support their marketing activities. The following levels of development of a web site can be identified:

- **Level 0.** No web site.
- **Level 1.** Company places an entry in a web site that lists company names such as Yellow Pages (www.yell.co.uk) to make people searching the web aware of the existence of a company or its products. There is no web site at this stage.
- **Level 2.** Simple static web site created containing basic company and product information (sometimes referred to as **brochureware**). With the average cost of a UK web site being £3000, many companies are currently in this category.
- **Level 3.** Simple interactive site where users are able to search the site and make queries to retrieve information such as product availability and pricing. Queries by e-mail may also be supported.
- **Level 4.** Interactive site supporting transactions with users. The functions offered will vary according to the company. If products can be sold direct then an electronic commerce option for online sales will be available. Other functions might include an interactive customer service helpdesk which is linked into direct marketing objectives.
- **Level 5.** Fully interactive site providing relationship marketing with individual customers and facilitating the full range of marketing functions.

Brochureware
Brochureware describes a web site in which a company has migrated its existing paper-based promotional literature on to the Internet without recognising the differences required by this medium.

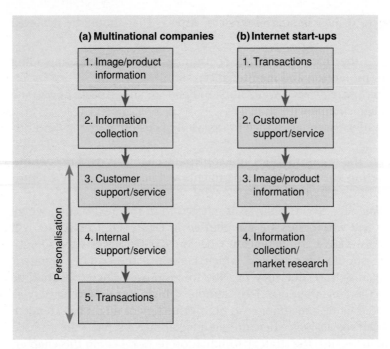

Figure 4.5 Levels of web site development in: (a) the information to transaction model and (b) the transaction to information model of Quelch and Klein (1996)

Quelch and Klein (1996) have noted how web sites develop for different types of company. They distinguish between existing major companies (see Figure 4.5(a)) and start-up companies (see Figure 4.5(b)) that start as Internet companies. The main difference is that Internet start-ups are likely to introduce transaction facilities earlier than existing companies. However, they may take longer to develop suitable customer service facilities.

Stage models have been criticised for a variety of reasons. First, as a generic model they may not apply to all types of services. Chaffey (2002) identifies a range of different types of online presence and business models each with different marketing objectives and different stage models. Four of the major different types of online presence are:

1 **Transactional e-commerce site**. Stage models are most appropriate to this type of presence. Examples: a car manufacturer such as Vauxhall (www.buypower.vauxhall.co.uk) or retailers such as Tesco (www.tesco.com).

2 **Services-oriented relationship-building web site**. For companies such as professional services companies, online transactions are inappropriate. Through time these sites will develop increasing information depth and question and answer facilities. Examples: PricewaterhouseCooper (www.pwcglobal.com), Accenture (www.accenture.com) and Arthur Andersen KnowledgeSpace (www.knowledgespace.com).

3 **Brand-building site**. These are intended to support the offline brand by developing an online experience of the brand. They are typical for low-value, high-volume fast moving consumer goods (FMCG brands). Examples: Tango (www.tango.com), Guinness (www.guinness.com).

4 **Portal site**. Information delivery as described in Chapter 2. Examples: Yahoo! (www.yahoo.com) and Vertical Net (www.verticalnet.com).

Table 4.1 A stage model for e-business development

	1. Web presence	2. E-commerce	3. Integrated e-commerce	4. E-business
Services available	Brochureware or interaction with product catalogues and customer service	Transactional e-commerce on buy-side or sell-side. Systems often not integrated	Buy- and sell-side integrated with ERP or legacy systems. Personalisation of services	Full integration between all internal organisational processes and elements of the value network
Organisational scope	Departments acting independently, e.g. marketing department, IS department	Coordination through steering committee or e-commerce manager	Cross-organisational	Across the enterprise and beyond (extraprise)
Transformation	Technological infrastructure	Technology and new responsibilities identified for e-commerce	Internal business processes and company structure	Change to e-business culture, linking of business processes with partners
Strategy	Limited	Sell-side e-commerce strategy, not well integrated with business strategy	E-commerce strategy integrated with business strategy using a value-chain approach	E-business strategy incorporated as part of business strategy

Source: Chaffey (2002)

Secondly, these stage models do not address the broader development of Internet marketing within an organisation. Key issues here are the broader issues associated with the move to e-business such as the extent of organisational transformation required and the integration of systems. Table 4.1 presents a synthesis of stage models for e-business development. Organisations can assess their position on the continuum between stages 1 and 4 for the different aspects of e-business development shown in the column on the left. When companies devise strategies they may return to the stage models to specify which level of innovation they are trying to achieve at future points in time. Varianini and Vaturi (2000) suggest plotting proposed site services on a matrix of degree of difficulty to implement from low to high and the perceived differentiation of the service from standard to distinctive. Priority should be given to those services that have a low difficulty (or cost) to implement and a standard or distinctive differentiation.

Despite these reservations, stage models still provide a general method for assessing the current position and for setting future targets of the services which will be provided online.

The internal audit is also likely to include the following assessment of the contribution of Internet marketing to an organisation. These different aspects are described in more detail in Chapter 9.

1 Business effectiveness

This will include the contribution of the site to revenue (*see* the section on the online revenue contribution), profitability and any indications of the corporate mission for the site. The relative costs of producing, updating and promoting the site will also be reviewed: that is, there will be a cost–benefit analysis.

2 Marketing effectiveness

These measures may include:

- leads (qualified enquiries);
- sales;
- customer retention and loyalty;
- market share;
- brand enhancement;
- customer service.

These measures will be assessed for each of the different product lines produced on the web site. The way in which the elements of the marketing mix are utilised will also be reviewed.

3 Internet effectiveness

These are specific measures that are used to assess the way in which the web site is used, and the characteristics of the audience. They are described in more detail in Chapter 9. According to Smith and Chaffey (2001) key performance indicators (KPIs) include:

- *unique visitors* – the number of separate, individual visitors who visit the site;
- total numbers of *sessions* or *visits* to a web site;
- *repeat visits* – average number of visits per individual;
- *duration* – average length of time visitors spend on your site;
- *subscription rates* such as the number of visitors subscribing for services such as an opt-in e-mail and newsletters;
- *conversion rates* – the percentage of visitors converting to subscribers (or becoming customers). Smith and Chaffey (2001) say:

  This is critical to e-marketing, let's take an example. Say 2% of 5000 visitors to a site in a month convert to 100 customers who place an order. £10 000 cost divided by 100 conversions = £100 cost per order. Now imagine you can double your conversion rate, or better still quadruple it to 8%, you then get £25 cost per order. The leverage impact caused by improved conversion rates is huge – revenues go up and % of marketing costs go down.

- *attrition rates* through the online buying process;
- *churn rates* – percentage of subscribers withdrawing or unsubscribing;
- *click-through rates (CTR)* from a banner ad or web link on another site to your own.

● External audits or analysis

External audits consider the business and economic environment in which the company operates. These include the economic, political, fiscal, legal, social, cultural and technological factors usually referred to by the STEP acronym and reviewed in Chapter 3. Of these various factors, it is worth noting how three of them are particularly relevant to the Internet and should be monitored regularly since the way in which they vary will directly affect the viability of the Internet channel. The three most significant factors, described in more depth in Chapter 3, are:

1 *Legal constraints*. What are the legal limitations to online promotion and trade?
2 *Ethical constraints*. What are the ethical implications?
3 *Technological constraints*. What is the current availability of technology to access the Internet and how is it likely to vary in the future?

The external audit should also consider the state of the market in terms of customers and competitors. Pertinent factors for the Internet include demand analysis, competitor analysis, intermediary analysis and channel structure. These are described only briefly here since they were discusssed in more depth in Chapter 2.

Demand analysis

A key factor driving e-marketing and e-business strategy objectives is the current level and future projections of customer demand for e-commerce services in different market segments. This will influence the demand for products online and this, in turn, should govern the resources devoted to different online channels. Customer activity covers current and projected customer use of each digital channel within different target markets. In a B2B context customer activity can be determined by asking for each market:

Demand analysis for e-commerce

Assessment of the demand for e-commerce services amongst existing and potential customer segments using the ratios Access : Choose : Buy online.

- What percentage of customer businesses have access to the Internet?
- What percentage of staff with the buying decision in these businesses have access to the Internet?
- What percentage of customers are prepared to purchase your particular product online?
- What percentage of customers with access to the Internet are not prepared to purchase online, but choose or are influenced by web-based information to buy products offline?
- What are the barriers to adoption and the facilitators amongst customers and how can we encourage adoption? Identifying the differences in psychographics between current online customers and those that are not offline can help inform strategy.

Thus the situation analysis as part of e-marketing planning must determine levels of access to the Internet in the marketplace and propensity to be influenced by the Internet to buy either offline or online.

Figure 4.6 summarises the type of picture the e-marketing planner needs to build up for each segment, including different geographic markets.

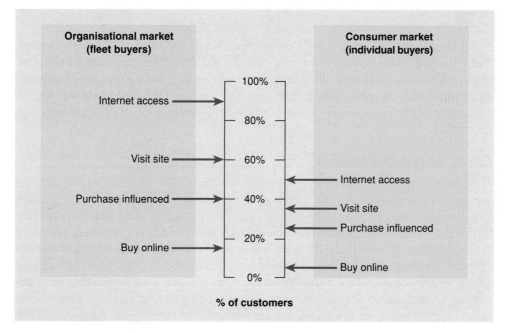

Figure 4.6 Customer demand analysis for the car market

Now refer to Activity 4.2 where this analysis is performed for the car market. This picture will vary according to different target markets, so the analysis will need to be performed for each of these. For example, customers wishing to buy 'luxury cars' may have web access and a higher propensity to buy than those for small cars.

Activity 4.2

Customer activity in the car market in your country

Purpose

To illustrate the type of marketing research needed to inform demand analysis for e-marketing planning and approaches to finding this information.

Activity

For your country update Figure 4.7 to reflect current and future projections for:

A. *Corporate buyers* (fleet market):
1. % of customers with Internet access;
2. % of customers who access web site;
3. % of customers who will be favourably influenced (may be difficult to determine);
4. % of customers who buy online.

If possible, try to gauge how these figures vary according to age, sex and social class.

B. *Individual buyers*:
1. % of customers with Internet access;
2. % of customers who access web site;
3. % of customers who will be favourably influenced;
4. % of customers who buy online.

If possible, try to gauge how these figures vary according to companies of different sizes and different members of the buying unit.

An alternative perspective on e-commerce demand analysis is to review demand from existing customers who migrate online, and those who are new to the company. For some companies, the e-commerce service may have more new customers than those who migrate online from the current user base. For example, 80% of customers of the Co-operative Bank's online bank Smile (www.smile.co.uk) were new customers.

Qualitative customer research

It is important that customer analysis is not restricted to quantitative demand analysis. Varianini and Vaturi (2000) point out that qualitative research provides insights that can be used to inform strategy. They suggest using graphic profiling, which is an attempt to capture the core characteristics of target customers – not only demographics, but also their needs, attitudes and how comfortable they are with the Internet. Online buyer behaviour should also be assessed as described in Chapter 7. We have seen that only a minority of consumers show a clear propensity to buy online. Organisations should understand how their offering can best cater to this group of customers. Additionally, market research concerning the barriers to adoption and the attitudes of the non-buyers can suggest how to overcome their fears.

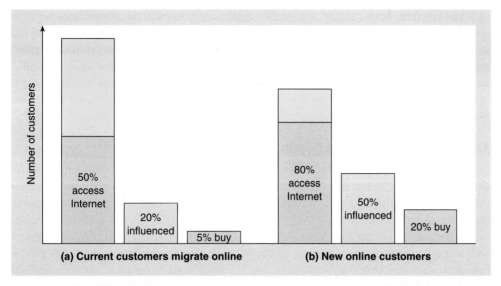

Figure 4.7 Demand analysis assessing the ratios Access : Choose : Buy for (a) new customers and (b) existing customers

Competitor analysis

Competitor analysis or the monitoring of competitor use of e-commerce to acquire and retain customers is especially important in the e-marketplace due to the dynamic nature of the Internet medium. This enables new services to be launched and prices and promotions changed much more rapidly than through print communications. Activity 4.3 highlights some of the issues in competitor benchmarking, and this topic is referred to in more detail in Chapter 2.

Competitor benchmarking   (Web)   **Activity 4.3**

Purpose

To understand the characteristics of competitor web sites it is useful to know how to benchmark and to assess the value of benchmarking.

Activity

Choose a B2C industry sector such as airlines, book retailers, book publishers, CDs or clothing, or a B2B sector such as oil companies, chemical companies, construction industry companies or B2B exchanges. Work individually or in groups to identify the type of information that should be available from the web site (and which parts of the site you will access it from) and will be useful in terms of competitor benchmarking. Once your criteria have been developed, you should then benchmark companies and summarise which you feel is making best use of the Internet medium.

Intermediary analysis

Chapter 2 highlighted the importance of web-based intermediaries such as portals in driving traffic to an organisation's web site. Situation analysis will also involve identifying relevant intermediaries for a particular marketplace and look at how the organisation and its competitors are using the intermediaries to build traffic and provide services. For example, an e-tailer needs to assess which comparison services such as Kelkoo (www.kelkoo.com) and Shopsmart (www.shopsmart.com) it and its competitors are represented on. Do competitors have any special sponsorship arrangements or microsites created with intermediaries. The other aspect of situation analysis for intermediaries is to consider the way in which the marketplace is operating. To what extent are competitors using disintermediation or reintermediation? How are existing channel arrangements being changed?

Assessing opportunities and threats

Companies should conduct a structured analysis of the external opportunities and threats that are presented by the Internet environment. They should also consider their own strengths and weaknesses in the Internet marketing environment. Summarising the results through SWOT analysis (internal Strengths and Weaknesses and external Opportunities and Threats) will clearly highlight the opportunities and threats. Appropriate planning to counter the threats and take advantage of the opportunities can then be built into the Internet marketing plan. An example of a typical SWOT analysis of Internet-marketing-related strengths and weaknesses is shown in Figure 4.8. As is often the case with SWOT analysis, the opportunities available to a company are the opposites of the threats presented by other companies. The strengths and weaknesses will vary according to the company involved, but many of the strengths and weaknesses are dependent on the capacity of senior management to acknowledge and act on change.

In order to exploit opportunities to gain competitive advantage it is essential for companies to act quickly. Competitive advantage tends to be short-lived on the Internet since it is easier for competitors to monitor each other and respond. When a company sees that its competitor has a better offer or service, it will counter with

Figure 4.8 A generic SWOT analysis showing typical opportunities and threats presented by the Internet

a similar service. However, if a company is the first with a truly innovative service, then this will be valuable in capturing market share. Once customers have used a service, and are happy with the service, they may not return to their original supplier. There are probably still opportunities for companies to 'Amazon their sector' or build up a clear market leadership on the Internet.

Assessing competitive threats

The application to the Internet of the analysis of the five competitive threats of Michael Porter's classic 1980 model was reviewed in Chapter 2.

Strategic goal setting

Any marketing strategy should be based on clearly defined corporate objectives, but there has been a tendency for Internet marketing to be conducted separately from other business and marketing objectives. This may be done because the Internet has not been integrated into company culture or management – it may be seen as a separate responsibility from marketing. It is best, of course, if the Internet marketing strategy is consistent with and supports business and marketing objectives. For example, business objectives such as increasing market share in an overseas market or introducing a new product to market can and should be supported by the Internet communications channel.

Goal setting for the Internet will be based on managers' view of the future relevance of the Internet to their industry. **Scenario-based analysis** is a useful approach to discussing alternative visions of the future prior to objective setting. Lynch (2000) explains that scenario-based analysis is concerned with possible models of the future of an organisation's environment. He says:

> *The aim is not to predict, but to explore a set of possibilities; scenarios take different situations with different starting points.*

He distinguishes qualitative scenario-based planning from quantitative prediction such as that of Activity 4.4 (see below). In an Internet marketing perspective, scenarios that could be explored include:

1 One player in our industry becomes dominant through use of the Internet ('Amazoning' the sector).
2 Major customers do not adopt e-commerce because of organisational barriers.
3 Major disintermediation (Chapter 2) occurs in our industry.
4 B2B marketplaces do or do not become dominant in our industry.
5 New entrants or substitute products change our industry.

Through performing this analysis, better understanding of the drivers for different views of the future will result, new strategies can be generated and strategic risks can be assessed. It is clear that the scenarios above will differ between worst-case and best-case scenarios.

When an Internet marketing strategy is being defined, the objectives should be clearly stated in the Internet marketing plan. Possible examples include:

- achieve 10 per cent online revenue contribution within 2 years;
- achieve first or second position in category penetration in the countries within which we operate (this is effectively online market share and can be measured through visitor rankings such as Hitwise (Chapter 2) or better by online revenue share);

Scenario-based analysis

Models of the future environment are developed from different starting points.

- achieve a cost reduction of 10 per cent in marketing communications within 2 years;
- increase retention of customers by 10 per cent;
- increase by 20 per cent within one year the number of sales arising from a certain target market, e.g. 18–25-year-olds;
- create value-added customer services not currently available;
- improve customer service by providing a response to a query within 2 hours, 24 hours per day, 7 days a week;
- all other objectives to be achieved profitably giving a return on investment in a 3-year period.

Note that these objectives have numerical targets and times attached to them. In this way everyone is sure exactly what the target is, and can work towards it. With quantification of targets and milestones for when they will be achieved it is possible to review progress towards these targets, and when there is a danger that they will not be achieved, appropriate action can be taken to put the company back on target.

Porter (2001) has criticised the lack of goal setting when many organisations have developed Internet strategies. He notes that many companies, responding to distorted market signals, have used 'rampant experimentation' that is not economically sustainable. This has resulted in the failure of many 'dot-com' companies and also poor investments by many established companies. He suggests that economic value or sustained profitability for a company is the final arbiter of business success. Thus objectives should also ensure that a positive return on investment is achieved.

When defining the aims of Internet marketing, a company should conduct a comprehensive review of all the business benefits that could accrue. It was mentioned in Chapter 1 that drivers can be divided into cost/efficiency drivers and competitiveness drivers. Companies will decide to adopt a combination of a cost/efficiency approach to strategy or a competiveness-driven approach which adds values to stakeholders. The types of benefits, and their relative importance, are highlighted in a 1998 report from Andersen Consulting (1999). Three hundred executives from European companies who were interviewed identified the following benefits as important:

- speed of transactions increased (73 per cent agreed);
- management of information improved (65 per cent agreed);
- increased service levels to customers (65 per cent agreed);
- removal of time constraints (65 per cent agreed);
- access to global markets (63 per cent agreed);
- removal of distance constraints (62 per cent agreed);
- ability to complete total transaction electronically (61 per cent agreed);
- access to full competitive arena (59 per cent agreed);
- opportunities for new revenues/services (57 per cent agreed);
- cost effectiveness (55 per cent agreed);
- more effective/closer relationships with business partnerships (54 per centagreed);
- improved understanding of customer requirements (50 per cent agreed).

Such benefits can be converted into objectives that become part of the business or marketing plan described in the previous section. In such a review of potential benefits, it is useful to identify both tangible benefits, for which monetary savings or revenues can be identified, and intangible benefits, for which it is more difficult to calculate cost savings. These benefits can then be put into the marketing plan as

Table 4.2 Tangible and intangible benefits from Internet marketing

Tangible benefits	Intangible benefits
Increased sales from new sales leads giving rise to increased revenue from: ● new customers, new markets ● existing customers (repeat-selling) ● existing customers (cross-selling) Cost reductions from: ● reduced time in customer service ● online sales ● reduced printing and distribution costs of marketing communications	● Corporate image communication ● Enhance brand ● More rapid, more responsive marketing communications including PR ● Improved customer service ● Learning for the future ● Meeting customer expectations to have a web site ● Identify new partners, support existing partners better ● Better management of marketing information and customer information ● Feedback from customers on products

critical success factors against which the success of the implementation can be based. Table 4.2 presents a summary of the benefits of Internet marketing.

As an example of how companies set specific targets and then record corresponding metrics to demonstrate the accountability of their web site, look at Mini Case Study 4.1.

Smith and Chaffey (2001) suggest there are five broad benefits, reasons or objectives of e-marketing. This framework is useful since it presents a comprehensive range of objectives, which can be summarised as the 5 Ss of e-marketing objectives. Marketers will decide whether all or only some will drive e-marketing:

Mini Case Study 4.1

Identifying tangible benefits for a B2B web site

Wallingford Software (www.wallingfordsoftware.com) supplies software to the water industry worldwide to enable design of facilities to manage water in a range of settings. Applications include modelling rivers in flood, wastewater management, coastal defence and water treatment. The software, which may cost thousands of pounds, is purchased by clients including civil engineers and central and local government agencies. The software is specialised and requires support to assist in how it is applied to engineering problems and also requires updates to enhance the models or correct errors.

Through using the Internet as a sales, distribution channel, the following tangible benefits can be identified:

● *Customer acquisition*. The Internet has been used to increase the reach of the company beyond those countries in which it has sales offices. Targets can be set for sales influenced by the web site.
● *Customer retention*. The use of e-mail newsletters linked to the web site is used to encourage renewal of support and maintenance contracts, which are an important revenue stream for the company.
● *Cost avoidance*. The cost of sales can be reduced since there is less need for sales visits to demonstrate the features and benefits of the software, as they can now be showcased online. Since software patches (upgrades) can now be downloaded by clients or supplied as e-mail attachments, costs of media, postage and packaging are avoided. The cost of support is also reduced since typical issues with applying the software can now be answered online.

- *Sell* – grow sales (through wider distribution to customers you can't service offline, or perhaps through a wider product range than in-store, or better prices).
- *Serve* – add value (give customers extra benefits online, or inform them of product development through online dialogue and feedback).
- *Speak* – get closer to customers by tracking them, asking them questions, conducting online interviews, creating a dialogue, monitoring chat rooms, learning about them.
- *Save* – save costs of service, sales transactions and administration, print and post. Can you reduce transaction costs and therefore either make online sales more profitable or use cost-savings to enable you to cut prices, which in turn could enable you to generate greater market share?
- *Sizzle* – extend the brand online. Reinforce brand values in a totally new medium. The Web scores very highly as a medium for creating brand awareness, recognition and involvement, as explained further in Chapter 5.

Specific objectives should be created for each of the 5 Ss. Consider Sales – a typical objective might be:

To grow the business with online sales, e.g. to generate at least 10% of sales online, within 6 months.

or

To generate an extra £100 000 worth of sales online by December.

These objectives can be further broken down, e.g. to achieve £100 000 of online sales means you have to generate 1000 online customers spending on average £100 in the time period. If, say, your conversion rate of visitors to customers was 1% then this means you have to generate 100 000 visitors to your site.

Specific communications objectives are described in Chapter 9.

● The online revenue contribution

Online revenue contribution

An assessment of the direct contribution of the Internet or other digital media to sales, usually expressed as a percentage of overall sales revenue.

A key objective for Internet marketing is the online revenue contribution. This is a measure of the extent to which a company's online presence directly impacts the sales revenue of the organisation. Online revenue contribution objectives can be specified for different types of products, customer segments and geographic markets. They can also be set for different digital channels such as web, mobile or interactive digital TV.

Companies that can set a high online revenue contribution objective of say 25% for 2 years' time will need to provide more resource allocation to the Internet than those companies that anticipate a contribution of 2.5%. Cisco Systems Inc (www.cisco.com), maker of computer networking gear, is now selling around 90% of its $20 billion sales online. This was achieved after senior executives at Cisco identified the significance of the medium, setting aggressive targets for the online revenue contribution and resourcing the e-commerce initiative accordingly. Note that through using the Internet Cisco has achieved strategic benefits beyond increased revenue. It has also dramatically increased profitability. This has partly been achieved through the web site which is thought to have been responsible for a 20% reduction in overall operating costs.

For some companies such as an FMCG manufacturer such as a beverage company, it is unrealistic to expect a high direct online revenue contribution. In this case, an indirect online contribution can be stated. This considers the Internet as part of the promotional mix and its role in reaching and influencing a proportion of customers to purchase the product or in building the brand. In this case a company could set an **online promotion contribution** of 5% of its target market visiting the web site and interacting with the brand.

Now complete Activity 4.4 to look at how the online contribution varies for different types of company.

Online promotion contribution

An assessment of the proportion of customers (new or retained) who are reached by online communications and are influenced as a result.

Activity 4.4

Variations in online revenue contribution

Table 4.3 Variations in online revenue contribution

Organisation	Sector	Online contribution	Overall turnover
Cisco	B2B Networking hardware	90%	$19bn
EasyJet	B2C Air travel	85%	£264m
Dell	B2B, B2C Computers	48%	$25bn
Lands End Clothing	B2C Clothing	11%	$1.3bn
Book Club Associates	B2C Books	10%	£100m
Electrocomponents	B2B Electronics	7%	£761m group
Domino's Pizza	B2C Food	3.4%	£76m
Tesco	B2C Grocery	1.4%	£18.4bn
Thomas Cook	B2C Travel	<1%	£1.8bn

Source: Company web sites, end 2000

Table 4.3 shows the online revenue contribution for some companies. Note that there is a wide variation in online contribution according to the market sector the company operates in.

Questions

1 Explain the varying percentage contribution to revenue according to the industry sector the companies operate in.

2 Comment on the variation in total Internet-based revenue for the companies shown.

3 What do you think are the strategic implications for other companies operating in a sector if they are not currently leaders in Internet contribution?

Case Study 4.1 shows a range of variation in online revenue contribution targets for Sandvik Steel that differs between different geographic markets. Annika Roos, marketing manager at Sandvik Steel, specified Sandvik's objectives as follows: 'by the end of December, 2001, we want a confirmation from at least 80 per cent of key customers that they consider the extranet to be a major reason to deal with Sandvik. Our aim is to have 200 key customers using the extranet at the end of June 2001.' Objectives involving key account customers are typical for B2B organisations.

Where sales are likely to be relatively homogeneous, as with a bookseller, the Internet contribution can be set in a general fashion for all products across the company. However, the Internet contribution may vary markedly for different product types or for different geographical or customer segments. In this case it may be useful to use a grid such as that in Table 4.4 to set objectives for the different product types.

CASE STUDY 4.1

Sandvik – setting the Internet revenue contribution

When dotcom mania was at its height, so-called old economy companies, such as Sweden's Sandvik, tended to be overshadowed as the brash new online stars took the limelight. But now that the collapse of internet and other technology stocks has injected a harsh dose of reality into the stock market and business scene, many established names are back in favour again.

As the experience of Sandvik, founded in 1862, shows, skilful use of the internet can lead to huge improvements in links with customers and suppliers, bringing considerable cost savings. Based north of Stockholm in Sandviken, the company's activities seem remote from the virtual world of the internet. It makes cutting tools, specialty steels and mining and construction equipment. However, the group – which last year raised turnover by 12 per cent to SKr44bn ($4.3bn) and earnings per share by 34 per cent – is a long-time advocate of IT. Its annual IT budget is some SKr1bn.

'We first formulated our IT strategy in 1969', says Clas Ake Hedstrom, the chief executive. 'We didn't foresee the internet.' Only recently, he adds, has IT moved from serving the company to benefitting customers. Transferring its 30-year-old IT experience to the age of the web requires more than a deep understanding of technology, says Arnfinn Fredriksson, director of internet business development at the group's Coromant tooling business. 'The major challenges are not IT and systems, but "soft" things such as attitudes, insights and getting people to understand and accept that this is part of their daily work.' This means focusing hard on business needs and cutting through the internet hype.

Sandvik Steel, the specialty steel operation, also goes beyond transactions to find solutions for its customers. Its extranet enables users to obtain worldwide stock information, catalogues and training aids, as well as take part in online discussions.

At both Coromant and Sandvik Steel, e-business activities are mainly directed towards enhancing links with customers. 'Customer value comes when our product is used, not when it is purchased', Mr Fredriksson says. Thus, Coromant allows customers not only to buy tools over the web but also to design their own products – within parameters set by Coromant – and receive advice on how best to use them. Choosing the right cutting tools and using them effectively can save around 10 per cent of the total cost of manufactured components. The e-business strategy had to take account of this. It also had to avoid channel conflict, the bypassing of its traditional sales outlets. Most Coromant tools are sold directly to customers, but 40 per cent goes through resellers. Moreover, there are big regional variations; more than 80 per cent of sales in the Nordic region are direct, while most North American sales are indirect. The company's approach was to work with the traditional sales channels. 'So many companies try to bypass traditional channels and lose sales and relationships', Mr Fredriksson says. It is the relationship with the customer – including greater personalisation and an extended reach into global markets – which will be the most important pillar of its e-business strategy in the long term, he says. This is what provides real competitive advantage. Shifting existing customers to the internet, winning new ones and saving costs are also important. But other companies will be doing the same.

At present, only a small part of Coromant's orders are transacted over the web. Nordic countries are leading the way. Around 20 per cent of all orders from Denmark are online and 31 per cent of those from Sweden. The proportion in the US, however, is only 3 per cent, since most business goes through distributors and is conducted by EDI (electronic data interchange), the pre-internet means of e-commerce. Over the next six months, the company hopes to raise the US figure to 40 per cent. Mr Fredriksson hopes that in two years, between 40 and 50 per cent of total orders will come via the web.

To enhance its online service to customers, Coromant plans to offer each one a personalised web page. This will enable the company to offer new products, materials and advice on productivity improvements. Training will also be part of this expanded web offering, which Coromant aims to have in place later this year.

For both Coromant and Sandvik Steel, the value of the web lies in strengthening and expanding relationships with customers. In the case of Coromant, with some 25 000 standard products, there are numerous customers buying low volumes. With Sandvik Steel, however, a small number of customers buys a high volume of products. 'Our aim is to have 200 key customers using the extranet at the end of June 2001', says Annika Roos, marketing manager at Sandvik Steel. 'By the end of December, 2001, we want a confirmation from at least 80 per cent of key customers that they consider the extranet to be a major reason to deal with Sandvik.'

By putting the internet at the heart of its business, the Sandvik group intends to penetrate deeply into the minds and ambitions of its customers. 'The challenge is not just doing e-business, it is *becoming* an e-business', she adds.

Source: Andrew Fisher, Sandvik – the challenge of becoming an e-business, *Financial Times*, 4 June 2001

Questions

1 Summarise how e-business has been used to transform Sandvik Steel.

2 What are some of the risks of e-business that need to be managed that are highlighted by the article?

Activity 4.5

Assessing the significance of digital channels

Purpose

To illustrate the issues involved with assessing the suitability of the Internet for e-commerce.

Table 4.4 Vision of online revenue contribution for different types of company

Products/services	Now	2 years' time	5 years' time	10 years' time
Example: Cars, US Direct online sales Indirect online sales	5% 50%	10% 70%	25% 90%	50% 95%
Financial services Direct online sales Indirect online sales				
Clothing Direct online sales Indirect online sales				
Business office supplies Direct online sales Indirect online sales				

Activity

For each of the products and services in Table 4.4, assess the suitability of the Internet for delivery of the product or service and position it on the grid in Figure 4.9 with justification. Make estimates in Table 4.4 for the direct and indirect online revenue contribution in 5 and 10 years' time for different products in your country. Choose specific products within each category.

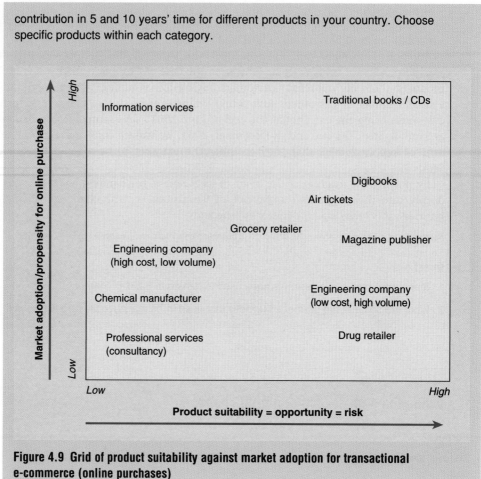

Figure 4.9 Grid of product suitability against market adoption for transactional e-commerce (online purchases)

Strategy formulation

Strategy formulation

Generation, review and selection of strategies to achieve strategic objectives.

Strategy formulation involves the identification of alternative strategies, a review of their merits and then selection of the best candidates. Since the Internet is a relatively new medium, and many companies are developing a strategy for the first time, a range of strategic factors must be considered, in order to make the best use of it. In this section we shall cover the main strategic options by defining eight key decisions. These decisions are:

- Decision 1: Target market strategies.
- Decision 2: Positioning and differentiation strategies.
- Decision 3: Resourcing – Internet marketing priorities – significance to organisation (replace or complement).
- Decision 4: Customer relationship management focus and financial control.
- Decision 5: Market and product development strategies.
- Decision 6: Business and revenue models including product development and pricing strategies.
- Decision 7: Organisational structure modifications.
- Decision 8: Channel structure modifications.

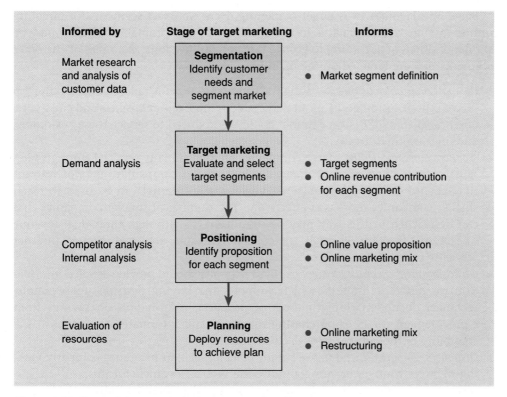

Figure 4.10 Stages in target marketing strategy development

● Decision 1: Target marketing strategy

Deciding on which markets to target is a key strategic consideration for Internet marketing strategy in the same way it is key to marketing strategy. Target marketing strategy involves the four stages shown in Figure 4.10.

In an Internet context, organisations need to target those customer groupings with the highest propensity to access, choose and buy online (see Figures 4.7 and 4.8).

The first stage in Figure 4.10 is segmentation. Segmentation involves understanding the groupings of customers in the target market in order to understand their needs and potential as a revenue source so as to develop a strategy to satisfy these segments while maximising revenue. Dibb et al. (2001) say that:

> *Market segmentation is the key of robust marketing strategy development . . . it involves more than simply grouping customers into segments . . . identifying segments, targeting, positioning and developing a differential advantage over rivals is the foundation of marketing strategy.*

In an Internet marketing planning context, market segments will be analysed to assess:

1 their current market size or value, future projections of size and the organisations current and future market share within the segment;
2 competitor market shares within segment;
3 needs of each segment, in particular, unmet needs;
4 organisation and competitor offers and proposition for each segment across all aspects of the buying process.

Target marketing strategy

Evaluation and selection of appropriate segments and the development of appropriate offers.

Segmentation

Identification of different groups within a target market in order to develop different offerings for each group.

Stage 2 in Figure 4.10 is target marketing. Here we select segments for targeting online that are most attractive in terms of growth and profitability. These may be similar or different according to groups targeted offline. Some examples of customer segments that are targeted online include:

- *the most profitable customers* – using the Internet to provide tailored offers to the top 20 per cent of customers by profit may result in more repeat business and cross-sales;
- *larger companies (B2B)* – an extranet could be produced to service these customers, and increase their loyalty;
- *smaller companies (B2B)* – large companies are traditionally serviced through sales representatives and account managers, but smaller companies may not warrant the expense of account managers. However, the Internet can be used to reach smaller companies more cost-effectively. The number of smaller companies that can be reached in this way may be significant, so although individual revenue of each one is relatively small, the collective revenue achieved through Internet servicing can be large;
- *particular members of the buying unit (B2B)* – the site should provide detailed information for different interests which supports the buying decision, for example, technical documentation for users of products, information on savings from e-procurement for IS or purchasing managers and information to establish the credibility of the company for decision makers;
- *customers who are difficult to reach using other media* – an insurance company looking to target younger drivers could use the Web as a vehicle for this;
- *customers who are brand-loyal* – services to appeal to brand loyalists can be provided to support them in their role as advocates of a brand as suggested by Aaker and Joachimstiler (2000);
- *customers who are not brand-loyal* – conversely, incentives, promotion and a good level of service quality could be provided by the web site to try and retain such customers.

Dibb et al. (2000) suggest these options for targeting strategy:

- Concentrate on a single segment with one product and marketing programme (this is a common approach when launching an online service).
- Offer one product and use one marketing programme across segments (again an appropriate online option).
- Target different segments with different products and marketing programmes.

A more rigorous B2B segmentation will follow that of Wind and Cardazo (1974), who identify three macro-segmentation bases for organisations, namely their size, location and usage rate of products. These can then be subdivided into micro-segmentation bases considering issues such as products, decision-making unit and the buyer–seller relationship. As would be expected, the macro level and micro level typically correspond to the hierarchy of menu choices on a web site. Consumer markets will also follow geographic segments, but are then broken down according to demographics, psychographics and behaviour segments. An online example of such segmentation is provided by Scottish Amicable, the financial services provider, which put three typical customer profiles, of increasing age and responsibilities, on its home page, as a means of providing more detailed information.

Positioning

Customers' perception of the product offer relative to those of competitors.

● Decision 2: Differentiation and positioning

Stage 2 in Figure 4.10 is positioning. Deise et al. (2000) suggest that in an online context, companies can position their products relative to competitor offerings according to four main variables: product quality, service quality, price and fulfilment time. They suggest it is useful to review these through an equation of how they combine to influence customer perceptions of value or brand:

$$\text{Customer value (brand perception)} = \frac{\text{Product quality} \times \text{Service quality}}{\text{Price} \times \text{Fulfilment time}}$$

Strategies should review the extent to which increases in product and service quality can be matched by decreases in price and fulfilment time. Chaston (2000) argues that there are four options for strategic focus to position a company in the online marketplace. It is evident that these are related to the different elements of Deise et al. (2000). He says that online these should build on existing strengths, and can use the online facilities to enhance the positioning as follows:

- *Product performance excellence.* Enhance by providing online product customisation.
- *Price performance excellence.* Use the facilities of the Internet to offer favourable pricing to loyal customers or to reduce prices where demand is low (for example, British Midland Airlines uses auctions to sell underused capacity on flights).
- *Transactional excellence.* A site such as that of software and hardware e-tailer dabs.com (Figure 4.11) offers transactional excellence through combining pricing information with dynamic availability information on products, listing number in stock, number on order and when they are expected.
- *Relationship excellence* – personalisation features to enable customers to review sales order history and place repeat orders. An example is RS Components (www.rswww.com).

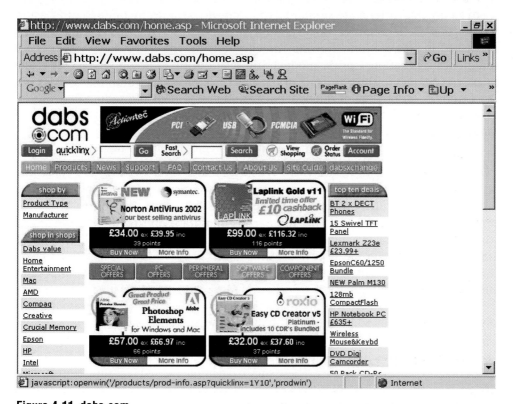

Figure 4.11 dabs.com

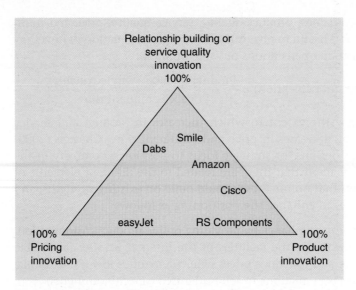

Figure 4.12 Alternative positionings for online services

These positioning options have much in common with Porter's competitive strategies of cost leadership, product differentiation and innovation (Porter, 1980). Porter has been criticised since many commentators believe that to remain competitive it is necessary to combine excellence in all of these areas. It can be suggested that the same is true for sell-side e-commerce. These are not mutually exclusive strategic options, rather they are prerequisites for success. Customers will be unlikely to judge on a single criterion, but on the balance of multiple criteria. It can be seen that Porter's original criteria are similar to the strategic positioning options of Chaston (2000) and Deise et al. (2000). Figure 4.12 summarises the positioning options described in this section, showing the emphasis on the three main variables for online differentiation – price, product and relationship-building services. The diagram can be used to show the mix of the three elements of positionings. EasyJet has an emphasis on price performance, but with a component of product innovation. Amazon is not positioned on price performance, but rather on relationship building and product innovation.

An alternative perspective on positioning strategies has been suggested by Picardi (2000). The first three of the six approaches suggested are generic:

1 *Attack e-tailing.* As suggested by the name, this is an aggressive competitive approach that involves frequent comparison with competitors' prices and then matching or bettering them. This approach is important on the Internet because of the transparency of pricing and availability information made possible through shopping comparison sites such as ShopSmart (www.shopsmart.com) and Kelkoo (www.kelkoo.com). As customers increasingly use these facilities then it is important that companies ensure their price positioning is favourable. High-street white-goods retailers have long used the approach of matching competitors' prices, but the Internet enables this to be achieved dynamically. Shopping sites such as Buy.com (www.buy.com) and Evenbetter.com (www.evenbetter.com) can now find the prices of all comparable items in a category but also guarantee that they will beat the lowest price of any competing product. These sites have implemented real-time adjustments in prices with small increments based on price policy algorithms that are simply not possible in traditional retailing.

2 *Defend e-tailing.* This is a strategic approach that traditional companies can use in response to 'attack e-tailing'. It involves differentiation based on other aspects of brand beyond price. The IDC research quoted by Picardi (2000) shows that while average prices for commodity goods on the Internet are generally lower, less than half of all consumers purchase the lowest-priced item when offered more information from trusted sources, i.e. price dispersion may actually increase online. Reasons why the lowest price may not always result in the sale are:

- ease of use of site and placing orders (e.g. Amazon One-Click makes placing an order with Amazon much easier than using a new supplier);
- ancillary information (e.g. book reviews contributed by other customers enhances Amazon service);
- after-sales service (prompt, consistent fulfilment and notification of dispatch from Amazon increases trust in the site);
- trust with regard to security and customer privacy.

These factors enable Amazon to charge more than competitors and still achieve the greatest sales volume of online booksellers (although not, to date, profitability). In summary, trust becomes the means of differentiation and loyalty. As a result, price comparison sites are being superseded by sites that independently rate the overall service such as Gomez (www.gomez.com) or use customers' opinions to rate the service such as Bizrate (www.bizrate.com) and Epinions (www.epinions.com).

3 *E2E (end-to-end) integration.* This is an efficiency strategy that uses the Internet to decrease costs and increase product quality and shorten delivery times. This strategy is achieved by moving towards an automated supply chain and internal value chain. A key issue in moving towards the automated supply chain is determining which processes should be owned internally, which should be achieved via partnerships, and which should be outsourced.

The online value proposition

The aim of positioning is to develop a **differential advantage** over rivals' products. In an e-marketing context the differential advantage and positioning can be clarified and communicated by developing an **online value proposition (OVP)**. This is similar to a unique selling proposition, but is developed for e-commerce services. Varianini and Vaturi (2000) conducted a review of failures in B2C dot-com companies in order to highlight lessons that can be learned. They believe that many of the problems have resulted from a failure to apply established marketing orientation approaches. They summarise their guidelines as follows:

> *First identify customer needs and define a distinctive value proposition that will meet them, at a profit. The value proposition must then be delivered through the right product and service and the right channels and it must be communicated consistently. The ultimate aim is to build a strong, long-lasting brand that delivers value to the company marketing it.*

Conversely, Agrawal et al. (2001) suggest that the success of leading e-commerce companies is often due to matching value propositions to segments successfully. In developing such propositions managers should:

- identify a clear differentiation of the online proposition compared to the company's conventional offline proposition;
- identify a clear differentiation of the online proposition from that of competitors, based on cost, product innovation or service quality;

Differential advantage

A desirable attribute of a product offering that is not currently matched by competitor offerings.

Online value proposition (OVP)

A statement of the benefits of e-commerce services that ideally should not be available in competitor offerings or offline offerings.

- target market segment(s) that the proposition will appeal to;
- identify how the proposition will be communicated to site visitors and in all marketing communications (developing a strap line can help this);
- identify how the proposition is delivered across different parts of the buying process;
- identify how the proposition will be delivered and supported by resources – is the proposition viable? Will resources be internal or external?

McDonald and Wilson (2002) suggest that to determine a value proposition marketers should first assess changes in an industries structure (see Chapter 2) since channel innovations will influence which proposition is possible. They then suggest sub-processes of first setting objectives for market share, volume or value by each segment and then defining the value to be delivered to the customer in terms of the marketing mix. They suggest starting with defining the price and value proposition using the 4 Cs and then defining marketing strategies using the 4 Ps (see Chapter 5).

Having a clear online value proposition has several benefits:

- it helps distinguish an e-commerce site from its competitors (this should be a web site design objective);
- it helps provide a focus to marketing efforts so that company staff are clear about the purpose of the site (Figure 4.13);
- if the proposition is clear it can be used for PR and word-of-mouth recommendations may be made about the company. For example, the clear proposition of Amazon on its site is that prices are reduced by up to 40% and that a wide range of 3 million titles are available;

Figure 4.13 Blackstar's online value proposition

- it can be linked to the normal product propositions of a company or its product.

Online value proposition

Visit the web sites of the following companies and, in one or two sentences each, summarise their Internet value proposition. You should also explain how they use the content of the web site to indicate their value proposition to customers.

Web

1 Blackstar (www.blackstar.co.uk).
2 Boots the Chemist Wellbeing (www.wellbeing.com).
3 NSK-RHP bearings (www.nsk-rhp.com).
4 Harrods (www.harrods.com).
5 Guinness (www.guinness.com).

Michael Porter's views on differentiation

We have seen that to achieve a sustainable competitive advantage online, differentiation of services is essential. Yet Porter (1996) argues that many organisations have used the wrong strategic approach to achieve this. He is critical of a tendency to rely on price performance through heavy discounting. He distinguishes between *operational effectiveness* and *strategic positioning*. Many organisations have focused on operational effectiveness, making activities such as new product development, distribution and promotional activities more effective. Porter argues that this does not readily confer a competitive advantage since it is difficult to sustain leads in operational effectiveness. Instead, Porter argues that strategic positioning is vital to sustainable competitive advantage.

Operational effectiveness

Performing similar activities better than rivals. This includes efficiency of processes.

Strategic positioning

Performing different activities from rivals or performing similar activities in different ways.

Porter (1996) suggests that to maintain a distinctive strategic positioning, a company must follow six principles:

1 the right goal: superior long-term return on investment;
2 a value proposition distinct from those of the competition;
3 a distinctive value chain to achieve competitive advantage;
4 trade-offs in products or services may be required to achieve distinction;
5 strategy defines how all elements of what a company does fit together;
6 strategy involves continuity of direction.

In an Internet marketing context we can pick out the value proposition, the value chain and the need to make trade-offs in products or services as being important.

Price reductions and discounting are approaches that some companies such as easyJet (www.easyjet.com) have used to build market share online. However, care must be taken that the discounts are sustainable. Porter (2001) says that

> many companies have subsidized the purchase of their products and services in the hope of staking out a position on the Internet and attracting a base of customers.

A different strategic option is to attempt to position the service as a premium service rather than a lowest-price service. Online brands such as Amazon (www.amazon.com) and RS (www.rswww.com) are not the lowest-price providers in their sectors, but have still managed to gain market share through delivering a quality service in terms of the on-site experience and product fulfilment. These attributes can also help build loyalty.

While it may be beneficial to have a unique value proposition for a web site, it may not be practical in some sectors. For example, a financial services provider that is competing in a very crowded sector, which has similar products, will find it difficult to make its proposition clear. Ideally, it should support the product, price or quality differentiation established as part of the core marketing strategy.

● Decision 3: Resourcing – Internet marketing prioritisation

Prioritisation

Assesses the strategic significance of the Internet relative to other marketing channels.

Bricks and mortar

A traditional organisation with limited online presence.

'Clicks and mortar'

A business combining an online and offline presence.

Clicks-only or Internet pureplay

A organisation with principally an online presence.

Prioritisation assesses the strategic significance of the Internet relative to other marketing channels.

Internet marketing priorities have been summarised by Gulati and Garino (2000) as 'getting the right mix of bricks and clicks'. This expression has been used to refer to traditional '**bricks and mortar**' enterprises with a physical presence, but limited Internet presence. In the UK, an example of a 'bricks and mortar' store would be the bookseller Waterstones (www.waterstones.co.uk), which when it ventured online would become '**clicks and mortar**'. As mentioned above, some virtual merchants such as Amazon that need to operate warehouses and shops to sustain growth have also become 'clicks and mortar' companies. An **Internet pureplay** which only has an online representation is referred to as '**clicks-only**'. In reality these are rare – most companies need inbound and outbound phone connections.

McDonald and Wilson (2002) suggest evaluating the strengths of a number of distribution channels using the channel curve which is a similar tool to the electronic shopping test of de Kare Silver (2000) described in Chapter 2. For a particular product category they suggest evaluating the Internet channel against store, mail-order and phone-ordering channels and in terms of cost, convenience, added-value, viewing and accessibility for the customer.

The general options for the mix of 'bricks and clicks' are shown in Figure 4.14. The online revenue contribution estimate is informed by the customer demand

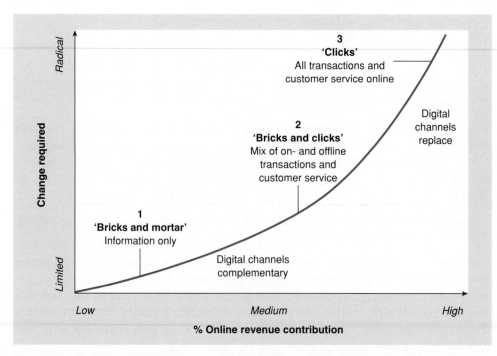

Figure 4.14 Strategic options for a company in relation to the importance of the Internet as a channel

analysis of propensity to purchase a particular type of product (see Figures 4.5 and 4.6). A similar diagram was produced by de Kare-Silver (2000) who suggested that strategic e-commerce alternatives for companies should be selected according to the percentage of the target market using the channel and the commitment of the company. The idea is that the commitment should mirror the readiness of consumers to use the new medium. If the objective is to achieve a high online revenue contribution of >70% then this will require fundamental change for the company to transform to a 'bricks and clicks' or 'clicks-only' company.

Arguably, the most important strategic decision taken by a company will be the extent of commitment given by the managing director, or senior management team, to the Internet. If the strength of this commitment (or a decision for more limited investment) is not clear, it will be very difficult for those implementing the system to have direction. Verbal and written commitment to the Internet medium is helpful in promoting the use of the Internet across the company, but of course it is financial commitment that is crucial. A 1998 report by KPMG consultants on the development of electronic commerce in Europe found that there was a correlation between the amount spent on the Internet and the revenues received. In a survey of 500 companies with a turnover of more than $300 million the leading 10 per cent of companies in terms of online revenues had an average expenditure on the Internet of $222 000 per year, compared with less than $130 000 in other companies (Baker, 1998). The leaders also tended to have the most management 'buy-in'.

To decide on an appropriate investment in the Internet is, in part, an act of faith by senior managers since it will be based on forecast levels of use of the Internet. There are, however, models available to assist them in deciding on the amount of investment. Kumar (1999) suggests that a company should decide whether the Internet will primarily *complement* the company's other channels or primarily *replace* other channels. Clearly, if it is believed that the Internet will primarily replace other channels, then it is important to invest in the promotion and infrastructure to achieve this. This is a key decision as the company is essentially deciding whether the Internet is 'just another communications and/or sales channel' or whether it will fundamentally change the way it communicates and sells to its customers.

Figure 4.15 summarises the main decisions on which a company should base its commitment to the Internet. Kumar (1999) suggests that replacement is most likely to happen when:

- customer access to the Internet is high;
- the Internet can offer a better value proposition than other media;
- the product can be delivered over the Internet (it can be argued that this condition is not essential for replacement, so it is not shown in the figure);
- the product can be standardised (the user does not usually need to view to purchase).

Only if all three conditions are met will there be primarily a replacement effect. The fewer the conditions met, the more likely is it that there will be a complementary effect.

From an analysis such as that in Figure 4.15 it should be possible to state whether the company strategy should be directed as a complementary or as a replacement scenario. As mentioned in relation to the question of the contribution of the Internet to its business, the company should repeat the analysis for different product segments and different markets. It will then be possible to state the company's overall commitment to the Internet. If the future strategic importance of the

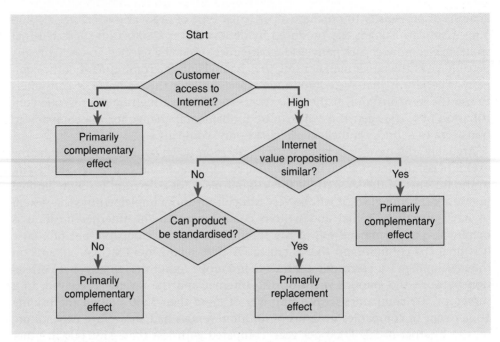

Figure 4.15 Flow chart for deciding on the significance of the Internet to a business
Source: After Kumar (1999)

Internet is high, with replacement likely, then a significant investment needs to be made in the Internet, and a company's mission needs to be directed towards replacement. If the future strategic importance of the Internet is low then this still needs to be recognised, and appropriate investment made.

Poon and Joseph (2000) have suggested that frameworks assessing the suitability of the Internet for sales, based solely on product characteristics are likely to be misleading. They surveyed Australian firms to assess the importance of product characteristics in determining online sales. They found that there was not a significant difference between physical goods and standardised, digital goods such as software.

They conclude:

> *Although it is logical to believe that firms who are selling search goods of low tangibility have a natural advantage in Internet commerce, it is important to understand that all products have some degree of tangibility and a mixture of search and experience components. The only difference is the relative ratio of such characteristics. For example, a pair of jeans is an experience good with high tangibility, but the size and fit can be easily described using standard descriptions. Similarly, a piece of software is a search good with low tangibility, but the functionality of a software package cannot be fully appreciated without 'test-driving' a beta release.*

Assessing different Internet projects

Typically, there will be a range of different Internet marketing alternatives to be evaluated. Limited resources will dictate that only some applications are practical. Portfolio analysis can be used to select the most suitable projects. For example, Daniel et al. (2001) suggest that potential e-commerce opportunities should be assessed for the value of the opportunity to the company against its ability to deliver.

Portfolio analysis

Identification, evaluation and selection of desirable marketing applications.

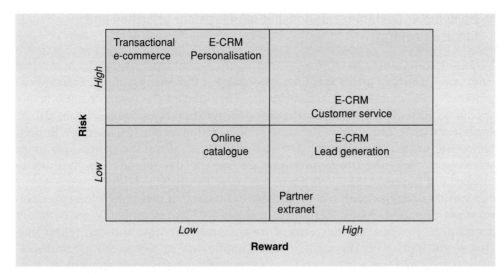

Figure 4.16 Example of risk–reward analysis

Typical opportunities for Internet marketing strategy for an organisation which has a brochureware site might be:

● online catalogue facility;
● e-CRM system – lead generation system;
● e-CRM system – customer service management;
● e-CRM system – personalisation of content for users;
● partner relationship management extranet for distributors or agents;
● transactional e-commerce facility.

Such alternatives can then be evaluated in terms of their risk against reward. Figure 4.16 shows a possible evaluation of strategic options. It is apparent that with limited resources, the e-CRM lead generation, partner extranet and customer services options offer the best mix of risk and reward.

For information systems investments, the model of McFarlan (1984) has been used extensively to assess the future strategic importance applications in a portfolio. This model has been applied to the e-commerce applications by Daniel et al. (2001) and Chaffey (2002). Potential e-commerce applications can be assessed as:

1 *key operational* – essential to remain competitive. Example: partner relationship management extranet for distributors or agents;
2 *support* – deliver improved performance, but not critical to strategy. Example: e-CRM system – personalisation of content for users;
3 *high potential* – may be important to achieving future success. Example: e-CRM system – customer service management;
4 *strategic* – critical to future business strategy. Example: e-CRM system – lead generation system is vital to developing new business.

A further portfolio analysis suggested by McDonald and Wilson (2002) is a matrix of attractiveness to customer against attractiveness to company, which will give a similar result to the risk–reward matrix. Finally, Tjan (2001) has suggested a matrix approach of viability (return on investment) against fit (with the organisation's capabilities) for Internet applications. He presents five metrics for assessing each of viability and fit.

● Decision 4: Customer relationship management priorities and financial control

Varianini and Vaturi (2000) suggest that many e-commerce failures have resulted from poor control of media spending. They suggest that many companies spend too much on poorly targeted communications. They suggest the communications mix should be optimised to minimise the cost of acquisition of customers. It can also be suggested that optimisation of the conversion to action on site (Chapter 1) is important to the success of marketing. The strategy will fail if the site design, quality of service and marketing communications are not effective in converting visitors to prospects or buyers.

A further strategic decision is the balance of investment between customer acquisition and retention. Many start-up companies will invest primarily on customer acquisition. This is a strategic error since customer retention through repeat purchases will be vital to the success of the online service. For existing companies, there is a decision on whether to focus expenditure on customer acquisition or on customer retention or to use a balanced approach.

Agrawal et al. (2001) suggest that the success of e-commerce sites can be modelled and controlled based on the customer lifecycle of customer relationship management (Chapter 6). They suggest using a scorecard, assessed using a longitudinal study analysing hundreds of e-commerce sites in the USA and Europe. The scorecard is based on the **performance drivers** or critical success factors for e-commerce such as the costs for acquisition and retention, conversion rates of visitors to buyers to repeat buyers together with churn rates. Note that to maximise retention and minimise churn there will be service-based service quality based drivers. These are discussed in Chapter 7. There are three main parts to their scorecard:

Performance drivers

Critical success factors that determine whether business or marketing objectives are met.

1 *Attraction.* Size of visitor base, visitor acquisition cost and visitor advertising revenue (e.g. media sites).
2 *Conversion.* Customer base, customer acquisition costs, customer conversion rate, number of transactions per customer, revenue per transaction, revenue per customer, customer gross income, customer maintenance cost, customer operating income, customer churn rate, customer operating income before marketing spending.
3 *Retention.* This uses similar measures to those for conversion customers.

The survey performed by Agrawal et al. (2001) shows that:

companies were successful at luring visitors to their sites, but not at getting these visitors to buy or at turning occasional buyers into frequent ones.

In the same study they performed a further analysis where they modelled the theoretical change in net present value contributed by an e-commerce site in response to a 10% change in these performance drivers. This shows the relative importance of these drivers or 'levers' as they refer to them:

1 **Attraction**
   ● Visitor acquisition cost: 0.74% change in NPV
   ● Visitor growth: 3.09% change in NPV

2 **Conversion**
   ● Customer conversion rate: 0.84% change in NPV
   ● Revenue per customer: 2.32% change in NPV

3 Retention

- Cost of repeat customer: 0.69 % change in NPV
- Revenue per repeat customer: 5.78 % change in NPV
- Repeat customer churn rate: 6.65 % change in NPV
- Repeat customer conversion rate: 9.49 % change in NPV

This modelling highlights the importance of on-site marketing communications and the quality of service delivery in converting browsers to buyers and buyers into repeat buyers. Case Study 4.2 provides an example of how marketing spend must be balanced through time. It is apparent that marketing spend is large relative to turnover initially, to achieve customer growth, but is then carefully controlled to achieve profitability.

CASE STUDY 4.2

Online bank Egg turns a profit

Launched in October 1998, Egg is an e-commerce company created as a start-up company by Prudential, the UK-based financial services company. By 2002, staff of over 2000 worked from offices in London, Dudley and Derby. In June 2000, it became listed on the London Stock Exchange and by the final quarter of 2001 Egg had made its first profit. It provides services through its web site (www.egg.com), interactive TV on Sky Interactive and via a contact centre. It has gained 2 million customers since inception, with 1.37m holding an Egg credit card which is 4% of total UK credit card balances. Customer growth is continuing with 600 000 new customers in 2002 (Figure 4.17).

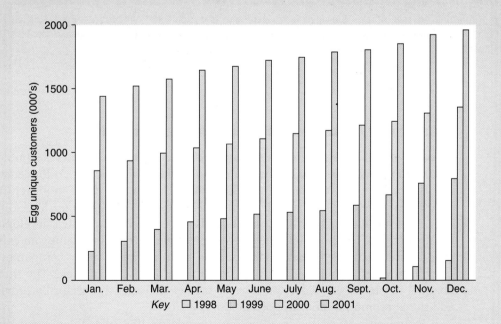

Figure 4.17 Number of Egg customers, 1998–2001

Compiled from Egg Investor relations (www.egg.com and www.investis.com/eggplc)

Future growth will be assisted by international expansion. In 2001 Egg acquired French online bank Zebank for 8 million euros and it plans to launch in France using Zebank's existing infrastructure, along with distribution partnerships with offline retailers. Egg says it will invest £100m in France, including a £50m marketing spend and £15m of development costs. It wants to have 1m customers and be profitable there by the end of 2004.

Financials

Table 4.5 shows that to achieve profitability Egg has reduced its brand development and marketing budget and operational expenses while revenues have grown. New customers are costing less money to win over with brand and marketing costs down 30% over 2001 at £35.8m.

Table 4.5 Key financial data for Egg, Q4 2000 to Q4 2001

	Q4 2000	Q1 2001	Q2 2001	Q3 2001	Q4 2001
Total revenues	32.0	36.5	39.7	50.8	62.4
Operational expenses	(31.5)	(30.9)	(32.6)	(32.5)	(30.8)
Brand and marketing	(15.6)	(15.1)	(6.0)	(6.6)	(8.2)
Development	(5.8)	(4.2)	(3.6)	(3.1)	(2.8)
Total admin expenses	(52.9)	(50.2)	(42.2)	(42.2)	(41.8)
Depreciation	(5.1)	(5.4)	(5.0)	(4.9)	(5.4)
Bad debts provisions	(12.4)	(16.6)	(16.4)	(19.5)	(15.5)
UK operating loss	(38.4)	(35.7)	(23.9)	(15.8)	(0.3)
Share of associates	(1.7)	(1.5)	(0.6)	(0.7)	(1.2)
UK loss before tax	(40.1)	(37.2)	(24.5)	(16.5)	(1.5)
International costs	–	(0.5)	(1.0)	(1.9)	(1.8)
Restructuring	–	–	–	–	(2.7)
Group loss before tax	(40.1)	(37.9)	(25.5)	(18.4)	(6.0)

Source: Compiled from Egg Investor relations (www.egg.com and www.investis.com/eggplc) and Dudley (2002)

Question

Through referring to this article, the investors' web site and additional sources at Find Articles (www.findarticles.com) summarise the Internet marketing strategy of Egg referring to concepts described in this chapter.

● Decision 5: Market and product development strategies

Managers of e-business strategy also have to decide whether to use new technologies to expand the scope of their business into new markets and products. As for decision 1 this is a balance between fear of the do-nothing option and fear of poor return on investment for strategies that fail. The model of Ansoff (1957) (Figure 1.5) is still useful as a means for marketing managers to discuss market and product development using electronic technologies. The Internet has great potential for selling an existing product into existing or new markets. As a starting point, many companies will use the Internet to help sell existing products into existing markets. The Internet channel can help consolidate or increase market share for this sector by providing additional promotion and support facilities.

It is, however, the other quadrants in the matrix that offer the greatest opportunities for companies to make new sales that would probably not be achieved without a web site (or certainly at a lower cost per sale). The top-left quadrant, indicating opportunities for selling existing products into new geographical markets, represents a common approach taken by companies, particularly small or medium-sized enterprises (SMEs) that do not have existing sales channels into other countries. When assessing this alternative, companies will consider three main objectives that will need to be fulfilled in order successfully to exploit the new market. The objectives are to achieve adequate promotion, sales and fulfilment of the product. Whether the objectives can be achieved should be carefully analysed by asking questions such as:

- Is an existing infrastructure in place for fulfilment?
- What will be the impact on the existing channel such as agents or distributors?
- Is the product standardised so that it is suitable for being purchased from a web site?

A less evident benefit of the Internet is that, as well as selling into new geographical markets, companies can also sell products to new market segments or different types of customer. This may happen simply as a by-product of having a web site. For example, RS Components, a company that is featured in Case Study 5.1, found that 10 per cent of its web-site sales were to individual consumers rather than traditional business customers. The retailer Argos found the opposite was true, with 10 per cent of web-site sales to businesses, its traditional market being consumer-based. The Internet may offer further opportunities for selling to market sub-segments that have not previously been targeted. For example, a product sold to large businesses may also appeal to SMEs, or a product targeted at young people could also appeal to some members of an older audience.

In addition to assessing how existing products can be sold via the Internet, companies should also evaluate whether new products can be developed that can be promoted or sold via the Internet (the two right-hand quadrants in Figure 1.5). These may differ from existing physical products and could include information products that can be delivered over the Web. Such products may not be charged for, but will add value to existing products. Product decisions are explored in more depth in Chapter 5.

The strategic options to be considered in an e-commerce context can be summarised as:

1 *Market penetration.* Digital channels can be used to sell more existing products into existing markets. Online channels can help consolidate or increase market share by providing additional promotion and customer service facilities amongst customers in an existing market. This is a relatively conservative use of the Internet.

2 *Market development.* Here online channels are used to sell into new markets, taking advantage of the low cost of advertising internationally without the necessity for a supporting sales infrastructure in the customer's country. This is a relatively conservative use of the Internet, but is a great opportunity for SMEs to increase exports at a low cost, but it does require overcoming the barriers to exporting.

A less evident benefit of the Internet is that as well as selling into new geographical markets, products can also be sold to new market segments or different types of customers. This may happen simply as a by-product of having a web site. For example, RS components (www.rswww.com), a supplier of a range of MRO (maintenance, repair and operations) items, found that 10% of the web-based sales were to individual consumers rather than traditional business customers. The UK retailer Argos found the opposite was true with 10% of web-site sales from businesses, when their traditional market was consumer based. The Internet may offer further opportunities for selling to market sub-segments that have not be previously targeted. For example, a product sold to large businesses may also appeal to SMEs, or a product targeted at young people could also appeal to some members of an older audience.

3 *Product development*. New digital products or services can be developed that can be delivered by the Internet. These are typically information products, for example online trade magazine *Construction Weekly* has diversified to a B2B portal Construction Plus (www.constructionplus.com) which has new revenue streams. This is innovative use of the Internet.

4 *Diversification*. In this sector, new products are developed which are sold into new markets. For example, Construction Plus is now international while formerly it had a UK customer-base.

The benefits and risks of market and product development are highlighted by the creation of Smile (www.smile.co.uk), an Internet-specific bank set up by the Co-operative Bank of the UK. Smile opened for business in October 1999 and its first year added 200 000 at a rate of 20 000 per month. Significantly, 80% of these customers were market development in the context of the parent, since they were not existing Co-op customers and typically belonged to a higher income segment. As well as the new online banking products available from Smile, a secure shopping zone (Figure 4.18) had been developed which is a new revenue model since each purchase made from the site will provide affiliate revenue (a small percentage of sales price paid by the retailer to Smile). Retailers also pay Smile for placing advertisements and promotions within the shopping zone. The risks of the new

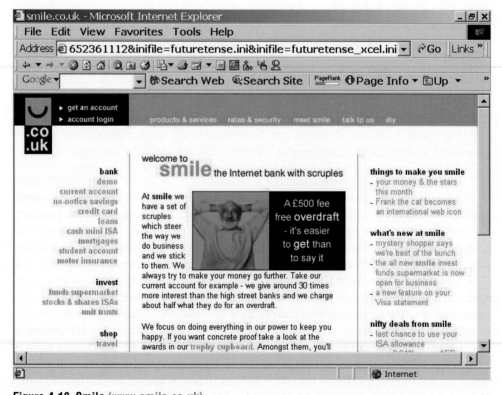

Figure 4.18 Smile (www.smile.co.uk)

approach are highlighted by the costs of these innovations. It is estimated that in its first year, costs of creation and promotion of Smile increased overall costs of the Co-op Bank by 5%. However, overheads are relatively low since Smile only employs 130 people and it is targeted for profit 3 years from launch.

The danger of diversification into new product areas is illustrated by the fortunes of Amazon, which is infamous for not delivering profitability despite multi-billion-dollar sales. Phillips (2000) reported that for books and records, Amazon sustained profitability through 2000, but it is following a strategy of product diversification into toys, tools, electronics and kitchenware. This strategy gives a problem through the cost of promotion and logistics to deliver the new product offering. Amazon is balancing this against its vision of becoming a 'one-stop shop' for online retailers.

● Decision 6: Business and revenue models

A further aspect of Internet strategy formulation is review of opportunities from new **business and revenue models** (Chapter 2). The options for introducing new product options for the core or extended product and pricing strategy is also related to this decision. These related issues are discussed in the next chapter in the sections on product and price.

Evaluating new models is important since if companies do not innovate then competitors and new entrants will and companies will find it difficult to regain the initiative. Equally, if inappropriate business or distribution models are chosen, then companies may make substantial losses.

One example of how companies can review and revise their business model is provided by Dell Computer. Dell gained **early-mover** advantage in the mid-1990s when it became one of the first companies to offer PCs for sale online. Its sales of PCs and peripherals grew from the mid-1990s with online sales of $1 million per day to 2000 sales of $50 million per day. Based on this success it has looked at new business models it can use in combination with its powerful brand to provide new services to its existing customer base and also to generate revenue through new customers. In September 2000, Dell announced plans to become a supplier of IT consulting services through linking with enterprise resource planning specialists such as software suppliers, systems integrators and business consulting firms. This venture will enable the facility of Dell's PremierPages to be integrated into the procurement component of ERP systems such as SAP and Baan, thus avoiding the need for rekeying and reducing costs.

In a separate initiative, Dell launched a B2B marketplace aimed at discounted office goods and services procurements including PCs, peripherals, software, stationery and travel (www.dellmarketplace.com). This strategic option did not prove sustainable.

To illustrate the importance of taking the right business model decision review Case Study 5.2. This article is informative since it shows how the online marketplace for car sales has changed during its five-year infancy from the initial success of new intermediaries to the increasing influence of the car manufacturers as they develop their e-business strategies. It again emphasises the need for a dynamic approach that produces new strategies to deal with changes in the marketplace.

To sound a note of caution, flexibility in the business model should not be to the company's detriment through losing focus on the core business. An example of business model flexibility is the diversification of Amazon from books and CDs to a range of products more typical of a department store. It remains to be seen whether this results in more profitability. A 2000 survey of CEOs of leading UK Internet

Business model

A summary of how a company will generate revenue, identifying its product offering, value-added services, revenue sources and target customers.

Revenue models

Describe methods of generating income for an organisation.

Early (first) mover

An early entrant into the marketplace.

companies such as Autonomy, Freeserve, NetBenefit and QXL (Durlacher, 2000) indicates that although flexibility is useful this may not apply to business models. The report states:

> *A widely held belief in the new economy in the past, has been that change and flexibility is good, but these interviews suggest that it is actually those companies who have stuck to a single business model that have been to date more successful . . . CEOs were not moving far from their starting vision, but that it was in the marketing, scope and partnerships where new economy companies had to be flexible.*

So with all strategy options, managers should also consider the 'do-nothing option'. Here a company will not risk a new business model, but adopt a 'wait-and-see' approach to see how competitors perform.

● Decision 7: Organisational structures

Organisational structure decisions form two main questions. The first is 'How should internal structures be changed to deliver e-marketing?' and the second 'How should the structure of links with other organisations be changed to achieve e-marketing objectives?'. Such decisions should balance the benefits of the changes against the disruption to business operations caused by the changes. Once structural decisions have been made attention should be focused on effective **change management**. Many e-commerce initiatives fail, not in their conceptualisation, but in their implementation. Chaffey (2002) describes approaches to change management and risk management in Chapter 10.

Change management

Controls to minimise the risks of project-based and organisational change.

Internal structures

There are also options for restructuring within a business such as the creation of an in-house division. This issue has been considered by Parsons et al. (1996) from a sell-side e-commerce perspective. They recognise four stages in the growth of what they refer to as the 'digital marketing organisation'. These are:

1 *Ad hoc activity*. At this stage there is no formal organisation related to e-commerce and the skills are dispersed around the organisation. It is likely that there is poor integration between online and offline marketing communications. The web site may not reflect the offline brand, and the web site services may not be featured in the offline marketing communications. A further problem with ad hoc activity is that the maintenance of the web site will be informal and errors may occur as information becomes out of date.

2 *Focusing the effort*. At this stage, efforts are made to introduce a controlling mechanism for Internet marketing. Parsons et al. (1996) suggest that this is often achieved through a senior executive setting up a steering group which may include interested parties from marketing and IT and legal experts. At this stage the efforts to control the site will be experimental, with different approaches being tried to build, promote and manage the site.

3 *Formalisation*. At this stage the authors suggest that Internet marketing will have reached a critical mass and there will be a defined group or separate business unit within the company that will manage all digital marketing.

4 *Institutionalising capability*. This stage also involves a formal grouping within the organisation, but is distinguished from the previous stage in that there are formal links created between digital marketing and a company's core activities. Baker (1998) argues that a separate e-commerce department may be needed as the company

may need to be restructured in order to provide the necessary levels of customer service over the Internet if existing processes and structures do not do this.

Although this is presented as a stage model with evolution implying all companies will move from one stage to the next, many companies will find that true formalisation with the creation of a separate e-commerce or e-business department is unnecessary. For small and medium companies with a marketing department numbering a few people and an IT department perhaps consisting of two people, it will not be practical to have a separate group. Even large companies may find it is sufficient to have a single person or small team responsible for e-commerce with their role to coordinate the different activities within the company using a matrix management approach. That many companies are not ready to move to a separate digital marketing department was indicated by the KPMG report (Baker, 1998). Here it was found that over three-quarters of respondents were against establishing a separate e-commerce department.

Activity 4.7 reviews different types of organisational structures for e-commerce. Table 4.6 reviews some of the advantages and disadvantages of each.

Which is the best organisation structure for e-commerce?

Activity 4.7

Purpose

To review alternative organisational structures for e-commerce.

Activity

1 Match the four types of companies and situations to the structures (a) to (d) in Figure 4.19.
   - A separate operating company. Example: Prudential and Egg (www.egg.com).
   - A separate business unit with independent budgets. Example: RS Components Internet Trading Company (www.rswww.com).
   - A separate committee or department manages and coordinates e-commerce. Example: Derbyshire Building Society (www.derbyshire.co.uk).
   - No formal structure for e-commerce. Examples: many small businesses and the Retail and Engineering Company.

2 Under which circumstances would each structure be appropriate?

3 Summarise the advantages and disadvantages of each approach.

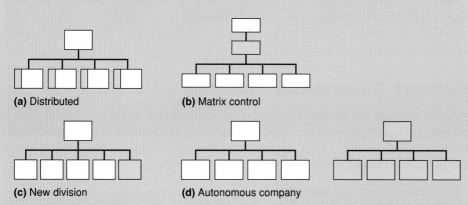

(a) Distributed   (b) Matrix control   (c) New division   (d) Autonomous company

Figure 4.19 Summary of alternative organisational structures for e-commerce suggested in Parsons et al. (1996)

Table 4.6 Advantages and disadvantages of the organisational structures shown in Figure 4.19

Organisational structure	Circumstances	Advantages	Disadvantages
(a) No formal structure for e-commerce	Initial response to e-commerce or poor leadership with no identification of need for change	Can achieve rapid response to e-commerce	Poor-quality site in terms of content quality and customer service responses (e-mail, phone). Priorities not decided logically. Insufficient resources
(b) A separate committee or department manages and coordinates e-commerce	Identification of problem and response in (a)	Coordination and budgeting and resource allocation possible	May be difficult to get different departments to deliver their input because of other commitments
(c) A separate business unit with independent budgets	Internet contribution (Chapter 6) is sizeable (>20%)	As for (b), but can set own targets and not be constrained by resources. Lower-risk option than (d)	Has to respond to corporate strategy. Conflict of interests between department and traditional business
(d) A separate operating company	Major revenue potential or flotation. Need to differentiate from parent	As for (c), but can set strategy independently. Can maximise market potential	High risk if market potential is overestimated due to start-up costs

Links with other organisations

Gulati and Garino (2000) identify a continuum of approaches from integration to separation for delivering e-marketing through working with outside partners. The choices are:

1 *In-house division (integration).* Example: RS Components Internet Trading Channel (www.rswww.com).
2 *Joint venture (mixed).* The company creates an online presence in association with another player.
3 *Strategic partnership (mixed).* This may also be achieved through purchase of existing dot-coms, for example, in the UK Great Universal Stores acquired e-tailer Jungle.com for its strength in selling technology products and strong brand while John Lewis purchased Buy.com's UK operations.
4 *Spin-off (separation).* Example: Egg bank is a spin-off from Prudential financial services company.

● Decision 8: Channel structure modifications

Strategies to take advantage in changes in marketplace structure should also be developed. These options are created through disintermediation and reintermediation (Chapter 2) within a marketplace. The strategic options for the sell-side downstream channels which have been discussed in Chapter 2 are:

- disintermediation (sell direct);
- create new online intermediary (countermediation);
- partner with new online or existing intermediaries;
- do nothing!

Prioritising strategic partnerships as part of the move from a value chain to a value network should also occur as part of this decision. For all options tactics will be needed to manage the channel conflicts that may occur as a result of restructuring.

Technological integration

To achieve strategic Internet marketing goals, B2B organisations will have to plan for integration with customers' and suppliers' systems. Chaffey (2002) describes how a supplier may have to support technical integration with a range of customer e-procurement needs, for example:

1 *Links with single customers*. Organisations will decide whether a single customer is large enough to enforce such linkage. For example, supermarkets often insist that their suppliers trade with them electronically. However, the supplier may be faced with the cost of setting up different types of links with different supermarket customers.
2 *Links with intermediaries*. Organisations have to assess which are the dominant intermediaries such as B2B marketplaces or exchanges and then evaluate whether the trade resulting from the intermediary is sufficient to set up links with this intermediary.

Strategy implementation

This forms the topic for subsequent chapters in this book:

- Chapter 5 – options for varying the marketing mix in the Internet environment;
- Chapter 6 – implementing customer relationship management;
- Chapter 7 – delivering online services via a web site;
- Chapter 8 – interactive marketing communications;
- Chapter 9 – monitoring and maintaining the online presence.

Summary

1 The development of the online presence follows stage models from basic static 'brochureware' sites through simple interactive sites with query facilities to dynamic sites offering personalisation of services for customers.

2 The Internet marketing strategy should follow a similar form to a traditional strategic marketing planning process and should include:
   - goal setting;
   - situation review;
   - strategy formulation;
   - resource allocation and monitoring.

   A feedback loop should be established to ensure the site is monitored and modifications are fed back into the strategy development.

3 Strategic goal setting should involve:
   - setting business objectives that the Internet can help achieve;
   - assessing and stating the contribution that the Internet will make to the business in the future, both as a proportion of revenue and in terms of whether the Internet will complement or replace other media;

● stating the full range of business benefits that are sought, such as improved corporate image, cost reduction, more leads and sales, and improved customer service.

4 The situation review will include assessing internal resources and assets, including the services available through the existing web site. External analysis will involve customer demand analysis, competitor benchmarking and review of the macro-environment STEP factors.

5 Strategy formulation will involve defining a company's commitment to the Internet; setting an appropriate value proposition for customers of the web site; and identifying the role of the Internet in exploiting new markets, marketplaces and distribution channels and in delivering new products and services. In summary:
● Decision 1. Target market strategies.
● Decision 2. Positioning and differentiation strategies.
● Decision 3. Resourcing Internet marketing priorities – significance to organisation (replace or complement).
● Decision 4. CRM focus and financial control.
● Decision 5. Market and product development strategies.
● Decision 6. Business and revenue models including product development and pricing strategies.
● Decision 7. Organisational restructuring required.
● Decision 8. Channel structure modifications.

EXERCISES

Self-assessment exercises

1 Draw a diagram that summarises the stages through which a company's web site may evolve.

2 What is meant by the 'Internet contribution', and what is its relevance to strategy?

3 What is the role of monitoring in the strategic planning process?

4 Summarise the main tangible and intangible business benefits of the Internet to a company.

5 What is the purpose of an Internet marketing audit? What should it involve?

6 What does a company need in order to be able to state clearly in the mission statement its strategic position relative to the Internet?

7 What are the market and product positioning opportunities offered by the Internet?

8 What are the distribution channel options for a manufacturing company?

Essay and discussion questions

1 Discuss the frequency with which an Internet marketing strategy should be updated for a company to remain competitive.

2 'Setting long-term strategic objectives for a web site is unrealistic since the rate of change in the marketplace is so rapid.' Discuss.

3 Explain the essential elements of an Internet marketing strategy.

4 Summarise the role of strategy tools and models in formulating a company's strategic approach to the Internet.

Examination questions

1 When evaluating the business benefits of a web site, which factors are likely to be common to most companies?

2 Use Porter's five forces model to discuss the competitive threats presented to a company by other web sites.

3 Which factors will affect whether the Internet has primarily a complementary effect or a replacement effect on a company?

4 Describe different stages in the sophistication of development of a web site, giving examples of the services provided at each stage.

5 Briefly explain the purpose and activities involved in an external audit conducted as part of the development of an Internet marketing strategy.

6 What is the importance of measurement within the Internet marketing process?

7 Which factors would a retail company consider when assessing the suitability of its product for Internet sales?

8 Explain what is meant by the online value proposition, and give two examples of the value proposition for web sites with which you are familiar.

References

Agrawal, V., Arjona, V. and Lemmens, R. (2001) E-performance: the path to rational exuberance, *McKinsey Quarterly*, No. 1, 31–43.

Andersen Consulting (1999) *Your choice. How eCommerce could impact Europe's future.* Andersen Consulting.

Ansoff, H. (1957) Strategies for diversification, *Harvard Business Review*, September–October, 113–24.

Baker, P. (1998) *Electronic Commerce. Research Report 1998.* KPMG Management Consulting, London.

Chaffey, D. (2002) *E-Business and E-Commerce Management.* Financial Times/Prentice Hall, Harlow.

Chaston, I. (2000) *E-marketing Strategy.* McGraw-Hill, Maidenhead.

Daniel, E., Wilson, H., McDonald, M. and Ward, J. (2001) *Marketing Strategy in the Digital Age.* Financial Times/Prentice Hall, Harlow.

Daniel, E., Wilson, H., Ward, J. and McDonald, M. (2002) Innovation @nd integration: developing an integrated e-enabled business strategy. Preliminary findings from an industry-sponsored research project for the Information Systems Research Centre and the Centre for E-marketing. Cranfield University School of Management, January.

Deise, M., Nowikow, C., King, P. and Wright, A. (2000) *Executive's Guide to E-Business. From Tactics to Strategy.* Wiley, New York.

de Kare-Silver, M. (2000) *EShock 2000. The Electronic Shopping Revolution: Strategies for Retailers and Manufacturers.* Macmillan, London.

de Kare-Silver, M. (2000) *EShock.* Macmillan, Basingstoke.

Dibb, S., Simkin, S., Pride, W. and Ferrel, O. (2001) *Marketing. Concepts and Strategies*, 4th European edn. Houghton Mifflin, New York.

Dudley, D. (2002) Egg hits profit, *New Media Age*, 25 February (www.newmediazero/nma).

Durlacher (2000) *Trends in the UK New Economy*, Durlacher Quarterly Internet Report, November, 1–12.

Gulati, R. and Garino, J. (2000) Getting the right mix of bricks and clicks for your company, *Harvard Business Review*, May–June, 107–14.

Kalakota, R. and Robinson, M. (2000) *E-Business. Roadmap for Success.* Addison-Wesley, Reading, MA.

Kumar, N. (1999) Internet distribution strategies: dilemmas for the incumbent, *Financial Times*, Special Issue on Mastering Information Management, no 7. Electronic Commerce (www.ftmastering.com).

Lynch, R. (2000) *Corporate Strategy*. Financial Times/Prentice Hall, Harlow.

McDonald, M. (1999) Strategic marketing planning: theory and practice, in M. Baker (ed.) *The CIM Marketing Book* (4th edn), pp. 50–77, Butterworth Heinemann, Oxford.

McDonald, M. and Wilson, H. (2002) *New Marketing: Transforming the Corporate Future*. Butterworth Heinemann, Oxford.

McFarlan, F.W. (1984) Information technology changes the way you compete, *Harvard Business Review*, May–June, 54–61.

Mintzberg, H. and Quinn, J.B. (1991) *The Strategy Process*, 2nd edn. Prentice Hall, Upper Saddle River, NJ.

Parsons, A., Zeisser, M. and Waitman, R. (1996) Organising for digital marketing, *McKinsey Quarterly*, No. 4, 183–92.

Phillips, S. (2000) Retailer's crown jewel is a unique customer database, *Financial Times*, 4 December.

Picardi, R. (2000) *EBusiness Speed: Six Strategies for eCommerce Intelligence*. IDC Research Report. IDC, Framlington, MA.

Poon, S. and Joseph, M. (2000) A preliminary study of product nature and electronic commerce. *Marketing Intelligence and Planning*, 19(7), 493–9.

Porter, M. (1980) *Competitive Strategy*. Free Press, New York.

Porter, M. (1996) What is strategy? *Harvard Business Review*, November–December, 61–78.

Porter, M. (2001) Strategy and the Internet, *Harvard Business Review*, March, 62–78.

Quelch, J. and Klein, L. (1996) The Internet and international marketing, *Sloan Management Review*, Spring, 61–75.

Smith, P.R. and Chaffey, D. (2001) *EMarketing Excellence: at the Heart of EBusiness*. Butterworth Heinemann, Oxford.

Tjan, A. (2001) Finally, a way to put your Internet portfolio in order, *Harvard Business Review*, February, 78–85.

Varianini, V. and Vaturi, D. (2000) Marketing lessons from e-failures, *McKinsey Quarterly*, No. 4, 86–97.

Wind, Y. and Cardazo, R. (1974) Industrial marketing segmentation, *Industrial Marketing Management*, 3 (March), 153–66.

Further reading

Baker, M. (ed.) (1999) *The Marketing Book*. Butterworth Heinemann, Oxford. Chapter 2, The basics of marketing strategy, and Chapter 3, Strategic marketing planning: theory and practice, are highly recommended. Chapter 4 describes environmental scanning.

Brassington, F. and Petitt, S. (2000) *Principles of Marketing*, 2nd edn. Financial Times/Prentice Hall, Harlow. *See* companion Prentice Hall web site (www.booksites.net/brassington2). Chapters 10 and 11 describe pricing issues in much more detail than that given in this chapter. Chapters 20, Strategic management, and 21, Marketing planning, management and control, describe the integration of marketing strategy with business strategy.

Daniel, E., Wilson, H., McDonald, M. and Ward, J. (2001) *Marketing Strategy in the Digital Age*. Financial Times/Prentice Hall, Harlow. Clear guidelines on strategy development based on and including industry case studies.

Deise, M., Nowikow, C., King, P. and Wright, A. (2000) *Executive's Guide to E-business. From Tactics to Strategy*. Wiley, New York. An excellent practitioners' guide.

de Kare-Silver, M. (1998) *eShock*. Macmillan, Basingstoke. This business book reviews the implications of the Internet and the strategic options available to retailers and manufacturers. At the time of writing de Kare-Silver had just been appointed as director responsible for e-commerce at retailer Great Universal Stores (GUS).

Dibb, S., Simkin, S., Pride, W. and Ferrel, O. (2001) *Marketing. Concepts and Strategies*, 4th European edn. Houghton Mifflin, New York. *See* companion Houghton Mifflin web site (www.busmgt.ulst.ac.uk/h_mifflin) *See* Chapter 22, Marketing strategy and competitive forces, and Chapter 19, Pricing concepts.

Ghosh, S. (1998) Making business sense of the Internet, *Harvard Business Review*, March–April, 127–35. This paper gives many examples of how US companies have adapted to the Internet and asks key questions that should govern the strategy adopted. It is an excellent introduction to strategic approaches.

Gulati, R. and Garino, J. (2000) Getting the right mix of bricks and clicks for your company, *Harvard Business Review*, May–June, 107–14. A different perspective on the six strategy decisions given in the strategic definition section with a road map through the decision process.

Hackbarth, G. and Kettinger, W. (2000) Building an e-business strategy, *Information Systems Management*, Summer, 78–93. An information systems perspective to e-business strategy.

Kotler, P., Armstrong, G., Saunders, J. and Wong, V. (1999) *Principles of Marketing*, 2nd edn. Prentice Hall Europe, Hemel Hempstead. *See* companion Prentice Hall web site for 8th US edn cw.prenhall.com/bookbind/pubbooks/kotler. *See* Chapter 3, Strategic marketing planning, and Chapter 12, Creating competitive advantage.

Kumar, N. (1999) Internet distribution strategies: dilemmas for the incumbent, *Financial Times*, Special Issue on Mastering Information Management, 7. Electronic Commerce (www.ftmastering.com). This article assesses the impact of the Internet on manufacturers and their distribution channels. The other articles in this special issue are also interesting.

Willcocks, L. and Sauer, C. (2000) Moving to e-business: an introduction. In L. Willcocks and C. Sauer (eds) *Moving to E-business*, 1–18. Random House, London. Combines traditional IS-strategy-based approaches with up-to-date case studies.

Web links

- BRINT.com (www.brint.com) A Business Researcher's Interests. Extensive portal with articles on e-business, e-commerce, knowledge management, change management and IS strategy.

- CIO Magazine E-commerce resource centre (www.cio.com/forums/ec) One of the best online magazines from business technical perspective – see other research centres also, e.g. intranets, knowledge management.

- E-commerce innovation centre (www.ecommerce.ac.uk) at Cardiff University. Interesting case studies for SMEs and basic explanations of concepts and terms.

- E-commerce Times (www.ecommercetimes.com) An online newspaper specific to e-commerce developments.

- Financial Times IT surveys (www.ft.com/ftit) Excellent monthly articles based on case studies. Also see Connectis for more European examples.

- E-commerce About.com (www.ecommerce.about.com) Portal about all aspects of e-commerce.

- E-consultancy (www.e-consultancy.co.uk) A good compilation of reports and white papers many of which are strategy-related.

- Mohansawney.com (www.mohansawney.com). Case studies and white papers from one of the leading IS authorities on e-commerce.

- US centre for e-business (www.ebusiness.mit.edu) Useful collection of articles.

- Net Academy (www.netacademy.org) Business resources including e-business articles.

Chapter 5

The Internet and the marketing mix

Links to other chapters

This chapter is related to other chapters as follows:

➤ Chapter 2 introduces the impact of the Internet on market structure and distribution channels

➤ Chapter 4 outlines how the Internet marketing strategy can be defined

➤ Chapters 6 and 7 explain the service elements of the mix in more detail

➤ Chapter 8 explains the promotion elements of the mix in more detail

Learning objectives

After reading this chapter, the reader should be able to:

● Apply the elements of the marketing mix in an online context

● Evaluate the opportunities that the Internet makes available for varying the marketing mix

● Define the characteristics of an online brand

Questions for marketers

Key questions for marketing managers related to this chapter are:

● How are the elements of the marketing mix varied online?

● What are the implications of the Internet for brand development?

● Can the product component of the mix be varied online?

● How are companies developing online pricing strategies?

● Does 'place' have relevance online?

Introduction

This chapter explores the implications the Internet has for marketers as they apply the marketing mix in the context of the Internet. It explores this key issue of Internet marketing strategy in more detail than was possible in Chapter 4.

The **marketing mix** – widely referred to as the 4 Ps of Product, Price, Place and Promotion – was originally proposed by Jerome McCarthy (1960) and is still used as an essential part of formulating implementing marketing strategy by many practitioners. The 4 Ps has since been extended to the 7 Ps which include three further elements that better reflect service delivery: People, Processes and Physical evidence (Booms and Bitner, 1981), although others argue that these are subsumed within the 4 Ps. Figure 5.1 summarises the different sub-elements of the 7 Ps.

Marketing mix
The series of seven key variables – Product, Price, Place, Promotion, People, Process and Physical evidence – that are varied by marketers as part of the customer offering.

The marketing mix is applied frequently since it provides a simple strategic framework for varying different elements of an organisation's product offering to influence the demand for products within target markets. For example, if the aim is to increase sales of a product, options include decreasing the price or changing the amount or type of promotion, or some combination of these elements. E-commerce provides many new opportunities for the marketer to vary the marketing mix. E-commerce also has far-reaching implications for the relative importance of different elements of the mix for many markets regardless of whether an organisation is involved directly in e-commerce. Given the implications of the Internet on the marketing mix, a whole chapter is devoted to examining its impact and strategies companies can develop to best manage this situation.

Activity 5.1

How can the Internet be used to vary the marketing mix?

Purpose

An introductory activity which highlights the vast number of areas which the Internet impacts.

Activity

Review Figure 5.1 and select the *two* most important ways in which the Internet gives new potential for varying the marketing mix *for each* of product, price, promotion, place, people and processes. State:

- new opportunities for varying the mix;
- examples of companies that have achieved this;
- possible negative implications (threats) for each opportunity.

The key issues related to different elements of the marketing mix that are discussed in this chapter are:

- *Product* – are there opportunities for modifying the core or extended product online?
- *Price* – the implications of the Internet for pricing and the adoption of new pricing models or strategies.
- *Place* – the implications for distribution.
- *Promotion* (what new promotional tools can be applied) – this is only discussed briefly in this chapter since it is described in more detail in Chapter 8.

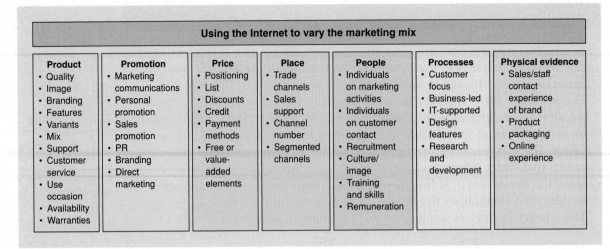

Figure 5.1 **The elements of the marketing mix**

- *People, process and physical evidence* – these are not discussed in detail in this chapter since their online application is covered in more detail in Chapters 6, 7 and 9 in connection with customer relationship management and managing and maintaining the online presence.

Before embarking on a review of the role of the Internet on each of the 7 Ps, it is worth briefly restating some of the well-known criticisms of applying the marketing mix as a solitary tool for marketing strategy. First and perhaps most importantly, the marketing mix, because of its origins in the 1960s, is symptomatic of a push approach to marketing and does not explicitly acknowledge the needs of customers. As a consequence, the marketing mix tends to lead to a product orientation rather than customer orientation – a key concept of market orientation and indeed a key Internet marketing concept (see Chapter 8, for example). To mitigate this effect, Lautenborn (1990) suggested the 4 Cs framework which considers the 4 Ps from a customer perspective. In brief, the 4 Cs are:

- customer needs and wants (from the product);
- cost to the customer (price);
- convenience (relative to place);
- communication (promotion).

It follows that the selection of the marketing mix is based on detailed knowledge of buyer behaviour collected through market research. Furthermore, it should be remembered that the mix is often adjusted according to different target markets or segments to better meet the needs of these customer groupings.

Product

Product variable

The element of the marketing mix that involves researching customers' needs and developing appropriate products.

The **product** element of the marketing mix refers to characteristics of a product, service or brand. Product decisions are informed by market research where customers' needs are assessed and the feedback is used to modify existing products or develop new products. There are many alternatives for varying the product in the online context when a company is developing its online strategy. Internet-related product decisions can be usefully divided into decisions affecting the core product and the extended product. The core product refers to the main product purchased by the consumer to fulfil their needs, while the extended or augmented product refers to additional services and benefits that are built around the core of the product.

The main implications of the Internet for the product aspect of the mix, which we will review in this section, are:

1 options for varying core product;
2 options for varying extended product;
3 conducting market research online;
4 velocity of new product development;
5 velocity of new product diffusion.

There is also a subsection which looks at the implications for migrating a brand online.

1 Options for varying the core product

For some companies, there may be options for new digital products which will typically be information products that can be delivered over the Web. Ghosh (1998) talks about developing new products or adding 'digital value' to customers. He says companies should ask the following questions:

1 Can I offer additional information or transaction services to my existing customer base?
2 Can I address the needs of new customer segments by repackaging my current information assets or by creating new business propositions using the Internet?
3 Can I use my ability to attract customers to generate new sources of revenue such as advertising or sales of complementary products?
4 Will my current business be significantly harmed by other companies' providing some of the value I currently offer?

Rayport and Sviokla (1994) describe transactions where the actual product has been replaced by information about the product, for example a company providing oil drilling equipment focusing instead on analysis and dissemination of information about drilling.

In some cases, an online version of the product may be more valuable to customers in that it can be updated more regularly. The advertising directory BRAD (Figure 5.2) has been changed from a large paper-based document to an online version with searching facilities that were not available in the paper-based version.

The Internet also introduces options for mass customisation of products. Levi's provide a truly personal service that dates back to 1994, when Levi Strauss initiated its 'Personal Pair' programme. Women who were prepared to pay up to $15 more than the standard price and wait for delivery could go to Levi's Stores and have themselves digitised – that is, have their measurements taken and a pair of custom jeans made and then have their measurements stored on a database for future purchases.

The programme achieved a repeat purchase rate significantly higher than the usual 10–12 per cent rate, and by 1997 accounted for a quarter of women's jean sales at Levi's Stores. In 1998 the programme was expanded to include men's jeans and the number of styles for each was doubled – to 1500 styles. This service has now migrated to the Web and is branded as Original Spin.

Mass customisation or personalisation of products in which a customer takes a more active role in product design is part of the move to the prosumer. An example is provided in Figure 5.3. Further details are given in the box.

Core product

The fundamental features of the product that meet the user's needs.

Extended product

Additional features and benefits beyond the core product.

Mass customisation

Using economies of scale enabled by technology to offer tailored versions of products to individual customers or groups of customers.

Prosumer

'Producer + consumer'. The customer is closely involved in specifying their requirements in a product.

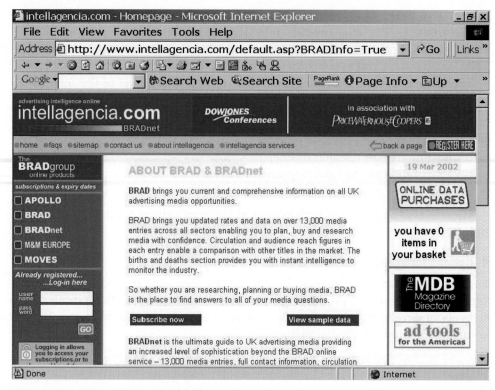

Figure 5.2 BRAD advertising directory (www.brad.co.uk)

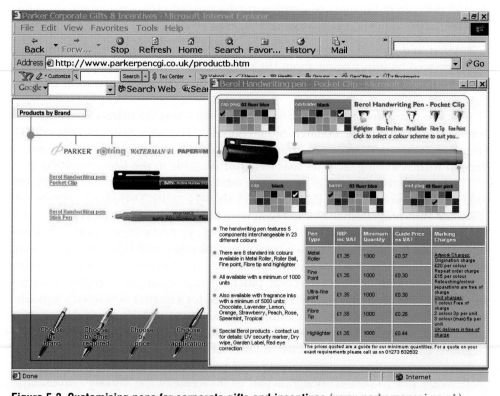

Figure 5.3 Customising pens for corporate gifts and incentives (www.parkerpencgi.co.uk)

The prosumer

The prosumer concept was introduced in 1980 by futurist Alvin Toffler in his book *The Third Wave*. According to Toffler, the future would once again combine production with consumption. In *The Third Wave*, Toffler saw a world where interconnected users would collaboratively 'create' products. Note that he foresaw this over 10 years before the Web was invented!

Alternative notions of the prosumer, all of which are applicable to e-marketing, are catalogued at Logophilia WordSpy (www.logophilia.com/WordSpy)

1 A consumer who is an amateur in a particular field, but who is knowledgeable enough to require equipment that has some professional features:
('professional' + 'consumer').

2 A person who helps to design or customise the products they purchase:
('producer' + 'consumer').

3 A person who creates goods for their own use and also possibly to sell:
('producing' + 'consumer').

4 A person who takes steps to correct difficulties with consumer companies or markets and to anticipate future problems:
('proactive' + 'consumer').

An example of the application of the prosumer is provided by BMW who used an interactive web site prior to launch of their Z3 roadster where users could design their own preferred features. The information collected was linked to a database and as BMW had previously collected data on its most loyal customers, the database could give a very accurate indication of which combinations of features were the most sought after and should therefore be put into production.

Companies can also consider how the Internet can be used to change the range or combination of products offered. Some companies only offer a subset of products online – for example, WH Smith interactive TV service only offers bestsellers at a discount. Alternatively, a company may have a fuller catalogue available online than is available through offline brochures. **Bundling** is a further alternative. For example, easyJet has developed a range of complementary travel-related services including flights, packages and car hire. McDonald and Wilson (2002) note how the potential for substituted or reconfigured products should be assessed for each marketplace.

Finally, it should also be noted that information about the core features of the product becomes more readily available online as pointed out by Allen and Fjermestad (2001). However, this has the greatest implications for price (downwards pressure caused by price transparency) and place and promotion (marketers must ensure they are represented favourably on the portal intermediaries) where the products will be compared with others in terms of core features, extended features and price.

Bundling
Offering complementary services.

2 Options for changing the extended product

When a customer buys a new computer, it consists not only of the tangible computer, monitor and cables, but also the information provided by the computer salesperson, the instruction manual, the packaging, the warranty and the follow-up technical service. These are elements of the extended product. Smith and Chaffey (2001) suggest these examples of how the Internet can be used to vary the extended product:

- endorsements
- awards
- testimonies
- customer lists
- customer comments
- warranties
- guarantees
- money-back offers
- customer service (see people, process and physical evidence)
- incorporating tools to help users during their use of the product. A good example of this is the Citroën ExCeed software which Citroën provides to fleet car managers (Figure 5.4)

The digital value referred to by Ghosh (1998) will often be free, in which case it will be part of the extended product. He suggests that companies should provide free digital value to help build an audience which can then be converted into customers. He refers to this process as building a 'customer magnet', today this would be known as a 'portal' or 'community'. There is good potential for customer magnets in specialised vertical markets served by business-to-business companies where there is a need for industry-specific information to assist individuals in their day-to-day work. For example, a customer magnet could be developed for the construction industry, agrochemicals, biotechnology or independent financial advisers. Alternatively the portal could be branded as an 'extranet' that is only available to key accounts to help differentiate the service. Dell Premier Pages is an example of such an extranet.

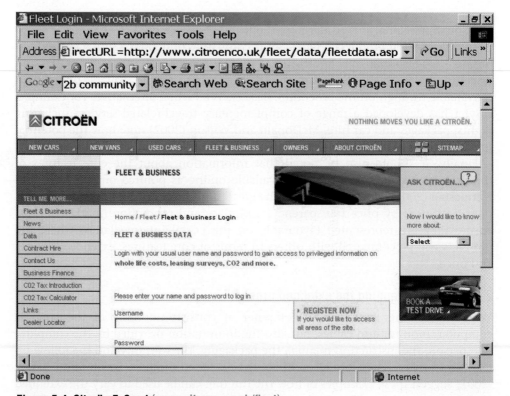

Figure 5.4 Citroën ExCeed (www.citroen.co.uk/fleet)

Extended product is not necessarily provided free of charge. In other cases a premium may be charged. Amazon (www.amazon.com), for instance, charges for its wrapping service.

3 Conducting research online

The Internet provides many options for learning about products. It can be used as a relatively low-cost method of collecting marketing research, particularly about customer perceptions of products and services. Typically these will complement rather than replace offline research. Options include:

- *Online focus group.* A moderated focus group can be conducted to compare customers' experience of product use.
- *Online questionnaire survey.* These typically focus on the site visitors' experience, but can also include questions relating to products.
- *Customer feedback or support forums.* Comments posted to the site or independent sites may give information on future product innovation.
- *Web logs.* A wealth of marketing research information is also available from the web site itself, since every time a user clicks on a link this is recorded in a transaction log file summarising what information on the site the customer is interested in. Such information can be used to indirectly assess customers' product preferences.

Approaches for undertaking these types of research are briefly reviewed in Chapter 12.

4 Velocity of new product development

Quelch and Klein (1996) note that the Internet can also be used to accelerate new product development since different product options can be tested online more rapidly. Indeed the network effect of the Internet enables companies to form partnerships more readily to launch new products. The subsection on virtual organisations in the section on 'Place' discusses this in a little more detail.

5 Velocity of new product diffusion

Quelch and Klein (1996) also noted that the implication of the Internet and concomitant globalisation is that to remain competitive, organisations will have to roll out new products more rapidly to international markets.

Assessing options online to vary product using the Internet

Purpose

To illustrate the options for varying the product element of the marketing mix online.

Activity

Select one of the sectors below. Use a search engine to find three competitors with similar product offerings. List ways in which each has used the Internet to vary its core and extended product. Which of the companies do you think makes best use of the Internet?

- Computer manufacturers
- Management consultants
- Children's toy sector
- Higher education.

● The Internet and branding

What comprises a successful online brand? Is it an e-commerce site with high levels of traffic? Is it a brand with good name recognition? Is it a profitable brand? Or is it a site with more modest sales levels, but one that customers perceive as providing good service? Although such sites meeting only some of these criteria are often described as successful brands, we will see that a successful brand is dependent on a wide range of factors.

The importance of building an effective online brand is often referred to when start-ups launch e-commerce sites, but what does branding mean in the online context and how important is online branding for existing companies?

Branding seems to be a concept that is difficult to grasp since it is often used in a narrow sense. Many think of branding only in terms of aspects of the brand identity such as the name or logo associated with a company or products, but branding gurus seem agreed that it is much more than that. A **brand** is described by Leslie de Chernatony and Malcolm McDonald in their classic book 1992 book *Creating Powerful Brands* as

> *an identifiable product or service augmented in such a way that the buyer or user perceives relevant unique added values which match their needs most closely. Furthermore, its success results from being able to sustain these added values in the face of competition.*

This definition highlights three essential characteristics of a successful brand:

- brand is dependent on customer perception;
- perception is influenced by the added-value characteristics of the product;
- the added-value characteristics need to be sustainable.

To summarise, a brand is dependent on a customer's psychological affinity for a product, and is much more than physical name or symbol elements of brand identity.

An alternative perspective on branding is provided by Aaker and Joachimstaler (2000) who refer to **brand equity**. These authors say that brand equity is made up of four dimensions:

1 *Brand awareness.* This is achieved through marketing communications to promote the brand identity and the other qualities of the brand. Aaker and Joachimstaler note that brand awareness is important not only in terms informing customers about a product, but also because people like the familiar and brand awareness links through to other aspects of brand equity. For example, the Intel Inside awareness campaign not only increased awareness but also provides a perception of technological innovation and quality. Ewing (2002) reports that compared to the previous Christmas shopping period, in 2001 twice as many British surfers visited the online presence of department stores or catalogue companies such as Littlewoods (www.littlewoods.com) and Argos (www.argos.co.uk). He suggests that these well-known brands are being used increasingly online because of the trust consumers place in companies they are familiar with.

2 *Perceived quality.* Awareness counts for little if the customer has a bad experience of a product or associated customer service. If quality of a brand is negatively perceived this affects its equity since word-of-mouth will quickly be relayed to many people.

3 *Brand associations.* There are many brand associations that connect a customer to a brand, including imagery, the situation in which a product is used and its

Branding

The process of creating and evolving successful brands.

Brand

The sum of the characteristics of a product or service perceived by a user.

Brand equity

The assets (or liabilities) linked to a brand's name and symbol that add to (or subtract from) a service.

personality and symbols. Intel Inside aims to create a fun and funky, but technical brand association through the use of dancing clean-lab technicians.

4 *Brand loyalty*. This refers to the commitment of customer segments to a brand. For example, Intel may have good brand awareness, quality and clear associations, but its brand equity is undermined if customers are happy to buy a computer with an AMD or Cyrix chip when they next upgrade their computer.

De Chernatony (2001) has evaluated the relevance of the brand concept on the Internet. He also believes that the main elements of brand values and brand strategy are the same in the Internet environment. However, he suggests that the classical branding model of the Internet where consumers are passive recipients of value is challenged online. Instead he suggests that consumers on the Internet become active co-producers of value where consumers can contribute feedback through discussion groups to add value to a brand. De Chernatony argues for a looser form of brand control where the company facilitates rather than controls customer discussion. An example of this looser control is the EggFreeZone (www.eggfreezone.com) created by bank Egg as an independent forum for discussion of the Egg brand and its partners. However, in 2001 this service was withdrawn.

A further method by which the Internet can change branding that was suggested by Jevons and Gabbott (2000) is that online, '*the first-hand experience of the brand is a more powerful token of trust than the perception of the brand*'. In the online environment, the customer can **experience** or interact with the brand more frequently and to a greater depth. As Dayal et al. (2000) say, '*on the world wide web, the brand is the experience and the experience is the brand*'. They suggest that to build successful online brands, organisations should consider how their proposition can build on these possible brand promises:

> **Brand experience**
> The frequency and depth of interactions with a brand can be enhanced through the Internet.

- *the promise of convenience* – making a purchase experience more convenient than the real-world one, or that with rivals;
- *the promise of achievement* – to assist consumers in achieving their goals, for example supporting online investors in their decision or supporting business people in their day-to-day work;
- *the promise of fun and adventure* – this is clearly more relevant for B2C services;
- *the promise of self-expression and recognition* – provided by personalisation services such as Yahoo! Geocities where consumers can build their own web site;
- *the promise of belonging* – provided by online communities.

Brand identity

Aaker and Joachimstaler (2000) also emphasise the importance of developing a plan to communicate the key features of the **brand identity** and increase brand awareness. Brand identity is again more than the name. These authors refer to it as a set of brand associations that imply a promise to customers from an organisation. See the 'Jungle.com's brand identity' case study to see the different elements of brand identity which are effectively a checklist of what many e-tailers are looking to achieve.

> **Brand identity**
> The totality of brand associations including name and symbols that must be communicated.

Options for changing brand identity online

A further decision for marketing managers is whether to redefine the name element of brand identity to support the move online. Brands that are newly created for the Internet such as Expedia.com and Quokka.com do not risk damaging existing brands, although it is suggested by de Chernatony and McDonald (1992) that new brand launches are risky activities and that even in the offline world less than 10%

Mini Case Study 5.1

Jungle.com's brand identity

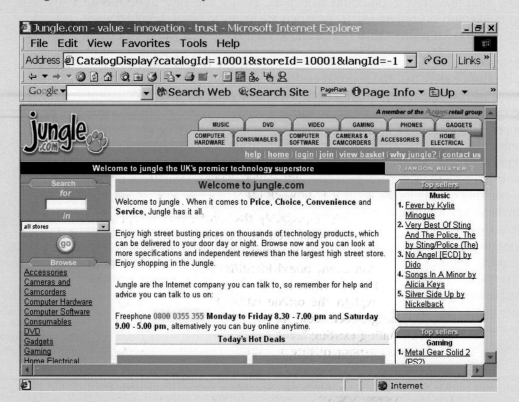

Figure 5.5 Jungle.com

Aaker and Joachimstaler (2000) suggest that the following characteristics of identity need to be defined at the start of a brand building campaign. Marketing communications can then be developed that create and reinforce this identity.

- *Brand essence (a summary of what the brand represents)*
  This is not necessarily a tag line, but for Jungle it could be 'Making technology fun and affordable'

- *Core identity (its key features)*
  - service quality – next-day delivery
  - value for money – price pledge policy
  - reliable, secure, backed by larger company (GUS/Argos) so support should be available
  - an entertaining, down-to-earth buying experience

- *Extended identity*
  - personality – flaunts what is standard for technology suppliers
  - symbols – Jungle.com logo and typeface and the Stanley monkey and footprint brand icons

- *Value proposition*
  - functional benefits – four reasons listed in catalogue are: 1. Huge stocks, 2. Next-day delivery, 3. Lines open 7 days a week, 4. Internet security – a member of the Argos group

- emotional benefits – good to make technology accessible and friendly, backed up by a larger company
- self-expressive benefit – willingness to go against the usual way of selling products

● *Relationship*
  - customers value and will be loyal to a company that isn't stuffy

This is an interpretation of Jungle.com's brand identity based on evaluation of their marketing communications. The intention is to indicate the depth to which brand identity is defined – interpretations may not be accurate for Jungle.com.

of new brands prove successful. There are four main options for a company migrating their brands online. When a company launches or relaunches an e-commerce site it has the following choices with regards to brand identity:

1 *Transfer traditional brand online.* This is probably the most common approach. Companies with brands that are well established in the real world can build on the brand by duplicating it online. Sites from companies such as Ford, Argos and Guinness (Figure 5.6) all have consistent brand identities and values that would be expected from experience of their offline brands. The Guinness site has some additional brand messages to explain the online value proposition (Chapter 4). Some companies, such as Orange, even replicate their offline branding campaigns online. The only risks of migrating existing brands online are that the brand equity may be reduced if the site is of poor quality in terms of performance, structure

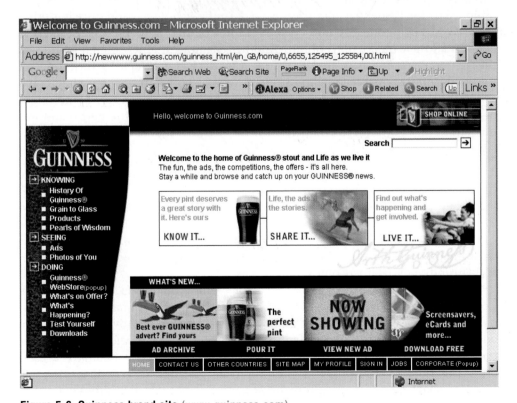

Figure 5.6 Guinness brand site (www.guinness.com)

or information content. There may also be a missed opportunity as explained below.

2 *Extend traditional brand: variant.* Some companies decide to create a slightly different version of their brand when they create their web site. The DHL site (www.dhl.co.uk) is based on an online brand 'Red Planet' which is based on a space-ship concept. Users order couriers and track using controls on a spaceship console. Through using this approach, the advantages of a brand variant are illustrated well. The company is able to differentiate itself from similar competing services and this can be used in online and offline promotion to distinguish the site from its rivals. Cisco uses a similar approach with its Cisco Online Connection brand. The use of an online brand variant helps raise the profile of the web site and helps the customer think of the site in association with the company. Aaker and Joachimstaler (2000) suggest that when a brand variant is created there may still be problems with recognition and also brand trust and quality associations may be damaged.

3 *Partner with existing digital brand.* It may be that a company can best promote its products in association in with a strong existing digital or Internet brand such as Yahoo! or Freeserve. For example, the shopping options for record and book sales on Freeserve are branded as Freeserve although they are actually based on sites from other companies such as record seller Audiostreet.com. Freeserve is given brand prominence since this is to the advantage of both companies.

4 *Create a new digital brand.* It may be necessary to create an entirely new digital brand if the existing offline brand has negative connotations or is too traditional for the new medium. An example of a new digital brand is the Egg banking service which is part of Prudential, a well-established company. Egg can take new approaches without damaging Prudential's brand, and at the same time, not be inhibited by the Prudential brand. Egg is not an entirely online brand since it is primarily accessed by phone. Egg now encourage some of their million-plus customers to perform all their transactions online. Another example of a new digital brand was the Go portal which was created by Disney, who desired to be able to 'own' some of the many online customers who are loyal to one portal. It was felt they could achieve this best through using a completely new brand. The Disney brand might be thought to appeal to a limited younger audience. However, the new brand was not sufficiently powerful to compete with the existing Yahoo! brand and has now failed.

Some of the characteristics of a successful brand name are suggested by de Chernatony and McDonald (1992): ideally it should be simple, distinctive, meaningful and compatible with the product. These principles can be readily applied to web-based brands. Examples of brands that fulfil most of these characteristics are CDNow, CarPoint, BUY.COM and e-STEEL. Others suggest that distinctiveness is most important: Amazon, Yahoo!, Expedia, Quokka.com (extreme sports), E*Trade, and FireandWater (HarperCollins) books.

Ries and Ries (2000) suggest two rules for naming brands. (a) The Law of the Common Name – they say 'The kiss of death for an Internet brand is a common name'. This argues that common names such as Art.com or Advertising.com are poor since they are not sufficiently distinctive. (b) The Law of the Proper Name – they say 'Your name stands alone on the Internet, so you'd better have a good one'. This suggests that proper names are to be preferred to generic names, e.g. Handbag.com against Woman.com or Moreover.com against Business.com. The authors suggest that the best names will follow most of these eight principles:

(1) short, (2) simple, (3) suggestive of the category, (4) unique, (5) alliterative, (6) speakable, (7) shocking and (8) personalised. Although these are cast as 'immutable laws' there will of course be exceptions!

Price

The **price variable** of the marketing mix refers to an organisation's pricing policies which are used to define **pricing models** and, of course, to set prices for products and services. The Internet has dramatic implications for pricing in many sectors and there is a lot of literature in this area. Baker et al. (2000) noted two approaches that have been commonly adopted for pricing on the Internet: start-up companies have tended to use low prices to gain a customer base, while many existing companies have transferred their existing prices to the web. These and other options are explored in this section.

The main implications of the Internet for the price aspect of the mix, which we will review in this section, are:

1   increased price transparency and its implications on differential pricing;
2   downward pressure on price (including commoditisation);
3   new pricing approaches (including dynamic pricing and auctions);
4   alternative pricing structure or policies.

● 1 Increased price transparency

Quelch and Klein (1996) describe two contradictory effects of the Internet on price that are related to **price transparency**. First, a supplier can use the technology for **differential pricing**, for example, for customers in different countries. However, if precautions are not taken about price, the customers may be able to quickly find out about the price discrimination and they will object to it.

So, customer knowledge of pricing is enhanced through the Internet. This is particularly the case for standardised goods sold through online retailers. Not only can customers visit sites of rival suppliers, but they can visit sites with price comparison engines provided by intermediaries such as ShopSmart (www.shopsmart.com) (Fig. 5.7), easyShop (www.easyshop.com) or MySimon (www.mysimon.com). These sites will list the best price from suppliers for a particular product ranked from highest to lowest. It is difficult to retain price differentials if all customers are aware of these differences. Currently, this is probably not the case. Research quoted by Marn (2000) suggests that only around 8% of active online consumers are 'aggressive price shoppers'. Furthermore, he notes that Internet price bands have remained broad. Online booksellers' prices varied by an average of 33% and those of CD sellers by 25%.

One strategy for companies in the face of increased price transparency is to highlight the other features of the brand, to reduce the emphasis on cost as a differentiator. In October 2000, *Revolution* magazine reported a dispute between Abbey National and financial comparison site Moneysupermarket.com (www.moneysupermarket.com). The bank had reportedly requested that several comparison sites including MoneySupermarket not list them and a legal dispute ensued.

For business commodities, auctions on business-to-business exchanges can also have a similar effect of driving down price. Purchase of some products that have not traditionally been thought of as commodities may become more price-sensitive. This process is known as **commoditisation**. Examples of goods that are becoming commoditised include electrical goods and cars.

Price variable

The element of the marketing mix that involves defining product prices and pricing models.

Pricing models

Describe the form of payment such as outright purchase, auction, rental, volume purchases and credit terms.

Price transparency

Customer knowledge about pricing increases due to increased availability of pricing information.

Differential pricing

Identical products are priced differently for different types of customers, markets or buying situations.

Commoditisation

The process whereby product selection becomes more dependent on price than differentiating features, benefits and value-added services.

Figure 5.7 ShopSmart (www.shopsmart.com)

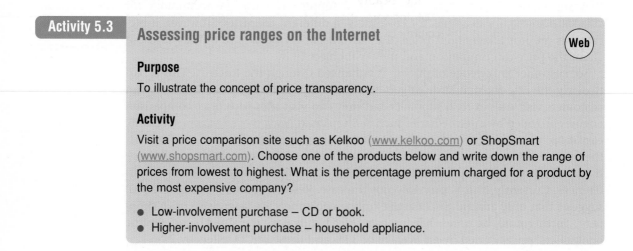

Activity 5.3

Assessing price ranges on the Internet

(Web)

Purpose

To illustrate the concept of price transparency.

Activity

Visit a price comparison site such as Kelkoo (www.kelkoo.com) or ShopSmart (www.shopsmart.com). Choose one of the products below and write down the range of prices from lowest to highest. What is the percentage premium charged for a product by the most expensive company?

● Low-involvement purchase – CD or book.
● Higher-involvement purchase – household appliance.

● 2 Downward pressure on price

Price transparency is one reason for downwards pressure on price. The Internet also tends to drive down prices since Internet-only retailers which do not have a physical presence do not have the overhead of operating stores and a distribution network. This means that online companies can offer lower prices than offline rivals. This phenomenon is marked in the banking sector where many banks have set up online companies offering better rates of interest on savings products.

A further reason for downward pressure on price is that companies looking to compete online may discount online prices. For example, easyJet discounted online prices in an effort to meet its growth objectives of online revenue contribution. Such discounts are possible since there is a lower overhead of processing a customer transaction online than for phone transactions. Note that there may be a danger in channel conflicts resulting from this approach.

Similarly, to acquire customers, online booksellers may decide to offer a discount of 50% on the top 25 best-selling books in each category, for which no profit is made, but offer a smaller discount on less popular books to give a profit margin.

Diamantopoulos and Matthews (1993) suggest there are two aspects of competition that affect an organisation's pricing. The first is the structure of the market – the greater the number of competitors and the visibility of their prices the nearer the market is to being a **perfect market**. The implication of a perfect market is that an organisation will be less able to control prices, but must respond to competitors' pricing strategies. It is clear that since the Internet is a global phenomenon and, as we have seen, it facilitates price transparency, it does lead to a move towards a perfect market. The second is the perceived value of the product. If a brand is differentiated in some way, it may be less subject to downward pressure on price. As well as making pricing more transparent, the Internet does lead to opportunities to differentiate in information describing products or through added-value services. Whatever the relative importance of these factors in influencing purchase decisions, it seems clear that the Internet will lead to more competition-based pricing.

Baker et al. (2000) suggest that companies should use the following three factors to assist in pricing.

Perfect market
An efficient market where there are an infinite number of suppliers and buyers and complete price transparency.

1 *Precision.* Each product has a price-indifference band, where varying price has little or no impact on sales. Baker et al. (2000) report that these bands can be as wide as 17% for branded consumer beauty products, 10% for engineered industrial components, but less than 10% for some financial products. The authors suggest that while the cost of undertaking a survey to calculate price indifference is very expensive in the real world, it is more effective online. They give the example of Zilliant, a software supplier that, in a price discovery exercise, reduced prices on four products by 7%. While this increased volumes of three of those by 5–20%, this was not sufficient to warrant the lower prices. However, for the fourth product, sales increased by 100%. It was found that this was occurring through sales to the educational sector, so this price reduction was just introduced for customers in that sector.

2 *Adaptablity.* This refers simply to the fact that it is possible to respond more quickly to the demands of the marketplace with online pricing. For some product areas such as ticketing it may be possible to dynamically alter prices in line with demand. Tickets.com adjusts concert ticket prices according to demand and has been able to achieve 45% more revenue per event as a result. The authors suggest that in this case and for other sought-after items such as video games or luxury cars, the Internet can actually increase the price since there it is possible to reach more people.

3 *Segmentation.* This refers to pricing differently for different groups of customers. This has not traditionally been practical for B2C markets since at the point of sale, information is not known about the customer, although it is widely practised for B2B markets. One example of pricing by segments would be for a car manufacturer to vary promotional pricing, so that rather than offering every purchaser discount purchasing or cash-back, it is only offered to those for whom it is thought necessary to make the sale. A further example is where a company can identify regular

customers and fill-in customers who only buy from the supplier when their needs can't be met elsewhere. In the latter case, up to 20% higher prices are levied.

What then are options available to marketers given this downward pressure on pricing? We will start by looking at traditional methods for pricing and how they are affected by the Internet. Bickerton et al. (2000) identify a range of options that are available for setting pricing.

1 *Cost-plus pricing.* This involves adding on a profit margin based on production costs. As we have seen above, a reduction in this margin may be required in the Internet era.

2 *Target-profit pricing.* This is a more sophisticated pricing method that involves looking at the fixed and variable costs in relation to income for different sales volumes and unit prices. Using this method the breakeven amount for different combinations can be calculated. For e-commerce sales the variable selling cost, i.e the cost for each transaction, is small. This means that once breakeven is achieved each sale has a large margin. With this model differential pricing is often used in a B2B context according to the volume of goods sold. Care needs to be taken that differential prices are not evident to different customers. One company, through an error on their web site, made prices for different customers available for all to see, with disastrous results.

3 *Competition-based pricing.* This approach is common online. The advent of price-comparison engines such as Kelkoo (www.kelkoo.com) for B2C consumables has increased price competition and companies need to develop online pricing strategies that are flexible enough to compete in the marketplace, but are still sufficient to achieve profitability in the channel. This approach may be used for the most popular products, e.g. the Top 25 CDs, but other methods such as target profit pricing used for other products.

4 *Market-oriented pricing.* Here the response to price changes by customers comprising the market are consider. This is known as the elasticity of demand. There are two approaches. *Premium pricing* (or *skimming the market*) involves setting a higher price than the competition to reflect the positioning of the product as a high-quality item. *Penetration pricing* is when a price is set below the competitors' prices to either stimulate demand or increase penetration. This approach was commonly used by dot-com companies to acquire customers. The difficulty with this approach is that if customers are price-sensitive then the low price has to be sustained – otherwise customers may change to a rival supplier. This has happened with online banks – some customers regularly move to reduce costs of overdrafts for example. Alternatively if a customer is concerned by other aspects such as service quality it may be necessary to create a large price differential in order to encourage a customer to change supplier.

Kotler (1997) suggests that in the face of price cuts from competitors in a market, a company has the following choices which can be applied to e-commerce:

A. Maintain the price (assuming that e-commerce-derived sales are unlikely to decrease greatly with price since other factors such as customer service are equally or more important).
B. Reduce the price (to avoid losing market share).
C. Raise perceived quality or differentiate product further by adding-value services.
D. Introduce new lower-priced product lines.

● 3 New pricing approaches (including auctions)

Figure 5.8 summarises different pricing mechanisms. While many of these were available before the advent of the Internet and are not new, the Internet has made some models more tenable. In particular, the volume of users makes traditional or forward auctions (B2C) and reverse auctions (B2B) more tenable – these have become more widely used than previously. Emiliani (2001) reviews the implications of B2B reverse auctions in detail, and Mini Case Study 5.2 provides an example. To understand auctions it is important to distinguish between offers and bids. An offer is a commitment for a trader to sell under certain conditions such as a minimum price. A bid is made by a trader to buy under the conditions of the bid such as a commitment to purchase at a particular price.

A further approach, not indicated in Figure 5.8, is aggregated buying. This approach was promoted by LetsBuyit.com, but the business model did not prove viable – the cost of creating awareness for the brand and explaining the concept was not offset by the revenue from each transaction.

Pitt et al. (2001) suggest that when developing a pricing strategy, the options will be limited by relative strengths of the seller and buyer. Where the buyer is powerful then reverse auctions are possible. Major car manufacturers fall into this category. See also, Mini Case Study 5.2. Where the seller is more powerful then a negotiation may be more likely where the seller can counter-offer. Nextag.com provides such a service.

Marn (2000) suggests that the Internet can be used to test new pricing policies. For example, if a company wants to know the sales impact of a 3 per cent price increase, it can try this on every 50th visitor to the site and compare the buy rates.

The Internet introduces new opportunities for dynamic pricing, for example new customers could be automatically given discounted purchases for the first three items. Care has to be taken with differential pricing since established customers will be unhappy if significant discounts are given to new customers. Amazon trialled such a discounting scheme in 2000 and it received negative press and had to be withdrawn when people found out that their friends or colleagues had paid less. If the scheme had been a clear introductory promotion this problem may not have arisen.

Forward auction
Item purchased by highest bid made in bidding period.

Reverse auction
Item purchased from lowest-bidding supplier in bidding period.

Offer
A commitment by a trader to *sell* under certain conditions.

Bid
A commitment by a trader to *purchase* under certain conditions.

Aggregated buying
A form of customer union where buyers collectively purchase a number of items at the same price and receive a volume discount.

Dynamic pricing
Prices can be updated in real time according to the type of customer or current market conditions.

Mini Case Study 5.2

GlaxoSmithKline reduces prices through reverse auctions

Healthcare company GlaxoSmithKline started using online reverse auctions in 2000 to drive down the price of its supplies. For example, it bought supplies of a basic solvent for a price 15 per cent lower than the day's spot price in the commodity market, and Queree (2000) reported that on other purchases of highly specified solvents and chemicals, SmithKline Beecham (prior to formation of GSK) is regularly beating its own historic pricing by between 7 and 25 per cent. She says:

> FreeMarkets, the company that manages the SmithKline Beecham auctions, quotes examples of savings achieved by other clients in these virtual market places: 42 per cent on orders for printed circuit boards, 41 per cent on labels, 24 per cent on commercial machinings and so on.

The reverse auction process starts with a particularly detailed Request for Proposals (RFP) from which suppliers ask to take part and then selected suppliers are invited to take part in the auction. Once the bidding starts, the participants see every bid, but not the names of the bidders. In the final stages of the auction, each last bid extends the bidding time by one more minute. One auction scheduled for 2 hours ran for 4 hours and 20 minutes and attracted more than 700 bids!

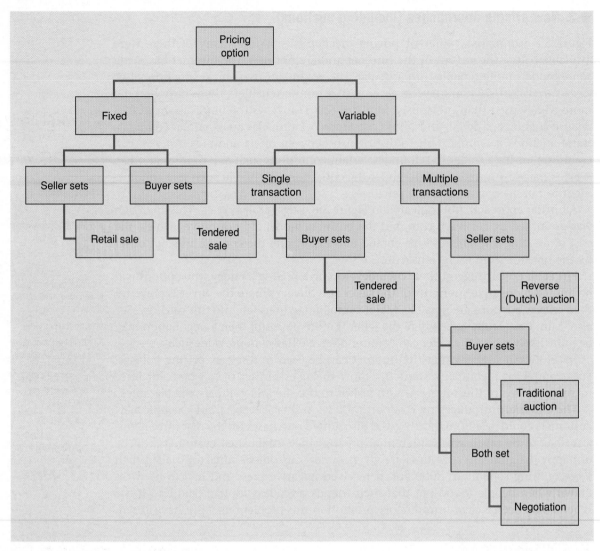

Figure 5.8 Alternative pricing mechanisms

● 4 Alternative pricing structure or policies

Different types of pricing may be possible on the Internet, particularly for digital, downloadable products. Software and music have traditionally been sold for a continuous right to use. The Internet offers new options such as payment per use, rental at a fixed cost per month or a lease arrangement. Bundling options may also be more possible. The use of applications service providers (ASPs) to deliver service such as web-site traffic monitoring also gives new methods of volume pricing. Companies such as Sitestats (www.sitestats.com) and RedSheriff (www.redsheriff.com) charge in price bands based on the number of visitors to the purchaser's site.

Further pricing options which could be varied online include:

● basic price
● discounts
● add-ons and extra products and services

- guarantees and warranties
- refund policies
- order cancellation terms.

CASE STUDY 5.1

An end to free content?

In a move to increase subscriber-bases, larger newspapers are offering 'premium content' services that are in some way exclusive to their publications.

The subscription is back in vogue on the internet. Web companies whose names were once synonymous with 'free' – including Yahoo and even Napster – are now beginning to flirt with paid-for services.

However, online news sites are not rushing to keep up with the trend. After all, many newspapers tried charging subscription fees in 1994 and 1995 when they first launched their online editions.

In most cases, the subscription plans were quickly scrapped after web users realised they could find free news elsewhere. Only the Wall Street Journal continues to have a substantial paid-up subscriber base.

But this does not mean that other online news sites have given up on the hope of making money on the internet. Many are beginning to experiment with means to complement their existing revenue streams, which in most cases consist of classified or other forms of advertising. Some, including the New York Times Digital, have begun charging for online access to archived stories, and others plan to follow suit.

Others, including The Financial Times and some newspapers owned by Tribune, are considering charging for premium content – meaning stories or features that are in some way exclusive to their newspapers.

'In many ways, these plans represent a return to pre-internet boom thinking. I'm not sure any of us expected we would be living in a totally free world', says Mike Silver, head of business development at Tribune.

'There was a desire from the beginning to have consumers pay for content. Now that we're in a more rational environment, were going back to the business planning of the sort when we first opened up.'

The online advertising recession – which began well before the rest of the ad market fell into a slump has forced companies to look for other sources of revenue on the internet. And there also has been a general re-examination of the tenets of the boom era, including the idea that charging fees for content somehow was an impediment to growth.

'If you are now used to paying for songs or financial data, are you more likely to pay for news from our sources? This is not an opportunity that we think is ripe', Mr Silver says. 'We did research that gets at the question of what is people's proclivity to pay. When we served up ideas, we got very little that looked like a solid winner for us.'

'The problem is that general news spreads quickly online and has a short shelf-life. It is also readily available in many places online for free. I've seen most of what daily newspapers have done, and I haven't seen anything I would pay for', says Jack Williams, vice president for business development at Gannett, the largest newspaper group in the US.

'We'd like to believe there's a paid mode out there, but I don't see it as this point.' Mr Williams says most of the news content in Gannett's papers is available for free on the web. But he says the company is making money on the internet from classified listings and from advertising.

▶

For most of the chain's smaller newspapers, the web division is a lean operation. Most of the local newspapers web units are run out of a centralised production facility in Washington, DC, which spares them the cost of maintaining expensive technology.

The exception is at Gannett's flagship newspaper, USA Today, which is the circulation leader in the US. USA Today's website maintains its own news, advertising and production staffs. 'USA Today is more like a national magazine in terms of ad sales, so this is the only way the model will work', he says.

Some news organisations hope that consumers will pay for access to 'premium' content on their sites. When sites such as TheStreet.com and Salon launched premium offerings, the plans were derided by some as desperate moves. But the idea appears to be gaining hold, and more news organisations are experimenting with 'premium' plans. For example, the New York Times, while a free site, charges $19.95 a year for online access to a premium crossword puzzle.

Sometimes, finding what people are willing to pay for is a matter of listening to readers' demands. Tony Uphoff, chief executive of religious site Beliefnet, launched an online education course last autumn called Understanding Islam. The course had 150 available positions, but 2600 people signed up.

In the end, 450 people took three separate Islam classes, which were offered for free. 'We sampled them later, and asked what would be appropriate pricing for this based on their experience', Mr Uphoff says. 'They came back saying that it was worth $25 to $30 a month. I was surprised.'

Still, the experience did not tempt Mr Uphoff into considering charging a subscription for the entire Beliefnet site. Our philosophy is that Beliefnet is not a fee-based service but a platform for fee-based products and services, he says.

Such specialised opportunities are limited for general news organisations, however. 'My view is that eventually there would be some things that it makes sense to charge for, but those will be few and far between', Mr Williams says. 'The free model will prevail for quite a while.'

Source: Christopher Grimes, Premium payments may boost web revenues, *Financial Times*, 6 February 2002

Question

Schemes to achieve revenue by charging for content on the Internet have had limited success in the past. Using the ideas in the article, supplemented by your own experience, evaluate whether future plans to charge for content will be successful.

Place

Place

The element of the marketing mix that involves distributing products to customers in line with demand and minimising cost of inventory, transport and storage.

The **place** element of the marketing mix refers to how the product is distributed to customers. The aim is typically to minimise costs of inventory, transport and storage while fulfilling demand from customers.

Allen and Fjermestad (2001) argue that the Internet has the greatest implications for place in the marketing mix since the Internet has a global reach. The main implications of the Internet for the place aspect of the mix, which we will review in this section, are:

1 place of purchase;
2 new channel structures;
3 channel conflicts;
4 virtual organisations.

Table 5.1 Different places for cyberspace representation

Place of purchase	Examples of sites
A. Seller-controlled	• Vendor sites, i.e. home site of organisation selling products, e.g. www.dell.com
B. Seller-oriented	• Intermediaries controlled by third parties to the seller such as distributors and agents, e.g. Opodo (www.opodo.com) represents the main air carriers
C. Neutral	• Intermediaries not controlled by buyer's industry, e.g. industry net (www.commerceone.com) • Product-specific search engines, e.g. CNET (www.computer.com) • Comparison sites, e.g. BarclaySquare/Shopsmart (www.barclaysquare.com) • Auction space, e.g. uBid (www.ubid.com)
D. Buyer-oriented	• Intermediaries controlled by buyers, e.g. Covisint represents the major motor manufacturers (www.tpn.geis.com) • Purchasing agents and aggregators
E. Buyer-controlled	• Web site procurement posting on company's own site, e.g. GE Trading Process Network (www.tpn.geis.com)

1 Place of purchase

Although the concept of place may seem peculiar for what is a global medium that transcends geographical boundaries, nevertheless, marketers still have several options for managing the place of purchase. The framework of Berryman et al. (1998), introduced in Chapter 2, is a simple framework for this. However, McDonald and Wilson (2002) introduce two additional locations for purchase which are useful (Table 5.1).

A. *Seller-controlled sites* are those that are the main site of the supplier company and are e-commerce-enabled.
B. *Seller-oriented sites* are controlled by third parties and are representing the seller rather than providing a full range of options.
C. *Neutral sites* are independent evaluator intermediaries that enable price and product comparison and will result in the purchase being fulfilled on the target site.
D. *Seller-oriented sites* are controlled by third parties on behalf of the seller.
E. *Seller-controlled sites* usually involve either procurement posting on buyer-company sites or on those of intermediaries that have been set up in such a way that it is the buyer who initiates the market making. This can occur through procurement posting, whereby a purchaser specifies what he or she wishes to purchase, this request is sent by e-mail to suppliers registered on the system and then offers are awaited. Aggregators are groups of purchasers who combine to purchase in bulk and thus benefit from a lower purchase cost.

Evans and Wurster (1999) have argued that there are three aspects of navigation that are key to achieving competitive advantage online. These are:

• *Reach*. This is the potential audience of the e-commerce site. Reach can be increased by moving from a single site to representation with a large number of different intermediaries. Allen and Fjermestad (2001) suggest that niche suppliers can readily reach a much wider market due to search-engine marketing (Chapter 8).

- *Richness*. This is the depth or detail of information which is both collected about the customer and provided to the customer. This is related to the product element of the mix.
- *Affiliation*. This refers to whose interest the selling organisation represents – consumers or suppliers. This particularly applies to retailers. It suggests that customers will favour retailers who provide them with the richest information on comparing compeititive products.

Localisation

Localisation

Tailoring of web site information for individual countries or regions.

Providing a local site, with or without a language-specific version, is referred to as localisation. A site may need to support customers from a range of countries with:

- different product needs;
- language differences;
- cultural differences.

Localisation will address all these issues. It may be that products will be similar in different countries and localisation will simply involve converting the web site to suit another country. However, in order to be effective, this often needs more than translation, since different promotion concepts may be needed for different countries. Examples of localised sites include Durex, B2C, and Gestetner, B2B. Note that each company prioritises different countries according to the size of the market, and this priority then governs the amount of work it puts into localisation.

Activity 5.4

Place of purchase on the Internet

Purpose

To illustrate the concept of representation and reach on the Internet.

Activity

For the same sector as you selected in Activity 5.2, find out which company has the best reach in terms of numbers of links from other sites. Go to a search engine such as Google and use the advanced search to find the number of sites that link to that site. Alternatively use the syntax: link:URL in the search box.

● 2 New channel structures

New channel structures enabled by the Internet have been described in detail Chapter 2. The main types of phenomena that companies need to develop strategies for are:

A. *Distintermediation*. Is there are an option for selling direct? Selling direct can lead to the channel conflicts mentioned in the next section. When assessing this option there will be a number of barriers and facilitators to this change. Research by Mols (2001) in the banking sector in Denmark suggests that important factors are senior management support, a willingness to accept some cannibalisation of existing channels and perceived customer benefits.

B. *Reintermediation*. The new intermediaries created through reintermediation described by Sarkar et al. (1996) should be evaluated for suitability for partnering with for affiliate arrangements. The intermediaries receive a commission on each sale resulting from a referral from their site.

C. *Countermediation*. Should the organisation partner with another independent intermediary, or set up its own independent intermediary? For example, a group of European airlines have joined forces to form Opodo (www.opodo.com) which is intended to counter independent companies such as Lastminute.com (www.lastminute.com) or eBookers (www.ebookers.com) in offering discount fares.

The distribution channel will also be affected. For instance, grocery retailers have had to identify the best strategy for picking customers' goods prior to home delivery. Options include in-store picking (selection of items on customer orders) and regional picking centres. The former is proving more cost-effective.

● 3 Channel conflicts

A significant threat arising from the introduction of an Internet channel is that while disintermediation gives a company the opportunity to sell direct and increase profitability on products, it can also threaten distribution arrangements with existing partners. Such channel conflicts are described by Frazier (1999), and need to be carefully managed. Frazier (1999) identifies some situations when the Internet should only be used as a communications channel. This is particularly the case where manufacturers offer an exclusive, or highly selective, distribution approach. To take an example, a company manufacturing expensive watches costing thousands of pounds will not in the past have sold direct, but will have used a wholesaler to distribute watches via retailers. If this wholesaler is a major player in watch distribution, then it is powerful, and will react against the watch manufacturer's selling direct. The wholesaler may even refuse to act as distributor and may threaten to distribute only a competitor's watches, which are not available over the Internet. Furthermore, direct sales may damage the product's brand or change its price positioning.

Further channel conflicts involve other stakeholders including sales representatives and customers. Sales representatives may see the Internet as a direct threat to their livelihood. In some cases such as Avon cosmetics and Enyclopaedia Britannica this has proved to be the case, with this sales model being partly or completely replaced by the Internet. For many B2B purchases, sales representatives remain an essential method of reaching the customer to support them in the purchase decision. Here, following training of sales staff, the Internet can be used as a sales support and customer education tool. Customers who do not use the online channels may also respond negatively if lower prices are available to their online counterparts. This is less serious than other types of channel conflict.

To assess channel conflicts it is necessary to consider the different forms of channel the Internet can take. These are:

1 a communication channel only;
2 a distribution channel to intermediaries;
3 a direct sales channel to customers;
4 any combination of the above.

To avoid channel conflicts, the appropriate combination of channels must be arrived at. For example, Frazier (1999) notes that using the Internet as a direct sales channel may not be wise when a product's price varies considerably across global markets. In the watch manufacturer example, it may be best to use the Internet as a communication channel only.

Internet channel strategy will, of course, depend on the existing arrangements for the market. If a geographical market is new and there are no existing agents or distributors, there is unlikely to be channel conflict, in that there is a choice of distribution through the Internet only or appointments of new agents to support Internet sales, or a combination of the two. Often SMEs will attempt to use the Internet to sell products without appointing agents, but this strategy will only be possible for retail products that need limited pre-sales and after-sales support. For higher-value products such as engineering equipment, which will require skilled sales staff to support the sale and after-sales servicing, agents will have to be appointed.

For existing geographical markets in which a company already has a mechanism for distribution in the form of agents and distributors, the situation is more complex, and there is the threat of channel conflict. The strategic options that are available when an existing reseller arrangement is in place have been described by Kumar (1999):

1 *No Internet sales*. Neither the company nor any of its resellers make sales over the Internet. This will be the option to follow when a company, or its resellers, feel that the number of buyers has not reached the critical mass thought to warrant the investment in an online sales capability.
2 *Internet sales by reseller only*. A reseller, who is selling products from many companies, may have sufficient aggregated demand (through selling products for other companies) to justify the expenditure of setting up online sales. The manufacturer may also not have the infrastructure to fulfil orders direct to customers without further investment, whereas the reseller will be set up for this already. In this case it is unlikely that a manufacturer would want to block sales via the Internet channel.
3 *Internet sales by manufacturer only*. It would be unusual if a manufacturer chose this option if it already had existing resellers in place. Were the manufacturer to do so, it would probably lead to lost sales as the reseller would perhaps stop selling through traditional channels.
4 *Internet sales by all*. This option is arguably the logical future for Internet sales. It is also likely to be the result if the manufacturer does not take a proactive approach to controlling Internet sales.

Strategy will need to be reviewed annually and the sales channels changed as thought appropriate. Given the fast rate of change of e-commerce, it will probably not be possible to create a five-year plan! Kumar (1999) notes that history suggests that most companies have a tendency to use existing distribution networks for too long. The reason for this is that resellers may be powerful within a channel and the company does not want to alienate them, for fear of losing sales.

● 4 Virtual organisations

Benjamin and Wigand (1995) state that 'it is becoming increasingly difficult to delineate accurately the borders of today's organisations'. A further implication of the introduction of electronic networks such as the Internet is that it becomes easier to outsource aspects of the production and distribution of goods to third parties (Kraut et al., 1998). This can lead to the boundaries within an organisation becoming blurred. Employees may work in any time zone, and customers are able to purchase tailored products from any location. The absence of any rigid boundary or hierarchy within the organisation should lead to a company's becoming more responsive and flexible, and having a greater market orientation.

Davidow and Malone (1992) describe the virtual corporation as follows:

To the outside observer, it will appear almost edgeless, with permeable and continuously changing interfaces between company, supplier and customer. From inside the firm, the view will be no less amorphous, with traditional offices, departments, and operating divisions constantly reforming according to need. Job responsibilities will regularly shift.

Kraut et al. (1998) suggest the following features of a virtual organisation:

1 Processes transcend the boundaries of a single form and are not controlled by a single organisational hierarchy.
2 Production processes are flexible, with different parties involved at different times.
3 Parties involved in the production of a single product are often geographically dispersed.
4 Given this dispersion, coordination is heavily dependent on telecommunications and data networks.

Introna (2001) notes that a key aspect of the virtual organisation is strategic alliances or partnering. The ease of forming such alliances in the value network as described in Chapter 2 is one of the factors that has given rise to the virtual organisation.

All companies tend to have some elements of the virtual organisation. The process whereby these characteristics increase is known as virtualisation. Malone et al. (1987) argued that the presence of electronic networks tends to lead to virtualisation since they enable the governance and coordination of business transactions to be conducted effectively at lower cost.

What are the implications for a marketing strategist of this trend towards virtualisation? Initially it may appear that outsourcing does not have direct relevance to market orientation. However, an example shows the relevance. Michael Dell relates (in Magretta, 1998) that Dell does not see outsourcing as getting rid of a process that does not add value, rather it sees it as a way of '*coordinating their activity to create the most value for customers*'. Dell has improved customer service by changing the way it works with both its suppliers and its distributors to build a computer to the customer's specific order within just six days. This *vertical integration* has been achieved by creating a contractual vertical marketing system in which members of a channel retain their independence, but work together by sharing contracts.

So, one aspect of virtualisation is that companies should identify opportunities for providing new services and products to customers who are looking to outsource their external processes. The corollary of this is that it may offer companies opportunities to outsource some marketing activities that were previously conducted in-house. For example, marketing research to assess the impact of a web site can now be conducted in a virtual environment by an outside company rather than by having employees conduct a focus group.

Marshall et al. (2001) provide useful examples of different structures for the virtual organisation. These are:

1 *Co-alliance model.* Effort and risk are shared equally by partners.
2 *Star-alliance model.* Here the effort and risk are centred on one organisation that subcontracts other virtual partners as required.
3 *Value alliance model.* This is a partnership where elements are contributed across a supply chain for a particular industry. This is effectively the value network of Chapter 2.
4 *Market alliance model.* This is similar to the value alliance, but is more likely to serve several different marketplaces.

Virtual organisation and virtualisation

A virtual organisation uses information and communications technology to allow it to operate without clearly defined physical boundaries between different functions. It provides customised services by outsourcing production and other functions to third parties. Virtualisation is the process whereby a company develops more of the characteristics of a virtual organisation.

Promotion

Promotion variable

The element of the marketing mix that involves communication with customers and other stakeholders to inform them about the product and the organisation.

The **promotion** element of the marketing mix refers to how marketing communications are used to inform customers and other stakeholders about an organisation and its products. This topic is discussed in more detail in Chapter 8 – it is only introduced here.

Promotion is the element of the marketing mix that is concerned with communicating the existence of products or services to a target market. Burnett (1993) defines it as:

the marketing function concerned with persuasively communicating to target audiences the components of the marketing program in order to facilitate exchange.

A broader view of promotion is given by Wilmshurst (1993):

Promotion unfortunately has a range of meanings. It can be used to describe the marketing communications aspect of the marketing mix or, more narrowly, as in sales promotion. In its very broad sense it includes the personal methods of communications, such as face to face or telephone selling, as well as the impersonal ones such as advertising. When we use a range of different types of promotion – direct mail, exhibitions, publicity etc. we describe it as the promotional mix.

The main elements of the promotional or communications mix can be considered to be (as stated by, for example, Fill (2000)):

1 advertising;
2 sales promotion;
3 personal selling;
4 public relations;
5 direct marketing.

Specification of the promotion element of the mix is usually part of a communications strategy. This will include selection of target markets, positioning and integration of different communications tools. The Internet offers a new, additional marketing communications channel to inform customers of the benefits of a product and assist in the buying decision. These are different approaches for looking at how the Internet can be used to vary the promotion element of the mix:

1 reviewing new ways of applying each of the elements of the communications mix such as advertising, sales promotions, PR and direct marketing;
2 assessing how the Internet can be used at different stages of the buying process;
3 using promotional tools to assist in different stages of customer relationship management from customer acquisition to retention. In a Web context this includes gaining initial visitors to the site and gaining repeat visits through these types of communications techniques:
   ● reminders in traditional media campaigns why a site is worth visiting such as online offers and competions;
   ● direct e-mail reminders of site proposition – new offers;
   ● frequently updated content including promotional offers or information that helps your customer do their job or reminds them to visit.

The promotion element of a marketing plan also requires three important decisions about investment for the online promotion or the online communications mix:

1 *Investment in site promotion compared to site creation and maintenance.* Since there is often a fixed budget for site creation, maintenance and promotion, the e-marketing plan should specify the budget for each to ensure there is a sensible balance and the promotion of the site is not underfunded.

2 *Investment in online promotion techniques in comparison to offline promotion.* A balance must be struck between these techniques. Typically, offline promotion investment often exceeds that for online promotion investment. For existing companies traditional media such as print are used to advertise the sites, while print and TV will also be widely used by dot-com companies to drive traffic to their sites.

3 *Investment in different online promotion techniques.* For example, how much should be paid for banner advertising as against online PR about online presence, and how much for search engine registration?

These issues are explored further in Chapter 9.

People, process and physical evidence

● People

The **people** element of the marketing mix refers to how an organisation's staff interact with customers and other stakeholders during sales and pre- and post-sale.

Smith and Chaffey (2001) suggest that, online, part of the consideration for the people element of the mix is the consideration of the tactics by which people can be replaced or automated. These are some of the options:

People variable

The element of the marketing mix that involves the delivery of service to customers during interactions with customers.

- *Autoresponders.* These automatically generate a response when a company e-mails an organisation or submits an online form.
- *E-mail notification.* Automatically generated by a company's systems to update customers on the status of their order, for example, order received, item now in stock, order dispatched.
- *Callback facility.* Customers fill in their phone number on a form and specify a convenient time to be contacted. Dialling from a representative in the call centre occurs automatically at the appointed time and the company pays, which is popular.
- *Frequently asked questions (FAQ).* For these, the art is in compiling and categorising the questions so customers can easily find (a) the question and (b) a helpful answer.
- *On-site search engines.* These help customers find what they're looking for quickly, and are popular when available. Site maps are a related feature.
- *Virtual assistants* come in varying degrees of sophistication and usually help to guide the customer through a maze of choices.

Organisations can test actions needed at each stage for different types of scenario, e.g. enquiry from a new or existing customer, enquiry about the web site or e-mails from different stages in the buying process such as pre-sales, sales or post-sales.

To manage service quality organisations must devise plans to accommodate the five stages shown in Figure 5.9. The stages are as follows.

Stage 1: Customer defines support query

Companies should consider how easily the customer can find contact points and compose a support request on site. Best practice is clear to find e-mail support

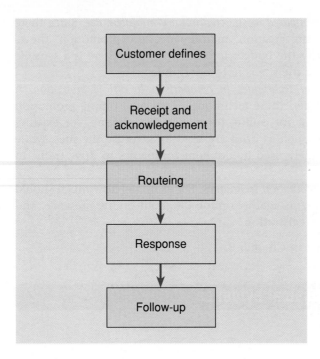

Figure 5.9 Stages in managing inbound e-mail

options. Often, finding contact and support information on a web site is surprisingly difficult. Standardised terminology on site is 'Contact Us' or 'Support'. Options should be available for the customer to specify the type of query on a web form or provide alternative e-mail addresses such as products@company.com or returns@company.com on-site, or in offline communications such as a catalogue. Utilities provider Servista (www.servista.com) provides a good example of such a form.

Providing FAQ or automated diagnostic tools should be considered at this stage to reduce the number of inbound enquiries. Epson (www.epson.co.uk) provides an online tool to diagnose problems with printers and to suggest solutions.

Finally, the web site should determine expectations about the level of service quality. For example, inform the customer that 'your enquiry will be responded to within 24 hours'.

Stage 2: Receipt of e-mail and acknowledgement

Best practice is that automatic message acknowledgement occurs. This is usually provided by **autoresponder** software. While many autoresponders only provide a simple acknowledgement, more sophisticated responses can reassure the customer about when the response will occur and highlight other sources of information. Blackstar (www.blackstar.co.uk) provides a good example of best practice here:

Autoresponders or 'mail-bots'

Software tools or 'agents' running on web servers which automatically send a standard reply to the sender of an e-mail message.

```
     Thanks for emailing blackstar.co.uk. There are currently 51 emails
        in the queue in front of yours,so our expected response time
                    is approximately 1 hour, 10 minutes.
           Don't forget that you can track your order status on line
     at:http://www.blackstar.co.uk/circle/order status(where you can also cancel
         your order if you've made a mistake, orhave just changed your mind)
        Many other common questions are also answered in our help section:
          click on the big question mark in the header bar or go direct to
                         http://www.blackstar.co.uk/help/
```

Stage 3: Routeing of e-mail

Best practice involves automated routeing or workflow. Routeing the e-mail to the right person is made easier if the type of query has been identified through the techniques described for Stage 1. It is also possible to use pattern recognition to identify the type of enquiry. For example, Nationwide (www.nationwide.co.uk), see Mini Case Study 5.3, use Brightware's 'skill-based message routeing' so that messages are sent to a specialist adviser where specific enquiries are made. Such software can also be used at Stage 1 to give an autoresponse appropriate for the enquiry. Using this approach, Mark Cromack says 40% of messages no longer reach their advisers.

Stage 4: Compose response

Best practice is to use a library of pre-prepared templates for different types of query. These can then be tailored and personalised by the contact centre employee as appropriate. The right type of template can again be selected automatically using the software referred to in Stage 2. Through using such auto-suggestion, the Nationwide has seen e-mail handling times reduced by 25% for messages requiring adviser intervention. Sony Europe identifies all new support issues and adds them with the appropriate response to a central knowledge base.

Mini Case Study 5.3

Customer service at the Nationwide

The Nationwide is a financial services organisation which has been active in using the Internet as a customer service tool. Bicknell (2002) reports that the volume of customer service is as follows:

- 900 000 registrants on-site with 2.4 million visits to the site in August 2001;
- of the 1.2 million who entered the online bank, 900 000 made transactions resulting in 60 000 online contacts which require customer service.

These figures highlight the number of transactions that will have reduced customer contacts in real-world branches and by phone, but this still leaves 60 000 online contacts. The Nationwide believed that customers should expect service to be fast and accurate. Mark Cromack, operations manager, said:

There was a huge demand for more and more information and an explosion in the level of information that people wanted. That had implications for staff morale. What we needed was an autoresponse facility which provided quality, compliant and consistent answers.

To reduce the volume of calls, Frequently Answered Questions (FAQ) was not sufficient. The company purchased two products from Firepond to improve service. *Concierge* is provided on the home page to provide a facility with natural-language searching to help customers find the answers to their queries more rapidly. *Answer* is an automated message-routeing tool that provides automated answers to simple questions which can be reviewed by contact centre staff before dispatch and yet is able to spot the phrasing of more complex queries for completion by call centre operators.

Using these solutions, the quality of answers improved to give a first-time resolution rate of 94%. With the reduced staff time involved, the cost per contact has been reduced from £4 to £2.

Stage 5: Follow-up

Best practice is that if the employee does not successfully answer the first response, then the e-mail should suggest callback from an employee or a live-chat. Indeed, to avoid the problem of 'e-mail ping-pong' where several e-mails may be exchanged, the company may want to proactively ring the customer to increase the speed of problem resolution, and so solve the problem. Finally, the e-mail follow-up may provide the opportunity for outbound contact and marketing, perhaps enquiring whether there are any further queries while advising about complementary products or offers.

This topic is examined in more depth in Chapter 7 with respect to managing service quality and in Chapter 8 with regard to marketing communications. Mini Case Study 5.3 gives an example of how inbound contacts are managed.

● Process

Process variable

The element of the marketing mix that involves the methods and procedures companies use to achieve all marketing functions.

The process element of the marketing mix refers to the methods and procedures companies use to achieve all marketing functions such as new product development, promotion, sales and customer service. The restructuring of the organisation and channel structures described in the previous chapter are part of the process variable.

● Physical evidence

Physical evidence variable

The element of the marketing mix that involves the tangible expression of a product and how it is purchased and used.

The physical evidence element of the marketing mix refers to the tangible expression of a product and how it is purchased and used. In an online context, physical evidence refers to the customers' experience of the company through the web site. It includes issues such as site ease of use or navigation, availability and performance which are discussed further in Chapter 7.

People, process and physical evidence are particularly important for service delivery. Since service delivery is an important aspect of Internet marketing and e-commerce, in particular, this topic is referred to in more detail in related coverage in future chapters. In Chapter 6, we relate the concept of service delivery to customer satisfaction and loyalty as part of customer relationship management and then in Chapters 7 and 9 we refer to how creation and maintenance of the online presence should be managed to deliver appropriate levels of service quality.

Summary

1 Evaluating the opportunities provided by the Internet for varying the marketing mix is a useful framework for assessing current and future Internet marketing strategy.

2 *Product.* Opportunities for varying the core product through new information-based services and also the extended product should be reviewed.

3 *Price.* The Internet leads to price transparency and commoditisation and hence lower prices. Dynamic pricing gives the ability to test prices or to offer differential pricing for different segments or in response to variations in demand. New pricing models such as auctions are available.

4 *Place*. Place refers to place of purchase and channel structure on the Internet. There are three main locations for e-commerce transactions: seller site, buyer site and intermediary. New channel structures are available through direct sales and linking to new intermediaries. Steps must be taken to minimise channel conflict.

5 *Promotion*. This aspect of the mix is discussed in more detail in Chapter 8.

6 *People, process and physical evidence*. These aspects of the mix are discussed in more detail in Chapters 6 and 7 where customer relationship management and service delivery are discussed.

EXERCISES

Self-assessment exercises

1 Select the two most important changes introduced by the Internet for each of the 4 Ps.
2 What types of product are most amenable to changes to the core and extended product?
3 Explain the differences in concepts between online B2C and B2B auctions.
4 Explain the implications of the Internet for Price.
5 What are the implications of the Internet for Place?

Essay and discussion questions

1 'The marketing mix developed as part of annual planning is no longer a valid concept in the Internet era.' Discuss.
2 Critically evaluate the impact of the Internet on the marketing mix for an industry sector of your choice.
3 Write an essay on pricing options for e-commerce.
4 Does 'Place' have any meaning for marketers in the global marketplace enabled by the Internet?

Examination questions

1 Describe three alternative locations for transactions for a B2B company on the Internet.
2 Explain two applications of dynamic pricing on the Internet.
3 How does the Internet impact an organisation's options for core and extended (augmented) product?
4 Briefly summarise the implications of the Internet on each of these elements of the marketing mix:
   (a) Product
   (b) Price
   (c) Place
   (d) Promotion
5 Explain the reasons why the Internet could be expected to decrease prices online.
6 How can an organisation vary its promotional mix using the Internet?

References

Aaker, D. and Joachimstaler, E. (2000) *Brand Leadership*. Free Press, New York.

Allen, E. and Fjermestad, J. (2001) E-commerce marketing strategies: a framework and case analysis, *Logistics Information Management*, 14(1/2), 14–23.

Baker, W., Marn, M. and Zawada, C. (2000) Price smarter on the Net, *Harvard Business Review*, February, 2–7.

Benjamin, R. and Wigand, R. (1995) Electronic markets and virtual value-chains on the information superhighway, *Sloan Management Review*, Winter, 62–72.

Berryman, K., Harrington, L., Layton-Rodin, D. and Rerolle, V. (1998) Electronic commerce: three emerging strategies, *McKinsey Quarterly*, No. 1, 152–9.

Bickerton, P., Bickerton, M. and Pardesi, U. (2000) *CyberMarketing*, 2nd edn. Butterworth Heinemann, Oxford.

Bicknell, D. (2002) Banking on customer service, *e.Businessreview*, January, 21–2.

Booms, B.H. and Bitner, M.J. (1981) Marketing strategies and organizational structures for service firms, in *Marketing of Services*, J. Donnelly and W. George, pp. 451–77. American Marketing Association, Chicago.

Burnett, J. (1993) *Promotional Management*. Houghton Mifflin, Boston.

Davidow, W.H. and Malone, M.S. (1992) *The Virtual Corporation. Structuring and Revitalizing the Corporation for the 21st Century*. HarperCollins, New York.

Dayal, S., Landesberg, H. and Zeissberg, M. (2000) Building digital brands, *McKinsey Quarterly*, No. 2.

de Chernatony, L. (2001) Succeeding with brands on the Internet, *Journal of Brand Management*, 8(3), 186–95.

de Chernatony, L. and McDonald, M. (1992) *Creating Powerful Brands*. Butterworth Heinemann, Oxford.

Diamantopoulos, A. and Matthews, B. (1993) *Making Pricing Decisions. A Study of Managerial Practice*. Chapman & Hall, London.

Emiliani, V. (2001) Business-to-business online auctions: key issues for purchasing process improvement, *Supply Chain Management: An International Journal*, 5(4), 176–86.

Evans, P. and Wurster, T. (1999) Getting real about virtual commerce, *Harvard Business Review*, November–December, 84–94.

Ewing. T. (2002) E-commerce settles down, *New Media Age*, 7 February.

Fill, C. (2000) *Marketing Communications – Contexts, Contents and Strategies*, 3rd edn. Financial Times/Prentice Hall, Harlow.

Frazier, G. (1999) Organising and managing channels of distribution, *Journal of the Academy of Marketing Science*, 27(2), 222–40.

Ghosh, S. (1998) Making business sense of the Internet, *Harvard Business Review*, March–April, 126–35.

Introna, L. (2001) Defining the virtual organization. In S. Barnes and B. Hunt (eds). *E-Commerce and V-Business. Business Models for Global Success*. Butterworth Heinemann, Oxford.

Jevons, C. and Gabbott, M. (2000) Trust, brand equity and brand reality in Internet business relationships: an interdisciplinary approach, *Journal of Marketing Management*, 16, 619–34.

Kotler, P. (1997) *Marketing Management: Analysis, Planning, Implementation and Control*, 9th international edn. Prentice Hall, Upper Saddle River, NJ.

Kraut, R., Chan, A., Butler, B. and Hong, A. (1998) Coordination and virtualisation: the role of electronic networks and personal relationships, *Journal of Computer Mediated Communications*, 3(4).

Kumar, N. (1999) Internet distribution strategies: dilemmas for the incumbent, *Financial Times*, Special Issue on Mastering Information Management, no 7. Electronic Commerce (www.ftmastering.com).

Lautenborn, R. (1990) New marketing litany: 4Ps passes; C-words take over, *Advertising Age*, 1 October, p. 26.

McCarthy, J. (1960) *Basic Marketing: A Managerial Approach*. Irwin, Homewood, IL.

McDonald, M. and Wilson, H. (2002) *New Marketing: Transforming the Corporate Future*. Butterworth Heinemann, Oxford.

Magretta, J. (1998) The power of virtual integration. An interview with Michael Dell, *Harvard Business Review*, March–April, 72–84.

Malone, T., Yates, J. and Benjamin, R. (1987) Electronic markets and electronic hierarchies: effects of information technology on market structure and corporate strategies, *Communications of the ACM*, 30(6), 484–97.

Marn, M. (2000) Virtual pricing, *McKinsey Quarterly*, No. 4.

Marshall, P., McKay, J. and Burn J. (2001) Structure, strategy and success factors in the virtual organisation. In S. Barnes and B. Hunt (eds). *E-Commerce and V-Business. Business Models for Global Success*. Butterworth Heinemann, Oxford.

Mols, N. (2001) Organising for the effective introduction of new distribution channels in retail banking, *European Journal of Marketing*, 35(5/6), 661–86.

Pitt, L., Berthorn, P., Watson, R. and Ewing, M. (2001) Pricing strategy and the Net, *Business Horizons*, March–April, 45–54.

Quelch, J. and Klein, L. (1996) The Internet and international marketing, *Sloan Management Review*, Spring, 61–75.

Queree, A. (2000) *Financial Times* Technology supplement, 1 March.

Rayport, J. and Sviokla, J. (1994) Managing in the marketspace, *Harvard Business Review*, July, 141–50.

Ries, A. and Ries, L. (2000) *The 11 Immutable Laws of Internet Branding*. HarperCollins Business, London.

Sarkar, M., Butler, B. and Steinfield, C. (1996) Intermediaries and cybermediaries. A continuing role for mediating players in the electronic marketplace, *Journal of Computer Mediated Communication*, 1(3).

Smith, P.R. and Chaffey, D. (2001) *EMarketing Excellence: at the Heart of EBusiness*. Butterworth Heinemann, Oxford.

Wilmshurst, J. (1993) *Below the Line Promotion*. Butterworth Heinemann, Oxford.

Further reading

Allen, E. and Fjermestad, J. (2001) E-commerce marketing strategies: a framework and case analysis, *Logistics Information Management*, 14(1/2), 14–23. Includes an analysis of how the 4 Ps are impacted by the Internet.

Baker, W., Marn, M. and Zawada, C. (2001) Price smarter on the Net, *Harvard Business Review*, February, 2–7. This gives a clear summary of the challenges and opportunities of Internet pricing.

Brassington, F. and Petitt, S. (2000) *Principles of Marketing*, 2nd edn. Financial Times/Prentice Hall, Harlow. *See* companion Prentice Hall web site (www.booksites.net/brassington2). Chapters 10 and 11 describe pricing issues in much more detail than that given in this chapter. Chapters 20, Strategic management, and 21, Marketing planning, management and control, describe the integration of marketing strategy with business strategy.

Dibb, S., Simkin, S., Pride, W. and Ferrel, O. (2001) *Marketing. Concepts and Strategies*, 4th European edn. Houghton Mifflin, New York. *See* companion Houghton Mifflin web site (www.busmgt.ulst.ac.uk/h_mifflin/). *See* Chapters 18 and 19 on Pricing decisions and Chapter 20 on Manipulating the marketing mix.

Ghosh, S. (1998) Making business sense of the Internet, *Harvard Business Review*, March–April, 127–35. This paper gives many examples of how US companies have adapted their products to the Internet and asks key questions that should govern the strategy adopted.

Kotler, P., Armstrong, G., Saunders, J. and Wong, V. (2001) *Principles of Marketing*, 3rd European edn. Financial Times/Prentice Hall, Harlow. Parts 4 to 7 contain further information on the marketing mix. *See* companion Prentice Hall web site for 8th US edn, cw.prenhall.com/bookbind/pubbooks/kotler. *See* Chapter 3, Strategic marketing planning, and Chapter 12, Creating competitive advantage.

Kumar, N. (1999) Internet distribution strategies: dilemmas for the incumbent, *Financial Times*, Special Issue on Mastering Information Management, 7. Electronic Commerce (www.ftmastering.com). This article assesses the impact of the Internet on manufacturers and their distribution channels. The other articles in this special issue are also interesting.

Web links

- ASCET Project (www.ascet.com) Excellent collection of articles coordinated by Accenture and Montgomery research which concern the effect of the Internet on pricing and purchasing.
- Clickz (www.clickz.com). An excellent collection of articles on online marketing communications. US-focused. Relevant sections for this chapter include: Brand marketing.
- Conspectus (www.conspectus.com) Industry studies on range of industry topics including procurement.
- The Purchasing web guide on About.com (http://purchasing.about.com) gives an excellent collection of links on the benefits and disadvantages of e-procurement.
- Marketing On The Internet (MOTI) by Greg Rich and colleagues from OhioLink educational establishments. This site provides a succinct summary, with examples, of how each of the 4 Ps of the Internet can be applied online. http://iws.ohiolink.edu/moti/.

Relationship marketing using the Internet

Links to other chapters

➤ Chapter 7 has guidelines on how to achieve suitable standards of service quality to assist in forming relationships

➤ Chapter 8 describes methods of acquiring customers for one-to-one marketing

➤ Chapters 10 and 11 give examples of relationship marketing in the business-to-consumer and business-to-business markets

Learning objectives

After reading this chapter, the reader should be able to:

● Assess the relevance of the concepts of relationship, direct and database marketing on the Internet

● Evaluate the potential of the Internet to support one-to-one marketing and the range of techniques and systems available to support dialogue with the customer over the Internet

● Assess the characteristics required of tools to implement one-to-one marketing

Questions for marketers

Key questions for marketing managers related to this chapter are:

● How can the Internet be used to support the different stages of the customer lifecycle?

● How do I implement permission marketing?

● What do personalisation and mass customisation mean and how should I apply them in my marketing?

Introduction

Relationship marketing, direct marketing and database marketing have combined to create a powerful new marketing paradigm. This paradigm is often referred to as customer relationship management (CRM). A related approach is one-to-one marketing, where relationships are managed on an individual basis. Owing to the costs of managing relationships on an individual level, many companies will apply CRM by approaches which tailor services to develop relationships with particular customer segments or groups, rather than individuals. This involves a company in developing a long-term relationship with each customer in order to better understand that customer's needs and then deliver services that meet these individual needs. The interactive nature of the Web combined with e-mail provides an ideal environment in which to conduct this relationship, and databases provide a foundation for storing information about the relationship and providing information to strengthen it by leading to improved, often personalised, services. Note that 'one-to-one' marketing is typically the goal rather than reality, since we will see that for many companies it is more cost-effective to target consumers in different segments using similar relationship building techniques for each segment.

Figure 6.1 summarises the linkages between CRM and existing marketing approaches. Direct marketing provides the tactics that deliver the marketing communications and sometimes the product itself to the individual customer. Relationship marketing theory provides the conceptual underpinning of CRM since it emphasises enhanced customer service through knowledge of the customer, and deals with markets segmented to the level of the individual. Database marketing provides the technological enabler allowing vast quantities of customer-related data to be stored and accessed in ways that create strategic and tactical marketing opportunities.

This chapter begins by exploring relationship and one-to-one marketing in the context of the evolution of marketing and then relates this to the new reality of the busy, confident and demanding customer, empowered by technology. We then review how one-to-one marketing on the Internet can be implemented using techniques such as personalisation, e-mail and push technology, married to more traditional direct marketing techniques such as data mining and neural networks.

Customer relationship management (CRM)

A marketing-led approach to building and sustaining long-term business with customers.

One-to-one marketing

A unique dialogue occurs between a company and individual customers (or groups of customers with similar needs).

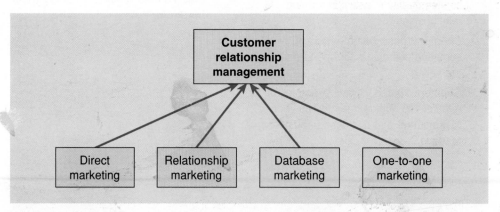

Figure 6.1 Linkages between customer relationship management and related marketing approaches

Relationship marketing

Relationship marketing is best understood within the context of the historical development of marketing. In medieval and feudal societies marketplaces were developed where people traded for agricultural purposes and to meet their basic needs. Suppliers mainly traded within a limited area and knew a small number of customers well. Effectively, one-to-one marketing was in operation. With the Industrial Revolution, the large-scale production of more widely distributed, standardised products changed the nature of marketing. Whereas marketing had previously been largely by word of mouth, it became a mass-marketing monologue from suppliers to customers with the aim of convincing customers of the need for standardised goods. The ultimate expression of this was, of course, the mass production of the Model T Ford. During the twentieth century, differentiation of products and services became more important, and this highlighted the need for feedback from customers about the type of product features required. This philosophy led to the promulgation by Jerome McCarthy at the University of Michigan in 1960 of the 4 Ps of Product, Price, Place and Promotion, which have long since been a mainstay of the teaching and practice of marketing. The 4 Ps model applies to the aggregate market: that is, where the market is considered as a homogeneous whole.

Since the late 1980s and the rise of the relationship approach to marketing, the limitations of the 4 Ps model have increasingly been highlighted. With increasing competition, the focus of marketers on meeting the customers' needs has increased, and the ultimate goal is to be able to hold details about each customer's preferences and produce customised products and services to meet this need. Gummesson (1987) argues that the 4 Ps approach to marketing is limited in theory, takes little notice of interrelationships and cooperation, and heavily exaggerates areas such as advertising and competition. Ultimately the 4 Ps model reveals itself as being product-centric rather than customer-centric, and a creature of the heyday of mass marketing.

Tailoring of products has been described as 'complicated simplicity' by Ira Matahia, chief executive officer of Brand Futures Group, as reported in *The Times* of 19 December 1998. He says:

> As consumers crave individually tailored products from DIY pottery shops to personalised perfume formulas to PC-generated greeting cards, there will be a strong demand for unique items. For businesses this means the end of a mass audience oriented approach and the beginning of an audience-of-one approach.

The need for more consumer choice has to be balanced against the concept of the accelerating lifestyle of the 'busy customer', who can be characterised by phrases such as:

- cash-rich, time-poor;
- time is money;
- value for *time*;
- personal disposable *time*.

According to Cross (1994), over 50 per cent of consumers feel too time-pressured to enjoy traditional shopping. Foley et al. (1997) comment on the lack of time available to sift through hundreds of television and print advertisements and 'a preference for communications which are personalised and directed specifically to their needs, typically based on past transactions'. Maling (1999) notes that 'A number of

Mass marketing
One-to-many communication between a company and potential customers, with limited tailoring of the message.

companies are beginning to withdraw from TV and return to other media and that shakedown will continue'.

The fragmentation of media audiences also makes the mass-marketing model untenable. The cosy scenario of the nuclear family sitting around the single television set watching family fare accompanied by mass-marketing communications is now becoming unrealistic. The first reason for this change involves social factors. In the 1960s, according to Schultz et al. (1994), 60 per cent of families included three or more members and 20 per cent included five or more. By the 1990s, the nuclear family of mother, father and two children comprised only 7 per cent of households, 60 per cent had two or fewer members, and more than half of all households were singles. Then there are the technological factors. The gradual increase in the number of television channels in the UK over the last few decades from one to five is being dwarfed by the hundreds of channels provided by digital television. A huge increase in the number of magazine titles available has also occurred in the last decade. The ability to reach large sections of the population through a small number of vehicles is now a thing of the past. This is not necessarily a problem for sophisticated marketing organisations as the audiences of the fragmented media are very tightly targeted to niche markets – thus aiding segmentation. A further, more intractable problem is the diversity of activities available that do not necessarily rely on advertising such as pay-per-view cable, videos, surfing the Internet and computer games. Additionally, 'channel hopping' with a remote control means that any advertising that is transmitted is easily avoided.

Relationship Marketing (McKenna, 1993) was a seminal text in bringing the approach of one-to-one marketing from the academic to the business domain. In this book McKenna describes the key elements of this approach as:

Relationship marketing

'Consistent application of up to date knowledge of individual customers to product and service design which is communicated interactively in order to develop a continuous and long term relationship which is mutually beneficial' (Cram, 1994).

● Own the market by selecting a specific market segment and attempting to dominate it by developing highly appropriate products and services for the market.
● Commit to a deep relationship with customers in this market to help develop appropriate products by integrating customers into the product design process.
● Be adaptive by using monitoring, analysis and feedback to respond flexibly to the environment.
● Develop partnerships with suppliers, vendors and users to help maintain an edge in the segment.

 Relationship marketing reflects the shift in attitude from 'making a sale' to 'gaining a client'. It is also referred to as *customer relationship management* (CRM).

● Benefits of relationship marketing

Relationship marketing is aimed at increasing customer loyalty, which has a number of benefits. Loyalty or retention within a current customer base is a highly desirable phenomenon for the following reasons:

● no acquisition costs (which are usually far higher than 'maintenance' costs);
● less need to offer incentives such as discounts, or to give vouchers to maintain custom (although these may be desirable);
● less price-sensitive (loyal customers are happy with the value they are getting);
● loyal customers will recommend the company to others ('referrals');
● individual revenue growth occurs as trust increases.

Rigby et al. (2000) have summarised a study by Mainspring and Bain & Company which evaluated the spending patterns and loyalty of consumers in online retail categories of clothing, groceries and consumer electronics. Their work shows that e-tailers could not break-even on 'one-time' shoppers. For grocery e-tailers, customers have to be retained for 18 months for break-even. The study also shows that repeat purchasers tend to spend more in a given time period and generate larger transactions. For example, online grocery shoppers spend 23% more in months 31–36 than in the first 6 months; this includes products in other categories (cross- and up-selling). A final effect is that repeat customers tend to refer more people, to bring in greater business. The impact of these referrals can be signficant – over a 3-year period, in each product category, more than 50% additional revenue of the referrer was generated. Each referrer also has a lower acquisition cost.

Table 6.1 summarises the differences between the two paradigms discussed in this section. Figure 7.2 shows that to build relationships and loyalty online, the quality of the online experience is significant. The topic of loyalty drivers is discussed further in Chapter 7.

Table 6.1 A summary of different concepts for the transactional and relationship paradigms

Transactional paradigm concept	Relationship paradigm concept	Comments and examples
Market segment	Individual customer	Raphel (1997) describes the success story of AMC Kabuki 8 movie theatres in San Francisco. Despite the competition from the giant multiplexes, AMC is flourishing because of its understanding of the cinematic preferences of its customers so they can be informed in advance of ticket sales. 'The most failure-prone fault-line in transactional marketing is the statistical customer – the hypothetical human who is composed of statistically averaged attributes drawn form research' (Wolfe, 1998)
Duration of transaction	Lifetime relationship	The pursuit of customer loyalty 'is a perpetual one – more of a journey than a destination' (Duffy, 1998)
Margin	Lifetime value	To support the Huggies product in the 1970s, Kimberley-Clark spent over $10m to construct a database that could identify 75 per cent of the four million expectant mothers every year in the USA, using information obtained from doctors, hospitals and childbirth trainers. During the pregnancy, mothers received a magazine and letters with advice on baby care. When the baby arrived a coded coupon was sent, which was tracked to learn which mothers had tried the product. The justification was the lifetime value of these prospective customers, not the unit sale (Shaw, 1996)
Market share	Most valued customers and customer share	Rather than waging expensive 'trench warfare' where profit objectives are linked automatically to overall market share, companies have now realised that, as 80 per cent of their business often comes from 20 per cent of their customers (the famous Pareto law), then retaining and delighting that 20 per cent will be much more cost-effective than trying to retain the loyalty of the 80 per cent. Reichheld (1996) conducted research indicating that an increase in customer retention of 5 per cent could improve profitability by as much as 125 per cent
Mass market monologue	Direct marketing dialogue	'The new marketing requires a feedback loop' (McKenna, 1993)
Passive consumers	Empowered clients	'Transactional marketing is all about seduction and propaganda and it depends on a passive, narcotised receptor, the legendary "couch potato"' (Rosenfield, 1998)

● Benefits of online relationship marketing

Using the Internet for relationship marketing involves integrating the customer database with web sites to make the relationship targeted and personalised. Through doing this marketing can be improved as follows.

- *Targeting more effectively.* Traditional targeting, for direct mail for instance, is often based on mailing lists compiled according to criteria that mean that not everyone contacted is in the target market. For example, a company wishing to acquire new affluent consumers may use postcodes to target areas with appropriate demographics, but within the postal district the population may be heterogeneous. The result of poor targeting will be low response rates, perhaps less than 1 per cent. The Internet has the benefit that the list of contacts is *self-selecting* or pre-qualified. A company will only aim to build relationships with those who have visited a web site and expressed an interest in its products by registering their name and address. The mere act of visiting the web site and browsing indicates a target customer. Thus the approach to acquiring new customers with whom to build relationships is fundamentally different, as it involves attracting the customers to the web site, where the company provides an offer to make them register. All of those who register are interested in the product (or offer). This is very different from contacting many customers, only a small proportion of whom may be interested.

- *Achieve mass customisation of the marketing messages* (and possibly the product). This tailoring process is described in a subsequent section. Technology makes it possible to send tailored e-mails or provide tailored web pages to smaller groups of customers (microsegments).

- *Increase depth, breadth and nature of relationship.* The nature of the Internet medium enables more information to be supplied to customers as required. For example, special pages such as Dell's PremierPages can be set up to provide customers with specific information. The nature of the relationship can be changed in that contact with a customer can be made more frequently. The frequency of contact with the customer can be determined by customers – whenever they have the need to visit their personalised pages – or they can be contacted by e-mail by the company.

- *A learning relationship can be achieved using different tools throughout the customer lifecycle.* For example: tools summarise products purchased on site and the searching behaviour that occurred before these products were bought; online feedback forms about the site or products are completed when a customer requests free information; questions asked through forms or e-mails to the online customer service facilities; online questionnaires asking about product category interests and opinions on competitors; new product development evaluation – commenting on prototypes of new products.

- *Lower cost.* Contacting customers by e-mail or through their viewing web pages costs less than using physical mail, but perhaps more importantly, information only needs to be sent to those customers who have expressed a preference for it, resulting in fewer mail-outs. Once personalisation technology has been purchased, much of the targeting and communications can be implemented automatically.

Despite these benefits, it should be noted that in 2000, it was reported that around 75% of CRM projects failed in terms of delivering a return on investment or completion on time. This is not necessarily indicative of weaknesses in the CRM concept, rather it indicates the difficulty of implementing a complex information system that requires substantial changes to organisations' processes and major impacts on the staff that conduct them. Such failure rates occur in many other information systems projects.

Key concepts of online customer relationship management (CRM)

The application of technology to achieve customer relationship management (CRM) is a key element of e-marketing. Building long-term relationships with customers is essential for any sustainable business. Failure to build relationships largely caused the failures of many dot-coms following huge expenditure on customer acquisition. Research summarised by Reichheld and Schefter (2000) shows that acquiring online customers is so expensive (20–30% higher than for traditional businesses) that start-up companies may remain unprofitable for at least 2 to 3 years. The research also shows that by retaining just 5% more customers, online companies can boost their profits by 25% to 95%. They say:

> but if you can keep customers loyal, their profitability accelerates much faster than in traditional businesses. It costs you less and less to service them.

Customer relationship management (CRM)
An approach to building and sustaining long-term business with customers.

● Marketing applications of CRM

A CRM system supports the following marketing applications:

1 *Sales force automation (SFA).* Sales representatives are supported in their account management through tools to arrange and record customer visits.
2 *Customer service management.* Representatives in contact centres respond to customer requests for information by using an intranet to access databases containing information on the customer, products and previous queries.
3 *Managing the sales process.* This can be achieved through e-commerce sites, or in a B2B context by supporting sales representatives by recording the sales process (SFA).
4 *Campaign management.* Managing advertising, direct mail, e-mail and other campaigns.
5 *Analysis.* Through technologies such as data warehouses and approaches such as data mining, which are explained further later in the chapter, customers' characteristics, their purchase behaviour and campaigns can be analysed in order to optimise the marketing mix.

● CRM technologies and data

Database technology is at the heart of delivering these CRM applications. Often the database is accessible through an intranet web site accessed by employees or an extranet accessed by customers or partners provides an interface onto the entire customer relationship management system. E-mail is used to manage many of the inbound, outbound and internal communications managed by the CRM system. Using technologies in this way is often referred to as e-CRM. A workflow system is often used for automating CRM processes. For example, a workflow system can remind sales representatives about customer contacts or can be used to manage service delivery such as the many stages of arranging a mortgage. The three main types of customer data held as tables in customer databases for CRM are typically:

e-CRM
Electronic customer relationship management involves integrating databases, personalised web access to the databases, e-mail and workflow to achieve CRM objectives.

1 *Personal and profile data.* These include contact details and characteristics for profiling customers such as age and sex (B2C), and business size, industry sector and individual's role in the buying decision (B2B).

2 *Transaction data.* A record of each purchase transaction including specific product purchased, quantities, category, location, date and time and channel where purchased.

3 *Communications data.* A record of which customers have been targeted by campaigns, and their response to them (outbound communications). Also includes a record of inbound enquiries and sales representative visits and reports (B2B).

Research completed by Stone et al. (2001a) illustrates how customer data collected through CRM applications can be used for marketing. The types of data that are held, together with the frequency of their usage, are:

- basic customer information (75%);
- campaign history (62.5%);
- purchase patterns (sales histories) (50%);
- market information (42.5%);
- competitor information (42.5%);
- forecasts (25%).

The data within CRM systems were reported to be used for marketing applications as follows:

- targeted marketing, 80%;
- segmentation, 65%;
- keeping the right customers, 47.5%;
- trend analysis, 45%;
- increased loyalty, 42.5%;
- customised offers, 32.5%;
- increase share of customer, 27.5%.

Case Study 6.1 shows an application of such a system. The Hewson Consulting Group (www.hewson.co.uk) identify the following benefits of CRM systems to customers:

- improved response times to customer requests for information;
- delivered product meets customer requirements;
- reduced costs of buying and using a product or service;
- immediate access to order status and more responsive technical support.

Customer self-service

Customers perform information requests and transactions through a web interface rather than by contact with customer support staff.

It is apparent that while many of these benefits could be achieved by phoning customer support staff who then access a CRM system, it may increase customer convenience if they can access the information through a web interface. This approach is referred to as customer self-service.

● The customer lifecycle

Customer lifecycle

The stages each customer will pass through in a long-term relationship through acquisition, retention and extension.

The correlation between relationship building and different stages of the customer lifecycle is shown in a schematic form in Figure 6.2. As the customer moves through the different stages from acquisition, through extension, to retention, the loyalty of the customer and their value to the organisation increases. Note that attempts to build customer loyalty at each stage of the customer lifecycle will start with identifying segments and then deciding which to target.

CASE STUDY 6.1

CRM at Deutsche Bank

Deutsche Bank is one of the largest financial institutions in Europe, with assets under management worth 100 billion euros (£60 billion). It operates in seven different countries under different names, although the company is considering consolidating into a single brand operating as a pan-European bank.

In 1999 its chairman, Dr Walther, said the company had to improve its cost-to-revenue ratio to 70 per cent from 90 per cent and add 10 million customers over the next four to eight years. That would be achieved by increasing revenues through growing customer value by cross and up-selling, reducing costs through more targeted communications, and by getting more new customers based on meaningful data analysis.

Central to this programme has been the introduction of an enterprise-wide database, analysis and campaign management system called DataSmart. This has brought significant changes to its marketing processes and effectiveness. Achieving this new IT infrastructure has been no mean feat – Deutsche Bank has 73 million customers, of which 800 000 are on-line and 190 000 use its on-line brokerage service, it has 19 300 employees, 1250 branches and 250 financial centres, plus three call centres supporting Deutsche Bank 24, its telebanking service. It also has e-commerce alliances with Yahoo!, e-Bay and AOL.

'DataSmart works on four levels – providing a technical infrastructure across the enterprise, consolidating data, allowing effective data analyses and segmentations, and managing multi-channel marketing campaigns', says Jens Fruehling, head of the marketing database automation project, Deutsche Bank 24.

The new database runs on the largest Sun server in Europe with 20 processors, 10 Gb of RAM and 5 terabytes of data storage. It is also mirrored. The software used comprises Oracle for the database, Prime Response for campaign management, SAS for data mining, Cognos for OLAP reporting, plus a data extraction, transformation, modelling and loading tool.

'Before DataSmart, we had a problem of how to get data from our operating systems where it was held in a variety of different ways and was designed only for use as transactional data. There are 400 million data sets created every month. We had a data warehouse which was good, but was not right for campaign management or data mining', says Fruehling.

The new data environment was developed to facilitate all of those things. It also brings in external data such as Experian's Mosaic. 'We have less information on new prospects, so we bought third party data on every household – the type of house, the number of householders, status, risk, lifestyle data, financial status, age, plus GIS coding', he says.

For every customer, over 1000 fields of data are now held. These allow the bank to understand customers' product needs, profile, risk, loyalty, revenue and lifetime value. That required a very sophisticated system. For every customer, there is also a whole bundle of statistical models, such as affinity for a product and channel, profitability overall and by type of product.

'These are calculated monthly so we can perform time-series analyses, so if their profitability is falling, we can target a mailing to them', says Fruehling. DataSmart has allowed Deutsche Bank to makes some important changes in its marketing process, allowing it to operate more quickly and effectively.

'We have a sales support system called BTV in our branches to communicate with each bank manager. They can see the customer data and are able to add information, such as lists of customers who should be part of a branch campaign, who to include or exclude, and response analyses', he says.

Previously, typical marketing support activity involved segmenting and selecting customers, sending these lists through BTV for veto by branch managers, making the final selection, then sending those lists to BTV and the lettershop for production. 'There were many disconnects in

▶

that process – we had no campaign history, nothing was automated. Our programmers had to write SAS code for every selection, which is not the best way to work. We had no event-driven campaigns', says Fruehling.

An interface has been developed between PrimeVantage, BTV and each system supporting the seven key channels to market. Now the database marketing unit simply selects a template for one of its output channels. This has allowed Deutsche Bank to become more targeted in its marketing activities, and also faster.

'Regular selections are very important because local branches do our campaigns. We may have up to 20 separate mailings per week for different channels. That is now much more profitable', says Fruehling. Customer surveys are a central part of the bank's measurement culture and these have also become much easier to run.

'Every month we run a customer opinion poll on a sample of 10 000. Every customer is surveyed twice in a year. That takes half a day to run, whereas previously it took one week and 30 people using SAS. If a customer responds, their name is then suppressed, if they do not, they are called by the call centre', he says.

The bank's customer acquisition programme, called AKM, now uses up to 30 mailings per year with as many as 12 different target groups and very complex selection criteria. 'We flag customers using SAS and PrimeVantage recognises those flags', he says. 'We are now looking to move to a higher communications frequency so every customer gets a relevant offer.'

Source: European Centre for Customer Strategies case study (www.uk.eccs.com), 2001

Question

Summarise the data types that Deutsche Bank collects and how they are used for customer relationship management.

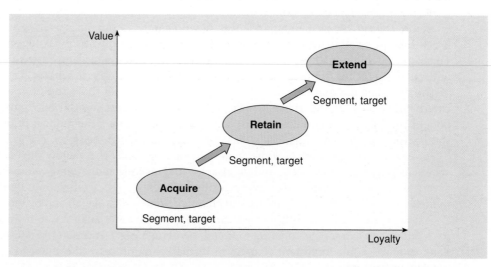

Figure 6.2 The relationship between the customer acquisition, retention and extension phases of the customer lifecycle and loyalty and customer value

We will now examine each of the stages of the customer lifecycle of Figure 6.2 in a little more detail. **Customer acquisition** involves techniques used to form relationships with new customers. Sargeant and West (2001) suggest the following seven stages in an acquisition or recruitment campaign:

Customer acquisition
Techniques used to gain new customers.

1 objectives;
2 segmentation and profiling;
3 targeting;
4 media planning;
5 development and communication of the offer;
6 fulfilment;
7 response analysis.

It is apparent that each of the first three stages will be informed by Internet marketing strategy development as described in Chapter 4.

In an online context, customer acquisition can have two meanings. First, it may mean the use of the web site to acquire new customers for a company as **qualified leads** that can be converted into sales. These will targeted as described in Chapter 4. Customer acquisition online involves converting site visitors who are not customers into leads and then into customers. Second, it may mean encouraging *existing* customers to engage in an online dialogue. Many organisations concentrate on the former, but where acquisition is well managed, campaigns will be used to achieve online conversion. For example, American Express developed a 'Go Paperless' campaign to persuade customers to receive and review their statements online rather than by post. Phone bank First Direct uses call-centre representatives to persuade customers the benefits of bypassing them by reviewing their statements online. The range of marketing options for communicating the offer to acquire new customers to use e-commerce services is reviewed in more detail in Chapter 8. The web site is also powerful as a low cost means of fulfilment of the offer and for response analysis.

Customer retention refers to the actions an organisation takes to retain existing customers. In an online context, e-mail and direct mail are important to encourage **repeat visits** and respond to online offers.

The phase of **customer extension** refers to increasing the depth or range of products that a customer purchases from a company. For example, an online bank may initially acquire a customer through use of a credit card. The relationship will be intensified if the customer can be persuaded to purchase other financial services such as loans or insurance.

Figure 6.2 also highlights the need for **customer selection** at each stage of customer relationship management. This links CRM with segmentation and target marketing. In an e-commerce context we may want to select for acquisition customers who belong to a particular segment, perhaps those having high disposable income. Our tactics for acquisition would then reflect that. Alternatively, if a customer is unprofitable there may not be a proactive approach to retention, i.e. special offers will not target unprofitable customers.

When discussing customer selection, Smith and Chaffey (2001) refer to ideal customers. They say:

> *Who are your ideal customers? You have good and bad customers. Bad ones continually haggle about prices, pay late, constantly complain, grab all your promotions and leave you as soon as another company comes along. The ideal customers, on the other hand, are the ones that pay on time, give you as much notice as possible, share information, become partners giving you useful feedback.*

There may also be ideal groups, or segments, of customers to target. Customer selection involves understanding the ideal customer's profile – who they are, where they

---

Qualified lead

Contact and profile information for a customer with an indication of their level of interest in product categories.

Customer retention

Techniques to maintain relationships with existing customers.

Repeat visits

If an organisation can encourage customers to return to the web site then the relationship can be maintained online.

Customer extension

Techniques to encourage customers to increase their involvement with an organisation.

Customer selection

Identifying key customer segments and targeting them for relationship building.

are, what they want and what they spend. Analytical tools for assessing customers, which are described in a little more detail later in the chapter, include:

- customer lifetime value calculation;
- CHAID;
- recency, frequency, monetary value and category (RFM) analysis.

We can then target these segments through using fields within the database to identify which segment customers belong to and then using mass customisation and personalisation to tailor offers to these customers, as described in the following section.

Customer selection can also be based on variations in online buyer behaviour and are related to the type of product. Read Case Study 6.2 below to review how companies can develop different tactics according to the type of product. The authors consider that customer behaviour should govern approaches to web marketing strategy.

We summarise this section on the customer lifecycle by reviewing the guidance provided by Peppers and Rogers (1993) in their book, subtitled *The One-to-One Future*, on how to prioritise actions on different customers. They say:

- Focus on share of the customer rather than market share – this means increasing the revenue from each customer as far as possible.
- Focus on customer retention, which is more cost-effective than acquisition.
- Concentrate on repeat purchases by cross- and up-selling; these also help margins increase.
- To achieve the above use dialogue at all stages to listen to customer needs and then *respond to them* in order to build trusting and loyal relationships

They also recommend stages to achieve these goals, which they popularise as the 5 Is (as distinct from the 4 Ps) (Peppers and Rogers, 1997):

- *Identification*. It is necessary to learn the characteristics of customers in as much detail as possible to be able to conduct the dialogue. In a business-to-business context, this means understanding those involved in the buying decision.
- *Individualisation*. Individualising means tailoring the company's approach to each customer, offering a benefit to the customer based on the identification of customer needs. The effort expended on each customer should be consistent with the value of that customer to the organisation.
- *Interaction*. Continued dialogue is necessary to understand both the customer's needs and the customer's strategic value. The interactions need to be recorded to facilitate the learning relationship.
- *Integration*. Integration of the relationship and knowledge of the customer must extend throughout all parts of the company.
- *Integrity*. Since all relationships are built on trust it is essential not to lose the trust of the customer. Efforts to learn from the customer should not be seen as intrusive, and privacy should be maintained. (Privacy issues are considered in the final section of this chapter.)

Though the books mentioned above predate the large-scale commercialisation of the Web the characteristics identified are remarkably compatible with the kind of dialogue-facilitated, customer-centric relationship that the Internet can support well. The web site representing Peppers and Rogers (Figure 6.3) is a good source of information about the concept of one-to-one and tools and techniques to achieve the goals.

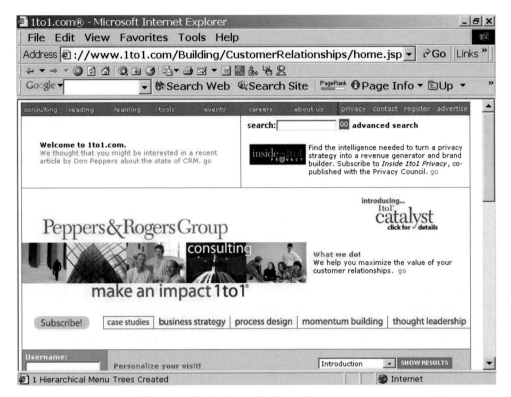

Figure 6.3 Peppers and Rogers web site (www.1to1.com)

CASE STUDY 6.2

Variations in online buyer behaviour and loyalty

Consumer behaviour should be the principal determinant of corporate e-commerce strategy. While technology will improve, consumer loyalty, for example, is likely to differ significantly between, say, online booksellers and providers of financial services. Two factors seem critical in predicting behaviour and determining an appropriate e-commerce strategy.

First, what is the duration of the relationship between buyer and seller? That is, does the buyer have a relationship with a favourite seller, in which they come to learn about each other, or does the buyer search for a different electronic vendor for each interaction? The former suggests an opportunity for tuning offerings; the latter precludes stable relationships.

Second, what is the scope of goods and services linking buyer and seller? Does the consumer purchase a single good or service, or a bundle of related goods and services? The former suggests the consumer searches for the provider of the best individual goods and services, while the latter suggests a search for the best provider of a collection of goods and services.

Combining these indicates that different companies, in different industries, will find themselves in one or more of four competitive landscapes.

Consumers buying products that can be described as opportunistic spot purchases exhibit no loyalty; each purchase may be from a different vendor and there is no one-stop shopping. They may buy a ticket from British Airways one day and United the next, and book their hotels separately.

Opportunistic store markets occur when consumers exhibit no loyalty or relationship continuity, to brands or stores. Unlike the spot market, however, they do use intermediaries to

▶

construct bundles of goods. They may shop at Sainsbury one day and Tesco another; they may use Amazon.com one day and Buy.com another.

Consumers buying in categories that may be described as loyal links exhibit continuity when choosing vendors and service providers, but have no desire to have bundles prepared for them. They may never leave home without their American Express cards, but see no reason for their card issuer to be their insurance provider or financial planner.

Finally, consumers buying in categories that may be described as loyal chains will have preferred providers. Additionally, they will count on these providers for a range of tightly coupled offerings. They may work with a financial consultant at Merrill Lynch who helps pick stocks, reminds them to draft a will and arranges guardians for their children, helps find a lawyer and reviews their insurance. The integrated service is so effective they seldom consider switching providers or taking the time to provide these things for themselves.

Each of these environments has a different competitive feel, requires a different strategy and use of different assets. This is as true in the physical world, where companies understand it pretty well, as it is in the dotcom world, where companies are struggling to develop profitable strategies.

Note that no e-commerce company occupies just one quadrant. There are, for instance, loyal link customers and companies may pursue them with loyal link strategies, but in reality some customers may use a website for spot purchases and others may show great loyalty. The challenge for companies is to guide the consumer to the behaviour matching the company's strategy; where this is not possible, companies should match the strategy to the customer's behaviour. The approach given here may help managers discover the forces that determine their best strategy.

Competition in opportunistic spot markets is based on price, since there is little loyalty to influence consumers' decisions. This brutal competition is exacerbated by nearly perfect web-based information. Thus, for standardised products such the latest Harry Potter, we observe both Amazon.com and BN.com selling at cost price. Where possible, companies try to soften competition by creating quality differences and ensuring consumers are aware of them. However, this branding must be based on real differences, since with nearly perfect information it is difficult to deceive consumers. There is a limited role for intermediaries. They may reduce risk in conducting transactions, but in most instances, consumers will buy from a set of trusted, well-known manufacturers and service providers.

The Internet will be used for supply chain management and logistics to ensure the lowest cost structure and the lowest prices. It will also support access to information on consumers, both current and potential new accounts, to allow the most accurate setting of prices where differential pricing is required. That means no applicant for insurance can be under-charged based on inaccurate risk assessment and no applicant for a credit card can be given too good a deal. In a market where no one can be overcharged without losing the account, there is little margin for error and little opportunity to recover from under-charging anyone. The ability to predict the profitability of a new customer, and so to determine a price to offer, is called predictive pricing.

It is essential to recognise consumers exhibiting opportunistic spot market behaviour and to develop an appropriate marketing and pricing strategy. For example, in markets that exhibit this behaviour, buying market share is unwise since it can be acquired only temporarily; when prices are raised to cover losses, customers will flee. Similarly, a policy of offering selected items below cost as loss leaders to attract traffic will be unwise, because consumers may easily purchase loss leaders from one site and the rest of their items elsewhere. Only time will tell whether the market for books, CDs or DVDs exhibits this behaviour, so it is too early to assess the validity of Amazon.com's customer acquisition strategy or the promotional items of other web retailers.

In the absence of consumer loyalty, competition in opportunistic store markets again is based on price; however, it is the pricing of bundles rather than individual items that attracts consumers. Unlike spot markets, there are opportunities for intermediaries to add value, through logistical savings (shipping a box of books), or through assembly or integration (selling a package tour or designing a digital imaging platform where camera, printer and computer work together).

In this scenario, intermediaries enjoy power over manufacturers because consumers select bundles with little attention to components. Thus, when filling an order for paper towels, a grocer will use the product with the highest margins. This pursuit of margins, in the absence of brand loyalty from customers, shifts economic power to intermediaries.

Manufacturers will attempt to use the web for branding, to create consumer awareness of product differences and to weaken intermediaries' power. While it is dangerous to antagonise the existing channel in the opportunistic store scenario by trying to sell directly, branding offers manufacturers the ability to counter some of the power of intermediaries. As in the spot markets, manufacturers will also use the internet to improve efficiency. Intermediaries will use the internet to create branding for their web stores, so weakening price competition. They will use customer information, as manufacturers did in spot markets, for predictive pricing.

As in spot markets, no consumer can consistently be overcharged, so it is difficult to recover from undercharging anyone. While loss leaders can work in these markets, since a customer may fill a basket or obtain a bundle of services, there is little loyalty to assure repeat business; thus, as in spot markets, buying market share is risky since there is no assurance that initial losses can be recouped by overcharging for later purchases.

Of course there may be reasons to buy share in a 'scale-intensive' industry where volume is needed to bring down unit costs. Indeed, some aspects of online retailing, such as grocery shopping, may be extremely scale-intensive, which could initially appear to justify buying share. However, without customer loyalty, the danger is that capital will be spent more on training users to accept online shopping and less on training users to accept your online shop.

Competition in loyal link markets is based on retaining the best customers through a careful blend of service and pricing. For the customer, relationship value and pricing improve over time. For example, anecdotal evidence suggests online PC seller Dell has succeeded in creating loyal link behaviour in customers, many of whom have bought several generations of computer from Dell.

In fact, no incumbent should ever lose desirable business to an attacker. If a less well-informed competitor were to attempt to persuade a loyal customer to transfer his or her business, the current supplier could decide whether or not to match the new offer. If the current supplier, with its detailed knowledge, were to choose not to match the new offer, odds are that the new supplier is making an offer that is too low. Successful attempts to get customers to switch in loyal link markets probably represent pricing mistakes by the attacker. Relationship pricing and value work to soften pure price competition in loyal link markets.

Buying market share will work under certain conditions, since it is possible to learn enough to price effectively. However, buying market share is ineffective without loyalty, as online brokerage firms are discovering; so it is critical to assess whether the company is operating in an opportunistic spot or loyal link market.

Using loss leaders in a link market will be unrewarding; offering online banking below cost to gain credit card business is unlikely to succeed in a link market, where customers will pick the best hotel and the best air service, or the best online banking and the best credit offers, independently.

Systems will be used for branding and attracting customers and to support relationship pricing and relationship service to keep the best accounts. These markets may appear to have only a limited role for intermediaries; however, intermediaries enjoy an advantage in controlling customer information and may end up owning customer relationships.

▶

Competition in loyal chain markets, as in loyal link markets, is based on attracting and retaining the best customers and, as in loyal link, relationship value and relationship pricing improve over time. However, in chain markets, which are composed of a tightly coupled set of links, pricing to individual customers and the value they receive are determined by a bundle of goods and services.

Taking the earlier example of the digital-imaging platform, it may not be necessary to replace all components when upgrading. However, if buying a higher-resolution camera and a faster laptop, it is helpful to determine if the new computer and the old printer are compatible, otherwise the customer may experience an unpleasant surprise if picking and choosing components in a spot or link fashion. If the previous chain supplier is used to update the components, unpleasant surprises are likely to be avoided, since this vendor can be relied upon to provide components that are compatible with those bought before. Evidence suggests Amazon has succeeded in encouraging a degree of loyal chain behaviour from its best customers, who value the book recommendations made to repeat buyers.

Loyal chain markets represent a power shift from producers to intermediaries. Online intermediaries can reconfigure the virtual store to show loyal purchasers the brands they wish to see; customers without a preference can be shown brands that earn the highest margins. Indeed, it is a small step from this relationship-based presentation to demanding rebates from manufacturers to ensure that their offerings will be shown to customers with no brand preference. While physical stores charge a fee for preferred locations such as displays near checkouts, they cannot reconfigure the store for each customer.

This shift in online power greatly increases the importance of branding for manufacturers, because a powerful brand is the best counter to pressure from retailers. It also suggests that, to the extent permitted by legislators, manufacturers should form consortia for web retailing. This would avoid loss of control to retailers with significant information advantage. However, a broad consortium is needed since online markets reward scope and breadth.

Intermediaries may effectively buy market share through pricing low, enabling them to pursue informed relationship pricing over time. Likewise, they may use loss leaders to increase traffic through their website, selling other items to consumers interested in a complete bundle.

Systems play many roles in chain markets. Intermediaries will use them for branding, to attract customers, and for informed relationship pricing and service. Likewise, manufacturers will use the internet for branding, so limiting price pressure from online retailers. However, efficient markets still place significant price pressure on retailers, assuring the role of systems for logistics and other forms of cost control. Likewise, manufacturers and service providers will use the web for their own cost control.

Conclusions

Three observations are true across all four competitive landscapes:

- Only differences between brands, and consumer awareness of them, can blunt pure price competition in an efficient market.
- Cost control is important: efficient access to information makes it almost impossible to overcharge.
- As online information makes markets more efficient, predictive pricing will be used in spot and store markets, and relationship pricing in link and chain markets. Pricing strategies will be limited by adverse publicity that companies receive from charging different prices for the same goods.

Other conclusions follow from these:

- The role of buying market share will vary. In opportunistic markets, buyers will leave when you raise prices.

● Similarly, the role of loss leaders will vary. In spot and link markets, consumers will pick off loss leaders and do the rest of their shopping elsewhere. Once customer traffic has been acquired, there is a chance to sell extra items.

Source: Clemons and Row (2000)

Questions

1 Summarise the characteristics of the four different types of customer behaviour by taking an example from a single market such as the financial services industry.

2 Evaluate the suitability of this framework as a method for generating e-marketing strategies.

● Permission marketing

Permission marketing is a significant concept that underpins online CRM. 'Permission marketing' is a term coined by Seth Godin. Godin (1999) notes that while research used to show we were bombarded by 500 marketing messages a day, with the advent of the web and digital TV this has now increased to over 3000 a day! From the marketing organisation's viewpoint, this leads to a dilution in the effectiveness of the messages – how can the communications of any one company stand out? From the customer's viewpoint, time is seemingly in ever-shorter supply, customers are losing patience and expect reward for their attention, time and information. Godin refers to the traditional approach as interruption marketing. Permission marketing is about seeking the customer's permission before engaging them in a relationship and providing something in exchange. The classic exchange is based on information or entertainment – a B2B site can offer a free report in exchange for a customer's sharing their e-mail address which will be used to maintain a dialogue, a B2C site can offer a screensaver in exchange.

From a practical e-commerce perspective, we can think of a customer agreeing to engage in a relationship when they agree by checking a box on a web form to indicate that they agree to receiving further communications from a company (see Figure 3.3 for further examples). This approach is referred to as opt-in. This is preferable to opt-out, the situation where a customer has to consciously agree not to receive further information.

The importance of incentivisation in permission marketing has also been emphasised by Seth Godin who likens the process of acquisition and retention to dating someone. Likening customer relationship building to social behaviour is not new, as O'Malley and Tynan (2001) note; the analogy of marriage has been used since the 1980s at least. They also report on consumer research that indicates that while marriage may be analogous to business relationships, it is less appropriate for B2C relationships. Moller and Halinen (2000) have also suggested that due to the complexity of the exchange, longer-term relationships are more readily formed for interorganisational exchanges. So, the description of the approaches that follow are perhaps more appropriate for B2B applications.

Godin (1999) suggests that dating the customer involves:

1 offering the prospect an *incentive* to volunteer;
2 using the attention offered by the prospect, offering a curriculum over time, teaching the consumer about your product or service;
3 reinforcing the *incentive* to guarantee that the prospect maintains the permission;

Permission marketing
Customers agree (opt in) to be involved in an organisation's marketing activities, usually as a result of an incentive.

Interruption marketing
Marketing communications that disrupt customers' activities.

Opt-in
A customer proactively agrees to receive further information.

Opt-out
A customer declines the offer to receive further information.

4 offering additional *incentives* to get even more permission from the consumer;

5 over time, using the permission to change consumer behaviour towards profits.

Notice the importance of incentives at each stage. The use of incentives at the start of the relationship and through it are key to successful relationships. As we shall see in a later section, e-mail is very important in permission marketing to maintain the dialogue between company and customer.

● Personalisation and mass customisation

Personalisation

Web-based personalisation involves delivering customised content for the individual, through web pages, e-mail or push technology.

The potential power of personalisation is suggested by these quotes from Evans et al. (2000) that show the negative effects of lack of targeting of traditional direct mail:

'Don't like unsolicited mail . . . haven't asked for it and I'm not interested' (Female, 25–34).

'Most isn't wanted, it's not relevant and just clutters up the table . . . you have to sort through it to get to the "real mail"' (Male, 45–54).

'It's annoying to be sent things that you are not interested in. Even more annoying when they phone you up. . . . If you wanted something you would go and find out about it' (Female, 45–54).

Mass customisation

Mass customisation is the creation of tailored marketing messages or products for individual customers or groups of customers typically using technology to retain the economies of scale and the capacity of mass marketing or production.

Personalisation and mass customisation can be used to tailor information content on a web site and opt-in e-mail can be used to deliver it to add value and at the same time remind the customer about a product. 'Personalisation' and 'mass customisation' are terms that are often used interchangeably. In the strict sense, personalisation refers to customisation of information requested by a site customer at an *individual* level. Mass customisation involves providing tailored content to a *group or individual* with similar interests. It uses technology to achieve this on an economical basis. An example of mass customisation is when Amazon recommends similar books according to what others in a segment have offered, or if it sent a similar e-mail to customers who had an interest in a particular topic such as e-commerce.

Mass customisation can range from minor cosmetic choices made by the customer (for example, the choice of colour, trim and specification available to the customer via the multimedia kiosks in Daewoo's car showrooms) to a collaborative process facilitated by ongoing dialogue. Peppers and Rogers (1993) give the example of Motorola, which could manufacture pagers to any of over 11 million different specifications.

Figure 6.4 summarises the options available to organisations wishing to use the Internet for mass customisation or personalisation. If there is little information available about the customer and it is not integrated with the web site then no mass customisation is possible (A). To achieve mass customisation or personalisation, the organisation must have sufficient information about the customer. For limited tailoring to groups of customers (B), it is necessary to have basic profiling information such as age, gender, social group, product category interest or, for B2B, role in the buying unit. This information must be contained in a database system that is directly linked to the system used to display web-site content. For personalisation on a one-to-one level (C) more detailed information about specific interests, perhaps available from a purchase history, should be available.

An organisation can use Figure 6.4 to plan their relationship marketing strategy. The symbols X_1 to X_3 show a typical path for an organisation. At X_1 information

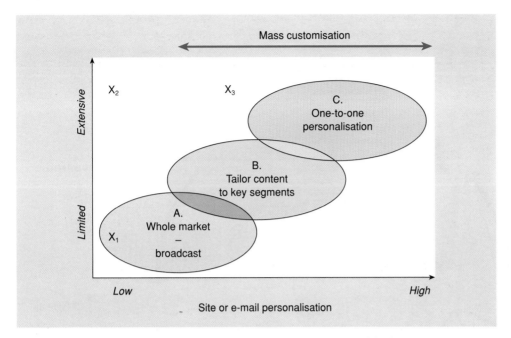

Figure 6.4 Options for mass customisation and personalisation using the Internet

collected about customers is limited. At X_2 detailed information is available about customers, but it is in discrete databases that are not integrated with the web site. At X_3 the strategy is to provide mass customisation of information and offers to major segments, since it is felt that the expense of full personalisation is not warranted.

● Online service quality

In the first section of Chapter 7, we review how the online presence can be managed in order to achieve online service quality which is also a key element leading to customer satisfaction and loyalty (Figure 7.1).

Approaches to implementing e-CRM

e-CRM uses common approaches or processes to achieve online customer acquisition and retention. Refer to Figure 6.5 for a summary of a common, effective process for online relationship building to achieve the different stages of the customer life-cycle shown in Figure 6.2. Stage 1 for building the relationship is visitor acquisition through traditional or new media as detailed in Chapter 8. Once the visitor is on-site it is essential to start a dialogue through permission marketing. This is usually achieved by providing incentives to convert a visitor into a prospect by obtaining their e-mail address, permission to contact and profile information (stage 2). Direct marketing in the form of e-mail (stage 3) and direct mail (stage 4) then follow to encourage repeat visits to the site to interact with the brand and learn more about the customer, leading to additional purchases as part of customer retention and extension.

In the following sections we proceed through the different stages in more detail.

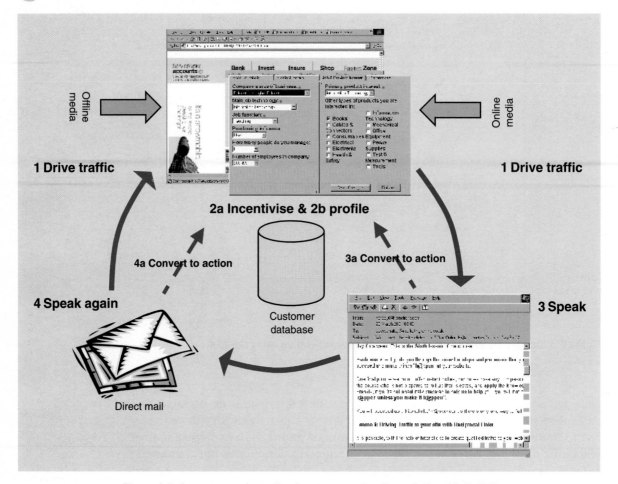

Figure 6.5 A summary of an effective process of online relationship building

● Stage 1: Attract new and existing customers to site

The strategy for achieving online customer relationship management should start with consideration of how to acquire customers who want to communicate in this way. These may be either new or existing customers. For new customers, the goal is to attract them to the site using all the methods of site promotion described in Chapter 8, such as search engines, portals and banner advertisements. These promotion methods should aim to highlight the value proposition of the site, for example incentives such as free information or competitions. To encourage new users to use the one-to-one facilities of the web site, information about the web site or incentives to visit it can be built into existing direct marketing campaigns such as catalogue mailshots.

The strategy to entice existing customers to use the web site as the start of e-CRM is complex. Companies can just leave them to find the site in the same way as new customers, but it is better, of course, to proactively encourage them to visit the site. To do this, marketing communications using other media are required as part of an integrated marketing campaign. In the business-to-business environment, mailshots can be sent to customers highlighting what is available on the site, whereas for consumers media campaigns should feature the web site prominently.

Table 6.2 Some examples of some offers intended to initiate one-to-one marketing

Offer	Example	Web sites
Free information	• Subscribing to a free monthly newsletter on one-to-one marketing • Downloading a report • Logging in to an extranet or password-restricted area such as the Virgin Megastore VIP Lounge (see Figure 6.6)	www.1to1.com www.ft.com www.virginmega.com
Access to a discussion forum	• A community with messages posted about industry or product topics	www.camcable.co.uk
Discounted product purchase	• Purchasing a product will enable a retailer to collect a customer's e-mail and real-world addresses, and these can subsequently be used for one-to-one marketing	www.rswww.com www.amazon.com www.outpost.com
Download of free software or screensaver	• The user has to fill in a form and give his or her e-mail address and contact details before being permitted to go to the file download area	www.cognos.com www.lotus.com www.oracle.com
Loyalty schemes	• These integrate well with one-to-one	www.webrewards.co.uk
Competitions and games	• Prize draws, treasure hunts, quizzes, etc.	www.vnunet.com www.disney.com

● Stage 2a: Incentivise visitors to action

The first time a visitor arrives at a site is the most important since if he or she does not find the desired information or experience, they may not return. We need to move from using the customer using the Internet in pull mode, to the marketer using the Internet in push mode through e-mail and traditional direct mail communications (Chapter 8). The quality and credibility of the site must be sufficient to retain the visitor's interest so that he or she stays on the site. To initiate one-to-one, offers or incentives must be prominent, ideally on the home page. It can be argued that converting unprofiled visitors to profiled visitors is a major design objective of a web site. Two types of incentives can be identified: lead generation offers and sales generation offers.

Types of offers marketers can devise include information value, entertainment value, monetary value and privileged access to information (such as that only available on an extranet). Identify these in Table 6.2, which illustrates common online incentives.

Lead generation offers

Offered in return for customers providing their contact details and characteristics. Commonly used in B2B marketing where free information such as a report or a seminar will be offered.

Sales generation offers

Offers that encourage product trial. A coupon redeemed against a purchase is a classic example.

● Stage 2b: Capture customer information to maintain relationship

Once the user has decided the incentive is interesting he or she will click on the option and will then be presented with an online form such as those shown in Figure 6.6. The user will be prompted to provide various items of information. The crucial information that must be collected is a method of contacting the customer. Ideally this will be both an e-mail address and a real-world address. The real-world address is important since from the postcode it may be possible to deduce the likely demographics of that person. Some companies, such as Peppers and Rogers (www.1to1.com), initially took the attitude that the e-mail address is the only piece of information that needs to be collected since this can be used to maintain the

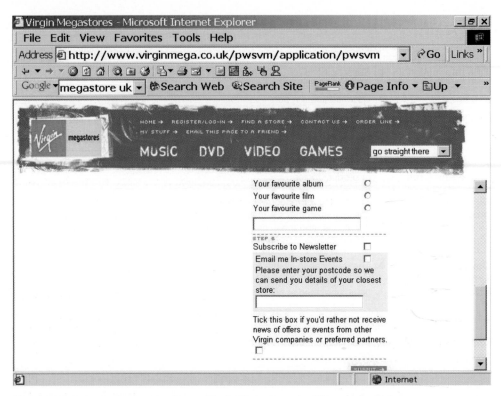

Figure 6.6 Form for data collection at Virgin Megastore for VIP membership
(www.virginmega.com)

Customer profiling

Using the web site to find out customers' specific interests and characteristics.

one-to-one relationship online. Apart from the contact information, the other important information to collect is a method of profiling the customer so that appropriate information can be delivered to the customer. For example, B2B company RS Components (Figure 3.6) asks for:

● industry sector;
● purchasing influence;
● specific areas of product interest;
● how many people you manage;
● total number of employees in company.

A company must decide carefully on the number of questions asked. It is, of course, a balance between the time taken to answer the questions and the value of the offer to the customer. If the offer is relevant and targeted, the customer is more likely to fill in a questionnaire accurately.

Collaborative filtering

Profiling of customer interest coupled with delivery of specific information and offers, often based on the interests of similar customers.

Other methods of profiling customers include collaborative filtering and monitoring the content they view. With collaborative filtering, customers are openly asked what their interests are, typically by checking boxes that correspond to their interests. A database then compares the customer's preferences with those of other customers in its database, and then makes recommendations or delivers information accordingly. The more information a database contains about an individual customer, the more useful its recommendations can be. An example of this technology in action can be found on the Amazon web site (www.amazon.com), where the database reveals that customers who bought book 'x' also bought books 'y' and 'z'. Moviecritic (www.moviecritic.com) is another example of this. This uses LikeMinds software from Andromedia (www.andromedia.com). An individual first spends time rating a minimum of 12 films. Then, comparing individual ratings with those of others with similar tastes, the site recommends films an individual is likely to enjoy. The more films an individual rates, the more appropriate the recommendations are.

Similar filtering is performed by 'intelligent agents'. For example, Autonomy (www.autonomy.com) monitors users' clicks and stores the results in a database to match the content with areas in which they have shown interest.

● Stage 3: Maintain dialogue using online communication

To build the relationship between company and customer there are three main Internet-based methods of physically making the communication. These are:

1 Send e-mail to customer.
2 Display specific information on web site when the customer logs in. This is referred to as 'personalisation'.
3 Use push technology to deliver information to the individual.

Dialogue will also be supplemented by other tools such as mailshots, phone calls or personal visits, depending on the context. For example, after a customer registers on the RS Components web site, the company sends out a letter to the customer with promotional offers and a credit-card-sized reminder of the user name and password to use to log in to the site.

As well as these physical methods of maintaining contact with customers, many other marketing devices can be used to encourage users to return to a site (see also Chapter 8). These include:

● loyalty schemes – customers will return to the site to see how many loyalty points they have collected, or convert them into offers. An airline such as American Airlines, with its Advantage Club, is a good example of this;
● news about a particular industry (for a business-to-business site);
● new product information and price promotions;
● industry-specific information to help the customer do his or her job. Snap-on Tools, a manufacturer of professional-grade tools for automobile repair businesses, adds new value for its customers by supplying them with regulatory information about subjects such as waste disposal at no fee. This strengthens Snap-on's relationship with its customers. Synetix provides technical information for chemical-plant designers to help with their day-to-day design work;
● personal reminders – the US company 1-800-Flowers has reminder programmes that automatically remind customers of important occasions and dates;
● customer support – Cisco's customers log on to the site over one million times a month to receive technical assistance, check orders or download software. The online service is so well received that nearly 70 per cent of all customer enquiries are handled online.

While adding value for their customers by means of these various mechanisms, companies will be looking to use the opportunity to make sales to customers by, for example, cross- or up-selling.

● Stage 4: Maintain dialogue using offline communication

Here, direct mail is the most effective form of communication since this can be tailored to be consistent with the user's preference. The aim here may be to drive traffic to the web site as follows:

- online competition;
- online web seminar (webinar);
- sales promotion.

● The IDIC approach to relationship building

An alternative process for building customer relationships online has been suggested by Peppers and Rogers (1998) and Peppers et al. (1999). They suggest the IDIC approach as a framework for customer relationship management and using the web effectively to form and build relationships (Figure 6.7). Examples of the application of IDIC include:

1 *Customer identification*. This stresses the need to identify each customer on their first visit and subsequent visits. Common methods for identification are use of cookies or asking a customer to log on to a site. In subsequent customer contacts, additional customer information should be obtained using a process known as **drip irrigation**. Since information will become out-of-date through time, it is important to verify, update and delete customer information.

2 *Customer differentiation*. This refers to building a profile to help segment customers. Appropriate services are then developed for each customer. Activities suggested are identifying the top customers, non-profitable customers, large customers who have ordered less in recent years and customers who buy more products from competitors.

3 *Customer interaction*. These are interactions provided on-site such as customer service questions or creating a tailored product. More generally, companies should listen to the needs and experiences of major customers. Interactions should be in the customer-preferred channel, for example e-mail, phone or post.

4 *Customer customisation*. This refers to dynamic personalisation or mass customisation of content or e-mails according to the segmentation achieved at the acquisition

Drip irrigation

Collecting information about customer needs through their lifetime.

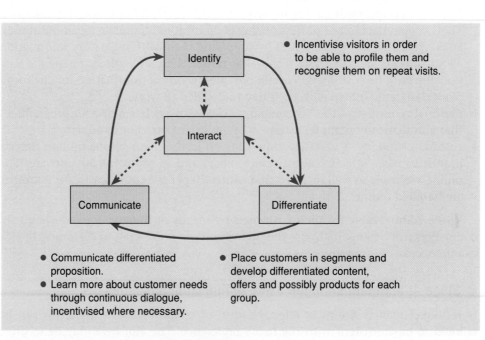

Figure 6.7 The elements of the IDIC framework

stage. Approaches for personalisation are explained in the section on *retention*. This stage also involves further market research to find out if products can be further tailored to meet customers' needs.

Techniques and technologies for implementing e-CRM

When reviewing the tools to implement one-to-one it is important to keep in mind that the relationship is more important than the technology. This was expressed well by Jim McCann, founder and president of 1-800-Flowers, in *Upside* magazine, November 1997:

> *Despite our name, 1-800-Flowers, we're in the 'social expression' business, like the people who sell greeting cards and chocolates. Flowers are symbolic, timeless, not hi-tech. And yet we conduct 10 percent of our business on-line. We're using this new channel to reach a growing market segment that is embracing new technology and is motivated by convenience. But we've never lost sight of customer satisfaction, which we handle the old-fashioned way: one-to-one.*

In this section, we describe the four techniques that support online customer relationship marketing. We start with the database, which underpins all interactive personalised communications. We then go on to look at how databases can be used to personalise the customers' web experience, e-mail and the creation of virtual communities.

● Databases

Databases effectively provide the 'brains' behind the web site, enabling customer profiling and personalisation and predictive analysis through techniques such as chi-squared automated interaction detectors (CHAID), neural networks and data mining. Without a database, a web server is 'dumb' and can only serve standard requested information. Personalisation is not possible. All of the reasons for which companies have applied **database marketing**, in order to assist them in learning about and targeting customers through other media, also apply to the Internet. This is clear from the definition of database marketing. Database marketing does not, however, constitute relationship marketing; it does provide 'the means by which a company identifies, maintains and builds up its network of customers' (DeTienne and Thompson, 1996).

Database marketing

The application of digital information collected about current and/or potential customers and their buying behaviour to improve marketing performance by formulating strategy and building personalised relationships with customers.

Analysing the customer base

According to Stone et al. (2001b), analysis of customer database and **data mining** can be used to answer questions such as the following.

Customer-based questions
- What type of customers does a company have?
- How do they behave?
- Which are most desirable and which are least desirable?

Product or price
- Which products are bought together?
- What is the best time to sell a product?
- Which combination of tariffs yields the maximum revenue?

Distribution and communications routes to market

- Which campaign design works best? A propensity analysis can determine which types are most likely to respond.
- Which distribution channel is most effective?

Combinations

- Which customers are responsive to which communications for which products?
- Is it possible to identify groups of customers that can be managed more profitably and less riskily if they are managed homogeneously within those groups?
- Why have some customers been lost for some products, but others gained?

Data fusion

The combining of data from different complementary sources (usually geodemographic and lifestyle or market research and lifestyle) to 'build a picture of someone's life' (Evans, 1998).

The customer data collected from the web site using the techniques described in Chapter 9 needs to be analysed in conjunction with data from other media. This process has been referred to as **data fusion** (Evans, 1998).

Historic data from disparate sources are increasingly being stored in a single place for analysis – the *data warehouse*. The data can be 'mined' to identify patterns which help a company understand its customers better.

Data warehousing and datamining

Extracting data from legacy systems and other resources; cleaning, scrubbing and preparing data for decision support; maintaining data in appropriate data stores; accessing and analysing data using a variety of end user tools and mining data for significant relationships. The primary purpose of these efforts is to provide easy access to specially prepared data that can be used with decision support applications such as management report, queries, decision support systems, executive information systems and datamining.

The Data Warehousing Institute (www.dw-institute.com)

Capital One Financial Corporation uses data mining to target low-rate loans at the appropriate targets so that it retains the customers, rather than having many customers leave after taking advantage of an initial offer (Souccar, 1999). Currently data mining is used in conjunction with direct mail, but as Internet access increases such communications will be made by e-mail and will appear on personalised web pages. The implication of this is that further integration is required between datamining tools and web sites.

A neural network is a data-mining approach that operates in a way that is similar to the functioning of neurons in the human brain. A neural network can be used to identify patterns within data.

Despite the potential of using databases referred to above, it is worth remembering that many web sites have not yet progressed beyond brochureware status. Of those sites that are making strides in personalisation, many are not yet exploiting the data they are collecting. Bayers (1998) reports that much of the data Amazon collects about its customers, it is unable to mine.

Belfer (1998) comments, 'Technologies such as datamining, datawarehousing and electronic commerce are lauded as the IT sledgehammer to crack the marketing walnut' in the article appropriately entitled 'IT are from Mars, Marketing are from Venus'. This article highlights the need for the marketing department to work closely with the IT department in the selection and implementation of personalisation tools.

● Web page personalisation

Personalisation involves delivering customised content for the individual through web pages, e-mail or push technology. To be able to display personalised web pages such as Dell's PremierPages, a web site needs to be able to identify an individual when he or she arrives at the site. There are three potential ways of doing this. The first is to use the IP or network address number of the computer accessing the site. This is not reliable since for many ISPs this number is generated dynamically each time a user logs on, so it will not be the same from one user session to the next. The second method is to use a cookie (see box 'What are cookies?', p. 89). This is more reliable, but will not work if the user logs on from a different location (from home rather than at work, for example). The most reliable, but most obtrusive, method is to require the user to log in using a user name and password. This extranet approach is used by many e-commerce sites such as RS Components (www.rswww.com) but some use only a cookie-based system. An example of personlisation achieved with a portal is shown in Figure 6.8.

Personalisation systems must provide not only a method of identifying the customer, but also a method of delivering appropriate content to the user. This is often delivered in line with predetermined rules based on the customer's profile. For example, a customer of the RS Components site may have specified an interest in office equipment. The database will then execute a rule: 'If customer is interested in office equipment, then display the office equipment sales promotions'. For a company that has a special account with a supplier, the database will display the account information for that customer. For instance, when a customer clicks the 'order history' button the database will perform a query that retrieves all orders for that specific customer.

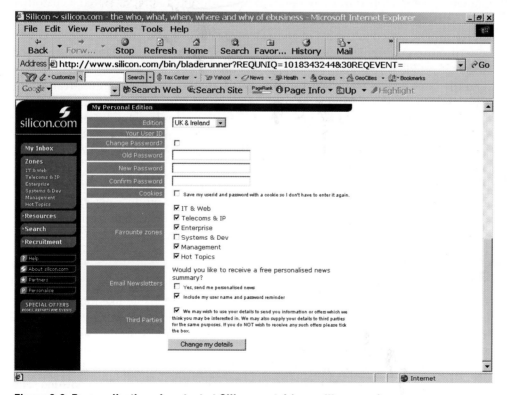

Figure 6.8 Personalisation of content at Silicon portal (wwwsilicon.com)

Tools for implementing personalisation

Some of the main tools used to implement personalisation include:

- Broadvision (www.broadvision.com);
- Engage Profileserver (www.engage.com);
- Bladerunner (www.bladerunner.com);
- LikeMinds (www.andromedia.com);
- GroupLens (www.netperceptions.com).

These sites provide good examples of the application of this technology as it develops.

One example of the use of personalisation is that by Messe Frankfurt as a means of enabling businesses around the world to access information about international trade fairs. The extranet, available in English and German, enables its members to access personalised information about trade shows and events, based on their industry and business objectives. Using the targeted information available on this site, members determine the most effective ways to display their products at trade shows around the world. Personalisation can be used either by those wishing to visit trade fairs or by companies exhibiting.

● E-mail

Outbound e-mails are sent out to customers, whose e-mail addresses are stored on a mail server. These are clearly analogous to direct postal mail. Approaches to e-mail marketing are described in more detail in a section in Chapter 8. When a customer registers interest in receiving a standard newsletter, for example, that customer's address will be added to the list of addressees on a mail server and the newsletter will be sent out regularly. For tailored e-mails, integration with a database storing the customer profile is required.

In the same way as mailing lists can be purchased for mailshots in the real world, lists of e-mail addresses can be bought-in that target particular types of users. Some of these are compiled by unscrupulous bulk mail operators, who obtain the e-mail addresses from web pages or newsgroups and then sell them in bulk – $500 for 100 000 addresses. These may give a low CPM, but are likely to be completely untargeted. Opt-in lists are the best approach. Here consumers can opt to receive information about particular topics. This approach also works well in a business-to-business context when Internet users will be interested in industry or product news.

Managing inbound e-mail has also become a major issue for companies operating over the Internet, and this is also described in Chapter 8.

● Virtual communities

Virtual community

An Internet-based forum for special-interest groups to communicate.

Virtual communities are a novel web concept in that they enable like-minded people from around the world to interact using e-mail or bulletin-board-type facilities. In a sense they are similar to user groups for some technical products such as software, or special-interest groups created to fight a cause or share a problem. What the Internet provides is an easy mechanism for sharing views over a wide area.

Since the publication of the article by Armstrong and Hagel in 1996 entitled 'The real value of online communities' and John Hagel's subsequent book (Hagel, 1997) there has been much discussion about the suitability of the Web for virtual communities. For companies they provide an opportunity to get closer to their customers, although not through a strictly one-to-one model.

The power of the virtual communities, according to Hagel (1997), is that they exhibit a number of positive-feedback loops (or 'virtuous circles'). Focused content attracts new members, who in turn contribute to the quantity and quality of the community's pooled knowledge. Member loyalty grows as the community grows and evolves. The purchasing power of the community grows and thus the community attracts more vendors. The growing revenue potential attracts yet more vendors, providing more choice and attracting more members. As the size and sophistication of the community grow (yet still remaining tightly focused) its data gathering and profiling capabilities increase – thus enabling better targeted marketing and attracting more vendors . . . and so on. In such positive-feedback loops there is an initial start-up period of slow and uneven growth until critical mass in members, content, vendors and transactions is reached. The potential for growth is then exponential – until the limits of the focus of the community as it defines itself are reached.

From this description of virtual communities it can be seen that they provide many of the attributes for effective relationship marketing – they can be used to learn about customers and provide information and offers to a group of customers.

When deciding on a strategic approach to virtual communities, companies have two basic choices if they decide to use them as part of their efforts in relationship building. First, they can provide community facilities on the site, or they can monitor and become involved in relevant communities set up by other organisations.

If a company sets up a community facility on its site, it has the advantage that it can improve its brand by adding value to its products. Sterne (1999) suggests that minimal intrusion should occur, but it may be necessary for the company to seed discussion and moderate out some negative comments. It may also be instrumental in increasing word-of-mouth promotion of the site. The community will provide customer feedback on the company and its products as part of the learning relationship. However, the brand may be damaged if customers criticise products. The company may also be unable to get sufficient people to contribute to a company-hosted community. Communities are best suited to high-involvement brands such as those related to sports and hobbies and business-to-business.

What is the reality behind Hagel and Armstrong's original vision of communities? How can companies deliver the promise of community? The key to a successful community is customer-centred communication. It is a customer-to-customer (C2C) interaction (Chapter 1). Consumers, not businesses, generate the content of the site, e-mail list or bulletin board. Its success and essential power can be gauged by the millions of customers who used Napster and Gnutella to download MP3 music files using the peer-to-peer (P2P) approach where these companies act as intermediaries to enable users to exchange files. As well as these high-profile examples of successful C2C community there is also often untapped potential for applying community on any organisation's web site. Remember that the C2C approach can be integrated into B2C and B2B sites.

According to Durlacher (1999), depending on market sector, an organisation has a choice of developing different types of community: communities of purpose, position and interest for B2C, and of profession for B2B.

1 *Purpose* – people who are going through the same process or trying to achieve a particular objective. Examples include those researching cars, e.g. at Autotrader

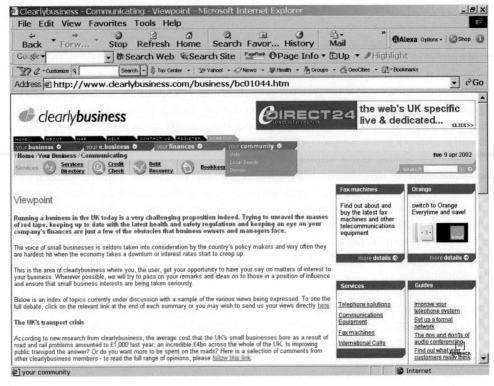

Figure 6.9 ClearlyBusiness community (www.clearlybusiness.com)

(www.autotrader.co.uk) or stocks online, e.g. at the Motley Fool (www.motleyfool.co.uk). Price or product comparison services such as MySimon, Shopsmart and Kelkoo serve this community. At sites such as Bizrate (www.bizrate.com), the Egg Free Zone (www.eggfreezone.com) or Alexa (www.alexa.com) companies can share their comments on companies and their products.

2 *Position* – people who are in a certain circumstance such as a health disorder or in a certain stage of life such as communities set up specifically for young people or old people. Examples are teenage chat site Dobedo (www.dobedo.co.uk), Cennet, www.cennet.co.uk 'New horizons for the over 50s', www.babycenter.com and www.parentcentre.com for parents and the Pet Channel (www.thepetchannel.com).

3 *Interest.* This community is for people who share an interest or passion such as sport (www.football365.com), music (www.pepsi.com), leisure (www.walkingworld.com) or any other interest (www.deja.com).

4 *Profession.* These are important for companies promoting B2B services. For example, Vertical Net has set up over 50 different communities to appeal to professionals in specific industries such as paints and coatings, the chemical industry or electronics. These B2B vertical portals can be thought of as 'trade papers on steroids'. In fact, in many cases they have been created by publishers of trade papers, for example, Emap Business Communications has created Construction Plus for the construction industry. Each has industry and company news and jobs as expected, but also offers online sales and auctions for buyers and sellers and community features such as discussion topics. Of course the trade papers such as Emap's *Construction Weekly* are responding by creating their own portals.

A further classification of communities is that of Armstrong and Hagel (1996) which is arguably less useful and identifies communities of transaction, communities of interest, communities of fantasy and communities of relationship.

You will notice that most of these examples of community are intermediary sites that are independent of a particular manufacturer or retailer. A key question to ask before embarking on a community-building programme is 'Can customer interests be best served through a company-independent community?'. If the answer to this question is 'yes', then it may be best to form a community that is a brand variant, differentiated from its parent. For example, Boots the Chemist has created Handbag.com as a community for its female customers. Another, and less costly, alternative is to promote your products through sponsorship or co-branding on an independent community site or portal or get involved in the community discussions.

What tactics can organisations used to foster community? Despite the hype and potential, many communities fail to generate activity, and a silent community isn't a community. Parker (2000) suggests eight questions organisations should ask when considering how to create a customer community:

1 What interests, needs or passions do many of your customers have in common?
2 What topics or concerns might your customers like to share with each other?
3 What information is likely to appeal to your customers' friends or colleagues?
4 What other types of business in your area appeal to buyers of your products and services?
5 How can you create packages or offers based on combining offers from two or more affinity partners?
6 What price, delivery, financing or incentives can you afford to offer to friends (or colleagues) that your current customers recommend?
7 What types of incentives or rewards can you afford to provide customers who recommend friends (or colleagues) who make a purchase?
8 How can you best track purchases resulting from word-of-mouth recommendations from friends?

A good approach to avoiding these problems is to think about the problems you may have with your community-building efforts. Typical problems are:

1 *Empty communities*. A community without any people isn't a community. The traffic-building techniques mentioned in the earlier section need to be used to communicate the proposition of the community.
2 *Silent communities*. A community may have many registered members, but community is not a community if the conversation flags. This is a tricky problem. You can encourage people to join the community, but how do you get them to participate? Here are some ideas.
   ● Seed the community. Use a moderator to ask questions or have a weekly or monthly question written by the moderator or sourced from customers. Have a resident independent expert to answer questions. Visit the communities on Monster (www.monster.co.uk) to see these approaches in action and think about what distinguishes the quiet communities from the noisy ones.
   ● Make it select. Limit it to key account customers or set it up as extranet service that is only offered to valued customers as a value-add. Members may be more likely to get involved.
3 *Critical communities*. Many communities on manufacturer or retailer sites can be critical of the brand – see the Egg Free Zone, for example (www.eggfreezone.com). Think about whether this is a bad thing. It could highlight weaknesses in your

service offer to customers and competitors, but enlightened companies use community as a means to better understand their customers' needs and failings with their services. Community is a key market research tool. Also, it may be better to control and contain these critical comments on your site rather than their being voiced elsewhere in newsgroups where you may not notice them and can less easily counter them. The computer-oriented newsgroup on Monster shows how the moderator lets criticisms go so far and then counters them or closes them off. Particular criticisms can be removed.

Finally, remember the *lurkers* – those who read the messages but do not actively contribute. There may be ten lurkers for every active participant. The community can also positively influence these people and build brand.

Integrating the Internet with other forms of direct marketing

Direct marketing

Marketing to customers using one or more advertising media and aimed at achieving a measurable response and/or transaction.

Direct marketing is closely linked to relationship marketing since the aim of both is to communicate directly with customers with information tailored for them. The difference is really one of emphasis. Direct marketing has been viewed as a tactical vehicle in the form of a single campaign such as a mailshot that is aimed at achieving a direct response. Relationship marketing is a longer-term strategic communication with the customer that is aimed at understanding the customer's needs and then responding to them. Implementing relationship marketing will contain elements of direct marketing. However, the distinction between relationship and direct marketing over a period of time is becoming blurred. Integrated direct marketing involves using different media over a longer time period to achieve a response. This is explored further in Chapter 8.

The popular conception of direct marketing is of torrents of junk mail pouring through letterboxes urging consumers to buy items they don't need. Direct marketing originated with the first trade catalogues, which appeared soon after the invention of movable type by Gutenberg in the 1400s. They later became popular among wealthy settlers in the New World wishing to purchase wine, china and furniture from Europe. It may appear as if direct marketing has not moved on since this, but direct marketing is becoming increasingly diverse and covers everything from direct mailshots, catalogue marketing and telemarketing to direct-response television advertisements and the use of web sites. One of the challenges for today's direct marketer is to integrate the Internet into other forms of direct marketing. We will now consider how this integration is occurring.

● Telemarketing and the Internet

In this section we briefly review the use of telephones in direct marketing and assess how the Internet can be used in conjunction with these.

Outbound telemarketing

Outbound telemarketing is known for its use for 'cold-calling' new prospects, but it is also used to increase the profitability of existing customers, either by encouraging them to spend more by up-selling or by cross-selling, often in conjuction with other media such as direct mail. If the target is accurate and a warm-up mailer has been sent this is a powerful technique. Misused, it has great potential to annoy and anger. Research by Datamonitor (*European Business Teleculture 98*) found that 70 per cent of customers have been annoyed by outbound calls, 20 per cent said it has destroyed their impression of a company, 14 per cent said that they would not use the company again, and 12 per cent told their families and friends about the experience, whilst 9 per cent were sufficiently annoyed to complain directly to the company. Outbound telemarketing can be thought of as the equivalent of 'spamming' on the Internet and there does not seem to be much potential to apply the Internet, other than by its decreasing the need for outbound telemarketing!

Inbound telemarketing

Inbound telemarketing is now widespread, and ranges from sales lines and carelines for goods and services to response handling for direct response campaigns. This technique can be used to up-sell and cross-sell to a customer who has called about something else. The Liederman and Roncorroni Group conducted a survey in 1995 showing that 22 per cent of all packaged goods in the UK now have a customer careline.

A web site can complement inbound telemarketing: product information may be available on the site and that obviates the need for the customer to call. Alternatively, the information may not be readily understandable on the web site (a complex financial product, for example) and it may be necessary for the customer to phone the company. In this situation callback facilities provide good synergy between telephone and Web. Callback facilities require integration between the web site and a call management system (using computer telephony integration – CTI) since the customer will specify a particular time he or she wants to be called. The callback is technically outbound since it originates from the company, but on a practical level it is inbound since it is initiated by the customer. Callback has the advantage that the customer does not pay for the phone call.

In some circumstances it may not be appropriate to encourage the use of the Web in conjunction with telemarketing. Imagine, for example, that you have designed a direct-response television advertisement. Would you want customers to call a human operator to explain the benefits of a product or use a web site that does not have the sales skills? Furthermore, someone following up an advertisement on the Web may be distracted and investigate competitors' offers or go to an intermediary site to find the best price! Advertisements from financial services companies, for example, may give prominence to the direct-response phone number, but may provide no web address. This may be deliberate.

Callback facility
A facility on the web site enabling the customer to request an outbound phone call from a company.

Computer telephony integration (CTI)
The combined use of software and telephones to facilitate communication between a business and its customers, particularly through call centres.

Call centres

According to Kislowski (1996) the renewed focus on the call centre is being driven primarily by three forces: customer demands for more convenient access to goods and services, business pressures to drive down costs, and the convergence of computers and telephones. The call centre is clearly important in supporting the outbound calls resulting from Internet callback systems.

An example of a company that has integrated its web site and call centre is the UK financial services company Clerical Medical, which set up a call centre in 1997 to manage requests arising from its promotional activity across all media, including its web site. This site is designed to enable independent financial advisers (IFAs) to find the information they need to service their clients. If they cannot find the information they need, they can request further information by clicking a screen button that triggers an e-mail message direct to the call centre. At the same time, customers can use a 'call-me' or callback button to get information from the call centre on their three nearest IFAs.

Finally, it should be noted that some commentators have predicted the 'death of call centres' at the hands of the Internet since many of the routine enquiries currently handled by call centres such as bank account enquiries and transfers can readily be performed by customers with web-enabled PCs, digital television or a telephone.

Summary

1 The three areas of relationship marketing, direct marketing and database marketing have converged to create a powerful new marketing paradigm known as customer relationship management.

2 Relationship marketing theory provides the conceptual underpinning of one-to-one marketing and customer relationship management since it emphasises enhanced customer service through customer knowledge.

3 The objective of customer relationship management (CRM) is to increase customer loyalty in order to increase profitability. CRM is aimed at improving all aspects of the level of customer service.

4 CRM tactics can be based around the acquisition, retention, extension model of the ideal relationship between company and customer.

5 Direct marketing provides the tactics that deliver the marketing communications (and sometimes the product itself) to the individual customer. This approach is evolving rapidly with the advent of the Internet, the rise of call centres and advances in logistics.

6 Database marketing provides the technological enabler, allowing vast amounts of data to be stored and accessed in ways that create business opportunities.

7 Online relationship marketing is effective since it provides an interactive, multimedia environment in which the customer opts in to the relationship.

8 Steps in implementing one-to-one on the Internet are:
   - Step 1. Attract customers to site.
   - Step 2a. Incentivise in order to gain contact and profile information.
   - Step 2b. Capture customer information to maintain the relationship and profile customer.
   - Step 3. Maintain dialogue through using online communications to achieve repeat site visits.
   - Step 4. Maintain dialogue consistent with customer's profile using direct mail.

9 Personalisation technologies enable customised e-mails to be sent to each individual (or related groups) and customised web content to be displayed or distributed using push technology.

10 Integration with databases is important for profiling the customer and recording the relationship.

11 Virtual communities have an important role to play in fostering relationships.

12 Marketers must be aware of the risk of infringing customer privacy since this is damaging to the relationship. Providing customers with the option to opt in and opt out of marketing communications is important to maintain trust.

13 Internet-based one-to-one marketing needs to be integrated with traditional communications by mail and phone as described in Chapter 8.

EXERCISES

Self-assessment exercises

1 Why is the Internet a suitable medium for relationship marketing?

2 Explain personalisation in an Internet marketing context.

3 What is meant by 'customer profiling'?

4 What is 'computer telephony integration'?

5 How can customer concerns about privacy be responded to when conducting one-to-one marketing using the Internet?

6 Explain the relationship between database marketing, direct marketing and relationship marketing.

7 What is a cookie?

8 How can a web site integrate with telemarketing?

Essay and discussion questions

1 'Direct response television advertisements are more effective if customers are directed to a call centre rather than a web site.' Discuss.

2 Compare and contrast traditional transaction-oriented marketing with one-to-one marketing using the Internet.

3 Write a report summarising for a manager the necessary stages for transforming a brochure-ware site to a one-to-one interactive site and the benefits that can be expected.

4 Explore the legal and ethical constraints upon implementing relationship marketing using the Internet.

Examination questions

1 Define and explain direct marketing within the Internet context.

2 What characteristics of the Internet make it so conducive to the direct marketing approach?

3 How does a company initiate one-to-one marketing with a company using the Internet?

4 Explain the concept of a 'virtual community' and how such communities can be used as part of relationship marketing.

5 Suggest three measures a company can take to ensure a customer's privacy is not infringed when conducting one-to-one marketing.

6 What is the role of a database when conducting one-to-one marketing on the Internet?

7 Describe how a web site can be integrated with inbound telemarketing.

8 Explore opportunities and methods for personalising the interactive web session and adding value for that individual customer.

References

Armstrong, A. and Hagel, J. (1996) The real value of online communities, *Harvard Business Review*, May–June, 134–41.

Bayers, C. (1998) The promise of one-to-one (a love story), *Wired*, 6 May.

Belfer, S. (1998) IT are from Mars, Marketing are from Venus, *Direct Marketing*, 61, 52–3.

Clemons, E. and Row, M. (2000) Behaviour is key to web retailing strategy, *Financial Times, Mastering Management Supplement*, 13 November.

Cram, T. (1994) *The Power of Relationship Marketing: Keeping Customers for Life*. Financial Times Management, London.

Cross, M. (1994) Internet: the missing marketing medium, *Direct Marketing*, 20(6) (October), 20–4.

DeTienne, K.B. and Thompson, J.A. (1996) Database marketing and organisational theory: towards a research agenda, *Journal of Consumer Marketing*, 13(5), 12–34.

Duffy, D. (1998) Customer loyalty strategies, *Journal of Consumer Marketing*, 15(5), 435–48.

Durlacher (1999) UK online community, *Durlacher Quarterly Internet Report*, Q3, 7–11, London.

ECCS (2001) Deutsche Bank Finds Value in its Customer Data. Case study on European Centre for Customer Strategies. Author: David Reed. www.eccs.uk.com.

Evans, M. (1998) From 1086 to 1984: direct marketing into the millennium, *Marketing Intelligence and Planning*, 16(1), 56–67.

Evans, M., Patterson, M. and O'Malley, L. (2000) Bridging the direct marketing–direct consumer gap: some solutions from qualitative research, *Proceedings of the Academy of Marketing Annual Conference*, 2000, Derby, UK.

Foley, D., Gordon, G.L., Schoebachler, D.D. and Spellman L. (1997) Understanding consumer database marketing, *Journal of Consumer Marketing*, 14(1), 5–19.

Godin, S. (1999) *Permission Marketing*. Simon and Schuster, New York.

Gummesson, E. (1987) The new marketing: developing long term interactive relationships, *Long Range Planning*, 20(4), 10–20.

Hagel, J. (1997) *Net Gain: Expanding Markets through Virtual Communities*. Harvard Business School Press, Boston.

Kislowski, M. (1996) The increasingly important role of cell centres: strategies for the future, *Direct Marketing*, 59(5), 34–8.

McCarthy, J. (1960) *Basic Marketing: A Managerial Approach*. Irwin, Homewood, IL.

McKenna, R. (1993) *Relationship Marketing: Successful Strategies for the Age of the Customer*. Addison-Wesley, Reading, MA.

Maling, N. (1999) TV money spirited down the pan, *Marketing Week*, 11(5), 26–9.

Moller, K. and Halinen, A. (2000) Relationship marketing theory: its roots and direction, *Journal of Marketing Management*, 16, 29–54.

O'Malley, L. and Tynan, C. (2001) Reframing relationship marketing for consumer markets, *Interactive Marketing*, 2(3), 240–6.

Parker, R (2000) *Relationship Marketing on the Web*, Adams Streetwise.

Peppers, D. and Rogers, M. (1993) *Building Business Relationships One Customer at a Time. The One-to-One Future*. Piatkus, London.

Peppers, D. and Rogers, M. (1997) *Enterprise One-to-One: Tools for Building Unbreakable Customer Relationships in the Interactive Age*. Piatkus, London.

Peppers, D. and Rogers, M. (1998) *One-to-One Fieldbook*. Doubleday, New York.

Peppers, D., Rogers, M. and Dorf, B. (1999) Is your company ready for one-to-one marketing? *Harvard Business Review*, January–February, 3–12.

Raphel, M. (1997) How a San Francisco movie complex breaks attendance records with database marketing, *Direct Marketing*, 59(11), 52–5.

Reichheld, F.F. (1996) *The Loyalty Effect*. Harvard Business School Press, Boston.

Reichheld, F. and Schefter, P. (2000) E-loyalty, your secret weapon, *Harvard Business Review*, July–August, 105–13.

Rigby, D., Bavega, S., Rastoi, S., Zook, C. and Hancock, S. (2000) The value of customer loyalty and how you can capture it. Bain and Company/Mainspring Whitepaper, 17 March. Published at www.mainspring.com.

Rosenfield, J.R. (1998) The future of database marketing, *Direct Marketing*, 60(10), 28–31.

Sargeant, A. and West, D. (2001) *Direct and Interactive Marketing*. Oxford University Press, Oxford.

Schultz, D.E., Tannenbaum, S.L. and Lauterborn, R.F. (1994) *The New Marketing Paradigm: Integrated Marketing Communications*. NTC, Lincolnwood, IL.

Shaw, R. (1996) How to transform marketing through IT, *Management Today*, Special Report.

Smith, P.R. and Chaffey, D. (2001) *EMarketing Excellence – at the Heart of EBusiness*. Butterworth Heinemann, Oxford.

Souccar, M.K. (1999) Epidemic of rate shopping spurs a search for remedies, *American Banker*, 164(4).

Sterne, J. (1999) *World Wide Web Marketing*, 2nd edn. Wiley, New York.

Stone, M., Abbott, J. and Buttle, F. (2001a) Integrating customer data into CRM strategy. In B. Foss and M. Stone (eds) *Successful Customer Relationship Marketing*. Wiley, Chichester.

Stone, M., Sharman, R., Foss, B., Lowrie, R. and Selby, D. (2001b) Data mining and data warehousing. In B. Foss and M. Stone (eds) *Successful Customer Relationship Marketing*. Wiley, Chichester.

Wolfe, D.B. (1998) Developmental relationship marketing: connecting messages with mind, an empathetic marketing system, *Journal of Consumer Marketing*, 15(5), 449–67.

Further reading

Kotler, P., Armstrong, G., Saunders, J. and Wong, V. (2001) *Principles of Marketing*, 3rd edn. Financial Times/Prentice Hall, Harlow. *See* companion Prentice Hall web site for 8th US edn: cw.prenhall.com/bookbind/pubbooks/kotler. *See* Chapter 11, Building customer relationships, customer satisfaction, quality, value and service, and Chapter 22, Direct and online marketing.

McCorkell, G. (1997) *Direct and Database Marketing*. Kogan Page, London.

Moller, K. and Halinen, A. (2000) Relationship marketing theory: its roots and direction, *Journal of Marketing Management*, 16, 29–54. A useful summary of the evolution of relationship marketing concepts.

Nash, E. (1993) *Database Marketing: The Ultimate Marketing Tool*. McGraw-Hill, New York.

Nash, E. (1995) *Direct Marketing: Strategy, Planning, Execution*. McGraw-Hill, New York.

Newells, F. (1996) *New Rules of Marketing: How to Use One-to-One Relationship Marketing*. Irwin, Homewood, IL.

Payne, A., Christopher, M. and Peck, M. (1995) *Relationship Marketing for Competitive Advantage*. Butterworth Heinemann, Oxford.

Peppers, D., Rogers, M. and Dorf, B. (1999) Is your company ready for one-to-one marketing? *Harvard Business Review*, January–February, 3–12. A fairly detailed summary of the IDIC approach.

Reichheld, F. and Schefter, P. (2000) E-loyalty, your secret weapon, *Harvard Business Review*, July–August, 105–13. An excellent review of the importance of achieving online loyalty and approaches to achieving it.

Sargeant, A. and West, D. (2001) *Direct and Interactive Marketing*. Oxford University Press, Oxford. An excellent coverage of traditional direct marketing, although the specific chapter on e-marketing is brief.

Tapp, A. (2000) *Principles of Direct and Database Marketing*, 2nd edn. Financial Times/Prentice Hall, Harlow.

Web links

- Clickz (www.clickz.com). An excellent collection of articles on online marketing communications. US-focused. Relevant sections for this chapter include: CRM strategies.

- Database Marketing Institute (www.dbmarketing.com). Useful collection of articles on best practice.

- European Centre for Customer Strategies (www.eccs.uk.com). Excellent collection of white papers and case studies, many on e-CRM.

- Peppers and Rogers One-to-One marketing web site (www.1to1.com). A site containing a lot of information on the techniques and tools of relationship marketing.

PART 3

Internet marketing: implementation and practice

In Part 3 particular issues of the execution of an Internet marketing strategy are described, including development of a web site and ensuring service quality (Chapter 7), marketing communications to promote a site (Chapter 8) and the maintenance and evaluation of an online presence (Chapter 9). In Chapters 10 and 11, specific examples are given of how business-to-consumer and business-to-business companies are using the Internet.

**Chapter 7
Achieving online service quality**

- ➤ Service quality
- ➤ Planning web site development
- ➤ Initiation of the web site project
- ➤ Researching site users' requirements
- ➤ Online buyer behaviour
- ➤ Designing the user experience
- ➤ Development and testing of content
- ➤ Promote site

**Chapter 8
Interactive marketing communications**

- ➤ The characteristics of interactive marketing communications
- ➤ Integrated Internet marketing communications
- ➤ Objectives for interactive marketing communications
- ➤ Offline promotion techniques
- ➤ Online promotion techniques
- ➤ Loyalty techniques and online incentive schemes
- ➤ Selecting the optimal communications mix
- ➤ Measuring effectiveness

**Chapter 9
Maintaining and monitoring the online presence**

- ➤ The maintenance process
- ➤ Responsibilities in web site maintenance
- ➤ Measuring Internet marketing effectiveness

**Chapter 10
Business-to-consumer Internet marketing**

- ➤ Business-to-consumer context
- ➤ Internet consumer markets
- ➤ Online retail activities
- ➤ Implications for Internet retail marketing strategy

**Chapter 11
Business-to-business Internet marketing**

- ➤ Business-to-business context
- ➤ Interorganisational exchanges
- ➤ Organisational markets
- ➤ E-marketing strategies

Achieving online service quality

Links to other chapters

Related chapters are:

➤ Chapters 4 and 5, which describe the development of the strategy and tactics that inform the design of the web site

➤ Chapter 8, which describes approaches to promoting web sites

➤ Chapter 9, which describes the maintenance of a site once it is created

Learning objectives

After reading this chapter, the reader should be able to:

● Describe the different stages involved in creating a new site or relaunching an existing site

● Describe the design elements that contribute to effective web site content

● Define the factors that are combined to deliver a quality online service

Questions for marketers

Key questions for marketing managers related to this chapter are:

● Which activities are involved in building a new site or updating an existing site?

● What are the key factors of online service quality and site design that will encourage repeat visitors?

● Which techniques can I use to determine visitors' requirements?

● Which forms of buyer behaviour do users exhibit online?

● What are the accepted standards of site design needed for consistency?

Introduction

This chapter essentially describes the marketing activity involved with creating an online presence. However, in the chapter title we refer to 'online service' since the visitors' online experience is affected by much more than the web site. The web site is what the customer can see, but behind this there is the supporting infrastructure of database, enquiry management and product fulfilment, all of which are vital to delivering a quality online service. The main stages that need to be managed when creating or updating an online presence are shown in Figure 7.1. The starting point is always having clear, identified objectives of what the new site should achieve. It should support the e-marketing objectives, strategy and tactics as described in Chapters 4, 5 and 6.

Of the stages shown in Figure 7.1, that of market research and design is described in most detail in this chapter since the nature of the web site content is, of course, vital in providing a satisfactory experience for the customer which leads to repeat visits. Testing and promotion of the web site are described in subsequent chapters. An alternative model can be found in a practical 'Internet marketing framework' presented by Ong (1995) and summarised by Morgan (1996).

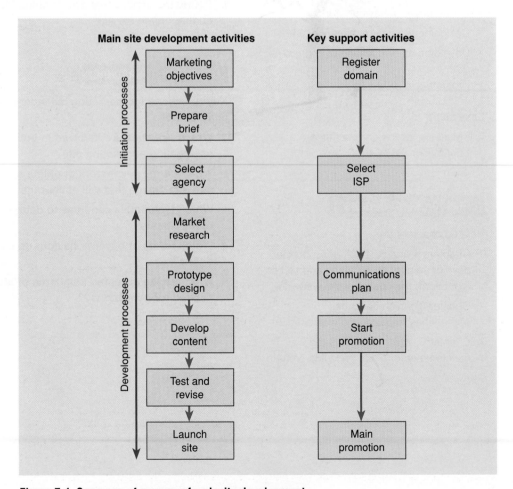

Figure 7.1 Summary of process of web site development

Service quality

Before examining the process for site and content development, we review the factors that affect the quality of service delivered by a site. Delivering service quality in e-commerce can be assessed through reviewing existing marketing frameworks for determining levels of service quality. Those most frequently used are based on the concept of a 'service-quality gap' that exists between the customer's expected level of service (from previous experience and word-of mouth communication) and their perception of the actual level of service delivery. We can apply the elements of service quality on which Parasuraman et al. (1985) suggest that consumers judge companies. Note that there has been heated dispute about the validity of this SERVQUAL instrument framework in determining service quality, see for example Cronin and Taylor (1992). Despite this it is still instructive to apply these dimensions of service quality to customer service on the web. They are:

- *reliability* – the ability to perform the service dependably and accurately;
- *responsiveness* – a willingness to help customers and provide prompt service;
- *assurance* – the knowledge and courtesy of employees and their ability to convey trust and confidence;
- *tangibles* – the physical appearance of facilities and communications;
- *empathy* – providing caring, individualised attention.

Online marketers should assess what customers' expectations are in each of these areas, and identify where there is an online service-quality gap between the customer expectations and what is currently delivered.

Online service-quality gap

The mismatch between what is expected and delivered by an online presence.

Research across industry sectors suggests that the quality of service is a key determinant of loyalty. Feinberg et al. (2000) report that when reasons why customers leave a company are considered, over 68% leave because of 'poor service experience', with other factors such as price (10%) and product issues (17%) less significant. Poor service experience was subdivided as follows:

- poor access to the right person (41%);
- unaccommodating (26%);
- rude employees (20%);
- slow to respond (13%).

This survey was conducted for traditional business contacts, but it is instructive since these reasons given for poor customer service have their equivalents online through e-mail communications and delivery of services on site.

We will now examine how the five determinants of online service quality apply online, based on the studies by Chaffey and Edgar (2000) and Kolesar and Galbraith (2000).

● Tangibles

It can be suggested that the tangibles dimension is influenced by ease of use and visual appeal based on the structural and graphic design of the site. Design factors that influence this variable are described later in this chapter. The importance customers attach to these different aspects of service quality is indicated by the compilation in Table 7.1 which considers the reasons why customers return to a site.

Table 7.1 Ten key reasons for returning to site

Reason to return	Percentage of respondents
1 High-quality content	75
2 Ease of use	66
3 Quick to download	58
4 Updated frequently	54
5 Coupons and incentives	14
6 Favourite brands	13
7 Cutting-edge technology	12
8 Games	12
9 Purchasing capabilities	11
10 Customisable content	10

Source: Forrester Research poll of 8600 online households, 1998

● Reliability

The reliability dimension is dependent on the availability of the web site or, in other words, how easy it is to connect to the web site as a user. Many companies fail to achieve 100% availability and potential customers may be lost for ever, if they attempt to use the site when it is unavailable (Table 7.1).

Reliability of e-mail response is also a key issue, Chaffey and Edgar (2000) report on a survey of 361 UK web sites across different sectors. Of those in the sample, 331 (or 92 per cent) were accessible at the time of the survey and, of these, 299 provided an e-mail contact point. E-mail enquiries were sent to all of these 299 web sites; of these nine undeliverable mail messages were received. It can be seen that at the time of the survey, service availability was certainly not universal. More recent surveys still indicate these types of problems.

● Responsiveness

The same survey showed that responsiveness was poor overall: of the 290 successfully delivered emails, a 62 per cent response rate occurred within a 28-day period. For over a third of companies there was zero response!

Of the companies that did respond, there was a difference in responsiveness (excluding immediately delivered automated responses) from 8 minutes to over 19 working days! Whilst the mean overall was 2 working days, 5 hours and 11 minutes, the median across all sectors (on the basis of the fastest 50 per cent of responses received) was 1 working day and 34 minutes. The median result suggests that response within one working day represents best practice and could form the basis for consumer expectations.

Responsiveness is also indicated by the performance of the web site: the time it takes for a page request to be delivered to the user's browser as a page impression. Data from monitoring services such as Keynote (www.keynote.com) indicate that there is a wide variability in the delivery of information and hence service quality from web servers hosted at ISPs, and companies should be careful to monitor this and specify levels of quality with suppliers in service level agreements (SLAs). Table 7.2 shows the standard set by the best-performing sites and the difference from the worst-performing site. Zona Research (1999) conducted an analysis that suggests that $4.35 billion may be lost in e-commerce revenues because of customer 'bailout' when customers are unwilling to wait for information to download. The report notes that many customers may not be prepared to wait longer than 8 seconds! Effective fulfilment is also an essential part of responsiveness.

Table 7.2 Variation in download performance and availability of top UK sites, February 2002

Site	Download performance (seconds)	Availability (%)
Yahoo	0.37	99.74
Go-Fly	0.47	99.68
BT	0.49	98.95
Iceland	0.59	99.74
easyJet	0.62	99.10
Worst	7.65	93.13

Source: www.keynote.com and Keynote Europe Ltd, Copyright © 2002 Keynote Systems, Inc., San Mateo, CA, The Internet Performance Authority®

● Assurance

In an e-mail context, assurance can best be considered as the quality of response. In the survey reported by Chaffey and Edgar (2000), of 180 responses received, 91 per cent delivered a personalised human response, with 9 per cent delivering an automated response which did not address the individual enquiry; 40 per cent of responses answered or referred to all three questions, with 10 per cent answering two questions and 22 per cent one. Overall, 38 per cent did not answer any of the specific questions posed!

A further assurance concern of e-commerce web sites is the privacy and security of customer information (see Chapter 3). A company that adheres to the UK Which? Web Trader (www.which.net/webtrader) or TRUSTe principles (www.truste.org) will provide better assurance than one that does not. Smith and Chaffey (2001) suggest that the following actions can be used to achieve assurance in an e-commerce site:

1 provide clear and effective privacy statements;
2 follow privacy and consumer protection guidelines in all local markets;
3 make security of customer data a priority;
4 use independent certification bodies;
5 emphasise the excellence of service quality in all communications.

● Empathy

Although it might be considered that empathy requires personal human contact, it can still be achieved, to an extent, through e-mail. Chaffey and Edgar (2000) report that of the responses received, 91 per cent delivered a personalised human response, with 29 per cent passing on the enquiry within their organisation. Of these 53, 23 further responses were received within the 28-day period: 30 (or 57 per cent) of passed-on queries were not responded to further.

Provision of personalisation facilities is also an indication of the empathy provided by the web site, but more research is needed as to customers perception of the value of web pages that are dynamically created to meet a customer's information needs.

An alternative framework for considering how service quality can be delivered through e-commerce is to consider how the site provides customer service at the different stages of the buying decision shown in Figure 7.9 below. Thus quality service is not only dependent on how well the purchase itself is facilitated, but also on how easy it is for customers to select products, and on after-sales service, including fulfilment quality. The Epson UK site (www.epson.co.uk) illustrates how the site can be used to help in all stages of the buying process. Interactive tools are available to help users select a particular printer, and diagnose and solve faults, and technical brochures can be downloaded. Feedback is solicited on how well these services meet customers' needs.

It can be suggested that for managers wishing to apply a framework such as SERVQUAL in an e-commerce context there are three stages appropriate to managing the process:

1 *Understanding expectations.* Customer expectations for the e-commerce environment in a particular market sector must be understood. The SERVQUAL framework can be used with market research and benchmarking of other sites to understand requirements such as responsiveness and empathy. Scenarios can also be used to identify the customer expectations of using services on a site.

2 *Setting and communicating the service promise.* Once expectations are understood, marketing communications can be used to inform the customers of the level of service. This can be achieved through customer service guarantees or promises. It is better to under-promise than over-promise. A book retailer that delivers the book in 2 days when 3 days were promised will earn the customer's loyalty better than the retailer who promises 1 day, but delivers in 2! The enlightened company may also explain what it will do if it doesn't meet its promises – will the customer be recompensed? The service promise must also be communicated internally and combined with training to ensure that the service is delivered.

3 *Delivering the service promise.* Finally, commitments must be delivered through on-site service, support from employees and physical fulfilment. Otherwise, online credibility is destroyed and a customer may never return.

Tables 7.3 and 7.4 summarise the main concerns of online consumers for each of the elements of service quality. Table 7.3 summarises the main factors in the

Table 7.3 Online elements of service quality

Tangibles	Reliability	Responsiveness	Assurance and empathy
• Ease of use	• Availability	• Download speed	• Contacts with call centre
• Content quality	• Reliability	• E-mail response	• Personalisation
• Price	• E-mail replies	• Callback	• Privacy
		• Fulfilment	• Security

Table 7.4 Summary of requirements for online service quality

E-mail response requirements	Web-site requirements
• Defined response times and named individual responsible for replies	• Support for customer-preferred channel of communication in response to enquiries (e-mail, phone, postal mail or in person)
• Use of autoresponders to confirm query is being processed	• Clearly indicated contact points for enquiries via e-mail mailto: and forms
• Personalised e-mail where appropriate	
• Accurate response to inbound e-mail by *customer-preferred channel*: outbound e-mail or phone callback	• Company internal targets for site availability and performance
	• Testing of site usability and efficiency of links, HTML, plug-ins and browsers to maximise availability
• Opt-in and opt-out options must be provided for promotional e-mail with a suitable offer in exchange for a customer's provision of information	• Appropriate graphic and structural site design to achieve ease of use and relevant content with visual appeal
	• Personalisation option for customers
• Clear layout, named individual and privacy statements in e-mail	• Specific tools to help a user answer specific queries such as interactive support databases and frequently asked questions (FAQ)

Source: Chaffey and Edgar (2000)

Service quality **263**

context of SERVQUAL and Table 7.4 presents the requirements from an e-commerce site that must be met for excellent customer service.

● The relationship between service quality, customer satisfaction and loyalty

Table 7.1 highlights the importance of online service quality. If customer expectations are not met, customer satisfaction will be poor and repeat site visits will not occur, which makes it difficult to build online relationships. Note, however, that online service quality is also dependent on other aspects of the service experience including the offline component of the service such as fulfilment and the core and extended product offer including pricing. If the customer experience is satisfactory, it can be suggested that customer loyalty will develop. The relationship between the drivers of customer satisfaction and loyalty is shown in Figure 7.2.

Reichheld and Schefter (2000) suggest that it is key for organisations to understand, not only what determines service quality and customer satisfaction, but loyalty or repeat purchases. From their research, they suggest five 'primary determinants of loyalty' online:

1 quality customer support;
2 on-time delivery;
3 compelling product presentations;
4 convenient and reasonably priced shipping and handling;
5 clear trustworthy privacy policies.

Figure 7.3 shows a more recent compilation of consumers' opinions of the importance of these loyalty drivers in the online context. It can be seen that it is the after-sales support and service which are considered to be most important – the ease of use and navigation are relatively unimportant.

Of course, the precise nature of the loyalty drivers will differ between companies. Reichheld and Schefter (2000) reported that Dell Computer has created a customer experience council that has researched key loyalty drivers, identified measures to

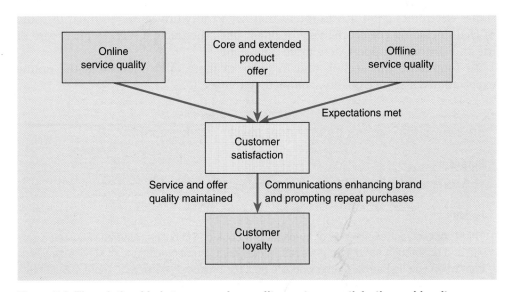

Figure 7.2 The relationship between service quality, customer satisfaction and loyalty

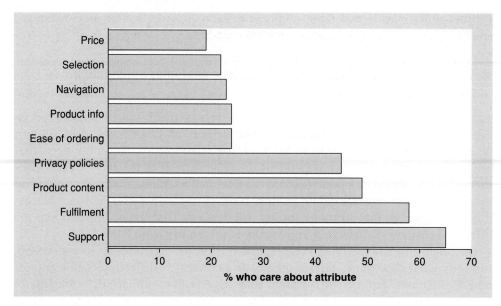

Figure 7.3 Customer ratings of importance of attributes of online experience
Source: J.P. Morgan report on e-tailing 2000

track these and put in place an action plan to improve loyalty. The loyalty drivers and their summary metrics were:

1 Driver: *order fulfilment*. Metrics: ship to target – percentage that ship on time exactly as the customer specified.
2 Driver: *product performance*. Metrics: initial field incident rate – the frequency of problems experienced by customers.
3 Driver: *post-sale service and support*. Metrics: on-time, first-time fix – the percentage of problems fixed on the first visit by a service rep who arrives at the time promised.

Rigby et al. (2000) assessed repeat-purchase drivers in grocery, clothing and consumer electronics e-tail. It was found that key loyalty drivers were similar to those of Dell, including correct delivery of order, but other factors such as price, ease of use and customer support were more important.

To summarise this section and in order to more fully understand the online expectations of service quality, complete Activity 7.1.

Activity 7.1

An example of factors determining online service quality

Purpose

To understand the elements of online service quality.

Activity

Think back to your experience of purchasing a book or CD online. Alternatively, visit a site and go through the different stages. Write down your expectations of service quality from when you first arrive on the web site until the product is delivered. There should be around ten different stages.

Planning web site development

It is a natural mistake amongst those creating a new web site for the first time to 'dive in' and start creating web pages without forward planning. Planning is necessary since design of a site must occur before creation of web pages – to ensure a good-quality site that does not need reworking at a later stage. Design involves analysing the needs of owners and users of a site and then deciding upon the best way to build the site to fulfil these needs. Without a structured plan and careful design, costly reworking is inevitable, as the first version of a site will not achieve the needs of the end-users or the business.

Conversely, it can be argued that not too much time should be spent on design and planning since web sites constantly evolve. Experience of developing information systems for marketing and other applications has shown that an approach that involves too much up-front planning, analysis and design before development is started does not usually work well (Bocij et al., 2003). The reason for this is that there may be a delay of several months between the time the users are involved in discussing their needs from a system and the time they start to use the software. Over this time, the needs of the users, or the business itself, may have changed as market forces dictate. Additionally, when using the 'finished' system, the users may become aware of the need for features that were not originally envisaged, or there may be many errors or 'bugs' in the software. The risk of encountering these types of problems can be reduced using the prototyping approach which is described in the next section.

The process of web site development summarised in Figure 7.1 is idealised, since for efficiency many of these activities have to occur in parallel. Figure 7.4 gives an indication of the relationship between these tasks, and how long they may take, for a typical initial web site. The content planning and development stages overlap in that HTML and graphics development are necessary to produce the prototypes. As a consequence, some development has to occur while analysis and design are under way. The main development tasks which need to be scheduled as part of the planning process are as follows:

1 *Pre-development tasks*. These include domain name registration and deciding on the company (ISP) to host the web site. They also include preparing a brief setting out the aims and objectives of the site, and then – if it is intended to outsource the site – presenting the brief to rival companies to bid and pitch their offering.
2 *Content planning*. This is the detailed analysis and design of the site, and includes market research and prototyping.
3 *Content development and testing*. Writing the HTML pages, producing the graphics and testing.
4 *Publishing or launching the site*. This is a relatively short stage.
5 *Pre-launch promotion or communications*. Search engine registration or optimisation is most important. This could include ensuring that all new stationery and advertising material show the web address. This stage will also include specific advertising for the web site using either banner advertisements or traditional advertisements. Briefing the PR company to publicise the launch is another source of promotion.
6 *Ongoing promotion*. The schedule should also allow for periodic promotion. This might involve discount promotions on the site or competitions. These are often reused each month. Many now consider search engine optimisation as a continuous process, and will employ a third party to help achieve this.

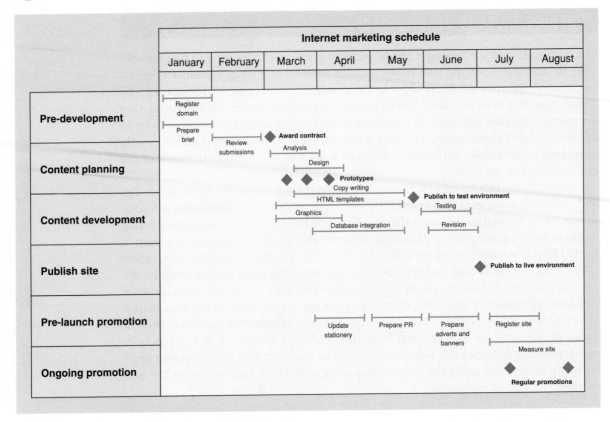

Figure 7.4 Example of web site development schedule

● Web site prototyping

Prototype

A preliminary version of
part or a framework of all
of a web site, which can
be reviewed by its target
audience or the marketing
team. Prototyping is an
iterative process in which
web site users suggest
modifications before
further prototypes and
the final version of the
site are developed.

Prototypes are initial versions of a web site that contain the basic features and structure of the web site, but without all the content in place. The idea is that the agency or development team and the marketing staff who commissioned the work can review and comment on the prototype, and changes can then be made to the site to incorporate these comments. A further version or iteration of the web site can be made and that too can be commented on. During prototyping, the prototype web pages are viewable only by staff inside the company – this is known as the test *environment*. This repeating or iterative approach is shown in Figure 7.5.

The stages involved in developing the prototype are described in more detail later in this chapter. In brief, they involve the following:

1 *Analysis.* Understanding the requirements of the audience of the site and the requirements of the business, defined by business and marketing strategy.
2 *Design.* Specifying different features of the site that will fulfil the requirements of the users and the business as identified during analysis.
3 *Development.* The creation of the web pages and the dynamic content of the web site.
4 *Testing and review.* Structured checks are conducted to ensure that different aspects of the site meet the original requirements and work correctly.

These are the four stages that are repeated during prototyping. There are also additional stages that occur at the start and end of the project and which are 'wrapped around' the prototyping effort (shown in Figure 7.1). There is an initial initiation

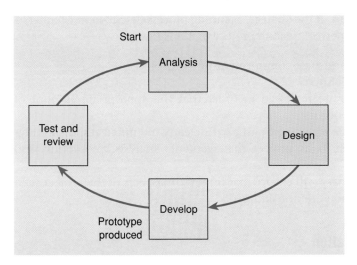

Figure 7.5 Four stages of web site prototyping

stage, where the feasibility of producing the web site is reviewed. After the prototype has been developed to the point where it can be made available to its audience, it is published on the Web in a live environment. A separate promotion activity also occurs during prototyping and when the site is completed.

The prototyping approach has the following benefits:

1 It prevents major design or functional errors being made during the construction of the web site. Such errors could be costly and time-consuming to fix once the web site becomes live and could also damage the brand. Such errors will hopefully be identified early on and then corrected.
2 It involves the marketers responsible for the web site and ideally the potential audience of the web site in proactively shaping the web site. This should result in a site that more closely meets the needs of the users.
3 The iterative approach is intended to be rapid, and a site can be produced in a period of months or weeks.

When using the prototyping approach for a web site, a company has to decide whether to implement the complete version of the web site before making it available to its target audience (hard launch) or to make available a more limited version of the site (soft launch). If it is necessary to establish a presence rapidly, the second approach could be used. This also has the benefit that feedback can be solicited from users and incorporated into later versions. Many companies will, however, prefer the security of the first approach in which the web site can be revised and market-tested before a professional and complete version of the site is made available. This approach is less likely to cause damage to the brand or corporate image. It will still be possible for the company to make subsequent changes to the site based on feedback from users.

Initiation of the web site project

Before the analysis, design and creation of the web site, all major projects will have an initial phase in which the aims and objectives of the web site are reviewed, to assess whether it is worthwhile investing in the web site, and to decide on the

Hard launch

A site is launched once fully complete with full promotional effort.

Soft launch

A trial version of a site is launched with limited publicity.

Initiation of web site project

The phase of the project that involves a structured review of the costs and benefits of developing a web site (or making a major revision to an existing web site). A successful outcome to initiation will be a decision to proceed with the site development with an agreed budget and target completion date.

amount to invest. This is part of the strategic planning process described in Chapters 4 and 5. This provides a framework for the project that ensures:

(a) there is management and staff commitment to the project;

(b) objectives are clearly defined;

(c) the costs and benefits are reviewed in order that the appropriate amount of investment in the site occurs;

(d) the project will follow a structured path, with clearly identified responsibilities for different aspects such as project management, analysis, promotion and maintenance;

(e) the implementation phase will ensure that important aspects of the project such as testing and promotion are not skimped.

● Domain name registration

Domain name registration

The process of reserving a unique web address that can be used to refer to the company web site, in the form of www.<company-name>.com or www.<company-name>.co.uk.

If the project involves a new site rather than an upgrade, it will be necessary to register a new domain name, more usually referred to as a web address or uniform resource locator (URL).

Domain names are registered using an ISP or direct with one of the domain name services, such as:

1 *InterNIC* (www.internic.net). Registration for the .com, .org and .net domains.

2 *Nominet* (www.nominet.org.uk). Registration for the .co.uk domain. All country-specific domains such as .fr (France) or .de (Germany) have their own domain registration authority.

3 *Nomination* (www.nomination.uk.com). An alternative registration service for the UK, allowing registration in the (uk.com) pseudo-domain.

The following guidelines should be borne in mind when registering domain names:

1 *Register the domain name as early as possible*. This is necessary since the precedent in the emerging law is that the first company to register the name is the one that takes ownership if it has a valid claim to ownership.

2 *Register multiple domain names* if this helps the potential audience to find the site. For example, British Midland may register its name as www.britishmidland.com and www.britishmidland.co.uk.

3 *Use the potential of non-company brand names* to help promote a product. For example, a 1998 traditional media campaign for British Midland used www.iflybritishmidland.com as a memorable address to help users find its site.

● Selecting an internet service provider (ISP)

Internet service provider (ISP)

Company that provides home or business users with a connection to access the Internet. It can also host web sites or provide a link from web servers to allow other companies and consumers access to a corporate web site.

Selecting the right partner to host a web site is an important decision since the quality of service provided will directly impact on the quality of service delivered to a company's customers. The partner that hosts the content will usually be an Internet service provider (or ISP) for the majority of small and medium companies, but for larger companies the web server used to host the content may be inside the company and managed by the company's IT department.

The quality of service of hosted content is essentially dependent on two factors: the performance of the web site and its availability.

The performance of the web site

The important measure in relation to performance is the speed with which a web page is delivered to users from the time when it is requested by clicking on a hyperlink (see Table 7.2 for examples). The length of time is dependent on a number of factors, some of which cannot be controlled (such as the number of users accessing the Internet), but primarily depends on the bandwidth of the ISP's connection to the Internet and the performance of the web server hardware and software.

Bandwidth gives an indication of the speed at which data can be transferred from a web server along a particular medium such as a network cable. In simple terms bandwidth can be thought of as the size of a pipe along which information flows. The higher the bandwidth, the greater the diameter of the pipe, and the faster information is delivered to the user. Bandwidth is measured in bits per second, where one character or digit, such as the number '1', would be equivalent to 8 bits. When selecting an ISP it is important to consider the speed of the link between the ISP and the Internet. Choices may be:

- ISDN – from 56 kbps to 128 kbps;
- Frame Relay – from 56 kbps to T1 (1.55 Mbps);
- Dedicated Point-to-Point – from 56 kbps to T3 (45 Mbps): connected to the Internet backbone.

Some ISPs are not connected directly to the Internet backbone and are linked to it via other providers. Their service will be slower than that of servers directly connected to the main Internet backbone since information has to 'jump' several different network links.

Bandwidth

The speed at which data are transferred using particular network media. Bandwidth is measured in bits per second (bps).

- Kbps (1 kilobit per second or 1000 bps – a modem operates at up to 56.6 kbps).
- Mbps (1 megabit per second or 1 000 000 bps – company networks operate at 10 or more Mbps).
- Gbps (1 gigabit per second or 1 000 000 000 bps – fibre-optic or satellite links operate at Gbps).

The speed of the site will also be affected by the speed of the response to a request by an end-user for information. The type of web server software will not greatly affect the speed at which queries are answered, but the factors that will are the amount of memory (RAM) installed in the server, the speed of retrieving data from the hard disk, and the speed of the processors. Many of the search engines now store all their index data in RAM since this is faster than reading data from the hard disk.

A major factor for a company to consider when choosing an ISP is whether the server is *dedicated* to one company or whether content from several companies is located on the same server. A dedicated server is best, but it will attract a premium price.

The availability of the web site

The availability of a web site is an indication of how easy it is for a user to connect to it. In theory this figure should be 100 per cent, but sometimes, for technical reasons such as failures in the server hardware or upgrades to software, the figure can drop substantially below this (see Table 7.2).

● Who is involved in a web site project?

The success of a web site will be heavily dependent on the range of people involved in its development, and how well they work as a team. As a result, the feasibility study will define how the project should be structured and what the different responsibilities will be. Typical profiles of team members follow:

- *Site sponsors*. These will be senior managers who will effectively be paying for the system. They will understand the strategic benefits of the system and will be keen that the site is implemented successfully to achieve the objectives they have set. Sponsors will also aim to encourage staff by means of their own enthusiasm and will stress why the introduction of the system is important to the business and its workers. This will help overcome any barriers to introduction of the web site.
- *Site owner*. 'Ownership' will typically be the responsibility of a marketing manager, who may be devoted full-time to overseeing the site in a large company; it may be part of a marketing manager's remit in a smaller company. The site owner is effectively the customer of the project manager for a web site in a larger company.
- *Project manager*. This person is responsible for the planning and coordination of the web site project. He or she will aim to ensure the site is developed within the budget and time constraints that have been agreed at the start of the project, and that the site delivers the planned-for benefits for the company and its customers. In smaller companies, the project manager may be the same person as the site owner.
- *Site designer*. The site designer will define the 'look and feel' of the site, including its layout and how company brand values are transferred to the web. Further details are given later in the chapter in the section on designing site content.
- *Content developer*. The content developer will write the copy for the web site and convert it to a form suitable for the site. In medium or large companies this role may be split between marketing staff or staff from elsewhere in the organisation who write the copy and a technical member of staff who converts it to the graphics and HTML documents forming the web page and does the programming for interactive content.
- *Webmaster*. This is a technical role. The webmaster is responsible for ensuring the quality of the site. This means achieving suitable availability, speed, working links between pages and connections to company databases. In small companies the webmaster may take on graphic design and content developer roles also.
- *Stakeholders*. The impact of the web site on other members of the organisation should not be underestimated. Internal staff may need to refer to some of the information on the web site or use its services.

While the site sponsor and site owner will work within the company, many organisations outsource the other resources since full-time staff cannot be justified in these roles. There are a range of different choices for outsourcing which are summarised in Activity 7.2.

Options for outsourcing different e-marketing activities

Purpose

To highlight the outsourcing available for e-business implementation and to gain an appreciation of how to choose suppliers.

Table 7.5 Options for outsourcing different e-business activities

E-marketing function	Traditional marketing agency	New media agency	ISP or traditional IT supplier	Management consultants
1. Strategy				✓
2. Design		✓		
3. Content and service development		✓		
4. Online promotion		✓		
5. Offline promotion	✓			
6. Infrastructure			✓	

Activity

A B2C company is trying to decide which of its e-business activities it should outsource. Select a single supplier that you think can best deliver each of these services indicated in Table 7.5. Justify your decision.

We are seeing a gradual blurring between these types of supplier as they recruit expertise so as to deliver a 'one-stop shop' service, but they still tend to be strongest in particular areas. Companies need to decide whether to partner with the best of breed in each, or to compromise and choose the one-stop shop that gives the best balance – this would arguably be the new media agency or perhaps a traditional marketing agency that has an established new media division. Which approach do you think is best?

Observation of the practice of outsourcing suggests that two conflicting patterns are evident:

1 *Outside-in.* A company starts an e-business initiative by outsourcing some activities where there is insufficient in-house expertise. These may be areas such as strategy or online promotion. The company then builds up skills internally to manage these areas as e-business becomes an important contributor to the business. The company initially partnered with a new media agency to offer online services, but once the online contribution to sales exceeded 20% the management of e-commerce was taken inside. The new media agency was, however, retained for strategy guidance. An outside-in approach will probably be driven by the need to reduce the costs of outsourcing, poor delivery of services by the supplier or simply a need to concentrate a strategic core resource in-house.

2 *Inside-out.* A company starts to implement e-business using existing resources within the IT department and marketing department in conjunction with recruitment of new media staff. They may then find that there are problems in developing a site that meets customers' needs or in building traffic to the site. At this point they may turn to outsourcing to solve the problems.

These approaches are not mutually exclusive, and an outside-in approach may be used for some e-commerce functions such as content development while an inside-out approach is used for other functions such as site promotion. It can also be suggested that these approaches are not planned – they are simply a response to prevailing conditions. However, in order to cost e-business and manage it as a strategic asset it can be argued that the e-business manager should have a long-term picture of which functions to outsource and when to bring them in-house.

Researching site users' requirements

Analysis phase

Analysis refers to the identification of the requirements of a web site. Techniques to achieve this may include focus groups, question-naires sent to existing customers or interviews to key accounts.

Analysis involves using different marketing research techniques to find out the needs of the site audience. These needs can then be used to drive the design and content of the web site.

It is not a 'one-off' exercise, but is likely to be repeated for each iteration of the prototype. Although analysis and design are separate activities, there tends to be considerable overlap between the two phases. In analysis we are seeking to answer the following types of questions:

- What are the key audiences for the site?
- What should the content of site be?
- Which customer service capabilities will we provide for customers?
- How will the site be structured?
- How will navigation around the site occur?

These questions will not be answered in relation to site structure and navigation until after we have looked at site design and assessed different alternatives. We will consider these issues in the section on design. In this section we will consider briefly how to collect information about the needs of users of the site.

● Methods of finding customer needs

There are a range of different market research methods for identifying customer needs – these are described in more detail in the following chapter. For pre-launch testing the focus group is one of the most common approaches. This can take two forms. First, a traditional concept-testing focus group can explore views about the proposition and positioning of the site. **Storyboards** may be used to discuss different alternatives. Secondly, a usability focus group can be used to assess the prototype. Here each member of the group is given a PC and is asked to follow certain **scenarios of use** such as finding product information, making a purchase or gaining product information. After the scenarios have been completed, experiences can then be discussed in the group.

Storyboard

An outline of the web page design either on paper or on screen.

Scenario of use

A particular path or flow of events or activities performed by a visitor to a web site.

Seybold (2001) also recommends using scenario-based design. She examines the example of how grocery retailer Tesco.com combined both online and offline activity for its online customers. She also give the example of Buzzsaw.com, a B2B service for construction projects where the high-level customer scenario which must be delivered by the web site is:

1 Set project scope, schedule and budget.
2 Gain financial backing.
3 Recruit the team.
4 Develop the design.

5 Produce the plans and specifications.
6 Manage the bidding and negotiations.
7 Manage the construction process.
8 Manage the facility.

In supporting this scenario, the web service also has to support a wide range of participants including the construction manager, architects, engineers and subcontractors.

When conducting focus groups, it is important to use a representative range of users. Analysts need to take into account variations in the backgrounds of visitors to the site. These can be thought of as four different types of familiarity:

1 *Familiarity with the Net.* Are short cuts provided for those familiar with the Net and for novices to help lead them through your site? Research by Netpoll in focus groups suggests that users pass through different stages of familiarity and confidence (see Figure 2.18). Site design should try to accommodate this. Jakob Nielsen (2000a) says this about novice users:

> *Web users are notoriously fickle: they take one look at a home page and leave after a few seconds if they can't figure it out. The abundance of choice and the ease of going elsewhere puts a huge premium on making it extremely easy to enter a site.*

But he notes that we also need to take account of experts. He says we may eventually move to interfaces where the average site visitor gets a simplified design that is easy to learn and loyal users get an advanced design that is more powerful. But for now *'in-depth content and advanced information should be added to sites to provide the depth expected by experts'*.

2 *Familiarity with organisation.* For customers who don't know an organisation, content is needed to explain who the company is and demonstrate credibility through 'About Us' options and customer testimonials.

3 *Familiarity with organisations' products.* Even existing customers may not know the full range of your product offering.

4 *Familiarity with your site.* Customers will be at different stages in adopting the web site (Breitenbach and van Doren, 1998): that is, they may be novices who need guidance or they may be experienced users who need short cuts to be productive. Site maps and Search and Help options are not 'nice-to-have' options for an e-commerce site since you may lose potential customers if they cannot be helped when they are lost.

Different types of online buyer behaviour should also be taken into account when conducting the analysis for a web site. In Chapter 2, different behaviour types such as directed information-seekers and undirected information-seekers (browsers) were identified. For the former group a search facility may be useful on the site, whereas a less formal approach will suit the browsers.

● Customer orientation

Customer orientation is one of the most important factors in achieving a successful web site. Analyst Patricia Seybold considers it sufficiently important that she has structured a whole book, *Customers.com* (Seybold, 1999), around the concept. Seybold (1999) offers eight guidelines for implementing an Internet strategy (available at Patricia Seybold Consulting (www.customers.com). She considers the first, and most important, to be to 'target the right customer'. What constitutes the 'right customer' will vary for different companies operating in different sectors, but some general principles can be established. First, some companies make the mistake of omitting some important types of site visitor. Table 7.6 summarises the different types of customers, staff or third parties that may visit a web site for information. For a web site to be effective, it should cater for all the different types of audience.

Customer orientation
Content and services on the web site are tailored for different audience types and customer segments.

Activity 7.3	Applying Patricia Seybold's Customers.com approach to customer orientation

Purpose

To highlight how the principles of customer orientation of services offered can be applied to site design.

Activity

Read the extract of the eight success factors outlined by US industry analyst Patricia Seybold in her book, *Customers.com* (Seybold, 1999). Explain how each of these could be applied to a B2B customer-oriented site of your choice.

The eight critical success factors she suggests are:

1 *Target the right customers*. This first, and most important, principle suggests concentrating on either the most profitable customers, which is one of the tenets of CRM (Chapter 6), or those that cannot be reached so well by other media. For example, UK car insurer Swinton wished to target the young-driver market so it trialled a web site with a special 'Streetwise' brand. Alternatively the right customers in the business-to-business context could be those who make the buying decisions. For management consultants such as those featured in the activity 'Tailoring the content for appropriate members of the buying decision' the web sites are aimed principally at the senior managers in the organisation.

2 *Own the customer's total experience*. By managing the customer's entire experience it should be possible to increase the quality of service and hence promote loyalty. The total experience can be considered as all parts of the fulfilment cycle from product selection, purchase, delivery, setup or installation and after-sales services. Examples of how the Internet can be used to improve the customer experience taken from across this cycle are provided in the final section of this chapter. Note that since many services such as delivery are now outsourced, this requires careful selection of partners to deliver this quality service.

3 *Streamline business processes that impact the customer*. Seybold (1999) gives the example of Federal Express as a company that has used the Internet to re-engineer the service it delivers to customers – ordering, tracking and payment are now all available from the Fedex web site. For a financial services company such as Eagle Star selling insurance via the web, streamlining the process has meant asking underwriters to reduce the complexity of the questions that are asked before a premium is calculated.

4 *Provide a 360-degree view of the customer relationship*. This means that different parts of the company must have similar information about the customer to provide a consistent service. It implies integration of the personalisation facilities of a web site with other databases holding information about the customer. If these databases are not integrated then customer trust may be lost. If, for example, the web site offers a customer a product they have already purchased offline it will appear that the company does not understand their needs. Integration of call centres with a web site are also an implication of this guideline.

5 *Let customers help themselves*. This has the benefit of reducing costs, while at the same time providing faster, more efficient customer service.

6 *Help customers do their jobs*. This guideline is similar to the previous one, but focuses more on providing them with the *information* needed to do their jobs. This is again a useful value-added facility of the web site which helps encourage loyalty.

7 *Deliver personalised service*. The importance of delivering personalised service to build a one-to-one relationship with the customer formed the basis for Chapter 6.

8 *Foster community*. Business web sites afford good opportunities to create communities of interest since information can be generated which helps customers in their work and again encourages returns to the web site. Independent business community sites are also important places for companies to have representation.

Table 7.6 Different potential audiences for a web site

Customers vary by	Staff	Third parties
New or existing prospects	New or existing	New or existing
Size of prospect companies (e.g. small, medium or large)	Different departments	Suppliers
Market type (e.g. different vertical markets)	Sales staff for different markets	Distributors
Location (by country)		Investors
Members of buying process (decision makers, influencers, buyers)	Location (by country)	Media
		Students

Although Activity 7.3 has suggested that it is useful to provide content suited to the breadth of a site's audience, Seybold's assertion is that the effort of developing content should not be equally distributed.

Localisation

A specific aspect of customer orientation or segmentation is the decision whether to include specific content for particular countries. This is referred to as localisation. A site may need to support customers from a range of countries with:

Localisation
Tailoring of web site information for individual countries.

- different product needs;
- language differences;
- cultural differences.

Localisation will address all these issues. It may be that products will be similar in different countries and localisation will simply involve converting the web site to suit another country. However, in order to be effective, this often needs more than translation, since different promotion concepts may be needed for different countries. Examples of a business-to-consumer site (Durex) and a business-to-business site (Gestetner) are featured in Activity 7.4. Note that each company prioritises different countries according to the size of the market, and this priority then governs the amount of work it puts into localisation.

Reviewing competitors' web sites

Benchmarking of competitors' web sites is vital in positioning your web site to compete effectively with competitors who already have web sites. Given the importance of this activity, criteria for performing benchmarking have been described in Chapters 2 and 5.

Benchmarking should not only be based on the obvious tangible features of a web site such as its ease of use and the impact of its design. Benchmarking criteria should include those that define the companies' marketing performance in the industry and those that are specific to web marketing as follows:

- *Financial performance* (available from About Us, investor relations and electronic copies of company reports). This information is also available from intermediary sites such as finance information or share dealing sites such as Interactive Trader International (www.iii.com) or Bloomberg (www.bloomberg.com) for major quoted companies.
- *Marketplace performance* – market share and sales trends and, significantly, the proportion of sales achieved through the Internet. This may not be available directly on the web site, but may need the use of other online sources. For example,

Accommodating international markets using localisation

Web

Visit one international consumer site such as Durex (www.durex.com) – *see* Figure 7.6 – and one business-to-business site such as Gestetner (www.gestetner.com). Review the information for a range of five countries from each site and evaluate the extent to which changes have been made to the type of information available.

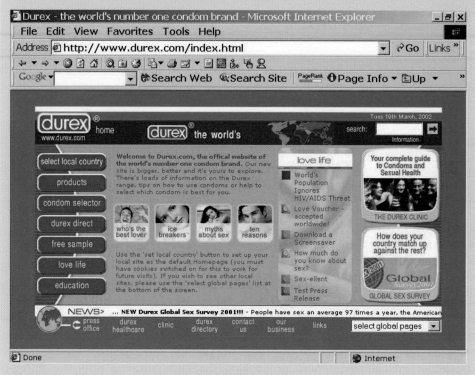

Figure 7.6 Durex.com, a site with an international flavour

new entrant to European aviation easyJet (www.easyjet.com) achieved over two-thirds of its sales via the web site and competitors needed to respond to this.

- *Business and revenue models (see Chapter 6)* – do these differ from other marketplace players?
- *Marketing communications techniques* – is the customer value proposition of the site clear? Does the site support all stages of the buying decision from customers who are unfamiliar with the company through to existing customers? Are special promotions used on a monthly or periodic basic? Beyond the competitor's site, how do they make use of intermediary sites to promote and deliver their services?
- *Services offered* – what is offered beyond brochureware? Is online purchase possible? What is the level of online customer support and how much technical information is available?
- *Implementation of services* – these are the practical features of site design that are described in this chapter, such as aesthetics, ease of use, personalisation, navigation, availability and speed.

A review of corporate web sites suggests that, for most companies, the type of information that can be included on a web site will be fairly similar. The box, 'A web site marketing communications checklist' suggests the type of information that should appear on the web site.

Many commentators such as Sterne (1999) make the point that some sites miss out the basic information that someone who is unfamiliar with a company may want to know, such as:

- Who are you? 'About Us' is now a standard menu option.
- What do you do? What products or services are available?
- Where do you do it? Are the products and services available internationally?

A web site marketing communications checklist

About the company

- ☐ History
- ☐ Contacts
- ☐ Office locations – addresses and maps
- ☐ Company annual reports (investor information)
- ☐ Financial performance (investor information)

Products and services

- ☐ Catalogue of products, prices?
- ☐ Online sales from product
- ☐ Current stock levels and delivery times
- ☐ Detailed technical specifications
- ☐ Customer testimonials and client list
- ☐ White papers
- ☐ Press releases
- ☐ Special offers
- ☐ Demonstrations
- ☐ Where to obtain them

(Consistent marketing message and branding applied throughout.)

Customer services

- ☐ Product returns
- ☐ Electronic help desk
- ☐ Frequently asked questions

Events

- ☐ Seminars
- ☐ Exhibitions
- ☐ Training

General information

- ☐ Contact us
- ☐ What's New or Media Centre (for PR)
- ☐ Job vacancies
- ☐ Index or site map
- ☐ Search
- ☐ Links to related sites

● Designing the information architecture

The information architecture describes how information is stored on the web site and how it is accessed by visitors. These are some observations. First, the information should be structured so that it can be accessed by different types of users without the need for duplication. Users with intranet, extranet and Internet facilities should all be able to gain access. Take the example of a computer supplier. Staff will need to answer many questions by phone from customers enquiring about product specifications and prices, and will need to provide support to customers who have purchased products and are experiencing difficulties. Information on these topics is likely to be available to staff on an intranet in order that they can answer the

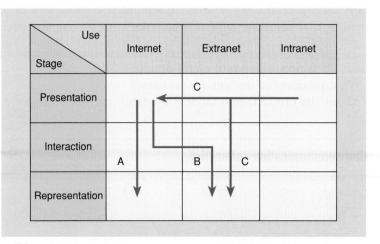

Figure 7.7 Options for developing different types of IP-based service
Source: Bickerton et al. (1998)

queries. It is logical to review this information for its relevance to customers and then make it available on the Internet web site. Why develop two customer support systems when one can be used by both staff and customers? Similarly, there will be an internal stock ordering system which will be linked with a manufacturing system for controlling the status of new machines being built, and the data may well be available through an intranet. Again, much of the information on the intranet may be of value to customers, and in particular to large corporate accounts which need to monitor the status and cost of their orders. In this case, why not make the information available to them as an extranet? This is precisely what Dell has done with its PremierPages service, which is available for large corporate customers.

We will now review two models which can help companies discuss their options for integrating the Internet web site information with intranets and extranets. Figure 7.7 shows the model of Bickerton et al. (1998). In order to understand this model, it is necessary to recognise three different levels of use of a web site, as defined in the book. These are similar to the increasing levels of sophistication of Quelch and Klein (1996) which were introduced in Chapter 5. The levels are as follows:

- *Presentation*. This is the delivery of static information on the web site. It can be thought of as a 'brochureware' site, but may have additional depth of information.
- *Interaction*. This stage involves methods of communicating with the customer such as the use of interactive forms and e-mail or discussion communities.
- *Representation*. Representation occurs where the Internet replaces customer's services that are normally delivered by human operators. In the case of a bank this stage would involve a customer's performing online money transfers between bank accounts or bill payment. IBM has referred to this concept as 'web self-service'.

The grid in Figure 7.7 shows three alternative strategies that a company could adopt. These strategies are more easily understandable and can be readily discussed through presentation in this form. Strategy A is that adopted by many small companies. They have a web site, which is initially an online brochure (presentation stage). The marketing plan may then indicate that, 6 months from launch, interaction facilities may be introduced, such as forms to give feedback on products. Finally, it may be planned that the site will be relaunched some 18 months to 2 years after

Table 7.7 Information and services mapping for the B2B company

Stage	Intranet (employees only)	Extranet (favoured partners)	Internet (public)
Presentation	Market research Contacts Sales reports	Technical information sheet Product/pricing information for agents	Company info Product info
Interaction	Access to sales rep reports on company visits Data mining E-mail briefings to staff	Key account user group Order filing	Product availability queries E-mail-based customer service
Representation	Online holiday and claims form submission and processing	Transactional e-commerce on buy-side and sell-side	Transactional e-commerce

inception and representation facilities will be included, such as online sales and customer service. Strategy B is one that is typically followed by larger companies. They may follow the initial stages of presentation and interaction, but will only provide their representation facilities to their largest customers. If an extranet is offered, with special login required, then this can be used to differentiate the service provided to favoured companies. This is the approach used by HR Johnson Tiles (www.johnson-tiles.com). They offer an extranet buying service that is only available to their larger customers. When the site was launched, they targeted 20 distributors with whom they wanted to do business over the Internet. So far, 12 have been persuaded to do that, resulting in £1 million in orders from the web site annually. A key feature of this extranet system is 'StockWatch': by clicking on this button customers get a picture of the amount of stock available for the items they regularly order. Finally, strategy C may occur where a company has a great deal of information that is available on the internal company network, and which can be usefully made available to customers, either select customers via the extranet or a wider audience. Strategy C might be one adopted by a technology company such as Dell. Note that the strategy adopted by any single company could involve elements of A, B and C.

The model of Bickerton et al. (1999) can be used to assess the different content and services offered to different audiences of a web site using intranets, extranets and the Internet. Using the model's three layers we can map content across different access levels to produce a site that is integrated with the needs of its audiences (Table 7.7). This also relates to the section on security since different access levels may be give for different information.

Figure 7.8 depicts an alternative model, derived from Friedman and Furey (1999), for comparing the role of open-access, Internet-based information with restricted extranet information. This model is best applied in a business-to-business context. It considers the different types of products a company sells, from lower-cost standardised products through to higher-cost customised products. These products are then considered in relation to the different sizes of company a company may serve. The core content of the site may appeal to smaller customers, which are perhaps unaware of the company or its products. This information will be provided by the Internet. At the other end of the spectrum, for key accounts which buy the full range of a company's products, an extranet may be appropriate. This is again the case with Dell's PremierPages and is similar to path B, shown in the figure.

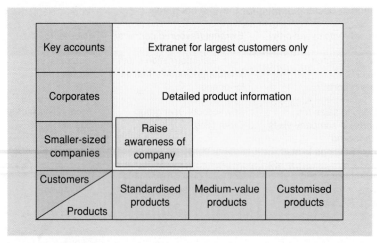

Figure 7.8 A matrix for segmenting customer information on the Internet according to size of customer

Source: Friedman and Furey (1999)

Online buyer behaviour

Insights into the different ways in which consumers use the Internet are provided by Table 7.8. It is apparent that using the Internet to inform buying decisions is the most common activity – almost twice as common as purchasing online. It is now estimated that over half of consumers purchasing a new car online will research it using the Internet, although the number actually purchasing online is very small. Clearly investment in Internet marketing is very important for the car manufacturers in order to persuade consumers of the features and benefits of their brands. So, the most significant point for marketers is that the Internet is significant in influencing purchases, particularly for high-involvement products. The popularity of e-mail use and general browsing show that socialising and entertainment are also common activities and suggests that FMCG brands can also use the Internet to reach their customers through supporting these activities.

Table 7.8 Internet usage activities in the UK

Note – respondents may give more than one answer

Finding information about goods and services	74
Using e-mail	71
General browsing or surfing	57
Finding information related to education	35
Buying or ordering tickets/goods/services	35
Personal banking, financial activities	27
Looking for work	21
Downloading software, including games	23
Using chat rooms/sites	18
Playing or downloading music	19
Accessing government services	19
Other	4

Source: National Statistics, 2001

The amount of Internet usage also appears to increase with familiarity. BMRB (2001) reports that those using the Internet for more than 2 years spent an average of 20 hours online per month. This compares to 14 hours for those who had been using the Internet for less than 2 years.

● Models of online buyer behaviour

Standard models of consumer buyer behaviour have been developed by Bettman (1979) and Booms and Bitner (1981). In these models, consumers process marketing stimuli such as the 4 Ps and environmental stimuli according to their personal characteristics such as their culture, social group and personal and psychological make-up. Together these characteristics will affect the consumers' response to marketing messages. For the Internet marketer, a review of the factors influencing behaviour is especially important since a single web site may need to accommodate consumers from different cultures and social backgrounds. Users will also have different levels of experience of using the Web.

Specific behavioural traits are evident on the Internet. Studies show that the World Wide Web is used quite differently by different groups of people. Lewis and Lewis (1997) identified five different types of web users:

- *Directed information-seekers*. These users will be looking for product, market or leisure information such as details of their football club's fixtures. This type of user tends to be experienced in using the Web and to be proficient in using search engines and directories. The GVU World Wide Web surveys (www.gvu.gatech.edu) indicate that more experienced users have a more focused way of using the Internet.
- *Undirected information-seekers*. These are the users, usually referred to as 'surfers', who like to browse and change sites by following hyperlinks. Members of this group tend to be novice users (but not exclusively so) and they may be more likely to click on banner advertisements.
- *Directed buyers*. These buyers are online to purchase specific products. For such users, brokers or cybermediaries that compare product features and prices will be important locations to visit.
- *Bargain hunters*. These users want to find the offers available from sales promotions such as free samples or prizes. For example, the Cybergold site (www.cybergold.com) pays users a small amount to read targeted advertising.
- *Entertainment seekers*. These are users looking to interact with the Web for enjoyment through entering contests such as quizzes (e.g. 'You Don't know Jack' at Won.net (www.won.net and www.bezerk.com)), puzzles or interactive multi-player games.

Styler (2001) describes four consumer buying behaviours derived from in-depth home interviews researching behaviour across a range of media, including the Internet. These behaviours are brand-focused, price-sensitive, feature-savvy and advice-led.

A more sophisticated, but similar, typology for online behaviour has been proposed by Kothari et al. (2001). They suggest that companies should adopt a segmentation based on a level of brand knowledge (low or high) and whether the user is seeking something specific or surfing. This then gives groups:

- *the expert* (knowledgeable about the brand and seeking something specific);
- *the wanderer* (neither);

Table 7.9 Alternative perspectives on online buyer behaviours

Range of behavioural traits	Sources referred to
1. Directed to undirected information-seekers	Lewis and Lewis (1997), Kothari et al. (2001)
2. Brand-knowledgeable to not knowledgeable	Kothari et al. (2001), Styler (2001)
3. Feature-led to not feature-led	Styler (2001)
4. Price-led to not price-led	Styler (2001)
5. Service-quality-led to not service-quality-led	—
6. Require advice to do not require advice	Styler (2001)
7. Brand-loyal to opportunistic	Clemons and Row (2000), Styler (2001)

- *the adventurer* (knowledgeable about the brand, but not seeking anything specific);
- *the investigator* (not knowledgeable, but seeking something specific).

These authors suggest that when designing a web site, marketers should provide information and navigation aids for each type of user profile within the target audience. For a retail site this might include all the types of user listed above, whereas for a business-to-business site visitors will mainly be directed information-seekers and buyers. Although it is suggested that there are generic types of users, the characteristics of users can, of course, vary with each session that they are logged on, varying for example according to whether they are using the Web for work or recreation.

A final aspect of consumer behaviour that must be taken into consideration when developing an online strategy is loyalty to a brand. Clemons and Row (2000) describe several alternative types of loyalty that can be exhibited online (see Case Study 6.1).

From this brief review of online buyer behaviours, we can suggest that online marketers need to take into account the range of behaviours shown in Table 7.9 both when developing an Internet marketing strategy and when executing it through site design.

Hierarchy of response models

An alternative view of how consumer behaviour in using a web site may vary relates to the stage they have reached in the adoption of a web site. The process of adoption (Rogers, 1983), summarised for example by Kotler et al. (2001), is made up of the following stages:

- awareness;
- interest;
- evaluation;
- trial;
- adoption.

Breitenbach and van Doren (1998) assess how a web user passes through each stage. While such a model may be suitable for some sites which will be visited repeatedly (such as a portal) it is less appropriate for a customer visiting a site a single time to make a one-off purchase.

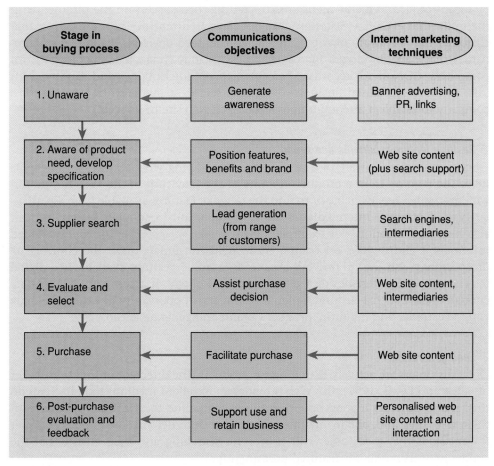

Figure 7.9 A summary of how the Internet can impact on the buying process for a new purchaser

The role of the Internet in supporting customers at different stages of the buying process should also be considered. Figure 7.9 indicates how the Internet can be used to support the different stages in the buying process. The boxes on the left show the typical stages that a new prospect passes through, according to, for example, Robinson et al. (1967). A similar analysis was performed by Berthon et al. (1998), who speculated that the relative communications effectiveness of using a web site in this process gradually increased from 1 to 6.

It is worthwhile reviewing each of the stages in the buying process referred to in Figure 7.9 in order to highlight how effective the Internet can be when used at different stages to support the marketing communications objectives.

1 Generate awareness (of need, product or service)

Generating awareness of need is conventionally achieved principally through mass media advertising. The Internet is not very effective at this since it has a more limited reach than television, radio or print media. Although banner advertising is widely used, it is limited in the message that it can convey. It can assist in generating brand awareness. Some companies have effectively developed brand awareness by means of PR and media mentions concerning their success on the Internet, with the result that even if a customer does not have a current need for a product, that customer may be aware of the source when the need develops. Examples of companies that have developed brand awareness include Amazon for books, Dell for computers, CDNow for records, Microsoft Expedia for Holidays and Autobytel for cars. In more specialised business-to-business sectors it may also be possible for a company to establish a reputation as a preferred web site in its sector.

2 Position features, benefits and brand

Once a consumer is aware of a need and is considering what features and benefits he or she requires from a product, then he or she may turn to the Web to find out which suppliers are available or to find the range of features available from a particular type of product. Intermediaries are very important in supplier search and can also help in evaluation. For example, CNET (www.computers.com) provides detailed information and reviews on computers to help consumers make the choice. The prospect may visit sites to find out about, for example, features available in a digital television or characteristics of a place to go on holiday. If a company is fortunate enough to have such a customer, then it has an early opportunity to enter a dialogue with a customer and build the product's brand and generate a lead.

3 Lead generation

Once customers are actively searching for products (the directed information-seeker of Lewis and Lewis, 1997), the Web provides an excellent medium to help them do this. It also provides a good opportunity for companies to describe the benefits of their web sites and obtain qualified leads. The Internet marketer must consider the methods that a customer will choose for searching and then ensure that the company or its product is featured prominently.

4 Assist purchase decision

One of the most powerful features of web sites is their facility to carry a large amount of content at relatively low cost. This can be turned to advantage when customers are looking to identify the best product. By providing relevant information in a form that is easy to find and digest a company can use its web site to help in persuading the customer. Brand issues are important here also, as a new buyer will prefer to buy from a supplier with a good reputation – it will be difficult for a company to portray itself in this way if it has a slow, poorly designed or shoddy web site.

5 Facilitate purchase

Once a customer has decided to purchase, then the company will not want to lose the custom at this stage! The web site should enable standard credit-card payment mechanisms with the option to place the order by phone or mail.

Table 7.10, which is based on audience panel data, suggests that the Web is more effective in supporting the purchase decision than in facilitating the purchase. In most countries, twice as many web users will browse for products compared to those who purchase them. There is also a wide variation between countries on the propensity to buy. It can be suggested that this is not only due to the use of the Internet being more established in some countries, such as the United States. There must be cultural reasons also.

Table 7.10 Worldwide online browsing and purchasing behaviour, six months to June 2001, adults 16+

Nation	Browsing for products	Purchasing products	Nation	Browsing for products	Purchasing products
Australia	24%	10%	New Zealand	29%	12%
Austria	25%	12%	Norway	24%	14%
Belgium/Luxembourg	12%	5%	Singapore	19%	7%
Denmark	39%	16%	South Korea	18%	11%
Finland	28%	11%	Spain	8%	3%
France	12%	6%	Sweden	46%	26%
Germany	22%	11%	Switzerland	32%	17%
Hong Kong	13%	4%	Taiwan	13%	4%
Ireland	17%	8%	UK	19%	11%
Italy	10%	3%	United States	74%	30%
Netherlands	28%	11%			

Source: Nielsen//NetRatings (www.netratings.com)

6 Support product use and retain business

The Internet also provides good potential for retaining customers since:

- value-added services such as free customer support can be provided by the web site and these encourage repeat visits and provide value-added features;
- feedback on products can be provided to customers; the provision of such information will indicate to customers that the company is looking to improve its service;
- e-mail can be used to give regular updates on products and promotions and encourage customers to revisit the site;
- repeat visits to sites provide opportunities for cross-selling and repeat selling through sales promotions owing to the amount of information that can be displayed on the web site.

Internet marketing techniques to support different aspects of marketing communications have been categorised by Breitenbach and van Doren (1998). Their categories include the supply of in-depth product or company information, open communications (a two-way dialogue with the customer), real-time transactions and catalogue browsing, demonstrations ('try before buy'), club membership (or discussion forum), give-aways, entertainment (games or quizzes), virtual tours, instructional support, and complementary services such as links and free customer support. The authors conducted a cross-industry survey of 50 company web sites, and found that of these techniques, those most commonly used include in-depth product or company information, open communications and complementary services.

Further insight into online buyer is available from audience panel data such as that shown in Table 7.11. An explanation of this type of data is given in Chapter 9. Complete Activity 7.5 to assess the implications of this information. These data should also be compared to other media. As would be expected, given that there are 24 hours in a day, Internet use appears to slightly reduce TV viewing. For example, UCLA (2001) reports that American Internet users tend to watch 4.5 hours less TV per week than they did before using the Internet.

Activity 7.5

Internet usage by consumer

Purpose

To understand the media consumption patterns of Internet users.

Activity

1 Visit the summary of Nielsen//NetRatings audience panel data (www.nielsen-netratings.com/hot_off_the_net_i).

2 Review the data for your country in comparison with that in Table 7.11. Can you suggest reasons for differences?

3 What are the implications for Internet marketers of the magnitude of each of the values in Table 7.11?

Table 7.11 Internet media consumption average – Nielsen//NetRatings (2002) Internet panel audience data

Number of sessions per month	17
Number of domains visited	43
Page views per month	778
Page views per surfing session	45
Time spent per month	9:20:27
Time spent during surfing session	0:32:28
Duration of a page viewed	0:00:43
Total Internet audience sample	164 648
Active Internet universe	254 017 978
Current Internet universe estimate	457 137 185

Published online at: www.nielsen-netratings.com/hot_off_the_net_i

Case Study 7.1 indicates the complexity of online buyer behaviour, suggesting that it is difficult to develop general models that define online buyer behaviour.

CASE STUDY 7.1

Multi-site online car purchase behaviour

Forrester (2002) has analysed online buyer behaviour in the car industry in detail. They estimate that different sites such as car manufacturers, dealers, and independent auto sites collectively invest more than $1 billion each year trying to turn online auto shoppers into buyers. They recommend that to effectively identify serious car buyers from the millions of site visitors, auto site owners must correlate car buyers' *multi-site* behaviour to near-term (within three months) vehicle purchases. In the research, Forrester analysed behaviour across sites from three months of continuous online behaviour data and buyer-reported purchase data provided by comScore Networks, extracted from comScore's Global Network of more than 1.5 million opt-in Internet users. To find the correlation between online shopping behaviour and car buying, Forrester observed 78 000 individual consumers' paths through 170 auto sites and interviewed 17 auto site owners and software providers. Behaviour patterns like frequency and intensity of online research sessions and cross-site comparison-shopping were strong purchase predictors.

By researching user paths from site to site, Forrester found that:

- Online auto marketing and retailing continues to see strong growth despite weak demand in 2001 from the car market. While independent sites remain popular with consumers, manufacturer sites saw a 59 per cent increase in traffic in 2001.
- Site owners currently lack the data and software tools to know where they fit in the online auto retail landscape – or even how individual customers use their sites.
- Roughly one in four auto site visitors buys a car within three months.
- Repeat visitors are rare. Sixty-four per cent of all buyers complete their research in five sessions or less.
- Auto shoppers' Web research paths predict their probability of vehicle purchase; on some paths, 46 per cent are near-term buyers.
- The theory of a «marketing funnel» doesn't map to actual car buyer behaviour. Conventional wisdom suggests that shoppers first visit information sites, then manufacturers, then e-retailers or dealer sites, as they go from awareness to interest, desire, and action. Mapping consumer data reveals a messier, more complex consideration process.

Summarising the research Mark Dixon Bünger, senior analyst, Forrester Research says:

Common assumptions about customer behavior when shopping for vehicles online are wrong. For example, loyalty and repeat visits are actually an anti-predictor of purchase. Most people who buy come in short, intense bursts, and don't hang out on auto sites. Single-site traffic analysis is not enough to understand and influence multisite, multisession auto shoppers. Today's Web site analysis tools weren't created to measure the complex nature of online auto shopping, which involves many sites over several episodes.

A segmentation of car buying profiles

Forrester developed what they call a 'site owner road map' to help car site owners better understand their customers and segment them into four distinct car buying profiles. Since this segmentation is not predictive, Forrester suggests that to sell more cars through a better site experience, companies need to help each type of buyer reach its different goals. The four types are:

- *Explorers*. Forrester suggests that car buying is a 'journey of discovery' for these users, so suggests giving them a guide tour or user guides. This should lead them through a convenient, explicit buying process.
- *Offroaders*. These perform detailed research before visiting showrooms, but often leave without purchasing. If dealers can identify these visitors through the number of configurations, comparisons and number of page views they have, then dealers should quickly respond to the number of quotes they require.
- *Drive-bys*. These are the largest segment of car site visitors. They visit four sites or fewer, but only 20 per cent buy online. Forrester suggests profiling these customers by incentivising them in order to better understand their purchase intentions.
- *Cruisers*. Frequent visitors, but only 15 per cent buy a car in the short-term. These are influencers who have a great interest in cars, but are not necessarily interested in purchase.

Question

Read the case, and discuss the practical value of buyer behaviour models and segmentation schemes given the variation in online buyer behaviour suggested by the case.

Designing the user experience

Design phase

The design phase defines how the site will work in the key areas of web site structure, navigation and security.

Once analysis has determined the information needs of the site, the site can be designed. **Design** is critical to a successful web site since it will determine the quality of experience users of a site have; if they have a good experience they will return, if not they will not! A 'good experience' is determined by a number of factors such as those that affect how easy it is to find information: for example, the structure of the site, menu choices and searching facilities. It is also affected by less tangible factors such as the graphical design and layout of the site.

Achieving a good design is important before too many web pages are developed since, if time is taken to design a site, less time will be wasted later when the site is reworked. Large sites are usually produced by creating templates comprising the graphical and menu elements to which content is added.

As mentioned previously, design is not solely a paper-based exercise, but needs to be integrated into the prototyping process. The design should be tested by review with the client and customer to ensure it is appropriate. The design of site layout, navigation and structure can be tested in two different ways. First, early designs can be paper-based – drawn by the designer on large pieces of paper – or 'mock-ups' can be produced on screen using a drawing or paint program. This process is referred to as **storyboarding**. Second, a working, dynamic prototype can be produced in which users can select different menu options on-screen that will take them to skeleton pages (minus content) of different parts of the site.

Storyboarding

Using static drawings or screenshots of the different parts of a web site to review the design concept with customers or clients.

Since the main reason given in Table 7.1 for returning to a web site is high-quality content, it is important to determine, through analysis, that the content is correct. However, the quality of content is determined by more than the text copy. It is important to achieve high-quality content through design. To help in this it is useful to consider the factors that affect quality content. These are shown in Figure 7.10. All are determined by the quality of the information.

● Developing customer-oriented content

Nigel Bevan (1999a) says:

Unless a web site meets the needs of the intended users it will not meet the needs of the organization providing the web site. Web site development should be user-centred, evaluating the evolving design against user requirements.

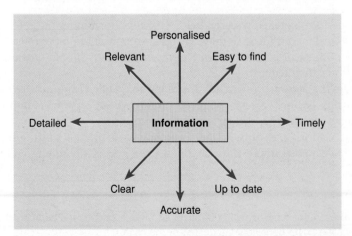

Figure 7.10 Different aspects of high-quality information content of a web site

How can this customer-oriented or user-centred content be achieved?

User-centred design starts with understanding the nature and variation within the user groups. According to Bevan (1999a), issues to consider include:

- Who are the important users?
- What is their purpose for accessing the site?
- How frequently will they visit the site?
- What experience and expertise do they have?
- What nationality are they? Can they read your language?
- What type of information are they looking for?
- How will they want to use the information: read it on the screen, print it or download it?
- What type of browsers will they use? How fast will their communication links be?
- How large a screen or window will they use, with how many colours?

Rosenfeld and Morville (1998) suggest four stages of site design that also have a user-centred basis:

1 Identify different audiences.
2 Rank importance of each to business.
3 List the three most important information needs of audience.
4 Ask representatives of each audience type to develop their own wish lists.

For an example of the principle of customer orientation in action visit retailer B&Q's DIY site (www.diy.com). This is targeted at a range of users of DIY products, so is designed around three zones: products, advice and inspiration. Experts who know what they want go straight to the product section and buy what they need. Less experienced users with queries on what to purchase can gain advice from an expert just as they would in-store and novices may visit the inspiration zone which includes room mock-ups with lists of the products needed to create a particular look. An alternative approach is used by Guinness (www.guinness.com, Figure 5.6) who formerly had three site zones: 'Like it, Live it, Love it'.

Evaluating designs

A test of effective design for usability is dependent on three areas according to Bevan (1999b):

1 *Effectiveness* – can users complete their tasks correctly and completely?
2 *Productivity (efficiency)* – are tasks completed in an acceptable length of time?
3 *Satisfaction* – are users satisfied with the interaction?

● Marketing-led site design

We have seen that there are many guidelines on how to approach web site design from a user or customer orientation. The marketing aims of the site should, however, always be remembered. Marketing-led site design is informed by marketing objectives and tactics. A common approach is to base the design on achieving the performance drivers of successful Internet marketing referred to in Chapter 4 and the loyalty drivers referred to at the start of this chapter. Design will be led by these performance drivers as follows:

- *Customer acquisition* – the online value proposition must be clear. Appropriate incentives for customer acquisition such as those described in Chapter 6 must be devised.

- *Customer conversion* – the site must engage first-time visitors. Call to action for customer acquisition and retention offers must be prominent with benefits clearly explained. The fulfilment of the offer or purchase must be as simple as possible to avoid attrition during this process.
- *Customer retention* – appropriate incentives and content for repeat visits and business must be available (see Chapter 6).
- *Service quality* – this has been covered in this chapter. Service quality is affected by site navigation, performance, availability and responsiveness to enquiries.
- *Branding* – the brand offer must be clearly explained and interaction with the brand must be possible.

Mini Case Study 7.1 gives an example of how a site was relaunched based on marketing-led design to achieve objectives for acquisition, conversion and retention.

Mini Case Study 7.1

CommonTime relaunch web site to increase online sales

CommonTime is a privately owned company formed in 1994 to produce software for enterprises that use mobile/handheld computers. CommonTime's audience is diverse but Internet-literate. Their market is reached through the CommonTime web site (www.commontime.com) and indirectly through a global network of resellers and partners such as Microsoft, Compaq, Palm and Infowave. Figure 7.11 shows an initial site; Figure 7.12 shows the relaunched site incorporating the enhancements referred to below.

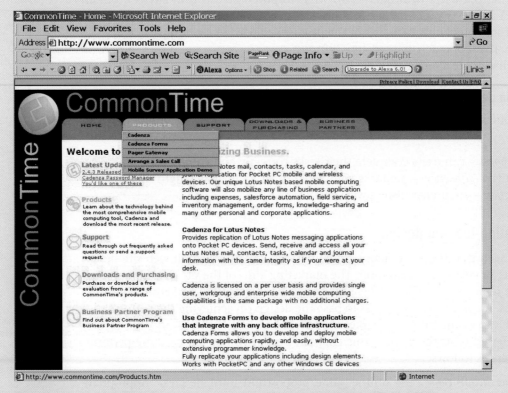

Figure 7.11 CommonTime (www.commontime.com) original web site, March 2002

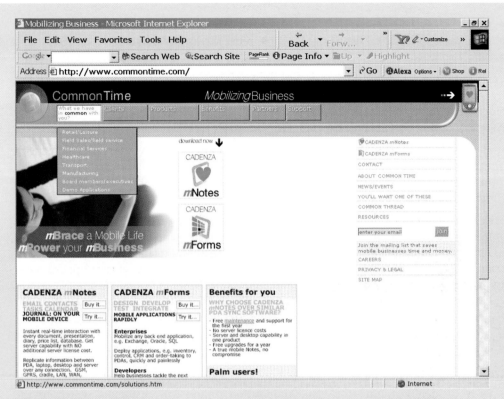

Figure 7.12 CommonTime (www.commontime.com) relaunched web site, May 2002

Product overview

CommonTime's Cadenza products, mNotes and MForms, enable a mobile workforce to work remotely on their handheld computers and access mail, contacts, tasks and calendar entries together with data from any back-end enterprise system, such as SAP, Siebel or Oracle.

Relaunch required

The web site relaunch was coordinated by Ollie Omotosho, Vice President Marketing, who was hired to enhance business development. This involved developing a new marketing strategy. He says:

> *It was clear from developing the marketing strategy that the site had to change. Yes, it was successful in achieving 40% of new business, but it could do so much more. Attempts had been made at automatic search engine submission, but like so many other businesses, this was not sustained when the site, for obvious reasons, didn't fly to the top of the listings.*

Linking marketing objectives to the new site design

The objectives and how they were achieved through the new site design are summarised below:

1 Dramatically increase awareness of CommonTime, particularly in Europe (UK, France, Germany, Spain and Scandinavia, where there is a high Lotus Notes business-user concentration) within the next six months.

   New site contained landing pages (destination of 'calls to action') and customer success stories native to a particular territory. Product value propositions clearly explained.

2 Raise web-based licence sales by a factor of ten in 8 months.

   On-site marketing communications support marketing objectives by converting visitors to achieve these key actions:

- request an evaluation;
- purchase online;
- refer a colleague;
- make a sales appointment;
- enter the loyalty programme.

Clear, intuitive navigation and clear calls to action were vital to achieving these actions. Dynamic facilities gave a menu of fast, automated responses to common enquiries, e.g. brochure requests, sales visit request etc. Page design and copy was also revised for search engine optimisation (Chapter 8).

3 Source and implement new e-CRM system within 3 months. The new site was designed with integration into the e-CRM system in mind. This included profiling of customers through forms data entry on-site and validation of postcode and address to aid sales and marketing effort offline using the CRM database.

4 Create a marketing information system (MIS) within two months that encourages the flow of market intelligence from customers, competitors, partners and employees.

The new customer-oriented web site was designed to appeal to all types of customers. For example, an area is included where developer partners can learn about new opportunities and give feedback on industry trends and competitor activity.

Part of the aim of the MIS was to collect statistical visitor data with visitor/evaluator and visitor/purchaser ratios and site exit ratios all monitored carefully against preset goals.

5 Have a product up-sell strategy in place within two months.

The site clearly explains the features and benefits of both products clearly.

6 Attack strategy in place by March for displacing product from competitors' customers.

Only by demonstrating the value proposition online will customers switch to the Cadenza brands. The new site would also have greatly enhanced aesthetics to increase the credibility of the CommonTime brand.

7 Share mission and develop enthused agents/partners in target territories and target market segments.

Clarity of copy for the new site was essential. It needed to transmit a message that all customer groups could believe in.

Summary of how the relaunched site helped achieve CRM objectives

To achieve acquisition objectives:

- high visibility on the Internet;
- communicate the value proposition;
- engage the customer, and build credibility;
- clear navigation, instinctive path to buying decision;
- obtain an opt-in e-mail address;
- obtain a referral.

To achieve conversion objectives:

- encourage the visitor to download free-trial software;
- encourage the visitor to buy the software;
- explain features and benefits, and USPs;
- capture accurate data.

To achieve retention objectives:

- demonstrate useful information worth coming back for;
- industry news;
- technology news;
- product news, free upgrades, advice and tips;
- case studies, white papers;
- e-mail opt-out questionnaire;
- customer service area, FAQ or user forum;
- special offer or loyalty reward programme.

● Elements of site design

Once the requirements of the user and marketer are established we turn our attention to the design of the human–computer interface. Nielsen (2000b) structures his book on web usability according to three main areas, which can be interpreted as follows:

1 *site design and structure* – the overall structure of the site;
2 *page design* – the layout of individual pages;
3 *content design* – how the text and graphic content on each page is designed.

● Site design and structure

The structures created by designers for web sites will vary greatly according to their audience and the site's purpose, but we can make some general observations about design and structure. We will review the factors designers consider in designing the style, organisation and navigation schemes for the site.

Site style

An effective web site design will have a style that is communicated through use of colour, images, typography and layout. This should support the way a product is positioned or its brand.

Site personality

The style elements can be combined to develop a personality for a site.

We could describe a site's personality in the same way we can described people, such as 'formal' or 'fun'. This personality has to be consistent with the needs of the target audience (Figure 7.13). A business audience often requires detailed information

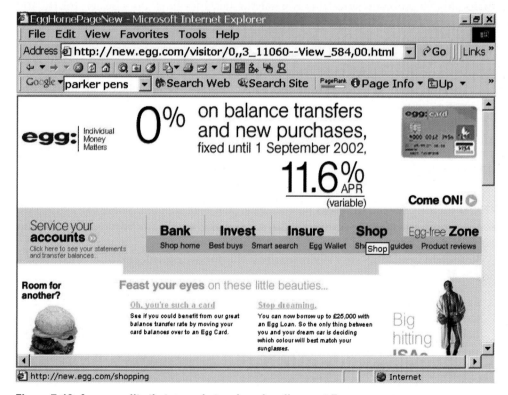

Figure 7.13 A personality that appeals to a broad audience at Egg.com

and prefers an information-intensive style such as that of the Cisco site (Figure 7.16 below) (www.cisco.com). A consumer site is usually more graphically intensive. Before the designers pass on the their creative designs to developers, they also need to consider the constraints on the user experience, such as screen resolution and colour depth, browser-used and download speed.

Graphic design

Graphic design of web sites represents a challenge since designers of web sites are severely constrained by a number of factors:

- *The speed of downloading graphics* – designers need to allow for home users who view sites using a slow modem across a phone line and who are unlikely to wait minutes to view a web site.
- *The screen resolutions of the computer* – designing for different screen resolutions is necessary, since some users with laptops may be operating at a low resolution such as 640 by 480 pixels, the majority at a resolution of 800 by 600 pixels, and a few at higher resolutions of 1064 by 768 pixels or greater.
- *The number of colours on screen* – some users may have monitors capable of displaying 16 million colours giving photo-realism, while other may have only 256 colours.
- *The type of web browser used* – different browsers such as Microsoft Internet Explorer and Netscape Navigator and different versions of browsers such as version 4.0 or 5.0 may display graphics or text slightly differently or may support different plug-ins (see the section in Chapter 12 on testing).

As a result of these constraints, the design of web sites is a constant compromise between what looks visually appealing and modern and what works for the older browsers, with slower connections. This is often referred to as the 'lowest common denominator problem' since this is what the designer must do – design for the old browsers, using slow links and low screen resolutions. One method for avoiding the 'lowest common denominator problem' is to offer the user a 'high-tech' or 'low-tech' choice: one for users with fast connections and high screen resolutions, and another for users who do not have these. This facility is mainly seen offered on sites produced by large companies since it requires more investment to effectively duplicate the site.

Despite these constraints, graphic design is important in determining the feel or character of a site. The graphic design can help shape the user's experience of a site and should be consistent with the brand involved.

Site organisation

Information organisation schemes

The structure chosen to group and categorise information.

In their book *Information Architecture for the World Wide Web*, Rosenfeld and Morville (1998) identify several different information organisation schemes. These can be applied for different aspects of e-commerce sites, from the whole site through to different parts of the site.

Rosenfeld and Morville (1998) identify the following information organisation schemes:

1 *Exact.* Here information can be naturally indexed. If we take the example of books, these can be alphabetical, by author or title; chronological – by date; or for travel books, for example, geographical – by place. Information on an e-commerce site may be presented alphabetically, but it is not suitable for browsing.
2 *Ambiguous.* Here the information requires classification, again taking the examples of books, the Dewey Decimal System is an ambiguous classification scheme since the librarians classify books into arbitrary categories. Such an approach is common

on an e-commerce site since products and services can be classified in different ways. Other ambiguous information organisation schemes that are commonly used on web sites are where content is broken down by topic, by task or by audience. The use of metaphors is also common, a metaphor being where the web site corresponds to a familiar real-world situation. The Microsoft Windows Explorer, where information is grouped according to Folders, Files and Trash is an example of a real-world metaphor. The use of the shopping basket metaphor is widespread within e-commerce sites. It should be noted though that Nielsen (2000b) believes that metaphors can be confusing if the metaphor isn't understood immediately or is misinterpreted.

3 *Hybrid.* Here there will be a mixture of organisation schemes, both exact and ambiguous.

Rosenfeld and Morville (1998) point out that using different approaches is common on web sites, but this can lead to confusion, because the user is not clear what mental model is being followed. We can say that is probably best to minimise the number of information organisation schemes.

Site navigation schemes

Devising a site that is easy to use is critically dependent on the design of the site navigation scheme. Hoffman and Novak (1997) stress the importance of the concept of flow in governing site usability. 'Flow' essentially describes how easy it is for the users to find the information they need as they move from one page of the site to the next, but it also includes other interactions such as filling in on-screen forms.

It can be suggested that there are three important aspects to a site that is easy to navigate. These are:

1 *Consistency.* The site will be easier to navigate if the user is presented with a consistent user interface when viewing the different parts of the site. For example, if the menu options in the support section of the site are on the left side of the screen, then they should also be on the left when the user moves to the 'news section' of the site.

2 *Simplicity.* Sites are easier to navigate if there are limited numbers of options. It is usually suggested that two or possibly three levels of menu are the most that are desirable. For example, there may be main menu options at the left of the screen that take the user to the different parts of the site, and at the bottom of the screen there will be specific menu options that refer to that part of the site. (Menus in this form are often referred to as 'nested'.)

3 *Context.* Context is the use of 'signposts' to indicate to users where they are located within the site – in other words to reassure users that they are not 'lost'. To help with this, the web site designer should use particular text or colour to indicate to users which part of the site they are currently using. Context can be provided by the use of JavaScript 'rollovers', where the colour of the menu option changes when the user positions the mouse over the menu option and then changes again when the menu option is selected. Many sites also have a site-map option that shows the layout and content of the whole site so the user can understand its structure. When using a well-designed site it should not be necessary to refer to such a map regularly.

Most navigation systems are based upon a hierarchical site structure. When creating the structure, designers have to compromise between the two approaches shown in Figure 7.14. The narrow and deep approach has the benefit of fewer choices on each page, making it easier for the user to make their selection, but more clicks

Site navigation scheme

Tools provided to the user to move between different information on a web site.

Flow

Flow describes how easy it is for users of a site to move between the different pages of content of the site.

Navigation

Navigation describes how easy it is to find and move between different information on a web site. It is governed by menu arrangements, site structure and the layout of individual pages.

Narrow and deep navigation

Fewer choices, more clicks to reach required content.

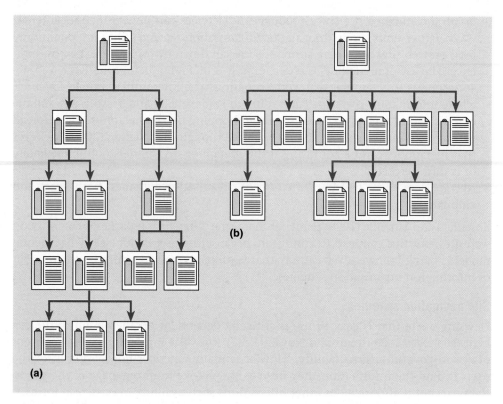

Figure 7.14 (a) Narrow and deep and (b) broad and shallow organisation schemes

Broad and shallow navigation
More choices, fewer clicks to reach required content.

are required to reach a particular piece of information. The broad and shallow approach requires fewer clicks to reach the same piece of information, but the design of the screen potentially becomes cluttered. Figures 7.14(a) and 7.15 depict the narrow and deep approach and Figures 7.14(a) and 7.16 the broad and shallow approach. Note that in these case the approaches are appropriate for the non-technical and technical audiences. A rule of thumb is that site designers should ensure it only takes three clicks to reach any piece of information on a site. This implies the use of a broad and shallow approach on most large sites. Lynch and Horton (1999) recommend a broad and shallow approach and note that designers should not conceive of a single home page where customers arrive on the site, but of different home pages according to different audience types. Each of the pages in the second row of Figure 7.14(b) could be thought of as an example of a home page which the visitors can bookmark if the page appeals to them. Nielsen (2000b) points out that many users will not arrive on the home page, but may be referred from another site or according to a print or TV advert to a particular page such as www.b2b.com/jancomp. He calls this process deep linking and site designers should ensure that navigation and context are appropriate for users arriving on these pages.

Deep linking
Jakob Nielsen's term for a user arriving at a site deep within its structure.

As well as compromises on depth of links within a site it is also necessary to compromise on the amount of space devoted to menus. Nielsen (1999) points out that some sites devote so much space to navigation bars that the space available for content is limited. Nielsen (1999) suggests that the designer of navigation systems should consider the following information that a site user wants to know:

● *Where am I?* The user needs to know where they are on the site and this can be indicated by highlighting the current location and clear titling of pages. This can

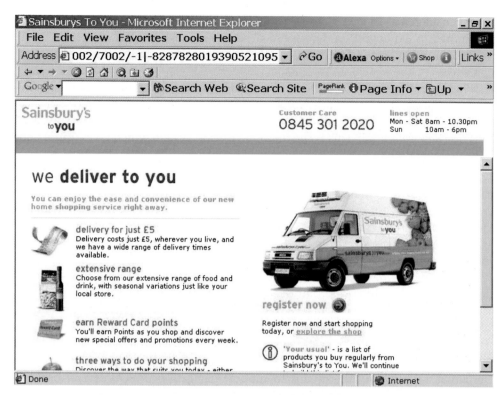

Figure 7.15 Narrow and deep organisation scheme for consumers at Sainsburys to You site (www.sainsburys.co.uk)

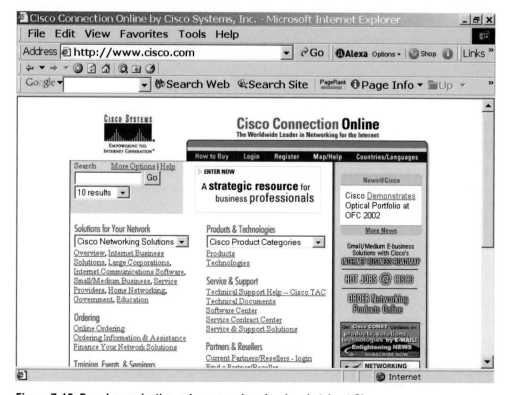

Figure 7.16 Broad organisation schemes and professional style at Cisco.com

be considered as *context. Consistency* of menu locations on different pages is also required to aid cognition. Users also need to know where they are on the Web. This can be indicated by a logo, which by convention is at the top or top left of a site.

- *Where have I been?* This is difficult to indicate on a site, but for task-oriented activities such as purchasing a product can show the user that they are at the *n*th stage of an operation such as making a purchase.
- *Where do I want to go?* This is the main navigation system which gives options for future operations.

To answer these questions, clear succinct labelling is required. Widely used standards such as Home, Main page, Search, Find, Browse, FAQ and Help and About Us are preferable. But for other particular labels it is useful to have what Rosenfeld and Morville (1998) call 'scope notes' – an additional explanation. These authors also argue against the use of iconic labels or pictures without corresponding text since they are open to misinterpretation and take longer to process.

Since using the navigation system may not enable the user to find the information they want rapidly, alternatives have to be provided by the site designers. These alternatives include search, advanced search, browse and site map facilities. Whatis.com (www.whatis.com) illustrates these features well.

Menu options

Designing and creating the menus to support navigation present several options, and these are briefly described here. The main options are the following.

1 Text menus, buttons or images

The site user can select menus by clicking on different objects. They can click on a basic text hyperlink, underlined in blue, by default. It should be noted that these will be of different sizes according to the size the user has selected to display the text. The use of text menus only may make a site look primitive and reduce its graphic appeal. Rectangular or oval buttons can be used to highlight menu options more distinctly. Images can also be used to show menu options. For instance, customer service could be denoted by a picture of a help desk. Whilst these are graphically appealing it may not be obvious that they are menu options until the user positions the mouse over them. A combination of text menu options and either buttons or images is usually the best compromise. This way users have the visual appeal of buttons or images, but also the faster option of text – they can select these menus if they are waiting for graphical elements to load, or if the images are turned off in the web browser. However, icons should have the advantage that their understanding is not language-dependent.

2 Rollovers

'Rollover' is the term used to describe colour changes – where the colour of the menu option changes when the user positions the mouse over the menu option and then changes again when the menu option is selected. Rollovers are useful in that they help achieve the context referred to in the previous section, by highlighting the area of the site the user is in.

3 Positioning

Menus can be positioned at any of the edges of the screen, with left, bottom or top being conventional for Western cultures. The main design aim is to keep the position consistent between different parts of the site.

4 Frames

Frames are a feature of HTML which enable menus to be positioned at one side of the screen in a small area (frame) while the content of the page is displayed in the main frame. Frames have their advocates and detractors, but they are commonly used on sites since they clearly and easily separate the menu from the content. Detractors point to poor display speed, difficulties in indexing content in search engines and inflexibility on positioning.

5 Number of levels

In a hierarchical structure there could be as many as ten different levels, but for simplicity it is normal to try and achieve a site structure with a nesting level of four or fewer. Even in an electronic commerce shopping site with 20 000 products it should be possible to select a product at four menu levels. For example:

- level 1 – drink;
- level 2 – spirits;
- level 3 – whisky;
- level 4 – brand x.

6 Number of options

Psychologists recommend having a limited number of choices within each menu. If a menu has more than seven, it is probably necessary to add another level to the hierarchy to accommodate the extra choices.

● Page design

The page design involves creating an appropriate layout for each page. The main elements of a particular page layout are the title, navigation and content. Standard content such as copyright information may be added to every page as a footer. Issues in page design include:

- *Page elements*. We have to consider the proportion of page devoted to content compared to all other material such as headers, footers and navigation elements. The location of these elements also needs to be considered. It is conventional for the main menu to be at the top or on the left. The use of a menu system at the top of the browser window allows more space for content below.
- *The use of frames*. This is generally discouraged since it makes search engine registration more difficult and makes printing and bookmarking more difficult for visitors.
- *Resizing*. A good page layout design should allow for the user to change the size of text or work with different monitor resolutions.
- *Consistency*. Page layout should be similar for all areas of the site unless more space is required, for example for a discussion forum or product demonstration. Standards of colour and typography can be enforced through cascading style sheets.
- *Printing*. Layout should allow for printing or provide an alternative printing format.

● Content design

The home page is particularly important in achieving marketing actions – if the customers do not understand or do not buy-into the proposition of the site, then they will leave. Gleisser (2001) states that is important to clarify what he refers to as the 'essentials' of: who we are, what we offer, what is inside and how to contact us.

A study of the advertising impact of web site content design has been conducted by Pak (1999). She reviewed the techniques on web sites used to communicate the message to the customer in terms of existing advertising theory. The study considered the creative strategy used, in terms of the rational and emotional appeals contained within the visuals and the text. As would be expected intuitively, the appeal of the graphics was more emotional than that for the text; the latter used a more rational appeal. The study also considered the information content of the advertisements using classification schemes such as that of Resnik and Stern (1977). The information cues are still relevant to modern web site design. Some of the main information cues, in order of frequency of use, were:

- performance (what does the product do?);
- components/content (what is the product made up of?);
- price/value;
- implicit comparison;
- availability;
- quality;
- special offers;
- explicit comparisons.

Aaker and Norris (1982) devised a framework in which the strategy for creative appeal is based on emotion and feeling, and that for rational and cognitive appeal is based on facts and logic.

Copywriting for the web is an evolving art form, but many of the rules for good copywriting are as for any media. Common errors we see on web sites are:

- too much knowledge assumed of the visitor about the company, its products and services;
- using internal jargon about products, services or departments – using undecipher-able acronyms.

Web copywriters also need to take account of the user reading the content on-screen. Approaches to dealing with the limitations imposed by the customer using a monitor include:

- writing more concisely than in brochures;
- chunking, or breaking text into units of 5–6 lines at most, which allows users to scan rather than read information on web pages;
- use of lists with headline text in larger font;
- never including too much on a single page, except when presenting lengthy information such as a report which may be easier to read on a single page;
- using hyperlinks to decrease page sizes or help achieve flow within copy, either by linking to sections further down a page or linking to another page.

Smith and Chaffey (2001) summarise the essentials of good copywriting for the web under the mnemonic CRABS. CRABS stands for chunking, relevance, accuracy, brevity and scannability.

Hofacker (2000) describes five stages of human information processing when a web site is being used. These can be applied to both page design and content design to improve usability and help companies get their message across to consumers. Each of the five stages summarised in Table 7.12 acts as a hurdle, since if the site design or content is too difficult to process, the customer cannot progress to the next stage. It is useful to consider the stages in order to minimise these difficulties.

Table 7.12 A summary of the characteristics of the six stages of information processing described by Hofacker (2000)

Stage	Description	Applications
1. Exposure	Content must be present for long enough to be processed	Content on banner ads may not be on screen long enough for processing and cognition
2. Attention	User's eyes will be drawn towards headings and content, not graphics and moving items on a web page (Nielsen, 2000b)	Emphasis and accurate labelling of headings is vital to gain a user's attention. Evidence suggests that users do not notice banner adverts, suffering from 'banner blindness'
3. Comprehension and perception	The user's interpretation of content	Designs that use common standards and metaphors and are kept simple will be more readily comprehended
4. Yielding and acceptance	Is information (copy) presented accepted by customers?	Copy should refer to credible sources and present counterarguments as necessary
5. Retention	As for traditional advertising, this describes the extent to which the information is remembered	An unusual style or high degree of interaction leading to flow and user satisfaction is more likely to be recalled

Completion of online forms – best practice

One specialist aspect of content design is that of online forms used for capturing customer contact details, profiles and needs as part of relationship building (Chapter 6). It can be suggested that these are the main elements of best practice.

1 *Information requested on forms should be kept to a minimum but must include contact information.* Early practice in relation to the information to collect through online forms seemed to be to collect as much as possible to help build up profiles of customers. There was a backlash against this, with users refusing to provide so much information. Many companies have now gone to the other extreme and capture the minimum information – usually just an e-mail address. Having this address will enable the company to keep in contact with the customer and work back to other information such as company name and position.

2 *Explain why information is being collected.* A customer will more readily provide personal information and spend time filling in a form if he or she knows why it is being collected. Alternatively, a suitable offering may be made, such as free information or a product trial, to provide an incentive to fill in the form.

3 *Indicate mandatory fields.* Extra information can be collected from customers if they have time by marking essential fields in a suitable way (perhaps by an asterisk).

4 *Validate.* Checks should be performed after the form is filled in to ensure that the user has filled in all mandatory fields. Fields should also be checked for validity – has the customer entered a valid e-mail address with the '@' symbol, is the postcode or zip code valid? The user should be clearly prompted with what information is wrong and why. Such validation can be performed using scripts such as Javascript.

5 *Provide 'opt-out'.* Check-boxes should be made available that the user can select if he or she does not want to receive further information through e-mail or communications through other media. This principle is important to 'permission

marketing', which is advocated by those such as Seth Godin of Yahoo! (Godin, 1999) and Patricia Seybold (Seybold, 1999). It is suggested that users should be able to 'opt in' to giving information and being placed on mailing lists and then easily 'opt out'.

6 *Provide prompt confirmation.* After a user has filled in a form, a company should respond to acknowledge confirmation of receipt as soon as possible and describe what the follow-up actions will be. For example, if a customer has ordered a product, the confirmation note should thank the customer for shopping with the company and state clearly when he or she can expect to receive the product by courier.

Figure 3.6 shows an example of well-laid-out forms used to collect customer information by RS Components. Note that mandatory fields are marked with a square symbol and that the company informs customers of its obligations under the Data Protection Act 1984. In this form, the company is collecting information about the needs of the customer in order that site content and promotions can be matched with the customer's interests.

Gleisser (2001) surveyed web site designers to identify consensus on what were success factors in web site design. The results of this research are used to summarise this section:

● *The home page essentials.* Segmentation, targeting and positioning play a key role in informing design. The essentials are: who we are, what we offer, what is inside and how to contact us.
● *Cater for the needs of anticipated users.* Web sites should be quick to download and easy to navigate. The users may not be able to incorporate the latest technical capabilities, such as plug-ins, so these should be used with care.
● *Update the web site frequently.* This is to encourage repeat visitors and keep customers informed of new products and offers.
● *Gathering customer information.* The web site should be used as part of a 'push' marketing strategy which includes gathering customer information and better targeting of direct marketing using a range of media.

Development and testing of content

Development phase

Development is the term used to describe the creation of a web site by programmers. It involves writing the HTML content, creating graphics, and writing any necessary software code such as JavaScript or ActiveX (programming).

It is not practical to provide details of the methods of developing content – for two reasons. First, to describe all the facilities available in web browsers for laying out and formatting text, and for developing interactivity, would require several books! Second, the programming standards and tools used are constantly evolving, so material is soon out of date.

● Testing content

Testing phase

Testing involves different aspects of the content such as spelling, validity of links, formatting on different web browsers and dynamic features such as form filling or database queries.

Marketing managers responsible for web sites need to have a basic awareness of web site **development** and **testing**. These testing steps are described further in Chapter 9 on maintenance of sites, since they are an ongoing part of web site maintenance. In brief, the testing steps necessary are:

● test content displays correctly on different types and versions of web browsers;
● test plug-ins;
● test all interactive facilities and integration with company databases;

- test spelling and grammar;
- test adherence to corporate image standards;
- test to ensure all links to external sites are valid.

Testing often occurs on a separate test web server (or directory) or *test environment*, with access to the test or prototype version being restricted to the development team. When complete the web site is released or published to the main web server or *live environment*.

● Tools for web-site development and testing

A variety of software programs are available to help developers of web sites. Some of these tools are listed below to illustrate the range of skills a web site designer will need; an advanced web site may be built using tools from each of these categories since even the most advanced tools may not have the flexibility of the basic tools.

Basic text editors

Text editors are used to edit HTML tags. For example, '<B>Products</B>' will make the enclosed text display bold within the web browser. Such tools are often available at low cost or free – including the Notepad editor included with Windows. They are very flexible, and all web site developers will need to use them at some stage in developing content since more automated tools may not provide this flexibility and may not support the latest standard commands. Entire sites can be built using these tools, but it is more efficient to use the more advanced tools described below, and use the editors for 'tweaking' content.

Specialised HTML and graphics editors

Specialised HTML and graphics editing tools provide facilities for adding HTML tags automatically. For example, adding the Bold text tag <B> </B> to the HTML document will happen when the user clicks the bold tag. Some of these editors are WYSIWYG. Examples of basic tools include:

- Microsoft FrontPage Express (www.microsoft.com);
- modern versions of word processors such as Microsoft Word and Lotus WordPro now have these facilities through using a Save As HTML option.

Examples of more advanced tools include:

- ColdFusion (www.allaire.com);
- Dreamweaver (www.macromedia.com);
- Fusion (www.netobjects.com);
- PageMill (www.adobe.com).

These advanced tools are often referred to as *content management tools*. This topic is discussed further in Chapter 9. They provide advanced HTML editing facilities, but also provide tools to help manage and test the site, including graphic layouts of the structure of the site – making it easy to find, modify and republish the page by sending the file to the web site using FTP. Style templates can be applied to produce a consistent 'look and feel' across the site. Tools are also available to create and manage menu options.

Examples of graphics tools include:

- Adobe Photoshop (extensively used by graphic designers, www.adobe.com);
- Macromedia Fireworks (a Web-specific graphics package, with more limited functionality than Photoshop, www.macromedia.com);
- Macromedia Flash and Director-Shockwave (used for graphical animations, www.macromedia.com).

Promote site

Promotion of a site is a significant topic that will be part of the strategy of developing a web site. It will follow the initial development of a site and is described in detail in Chapter 8.

Summary

1 Careful planning and execution of web site implementation is important, in order to avoid the need for extensive reworking at a later stage if the design proves to be ineffective.

2 Implementation is not an isolated process; it should be integrated with the Internet marketing strategy. Analysis, design and implementation should occur repeatedly in an iterative, prototyping approach that involves the client and the user in producing an effective design.

3 A feasibility study should take place before the initiation of a major web site project. A feasibility study will assess:
   - the costs and benefits of the project;
   - the difficulty of achieving management and staff commitment to the project;
   - the availability of domain names to support the project;
   - the responsibilities and stages necessary for a successful project.

4 The choice of host for a web site should be considered carefully since this will govern the quality of service of the web site.

5 Options for analysis of users' requirements for a web site include:
   - interviews with marketing staff;
   - questionnaire sent to companies;
   - informal interviews with key accounts;
   - focus groups;
   - reviewing competitors' web sites.

6 According to surveys the main factors governing whether customers will return to a site are (in order of importance):
   - high-quality content;
   - ease of use;
   - it is quick to download;
   - it is updated frequently.

7 The design phase of developing a web site includes specification of:
   - the structure of the web site;
   - the flow, controlled by the navigation and menu options;
   - the graphic design and brand identity;
   - country-specific localisation;
   - the service quality of online forms and e-mail messages.

EXERCISES

Self-assessment exercises

1 Explain the term 'prototyping' in relation to web site creation.
2 What tasks should managers undertake during initiation of a web page?
3 What is domain name registration?
4 List the factors that determine web site 'flow'.
5 Explain the structure of an HTML document and the concept of 'tags'.
6 List the options for designing web site menu options.
7 What is a hierarchical web site structure?
8 What are the factors that control the performance of a web site?

Essay and discussion questions

1 Discuss the relative effectiveness of the different methods of assessing the customers' needs for a web site.
2 Select three web sites of your choice and compare their design effectiveness. You should describe design features such as navigation, structure and graphic design.
3 Explain how strategy, analysis, design and implementation of a web site should be integrated through a prototyping approach. Describe the merits and problems of the prototyping approach.
4 When designing the interactive services of a web site such as online forms and e-mails to customers, what steps should the designer take to provide a quality service to customers?

Examination questions

1 What is web site prototyping? Give three benefits of this approach.
2 What controls on a web site project are introduced at the initiation phase of the project?
3 A company is selecting an ISP. Explain:
   (a) what an ISP is;
   (b) which factors will affect the quality of service delivered by the ISP.
4 How are focus groups used to gain understanding of customer expectations of a web site?
5 Name, and briefly explain, four characteristics of the information content of a site that will govern whether a customer is likely to return to that web site.
6 When the graphic design and page layout of a web site are being described, what different factors associated with type and set-up of a PC and its software should the designer take into account?
7 What is meant by 'opt-in'? Why should it be taken into account as part of web site design?

References

Aaker, D. and Norris, N. (1982) Characteristics of TV commercials perceived as informative, *Journal of Advertising*, 25(2), 22–34.

Berthon, B., Pitt, L. and Watson, R. (1998) The World Wide Web as an industrial marketing communication tool: models for the identification assessment of opportunities, *Journal of Marketing Management*, 14, 691–704.

Bettman, J. (1979) *An Information Processing Theory of Consumer Choice*. Addison-Wesley, Reading, MA.

Bevan, N. (1999a) Usability issues in web site design. Proceedings of the 6th Interactive Publishing Conference, November 1999. Available online at www.usability.serco.com.

Bevan, N. (1999b) Common industry format usability tests. Proceedings of UPA'98, Usability Professionals Association, Scottsdale, Arizona, 29 June – 2 July 1999. Available online at www.usability.serco.com.

Bickerton, P., Bickerton, M. and Simpson-Holey, K. (1998) *Cyberstrategy*. Butterworth Heinemann, Oxford. Chartered Institute of Marketing series.

BMRB (2001) *Internet Monitor, November 2001*. BMRB International, Manchester, UK. Available online at www.bmrb.co.uk.

Bocij, P., Chaffey, D., Greasley, A. and Hickie, S. (2003) *Business Information Systems. Technology, Development and Management in E-Business*, 2nd edn. Financial Times/Prentice Hall, Harlow.

Booms, B. and Bitner, M. (1981) Marketing strategies and organisation structure for service firms, in J. Donelly and W. George (eds) *Marketing of Services*. American Marketing Association, New York.

Breitenbach, C. and van Doren, D. (1998) Value-added marketing in the digital domain: enhancing the utility of the Internet, *Journal of Consumer Marketing*, 15(6), 559–75.

Chaffey, D. and Edgar, M. (2000) Measuring online service quality, *Journal of Targeting, Analysis and Measurement for Marketing*, 8(4) (May), 363–78.

Clemons, E. and Row, M. (2000) Behaviour is key to web retailing strategy, *Financial Times, Mastering Management Supplement*, 13 November.

Cronin, J. and Taylor, S. (1992) Measuring service quality: a reexamination and extension, *Journal of Marketing*, 56, 55–63.

Feinberg, R., Trotter, M. and Anton, J. (2000) At any time – from anywhere – in any form. In D. Renner (ed.) *Defying the Limits, Reaching New Heights in Customer Relationship Management*. Report from Montgomery Research Inc, San Francisco, CA. http://feinberg.crmproject.com.

Forrester (2002) Mapping customer paths across multiple sites helps site owners predict which consumers are likely to buy and when. Forrester Research Press Release, Cambridge, MA, 19 February.

Friedman, L. and Furey, T. (1999) *The Channel Advantage*. Butterworth Heinemann, Oxford.

Gleisser, G. (2001) Building customer relationships online: the web site designer's perspective, *Journal of Consumer Marketing,* 18(6), 488–502.

Godin, S. (1999) *Permission Marketing*. Simon and Schuster, New York.

Hofacker, C. (2000) *Internet Marketing*. Wiley, New York.

Hoffman, D.L. and Novak, T.P. (1997) A new marketing paradigm for electronic commerce, *The Information Society*, Special issue on electronic commerce, 13, 43–54.

Kolesar, M. and Galbraith, R. (2000) A services-marketing perspective on e-retailing, *Internet Research: Electronic Networking Applications and Policy*, 10(5), 424–38.

Kothari, D., Jain, S., Khurana, A. and Saxena, A. (2001) Developing a marketing strategy for global online customer management, *International Journal of Customer Relationship Management,* 4(1), 53–8.

Kotler, P., Armstrong, G., Saunders, J. and Wong, V. (2001) *Principles of Marketing*, 3rd edn. Financial Times/Prentice Hall, Harlow.

Lewis, H. and Lewis, R. (1997) Give your customers what they want, *Selling on the Net. Executive book summaries*, 19(3), March.

Lynch, P. and Horton, S. (1999) *Web Style Guide. Basic Design Principles for Creating Web Sites.* Yale University Press, New Haven, CT.

Morgan, R. (1996) An Internet marketing framework for the World Wide Web, *Journal of Marketing Management*, 12, 757–75.

National Statistics (2001) Internet Access Survey, National Statistics Omnibus Survey, July. London.

Nielsen, J. (1999) Details in study methodology can give misleading results. Jakob Nielsen's Alertbox, 21 February. www.useit.com/alertbox/990221.html

Nielsen, J. (2000a) Novice vs. expert users, Jakob Nielsen's Alertbox, 6 February. www.useit.com/alertbox/20000206.html

Nielsen, J. (2000b) *Designing Web Usability*. New Riders Publishing, USA.

Nielsen, J. (2002) Nielsen//Net Ratings: Internet panel audience data. www.nielsen-netratings.com/hot-off-the-net-i

Ong, C. (1995) Practical aspects of marketing on the WWW, MBA Dissertation, University of Sheffield, UK.

Pak, J. (1999) Content dimensions of web advertising: a cross national comparison, *International Journal of Advertising*, 18(2), 207–31.

Parasuraman, A., Zeithaml, V. and Berry, L. (1985) A conceptual model of service quality and its implications for future research, *Journal of Marketing*, 49, Fall, 48.

Quelch, J. and Klein, L. (1996) Intermediaries and cybermediaries. A continuing role for mediating players in the electronic marketplace, *Journal of Computer Mediated Communication*, 1(3).

Reichheld, F. and Schefter, P. (2000) E-loyalty, your secret weapon, *Harvard Business Review*, July–August, 105–13.

Resnik, A. and Stern, A. (1977) An analysis of information content in television advertising, *Journal of Marketing*, January, 50–3.

Rigby, D., Bavega, S., Rastoi, S., Zook., C. and Hancock, S. (2000) The value of customer loyalty and how you can capture it. Bain and Company/Mainspring white paper, 17 March. Published at www.mainspring.com.

Robinson, P., Faris, C. and Wind, Y. (1967) *Industrial Buying and Creative Marketing*. Allyn and Bacon, Boston.

Rogers, E. (1983) *Diffusion of Innovations*, 3rd edn. Free Press, New York.

Rosenfeld, L. and Morville, P. (1998) *Information Architecture for the World Wide Web*. O'Reilly, Sebastopol, CA.

Seybold, P. (1999) *Customers.com*. Century Business Books, London.

Seybold, P. (2001) Get inside the lives of your customers, *Harvard Business Review*, May, 80–9.

Siegel, D. (1997) *Creating Killer Web Sites*, 2nd edn. Hayden Books, Indianapolis, IN.

Smith, P.R. and Chaffey, D. (2001) *EMarketing Excellence – at the Heart of EBusiness*. Butterworth Heinemann, Oxford.

Sterne, J. (1999) *World Wide Web Marketing*, 2nd edn. Wiley, New York.

Styler, A. (2001) Understanding buyer behaviour in the 21st century, *Admap*, September, 23–6.

UCLA (2001) The UCLA Internet Report 2001: Surveying the Digital Future.

University of California Los Angeles (UCLA). Available online at: ccp.ucla.edu/pdf/UCLA-Internet-Report-2001.pdf

Zona Research (1999) The economic impacts of unacceptable web-site download speeds. White paper, April (www.zonaresearch.com).

Further reading

Bevan, N. (1999) Usability issues in web site design, *Proceedings of the 6th Interactive Publishing Conference, November*. Available online at www.usability.serco.com. Accessible, lists of web-design pointers.

Brassington, F. and Petitt, S. (2000) *Principles of Marketing*, 2nd edn. Financial Times/Prentice Hall, Harlow. *See* companion Prentice Hall web site (www.booksites.net/brassington2). Chapter 3, Customer behaviour, describes the stages in the buying-decision process and reviews psychological and environmental inpacts on this. Chapter 5, Customer segmentation, describes methods of identifying different groupings of customers and communicating with them accordingly.

Noyes, J. and Baber, C. (1999) *User-centred Design of Systems*. Springer-Verlag, Berlin. Details the user-centred design approach.

Preece, J., Rogers, Y. and Sharp, H. (2002) *Interaction Design*. Wiley, New York. Clearly describes a structured approach to interaction design, including web interaction.

Siegel, D. (1997) *Creating Killer Web Sites*, 2nd edn. Hayden Books, Indianapolis, IN. Was the state-of-the-art guide to practical web site design and implementation issues when it was published. Useful information online at www.killersites.com.

Web links

- Clickz (www.clickz.com). An excellent collection of articles on online marketing communications. US-focused. Relevant sections for this chapter include: Site design, content development and converting web site traffic.

- Killer sites (www.killersites.com). Site to support David Siegel's book (see Further reading, above). Contains many useful tips.

- Web Pages That Suck (www.webpagesthatsuck.com). Gives a light-hearted review of design best practice by 'learning good web site design through viewing bad web site design'.

- Yale University Press (info.med.yale.edu/caim/manual/contents.html). Supporting site for Lynch, P. and Horton, S. (1999) *Web Style Guide. Basic Design Principles for Creating Web Sites.* Yale University Press, New Haven, CT. Provides a large amount of detail on design.

- Jakob Nielsen's UseIt (www.useit.com). Detailed guidelines (alertboxes) and summaries of research into usability of web media.

- Serco usability (www.usability.serco.com). Articles on design for usability.

- ZD Net (www.zdnet.com/enterprise/e-business/bphome). Summaries of best practice in page design.

Chapter 8

Interactive marketing communications

Chapter at a glance

Main topics

Case studies

Links to other chapters

- Chapter 1 describes the 6 Is, a framework that introduces the characteristics of Internet marketing communications
- Chapter 2 introduces portals and search engines – one of the methods of online traffic building discussed in this chapter
- Chapter 3 introduces some of the legal and ethical constraints on online marketing communications
- Chapter 4 provides the strategic basis for Internet marketing communications
- Chapter 6 describes on-site communications
- Chapter 9 also considers the measurement of communications effectiveness

Learning objectives

After reading this chapter, the reader should be able to:

- Assess the difference in communications characteristics between digital and traditional media
- Identify effective methods for online and offline promotion
- Understand the importance of integrating online and offline promotion
- Relate promotion techniques to methods of measuring site effectiveness

Questions for marketers

Key questions for marketing managers related to this chapter are:

- What are the new types of interactive marketing communications tools I can use?
- How do their characteristics differ from those of traditional media?
- What are the strengths and weaknesses of these promotional tools?
- How do I choose the best mix of online and offline communications techniques?

Introduction

A company that has developed an easy-to-use web site with content and appropriate services to its audience is only part-way to achieving successful Internet marketing outcomes. The idea 'build a great site, and they will come' is not valid – effective marketing communications are necessary to promote the site in order to generate visitors or traffic to the site. Berthon et al. (1998) make the analogy with a trade fair. Here, there will be many companies at different stands promoting their products and services. Effective promotion of a stand is necessary to attract some of the many show visitors to that stand. The concept of 'visibility' can be applied to both the trade show and the Web. From those people noticing and visiting the stand it is then necessary to achieve a successful marketing outcome. In the context of the trade show this is done by capturing the stand visitor's interest for long enough to be able to offer something in order to be able to obtain a person's contact details so that marketing communications can continue – a traditional form of permission marketing. In the context of the web site the aim is similar: to give the visitor an incentive in order to capture their e-mail address and profile their interests as the start of the customer lifecycle.

Using marketing communications tools to promote a web site is challenging. First, the Web is a large place: there are estimated to be over 30 million commercial web sites and several billion web pages, so it is not easy for potential visitors to find out about its existence or for the company to differentiate its offering. Secondly, web site promotion is not straightforward – there are a host of new issues in using traditional communications tools such as advertising and PR, plus novel approaches such as banner advertising and search engine optimisation. Web marketers are still learning what works and what does not. What works this year may not work next year. For example, search engines change in popularity and change payment models.

Figure 8.1 shows the main elements of the traditional communications mix. Where would you place the Internet and other digital media on this diagram? The Internet is not shown since it is simply another medium, like traditional media such as TV, radio, print, and ambient, used for transmission of these communications tools.

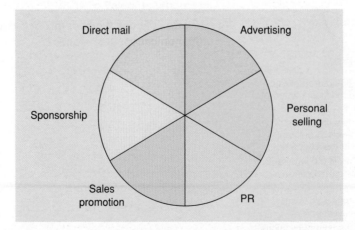

Figure 8.1 The main elements of the communications mix

Most organisations use a combination of the communications tools shown in Figure 8.1 to communicate with their target audiences in order to differentiate their products, remind, reassure, inform and persuade their customers and potential customers. The Internet provides organisations with a new media outlet that offers the opportunity to integrate all promotional mix elements. It has the benefit that a great depth and breadth of information can be readily provided on the web site.

In this chapter, we will explore how the Internet and other digital media can be used to achieve marketing objectives by applying the communications tools of Figure 8.1 in new ways. In the context of Internet marketing, the three main objectives of developing an interactive marketing communications programme are to:

1 use online and offline promotion to drive visitors or traffic to a web site;
2 use on-site communications to deliver an effective message to the visitor which helps shape customer behaviour or achieve a required marketing outcome through conversion marketing;
3 integrate all communications channels to help achieve marketing objectives by supporting mixed-mode buying.

This chapter focuses on the first of these objectives. We start by reviewing the characteristics of digital media such as the Internet, mobile communications and interactive TV since an understanding of this is required to select the most appropriate tools. We then look at techniques of integrated marketing communications and then review the suitability of the full range of tools for online and offline promotion. The chapter is concluded by a section which explores how marketers can decide on the best mix of communications tools as part of communications planning.

The second objective has been covered in the previous chapter, so is not discussed in depth. We introduced the third objective in Chapter 1 (Figure 1.13). The ultimate aim of Internet marketing communications is to achieve sales of products or service regardless of whether the final purchase occurs through the web site or the other media – this is referred to in the sections on integrated marketing communications.

Online site promotion
Internet-based techniques used to generate web site traffic.

Offline site promotion
Traditional techniques such as print and TV advertising used to generate web site traffic.

Mixed-mode buying
The customer's purchase decision is influenced by a range of media such as print, TV and Internet.

The characteristics of interactive marketing communications

Through understanding the key interactive communications characteristics enabled through digital media we can exploit these media while guarding against their weaknesses. In this section, we will describe eight key changes in the media characteristics between traditional and new media. Note that the 6 Is in Chapter 1 provide an alternative framework that is useful for evaluating the differences between traditional media and new media. The eight key changes in communications characteristics as marketers move from exploiting traditional to new media will now be described.

1 From push to pull
Traditional media such as print, TV and radio are push media, one-way streets where information is mainly unidirectional, from company to customer unless direct response elements are built in. In contrast, the Web is an example of pull media. This is its biggest strength and its biggest weakness. It is a strength since pull means that prospects and customers only visit a web site when it enters their head to do so – when they have a defined need – they are proactive and self-selecting. But this is a

Push media
Communications are broadcast from an advertiser to consumers of the message who are passive recipients.

Pull media
The consumer is proactive in selection of the message through actively seeking out a web site.

weakness since online pull means marketers have less control than in traditional communications where the message is pushed out to a defined audience. What are the e-marketing implications of the pull medium? First, we need to provide the physical stimuli to encourage visits to web sites. This may mean traditional ads, direct mail or physical reminders. Second, we need to ensure our site is optimised for search engines – it is registered and is ranked highly on relevant keyword searches. Third, e-mail is important – this is an online push medium, and it should be a priority objective of web site design to capture customers' e-mail addresses in order that opt-in e-mail can be used to push relevant and timely messages to customers. All these techniques are described further later in this chapter.

2 From monologue to dialogue

Interactivity

The medium enables a dialogue between company and customer.

Creating a dialogue through interactivity is the next important feature of the Web and new media. Since the Internet is a digital medium and communications are mediated by software on the web server that hosts the web content, this provides the opportunity for two-way interaction with the customer. This is a distinguishing feature of the medium (Peters, 1998). For example, if a registered customer requests information, or orders a particular product, it will be possible for the supplier to contact them in future using e-mail with details of new offers related to their specific interest. Deighton (1996) proclaimed the interactive benefits of the Internet as a means of developing long-term relationships with customers.

A web site, interactive digital TV and even a mobile phone can enable marketers to enter dialogue with customers. These can be short-term, perhaps an online chat to customer support, or long-term, lifelong dialogues discussing product and supply requirements. These dialogues can enhance customer service, deepen relationships and trust and so build loyalty as described in Chapters 6 and 7.

But digital dialogues have a less obvious benefit also – intelligence. Interactive tools for customer self-help can help collect intelligence – clickstream analysis recorded in the web log file can help us build up valuable pictures of customer preferences. If we profile customers, placing them into different segments we can then build a more detailed picture that is used to refine our products and offers.

3 From one-to-many to one-to-some and one-to-one

Traditional push communications are one-to-many, from one company to many customers, often the same message to different segments and often poorly targeted. With new media 'one-to-some' – reaching a niche or microsegment becomes more practical – e-marketers can afford to tailor and target their message to different segments through providing different site content or e-mail for different audiences through mass customisation. We can even move to one-to-one communications where personalised messages can be delivered according to customer preferences.

Personalisation

Web-based personalisation involves delivering customised content for the individual through web pages, e-mail or push technology.

The interactive nature of the Internet lends itself to establishing dialogues with individual customers. Thus potentially it is a one-to-one communication (from company to customer) rather than the one-to-many communication (from company to customers) that is traditional in marketing using the mass media, such as newspapers or television. Figure 8.2 illustrates the interaction between an organisation (O) communicating a message (M) to customers (C) for a single-step flow of communication. It is apparent that for traditional mass marketing in (a) a single message (M_1) is communicated to all customers (C_1 to C_5). With a web site with personalisation facilities (b) there is a two-way interaction, with each communication potentially being unique. Note that many brochureware sites do not take full advantage of the Internet

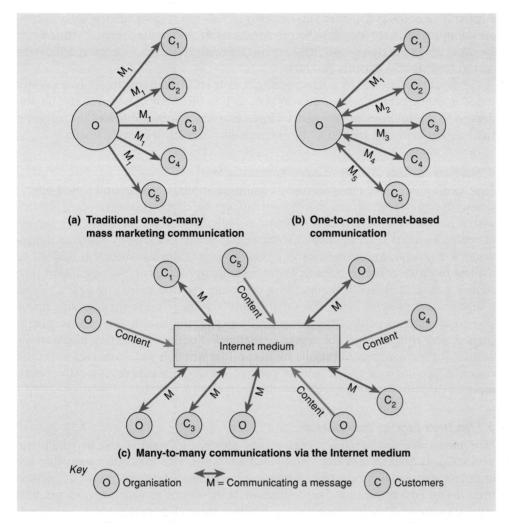

(a) **Traditional one-to-many mass marketing communication**

(b) **One-to-one Internet-based communication**

(c) **Many-to-many communications via the Internet medium**

Key: O Organisation M = Communicating a message C Customers

Figure 8.2 The differences between one-to-many and one-to-one communication using the Internet (organisation (O), communicating a message (M) to customers (C))

and merely use the Web to replicate other media channels by delivering a uniform message.

Hoffman and Novak (1997) believe that this change is significant enough to represent a new model for marketing or a new marketing paradigm. They suggest that the facilities of the Internet including the Web represent a computer-mediated environment in which the interactions are not between the sender and receiver of information, but with the medium itself. They say:

consumers can interact with the medium, firms can provide content to the medium, and in the most radical departure from traditional marketing environments, consumers can provide commercially-oriented content to the media.

This situation is shown in Figure 8.2(c). This potential has not yet been fully developed since many companies are still using the Internet to provide standardised information to a general audience. However, some companies provide personalised Internet-based services to key accounts. An example is Dell (www.dell.com), with its PremierPages.

Furthermore some companies such as eBay (www.ebay.com) or uBid (www.uBid.com) are adopting the new paradigm by offering bespoke auction facilities. Hoffman and Novak (1997) note that consumers can also take part in product design specification and in feedback on existing products.

Despite the reference to a new paradigm, it is still important to apply tried and tested marketing communications concepts such as hierarchy of response and buying process to the Internet environment. However, some opportunities will be missed if the Internet is merely treated as another medium similar to existing media.

4 From one-to-many to many-to-many communications

New media also enable many-to-many communications. Hoffman and Novak (1996) noted that new media are many-to-many media. Here customers can interact with other customers via your web site or in independent communities. The success of online auctions such as eBay also shows the power of many-to-many communications. However, online discussion groups represent a threat since it is difficult to control negative communications about a company. For example, one recent post to newsgroup 'uk.food+drink.misc' by a consumer referred to finding a rat's foot in a supermarket product. Since the supermarket was monitoring these groups it was able to attempt to control the situation by explaining that it was 'an irregularly shaped, very thin fragment of vegetable material'. So, the e-marketing implications of many-to-many communications are to consider whether you should set up online communities on your site or with a partner, or whether you deploy resources to monitor other independent communities on specialist portals.

5 From 'lean-back' to 'lean-forward'

New media are also intense media – they are lean-forward media in which the web site usually has the visitor's undivided attention. This intensity means that the customer wants to be in control and wants to experience flow and responsiveness to their needs. First impressions are important. If the visitor to your site does not find what they are looking for immediately, whether through poor design or slow speed, they will move on, probably never to return.

6 The medium changes the nature of standard marketing communications tools such as advertising

In addition to offering the opportunity for one-to-one marketing, the Internet can be, and still is widely, used for one-to-many advertising. On the Internet the overall message from the advertiser becomes less important, and typically it is detailed information the user is seeking. The web site itself can be considered as similar in function to an advertisement (since it can inform, persuade and remind customers about the offering, although it is not paid for in the same way as a traditional advertisement). Berthon et al. (1996) consider a web site as a mix between advertising and direct selling since it can also be used to engage the visitor in a dialogue. Constraints on advertising in traditional mass media such as paying for time or space become less important. A later section in this chapter explores the differences the Internet implies for different elements of the communications mix including advertising.

Peters (1998) suggests that communication via the new medium is differentiated from communication using traditional media in four different ways. First, *communication style* is changed, with *immediate*, or synchronous transfer of information through

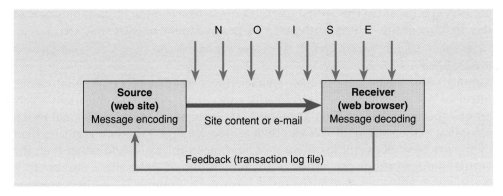

Figure 8.3 The communications model of Schramm (1955) applied to the Internet

online customer service being possible. Asynchronous communication, where there is a time delay between sending and receiving information as through e-mail, also occurs. Second, *social presence* or the feeling that a communications exchange is sociable, warm, personal and active may be lower if a standard web page is delivered, but can be enhanced, perhaps by personalisation. Third, the consumer has more *control of contact*, and finally the user has control of *content*, for example through personalisation facilities such as Silicon (Figure 6.8).

Although Hoffman and Novak (1996) point out that with the Internet the main relationships are not *directly* between sender and receiver of information, but with the web-based environment, the classic communications model of Schramm (1955) can still be used to help understand the effectiveness of marketing communication using the Internet. Figure 8.3 shows the model applied to the Internet. Four of the elements of the model that can constrain the effectiveness of Internet marketing are:

- *encoding* – this is the design and development of the site content or e-mail that aims to convey the message of the company, and is dependent on understanding of the target audience;
- *noise* – this is the external influence that affects the quality of the message; in an Internet context this can be slow download times, the use of plug-ins that the user cannot use or confusion caused by too much information on-screen;
- *decoding* – this is the process of interpreting the message, and is dependent on the cognitive ability of the receiver, which is partly influenced by the length of time they have used the Internet;
- *feedback* – this occurs through online forms and through monitoring of on-site behaviour through log files (Chapter 9).

7 Increase in communications intermediaries

If we consider advertising and PR, with traditional media, this increase occurs through a potentially large number of media owners such as TV and radio channel owners and the owners of newspaper and print publications such as magazines. In the Internet era there is a vastly increased range of media owners or publishers through which marketers can promote their services and specifically gain links to their web site. Traditional radio channels, newspapers and print titles have migrated online, but in addition there are a vast number of online-only publishers including horizontal portals (Chapter 2) such as search engines and vertical portals such as industry-specific sites. The online marketer needs to select the most appropriate of this plethora of sites which customers visit to drive traffic to their web site.

8 Integration

Although new media have distinct characteristics compared to traditional media, this does not mean we should necessarily concentrate our communications solely on new media. Rather we should combine and integrate new and traditional media according to their strengths. We can then achieve synergy – the sum is greater than their parts. Most of us still spend most of our time in the real world rather than the virtual world, so offline promotion of the proposition of a web site is important. It is also important to support mixed-mode buying. For example, a customer wanting to buy a computer may see a TV ad for a certain brand which raises awareness of the brand and then see an advert in a print ad that directs them across to the web site for further information. However, the customer does not want to buy online, preferring the phone, but the site allows for this by prompting with a phone number at the right time. Here all the different communications channels are mutually supporting each other.

Similarly inbound communications to a company need to be managed. Consider if the customer needs support for an error with their system. They may start by using the on-site diagnostics which do not solve the problem. They then ring customer support. This process will be much more effective if support staff can access the details of the problem as previously typed in by the customer to the diagnostics package.

Evans and Wurster (1999) have suggested an alternative framework for how the balance of marketing communications may be disrupted by the Internet. They consider three aspects of consumer navigation that they refer to as reach, affiliation and richness. *Reach* refers to the number of different categories and products a consumer interface (e.g. store, catalogue or web site) can cover. It can be argued that the Web offers the greatest potential for communicating the full range of products. Reach also refers to the number of customers a business can interact with. Again the Web enables the reach to be increased through its global nature. Potential customers can also be potentially reached at a lower cost through technologies such as search engines. *Affiliation* refers to whose interests are most important to an online merchant – the customer's, the retailer's or the supplier's? *Richness* is how much information can be exchanged between a producer and consumer. Richness has two aspects: customer information and product information. In a marketing communications context, we can say that the Internet offers the customer a greater depth or richness of information when making product and supplier selections. Evans and Wurster (1999) say that this may decrease the value of some brands where selection is based on information. Additionally, online marketing communications involves increasing the amount of information that can be obtained about the customer and their behaviour in order to better profile them as part of CRM.

● Differences in advertising between traditional and new media

Evaluation of the differences between traditional and new media for advertising is necessary in order to select the best media for promoting the online presence. Janal (1998) considers how Internet advertising differs from traditional advertising in a number of key areas. These are summarised in Table 8.1.

Table 8.1 Key concepts of advertising in the new and old media

	Old media	New media
Space	Expensive commodity	Cheap, unlimited
Time	Expensive commodity for marketers	Expensive commodity for users
Image creation	Image most important Information is secondary	Information most important Image is secondary
Communication	Push, one-way	Pull, interactive
Call to action	Incentives	Information (incentives)

Source: After Janal (1998)

The main differences that should be noted are:

- The cost of advertising in the new medium reduces as more space becomes available.
- It is the customer who initiates the dialogue and who will expect his or her specific needs to be addressed. Web marketers need to promote their web sites effectively in order that customers find the information they are looking for.
- The user's time is valuable and the time interacting with the user will be limited. So this time must be maximised.
- Information is the main currency. Supplying information is arguably more important than appealing to emotions.

We can extend this analysis by considering the effectiveness of offline media in comparison with online media. We can make the following observations:

1 *Reach of media*. We saw in Chapters 2 and 3, that access to the Internet has exceeded 50% in many developed countries. While this indicates that the Internet is now a mass medium, there are a significant minority that don't have access and cannot be reached via this medium. As we saw in Chapter 2, reach varies markedly by age and social group, so the Internet is innappropriate for reaching some groups.
2 *Media consumption*. Most customers spend more of their time in the real world than the virtual world so it follows that it may be the best method to reach them. The panel data referred to in Table 2.5 (p. 79) suggested that web users are spending an average of 9 hours per month online – significantly less than the time they spend watching TV or reading newspapers each month. However, a counter-argument to this is that the intensity and depth of online interactions are greater.
3 *Involvement*. Use of the Internet has been described as a 'lean-forward' experience, suggesting high involvement based on the interactivity and control exerted by web users. This means that the user is receptive to content on a site. However, there is evidence that certain forms of graphic advertising such as banner adverts are filtered out when informational content is sought. A study of online newspaper readers (Poynter, 2000) found that text and captions were read first, with readers then later returning to graphics.
4 *Building awareness*. It can be argued that because of the form of their creative, some forms of offline advertising such as TV are more effective at explaining concepts and creating retention (Branthwaite et al., 2000).

We conclude this section with a review of how consumers perceive the Internet in comparison to traditional media. Refer to Mini Case Study 8.1 for the summary of the results of a qualitative survey.

Consumer perceptions of the Internet and different media

Branthwaite et al. (2000) conducted a global qualitative project covering 14 countries, across North and South America, East and West Europe, Asia and Australia to investigate consumer perceptions of the Internet and other media. In order to reflect changing media habits and anticipate future trends, a young, dynamic sample were selected in the 18–35 age range, with access to the Internet, and regular users of all four media. Consumers' perceptions of the Internet, when asked to explain how they felt about the Internet in relation to different animals, was as follows:

The dominant sense here was of something exciting, but also inherently malevolent, dangerous and frightening in the Internet.

The positive aspect was expressed mainly through images of a bird but also a cheetah or dolphin. These captured the spirit of freedom, opening horizons, versatility, agility, effortlessness and efficiency. Even though these impressions were relative to alternative ways of accomplishing goals, they were sometimes naive or idealistic. However, there was more scepticism about these features with substantial experience or great naivety.

Despite their idealism and enthusiasm for the Internet, these users found a prevalent and deep-rooted suspicion of the way it operated. The malevolent undertones of the Internet came through symbols of snakes or foxes predominantly, which were associated with cunning, slyness, and unreliability. While these symbols embodied similar suspicions, the snake was menacing, intimidating, treacherous and evasive, while the fox was actively deceptive, predatory, surreptitious, plotting, and persistent. For many consumers, the Internet was felt to have a will of its own, in the form of the creators of the sites (the ghosts in the machine). A snake traps you and then tightens its grip. A fox is mischievous.

In comparison with other media, the Internet was described as follows:

The Internet seemed less like a medium of communication than the others, and more like a reservoir of information.

This distinction was based on differences in the mode of operating: other media communicated to you whereas with the Internet the user had to actively seek and extract information for themselves. In this sense, the Internet is a recessive medium that sits waiting to be interrogated, whereas other media are actively trying to target their communications to the consumer.

- This meant that these users (who were not addicted or high internet users) were usually task orientated and focussed on manipulating their way around (tunnel vision). The more inexperienced you were, the more concentration was needed, but irritation or frustration was never far away for most people.
- Everywhere, regardless of experience and availability, the Internet was seen as a huge resource, with futuristic values, that indicated the way the world was going to be. It was respected for its convenience and usefulness. Through the Internet you could learn, solve problems, achieve goals, travel the world without leaving your desk, and enter otherwise inaccessible spaces. It gave choice and control, but also feelings of isolation and inadequacy. There was an onus on people wherever possible to experience this medium and use it for learning and communicating.
- The most positive attitudes were in North America. Slick and well-structured Web-sites made a positive impression and were a valuable means of securing information through the links to other sites and to carry out e-commerce. However, even here there was frustration at slow downloading and some uncooperative sites.

- In other countries, there was concern at the irresponsibility of the medium, lack of serious-ness and dependability. There was desire for supervisory and controlling bodies (which are common for Print and TV).
- Banner ads were resented as contributing to the distractions and irritations. Sometimes they seemed deliberately hostile by distracting you and then getting you lost. Internet advertising had the lowest respect and status, being regarded as peripheral and trivial.
- In the least economically advanced countries, the Internet was considered a divisive medium which excluded those without the resources, expertise or special knowledge.

Table 8.2 presents the final evaluation of the Internet against other media.

Table 8.2 Comparison of the properties of different media

	TV	Outdoor	Print	Internet
Intrusiveness	High	High	Low	Low
Control/selectivity of consumption	Passive	Passive	Active, selective	Active, selective
Episode attention span	Long	Short	Long	Restless, fragmented
Active processing	Low	Low	High	High
Mood	Relaxed Seeking emotional gratification	Bored, under-stimulated	Relaxed Seeking interest, stimulation	Goal-orientated Needs-related
Modality	Audio/visual	Visual	Visual	Visual (auditory increasing)
Processing	Episodic Superficial	Episodic/semantic	Semantic Deep	Semantic Deep
Context	As individual in interpersonal setting	Solitary (in public space)	Individual Personal	Alone Private

Source: Branthwaite et al. (2000)

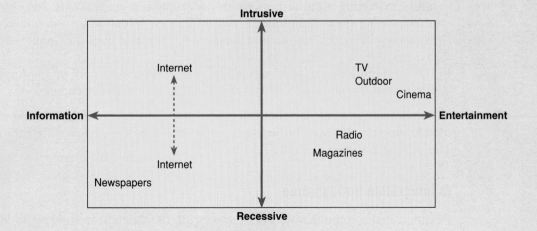

Figure 8.4 Summary of the different characteristics of media
Source: Millward Brown Qualitative

Integrated Internet marketing communications

Integrated marketing communications

The coordination of communications channels to deliver a clear, consistent message.

In common with other communications media, the Internet will be most effective when it is deployed as part of an integrated marketing communications approach. Kotler et al. (2001) describe integrated marketing communications as:

the concept under which a company carefully integrates and co-ordinates its many communications channels to deliver a clear, consistent message about the organisation and its products.

The characteristics of integrated marketing communications have been summarised by Pickton and Broderick (2000) as the 4 Cs of:

- *Coherence* – different communications are logically connected.
- *Consistency* – multiple messages support and reinforce, and are not contradictory.
- *Continuity* – communications are connected and consistent through time.
- *Complementary* – synergistic, or the sum of the parts is greater than the whole!

The 4 Cs also act as guidelines for how communications should be integrated.

Further guidelines on integrated marketing communications from Pickton and Broderick (2000) that can be usefully applied to Internet marketing are the following.

1 Communications planning is based on *clearly identified marketing communications objectives* (see later section).
2 Internet marketing involves the *full range of target audiences* (see the section on customer orientation in Chapter 7). The full range of target audiences is the customer segments plus employees, shareholders and suppliers).
3 Internet marketing should involve *management of all forms of contact*, which includes management of both outbound communications such as banner advertising or direct e-mail and inbound communications such as e-mail enquiries.
4 Internet marketing should utilise a *range of promotional tools*. These are the promotional tools illustrated in Figure 8.1.
5 *A range of media* should be used to deliver the message about the web site. Marketing managers need to consider the most effective mix of media to drive traffic to their web site. The different techniques can be characterised as traditional offline marketing communications or new online communications. The objective of employing these techniques is to acquire new traffic on an e-commerce site using the techniques summarised in Figure 8.5. Many of these techniques can also be used to drive customers to a site for retention.
6 The communications plan should involve careful selection of *most effective promotional and media mix*. This is discussed at the end of the chapter.

Additionally, we can say that integrated marketing communications should be used to support customers through the entire buying process, across different media. This process is shown in Figure 7.10.

● Integration through time

For integrated communications to be successful, the different techniques should be successfully integrated through time as part of a campaign or campaigns.

Figure 8.6 shows how communications can be planned around a particular event. (SE denotes 'search engine'; C1 and C2 are campaigns 1 and 2.) Here we have chosen the launch of a new version of a web site, but other alternatives include a

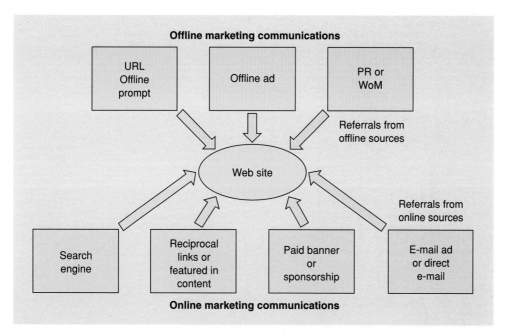

Figure 8.5 Common offline and online communications techniques used to drive visitors to a web site

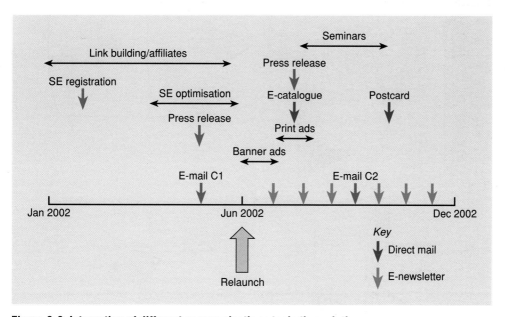

Figure 8.6 Integration of different communications tools through time

new product launch or a key seminar. This planning will help provide a continuous message to customers. It also ensures a maximum number of customers are reached using different media over the period.

Communications can also be integrated through time during a particular campaign. The web response model (Hughes, 1999) is one that is frequently used today in direct marketing. This is usually a permission-based model (Chapter 6) and an example is shown in Figure 8.7. It starts with a direct mail drop or e-mail shot. The

Web response model

The web site is used as the response mechanism for a direct marketing campaign delivered by e-mail or by post.

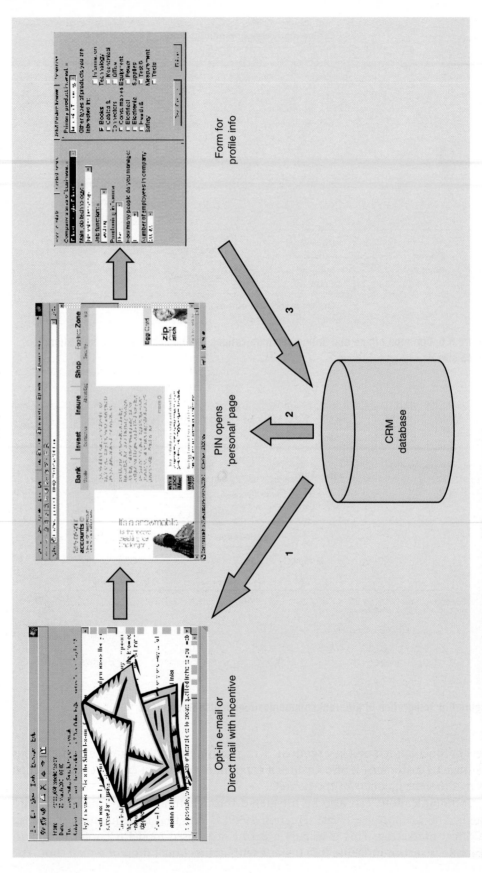

Figure 8.7 Communications supporting retention through the Web response model

web site is used as the direct response mechanism, hence 'web response'. Ideally, this approach will use targeting of different segments. For example, a Netherlands bank devised a campaign targeting six different segments based on age and income. The initial letter was delivered by post and contained a PIN (personal identification number) which had to be typed in when the customer visited the site. The PIN had the dual benefit that it could be used to track responses to the campaign, while at the same time personalising the message to the consumer. When the PIN was typed in, a 'personal page' was delivered for the customer with an offer that was appropriate to their particular circumstances.

In keeping with planning for other media, Pincott (2000) suggests there are two key strategies in planning integrated Internet marketing communications. First, there should be a media strategy which will mainly be determined by how to reach the target audience. This will define the online promotion techniques described in this chapter and where to advertise online. Second, there is the creative strategy. Pincott says that 'the dominant online marketing paradigm is one of direct response'. However, he goes on to suggest that all site promotion will also influence perceptions of the brand.

● Callback services

Television and newspaper advertisements commonly feature a direct response option via a freephone number. This concept has translated to the Web and is increasingly being used by companies with call-centre operations that can handle this type of enquiry in volume. It is usually referred to as a **callback service** and integrates Web and phone. RealCall is a service offered by several rival suppliers to any company with a web site. It can be seen from Figure 8.8 that it provides a form, to be filled in

Web callback service

A facility available on the web site for a company to contact a customer at a later time as specified by the customer.

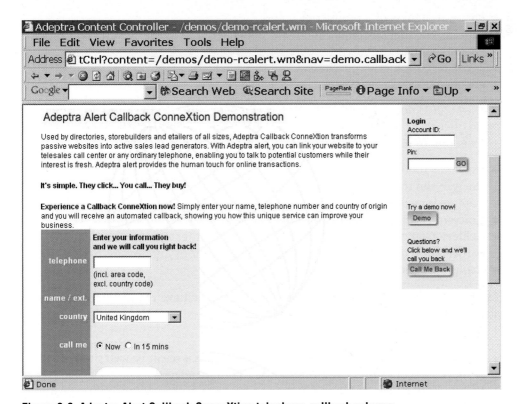

Figure 8.8 Adeptra Alert Callback ConneXtion telephone callback scheme

by the customer so that he or she can be called by a service representative at a later time. This has the advantage, for the customer, that the company pays the phone bill, but on a practical level, home users accessing the Internet from home using a modem and a single phone line will be unable to receive a phone call while online, and may forget about the request later. The callback mechanism is consistent with the general philosophy of using the Internet to facilitate communications with the customer and of using the method that suits the customer best.

Objectives for interactive marketing communications

As was mentioned in the introduction to this chapter, an interactive marketing communications plan usually has three main goals:

Traffic building
Using online and offline site promotion techniques to generate visitors to a site.

SMART
Specific, Measurable, Actionable, Relevant and Time-related.

(1) Use online and offline communications to drive or attract visitors traffic to a web site. This process is commonly referred to as **traffic building**.
Examples of SMART traffic building objectives:

- Generate awareness of Web offering in 80% of existing customer base in one year.
- Generate awareness of Web offering in each market within 1 year.
- Achieve 10 000 new site visitors within one year.
- Convert 30% of existing customer base to regular site visitors.

(2) Use on-site communications to deliver an effective message to the visitor which helps shape customer behaviour or achieve a required marketing outcome. The message delivered on-site will be based on traditional marketing communications objectives for a company's products or services. For example:

- create awareness of a product or brand;
- inform potential customers about a product;
- encourage trial;
- persuade customer to purchase;
- encourage further purchases.

Rowley (2001) notes that while the Internet is generally effective in supporting these types of goals, it seems to be less effective in changing and maintaining attitudes.
Examples of on-site communications objectives:

- Generate 1000 new potential customers in Europe by converting new visitors to the web site to qualified leads.
- Capture e-mail addresses and profile information for 100 leads in first 6 months.
- Convert 3% of visitors to a particular part of site to buyers across the year.
- Achieve relationship building and deepen brand interaction by encouraging 10% participation of customer base in online competitions and forums.
- Acquire 100 new contacts through viral referrals.

(3) Integrate all communications methods to help achieve marketing objectives by supporting mixed-mode buying.
Examples of mixed-mode buying objectives.

- Achieve 20% of sales achieved in the call centre as a result of web site visits.
- Achieve 20% of online sales in response to offline adverts.
- Reduce contact-centre phone enquiries by 15% by providing online customer services.

It is evident that companies will develop specific objectives in each area such as the number of new visitors directed to the site. Although traffic-building objectives and measures of effectiveness are often referred to in terms of traffic *quantity*, such as the number of visitors or page impressions, it is the traffic *quality* that really indicates the success of interactive marketing communications (e.g. van Doren et al., 2000); Smith and Chaffey, 2001). Traffic quality is determined by:

- whether the visitors are within the target audience for the web site;
- whether the visitors respond on-site in line with the communications objectives.

● Conversion marketing objectives

Internet marketing objectives can also be stated in terms of conversion marketing. This technique of objective setting uses a bottom-up approach to objective setting as shown in Figure 8.9. Take, for example, the objectives of a campaign for a B2B services company such as a consultancy company, where the ultimate objective is to achieve 100 new clients using the web site in combination with traditional media to convert leads to action. To achieve this level of new business, the marketer will need to make assumptions about the level of conversion that is needed at each stage of converting prospects to customers. This gives a core objective of 100 new clients and different critical success factors based on the different conversion rates.

It is also worth noting that communications objectives will differ according to the stage of development of an e-commerce service. Rowley (2001) suggests that the general goals of these four stages are:

- *Contact* – promoting corporate image, publishing corporate information and offering contact information. Content.
- *Interact* – embed information exchange. Communication.
- *Transact* – online transactions and interaction with trading partners. Commerce.
- *Relate* – two-way customer relationship. Community.

Four similar levels of intensity of promotional activity are also identified by van Doren et al. (2000).

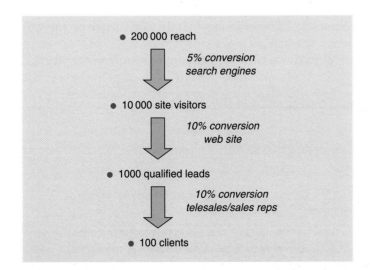

Figure 8.9 Conversion marketing approach to objective setting

● Timescales for objective setting

Smith and Chaffey (2001) refer to the relevance of timing for traffic building. They say:

> *Some e-marketers may consider traffic building to be a continuous process, but others may view it as a specific campaign, perhaps to launch a site or a major enhancement. Some methods tend to work best continuously; others are short term. Short-term campaigns will be for a site launch or an event such as an online trade show.*

Accordingly, online marketers can develop communications objectives for different timescales:

- *Annual marketing communications objectives*. For example, achieving new site visitors or gaining qualified leads could be measured across an entire year since this will be a continuous activity based on visitor building through search engines and other campaigns. Annual budgets are set to help achieve these objectives.
- *Campaign-specific communications objectives*. Internet marketing campaigns such as a direct e-mail campaign will help fulfil the annual objectives. Specific objectives can be stated for each in terms of gaining new visitors, converting visitors to customers and encouraging repeat purchases. Campaign objectives should build on traditional marketing objectives, have specific target audience and have measurable outcomes which can be attributed to the specific campaign.

● Costs

The final aspect of objective setting to be considered is the constraints on objectives placed by the cost of traffic building activities. A campaign will not be successful if it meets its objectives of acquiring site visitors and customers but the cost of achieving this is too high. This constraint is usually imposed simply by having a campaign budget – a necessary component of all campaigns. However, in addition it is also useful to have specific objectives for the cost of getting the visitor to the site, and the cost of achieving the outcomes during their visit. Typical cost measures include:

Cost of acquisition

Marketing communications costs incurred in gaining visitors or customers.

- cost of acquisition per visitor;
- cost of acquisition per lead or enquiry;
- cost of acquisition per sale (customer acquisition cost).

Costs within the campaign can be compared for different sources of traffic such as referrals from banner adverts on different sites. To be able to measure cost per action we need to be able to track a customer from when they first arrive on the web site through to when the action is taken.

To see further examples of objective setting for campaigns, complete Activity 8.1.

Activity 8.1   **Objectives from *Revolution* campaign of the month**   **Web**

Purpose

To provide examples of objectives for different Internet marketing campaigns.

Activity

Visit *Revolution* (www.revolutionmagazine.com) and summarise each campaign by creating a table with these columns:

- name of client;
- objectives of campaign;
- creative;

- Internet marketing promotion technique used;
- results or how success was measured.

Mini Case Study 8.2 is an example of the type of information you should find.

Mini Case Study 8.2

Thistle hotels

This case study shows how objectives can be stated, how these link through to the execution of the campaign and how its success is evaluated.

Aim of campaign

- Generate bookings and qualified leads.
- Increase unique users by 25% and increase business traveller database by 25%.

Creative

Campaign message pushed the central location of Thistle and the ease of booking online. Targeted at business travellers and personal assistants (PAs).

Execution

Drop-down banner ads were used on Freeserve and Ask Jeeves and e-mails were sent to opt-in subscriber databases of people interested in business travel. Relevant keyword search terms were reserved on Ask Jeeves, Freeserve, Streetmap and Yahoo!.

Results

Using data from Engage's DataDNA, Thistle found that revenue had increased by 23% as a direct result of the campaign. People who saw the ads and did not click on them, but still went to the Thistle web site and booked, made up half of the bookings. At the end of the campaign, the number of unique users visiting the Thistle site had grown by 37.5% and the customer database had increased by 98%.

Source: *Revolution* campaign of the week (www.revolutionmagazine.com), 2001

Offline promotion techniques

Online promotion techniques such as search engine registration and banner advertising often take prominence when discussing methods of traffic building, but we start here with offline traffic building since it is one of the main techniques used to generate site traffic. **Offline promotion** refers to using different communications tools such as advertising and PR delivered by traditional media such as TV, radio and print in order to direct visitors to an online presence.

Offline promotion

Using traditional media such as TV, radio and print to direct visitors to an online presence.

Jay Walker, co-founder of Priceline.com, an online intermediary for travel products, has said:

> *Priceline.com has been about building a brand as opposed to building traffic. In advertising, you're building a larger context around who you are as a company. To do that, online advertising just doesn't cut it.*

In its first 12 months, Priceline.com spent $40 million to $50 million on old-media advertising. This example highlights the importance of offline media in creating awareness and brand-building for start-up Web companies. But, what about existing companies who are seeking to promote their online presence? These companies can modify their existing use of offline media for advertising as explained in the section below on incidental and specific advertising.

The offline promotion methods used by existing companies usually involve highlighting the existence of the web site. The normal technique will involve printing the web address (URL) of the web site in a printed or television advertisement. Here, the Internet is acting as an alternative method of facilitating a direct response. Rather than viewers of the advertisement being encouraged to ring a freephone number to give their name to obtain further information, they can be directed to the web site instead. The Internet provides a more informal type of direct response advertising, which may appeal to some people. However, it can be argued that the Internet is not as effective at establishing a dialogue as asking a person to ring a freephone number, in that the phone approach is more immediate and has a better opportunity for capturing a person's contact details. If the customer ventures on to the web they may well be diverted from the advertising organisation's site to a competitor's site by a search engine or comparison site. This could explain why many financial services advertisements in newspapers often contain a prominent freephone number, but a much smaller web address!

We saw in Chapter 1 that one of the key benefits of the Internet as a communications tool, is the ability to target more precisely than traditional media. Visitors to a site or part of a site with particular informational content will be self-selecting. For example, a visitor to a used car site can only be interested in purchasing a used car. However, the targeting possible through traditional offline media such as advertising during a niche programme or in a particular trade magazine is equivalent and may be sufficient for an advertiser's needs.

● Incidental and specific advertising of the online presence

Incidental offline advertising

Driving traffic to the web site is not a primary objective of the advert.

Specific offline advertising

Driving traffic to the web site or explaining the online proposition is a primary objective of the advert.

Two types of offline advertising can be identified: incidental and specific. Reference to the web site is incidental if the main aim of the advert is to advertise a particular product and the web site is available as an ancillary source of information if required by the viewer. Traditionally, much promotion of the web site in the offline media by traditional companies has been incidental – simply consisting of highlighting the existence of the web site by including the URL at the bottom of an advertisement. Reference to the web site is specific if it is an objective of the advert to explain the proposition of the web site in order to drive traffic to the site to achieve direct response. Here the advert will highlight the offers or services available at the web site, such as sales promotions or online customer service. Amazon commonly advertises in newspapers to achieve this. Naturally, this approach is most likely to be used by companies that only have an online presence, but existing companies can develop strap lines to use which explain the web-site value proposition (Chapter 4). Many state 'Visit our web site!!', but clearly, a more specific strap line can be developed which describes the overall proposition of the site ('detailed information and product guides to help you select the best product for you') or is specific to the campaign ('we will give you an instant quote online, showing how much you save with us').

Publicising the URL offline

There are some specialist techniques of specifying the URL (web address) that can be used to help customers in finding the information they need on the web site. When advertising in traditional media such as a newspaper or magazine it is beneficial not to give as the address the home page, but a specific page that is related to the offline promotion and the interests of the audience. For example:

- in an American magazine: Jaguar (www.jaguar.com/us);
- in an advertisement for a phone from a company that sells other products: Ericsson (www.ericsson.com/us/phones);
- for a specific digital camera: Agfa (www.agfahome.com/ephoto).

Providing the specific page enables the user to be sent direct to the relevant information without having to navigate through the corporate site – which can be difficult for companies with a diverse product range. A further advantage of using a specific web address is for measuring advertising effectiveness. If there is no other way of navigating to that page on the site, it can then be established how many people arriving at a site on this page have viewed the orginal advertisement. For brand building and establishing the credibility of a site, it is, however, more normal not to give a specific web address.

A similar technique is to use a sub-domain different from the main domain, or to register a completely different domain name that is in keeping with the campaign, as in the following examples:

- Canon's www.csci.canon.com/6000 rather than www.canon.com;
- Honda's www.drivehonda.com rather than www.honda.com;
- HarperCollins's www.fireandwater.com rather than www.collins.co.uk;
- ntl www.askntl.com to highlight that the site has the answers to questions such as: Who are ntl? What are their services?

Dell and other e-tailers use 'e-codes' in print media to help users find particular products online by typing in a code.

● Public relations

Public relations can be an important tool for driving traffic to the web site if changes to online services or online events are significant. The days of the launch of a web site being significant are now gone, but if a site is relaunched with significant changes to its services, this may still be worthy of mention. Many newspapers have regular features listing interesting entertainment or leisure sites or guides to specific topics such as online banking or grocery shopping. Trade magazines may also give information about relevant web sites.

Public relations (PR) activity on the Web also offers organisations scope for corporate communications, sponsorship, publicity and a direct vehicle for communicating press releases. The Internet provides scope for two-way interaction, clear targeting of key opinion-formers and journalists and the potential for communicating strong corporate brand messages.

The Internet can be used to facilitate traditional methods of PR. It can also be used to expand the depth and breadth of PR.

Most press agencies now use the Internet as a primary source of information. Press releases can be sent by e-mail to agencies with which a company is registered, and can also be made available on a company's web site.

With this new method of PR, a key difference is that a company can talk direct to the market via the corporate web site. Third-party agencies and old media still have a role, because of their credibility as independent sources of information and their wider circulation. Agency information can be supplemented by more detailed and timely information direct from the corporate web site. Another way in which the new PR is different is that traditional weekly and monthly publishing deadlines disappear as new stories appear by the minute. This has the obvious benefit that a company can make an immediate impact and be better aware of the changing marketing environment. The obvious problem of the new PR is that a company's competitors have these advantages too. So it is likely that there will be an increased need for defensive PR.

Jenkins (1995) argues that one key objective for public relations is its role in transforming a negative situation into a positive achievement. The public relations transfer process he suggests is as follows:

- from ignorance to knowledge;
- from apathy to interest;
- from prejudice to acceptance;
- from hostility to sympathy.

Based on an assessment of the biotechnology sector, Ranchod et al. (2002) suggest that a web site can be used to support each element of the public relations transfer process. Their assessment of biotechnology companies suggested that PR-related web content was provided in these areas: general profile (About Us), newsletter, educational information, special events, discussion forum, external links and investor relations.

● Direct marketing

Direct marketing can be an effective method of driving traffic to the web site. As mentioned in Chapter 6 and the section on integrated communications, a web response model can be used where the web site is the means for fulfilling the response, but a direct mail campaign is used to drive the response. Many catalogue companies will continue to use traditional direct mail to mail-out a subset of their offering, with the recipient tempted to visit the site through the fuller offering and incentives such as competitions or web-specific offers.

An example of an offline adverts for an online sales promotion is that reported in *Revolution* (2000). EasyJet ran its first Internet-only promotion in a newspaper in *The Times* in February 1999. Some 50 000 seats were offered to readers and 20 000 of them were sold on the first day, rising to 40 000 within three days. The scalability of the Internet helped deal with demand since everyone was directed to a *Times* microsite (www.times.easyjet.com) web site rather than the company needing to employ an extra 250 telephone operators. A subsequent five-week promotion within *The Times* and *The Sunday Times* newspapers offered cheap flights to a choice of all easyJet destinations when 18 tokens were collected. In total, 100 000 seats were sold during the promotion, which was worth more than £2m to the airline.

● Other physical reminders

Since we all spend more time in the real rather than the virtual world, physical reminders explaining why customers should visit web sites are significant. What is in customers' hands and on their desk top will act as a prompt to visit a site and counter the weakness of the Web as a pull medium. This is perhaps most important in the B2B context where a physical reminder in the office can be helpful. Examples, usually delivered through direct marketing, include brochures, catalogues, business cards, point-of-sale material, pens, etc. from trade shows, postcards, inserts in magazines and password reminders for extranets. In a B2C context on-pack promotions can be used to direct customers to web sites. *Revolution* (2000) reported that

Bestfoods, the Marmite brand owner, wanted to create an on-pack dialogue allowing customers to interact with the brand through the internet. The activity aimed to use the pack space to promote innovative serving suggestions, to increase frequency of use among light users and to build penetration among lapsed users. Point-of-sale materials can be useful to retailers in promoting online offers for retailers. For example, retailers such as Dixons and WH Smith have successfully used CDs available in-store to build use of their ISP service.

● Word of mouth

It is worth remembering that, in addition to the methods above, word of mouth is playing an important role in promoting sites, particularly consumer sites, where the Internet is currently a novelty. A report by Opinion Research Corporation International, ORCI, reported on a study amongst US consumers that showed that the typical Internet consumer tells 12 other people about his or her online shopping experience. This compares with the average US consumer, who tells 8.6 additional people about a favourite film and another 6.1 people about a favourite restaurant! It has been said that if the online experience is favourable a customer will tell 12 people, but if it is bad, they will tell twice as many, so word of mouth can be negative also. Parry (1998) reported that for European users, word of mouth through friends, relatives and colleagues was the most important method by which users found out about web sites, being slightly more important than search engines and directories or links from other sites.

Thus the role of opinion leaders and multi-step communications with target audiences receiving information about the Internet experience from opinion leaders, the mass media and the Internet, appear to be perhaps even more important in relation to the Internet than for other media. Dichter (1966) summarised how word-of-mouth communications work. To exploit such communications, it is necessary for marketers to use appropiate techniques to target and adapt the message for the opinion leaders when a product or service is at an early stage of diffusion (Rogers, 1983). Viral marketing (see later) will often target these opinion leaders to advocates in initial contacts.

Online promotion techniques

In this section we will review approaches to online promotion using the different tools of Figure 8.4, including banner advertisements, e-mail and other methods of linking to sites. These techniques are often combined in what is known as a **traffic-building campaign**; this is a method of increasing the audience of a site using different online (and possibly offline) techniques.

The relative importance of online promotion techniques is indicated by a European study that shows that nearly half of European marketers are participating in online marketing (Doubleclick, 2001). The study surveyed 3000 marketers from France, Germany, Italy, Scandinavia, Spain and the UK. In some countries, such as the UK, this increases to 73%. The level of spending as part of the marketing marketing budget is significant: 49% of UK marketers, 38% of Spanish marketers and 39% of Scandinavian marketers planned to spend 15% or more of their total budget on online marketing in 2001. The types of spend on different communications tools are as follows:

Traffic-building campaign

The use of online and offline promotion techniques such as banner advertising, search engine promotion and reciprocal linking to increase the audience of a site (both new and existing customers).

- in the UK, 58% of marketers use e-mail marketing and 50% participate in targeted banner advertising;
- in Spain, 54% of marketers engage in e-mail marketing and 37% engage in targeted banner advertising;
- France is the only country citing higher usage of targeted banner advertising (10%) compared with e-mail marketing (9%).

Online promotion – banner advertising

Ad serving

The term for displaying an advertisement on a web site. Often the advertisement will be served from a web server different from the site on which it is placed.

Banner advertisement

A rectangular graphic displayed on a web page for the purposes of advertising. It is normally possible to perform a clickthrough to access further information. Banners may be static or animated.

Destination site

The site reached on clickthrough.

Microsite

A small-scale destination site reached on click-through which is part of the media owner's site.

It can be contended that each web site is in itself an advertisement since it can inform, persuade and remind customers about a company or its products and services. However, a company web site is not strictly an advertisement in the conventional sense, since money is not exchanged to place the content of the web site on a medium owned by a third party. Advertising on the World Wide Web is generally acknowledged to take place when an advertiser pays to place advertising content on another web site. The process usually involves ad serving from a different server from that on which the page is hosted. The simplest and most common model of advertising is shown in Figure 8.10, where the advertiser places a banner advertisement on a range of sites in order to drive traffic to an organisation's destination site or alternately a microsite or nested ad-content. These are so called since they are usually placed across the top of the web page, as shown in Figure 8.11. Access to a microsite or nested ad-content occurs when the person undertaking the clickthrough is not redirected to a corporate or brand site, but is instead taken to a related page on the same site as that on which the advertisement is placed. For example, the nappy supplier Huggies placed an advertisement on a childcare site that led the parents clicking on this link to more detailed information on Huggies contained on the site.

The destination page from a banner ad will usually be designed as a specifically created direct-response page to encourage further action.

For example, a banner can be targeted at customers looking for travel insurance, on the basis of the two keywords they have typed into Yahoo! (holiday insurance).

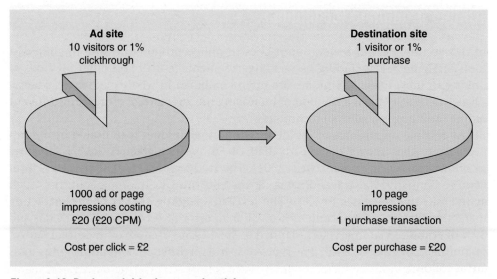

Figure 8.10 Basic model for banner advertising

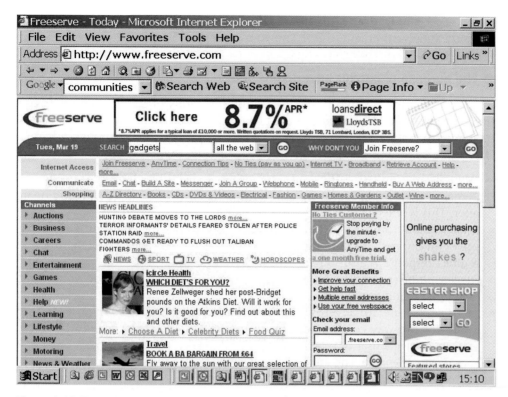

Figure 8.11 Typical placement of a banner advertisement (www.freeserve.com)

Companies will pay for banner advertising for two main reasons: (a) in the hope that the customer will click on the advertisement and then will be exposed to more detailed brand information on the company's web site; (b) all visitors to a page will see an advertisement, either noting it consciously or viewing it subconsciously.

● Measurement of banner ad effectiveness

Figure 8.11 summarises the different terms used for measuring banner ad effectiveness.

Each time an advertisement is viewed, this is referred to as an **advertisement or ad impression**. **Page impressions** and 'page views' are other terms used. 'Ad impressions' is used rather than 'hits' since, as explained in Chapter 9, referring to hits overestimates the number of people actually viewing a page. Since some people may view the advertisement more than one time, marketers are also interested in the **reach**, which is the number of unique individuals who view the advertertisement. This will naturally be a smaller figure than that for ad impressions.

There is much discussion about how many impressions of an advertisement an individual has to see for it to be effective. Novak and Hoffman (1997) note that for traditional media it is thought that fewer than three exposures will not give adequate recall. For new media, because of the greater intensity of viewing a computer screen, recall seems to be better with a smaller number of advertisements compared with old media. The technical term for adequate recall is **effective frequency**.

When a user clicks on the advertisement, he or she will normally be directed to further information, viewing of which will result in a marketing outcome. Usually the user will be directed through to part of the corporate web site that will have been

Page and ad impressions and reach

One page impression occurs when a member of the audience views a web page. One ad impression occurs when a person views an advertisement placed on the web page. Reach defines the number of unique individuals who view an advertisement.

Effective frequency

The number of exposures or ad impressions (frequency) required for an advertisement to become effective.

Clickthrough and clickthrough rate

A clickthrough (or an advertisement click) occurs each time a user clicks on a banner advertisement with the mouse to direct him or her to a web page that contains further information.

The clickthrough rate is expressed as a percentage of total ad impressions, and refers to the proportion of users viewing an advertisement who click on it. It is calculated as the number of clickthroughs divided by the number of ad impressions.

set up especially to deal with the response from the advertisement. When a user clicks on an advertisement, this is known as a **clickthrough**.

● The purpose of banner advertising

Banner advertising is often thought of simply in terms of its function in driving traffic to a web site, as described in the previous section. There are, however, several outcomes that a marketing manager may be looking to achieve through a banner advertising campaign. Cartellieri et al. (1997) identify the following objectives:

- *Delivering content.* This is the typical case where a clickthrough on a banner advertisement leads through to a corporate site giving more detailed information on an offer. This is where a direct response is sought.
- *Enabling transaction.* If a clickthrough leads through to a merchant such as a travel site or an online bookstore the advertisement is placed to lead directly to a sale. A direct response is also sought here.
- *Shaping attitudes.* An advertisment that is consistent with a company brand can help build brand awareness.
- *Soliciting response.* An advertisement may be intended to identify new leads or as a start for two-way communication. In these cases an interactive advertisement may encourage a user to type in an e-mail address.
- *Encouraging retention.* The advertisement may be placed as a reminder about the company and its service and may link through to on-site sales promotions such as a prize draw.

These objectives are not mutually exclusive, and more than one can be achieved with a well-designed banner campaign. Zeff and Aronson (2001) stress the unique benefits of banner advertising as compared with those of other media. Using banners makes it possible to target Internet advertisements to groups of people, sometimes in a more sophisticated way than is possible with other media, as is shown by the example in Mini Case Study 8.3 on DoubleClick later in the chapter. The response to web-based advertisements can be tracked in more detail than that for advertisements in other media. Zeff and Aronson (2001) also note that a web-based advertising campaign can be more responsive than a campaign in other media since it is possible to place an advertisement more rapidly and make changes as required. Finally, since the advertisement can lead straight to a web site where more information and interactivity are available it should be possible to convey a more powerful message about a product.

● Banner ad formats

Formats for banner ads in which the creative must be displayed is mainly limited in size to the CASIE standards (in December 1996 the Internet Advertising Bureau, IAB, and the Coalition for Advertising Supported Information, CASIE, put together eight specific banner ad sizes as standards to be used on the WWW). The full banner ad is most important. Banner ads are based on .GIF graphic files which are usually hosted on a separate server. To the user, these appear as part of the web page. As for traditional advertising, testing creative is important, but banner ads have the benefit that they can be updated during the campaign in line with clickthrough response.

The top 10 banner adverts in the USA can be viewed at www.nielsennetratings.com, which illustrates the forms of banner and creative techniques that seem to be popular.

Banners can be:

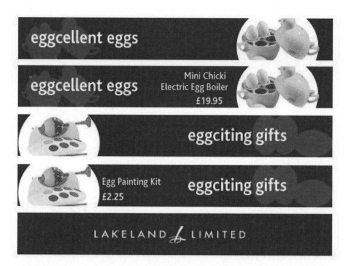

Figure 8.12 Five different elements of an animated banner advertisement

- *static* – they don't change through time;
- *animated* – the norm with a typical rotation of three to five different images;
- *interactive* – the user can type in an e-mail address to register for information;
- *pop-up* – superstitials and interstitials;
- *rich-media* – using a combination of animation, video or even sound.

We will now review the merits of these different types in a little more detail.

Animated banner advertisements

Early banner advertisements featured only a single image, but today they will typically involve several different images, which are displayed in sequence to help to attract attention to the banner and build up a theme, often ending with a call to action and the injunction to click on the banner. An example is shown in Figure 8.12. This type of advertisement is achieved through supplying the creative elements of the advertisement as an animated GIF file with different layers, usually a rectangle of 468 by 60 pixels.

A further type of animated banner ad is the overt. Examples include Microsoft using a butterfly fluttering around the page to advertise MSN and a Reebok campaign of a belly moving around the screen.

Overt

Typically an animated ad that moves around the page and is superimposed on the web site content.

Pop-up adverts

Pop-up adverts tend to have the biggest impact, but they can also cause annoyance since they sometimes have to be proactively removed. Interstitials are literally 'in between' other screens of information. They are usually displayed as part of the main browser window, for example Yahoo! Mail displays interstitials after you have sent an e-mail. Superstitials take the form of an additional 'pop-up' browser window that is displayed when a new web page is opened. Since they have to be removed by the user they are intrusive and have been reported as unpopular. However, some advertisers have found them to be quite effective.

Interstitial ads

Ads that appear between one page and the next.

Superstitials

Pop-up adverts that require interaction to remove them.

Interactive banner advertisements

The use of interactive banners is also increasing. These are intended to add value to the advertisement by providing a service that would normally only be available on the web site. Uses of interactive banners might include:

- entering the amount of loan required to give an indication of its cost;
- entering the destination of a flight to show the cheapest fare available;
- buying a product;
- filling in an e-mail address for further information on a product.

It can be seen that interactive advertisements may increase response since someone may fill in the form even though they might not bother to click on an advertisement.

● Making banner advertising work

As with any form of advertising, certain techniques will result in a more effective advertisement. Discussions with those who have advertised online indicate the following are important to effective advertising:

1 *Appropriate incentives are needed to achieve clickthrough.* Banner advertisements with offers such as prizes or reductions can achieve higher clickthrough rates by perhaps as much as 10 per cent.

2 *Creative design needs to be tested extensively.* Alternative designs for the advertisement need to be tested on representatives of a target audience. Anecdotal evidence suggests that the clickthrough rate can vary greatly according to the design of the advertisement, in much the same way that recall of a television advertisement will vary in line with its concept and design. Different creative designs may be needed for different sites on which advertisements are placed. Zeff and Aronson (2001) note that simply the use of the words 'click here!' or 'click now' can dramatically increase clickthrough rates because new users do not know how banners work! Animated banners, or those that change during a campaign, may also provide a better response.

3 *Appropriate keywords are needed.* Testing is also needed to ensure that the keywords typed into a search engine fit the required profile of audience for the advertisement. An example of this is displaying an advertisement for IBM's Lotus Notes product if the user types in the name of the competing product, 'Microsoft Exchange'. This could appeal to members of an audience who were not loyal to Microsoft.

4 *Placement of advertisement and timing need to be considered carefully.* The different types of placement option available have been discussed earlier in the chapter, but it should be remembered that audience volume and composition will vary through the day and the week.

5 *Consider the clickthrough quality, not just the quantity.* A UK bank stated that having a clickthrough rate of 10 per cent is of limited value if the profile of the person clicking through does not fit a certain investment product. It is much better to have a 0.1 per cent clickthrough rate with a good match, resulting in qualified customers signing up for the new product.

6 *Build the infrastructure to deal with the response.* A successful advertising campaign will naturally lead to visits to the company web site. The content should be right to give the audience what they expect after clicking on the creative components, and the company should be able to follow up any subsequent communications with customers. Are there people in place to deal with e-mails or send out promotional materials?

● Buying advertising

Banner advertising is typically paid for according to the number of web users who view the web page and the advertisement on it. These are the 'ad impressions' referred to earlier. Cost is then calculated as **CPM** or cost per thousand (*mille*) ad impressions.

When payment is made according to the number of viewers of a site it is important that the number of viewers be measured accurately. To do this independent **web site auditors** are required. The main auditing bodies are:

CPM (cost per thousand)
The cost of placing an ad viewed by 1000 people.

- the international auditing body BPA (www.bpai.com);
- Audit Bureau of Circulation, ABC (www.abc.org.uk);
- Internet Advertising Bureau, IAB (www.iab.net).

Web site auditors
Auditors accurately measure the usage of different sites in terms of the number of ad impressions and clickthrough rates.

Banner advertising is purchased for a specific period. It may be purchased for the ad to be served on:

- the **run of site** (the entire site);
- a section of site;
- according to keywords entered on a search engine.

Run of site
Cost per 1000 ad impressions. CPM is usually higher for run-of-site advertisements where advertisements occur on all pages of the site.

Traditionally, the most common payment is according to the number of customers who view the page as a cost per thousand (CPM) ad or page impressions. Typical CPM is in the range £10–£50. Other options that benefit the advertiser if they can be agreed are per-clickthrough or per-action such as a purchase on the destination site.

Other payment models

Cartellieri et al. (1997) and Sterne (1999) note that other payment models are possible. They identify payment options as:

- *per exposure* – typically through ad impressions or possibly through the length of time the user views an advertisement;
- *per response* – payment only occurs according to the number of clickthroughs that occur (pay per click);
- *per action* – payment according to a marketing outcome such as downloading a product factsheet, a new sales lead received when the user fills in an online form giving his or her name and address, or an actual purchase placed online.

Media owners and those selling advertising space prefer the CPM/**exposure-based payment model** since the cost is not related to the quality of the creative content. This model is similar to that used for payment in other media. Media owners are wary of the other two methods since these will be governed directly by the quality of the creative content; if this is poor there would be a low clickthrough, resulting in lower revenue for the media owner. Similarly if the offer is poor or the user is led through to a poor-quality corporate site, then there are less likely to be follow-up actions. Media owners point out that the quality of the creative content or the destination web site is beyond their control – their function is merely to deliver viewers to the advertisement. Although initially media owners were able to control charging rates and largely used a per-exposure model with the increase in unused ad inventory, there has been an increase in **results-based payment** methods. Organisations such as Valueclick (www.valueclick.com), now operate ad networks where the advertiser only pays for each response. This advertising model is similar to the affiliate method (see the later section) except that with the affiliate method, the referring site is usually paid a commission based on the cost of the item sold.

Exposure-based payment
Advertisers pay according to the number of times the ad is viewed.

Results-based payment
Advertisers pay according to the number of times the ad is clicked on.

Mini Case Study 8.4 provides a snapshot of the current use of different payment models and formats.

● Locations for placing banner advertising

Banner advertising is not usually directed at a single site; rather a banner campaign will be organised in which advertisements are placed in a range of locations. Banner advertisements can be placed through traditional advertising agencies since many are now seeking to integrate the Internet into their work. There is also a range of specialist services known as *advertising networks* that undertake this type of work.

Banner advertising requires a good knowledge of the media owners and their rates. Advertising networks such as Doubleclick (www.doubleclick.net) organise co-ordinated campaigns across several sites (see the section on advertising networks later in the chapter). There are three main different locations for placing banner adverts. These alternatives will now be examined in more detail, in order to understand why the different alternatives are used. The main criteria on which the sites are chosen for advertising will of course be the size of the audience (or reach) and the composition of the audience. There are three main types of locations.

1 Portals

It was shown in Chapter 4 that there are different types of portal, but they are similar in that they all tend to have large audiences who visit the portals to gain access to the information on the Internet. This may be through search services such as Excite (www.excite.com) or AltaVista (www.altavista.com), or more structured directories such as Yahoo! (www.yahoo.com) or Yellow Pages (www.yell.co.uk). Alternatively the portals may be the home pages of ISPs such as AOL, Freeserve or VirginNet (www.virgin.net), to which the ISPs' users are directed when they first join the Web. By placing banner advertising on the home page of portals, advertisers get access to large but relatively undifferentiated audiences. This is similar to an advertiser placing a traditional advertisement in a prime-time television slot. A banner advertisement placed to reach a large, but non-specific, audience will be that displayed when the user first visits the portal. Yet portals offer greater advertising potential than other media since it is possible for companies to place specific advertisements that are related to the keywords that the user types in when performing a search. For example, if a user types in 'cheap flights', an airline such as British Airways or a flight broker can pay to display their banner advertisement. This has the benefit that the advertisement is delivered to an audience that is pre-qualified as being interested in it. This is much less easy to achieve in other media, although it is possible to place advertisements in keeping with a special-interest TV programme, such as golf club advertisements in a live broadcast from a golf competition.

2 Generalised news services

It can be argued that news services overlap with the other two categories described here, but news services are presented separately since this type of site is commonly used. Such services are similar in audience to portals in that they have quite large audiences, but the audiences are arguably better differentiated, in that a certain type of person is likely to visit a certain type of news site. For example, the audience of the *Sunday Times* web site or the *Electronic Telegraph* web site is likely to be similar to that of their real-world equivalent. On this type of site, banners are not usually offered in response to keywords, but advertisements may be varied according to which section of the online newspaper is being read.

3 Specialised-interest site

This category covers a range of sites, but special-interest online magazine sites are popular for banner advertising. Examples could include:

- men's lifestyle magazines – *FHM*, *GQ*;
- women's lifestyle magazines – *Vogue* and *Tatler*;
- science fiction – *Fortean Times*;
- 'vertical portals', for example the online computing trade press – *Computer Weekly* and *Computing*.

Novak and Hoffman (1997) also identify three major types of advertiser supported sites. These are:

1 sponsored content sites such as newspapers;
2 sponsored search engines such as Infoseek and Excite;
3 entry portals such as Netscape.

As noted above, it is increasingly difficult to distinguish between the second and third types identified by Novak and Hoffman, so it is felt that the classification mentioned given in this chapter is more appropriate for the type of sites on which advertisement placements occur.

To target a particular segment with a banner ad, the following options are possible:

- purchasing on a site (or part of site) with a particular visitor profile;
- purchasing at a particular time of day or week;
- buying a keyword-based advert on a portal.

Banner ad campaigns can be rated by:

- reach (the percentage of Web users who see the advert);
- recognition (spontaneous and prompted recall of advert from Web users);
- clickthrough;
- traffic quantity (thousands of visitors);
- traffic quality (those who proactively use the site);
- cost.

Advertising networks

Advertising networks are collections of independent web sites from different companies and media networks, each of which has an arrangement with an advertising broker to place banner advertisements. The advantage for the companies that are part of the network is that they do not need to deal directly with different companies wishing to advertise on their site. They simply have the broker, who acts as a single contact point. In addition, they do not need to manage the technical process of serving banner advertisements and monitoring their usage. Companies wishing to place advertisements benefit by being able to deal with a single agency or broker. Mini Case Study 8.3 shows DoubleClick, one of the best-known advertising networks, which operates both in the USA and through worldwide franchises. The network offers advertisements in a range of different areas such as automotive, finance, health and entertainment.

The DoubleClick advertising network

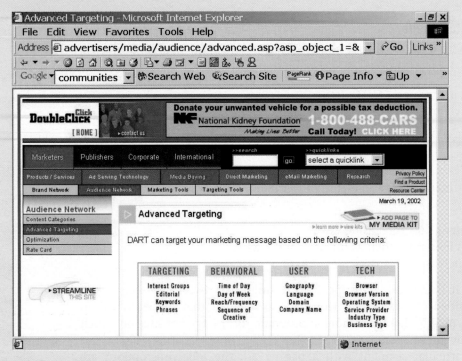

Figure 8.13 The DoubleClick advertising network site, showing affiliated sites in the Entertainment category

DoubleClick offers advertisers the ability to dynamically target advertisements on the Web through its 'DART' targeting technology. This gives advertisers a core objective – that of reaching specific audiences. There are four basic categories of targeting criteria:

1 *Content targeting*. Allows placement of advertising message on a particular interest site or within an entire interest category such as:

- Automotive
- Business and Finance
- Entertainment
- Health
- News, Information and Culture
- Search, Directories and ISPs
- Sports
- Technology
- Travel
- Women and Family

2 *Behavioural targeting*. An audience can be targeted according to how they use the Web. For example, advertisers can select business users by delivering advertisements on Monday to Friday between 9 and 5, or leisure users by targeting messages in the evening hours. Behavioural targeting includes psychographic aspects of advertising. For example, it has been shown that the impact of advertisements tends to decline after they have been viewed three or four times. It is possible through DoubleClick to save money on the total number of ad impressions by showing an advertisement to an individual up to a maximum number of times.

3 *User targeting*. This enables advertisements to be placed according to specific traits of the audience including their geographic location (based on country or postal code), domain type (for example, educational users with addresses ending in .edu or .ac.uk can be targeted), business size or type according to SIC code or even by the company for which they work, based on the company domain name.

4 *Technical targeting*. This is based on user hardware, software and Internet access provider. For example, engineers tend to use UNIX operating systems and graphic designers tend to use Macintosh systems.

A snapshot of Internet advertising practice

Level of expenditure

Expenditure on Internet advertising in the first nine months of 2001 stood at $5.55 billion. This was a slight decline compared to the previous year, but smaller than the reduction in offline advertising expenditure.

Categories of advertiser spend

The consumer-targeted category continues to be the largest overall segment with the retail segment of this being the largest:

- Consumer, 29%
- Computing, 19%
- Business Services, 10%
- Financial Services, 12%
- Media, 14%

Pricing model

There has been an increase in the use of performance payment models, but the exposure model is still predominant.

- Straight CPM (cost per thousand), 48%
- Hybrid, 39%
- Straight performance (payment according to clickthrough), 13%

Ad formats

The range and relative popularity of different Internet advertising formats is indicated by an IAB report of the US marketplace for Q3, 2001 (IAB, 2001):

- Banners (standard banners), 35%
- Sponsorships (sponsorship of a site or part-site), 25%
- Classifieds (equivalent of traditional adverts), 17%
- Slotting fees (the fees charged for premium ad placement and/or exclusivity), 7%
- Interstitials/superstitials (specialised format ads), 3%
- Key word search (banners served in response to search engine keywords), 5%
- Rich media (animated and audio components to banners), 3%
- E-mail (banners in newspaper adverts), 3%
- Referrals, 2%

Source: IAB (2001)

● How effective are banner ads?

A key question that marketers have asked since the first use of banner ads is: 'How effective are banner advertisements in comparison with other media?' In a study conducted in 1997 for the Internet Advertising Bureau (ww.iab.net) in the USA, MBinteractive (www.mbinteractive.com) concluded that 'online advertising is more likely to be noticed than television advertising'. It was suggested that advertising banners performed so well because of the lower advertisement-to-editorial ratio on web pages (typically 90 per cent text to 10 per cent advertising for a single banner advertisement on a page) and because Web users use the medium actively rather than passively receiving information. Boyce (1998) notes that for a television audience, the proportion who actually watch the advertisement may be as low as 25 per cent! Further evidence on the effectiveness of the Web for advertising, in comparison with television, is provided by an IPSOS-ASI survey published in February 1999, which suggested that banner advertisements and television advertisements are equally memorable. This conclusion was based on a survey of 7000 US consumers testing their recall of 45 banner advertisements on AOL sites, across a range of categories. The study tested consumers' advertisement recall after one viewing. It found that while 41 per cent recalled a 30-second television commercial after one viewing, 40 per cent recalled a static online banner advertisement. However, Marianne Foley, senior vice president of IPSOS-ASI Interactive, acknowledged that the study does not take into account the advanced features of advertisement impact such as communication and brand imagery and persuasion. More recent studies, however, indicate 'banner blindness' we subsconsiously filter out adverts.

The death of banner advertisements has been forecast since their first use, but the global value of banner advertising has increased year on year. According to eMarketer (2002), although advertising in print, TV and radio is not predicted to increase over the next few years, it is predicted that the US online advertising market will grow from $7.9 billion in 2001 to $18.8 billion by 2005. However, online advertising still represents only 3% of the total US ad market. In Europe there is a similar picture of growth with IABUK (2001) reporting that the total online advertising expenditure figure for all participating European member states in 2000 was £1.2 billion, an increase of more than 700% from a figure of £164 million in 1999. Figures in individual countries are UK £154 million, France £96.2, Italy £85.2 million, Germany £56.8 million, Netherlands £23.7 million and Belgium £8 million. Again the overall figure is a small percentage of total advertising at 1%.

One argument for why banner ads will decline in importance is that there is currently a 'novelty value' in banner ads. New Internet users, of which there are millions each month, may click on banners out of curiosity or ignorance. More experienced users tend to filter out banner adverts concentrating mainly on the text content of the site where the ad placement is. Data at eMarketer (www.emarketer.com) shows a dramatic decline in average clickthrough rate from over 2% to less than 0.2% through time. Much ad inventory also remains unsold, suggesting that supply outstrips demand. The counter-argument is that new large ad formats such as skyscrapers (large online ads of a vertical column orientation), interstitials and rich-media techniques will be more effective than traditional banner advertisements.

Despite negative reporting of the effectiveness of banner advertising, clearly banner ads are still found to be cost effective by some advertisers. Mini Case Study 8.5 provides some insight into how consumers perceive banner ads. Marketers are likely to rise to the challenge to increase the effectiveness of banner advertising. A range of approaches will probably be used to increase the effectiveness of advertising. Such approaches include the use of larger-format ads such as skyscraper ads and interstitials, the use of text ads (see Case Study 8.2) and more use of rich-media adverts, particularly once broadband Internet connections become more widespread.

Mini Case Study 8.5

Dual standards of banner ads

Over half of Internet users agree that 'all web advertising annoys me' but two-fifths have clicked a banner in the last month, with heavy users clicking more. Increasing its contribution to traffic numbers, TV advertising has become more effective over the last year.

On balance Internet users have a negative attitude to web advertising, with nearly half of all users agreeing with the statements: 'I think quite a lot of web advertising is devious' and 'nearly all web advertising annoys me'. The remainder of respondents either disagreed with these statements or were neutral. Heavy Internet users and more experienced users are more likely to agree with these negative statements.

Only a fifth of Internet users expressed agreement with positive statements about web advertising such as: 'I find web advertising interesting' and 'I find web advertising entertaining'.

When asked, nearly two-fifths (37%) of Internet users claim to have been prompted to visit a web site by a banner ad during the last month. This suggests that whilst banners may be seen in a negative light by some, they are useful to many and do drive traffic to sites. It is worth noting, however, that 12 months ago this figure was just over a half (51%) so banner ads do appear to be declining in value to net users.

Heavy and more experienced users are more likely than other users to have clicked on banner ads in the last month, which suggests they still respond to banners and find them useful. However, given the amount of time these people spend online and the high exposure they have to banner ads, we would expect them to click on far more banner ads than they do. This group clicks on a much smaller proportion of the banners that they see. Therefore, both their overall attitude and actual behaviour towards web advertising are negative relative to less frequent and less experienced users.

According to Internet users, TV adverts have increased in effectiveness over the last 12 months in terms of generating site visits. The relative novelty of banner ads is wearing off whereas TV creative treatments are increasing their appeal.

Source: BMRB (2001)

Online promotion – affiliate networks

An **affiliate network** is different from an advertising network although the broad aim of the two is the same: to use graphic or text link advertisements placed on many sites to generate traffic by referring links to a destination web site. The use of affiliate networks is best illustrated by the example of the Amazon bookshop, which is perhaps the best exponent of this online marketing technique. According to Schiller (1999), Amazon has over 300 000 affiliates, who offer small banner advertisements on their sites that when clicked will take the user of their site through to the Amazon site (www.amazon.com). The network includes many major portals, for example, Yahoo! (Fig. 9.2). Each partner earns up to 15 per cent commission every time a customer clicks on the advertisement and then buys a book or other item at Amazon. Amazon claims that nearly a quarter of its revenue is derived in this way, which illustrates the effectiveness of this method. This is effectively a no-cost method of advertising or one in which payment is only made where there is a definite outcome – the purchase of an item.

Links to Amazon also occur on portals such as Yahoo! (www.yahoo.com), where links to Amazon are given according to the types of keywords typed in. Further examples of affiliate marketing are supplied in Case Study 8.1.

Affiliate network
Collection of web sites that link to an online retailer in exchange for commission on purchases made from the retailer.

CASE STUDY 8.1

Affiliate marketing

There is safety in numbers. At least, so hundreds of thousands of websites are hoping. Faced with a softening advertising market and rabid price competition driving yields ever lower, many are choosing to band together in schemes known as affiliate marketing, in the hope that, by combining forces, they can attract a greater share of the dwindling marketing dollars.

Simply put, affiliate marketing means sites of a vaguely similar nature clubbing together to accept the same set of ads from advertisers. For the advertisers, it looks like a convenient way of getting greater exposure – instead of having to go and hunt out sites with the kind of visitors they want to target, they can gain access to groups of suitable sites at one swoop.

For the sites, it's convenient because they are fed ads through their affiliate networks, instead of having to go out and laboriously track down the advertisers themselves. It is easy to see the appeal.

'Affiliate marketing is a good thing', declares Staffan Engdegard, analyst at Jupiter MMXI, the internet research specialist. 'It's especially good for smaller sites, which wouldn't be able to sell to big advertisers otherwise, and it's good for advertisers, because they would find it too time-consuming to go out and find these smaller sites, and to manage (their relationship with) them.'

There is no shortage of affiliate networks to agree with him. Commission Junction, which claims to be the world's biggest such network with 470 000 sites affiliated to it, UK Affiliates, with 48 000 sites, and a host of smaller names are targeting the UK. These middlemen claim to take the hassle out of marketing for advertisers. Adrian Moss, group managing director of the Deal Group, parent of UK Affiliates, says: 'We tell the clients just what to do – breathe in, breathe out – we take the targeted banner creative off them and (put it) in the most efficient sales route.'

Advertisers are always in charge, stresses Susan Kingston, business development manager at Commission Junction. 'Advertisers can either handpick the sites from our network or it can be automated, but at any point, they can reject any sites that they do not feel fit with their brand values', she explains. While it is easy to see why sites desperate to get rid of their excess ad space at any price should find affiliate marketing attractive, it could turn out to be a dangerous game. The risk is that this method of selling advertising merely cheapens the whole web as a medium, driving down prices even further.

In addition, affiliate networks – where ads are dished out to thousands of websites that share only vague connections in content and audience profiles – seem to make a mockery of that prized tenet of web advertising: the ability to personalise and closely target ads to exactly the demographic you seek.

The most important aspect of affiliate marketing, however, is its close association with the pay-per-result model. This strikes right to the core of the key debate on internet marketing: how should the medium be priced for advertisers?

Pay-per-view, where advertisers pay according to the number of people who see their ads, and click-through rates, where they pay according to the number of people who click on the ads, used to be the standard method of calculating payment. The problem is that people don't click on banner ads any more.

So media sellers deriving commissions on the basis of click-through rates are finding the bottom falling out of their market. Finding they have the advantage, advertisers have pushed this model further and are frequently refusing to pay for mere click-through and demanding deals where they only pay where a purchase is made or a customer requests further information.

William Hill, the bookmaker, for instance, pays between £10 and £20 for new accounts generated through UK Affiliates.

Paul Longhurst, chief executive of media buyer Quantum Media, sums it up: 'This is OK for small sites that have good quality visitors where users spend significant amounts of money on their (interests). But in the bland dotcom world, this model is not going to help sites out of their problems.'

There is no reason why affiliate networks have to tie their fate to per-result payment methods. In theory, at least, advertisers should be willing to pay for the exposure of their brands on a wide range of websites, based on the number of visitors they garner, irrespective of whether those visitors go on to make purchases. But as advertisers have used their muscle to squeeze concessions from hard-pressed internet sites, the two terms have become synonymous in the minds of many web experts.

'Affiliate marketing is very focused on performance-based pricing', says Engdegard. The Deal Group's Moss goes further: 'Affiliate marketing means performance-based pricing.' Do advertisers really need affiliate networks on any other basis than pay-per-results? Probably not. It's not as if there is a shortage of websites with cheap ad space, forcing the would-be advertiser to ferret through the undergrowth of the web in the hope of finding an unused banner space.

For struggling sites, affiliate marketing may not be the lifeline it seems. The higher value websites will tend to shun affiliate marketing deals anyway because they detract from the value of their carefully cultivated brand identity. Only smaller sites will really benefit from affiliate schemes, and these mass, commoditised deals with their meagre returns may not be enough to save them. Drowning men may cling together, but it doesn't make them any more able to swim.

Source: Fiona Harvey, Survey – creative business: affiliate marketing, *Financial Times*, 31 July 2001

Questions

1 Distinguish between affiliate networks and banner advertising networks.

2 What are the benefits of affiliate networks in comparison with advertising networks?

Online promotion – search engine registration and optimisation

Portals, which include search engine and directory services, are the primary method of finding information about a company and its products. Over 80% of web users state that they use search engines to find information. It follows that if search engine registration has not occurred for an organisation, then traffic volume will be less than optimal.

● How do search engines work?

Search engine users are most likely to select sites to visit that are near the top of a search engine listing or ranking – typically within the first screen.

To optimise your position in different search engines, it helps to understand the basis on which search engine listings are generated and ordered. By understanding this you can boost your position higher than your competitors' and so achieve higher levels of traffic. Search engines compile an index by sending out spiders or robots to crawl around sites that are registered with that search engine (Figure 8.14). The spider compiles an index containing every word on every page against the page address. It weights the index according to different parameters and then stores the index as part of a database on a web server. This index is what is searched

Search engine

Provides an index of content on registered sites that can be searched by keyword.

Search engine registration (submission)

A request to a search engine that a site be included within its index.

Search engine listing

The list of sites and descriptions returned by a search engine after a user types in keywords.

Search engine ranking

The position of a site on a particular search engine, e.g. third.

Spiders and robots

Antomated software tools that index keywords on web pages.

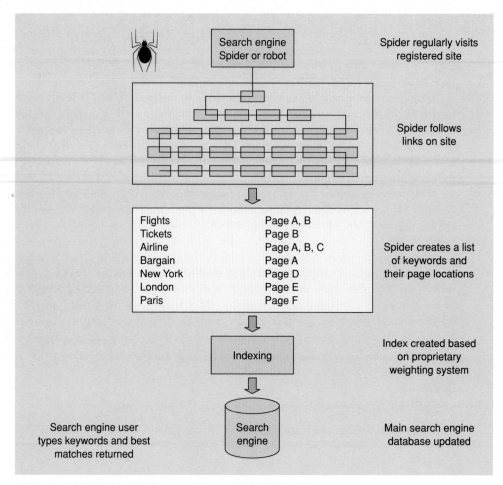

Figure 8.14 Stages involved in creating a search engine listing

when potential customers type in keywords. Danny Sullivan, editor of respected Search Engine Watch (www.searchenginewatch.com), says: 'Search engines prefer 'big, dumb and ugly pages'. He also emphasises the importance of the title HTML tag (<TITLE>):

After the page content itself, the title tag is the most important. Keep the title short, attractive, and enticing, and it will work well both for search engines and people reading a description of your page.

Employees who are involved with promoting a web site will want to optimise its position in listings from different search engines, aiming for it to be within the top 10 for certain keywords, so some of the factors that impact this are outlined here. There are five main parameters on which search engines base the order of their ranking. These are mainly based on how well the keywords typed in by the searcher match against the same words on the page of your website. They are summarised in Table 8.3 in approximate order of importance, but note that some such as frequency of occurrence and links-in are becoming more important. For a review of current techniques refer to www.searchenginewatch.com. There now many specialist **search engine optimisation (SEO)** companies. Figure 8.15 gives an example of the increase in traffic that can be achieved through search engine optimisation.

Search engine optimisation (SEO)

A structured approach used to enhance the position of a company or its products in search engine results according to selected keywords.

Table 8.3 Techniques to boost position of a web site in search engine listings

Factor	Description	Interpretation
1. Title	The keywords in the title of a web page that appear at the top of a browser window are indicated in the HTML code by the <TITLE></TITLE> keyword.	This is significant in search engine listings since if a keyword matches a title it is more likely to be listed highly than if it is only in the body text of a page.
2. Meta tags	Meta tags are part of a web page, hidden from users, but used by search engines when robots or spiders compile their index. There are two types of meta tag. Example: <meta name='keywords' content='book, books, shop, store'> <meta name='description' content='The largest online book store in the world.'>	In most search engines, if a keyword typed in by the user matches the meta tag on a site, then this site will be listed higher up the search engine listing than a site that doesn't use meta tags.
3. Frequency of occurrence	The number of occurrences of the keyword in the text of the web page will also determine the listing. Higher listings will also occur if the keyword is near the top of the document.	Copy can be written to increase the number of times a word is used and boost the position in the search engine listing. Doorway pages which feature relevant keywords are used to attract visitor segments with a particular interest.
4. Hidden graphic text	For example, text about a company name and products can be assigned to a company logo using the 'ALT' tag as follows: <IMG NAME='Logo' SRC='logo.gif' ALT='The B2B Company for chemical products'>	A site that uses a lot of graphical material or is less likely to be listed high, but it is essential that the hidden graphic text keyword be used.
5. Links	Some search engines rank more highly when keywords entered are included as links. Others such as Google rank more highly when there are links in from other sites.	A link-building campaign can help increase position in search engines also.

Directories

Web directories or catalogues are constructed and presented differently from search engines. Directories are not constructed automatically by robots and spiders, but are human-generated. A human being will place each reference to a site in a category. After you submit your URL to a site such as Yahoo! it will be reviewed by a human and then included if it is thought to be of a suitable standard. Another difference is that directories do not give comprehensive access to all web pages. When you search a directory, you are not searching the entire Web, but the list of company names, categories and, for Yahoo!, the 25-word description of the site. Yahoo! is notoriously difficult to be listed on, so it may be worthwhile arranging for a third party to do this for you.

Site registration and search engine optimisation are not straightforward – there are a number of barriers that make this difficult:

1 The site has to be registered with each of the main search engines, and there are hundreds of potential search engines that customers may use. In practice it is only necessary to be listed in all the main search engines. Typically the top 10 will cover over 95% of all search engine traffic.
2 Each of the search engines uses different criteria such as those of Table 8.3 to order the list of results or 'hits' associated with the keywords the user types in.

Meta tags

Keywords that are part of an HTML page that result in a higher search listing if they match the typed keyword.

Doorway pages

Specially constructed pages which feature keywords for particular product searches. These often redirect visitors to a home page.

Directory or catalogue

Provides a structured listing of registered web sites and their purpose in different categories.

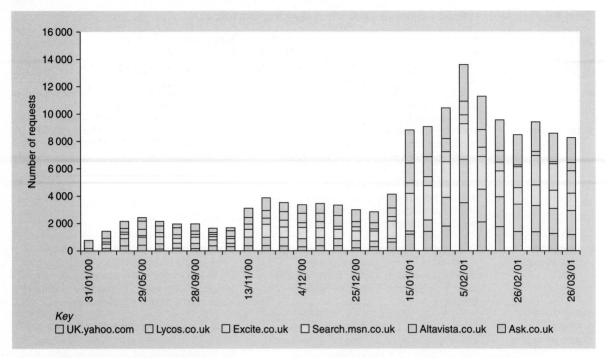

Figure 8.15 Variation in number of requests from .co.uk sites before and after search engine optimisation
Source: Senior Internet (www.senior.co.uk)

3 The techniques used to register and the procedures for producing the listings vary through time, so a repeat registration with a search engine may be necessary quite frequently.

4 There are a large number of web sites indexed by search engines. The webmaster may be competing for visibility with more than 1 billion web pages, as listed in Google. Imagine the position of a company selling home insurance: if a user types in the keywords 'home insurance' there may be hundreds of companies offering this service, but users are not likely to view any more than the first ten in the search engine listing. Colborn (2002) uses the examples of the search term 'flights'. He says:

> *Optimising the keyword 'flights' will not necessarily drive searchers who are looking to buy a ticket. Instead you could receive traffic from people wanting to know a range of possible enquiries such as flight times, flight arrivals, flight destinations not just purchasable flight tickets. The term 'flights' is one of the most expensive cost per click terms available and based upon the variables mentioned above may not necessarily yield the most lucrative return on investment from the received click through amount.*

If, instead, a more targeted key phrase or search term such as 'online flight tickets uk' is used, he says:

> *Optimising the keyphrase 'online flight tickets uk' will not drive nearly as much traffic as the example of 'flights' given above, however, this phrase targets individuals looking for flight tickets online and has segmented the search market by using the uk suffix. Therefore, despite the traffic levels being lower your average cost per click will be less and those who do click are better qualified searchers actually wanting to buy tickets online.*

5 Note also that dynamic content generated 'on the fly' when a user requests a page from a database will not be featured at all in the search engine index. Similarly, Macromedia Flash components of a site will not be indexed. Information from a database can be mirrored (duplicated) on a server where it will be indexed by search engines. This is sometimes referred to as **deep linking**. An example of such as service is provided by Excedia (www.excedia.com). The use of frames (Chapter 7) can make it difficult for search engines to index a site. Information on the subsidiary frames is not available in the home page for indexing. No relevant words such as holidays or flights are available on which the search index can build its index.

Deep linking

Search engines index a mirrored copy of content normally inaccessible by search engine spiders.

Given these difficulties, many companies find that the webmaster may not have the time to keep up with the changing techniques, so a better solution is to outsource the promotion of a site through search engines to other companies. For example, in the UK the following companies offer what they call 'traffic-generating' or 'visibility' programs:

- Sitelynx (www.sitelynx.co.uk);
- Web Promote (www.webpromote.co.uk);
- Web Marketing (www.web-marketing.co.uk);
- Hyperlink Services (www.hyperlink.co.uk).

A monthly payment will ensure that a company and its products are visible via search engines and may include other services such as ensuring links refer to the site from other web sites (other than search engines). Companies or individuals who are unable to pay for such a service can register manually, or use free submission engines which provide submission to several search engines.

● Paid-for search engine positioning

There has been a dramatic shift from free registration with search engines to paid-for placements where companies pay to be listed with search engines. Two distinct types of payment scheme operate:

1 *Express inclusion schemes*. Here, search engine companies charge to rapidly index and include a new site registration in their listing. Alternatively, the company wishing to register may have to wait several months. For example, Yahoo! now requires payment for rapid inclusion in its directory listings. There are relatively few companies that do not now operate in this way, although Google is one of them.

2 *Payment-by-position or pay-per-placement programmes*. Here, the more a company pays to the search engine owner, the higher their ranking. The most widely used services are Overture (www.overture.com) and Espotting (www.espotting.com). Figure 8.16 shows how companies who bid the most money are placed at the top of the list, resulting in a higher probability of the customer clicking through. If this is an explicit arrangement where the consumer is aware why the company is top, it may not be a problem. However, often the user of the service may not be aware they are using a payment-by-position search engine. For example, Overture search is used on Freeserve (www.freeserve.com) although the users may believe the top listing is for the most relevant company. In Yahoo! (www.yahoo.co.uk) Espotting sites are clearly featured as sponsored links.

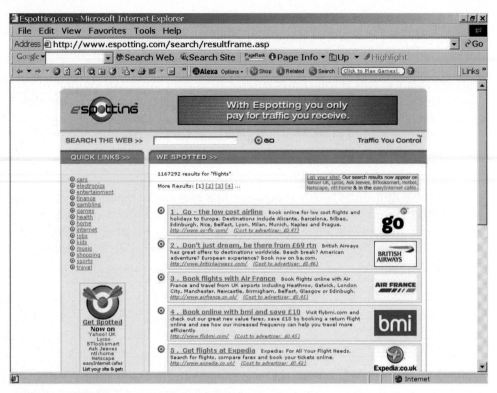

Figure 8.16 Espotting (www.espotting.com)

CASE STUDY 8.2

Options for building traffic from Google

Just inside the front doors of Google.com's Silicon Valley headquarters, real-time queries entered by the search engine's 12m-odd users stream by on the wall above the receptionist's head – 'flamingos', 'cataract surgery complications', 'JPEG file plug-in filter', 'greetings, earthlings', 'watermelon pickle', and . . . 'Anna Kournikova pictures'.

Internet user surveys have revealed that Google's users enter these queries because of its uncanny ability to offer accurate results on its first page of returns. In April, according to internet marketing company Jupiter Media Metrix, Google reached a milestone when – for the first time – it was named the number one US search engine, beating rivals such as Ask Jeeves, GoTo and AltaVista.

Google has 200 employees, and investment bankers believe its revenues could reach Dollars 50m in 2002. It is thought that given comparable valuations, the company could achieve a market capitalisation of Dollars 250m.

Google is now hoping to parlay its domestic popularity into a larger international presence. It has recently struck deals with companies such as the UK's Vodafone, Fujitsu of Japan's Nifty, NTT DoCoMo, as well as Malaysia's E-Chilipadi, to provide its search capabilities to international desktop and wireless users. It is also opening its first overseas offices for advertising in the UK, Germany and Japan.

Omid Kordestani, vice-president of business development and sales, admitted Google's wireless deals were not meant as an immediate revenue builder. 'We're focused on (wireless) as a place where the customers are', he said.

While industry insiders and users agree that Google is the best search engine, the challenge still remains: how to monetise search.

The company relies on two revenue streams, advertising and licensing. By running text-based ads instead of banner ads, Google has eschewed a staple of online advertising, and user response suggests it is on to something. It claims it achieves click-through rates four to five times the industry average, which is roughly 1 per cent.

'I think the guys at Google are being extremely smart', says Louis Monier, founder of AltaVista. 'Instead of banner ads and making your site look like the side of a race car, they are staying with the small text advertisements.'

The balance of Google's revenue comes from licensing its search technology to companies such as Yahoo, AOL/Netscape and Cisco, along with the recent international deals it has forged. Yahoo's decision last year to adopt Google's search engine was a huge validation of Google's technology.

Its technological lead is thanks to its co-founders, Larry Page and Sergey Brin. While pursuing their doctoral degrees, the two realised that the existing search technology, which was based on text searches within web pages, returned too many irrelevant results. They devised an algorithmic formula, called link analysis, to streamline searches, a method that used internal links within relevant web pages to determine results.

This initial focus on technology has remained central to philosophy, Mr Kordestani says. 'We still view ourselves as a start-up. We feel we can't take our eyes off the ball.'

He says Google sees search as an ever-important tool, one that will only gain importance as the number of web pages increases. (The name Google itself is a play on this. It is based on 'googol', the number one followed by 100 zeros.)

Unlike previous search engine leaders such as AltaVista, which stumbled when it tried to be all things to all people and lost focus, Google has kept its brand synonymous with search, Mr Kordestani says.

For the moment that strategy appears to be paying off. Google has said it expects to be profitable by the third quarter this year. However, unlike many other dotcoms, Google has so far resisted the temptation to go public.

Silicon Valley venture capital heavyweights John Doerr and Michael Moritz, of Kleiner Perkins Caufield & Byers and Sequoia Capital respectively, are investors and sit on Google's board. For now it appears Google's cash position is strong enough to ride the slowdown. (As a private company Google does not release financial details.) Rumours of an initial public offering swirl through the Valley, but the company, while saying it will eventually go public, will not say when.

Keeping eventual investors happy, of course, will be Google's biggest challenge, and that means growth in a dotcom market still defining itself. 'You can probably build a nice little company based on web search technology', Mr Monier cautioned, 'but you can't build an empire on it.'

Source: Matthew Leising, Companies and finance international, *Financial Times*, 9 June 2001

Question

Evaluate the business model of Google in the context of online buyer behaviour.

Online promotion – link building

Given the large number of web sites indexed in search engines and the difficulty this causes in providing visibility for a web site, it is important for companies to consider other low-cost methods of generating web site traffic. A relatively straightforward method is for them to make sure that their site has links from as many other related sites as possible, using hyperlinks. This is sometimes referred to as a 'link-building campaign'. A good starting-point for this process is to see how many sites are currently

Link-building campaign

A structured approach to gaining as many links as possible from other Web-related web sites.

linking to a given site. There are two methods for achieving this. First, a log-file analyser program such as WebTrends (see Chapter 9) can be used to indicate what are known as the *referring sites*. Second, some search engines such as AltaVista and Infoseek provide a facility that allows the user to type 'link:' followed by the URL, which then lists other web sites that are linked to the site specified.

Techniques that can be used to increase the number of links include:

Reciprocal links

A free exchange of links between site owners.

- Reciprocal links. These are two-way links agreed between two organisations. They have the benefit that they are free. A 'web ring' is a similar arrangement involving more than two sites.
- *PR – content mentions*. If links to your site are featured in media sites like online newspapers or trade magazines, then this will also increase traffic.

Affiliate network

A reciprocal arrangement between a company and third-party sites where traffic is directed to the company from third-party sites through banner advertisements and links and incentives.

- *Affiliates*. Affiliate networks are widely used by e-tailers to drive traffic to a site. Reviewed in a previous section.
- *Sponsorship*. Paid-for sponsorship of another site, or part of it, especially a portal, for an extended period is another way to develop permanent links. Co-branding is a similar method of sponsorship and can exploit synergies between different companies, but is a reciprocal arrangement.
- *Banner advertising*. This technique is widely used by large B2C companies to drive traffic to their sites and has been explained in a previous section.

Co-branding

An arrangement between two or more companies where they agree to jointly display content and to conduct joint promotions using brand logos or banner advertisements.

- *Price-comparison portals*. These are for companies selling commodity products using e-commerce to ensure that the products are listed on infomediary or portal sites offering product and price comparison. The promoter of a site needs to check that a company's products or distributors selling its products are represented in as wide a range of these as is practical.

Co-branding or promotion partnering is seen as a cost-effective method of promotion which can be used for longer periods than banner advertisments. The practice has become so widespread that *Revolution* magazine now has a monthly feature that lists co-branding arrangements. Examples from the June 1999 'dealwatch' include:

- *WhatCar* magazine and *AutoHunter* have joined together to encourage online car sales through reciprocal links between their sites (this is an example of two-way co-branding).
- The British Tourist Authority has signed a contract with Avis to offer visitors to the BTA web site special offers on UK car rental. The deal involves banner advertisements and sponsorship on 29 pages of the BTA sites linking to a special offer page on the Avis site (this is an example of one-way co-branding).
- The portal and ISP, AOL UK, has formed links with the online wine retailer Chateau online and the travel agency Thomas Cook, who are both 'anchor tenants', providing promotion of both companies in the relevant shopping channels.

Sponsorship, as well as taking the form of a promoter sponsoring a site, for example the sponsorship of the *Guardian* site (www.footballunlimited.co.uk) by the brewer Carling, which also sponsors the Football Premiership, can also make use of opportunities for involving individual personalities in sponsorship. For example, an investment bank in the Isle of Man sponsored a round-the-world yachtsman. This generated a lot of traffic to the bank's site amongst people interested in yachting, who also had the correct profile for investing (mainly mature, with high disposable incomes). It can be seen from these examples that there needs to be good synergy between the sponsored site and the sponsor for it to be effective. The motoring information organisation TrafficMaster, which provides traffic news and co-branding on the Vauxhall car site, is a good example of such synergy.

Online promotion – e-mail marketing

E-mail is increasing in importance as part of the online communications mix. Doubleclick (2001) reported that in most European countries more is spent on e-mail marketing than banner advertising. E-mail is a significant communications medium since it is widely used. Surveys in many countries show that it is a significant method of Internet communication. For example, ONS (2001) shows that, in the UK, 71% of Internet users use e-mail. Globally, around 4 billion e-mail messages are sent daily, not to mention 300 million SMS messages.

The impact of e-mail on the modern organisation can also be significant. Iconocast (2001) reported that Dell Computer achieve more than $1 million in revenue per week through e-mail marketing campaigns. Each month in 2000, Dell received 50 000 e-mail messages and 100 000 order-status requests. This example shows that when devising plans for e-mail marketing communications, marketers need to plan for:

- **outbound e-mail marketing**, where e-mail campaigns are used as a form of direct marketing to encourage trial and purchases and as part of a CRM dialogue;
- **inbound e-mail marketing**, where e-mails from customers such as support enquiries are managed.

Outbound e-mail marketing
E-mails are sent to customers and prospects from an organisation.

E-mail can also be used for paid-for advertising since it is possible to buy space for an advertisement within an e-mail newsletter or sponsor it. Such newsletters have the benefit that they are highly targeted, and the audience will view the advertisement as part of the e-mail (although they may skim over it). Such advertising can be graphical or text-based depending on whether the e-mail is HTML-based or not. An example is the Search Engine Watch newsletter (from www.searchenginewatch.com), an e-mail newsletter that gives advice on how to boost a site's position in search engines and is read by over 100 000 marketers and webmasters. We will not discuss advertising in other organisations further in this section since the issues are similar to banner advertising. Instead we will focus on e-mail campaigns and management of inbound e-mail.

Inbound e-mail marketing
Management of e-mails from customers by an organisation.

Note that the web site is a vital part of integrated e-mail marketing as explained in Figure 6.4. It is used to collect e-mail addresses as part of permission marketing and manage responses to e-mail address on a landing page or microsite. Additionally, e-mail campaigns can be integrated with direct postal campaigns.

Landing page
Part of a web site used for direct responses from an e-mail campaign.

E-mail benefits

For the e-marketer, e-mail offers many advantages as a communications tool – it offers immediacy, targeting, accountability and is relatively cheap. Perhaps its key advantage is that unlike the web site it is a push communication tool. A key limitation of web site marketing is that since it is a pull medium visitors will only visit a site when it enters their mind, typically through typing in a URL in response to an offline stimulus or following a hyperlink. In contrast, e-mail provides a push mechanism. The marketer can devise appropriate copy to deliver targeted messages to selected customers or prospects. The message arrives in the recipient's inbox and it can't be ignored – the message header must be read – even if the decision is to delete the e-mail.

E-mail also offers more effective direct marketing campaigns, since it is possible to send more messages because lower-cost follow-ups can occur that are impractical with the cost of printing and postage. E-mail can be used to send reminders about a sales promotion and messages can be sent to those who fail to win, offering further benefits. Figure 8.17 gives an example of a campaign structure used with a rented

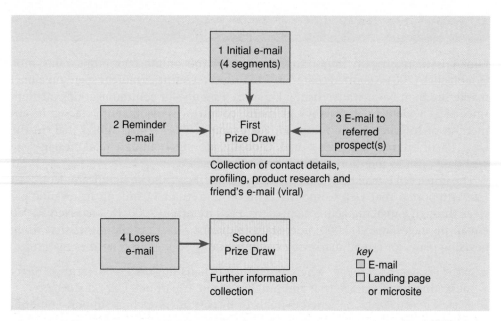

Figure 8.17 Example of a campaign structure for an e-mail campaign. Supplied by UK-based e-mail marketing specialists Harvest Digital (www.harvestdigital.com)

opt-in list. It shows that following an initial e-mail (1) with different creative for each of four segments offering entry into a prize draw, a reminder (2) was sent to those who had not entered. Those entering the prize draw had the opportunity to provide the e-mail addresses and names of friends or colleagues who were sent an e-mail offering them the opportunity to take part in the campaign (3). This can be described as a **viral referral**. Finally, an e-mail was sent to losers (4) which offered participation in a further draw. Clearly such a campaign structure would not be possible in conventional direct marketing because of cost constraints.

Additionally, it is more cost-effective to target niche groups. For example, a bank could e-mail an 18–25 female customer who reads a particular newspaper and who has a credit card and has responded to an e-mail campaign within the last 6 months. Such precision targeting is known as 'using multiple selects'. For house lists the cost per thousand is increased for multiple selects.

Of course, e-mail marketing also provides new challenges for marketers. Managing lists, producing a new form of creative, response rates and privacy issues all need to be considered as they are for conventional direct marketing.

Using e-mail marketing to support CRM

An effective way to formulate an e-mail marketing strategy is to apply it to achieving customer lifecycle objectives as part of CRM. Companies with limited resources may decide to focus on using acquisition or retention according to their marketing objectives. Questions arising include:

- *Selection* – Which are the ideal customer segments we should target? Can we use an existing database to profile customers? Which offers and creative should we use for different segments?
- *Acquisition* – How do we build a list of new prospects using the web site? How can we use e-mail in conjunction with other techniques to help convert prospects to customers?

Viral referral

An 'e-mail a friend or colleague' component to an e-mail campaign or part of web site design.

- *Retention* – How can we manage inbound e-mail service quality to increase customer loyalty?
- *Extension* – How can direct e-mail campaigns be used to extend the range and depth of products and services used by customers?

● E-mail for customer acquisition

To participate in outbound e-mail marketing, companies need to obtain e-mail addresses together with names and profile information for segmenting both prospects and existing customers. To obtain e-mail addresses of prospects there are two approaches:

1 Purchase of opt-in bought-in lists

Here, as for conventional postal direct marketing, the company will contact a list broker or list owner and purchase e-mail addresses of individuals who have agreed to receive marketing e-mails. They will rent a list of e-mail addresses which will be used to run the campaign. Potential customers may have agreed to receive e-mails if they are subscribers to a magazine, or have entered an online competition on a web site such as E-mail Inform (www.emailinform.com) which is owned by Claritas Interactive and has been used to obtain around approximately 1 million e-mail addresses in return for entry into a prize draw.

List broker

Will source the appropriate e-mail list(s) from the list owner.

List owner

Has collected e-mail addresses which are offered for sale.

2 Building a house list

A house list can be built using a company web site combined with permission-based marketing opt-in techniques (Chapter 6). A relevant incentive, such as free information or a discount, is offered in exchange for a prospect's providing their e-mail address by filling in an online form. Further best-practice in e-mail capture is contained in the box. Careful management of e-mail lists is required since, as the list ages, the addresses of customers and their profiles will change, resulting in many bounced messages and lower response rates Data protection law also requires the facility for customers to update their details.

House list

A list of prospect and customer names, e-mail addresses and profile information owned by an organisation.

Opt-in

An individual agrees to receive e-mail communications.

E-mail-capture best practice

1. Verify the accuracy of the e-mail address provided by delivering the offer by e-mail – for example, the link to free information is contained in an e-mail.
2. In 'double opt-in' a second confirmation is used to check that the person wishes to receive further information.
3. Explain why information is being collected. A customer will more readily give up their time and information if they know why it is being collected and how it may benefit them.
4. Keep information requested to a minimum. The bare minimum is the e-mail address, but additional profiling of product category preferences and basic demographics or company characteristics are typical. For existing customers, the e-mail address should be integrated with existing data – a customer account number can be requested to avoid repetition of information. 'Drip irrigation' to collect different data from different contacts.
5. Provide a privacy statement. This should explain that the data will not be shared with a third party and can increase e-mail capture rate.
6. Indicate mandatory fields. These are fields it is essential the customer fills in such as e-mail address and postcode.
7. Validate completion of form. Accuracy of information such as e-mail addresses and postcodes is again important, so perform a check on the fields in the form and prompt visitors to make amendments.
8. Provide prompt confirmation. After a visitor has filled in a form, a company should start the dialogue using an autoresponder to acknowledge receipt and describe follow-up actions.

The house list can also be built offline through collecting e-mail addresses where there is a customer contact such as a sales representative visit, at a point of sale or during a phone contact. For existing customers, companies should aim to increase the percentage of customers for whom e-mail addresses are held.

● E-mail for customer retention and extension

Once an e-mail address has been collected, the e-mail can be used to communicate with the customer in a variety of ways. While using a campaign to a house list to encourage repeat sales is typical, e-mail can also be used to inform about new products and events and also to learn by inviting the customer to participate in an online survey. As with any direct marketing campaign the results are mainly determined by the offer, targeting, creative and timing. Reference to the box 'Best practice for effective e-mail campaigns' highlights this.

● E-mail creative

Designing a direct e-mail requires just as much care as designing a traditional mailer and many similar principles apply. Effective e-mail should follow these guidelines:

- Grab attention in subject line and body. Don't leave the best to last.
- For newsletters use a standard header, but highlight specific content each month. Run articles over several months to maintain interest.
- Be relevant to target.
- Be brief, but contain sufficient information to be of interest as a standalone communication.
- Hyperlink to web site for more detailed content
- Be personalised – not Dear Valued Customer, but Dear Ms Smith.
- Have a clear call to action, which should be repeated at the start and end of e-mail as a link to a specific landing page on a web site.
- Test for effectiveness by sending trial mailings which vary the different elements of the campaign such as subject line, offer and close.
- Provide an opt-out or unsubscribe option that works.
- Operate within the legal and ethical constraints of the country.

Achieving an eye-catching e-mail is difficult using a plain text e-mail. For greater impact and branding, many marketers are turning to HTML mail which tends to have higher response rates. But there are many pitfalls in using HTML mail that may result in customers' not being able to read a message. Care is required by mailing house tests for the full range of e-mail reader software – e-mails can be coded to display either HTML or text according to the capability of the reader. Ideally, give subscribers a choice of e-mail or plain text. In the future broadband Internet rich-media e-mails using audio and Flash will be used increasingly.

● Managing inbound e-mail communications

For large organisations, e-mail volumes are already significant. For example, Bicknell (2002) reports that the Nationwide Bank Web contact centre receives nearly 20 000 e-mails each month. According to Mark Cromack, Nationwide's senior operations manager, customer contacts by e-mail have increased fourfold within the last year, but through choosing the right process and tools, it has only been necessary to double the number of operators. See Mini Case Study 5.3 (p. 211) for further information on this topic.

Best practice for effective e-mail campaigns

1 *Review the full range of options for the type of outbound e-mail and integrate them into the communications mix.* Options include:
- regular newsletter e-mail to keep customers informed about industry, company or product news;
- e-mail discussion list, perhaps about product support;
- viral e-mails: for example, customers are encouraged to enter the e-mail of a friend or colleague to forward information or entertainment to them;
- Small Message Service (SMS) messages to mobile phones can be used in a similar way to standard e-mail for a direct response approach.

2 *Select the appropriate frequency.* Marketers are currently learning about the optimum frequency. If messages are received too frequently from an organisation, their effectiveness will fall. Frequency options include:
- regular newsletter type. For example, daily, weekly, monthly. Let customers choose the frequency;
- event-related. These tend to be less regular, but give a higher impact. They are sent out perhaps every 3 or 6 months when there is news of a new product launch or an exceptional offer;
- multi-stage messaging is one of the most exciting applications of e-mail which can be deployed according to different events on site, for example after subscription to a trial version of an online magazine, e-mails will be sent out at 3, 10, 25 and 28 days to encourage a subscription before the trial lapses.

3 *Choose the optimum time.* This may be time of year, month, week or even day. For example, a monthly offer or newsletter may be best on a regular date such as the first of the month. Response rates may differ through the week, for example a Monday am B2B mailing is likely to have a lower response than a Wednesday pm mailing. Some B2B agencies send out e-mails at 11 or 3, when research suggests people are most likely to be at their desk.

4 *Ensure e-mail communications are relevant and targeted.* As for any direct marketing effort the offer and creative must be of interest to the recipient.

5 *Personalise.* Offer choice. Refer to the customer by name, where possible tailor for their preferences (e.g. type of content, frequency, HTML or plain text) or use mass customisation to give specific offers to different segments based on their past behaviour.

6 *Consider web response.* Here the power of e-mail and the Web are integrated. The web page is used as a direct response to the e-mail offer in the same way a TV ad provides a freephone number as a call to action. Web response can use a single page for all respondents or for each segment, or it can be personalised. A PIN or a user name and password can be used to identify respondents.

7 *Be distinctive.* Be the best. Research other e-mail offerings in your sector carefully and aim to better them. There are now tens of thousands of e-mail newsletters and other forms of opt-in e-mail. Make sure your offering stands out.

8 *Respect opt-out.* The procedure for opt-out or unsubscribe should be explained at the base of the message, and it should work. Privacy policy should be explained. Stay within the law, for example different regulations apply to minors.

9 *Test.* The mantra of direct marketing. Test. Test. Test. This medium is well suited to testing. How do you test?

10 *Tracking.* Plan to measure response or clickthrough rates and conversion to follow-up actions such as sales.

Inbound customer contact strategies

Approaches to managing the cost and quality of service related to management of customer enquiries.

Successful management of inbound communications is important to service quality as perceived by customers. In order to manage these communications, organisations need to develop **inbound customer contact strategies**.

Customer contact strategies are a compromise between delivering quality customer service with the emphasis on customer choice and minimising the cost of customer contacts. Typical operational objectives that should drive the strategies and measure their effectiveness are:

● Minimise average response time per e-mail and range of response time from slowest to fastest. This should form the basis of an advertised service quality level.
● Minimise clear-up (resolution) time – e.g. number of contacts and elapsed time to resolution.
● Maximise customer satisfaction ratings with response.
● Minimise average staff time and cost per e-mail response.

Customer contact strategies for integrating Web and e-mail support into existing contact centre operations usually incorporate elements of both of the following options.

1 *Customer-preferred channel*. Here the company uses a customer-led approach where customers use their preferred channel for enquiry whether it be phone callback, e-mail or live-chat. There is little attempt made to influence the customer as to which is the preferable channel. Note that while this approach may give good customer satisfaction ratings, it is not usually the most cost-effective approach, since the cost of phone support will be higher than customer self-service on the Web, or an e-mail enquiry.
2 *Company-preferred channel*. Here the company will seek to influence the customer on the medium used for contact. For example, easyJet encourages customers to use online channels rather than using voice contact to the call centre for both ordering and customer service. Customer choice is still available, but the company uses the web site to influence the choice of channel. Visit the easyJet web site (www.easyjet.com) and look at the box below to see how this is achieved.

Inbound contact management at easyJet (www.easyJet.com)

If an easyJet customer selects the 'Contact Us' option, rather than listing phone numbers and e-mail addresses, the customer is led through the three steps shown below which are intended to reduce the need for them to call the contact centre:

● **Step 1: Links or 'frequently asked questions (FAQ)'.** These are based on careful analysis of phone calls and e-mails received by the contact centre. Examples include questions concerning use of the site and booking online, fares, availability and pricing, airports, check-in, and travel information.

● **Step 2: E-mail enquiry through web form completion.** Examples include technical queries relating to the site, customer service, route feedback and general feedback – for comments and suggestions. (These e-mails are categorised to help prioritisation and routeing to the right person.)

● **Step 3: Telephone numbers.** Phone contact is only encouraged at the final stage. As easyJet explain, 'We've tried to make the FAQ and email service as simple and efficient as possible in order to keep the cost down and provide you with a good service, but if you're really stuck then, of course, you can call us'.

Other management options for contact management strategy that concern resourcing include:

- *Call-centre staff multi-skilling or separate Web contact centre.* Many companies start with a separate Web contact centre and then move to multi-skilling. Multi-skilling is the best way of effectively answering queries from customers whose support query may refer to a combination of online or offline activities. Multi-skilling also reduces hand-offs and can increase variety for contact-centre staff.
- *Balance between automation and manual processes.* Automated responses, intelligent routeing and autosuggestion are all techniques described in the next section which can be used to reduce the number of queries handled by human operators. If the automated approach fails, however, then inappropriate responses may be received by customers.
- *Insourcing or outsourcing.* Software, hardware and staff can be deployed internally or can be outsourced to an application service provider who will work according to a service level agreement to achieve quality standards.

Online promotion – viral marketing

Viral marketing harnesses the network effect of the Internet and can be effective in reaching a large number of people rapidly in the same way as a computer virus can affect many machines around the world. It is effectively an online form of word-of-mouth communications. Although the best-known examples of viral activity are of compromising pictures or jokes being passed around offices worldwide, viral marketing is increasingly being used for commercial purposes. At the time of writing, examples were a viral game from bank First Direct inviting users to 'Stuff the Cat' with varying sums of money. Success results in the cat exploding. E-mail addresses are collected as part of the campaign. A further example is 'Wax the Wimp' from Vauxhall cars which is targeted at a young female audience. It invites players to strip chest-hair off a model accompanied by squeals. A banner advert is displayed while the game is operational.

> **Viral marketing**
> E-mail is used to transmit a promotional message to another potential customer.

Godin (2001) writes about the importance of what he terms 'the ideavirus' as a marketing tool. He describes it as 'digitally augmented word-of-mouth'. What differences does the ideavirus have from word of mouth? First, transmission is more rapid, second, transmission tends to reach a larger audience, and third, it can be persistent – reference to a product on a service such as Epinions (www.epinions.com) remains online on a web site and can be read at a later time. Godin emphasises the importance of starting small by **seeding** a niche audience he describes as a 'hive' and then using advocates in spreading the virus – he refers to them as 'sneezers'. Traditionally, marketers would refer to such grouping as 'customer advocates' or 'brand loyalists'.

> **Seeding**
> The viral campaign is started by sending an e-mail to a targeted group that are likely to propagate the virus.

The speed of transmission and impact of the message must be balanced by naturally negative perceptions of viruses. A simple, yet elegant method of customer acquisition is the 'e-mail a friend' facility where a form is placed on an article that enables a customer to forward the page to a colleague. Other techniques include forwarding particular information such as a screensaver or an online postcard.

An example of a viral campaign is discussed in Mini Case Study 8.6. This shows that viral campaigns can be enhanced by other communications tools such as PR and search engine registration.

Crackermatic case study

(a)

(b)

Figure 8.18 Crackermatic viral campaign

(c)

Figure 8.18 (*continued*)

The site allowed web users to create and send single or multiple Christmas crackers by e-mail. Recipients would likewise be encouraged to make and send their own. The site was launched on 29 November 2001, and by 3 January 2002 had delivered a total of over 200 000 crackers.

Promotion

Seeded at different sources:

- company list;
- discussion groups;
- PR profile on Radio 2.

Also registered on search engines, for those looking in response to word of mouth.

Results

Total days of activity	36
Total number of crackers sent	200 667
Unopened crackers	76 195
Visitors to main site	91 353
Total number of unique senders	58 735
Propagation rate	110%
Average number of crackers sent	3.4
Most crackers sent by one person	110
Longest unbroken viral chain	14 users

Further examples of viral campaigns can be found at the Viral Bank www.viralbank.com.

Loyalty techniques and online incentive schemes

Air Miles and storecards are well known as methods of generating loyalty from customers by offering special promotional offers or the perception of 'getting something for nothing'. Given the success of these techniques, it is no surprise that many companies have tried to use these marketing concepts online. However, the model has not transferred successfully to the Internet for many new brands. For example, Beenz received millions of dollars of venture funding for its 'online currency' that could be gained through purchases at some sites while redeemed towards purchases at others. It was unable to successfully balance the expenses of brand-building and delivering the service with the commission it received from the companies using its service. However, traditional loyalty schemes, which have not had the large set-up costs, have transferred online successfully.

● On-site promotional techniques

In addition to ensuring promotion on other sites to attract an audience to a site, communications plans should consider how to convert visitors to action and to encourage repeat visits. Online media sites will aim to deploy content to maximise the length of visits. Approaches for increasing conversion of customers include:

- relevant incentive or option, clearly explained;
- clear call to action using a prominent banner ad or text heading;
- position of call to action in a prime location on screen, e.g. top left or top right.

To achieve this a variety of devices can be used, both to increase the length of site visit, and to make users return. A measure of a site's ability to retain visitors has been referred to as 'site stickiness' since a 'sticky' site is difficult to drag oneself away from. Activity 8.2 is intended to highlight some of the methods that can be used to achieve the objective of repeat visits.

Activity 8.2

Methods for enhancing site stickiness and generating repeat visits

This activity is intended to highlight methods of on-site promotion which may cause people to visit a web site, stay for longer than one click and then return. For each of the following techniques, discuss:

1 how the incentives should be used;
2 why these incentives will increase the length of site visits and the likelihood of return to the site;
3 the type of company for which these techniques might work best.

Techniques

- Sponsorship of an event, team or sports personality.
- A treasure hunt on different pages of the site, with a prize.
- A screensaver.
- A site-related quiz.
- Monthly product discount on an e-commerce site.
- Regularly updated information indicated by the current date or the date new content is added.

Note that as well as 'up-front' incentives there are some simple techniques that make a site 'fresh', which can be used to generate repeat visits. These include:

- daily or weekly update of pages with a date on the web site to highlight that it is updated regularly;
- regular publication of industry- or product-specific news;
- the use of e-mails to existing customers to highlight new promotions.

● Purchase follow-up activities

Offline communications or e-mail following a purchase offer good prospects for repeat business. However, it seems that not all online retailers are taking full advantage of this opportunity. Petersen (1999) reports on a survey by US consultants Rubric in which mystery shoppers shopped at 50 high-profile e-commerce sites. The mystery shoppers reported that 84 per cent of the sites did not follow up a sale with a related marketing offer, 96 per cent did not employ personalisation and 75 per cent did not recognise a 'repeat customer', that is one who visited the site again. One of the best sites was that of Cyberian Outpost, www.outpost.com.

Selecting the optimal communications mix

The promotion element of a marketing plan requires three important decisions about investment for the online promotion or the online communications mix.

1 Investment in promotion compared to site creation and maintenance

Since there is a fixed budget for site creation, maintenance and promotion, the e-marketing plan should specify the budget for each to ensure there is a sensible balance and the promotion of the site is not underfunded. The amount spent on maintenance for each major revision of a web site is generally thought to be between a quarter and a third of the original investment. The relatively large cost of maintenance is to be expected, given the need to keep updating information in order that customers return to a web site. Figure 8.19 shows two alternatives for balancing these three variables. Figure 8.19(a) indicates a budget where traffic-building expenditure exceeds service and design. This is more typical for a dot company that needs to promote its brand. Figure 8.19(b) is a budget where traffic-building expenditure is less than service and design. This is more typical for a traditional bricks-and-mortar company that already has a brand recognition and an established customer base.

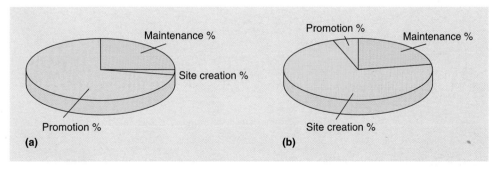

Figure 8.19 Alternatives for balance between different expenditure on Internet marketing

Analysis by Kemmler et al. (2001) of US and European e-commerce sites provides a cross-industry average of the spend on different components of Internet marketing. The top performers achieved an average operating profit of 18%. Costs were made up as follows:

- cost of goods sold (44%);
- maintenance costs (24%);
- marketing costs (14%).

2 Investment in online promotion techniques in comparison to offline promotion

A balance must be struck between these techniques. Figure 8.20 summarises the tactical options that companies have. Which do you think would be the best option for an established company as compared to a dot-com company? It seems that in both cases, offline promotion investment often exceeds that for online promotion investment. For existing companies, traditional media such as print are used to advertise the sites, while print and TV will also be widely used by dot-com companies to drive traffic to their sites.

3 Investment in different online promotion techniques

We have reviewed a wide range of techniques that can be used to build traffic to web sites. Agrawal et al. (2001) suggest that e-commerce sites should focus on narrow segments that have demonstrated their attraction to a business model. They believe that promotion techniques such as affiliate deals with narrowly targeted sites and e-mail campaigns targeted at segments grouped by purchase histories and demographic traits are 10 to 15 times more likely than banner ads on generic portals to attract prospects who click through to purchase. Alternatively, text banners on Google may have a higher success rate.

Marketing managers have to work with agencies to agree the balance and timing of all these methods. Perhaps the easiest way to start budget allocation is to look at those activities that need to take place all year. These include search engine registration, link building, affiliate campaigns and long-term sponsorships. These are often now outsourced to third-party companies because of the overhead of retaining specialist skills in-house.

Other promotional activities will follow the pattern of traditional media-buying with spending supporting specific campaigns which may be associated with new product launches or sales promotions: for example how much to pay for banner advertising as against online PR about online presence and how much to pay for search engine registration. Such investment decisions will be based on the strengths

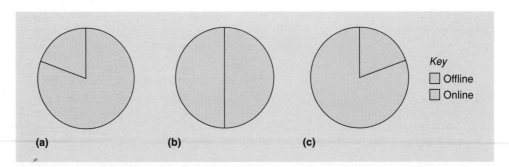

Figure 8.20 Options for the online v offline communications mix: (a) online > offline, (b) similar online and offline, (c) offline > online

Table 8.4 Summary of the strengths and weaknesses of different communications tools for promoting an online presence

Promotion technique	Main strengths	Main weaknesses
Search engine registration	Large online reach – used by high proportion of web users. Visitors are self-selecting. Relatively low cost, but increasing	Works best for specialist products rather than generic products, e.g. insurance. Cost – search engine optimisation is continuous as techniques change
Link-building campaigns	Relatively low cost and good targeting	Setting up a large number of links can be time-consuming
Affiliate campaigns	Payment is by results (e.g. 10% of sale goes to referring site)	Further payment to affiliate manager required for large-scale campaigns
Banner	Main intention to achieve visit, i.e. direct response model. Useful role in branding also	Response rates have declined historically because of banner blindness
Sponsorship	Most effective if low-cost, long-term co-branding arrangement with synergistic site	May increase mind-share, but does not directly lead to sales
E-mail marketing	Push medium – can't be ignored in user's in-box. Can be used for direct response link to web site	Requires opt-in list for effectiveness. Better for customer retention than for acquisition? Message diluted amongst other e-mails
Viral marketing	With effective creative possible to reach a large number at relatively low cost	Risks damaging brand since unsolicited messages may be received
PR	Relatively low-cost vehicle for PR. Many alternatives for innovation	Offline PR may give higher impact and reach
Traditional offline advertising (TV, print, etc.)	Larger reach than most online techniques. Greater creativity possible, leading to greater impact	Targeting arguably less easy than online. Typically high cost of acquisition

and weaknesses of the different promotion online. Table 8.4 presents a summary of the different techniques.

Deciding on the optimal expenditure on different communication techniques will be an iterative approach since past results should be analysed and adjusted accordingly. A useful analytical approach to help determine overall patterns of media buying is presented in Table 8.5. Marketers can analyse the proportion of the promotional budget that is spent on different channels and then compare this with the contribution from customers who purchase that originated using the original channel. This type of analysis, reported by Hoffman and Novak (2000), requires two different types of marketing research. First, **tagging** of customers can be used. We can monitor, using cookies, the numbers of customers who are referred to a web site through a particular online technique such as search engines, affiliate or banner ads, and then track the money they spend on purchases. Secondly, for other promotional techniques, tagging will not be practical. For word-of-mouth referrals, we would have to extrapolate the amount of spend for these customers through traditional market research techniques such as questionnaires. The use of tagging enables much better feedback on the effectiveness of promotional techniques than is possible in traditional media, but it requires a large investment in tracking software to achieve it.

Tagging

Tracking of origin of customers and their spending patterns.

Table 8.5 Relative effectiveness of different forms of marketing communications for the B2C company

Medium	Budget %	Contribution %	Effectiveness
Print (off)	20%	10%	0.5
TV (off)	25%	10%	0.25
Radio (off)	10%	5%	0.5
PR (off)	5%	15%	3
Word of mouth (off)	0%	25%	Infinite
Banners (on)	20%	20%	1
Affiliate (on)	20%	10%	0.5
Links (on)	0%	3%	Infinite
Search engine registration (on)	0%	2%	Infinite

Activity 8.3

Selecting the best promotion techniques

Suggest the best mix of promotion techniques to build traffic for the following applications:

1 well-established B2C brand with high brand awareness;
2 dot-com start-up;
3 small business aiming to export;
4 common B2C product, e.g. household insurance;
5 specialist B2B product.

---

4 Setting overall expenditure levels

We can use traditional approaches such as those suggested by Kotler et al. (2001). For example:

- *Affordable method* – the communications budget is set after subtracting fixed and variable costs from anticipated revenues.
- *Percentage-of-sales methods* – the communications budget is set as a percentage of forecast sales revenues.
- *Competititive parity methods* – expenditure is based on estimates of competitor expenditure. For example, e-marketing spend is typically 10–15% of the marketing budget.
- *Objective and task method* – this is a logical approach where budget is built up from all the tasks required to achieve the objectives in the communications plan.

● Acquisition costs

Varianini and Vaturi (2000) have suggested that many online marketing failures have resulted from poor control of media spending. The communications mix should be optimised to minimise the cost of acquisition. If an online intermediary has a cost acquisition of €100 per customer while it is gaining an average commission on each sale of €5 then, clearly, the company will not be profitable unless it can achieve a large number of repeat orders from the customer. For example, Figure 8.21 shows how Egg has managed its cost of customer acquisition.

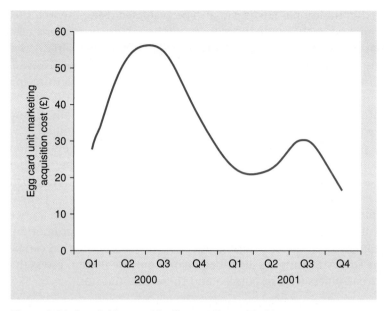

Figure 8.21 Acquisition cost for Egg credit card holders

Source: Egg investor relations www.investis.com/eggplc

Measuring effectiveness

Assessing the effectiveness of the methods to lead customers to the web site, or the impact of the web site itself, can be carried out by traditional methods used to assess non-digital advertising. For example, *post-testing* methods of evaluating traditional advertisements can be used for banner advertisements, or for the web site itself. These methods include recall and recognition tests. The impact on brand awareness and activity amongst potential and current customers can be reviewed in terms of the following scale:

● unaware;
● aware;
● attitude;
● preference;
● intention;
● trial;
● repeat.

Kotler (1997) summarises the *communication effects* of copy by asking questions such as:

● How well does the page catch the reader's attention?
● How well does the page lead the reader to go further?
● How effective is the particular appeal?
● How well does the page suggest follow-through or call to action?

Such questions can be applied to banner advertisements or the web site.

Pak (1999) has studied the advertising impact of web site content and its design (copy-testing). She reviewed the techniques on web sites used to communicate the message to the customer in terms of existing advertising theory. The impact of advertisements placed in traditional media can also be evaluated using the web site. In a crude form, a company might see an increase in number of site visits after a television campaign that promotes the web site URL, or even immediately after it was shown. If a company publicises a specific web address particular to one advertisement, it can then directly monitor how many enter the site in response to seeing that advertisement using the web log analysis techniques described in Chapter 9. The use of a web site can also be indicated by the number of phone calls arising directly from the site (with a callback system or a web-specific phone number).

A company such as DoubleClick (www.doubleclick.net) provides direct evaluation reports of banner advertisements in terms of number of clickthroughs. Further follow-up should take place, to see the behaviour of these customers when they visit the web site.

For specific sales promotions that take place over a period of time, such as a price reduction, it is possible to use the web site to directly evaluate the promotion. The number of page impressions before, during and after the sales promotion can be assessed. Some of the survey techniques described below could be used to assess the characteristics of the customers who responded and those who did not.

● Relative effectiveness of referrers

Overture (2002) suggests that its advertisers use three approaches to measure the effectiveness of online advertising spend with each advertiser.

- *Conversion rate.* This indicates the targeting of advertising since a more targeted audience from the referrer should result in a higher conversion rate to action.

$$\text{Conversion rate} = \frac{\text{Number of actions (sales) from referrer}}{\text{Number of site visitors from referrer}}$$

- *Return on advertising spend (ROAS).* This indicates amount of revenue generated from each referrer.

$$\text{ROAS} = \frac{\text{Total revenue generated from referrer}}{\text{Amount spent on advertising with referrer}}$$

- *Return on investment (ROI).* This indicates the profitability of each referrer.

$$\text{ROI} = \frac{\text{Profit generated from referrer}}{\text{Amount spent on advertising with referrer}}$$

To calculate these values, tracking systems must be put in place to measure the number of visits to your site from each referrer, and it must be also possible to measure the referrer source at the point of sale or action.

Summary

1 Online promotion techniques include:
   - banner advertising;
   - advertising in e-mail newsletters;
   - co-branding and sponsorship.

2 Offline promotion involves promoting the web site address and highlighting the value proposition of the web site in traditional media advertisements in print, or on television.

3 Banner advertising is used to drive traffic to sites by placing advertisements on specific-interest sites or displaying advertisements when particular keywords are entered. Advertising can also occur through sponsorship of a web site. When a user clicks on an advertisement (a clickthrough) he or she is taken to a web site that provides further information. Banner advertising can also be used for other purposes such as brand building or offering incentives.

Banner advertisements are usually paid for according to the cost per 1000 people viewing the advertisement (CPM).

4 Companies should ensure their web sites are listed as near to the top as possible in the most popular search engines. This task is best outsourced since search engine listings are dependent on several factors.

5 Referring links from related sites are also important in building traffic to a site.

6 For companies selling products online it is vital that their products be included in as many as possible of the price comparison shopping sites such as Yahoo Shopping.

7 Reciprocal links or co-branding, whereby companies agree to promote each other's site and services, are relatively low-cost forms of online advertising.

8 In addition to using the various methods for driving traffic to the web site, companies must ensure that the content and promotional offers on the site are sufficient when the user arrives. Methods such as loyalty schemes should be devised to keep the content and offers fresh and relevant.

9 Promotion works most effectively when online and offline techniques are combined to give a consistent marketing message.

EXERCISES

Self-assessment exercises

1 Briefly explain and give examples of online promotion and offline promotion techniques.
2 Explain the different types of payment model for banner advertising.
3 Which factors are important in governing a successful online banner advertising campaign?
4 How can a company promote itself through a search engine web site?
5 Explain the value of co-branding.
6 Explain how an online loyalty scheme may work.
7 How should web sites be promoted offline?
8 What do you think the relative importance of these Internet-based advertising techniques would be for an international chemical manufacturer?
   (a) Banner advertising.
   (b) Reciprocal links.
   (c) E-mail.

Essay and discussion questions

1 Discuss the analogy of Berthon et al. (1998) that effective Internet promotion is similar to a company exhibiting at an industry trade show attracting visitors to its stand.
2 Discuss the merits of the different models of paying for banner advertisements on the Internet for both media owners and companies placing advertisements.

3 'Online promotion must be integrated with offline promotion.' Discuss.

4 Compare the effectiveness of different methods of online advertising including banner advertisements, e-mail inserts, site co-branding and sponsorship.

Examination questions

1 Give three examples of online promotion and briefly explain how they function.

2 Describe four different types of site on which online banner advertising for a car manufacturer's site could be placed.

3 Clickthrough is one measure of the effectiveness of banner advertising. Answer the following:
   (a) What is clickthrough?
   (b) Which factors are important in determining the clickthrough rate of a banner advertisement?
   (c) Is clickthrough a good measure of the effectiveness of banner advertising?

4 What is meant by co-branding? Explain the significance of co-branding.

5 What are 'meta tags'? How important are they in ensuring a web site is listed in a search engine?

6 Name three ways in which e-mail can be used for promotion of a particular web site page containing a special offer.

7 Give an example of an online loyalty scheme and briefly evaluate its strengths and weaknesses.

8 Which techniques can be used to promote a web site in offline media?

References

Agrawal, V., Arjona, V. and Lemmens, R. (2001) E-performance: the path to rational exuberance, *McKinsey Quarterly*, No. 1, 31–43.

Berthon, P., Pitt, L. and Watson, R. (1996) Resurfing W³: research perspectives on marketing communication and buyer behaviour on the World Wide Web, *International Journal of Advertising*, 15, 287–301.

Berthon, P., Lane, N., Pitt, L. and Watson, R. (1998) The World Wide Web as an industrial marketing communications tool: models for the identification and assessment of opportunities, *Journal of Marketing Management*, 14, 691–704.

Bicknell, D. (2002) Banking on customer service, *e.Businessreview*, January, 21–2.

BMRB (2001) Users ignore banners, but off-line makes up the difference. Bytesize e-mail newsletter (www.bmrb.co.uk).

Boyce, R. (1998) Exploding the web CPM myth, IAB web site (www.iab.net).

Branthwaite, A., Wood, K. and Schilling, M. (2000) The medium is part of the message – the role of media for shaping the image of a brand. *ARF/ESOMAR Conference, Rio de Janeiro, Brazil, 12–14 November*.

Cartellieri, C., Parsons, A., Rao, V. and Zeisser, M. (1997) The real impact of Internet advertising, *McKinsey Quarterly*, No. 3, 44–63.

Colborn, J. (2002) Search engines – developing an effective strategy. *What's New in Marketing?*, 7 May. Online newsletter: www.wnim.com.

Deighton, J. (1996) The future of interactive marketing, *Harvard Business Review*, Nov–Dec, 151–62.

Dichter, E. (1966) How word-of-mouth advertising works, *Harvard Business Review*, 44 (November–December), 147–66.

Doubleclick (2001) Doubleclick's digital marketing study involving research of reveals that nearly half of European marketers are engaging in online marketing, *Doubleclick Press release* 12/11/01. www.doubleclick.net.

eMarketer (2002) E-advertising will grow despite general ad flatline. eStats report 22 January, www.emarketer.com.

Evans, P. and Wurster, T.S. (1999) Getting real about virtual commerce, *Harvard Business Review*, November, 84–94.

Godin, S. (2001) *Unleashing the Ideavirus*. Available online at: www.ideavirus.com.

Hoffman, D.L. and Novak, T.P. (1996) Marketing in hypermedia computer-mediated environments: conceptual foundations, *Journal of Marketing*, 60 (July), 50–68.

Hoffman, D.L. and Novak, T.P. (1997) A new marketing paradigm for electronic commerce. *The Information Society*, Special issue on electronic commerce, 13 (Jan–Mar), 43–54.

Hoffman, D.L. and Novak, T.P. (2000) How to acquire customers on the web, *Harvard Business Review*, May–June, 179–88. Available online at: http://ecommerce.vanderbilt.edu/papers.html

Hughes, A. (1999) Web Response – Modern 1:1 marketing. Database Marketing Institute article. www.dbmarketing.com/articles/Art196.htm.

IAB (2001) *Internet Advertising Revenue Holds Steady as All Ad Sectors Decline*. New release Interactive Advertising Bureau (www.iab.net) 4 December.

IABUK (2001) UK online advertising business fastest growing in history. Internet Advertising Bureau UK. Press briefing. 9-10-2001. www.iabuk.net.

Iconocast (2001) E-mail Strategy, Part 1. ICONOCAST e-newsletter 12-Jul-01. www.iconocast.com.

IPSOS-ASI (1999) Banner ads and TV ads equally memorable. Press release of survey reported at Nua Internet Surveys (www.nua.ie/surveys) 14 February. See also www. ipsosasi.com.

Janal, D. (1998) *Online Marketing Handbook. How to Promote, Advertise and Sell your Products and Services on the Internet*. Van Nostrand Reinhold, ITC, New York.

Jenkins, F. (1995) *Public Relations Techniques*, 2nd edn. Butterworth Heinemann, Oxford.

Kemmler, T., Kubicová, M., Musslewhite, R. and Prezeau, R. (2001) E-performance II: the good, the bad and the merely average, *McKinsey Quarterly*, No. 3. Online only.

Kotler, P. (1997) *Marketing Management – Analysis, Planning, Implementation and Control*. Prentice Hall, Englewood Cliffs, NJ.

Kotler, P., Armstrong, G., Saunders, J. and Wong, V. (2001) *Principles of Marketing*, 3rd European edn. Financial Times/Prentice Hall, Harlow.

Novak, T. and Hoffman, D. (1997) New metrics for new media: towards the development of web measurement standards, *World Wide Web Journal*, 2(1), 213–46.

ONS (2001) Internet Access Households and individuals. Office of National Statistics report 26 September 2001 of July 2001 survey. www.statistics.gov.uk.

Overture (2002) Overture Frequently Asked Questions (www.uk.overture.com)

Pak, J. (1999) Content dimensions of web advertising: a cross national comparison, *International Journal of Advertising*, 18(2), 207–31.

Parry, K. (1998) *Europe Gets Wired. A Survey of Internet Use in Great Britain, France and Germany, Research Report 1998*. KPMG Management Consulting, London.

Peters, L. (1998) The new interactive media: one-to-one but to whom? *Marketing Intelligence and Planning*, 16(1), 22–30.

Petersen, S. (1999) Handle e-customers gently, *PC Week*, 13 July, p. 19.

Pickton, A. and Broderick, D. (2000) *Integrated Marketing Communications*. Financial Times/Prentice Hall, Harlow.

Pincott, G. (2000) Web site promotion strategy. White paper from Millward Brown Intelliquest. Available online at www.intelliquest.com.

Poynter (2000) Eye Tracking Study (www.poynter.org/eyetrack2000).

Ranchhod, A., Gurau, C. and Lace, J. (2002) On-line messages: developing an integrated communications model for biotechnology companies, *Qualitative Market Research: An International Journal*, 5(1), 6–18.

Revolution (2000) Online promotions – campaign of the week, *Revolution Magazine*, 19 April.

Revolution (2001) Campaign of the week, *Revolution*, 16 May, p. 38.

Rogers, E. (1983) *Diffusion of Innovations*, 3rd edn. Free Press, New York.

Rowley, J. (2001) Remodelling marketing communications in an Internet environment, *Internet Research: Electronic Networking Applications and Policy*, 11(3), 203–12.

Schiller, B. (1999) Online alliances help firms spread their reach, *Net Profit*, June, p. 9.

Schramm, W. (1955) How communication works. In *The Process and Effects of Mass Communications*, W. Schramm (ed.), pp. 3–26. University of Illinois Press, Urbana, IL.

Smith, P.R. and Chaffey, D. (2001) *EMarketing Excellence: at the Heart of EBusiness*. Butterworth Heinemann, Oxford.

Sterne, J. (1999) *World Wide Web Marketing*, 2nd edn. Wiley, New York.

Van Doren, D., Flechner, D. and Green-Adelsberger, K. (2000) Promotional strategies on the world wide web, *Journal of Marketing Communications*, 6, 21–35.

Varianini, V. and Vaturi, D. (2000) Marketing lessons from e-failures, *McKinsey Quarterly*, No. 4, 86–97.

Zeff, R. and Aronson, B. (2001) *Advertising on the Internet*, 3rd edn. Wiley, New York.

Further reading

Brassington, F. and Petitt, S. (2000) *Principles of Marketing*, 2nd edn. Financial Times/Prentice Hall, Harlow. *See* companion Prentice Hall web site (www.booksites.net/brassington2). Chapter 15, Advertising, provides the conceptual underpinning of and describes best practice in advertising in traditional media. Chapter 16, Sales promotion, introduces traditional methods of sales promotion, many of which can be applied to the Internet.

Fill, C. (2002) *Marketing Communications – Contexts, Contents and Strategies*, 3rd edn. Financial Times/Prentice Hall, Harlow. The entire book is recommended for its integration of theory, concepts and practice.

IAB Internet Advertising revenue report Q3, 2001. www.iab.net/news/content/12_04_01b.html

Kotler, P., Armstrong, G., Saunders, J. and Wong, V. (2001) *Principles of Marketing*, 3rd edn. Financial Times/Prentice Hall, Harlow. *See* Chapter 18, Integrated marketing communications strategy and Chapter 19, Mass communications: advertising, sales promotion and public relations.

Novak, T. and Hoffman, D. (1997) New metrics for new media: towards the development of web measurement standards, *World Wide Web Journal*, 2(1), 213–46. This paper gives detailed, clear definitions of terms associated with measuring advertising effectiveness.

Zeff, R. and Aronson, B. (2001) *Advertising on the Internet*, 3rd edn. Wiley, New York. A comprehensive coverage of online banner advertising and measurement techniques and a more limited coverage of other techniques such as e-mail-based advertising.

Web links

Internet-marketing-related e-mail newsletters

- Iconocast (www.iconocast.com). US-based newsletter of Internet marketing news.
- Nua: e-mail (www.nua.ie/surveys). A digest of research reports on Internet marketing.
- Marketing Sherpa (www.marketingsherpa.com). Articles and links on Internet marketing communications including e-mail and online advertising.
- Whats New in Marketing (www.wnim.com). A monthly newsletter from the Chartered Institute of Marketing including many e-marketing features.

E-mail-related links

- Clickz (www.clickz.com). Has columns on e-mail marketing, e-mail marketing optimisation and e-mail marketing case studies.
- EMMA – E-Mail Marketing Association, formed in July 2001 to support best practice amongst agencies and clients (www.emmacharter.org).
- Opt-in News (www.optinnews.com). An online magazine focusing on permission-based e-mail marketing.

Internet-advertising-related links

- Bluestreak (www.adknowledge.com). Has acquired AdKnowledge, which specialised in measurement of online advertising campaigns.

- Advertising Age (www.adage.com).

- Clickz (www.clickz.com). An excellent collection of articles on online marketing communications. US-focused. Relevant sections for this chapter include: Affiliate marketing, Advertising technology, E-mail marketing, Media buying.

- DoubleClick (www.doubleclick.net). The main advertising network worldwide, with offices in many countries. Its site describes how it uses its 'DART' technolology to target customers. Also major e-mail marketing agency.

- eMarketer (www.emarketer.com). Includes reports on media spend based on compilations of other analysts.

- Internet Advertising Bureau (www.iab.net). The widest range of studies about Internet advertising effectiveness. In UK: www.iabuk.net.

- Jupiter MMXI (www.jupitermmxi.com). Resources include audience panels.

- Nielsen-Netratings (www.nielsen-netratings.com). Nielsen has acquired NetRatings, and this site is an interesting resource on the current levels of activity and success of banner advertising. The site shows the creative content of the ten most popular banners each week and gives information on the main advertisers.

Search-engine-related links

- Searchenginewatch (www.searchenginewatch.com). A complete resource.

- WebSearch at About.com (http://websearch.about.com). Articles and resources.

Chapter 9

Maintaining and monitoring the online presence

Links to other chapters

This chapter should be read in conjunction with these chapters:

➤ Chapter 4 describes the development of an Internet marketing strategy. The aim of measurement is to quantify whether the objectives of this strategy have been achieved

➤ Chapter 7 describes how to set up a web site, and should be read before this chapter to introduce the reader to concepts of web site development

➤ Chapter 8 describes methods of promoting a web site. It should be read before this chapter since one aspect of measuring the effectiveness of Internet marketing is aimed at assessing the different promotional methods

Learning objectives

After reading this chapter, the reader should be able to:

● Identify the tasks necessary when managing an online presence

● Understand terms used to measure and improve site effectiveness

● Develop an appropriate process to collect measures for Internet marketing effectiveness

Questions for marketers

Key questions for marketing managers related to this chapter are:

● How much resource do I need to put into maintaining and monitoring the site?

● What processes should I use to maintain the web site?

● How do I measure the effectiveness of web marketing?

Introduction

In the mid-1990s, a common sight when one viewed web sites was an 'under construction' logo showing a person digging a hole. Such logos are seen much less frequently nowadays, since it has been realised that effective web sites are always under construction. The need for frequent updating does not necessarily indicate a poor site: it was shown in Chapter 7 that high-quality, up-to-date content was one of the key factors visitors gave for returning to web sites. This chapter discusses issues in managing the update process for an online presence, answering questions such as:

- How often does a web site need to be updated?
- What is a suitable process for managing maintenance of the site?
- Who is responsible for updating?
- What needs to be tested?
- How do we monitor and measure Internet marketing effectiveness?

Measuring the effectiveness of Internet marketing in achieving marketing goals is considered in some detail since a key part of managing the site is to see how popular the different areas of the site are, and then to adjust the content accordingly. Measuring effectiveness goes beyond this to ask whether the site is helping to achieve the strategic goals of the company.

The maintenance process

For effective control of a web site, it is important to have a clearly defined process for making changes to the content of the web site. This process should be understood by all staff working on the site, with their responsibilities clearly identified in their job descriptions. The main stages involved in producing a web page are to design it, write it, test it and publish it. A more detailed process is set out here, which distinguishes between review of the content and technical testing of the completed web page. A simple model of the work involved in maintenance is shown in Figure 9.1. It is assumed that the needs of the users and design features of the site have already been defined when the site was originally created, as described in Chapter 7. The model only applies to minor updates to copy, or perhaps updating product or company information. The different tasks involved in the maintenance process are as follows:

1 *Write*. This stage involves writing the marketing copy and, if necessary, designing the layout of copy and associated images.
2 *Review*. An independent review of the copy is necessary to check for errors before a document is published. Depending on the size of organisation, review may be necessary by one person or several people covering different aspects of site quality such as corporate image, marketing copy, branding and legality.
3 *Correct*. This stage is straightforward, and involves updates necessary as a result of stage 2.
4 *Publish (to test environment)*. The publication stage involves putting the corrected copy on a web page that can be checked further. This will be in a test environment that can only be viewed from inside a company.
5 *Test*. Before the completed web page is made available over the World Wide Web a final test will be required for technical issues such as whether the page loads successfully on different browsers.

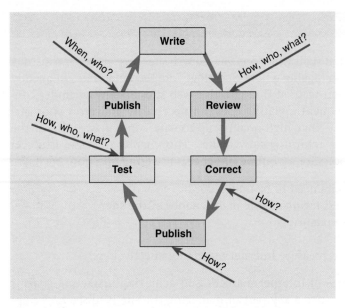

Figure 9.1 A web document review and update process

6 *Publish (to live environment).* Once the material has been reviewed and tested and is signed off as satisfactory it will be published to the main web site and will be accessible by customers.

● How often should material be updated?

Web site content needs to be up-to-date, in line with customer expectations. The Web is perceived as a dynamic medium, and customers are likely to expect new information to be posted to a site straight away. If material is inaccurate or 'stale' then the customer may not return to the site.

After a time, the information on a web page naturally becomes outdated and will need to be updated or replaced. It is important to have a mechanism defining what triggers this update process and leads to the cycle of Figure 9.1. The need for material to be updated has several facets. For the information on the site to be accurate it clearly needs to be up to date. Trigger procedures should be developed such that when price changes or product specifications are updated in promotional leaflets or catalogues, these changes are also reflected on the web site. Without procedures of this type, it is easy for there to be errors on the web site. This may sound obvious, but the reality is that the people contributing the updates to the site will have many other tasks to complete, and the web site could be a low priority.

A further reason for updating the site is to encourage repeat visits. For example, a customer could be encouraged to return to a business-to-business site if there is some industry news on the site. Such information needs to be updated at least weekly, and possibly daily, to encourage the customer to return. Again, a person has to be in place to collate such news and update the site frequently. The facility of being able to update prices regularly should be taken advantage of where possible. Some companies such as RS Components have monthly promotions, which may encourage repeat visits to the site. It is useful to emphasise to the customer that the information is updated frequently. This is possible through simple devices such as putting the date on the home page, or perhaps just the month and year for a site that is updated less frequently.

As part of defining a web site update process, and standards, a company may want to issue guidelines that suggest how often content is updated. This may specify that content is updated as follows:

- within two days of a factual error being identified;
- a new 'news' item is added at least once a month;
- when product information has been static for two months.

Responsibilities in web site maintenance

Maintenance is easy in a small company with a single person updating the web site. That person is able to ensure that the style of the whole site remains consistent. For a slightly larger site with perhaps two people involved with updating, the problem more than doubles since communication is required to keep things consistent. For a large organisation with many different departments and offices in different countries, site maintenance becomes very difficult, and production of a quality site is only possible when there is strong control to establish a team who all follow the same standards. Sterne (1999) suggests that the essence of successful maintenance is to have clearly identified responsibilities for different aspects of updating the web site. The questions to ask are:

- Who owns the process?
- Who owns the content?
- Who owns the format?
- Who owns the technology?

We will now consider these in more detail, reviewing the standards required to produce a good-quality web site and the different types of responsibilities involved.

● Who owns the process?

One of the first areas to be defined should be the overall process for updating the site. But who agrees this process? For the large company it will be necessary to bring together all the interested parties such as those within the marketing department and the site developers – who may be an external agency or the IT department. Within these groupings there may be many people with an interest such as the marketing manager, the person with responsibility for Internet or new-media marketing, a communications manager who places above-the-line advertising, and product managers who manage the promotion of individual products and services. All of these people should have an input in deciding on the process for updating the web site. This is not simply a matter of updating the web site; there are more fundamental issues to consider, such as how communications to the customer are made consistent between the different media. Some companies such as Orange (www.orange.net) and Ford (www.ford.co.uk) manage this process well, and the content of the web site is always consistent with other media campaigns in newspapers and on television. In Ford this has been achieved by breaking down the barriers between traditional-media account managers and the Internet development team, and both groups work closely together. In other organisations, a structure is adopted in which there is a person or group responsible for customer communications, and they then ensure that the message conveyed by different functions such as the web site developers and the advertisement placers is consistent. Options for structuring an organisation to integrate new and old media are given in Parsons et al. (1996).

What, then, is this process? The process will basically specify responsibilities for different aspects of site management and detail the sequence in which tasks occur for updating the site. A typical update process is outlined in Figure 9.1. If we take a specific example we can illustrate the need for a well-defined process. Imagine that a large organisation is launching a new product, promotional literature is to be distributed to customers, the media are already available, and the company wants to add information about this product to the web site. A recently recruited graduate is charged with putting the information on the site. How will this process actually occur? The following process stages need to occur:

1 Graduate reviews promotional literature and rewrites copy on a word processor and modifies graphical elements as appropriate for the web site. This is the *write* stage in Figure 9.1.
2 Product and/or marketing manager reviews the revised web-based copy. This is part of the *review* stage in Figure 9.1.
3 Corporate communications manager reviews the copy for suitability. This is also part of the *review* stage in Figure 9.1.
4 Legal adviser reviews copy. This is also part of the *review* stage in Figure 9.1.
5 Copy revised and corrected and then re-reviewed as necessary. This is the *correct* stage in Figure 9.1.
6 Copy converted to web and then published. This will be performed by a technical person such as a site developer, who will insert a new menu option to help users navigate to the new product. This person will add the HTML formatting and then upload the file using FTP to the test web site. This is the first *publish* stage in Figure 9.1.
7 The new copy on the site will be reviewed by the graduate for accuracy, and needs to be tested on different web browsers and screen resolutions if it uses a graphical design different from the standard site template. This type of technical testing will need to be carried out by the webmaster. The new version could also be reviewed on the site by the communications manager or legal adviser at this point. This is part of the *test* stage in Figure 9.1.
8 Once all interested parties agree the new copy is suitable, the pages on the test web site can be transferred to the live web site and are then available for customers to view. This is the second *publish* stage in Figure 9.1.

Note that, in this scenario, review of the copy at stages 2 to 4 happens before the copy is actually put on to the test site at stage 6. This is efficient in that it saves the technical person or webmaster having to update the page until the copy is agreed. An alternative would be for the graduate to write the copy at stage 1 and then the webmaster publish the material before it is reviewed by the various parties. Each approach is equally valid.

It is apparent that this process is quite involved, so the process needs to be clearly understood within the company or otherwise web pages may be published that do not conform to the look and feel for the site, have not been checked for legal compliance, or may not work. The only way such a process can be detailed is if it is written down and its importance communicated to all the participants. It will also help if technology facilitates the process. In particular, a workflow system should be set up that enables each of the reviewers to comment on the copy as soon as possible and authorise it. Content management tools such as Lotus Notes are increasingly used to help achieve this. The copy can be automatically e-mailed to all reviewers and then the comments received by e-mail can be collated.

The detailed standards for performing a site update will vary according to the extent of the update. For correcting a spelling mistake, for example, not so many people will need to review the change! A site re-design that involves changing the look and feel of the site will require the full range of people to be involved.

Once the process has been established, the marketing department, as the owners of the web site, will insist that the process be followed for every change that is made to the web site.

To conclude this section refer to Activity 9.1 which shows a typical web site update process and considers possible improvements.

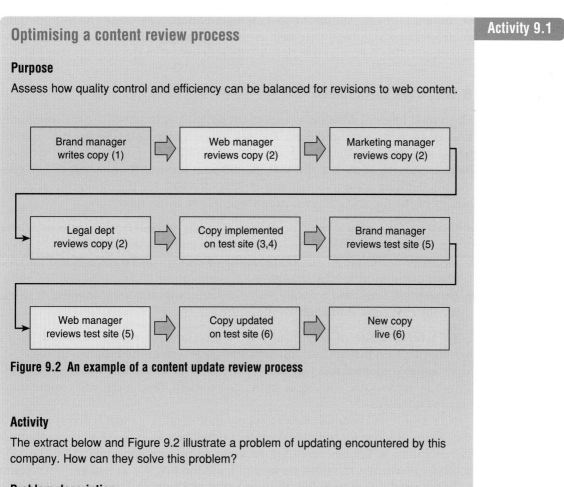

Activity 9.1

Optimising a content review process

Purpose

Assess how quality control and efficiency can be balanced for revisions to web content.

Figure 9.2 An example of a content update review process

Activity

The extract below and Figure 9.2 illustrate a problem of updating encountered by this company. How can they solve this problem?

Problem description

From when the brand manager identifies a need to update copy for their product, the update might happen as follows: brand manager writes copy (half a day), one day later the web manager reviews copy, three days later the marketing manager checks the copy, seven days later the legal department checks the copy, two days later the revised copy is implemented on the test site, two days later the brand manager reviews the test site, the next day the web manager reviews the web site followed by updating and final review before the copy is added to the live site two days later and over a fortnight from when a relatively minor change to the site was identified!

● Who owns the content?

For a medium to large site where the content is updated regularly, as it should be, it will soon become impossible for one person to be able to update all the content.

It is logical and practical to distribute the responsibility for owning and developing different sections of the site to the people in an organisation who have the best skills and knowledge to develop that content. For example, for a large financial services company, the part of the business responsible for a certain product area should update the copy referring to their products. One person will update copy for each of savings accounts, mortgages, travel insurance, health insurance and investments. For a PC supplier, different content developers will be required for the product information, financing, delivery information and customer service facilities. Once the ownership of content is distributed throughout an organisation, it becomes crucial to develop guidelines and standards that help ensure that the site has a coherent 'feel' and appearance. The nature of these guidelines is described in the sections that follow.

Content developer
A person responsible for updating web pages within part of an organisation.

● Who owns the format?

The format refers to different aspects of the design and layout of the site commonly referred to as its 'look and feel'. The key aim is consistency of format across the whole web site. For a large corporate site, with different staff working on different parts of the site, there is a risk that the different areas of the site will not be consistent. Defining a clear format or site design template for the site means that the quality of the site and customer experience will be better since:

Site design template
A standard page layout format which is applied to each page of a web site.

- *the site will be easier to use* – a customer who has become familiar with using one area of the site will be able to confidently use another part of the site;
- *the design elements of the site will be similar* – a user will feel more at home with the site if different parts look similar;
- *the corporate image and branding will be consistent with real-world branding* (if this is an objective) and similar across the entire site.

To achieve a site of this quality it is necessary for written standards to be developed. These may include different standards such as those shown in Table 9.1. The standards adopted will vary according to the size of the web site and company. Typically, larger sites, with more individual content developers, will require more detailed standards.

Note that it will be much easier to apply these quality standards across the site if the degree of scope for individual content developers to make changes to graphics or navigation is limited and they concentrate on changing text copy. To help achieve consistency, the software used to build the web site should allow templates to be designed that specify the menu structure and graphical design of the site. The content developers are then simply adding text- and graphics-based pages to specific documents and do not have to worry about the site design.

● Who owns the technology?

The technology used to publish the web site is important if a company is to utilise fully the power of the Internet. This may not be evident when a simple brochure-ware site is produced, as this may require just an HTML editor. It becomes more significant when a company wants to make its product catalogue available for queries or to take orders online. As these facilities are added the web site changes from an isolated system to one that must be integrated with other technologies such as the customer database, stock control and sales order processing systems. Given this integration with corporate IS, the IT department (or the company to which IT has been outsourced) will need to be involved in the development of the site and its strategy.

Table 9.1 Web site standards

Standard	Details	Applies to
Site structure	Will specify the main areas of the site, for example products, customer service, press releases, how to place content and who is responsible for each area.	Content developers
Navigation	May specify, for instance, that the main menu must always be on the left of the screen with nested (sub-) menus at the foot of the screen. The home button should be accessible from every screen at the top left corner of the screen. See Lynch and Horton (1999) for guidelines on navigation and site design.	Web site designer/webmaster usually achieves these through site templates
Copy style	General guidelines, for example reminding those writing copy that web copy needs to be briefer than its paper equivalent. Where detail is required, perhaps with product specifications, it should be broken up into chunks that are digestible on-screen.	Individual content developers
Testing standards	Check site functions for: ● different browser types and versions ● plug-ins ● invalid links ● speed of download of graphics ● spellcheck each page See text for details.	Web site designer/webmaster
Corporate branding and graphic design	Specifies the appearance of company logos and the colours and typefaces used to convey the brand message.	Web site designer/webmaster
Process	The sequence of events for publishing a new web page or updating an existing page. Who is responsible for reviewing and updating?	All
Performance	Availability and download speed figures.	

A further technology issue to be addressed is providing an infrastructure which allows the content developers throughout the company to update copy from their own desktop computer. For example, companies that have standardised on Lotus Notes can use this so that individual content developers can readily contribute their copy and the process of checking can be part-automated, using workflow facilities, to send messages to testers and reviewers who can then authorise or reject the content.

As well as issues of integrating systems, there are detailed technical issues for which the technical staff in the company need to be made responsible. These include:

● availability and performance of web site server;
● checking HTML for validity and correcting broken links;
● managing different versions of web pages in the test and live environments.

● Content management

Content management refers to when software tools (usually browser-based software running on a server) permit business users to contribute web content while an administrator keeps control of the format and style of the web site and the approval

Content management
Software tools for managing additions and amendment to web site content.

process. Theses tools are used to organise, manage, retrieve and archive information content throughout the life of the site.

Content management tools provide these facilities:

- *structure authoring*: the design and maintenance of content structure (sub-components, templates, etc.), web page structure and web site structure;
- *link management*: the maintenance of internal and external links through content change and the elimination of dead links;
- *input and syndication*: the loading (spidering) of externally originating content and the aggregation and dissemination of content from a variety of sources, including multimedia binary large objects (BLOBs) such as MPEG movie files;
- *versioning*: the crucial task of controlling which edition of a page, page element or the whole site is published. Typically this will be the most recent, but previous editions should be archived and it should be possible to roll back to a previous version at the page, page element or site level;
- *publication*: content destined for a web site needs to pass through a publication process to move it from the management environment to the live delivery environment. The process may involve tasks such as format conversion (e.g. to PDF, or to WAP), rendering to HTML, editorial authorisation and the construction of composite documents in real time (personalisation and selective dissemination);
- *tracking and monitoring*: providing logs and statistical analysis of use to provide performance measures, tune the content according to demand and protect against misuse;
- *navigation and visualisation*: providing an intuitive, clear and attractive representation of the nature and location of content using colour, texture, 3D rendering or even virtual reality (thereby visualising cyberspace, as portrayed in the book *Neuromancer* by William Gibson and movies such as *Tron* and *The Matrix*).

Measuring Internet marketing effectiveness

Measurement is one of the most important activities that occur once a web site is published. As explained in Chapter 1 in the section on conversion marketing, analysing the effectiveness of a site is crucial in assessing the strategy and then improving it to overcome problems. Given this, we will examine how we can measure the effectiveness of the Internet channel in some detail.

Measurement for assessing the effectiveness of Internet marketing can be thought of as answering these questions:

1 Are corporate objectives identified in the Internet marketing strategy being met?
2 Are marketing objectives defined in the Internet marketing strategy and plan achieved?
3 Are marketing communications objectives identified in the Internet marketing plan achieved? How effective are the different promotional techniques used to attract visitors to a site?

The measures can also be related to the different levels of marketing control specified by Kotler (1997). These include strategic control (question 1), profitability control (question 1), annual-plan control (question 2) and efficiency control (question 3).

We will describe measurement by examining three key elements of an Internet marketing measurement system. These are, first, the process for the performance measurement system, secondly, the measurement framework which specifies groups of relevant Internet marketing metrics and, finally, an assessment of the suitability of tools and techniques for collecting, analysing, disseminating and actioning results.

Although we have stated that measurement is an important part of maintaining a web site, it is worth noting that the reality is that measurement is often neglected when a web site is first created. This is natural since, when designing the first version of a site, the designers are concerned with issues such as what content to put on the site, how it will be laid out, and how users can navigate between the different pages. With many immediate issues such as these to be settled it is understandable that measurement is often not considered. Measurement will often become an issue once the first version of a site has been 'up and running' for a few months, and people start to ask questions such as 'How many customers are visiting our site, how many sales are we achieving as a result of our site and how can we improve the site to achieve a return on investment?' The consequence of this is that measurement is something that is added after the first versions of a web site have been created. Fortunately, it is possible to do this, but it is probably easier and site performance information can be obtained earlier if measurement is built into site management from the start.

Internet marketing metrics
Measures that indicate the effectiveness of Internet marketing activities in meeting customer, business and marketing objectives.

● Stage 1: Creating a performance measurement system

Many organisations now have an established online presence, but there are many unanswered questions about the process by which the marketing performance of this presence is evaluated and how it is modified with a view to improving its performance. Adams et al. (2000), for example, asked managers to name their priorities for improvements to e-business performance measurement systems. Results differed for different types of organisation, reflecting the stage of evolution in their measurement. For bricks-and-mortar companies, developing or introducing a more comprehensive measurement system and enhancing analysis capabilities to establish what really drives business performance was most important. For clicks-and-mortar, integrating new systems with legacy systems and benchmarking against best practice were most important. Finally dot-coms, as start-ups, were concerned with improving clickstream analysis and customer tracking and profiling and improving the entire company's performance measurement system.

Performance measurement system
The process by which metrics are defined, collected, disseminated and actioned.

Bourne et al. (2000) suggest that the development of a performance measurement system can be divided into three main phases: (1) the design of the performance measures, (2) the implementation of the performance measures and (3) the use of the performance measures. The need for a structured measurement process is clear if we examine the repercussions if an organisation does not have one. These include: poor linkage of measures with strategic objectives or even absence of objectives; key data not collected; data inaccuracies; data not disseminated or analysed; or no corrective action. Many of the barriers to improvement of measurement systems reported by respondents in Adams et al. (2000) also indicate the lack of an effective process. The barriers can be grouped as follows:

- senior management myopia – performance measurement not seen as a priority, not understood or is targeted at the wrong targets – reducing costs rather than improving performance;
- unclear responsibilities for delivering and improving the measurement system;

- resourcing issues – lack of time (perhaps suggesting lack of staff motivation), the necessary technology and integrated systems;
- data problems – data overload or of poor quality, limited data for benchmarking.

These barriers are reinforced by the survey by Cutler and Sterne (2000) which describes the main obstacles to metrics development as lack of qualified personnel (31%), data overload (19%), lack of technical resources (software) (19%).

To avoid these pitfalls, a coordinated, structured measurement process such as that shown in Figure 9.3 is required. Figure 9.3 indicates four key stages in a measurement process. These were defined as key aspects of annual plan control by Kotler (1997). Stage 1 is a goal-setting stage where the aims of the measurement system are defined – this will usually take the strategic Internet marketing objectives as an input to the measurement system. The aim of the measurement system will be to assess whether these goals are achieved and specify corrective marketing actions to reduce variance between target and actual key performance indicators. Stage 2, performance measurement, involves collecting data to determine the different metrics that are part of a measurement framework as discussed in the next section. Stage 3, performance diagnosis, is the analysis of results to understand the reasons for variance from objectives (the 'performance gap' of Friedman and Furey, 1999) and selection of marketing solutions to reduce variance. The purpose of stage 4, corrective action, according to Wisner and Fawcett (1991), is

> to identify competitive position, locate problem areas, assist the firm in updating strategic objectives and making tactical decisions to achieve these objectives and supply feedback after the decisions are implemented.

In an Internet marketing context, corrective action is the implementation of these solutions as updates to web site content, design and associated marketing communications. At this stage the continuous cycle repeats, possibly with modified goals. Bourne et al. (2000) and Plant (2000) suggest that in addition to reviewing objectives, the suitability of the metrics should also be reviewed and revised.

Measurement is not something that can occur on an ad hoc basis because if it is left to the individual they may forget to collect the data needed. A 'measurement culture' is one in which each employee is aware of the need to collect data on how well the company is performing and on how well it is meeting its customer's needs.

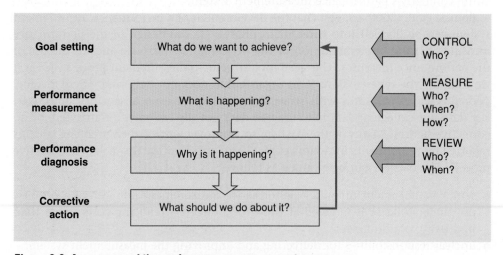

Figure 9.3 A summary of the performance measurement process

● Stage 2: Defining the performance metrics framework

Chaffey (2000) suggests that organisations define a measurement framework which defines groupings of specific metrics used to assess Internet marketing performance. He suggests that suitable measurement frameworks will fulfil these criteria:

A. Include both macro-level metrics which assess whether strategic goals are achieved and indicate to what extent e-marketing contributes to the business (revenue contribution and return on investment). This criterion covers the different levels of marketing control specified by Kotler (1997) including strategic control, profitability control annual-plan control.

B. Include micro-level metrics which assess the effectiveness and efficiency of e-marketing tactics and implementation. Wisner and Fawcett (1991) note that typically organisations use a hierarchy of measures and they should check that the lower-level measures support the macro-level strategic objectives. Such measures are often referred to as *performance drivers*, since achieving targets for these measures will assist in achieving strategic objectives. E-marketing performance drivers help optimise e-marketing by attracting more site visitors and increasing conversion to desired marketing outcomes. These achieve the marketing efficiency control specified by Kotler (1997). The research by Agrawal et al. (2001), who assessed companies on metrics defined in three categories of attraction, conversion and retention as part of an e-performance scorecard, uses a combination of macro- and micro-level metrics.

C. Assess the impact of the e-marketing on the satisfaction, loyalty and contribution of key stakeholders (customers, investors, employees and partners) as suggested by Adams et al. (2000).

D. The framework must be flexible enough to be applied to different forms of online presence whether business-to-consumer, business-to-business, not-for-profit or transactional e-tail, CRM-oriented or brand-building. Much discussion of e-marketing measurement is limited to a transactional e-tail presence. Adams et al. (2000) note that a 'one-size-fits-all' framework is not desirable.

E. Enable comparison of performance of different e-channels with other channels as suggested by Friedman and Furey (1999).

F. The framework can be used to assess e-marketing performance against competitors' or out-of-sector best practice.

When identifying metrics it is common practice to apply the widely used SMART mnemonic (see, for example, Obolensky, 1994). SMART metrics must be:

- Specific;
- Measurable;
- Actionable;
- Relevant;
- Timely.

Using SMART metrics avoids the following types of problem:

(a) developing metrics for which accurate or complete data cannot be collected;
(b) developing metrics that measure the right thing, but cause people to act in a way contrary to the best interests of the business to simply 'make their numbers';
(c) developing so many metrics that excessive overhead and red tape are created. Friedman and Furey (1999) contend that minimising the number of metrics to the key factors is important;
(d) developing metrics that are complex and difficult to explain to others.

An Internet marketing measurement framework

Berthon et al. (1998) proposed a conceptual measurement framework based on the industrial marketing concepts of purchasing decision processes and hierarchy of effects models. An enhanced version of this framework, which can be used to assess conversion to different goals was presented as Figure 1.15. While Figure 1.15 can be used to assess the success of Internet marketing tactics, it does not achieve all the criteria of a measurement framework presented as criteria A to E above. Chaffey (2000) presents a more comprehensive measurement framework, shown in Figure 9.4. This framework was also developed to use readily collectable metrics to enable comparison across channels whether online (web, mobile or digital TV) or offline, such as mail order, sales team or call centre. These metrics can also be used for benchmarking against competitors. Specific examples of metrics in each category are provided later in the chapter.

Metrics for the categories are generated as objectives from Internet marketing planning which then need to be monitored to assess the success of strategy and its implementation. Objectives can be devised in a top-down fashion, starting with strategic objectives for business contribution and marketing outcomes leading to tactical objectives for customer satisfaction, behaviour and site promotion. An alternative perspective is bottom-up – success in achieving objectives for site promotion, on-site customer behaviour and customer satisfaction lead sequentially to achieving objectives for marketing outcomes and business contribution.

A broader framework for e-business performance measurement has been suggested by Adams et al. (2000). A survey was conducted of how companies monitored e-business performance by using the Performance Prism, an integrative framework which is an alternative to the balanced scorecard. The five areas of the performance measurement of the performance prism are: (1) stakeholder satisfaction (customer, employee and investor satisfaction); (2) stakeholder contribution (customer, employee and investor contribution); (3) strategies adopted (objective setting); (4) processes

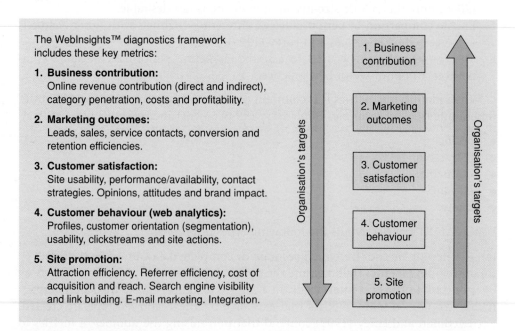

Figure 9.4 The five diagnostic categories for e-marketing measurement from the framework presented by Chaffey (2000)

(efficiency and effectiveness, which includes the measures shown in Figure 9.4); and (5) capabilities (technology and people skills). Another section of the survey dealt with measuring specific aspects of Web-related performance. This included maintenance costs, clickstream patterns, trends and forecasting, level of web site visits not consummated, web site downtime, level of web site security.

● Stage 3: Introducing techniques to collect metrics and summarise results

Techniques to collect metrics include the collection of site-visitor activity data such as that collected from site log-files, the collection of metrics about outcomes such as online sales or e-mail enquiries and traditional marketing research techniques such as questionnaires and focus groups which collect information on the customer's experience on the web site. We start by describing methods for collecting site visitor activity and then review more traditional techniques of market research which assess the customer experience.

Collecting site-visitor activity data

Site-visitor activity data records the number of visitors on the site and the paths or clickstreams they take through the site as they visit different content. There are a wide variety of technical terms to describe this activity data which Internet marketers need to be conversant with.

Traditionally this information has been collected using log file analysis. The server-based log file is added to every time a user downloads a piece of information (a hit) and is analysed using a log file analyser as illustrated by Figure 1.9. Examples of transactions within a log file are:

www.marketing-insights.co.uk - [05/Oct/2001:00:00:49 -000] "GET /index.html HTTP/1.0" 200 33362
www.marketing-insights.co.uk - [05/Oct/2001:00:00:49 -000] "GET /logo.gif HTTP/1.0" 200 54342

Hits are not useful measures of web site effectiveness since if a page consists of 10 graphics, plus text, this is recorded as 11 hits. Page impressions and site visits are better measures of site activity.

An example of the output reporting following analysis of the log file is illustrated by Figure 9.5.

Other information giving detailed knowledge of customer behaviour that can be reported by log file analysis packages, of which WebTrends (www.webtrends.com) is the market leader by volume, includes:

● page impressions;
● entry and exit pages;
● path or click-stream analysis;
● user (visitor) sessions;
● unique users (visitors), the number of unique visitors to a web site within a set period;
● visitor frequency report (repeat visitors);
● session duration or the length of time a visitor spends on a site (a session ends after inactivity for a time set in the analyser preferences, e.g. 30 minutes) and page duration;
● country of origin;
● browser and operating system used;
● referring URL and domain (where the visitor came from).

Site-visitor activity data

Information on content and services accessed by e-commerce site visitors.

Hit

Recorded for each graphic or text file requested from a web server. It is not a reliable measure for the number of people viewing a page.

Log file analyser

A separate program such as WebTrends that is used to summarise the information on customer activity in a log file.

Page impression

A more reliable measure than a hit, denoting one person viewing one page.

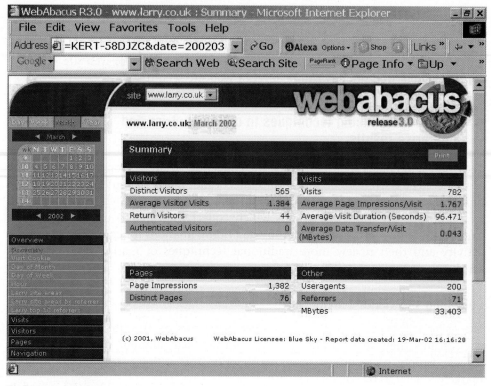

Figure 9.5 Webabacus (www.webabacus.com)

Complete Activity 9.2 to understand how some of these terms are related.

Activity 9.2

Measurement terms

(Web)

Refer to the data below, which define the level of usage of a site.

Measure	Value
Number of hits for home page	8 398
Number of successful hits for entire site	57 868
Number of page views (impressions)	24 437
Number of user sessions	2 598
User sessions from United States	52.61%
International user sessions	20.51%
User sessions of unknown origin	26.86%
Average number of hits per day	4 822
Average number of page views per day	2 036
Average number of user sessions per day	216
Average user session length	00:14:17
Number of unique users	2 096
Number of users who visited once	1 824
Number of users who visited more than once	272

Source: Based on WebTrends summary statistics (www.webtrends.com)

Activity

1 For the following measures explain the difference between the terms and how the numbers differ. For example, why is the number of hits greater than the number of site visits?
   - Hits
   - Page impressions/views *
   - Site visits/user sessions *
   - Unique users *
   - E-mails
   - Registrations
   - Online sales

2 Visit the site of a supplier of a web site analysis tool and summarise the different facilities available. Which do you think would be valuable to a marketer and which could be disregarded?

Managers of e-commerce systems know that log file analysis has a number of potential weaknesses. Perhaps the worst problem is the problems of undercounting and overcounting. These are reviewed in Table 9.2.

A relatively new approach to the problems of undercounting and overcounting of server-based log file analysis described in Table 9.3 is to use a different *browser-based* measurement system that records access to web pages every time a page is loaded into a user's web browser through running a short script or program inserted into the web page. The key benefit of the browser-based approach is that potentially it is more accurate than server-based approaches. Figure 9.6 shows how the browser-based approach works. One of the pioneers of this technique is Australian company RedSheriff (www.redsheriff.com). Their RedMeasure approach counts pages every time they're *viewed* by customers. It does this because a small piece of JavaScript code is inserted into each web page and this is automatically run every time the page is loaded into the browser by the user. RedSheriff refer to this as *instrumentation*. This JavaScript sends details about the page views to a remote server.

Table 9.2 Inaccuracies caused by server-based log-file analysis

Sources of undercounting	Sources of overcounting
Caching in user's web browsers (when a user accesses a previously accessed file, it is loaded from the user's cache on their PC)	Frames (a user viewing a framed page with three frames will be recorded as three page impressions on a server-based system)
Caching on proxy servers (proxy servers are used within organisations or ISPs to reduce Internet traffic by storing copies of frequently used pages)	Spiders and robots (traversing of a site by spiders from different search engines is recorded as page impressions. These spiders can be excluded, but this is time-consuming)
Firewalls (these do not usually exclude page impressions, but they usually assign a single IP address for the user of the page, rather than referring to an individual's PC)	Executable files (these can also be recorded as hits or page impressions unless excluded)
Dynamically generated pages, generated 'on the fly', are difficult to assess with server-based log files	

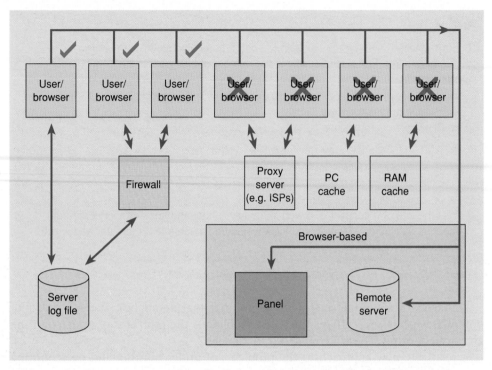

Figure 9.6 Differences between browser-based and server-based measurement systems

Collecting site outcome data

Site outcome data is about when a customer performs a significant action. This is usually a transaction that is recorded. It involves more than downloading a web page, and is proactive. Key marketing outcomes include:

- registration to site or subscriptions to an e-mail newsletter;
- requests for further information such as a brochure or a request for a callback from a customer service representative;
- responding to a promotion such as an online competition;
- a sale influenced by a visit to the site;
- a sale on-site.

An important aspect of measures collected offline is that the marketing outcomes may be recorded in different media according to how the customer has performed mixed-mode buying. For example, a new customer enquiry could arrive by e-mail, fax or phone. Similarly, an order could be placed online using a credit card, or by phone, fax or post. For both these cases what we are really interested in is whether the web site influenced the enquiry or sale. This is a difficult question to answer unless steps are put in place to answer it. For all contact points with customers staff need to be instructed to ask how they found out about the company, or made their decision to buy. Although this is valuable information it is often intrusive, and a customer placing an order may be annoyed to be asked such a question. To avoid alienating the customer, these questions about the role of the web site can be asked later, perhaps when the customer is filling in a registration or warranty card. Another device that can be used to identify use of the web site is to use a specific phone number on the web site, so when a customer rings to place an order, it is known that the number was obtained from the web site. This approach is used by Dell on its site.

It will be apparent that to collect some of these measures we may need to integrate different information systems. Where customers provide details such as an e-mail address and name in response to an offer, these are known as 'leads' and they may need to be passed on to a direct-sales team or recorded in a customer relationship management system. For full visibility of customer behaviour, the outcomes from these systems need to be integrated with the site-visitor activity data. Analysis tools such as Accrue (www.accrue.com) and NetGenesis (www.netgen.com) assist in integrating information from these different sources. The field of measurement is now sometimes referred to as **web analytics**. Refer to Case Study 9.1 for a summary of the issues this presents to managers.

Web analytics

Reporting and analysis of data on web site visitor activity.

CASE STUDY 9.1

Web analytics

Web analytics software used to be the province of company IT departments, where it was deployed to help predict the load on internet servers. But the market has been changing, and its importance is now much broader.

'Businesses with a web presence have to handle more information than ever before', says Geoff McClure, managing director of Tahola, which specialises in extracting information from a company's data.

Companies also need to know how their internet-based marketing campaigns are working. 'Marketing people are increasingly driving the need for web analytics', says John Shumway, global vice president of product management at Akamai, the US internet content delivery and services company.

One way that information can be collected is through log files. These are created by recording the information that is sent in the so-called 'http headers' every time a browser requests a web page. These data include the internet address of the computer the browser is on and the referring page.

Being lists of text, these web logs are virtually impossible to understand. So companies such as WebTrends and Sane Solutions produce software that converts the data into formats that managers can understand, using combinations of tables and graphs.

Sane Solutions says that by using its NetTracker software, it is possible to test the effectiveness of ad campaigns, see how visitors come to a site by checking the referrer pages, and track visitors' progress as they click through the site.

The software also allows reports to be compiled from logs where the website is 'distributed' or exists on several servers.

However, collecting data on how visitors use sites does not have to depend on log files. After all, many web masters may not have access to log files, especially when their site is hosted 'virtually' on a server that is home to thousands of others.

For sites such as this, there are companies such as Web Tracking Services LLC, which runs two separate but similar services, Web-Stat and 123Count. The latter is slightly more expensive and is somewhat faster.

Olivier Galy, founder of Web-Stat, says its market is the small- to medium-sized site owner who does not want to be drowned in complex reports. One of Web-Stat's main features is 'referrer tracking' or recording the site which referred the browser to their current site. The aim is to produce easy-to-understand reports at very competitive rates, says Mr Galy.

▶

As with Web-Stat, Akamai has a service that does not depend on access to web logs, but provides a managed service in web reporting, following an ASP model. The service is particularly apt for sites which run off multiple servers or have a presence in multiple locations, says Mr Shumway. Busy sites often do this so that users are serviced by a server close to their location.

Rather than read the web logs that servers produce, Akamai's clients embed a small amount of code into their web pages in a language called JavaScript. This communicates data about the user back to Akamai where real-time reports can be compiled.

One technique for getting information about visitors to sites is to use 'cookies', the computer code that identifies a user. It is sent back to the website as part of the http header whenever a browser requests a page. This system allows 'session tracking', that is, identifying precisely the user as he or she moves through the website. Another advantage of cookies is that a user can be identified the next time they visit a website.

Alison Bryant, marketing director of iLux, which makes personalised marketing software and uses cookies in its product, says customers who come to a site leave an electronic footprint. This can be correlated with what they visited and therefore it is possible to market to them whether they registered with the site or not.

'The log file will tell where the customer came from, which pages were visited and where they left', says Ms Bryant. For example, one place where customers may leave is just before they have to enter their credit card details.

Cookies have received some negative publicity because some net users have been worried about privacy implications. For this reason, around 1.9 per cent of users turn them off, says Ms Bryant. However, for most, the dangers of privacy invasion seem to be outweighed by the convenience.

Guy Creese, an analyst at Aberdeen Group, the technology market consultants, says web analytics is also providing a basis for developing sophisticated applications which bring together not only data from companies' websites but also their other distribution and retail channels. This has been especially true in the area of customer relationship management (CRM). Dixit Shah, head of eCRM business development for Hyperion UK, says the company's software can quantify the value of the customer relationship and each click.

This, however, goes beyond analysis of web logs and involves understanding what the business of the customer is. 'Web log data can be combined from advertisement servers, personalisation engines, profiling engines, e-commerce servers and ERP (enterprise resource planning)', says Mr Shah.

Source: Paul Talacko, Survey – FT-IT: Useful aid for internet marketing campaigns: web analytics software, *Financial Times*, 4 April 2001

Question

Summarise the relevance of web analytics to an organisation and make recommendations on the alternative methods outlined in the case study.

Collecting market research data

We can divide market research for e-commerce into primary research where we collect our own data and secondary data where we use published research. Market research data are intended to reveal profiles of customers and their opinion of the e-commerce experience. There are several different methods of collecting primary data. These are compared in Table 9.3. Internet panel data are collected in a similar way to home-based TV panels. Panel members agree to have installed on their PC software that sends data that are collected by the monitoring organisation. This approach is similar to the browser-based activity measurement shown in Figure 9.7. Critics note that there may be a problem with panel accuracy since the type of

Table 9.3 A comparison of different online metrics collection methods

Technique	Strengths	Weaknesses
1. **Server-based log-file analysis of site activity**	• Directly records customer behaviour on site plus where they were referred from • Low cost	• Not based around marketing outcomes such as leads, sales • Size, even summaries may be over 50 pages long • Doesn't directly record channel satisfaction • Undercounting and overcounting • Misleading unless interpreted carefully
2. **Browser-based site activity data**	• Greater accuracy than server-based analysis • Counts all users, cf. panel approach	• Relatively expensive method • Similar weaknesses to server-based technique apart from accuracy • Limited demographic information
3. **Panel activity and demographic data**	• Provides competitor comparisons • Gives demographic profiling • Avoid undercounting and overcounting	• Depends on extrapolation from limited sample that may not be representative
4. **Outcome data**, e.g. enquiries, customer service e-mails	• Records marketing outcomes	• Difficulty of integrating data with other methods of data collection when collected manually or in other information systems
5. **Online questionnaires.** Customers are prompted randomly – every *n*th customer or after customer activity or by e-mail	• Can record customer satisfaction and profiles • Relatively cheap to create and analyse	• Difficulty of recruiting respondents who complete accurately • Sample bias – tend to be advocates or disgruntled customers who complete
6. **Online focus groups.** Synchronous recording	• Relatively cheap to create	• Difficult to moderate and coordinate • No visual cues, as from offline focus groups
7. **Mystery shoppers.** Example is customers are recruited to evaluate the site, e.g. www.emysteryshopper.com	• Structured tests give detailed feedback • Also tests integration with other channels such as e-mail and phone	• Relatively expensive • Sample must be representative

person who agrees to have the software installed may not be representative of the wider population. Web site auditing is performed by independent auditing bodies which have traditionally audited print media. Analysis is based on analysis of server-based log-files. An example of an audit is that conducted by ABC Electronic's auditors (www.abc.org) who audited the site of the Periodical Publishers Association during an audit period 1–31 October 1999 and found that site activity reached 33 000 page impressions with 4425 users and 8504 user sessions. This suggests that on average the users make around two visits per month.

Despite the range of available methods evident from Table 9.3, care still needs to be exercised when interpreting activity data to base revenue estimates for forecasting. For example, three different approaches yielded widely differing estimates for activity on the Britannica.com web site for July 2000:

Net Ratings panel data	4 million visitors
MediaMetrix panel data	2.8 million
Server-based log-file data	2.9 million

Types of data collected

E-commerce site managers collect the following data which are part of the framework shown in Figure 9.4. The five categories of measures shown in Figure 9.4 have differing significance to a manager according to the level of managerial decision making. But, we can identify three additional levels of metrics.

1 *Level 1: Business effectiveness measures*. This type of measure assesses how the Internet is affecting the performance of the whole business: in other words, what is the impact of the Internet on the business. Such measures include channel profitability measures.

2 *Level 2: Marketing effectiveness measures*. Marketing effectiveness measures will reflect how well the e-commerce site is fulfilling marketing objectives. These are mainly the channel satisfaction and channel outcome measures.

3 *Level 3: Internet marketing effectiveness*. The Internet marketing effectiveness measures involve assessing how well the particular online Internet marketing techniques required for effective Internet marketing are working. These include channel promotion, channel behaviour and satisfaction from Figure 9.4.

The five categories of e-commerce metrics are as follows.

Channel promotion

Measures that assess why customers visit a site – which adverts they have seen, which sites they have been referred from.

1 Channel promotion

These measures consider where the web site users originate – online or offline, and what are the sites or offline media that have prompted their visit. Log file analysis can be used to assess which intermediary sites customers are referred from and even which keywords they typed into search engines when trying to locate product information. Promotion is successful if traffic is generated that meets objectives of volume and quality. Quality will be determined by whether visitors are in the target market and have a propensity for the service offered. Overall hits or page views are not enough – inspection of log files for companies shows that a high proportion of visitors get no further than the home page! Differences in costs of acquiring customers via different channels can also be assessed.

Referrer

The site that a visitor previously visited before following a link.

Key measure:

Referral mix. For each referral source such as offline or banner ads online it should be possible to calculate:

- % of all referrals (or visitors);
- cost of acquisition;
- contribution to sales or other outcomes.

Channel buyer behaviour

Describes which content is visited, time and duration.

2 Channel buyer behaviour

Once customers have been attracted to the site we can monitor content accessed, when they visit and how long they stay, and whether this interaction with content leads to satisfactory marketing outcomes such as new leads or sales. If visitors are incentivised to register on-site it is possible to build up profiles of behaviour for different segments. It is also important to recognise return visitors for whom cookies or login are used.

Key ratios are:

Stickiness

An indication of how long a visitor stays on site.

Home page interest	Home Page Views/All page views e.g.	20%	= (2358/11 612)
Stickiness	Page views/visitor sessions e.g.	6	= 11 612/2048
Repeats	Visitor sessions/visitors e.g.	2	= 2048/970

3 Channel satisfaction

Customer satisfaction with the online experience is vital in achieving the desired channel outcomes, although it is difficult to set specific objectives. Online methods such as online questionnaires, focus groups and interviews can be used to assess customers' opinions of the web site content and customer service and how it has affected overall perception of brand.

Key measure:

Customer satisfaction indices. These are discussed in Chapter 7 and include ease of use, site availability and performance, and e-mail response. To compare customer satisfaction with other sites, benchmarking services such as that of Gomez (www.gomez.com) can be used.

Bevan (1999) says that from a usability viewpoint, there are three key measures in determining usability for each task:

1 The percentage of participants who completely and correctly achieved each task goal.
2 If it is necessary to provide participants with assistance, efficiency and effectiveness metrics must be determined for both unassisted and assisted conditions.
3 The mean time taken to complete each task, together with the range and standard deviation of times across participants.

Marketing research

Marketing research will help determine the influence of the web site and related communications on customer perception of the company and its products and services. The options for conducting survey research include interviews, questionnaires and focus groups. Each of these techniques can be conducted offline or online. Offline methods are especially appropriate for companies with a smaller number of customers, who can be easily accessed, for example by sales staff. When surveys such as interviews are conducted they may not solely concern the impact of the web site, but questions about this could be part of a wider survey on customer perception of the company or its product.

This type of measurement will use the traditional techniques of survey-based marketing research, which seeks to collect primary data for gathering descriptive information about people's attitudes, preferences or buying behaviour.

The techniques that are appropriate for conducting this type of research will need to target a sample of people who actively use the web site. The best place to find these customers is on the web site! As a result, online focus groups and questionnaires administered online are becoming more common. The use of Internet-based market research is relatively new, so there is little research on what works, and what does not. However, some general comments can be made for the different survey types.

Questionnaires

Malhotra (1999) suggests that Internet surveys using questionnaires will increase in popularity since the cost is generally lower, they can be less intrusive and the ability to target specific populations. Questionnaires often take the form of pop surveys. The key issues are:

A. *Encouraging participation*. Techniques that can be used are:
  - interruption on entry – a common approach where every 100th customer is prompted;

Channel satisfaction
Evaluation of the customer's opinion of the service quality on the site and supporting services such as e-mail.

Internet-based market research
The use of online questionnaires and focus groups to assess customer perceptions of a web site or broader marketing issues.

- continuous, for example click on the button to complete survey;
- on registration on site the customer can be profiled;
- after an activity such as sale or customer support the customer can be prompted for their opinion about the service;
- incentives and promotions (this can also be executed on independent sites);
- by e-mail (an e-mail prompt to visit a web site to fill in a survey or a simple e-mail survey).

B. *Stages in execution.* It can be suggested that there are five stages to a successful questionnaire survey:
   1 attract (button, pop-up, e-mail as above);
   2 incentivise (prize or offer consistent with required sample and audience);
   3 reassure (why the company is doing it – to learn, not too long and that confidentiality is protected);
   4 design and execute (brevity, relevance, position);
   5 follow-up (feedback).

C. *Design.* Grossnickle and Raskin (2001) suggest the following approach to structuring questionnaires:
   - easy, interesting questions first;
   - cluster questions on same topic;
   - flow topic from general to specific;
   - flow topic from easier behavioural to more difficult attitudinal questions;
   - easy questions last, e.g. demographics or offputting questions.

Focus groups

Malhotra (1999) notes that the advantage of online focus groups is that they can be used to reach segments that are difficult to access, such as doctors, lawyers and professional people. These authors also suggest that costs are lower, they can be arranged more rapidly and can bridge the distance gap when recruiting respondents. Traditional focus groups can be conducted, where customers are brought together in a room and assess a web site; this will typically occur pre-launch as part of the prototyping activity. Testing can take the form of random use of the site, or more usefully the users will be given different scenarios to follow. It is important that focus groups use a range of familiarities (Chapter 8). Focus groups tend to be relatively expensive and time-consuming, since rather than simply viewing an advertisement, the customers need to actually interact with the web site. This may be unrealistic if they are rushed. Mike Bloxham of Netpoll (www.netpoll.net), an organisation specialising in measuring online marketing effectiveness for companies such as Microsoft and Sky.com, believes that conducting real-world focus groups has the benefit that the reactions of site users can be monitored; the scratch of the head and the fist hitting the desk cannot be monitored in the virtual world!

Mystery shoppers

Real-world measurement is also important since the Internet channel does not exist in isolation. It must work in unison with real-world customer service and fulfilment. Chris Russell of eMysteryShopper (www.emysteryshopper.com), a company that has completed online customer service surveys for major UK retailers and travel companies, says 'we also needed to make sure the bricks-and-mortar customer service support was actually supporting what the clicks-and-mortar side was promising. There is no doubt that an e-commerce site has to be a complete customer service fulfilment picture, it can't just be one bit working online that is not supported offline'. An eMysteryShopper survey involves shoppers commenting on site usability, but also on the service quality of e-mail and phone responses together with product fulfilment. Mystery shoppers test these areas:

- site usability;
- e-commerce fulfilment;
- e-mail and phone response (time, accuracy);
- impact on brand.

4 Channel outcomes

Traditional marketing objectives such as number of sales, number of leads, **conversion rates** and targets for customer acquisition and retention should be set and then compared to other channels. Dell Computer (www.dell.com) records on-site sales and also orders generated as a result of site visits, but placed by phone. This is achieved by monitoring calls to a specific phone number unique to the site.

Key measure:
Channel contribution (direct and indirect).

A widely used method of assessing channel outcomes is to review the conversion rate, which gives an indication of the percentage of site visitors who take a particular outcome. For example:

Conversion rate, visitors to purchase = 2% (10 000 visitors, of which 200 make purchases).
Conversion rate, visitors to registration = 5% (10 000 visitors, of which 500 register).

A related concept is the **attrition rate** which describes how many visitors are lost at each stage of visiting a site. Figure 9.7 shows that for a set time period, only a proportion of site visitors will make their way to product information, a small proportion will add an item to a basket and a smaller proportion still will actually make the purchase. A key feature of e-commerce sites is that there is a high attrition rate between a customer's adding an item to a basket and subsequently making a purchase. It is surmised that this is due to fears about credit card security, and that customers are merely experimenting.

5 Channel profitability

A contribution to business profitability is always the ultimate aim of e-commerce. To assess this, leading companies set an Internet contribution target of achieving a certain proportion of sales via the channel. When easyJet (www.easyjet.com) launched

Channel outcomes
Record customer actions taken as a consequence of a site visit.

Conversion rate
Percentage of site visitors who perform a particular action such as making a purchase.

Attrition rate
Percentage of site visitors who are lost at each stage in making a purchase.

Channel profitability
The profitability of the web site, taking into account revenue and cost and discounted cash flow.

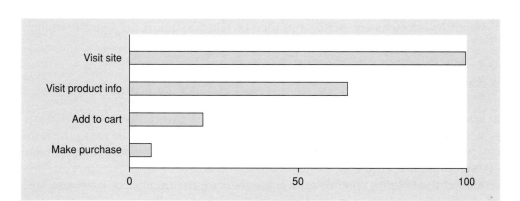

Figure 9.7 Attrition through e-commerce site activities

Table 9.4 Some offline measures of Internet marketing effectiveness

Measure	Measured through
Enquiries or leads (subdivided into new customers and existing customers)	• Number of online e-mails • Phone calls mentioning web site • Faxed enquiries mentioning web site
Sales	• Online sales or sales in which customers state they found out about the product on the web site. Sales received on a phone number only publicised on a web site
Conversion rate	• Can be calculated separately for customers who are registered online and those who are not
Retention rates	• Is the 'churn' of customers using the web site lower?
Customer satisfaction	• Focus groups, questionnaires and interviews • Mystery shoppers
Brand enhancement	• Focus groups, surveys

its e-commerce facility in 1998, it set an Internet contribution target of 30% by 2000. They put the resources and communications plan in place to achieve this and their target was reached in 1999. Assessing contribution is more difficult for a company that cannot sell products online, but the role of the Internet in influencing purchase should be assessed. Discounted cash flow techniques are used to assess the rate of return over time.

To conclude the chapter, Table 9.4 summarises key offline measures of Internet marketing effectiveness.

Summary

1 Maintaining a web site requires clear responsibilities to be identified for different roles. These include the roles of content owners and site developers, and those ensuring that the content conforms with company and legal requirements.

2 To produce a good-quality web site, standards are required to enforce uniformity in terms of:
   • site look and feel;
   • corporate branding;
   • quality of copy.

3 A structured measurement programme is necessary to collect measures to assess a web site's effectiveness. Action can then be taken to adjust the web site strategy or promotional efforts. A measurement programme involves:
   • *Stage 1: Defining a measurement process.*
   • *Stage 2: Defining a metrics framework.*
   • *Stage 3: Selecting of tools for data collection, reporting and analysis.*

4 Measures of Internet marketing effectiveness can be categorised as assessing:
   • *Level 1: Business effectiveness* – these measure the impact of the web site on the whole business, and look at financial measures such as revenue and profit and promotion of corporate awareness.
   • *Level 2: Marketing effectiveness* – these measure the number of leads and sales achieved via the Internet and effect of the Internet on retention rates and other aspects of the marketing mix such as branding.

- *Level 3: Internet marketing effectiveness* – these measures assess how well the site is being promoted, and do so by reviewing the popularity of the site and how good it is at delivering customer needs.

5 The measures of effectiveness referred to above are collected in two main ways – online or offline – or in combination.

6 Online measures are obtained from a web-server log file or using browser-based techniques. They indicate the number of visitors to a site, which pages they visit, and where they originated from. These also provide a breakdown of visitors through time or by country.

7 Offline measures are marketing outcomes such as enquiries or sales that are directly attributable to the web site. Other measures of the effectiveness are available through surveying customers using questionnaires, interviews and focus groups.

EXERCISES

Self-assessment exercises

1 Why are standards necessary for controlling web site maintenance? What aspects of the site do standards seek to control?

2 Explain the difference between hits and page impressions. How are these measured?

3 Define and explain the purpose of test and live versions of a web site.

4 Why should content development be distributed through a large organisation?

5 What is the difference between online and offline metrics?

6 How can focus groups and interviews be used to assess web site effectiveness?

7 Explain how a web log file analyser works. What are its limitations?

8 Why is it useful to integrate the collection of online and offline metrics?

Essay and discussion questions

1 'Corporate standards for a web site's format and update process are likely to stifle the creative development of a site and reduce its value to customers.' Discuss.

2 'There is little value in the collection of online metrics recorded in a web server log file. For measurement programmes to be of value, measures based on marketing outcomes are more valuable.' Discuss.

3 You have been appointed as manager of a web site for a car manufacturer and have been asked to refine the existing metrics programme. Explain, in detail, the steps you would take to develop this programme.

4 The first version of a web site for a financial services company has been live for a year. Originally it was developed by a team of two people, and was effectively 'brochureware'. The second version of the site is intended to contain more detailed information, and will involve contributions from 10 different product areas. You have been asked to define a procedure for controlling updates to the site. Write a document detailing the update procedure, which also explains the reasons for each control.

Examination questions

1 Why are standards necessary to control the process of updating a web site? Give three examples of different aspects of a web site that need to be controlled.

2 Explain the following terms concerning measurement of web site effectiveness:
(a) hits;
(b) page impressions;
(c) referring pages.

3 Measurement of web sites concerns the recording of key events involving customers using a web site. Briefly explain five different types of event.

4 Describe and briefly explain the purpose of the different stages involved in updating an existing document on a commercial web site.

5 Distinguish between a test environment and a live environment for a web site. What is the reason for having two environments?

6 Give three reasons explaining why a web site may have to integrate with existing marketing information systems and databases within a company.

7 You have been appointed as manager of a web site and have been asked to develop a metrics programme. Briefly explain the steps you would take to develop this programme.

8 If a customer can be persuaded to register his or her name and e-mail address with a web site, how can this information be used for site measurement purposes?

References

Adams, C., Kapashi, N., Neely, A. and Marr, B. (2000) Managing with measures. Measuring ebusiness performance. *Accenture white paper*. Survey conducted in conjunction with Cranfield School of Management.

Agrawal, V., Arjona, V. and Lemmens, R. (2001) E-performance: the path to rational exuberance, *McKinsey Quarterly*, No. 1, 31–43.

Berthon, P., Lane, N., Pitt, L. and Watson, R. (1998) The World Wide Web as an industrial marketing communications tool: models for the identification and assessment of opportunities, *Journal of Marketing Management*, 14, 691–704.

Bevan, N. (1999) Common industry format usability tests. *Proceedings of UPA'98, Usability Professionals Association, Scottsdale, Arizona, 29 June – 2 July, 1999*. Available online at www.usability.serco.com.

Bourne, M., Mills, J., Willcox, M., Neely, A. and Platts, K. (2000) Designing, implementing and updating performance measurement systems, *International Journal of Operations and Production Management*, 20(7), 754–71.

Chaffey, D. (2000) Achieving Internet marketing success, *The Marketing Review*, 1(1), 35–60.

Cutler, M. and Sterne, J. (2000) E-metrics. Business metrics for the new economy. *Netgenesis white paper*.

Friedman, L. and Furey, T. (1999) *The Channel Advantage*. Butterworth Heinemann, Oxford.

Grossnickle, J. and Raskin, O. (2001) *The Handbook of Online Marketing Research: Knowing your Customer using the Net*. McGraw-Hill, New York.

Kotler, P. (1997) *Marketing Management – Analysis, Planning, Implementation and Control*. Prentice Hall, Englewood Cliffs, NJ.

Lynch, P. and Horton, S. (1999) *Web Style Guide. Basic Design Principles for Creating Web Sites*. Yale University Press, New Haven, CT.

Malhotra, N. (1999) *Marketing Research: An Applied Orientation*. Prentice Hall, Upper Saddle River, NJ.

Obolensky, N. (1994) *Practical Business Re-engineering. Tools and Techniques for Achieving Effective Change*. Kogan Page, London.

Parsons, A., Zeisser, M. and Waitman, R. (1996) Organising for digital marketing, *McKinsey Quarterly*, No. 4, 183–92.

Sterne, J. (1999) *World Wide Web Marketing*, 2nd edn. Wiley, New York.

Wisner, J. and Fawcett, S. (1991) Link firm strategy to operating decisions through performance measurement, *Production and Inventory Management Journal*, Third Quarter, 5–11.

Further reading

Berthon, P., Pitt, L. and Watson, R. (1998) The World Wide Web as an industrial marketing communication tool: models for the identification and assessment of opportunities, *Journal of Marketing Management*, 14, 691–704. This is a key paper assessing how to measure how the Internet supports purchasers through the different stages of the buying decision.

Brassington, F. and Petitt, S. (2000) *Principles of Marketing*, 2nd edn. Financial Times/Prentice Hall, Harlow. *See* companion Prentice Hall web site (www.booksites.net/brassington2). Chapter 6, Marketing information and research, describes the marketing research process and techniques for collection of primary and secondary data.

Burnett, J. and Moriarty, S. (1999) *Introduction to Marketing Communications. An Integrated Approach*. Prentice Hall, Upper Saddle River, NJ. *See* companion Prentice Hall web site (cw.prenhall.com/bookbind/pubbooks/burnett). *See* Chapter 18, Measuring IMC performance.

Dibb, S., Simkin, S., Pride, W. and Ferrel, O. (1997) *Marketing. Concepts and Strategies*, 3rd European edn. Houghton Mifflin, Boston. *See* Chapter 24, Implementing strategies and measuring performance.

Friedman, L. and Furey, T. (1999) *The Channel Advantage*. Butterworth Heinemann, Oxford. Chapter 12 is on managing channel performance.

Sterne, J. (1999) *World Wide Web Marketing*, 2nd edn. Wiley, New York. Chapter 11 is entitled 'Measuring your success'. It mainly reviews the strengths and weaknesses of online methods.

Web links

- ABC Home Page (www.abce.org.uk). Audited Bureau of Circulation is standard for magazines in the UK. This is the electronic auditing part. Useful for definitions and examples of traffic for UK organisations.

- Analog (www.analog.cx). Basic, but popular freeware.

- Hitbox (www.hitbox.com). Browser-based metrics.

- Hitwise (www.hitwise.co.uk). Novel method of monitoring site visitor volume compared to competitors using ISP data.

- IBM (www.ibm.com/software/data/pubs/papers). IBM articles on databases and data management.

- Intranet Journal (www.intranetjournal.com). Articles on content management.

- I/PRO (www.ipro.com). Provides services to audit web site effectiveness through studies of the site traffic. Sample reports held on this site indicate the types of approach used.

- Marketing Insights (www.marketing-insights). Contains resources to assist in assessing online marketing performance.

- MediaMetrix (www.mediametrix.com). Now merged with RelevanKnowledge (www.relevantknowledge.com), claims to be the world leader in 'media measurement'.

- net.Genesis (www.netgen.com). Analysis tool supplier, now part of SPSS, has useful papers on approaches to measurement.

- Vignette (www.vignette.com). CM vendor with articles on best practice.

- Webabacus (www.webabacus.com). Analysis of log files with flexible reporting.

- WebTrends Web analysis (www.webtrends.com). Most popular analysis software by numbers shipped. Includes server-based and browser-based versions (WebTrends Live).

Business-to-consumer Internet marketing

Links to other chapters

This chapter builds on concepts and frameworks introduced earlier in the book. The main related chapters are:

Learning objectives

After reading this chapter, the reader should be able to:

● Understand the potential of online business-to-consumer markets

● Identify the key uses of the Internet within a business-to-consumer context

● Identify Internet retail formats and understand the implications of business models applied to the Internet by retail organisations

● Consider the strategic implication of operating online

● Give examples of best practice in Internet retailing

Questions for marketers

Key questions for marketing managers related to this chapter are:

● Which factors affect demand for online B2C services?

● What services can be provided online?

● How can an Internet retail strategy be developed?

Introduction

The Internet provides access to a new trading environment – a marketspace, which thrives on the exchange of digital data. During the last decade this marketspace has become widely accessible to consumers around the globe but in doing so has presented businesses with many difficult decisions about how they should proceed; whether to invest heavily in developing Internet-based operations or not.

In the early days (*c.* 1992), the commercial Internet was largely considered to be an arcane geekish environment used by computer experts and scientists. Even as levels of awareness grew, companies could be broadly divided into two groups:

1 *Non-adopters*: companies that perceived the Internet to be a potentially dangerous environment as it gave **crackers** a means of entry to a company's most valuable knowledge-based assets. For such companies the approach towards Internet adoption was to do nothing perhaps with the hope that the Internet like Citizen Band radio would fade into obscurity.
2 *Proactive adopters*: companies that saw the Internet as a tremendous opportunity to access new markets around the globe. For these companies the approach towards Internet adoption was more complex as the opportunity to trade was believed to be limitless. However, significant investments were required in newly developing Internet technologies, which had (as yet) unproven capabilities.

A **cracker** is a malicious meddler who tries to discover sensitive information by poking around computer networks. This term is sometimes confused with 'hacker'. According to *The New Hacker's Dictionary* (Raymond, 1996), a hacker (originally, someone who makes furniture with an axe) is a person who enjoys exploring the details of programmable systems and how to stretch their capabilities, as opposed to most users, who prefer to learn only the minimum necessary.

So what choice should a company currently make when considering whether or not to adopt the Internet? On the one hand, for the non-adopters, pressure to accept the Internet as a durable trading environment has increased significantly, whereas on the other hand, proactive adopters are having to deal with many difficulties associated with their early investment into the Internet: logistics, distribution and increased financial demands, which they may not have originally envisaged.

Furthermore, the reality is that few businesses operating in business-to-consumer markets have shown their online operations to be consistently profitable during the last decade, e.g. Peapod and Webvan (Kämäräinen et al., 2001). This fact perhaps provides evidence for the non-adopters to cry 'we told you so – online retailing is destined to remain at best limited to niche markets'. Indeed, some household names have ceased to trade online and now offer information-only websites. However, a five-year study examining the extent of Internet adoption in the UK by Ellis-Chadwick et al. (2002) has found that retailers are increasingly likely to have a web site and offer online trading facilities, a trend which is somewhat endorsed by the success of Tesco.com, which is now the world's largest online grocer.

This chapter examines how companies operating in business-to-consumer markets are currently adopting the Internet. The chapter begins by examining the context of business-to-consumer use of the Internet. It then discusses the various Internet-based retail formats that a company may choose from and the different functions that Internet applications might be used to perform for a company operating in business-to-consumer markets. This is followed by a review of online product and service availability. The chapter concludes with consideration of the implications of Internet adoption for retail strategy and a final summary.

Business-to-consumer context

This section examines the situation in which Internet retailing occurs, from a historical and geographical perspective. Each view aims to contribute towards an overview of the nature of Internet retailing.

● Internet retailing history

Using the Internet as a retail channel is far removed from its original purpose as a military communication tool which could operate without central authority in order to withstand nuclear attack. The Internet has rapidly evolved into a commercial trading environment during the last decade. The expansion has spawned new business formats and models, and products and services in order to tempt customers to embrace the new virtual environment. Indeed, the Internet has been described as a new '**retail channel**'.

> **Retail channel** is a term introduced by Doherty et al. (1999) to describe companies' multi-purpose adoption of the Internet, using it as both a communication and transactional channel concurrently in business-to-consumer markets. Traditionally the term *channel* describes the flow of a product from source to end-user. This definition implies a passive unidirectional system whereby the manufacturer or producer markets through a wholesaler or retailer to the consumer. Recent developments in information technology are changing this orientation by enabling retailers to focus their marketing efforts on managing customers more effectively (Mulhern, 1997). Therefore, the Internet brings the customer even closer to the retailers via a new combined marketing and distribution channel, in effect an interactive '*retail channel*'. This move may also suggest a shift towards a bidirectional retailer–consumer relationship, in which more power accrues to the customer (Hagel and Armstrong, 1997).

Commercial use of the Internet has been possible since 1989: electronic mail communications provided the first practical example (Kahin, 1995). By 1992, Tim Berners-Lee had perfected Hypertext Transfer Protocol and the World Wide Web. Marc Andersen's Web browser MOSAIC helped a new type of user navigate around this new digital environment. By now companies were beginning to realise that the Internet could be used for trade. This sparked off a decade of online activity, which has been likened to the gold rush era of the 1870s. Like their earlier counterparts who profited from selling picks and shovels, computer manufacturers, resellers, and network and Internet service providers were eager to highlight the opportunities afforded by the Internet. By early 1994, companies around the world were being bombarded with marketing communication messages extolling the virtues of the latest innovations in Internet technologies. The response was incredible. Internet adoption and Web-based activities grew exponentially year on year. In 1994, the US-based Flowers Direct was one of the first companies to offer consumers the opportunity to order flowers via the Internet.

In Europe, Blackwell's Bookshop and Victoria Wine were among the first retailers to give consumers the opportunity to buy online via the Internet. Both of these companies were also the original **core tenants** in Barclay's electronic mall, called 'BarclaySquare'. Electronic malls followed the format of fixed-location malls in the physical world, grouping together an assortment of retailers in one virtual destination on the Internet. However, unlike their real-world counterpart, online malls offered few advantages to potential customers who could view the product assortment of retailers located anywhere in the world from their workstations and laptops without the need to travel, and so the advantages for the consumer of retailers being grouped together in one destination were lost. Speciality malls appeared which brought together retailers with similar product ranges. This approach was soon abandoned, as individual retailers were not willing to participate in an online mall, which facilitated comparison shopping.

Core tenants: a shopping centre or mall is usually a centrally owned managed facility. In the physical world, the management will aim to include in the mall stores that sell a different but complementary range of merchandise and include a variety of smaller and larger stores. The core tenants or 'anchor stores', as they are often called, are the dominant large-scale store operators that are expected to draw customers to the centre (Dunne and Lusch, 1999).

From 1995 onwards, retailers continued to develop their own Web presence in the form of *destination* web sites in a similar way to the development of a fixed-location destination store in the real world. Nevertheless, European consumers struggled to locate their favourite retailers online. In an attempt to increase web site traffic, 1997 saw a notable increase in offline marketing communication activity aimed at promoting retail-company web sites. Companies began to add their URLs to television adverts and on real-world point-of-sales materials and packaging, e.g. the Co-op Group and Debenhams printed their company URLs on carrier bags.

Destination store

A retail store in which the merchandise, selection, presentation, pricing or other unique features act as a magnet for the customer (Levy and Weitz, 1995).

The following year saw more products and services becoming available from more online retailers. Despite such increases, very few organisations were reporting profits from their online operations. Even the launch of digital television, which was heralded as the channel to mass-market Internet sales did little to boost profitability. Interestingly, this is still largely the case at the time of writing, and some retailers are even turning away from offering shopping services via digital television altogether, e.g. both Woolworths and Argos have discontinued their iDTV services offered by Sky Digital.

From the end of 1999 and the first half of 2000, there was a period of frenzied activity by companies around the globe, driven by media hype and financial analysts' positive forecasts. Billions of dollars were invested into Internet start-ups. However, the dot-com boom was largely created by a lack of Internet stocks. As a result *demand* for such stocks was high but *supply* was low – venture capitalists began funding almost any seemingly innovative idea associated with the Internet and the Web. Many of these start-ups were operating in business-to-consumer markets without sound financial plans and many businesses collapsed due to lack of profits (see Case Study 10.1). In fact, in mid-2000, PricewaterhouseCoopers predicted that a quarter of the Internet stock quoted on the London Stock Exchange would run out of money within six months.

CASE STUDY 10.1

The online shopping boom (and bust)

By the end of 1999 specialist business consultants were producing compelling findings suggesting that Internet trade was set to expand significantly. Every aspect of Internet trade received wide coverage in both broadcast and print media:

> **Online shopping set to boom**
> 'UK spending on the Internet is set to boom over the next two years, according to a survey by professional services firm Ernst and Young. It says online shopping will treble by 2002, with retailers facing intense competition from US companies which already have an established online presence'.
>
> (*BBC Business News*, 2000a)

To join in with the spirit of this period of intense growth in Internet businesses, the UK's Channel 4 Television even ran a competition to find the best business idea, offering a prize of £1,000,000 as start-up capital. Henrietta Conrad, the show's co-executive producer, said: '*We're basically conducting a massive talent scout . . . We want to find a granny in Huddersfield who's got an idea but not the first clue how to go about it*' (Wells, 2000).

Perhaps the television competition really did succeed in identifying a winning idea where speculators and venture capitalists failed. At the time of writing one of the competition's winning ideas – www.yourable.com – continues to operate as a functioning web portal offering information, products and services for the disabled.

However, other high-profile dot-com start-ups were not so fortunate:

> **Top web retailer collapses**
> 'European online clothing retailer Boo.com has just collapsed through lack of funds, just six months after it was launched to a huge fanfare of publicity.'
>
> (*BBC Business News*, 2000b)

Boo.com had received funding of around £80 million to establish its business. Some of its shareholders were very well-respected established business leaders and financiers. The collapse was blamed on poor application of Internet technologies and operational problems particularly associated with delivery.

The failure of this high-profile start-up did not help to reassure technology-stock investors, who were becoming increasingly concerned about the inability of Internet companies to demonstrate when they might produce profitable returns. Neither did the collapse of Clickmango, which had also enjoyed generous financial backing from experienced business people.

> **Clickmango rescue effort fails**
> 'Clickmango, the natural health website fronted by actress Joanna Lumley, said yesterday that 11th-hour attempts to find a backer willing to keep the business going had failed.'
>
> (Teather, 2000)

Discussion points

- Suggest why a competition-winning idea with comparatively limited start-up capital and business knowledge has succeeded, where well-funded ideas supported by experienced business knowledge have failed.

- Do you think that if a similar competition were launched now (during a period of general economic slowdown) it would still produce successful and sustainable business ideas. Justify your position whether it be positive or negative.

Currently, Internet retailers are focusing on producing sustainable and profitable business strategies for their Internet-based operations. Established retailers using physical channels to market as well as the Internet are now demonstrating that they can compete and in many instances surpass dot-com start-ups (pureplays), which only use the Internet as a route to market. However, some of the more durable Internet-based companies like Amazon.com and Lastminute.com are on the brink of showing profitable returns. Indeed, it is quite possible that in ten to fifteen years' time the pureplays (discussed later in this chapter) will account for the majority of trade in business-to-consumer markets.

● Internet geography

This section aims to explore the size of the Internet and current geographic dispersion of Internet users in order to provide better understanding of the potential Internet markets.

Technological infrastructure

The Internet is a loose collection of networks, so it is hard to decide what to include when estimating its size. The solution for the Internet Software Consortium (ISC), which has been measuring the size of the Internet since 1993, is currently to survey the number of Internet hosts. In the latest survey, January 2002, 147 344 723 hosts were recorded, an increase of just under 36 million hosts since the January 2001 survey. To put this into perspective, in July 1998 there were just 36.7 million hosts in total recorded. This phenomenal rate of growth is noteworthy but perhaps the actual size *per se* is not as important from a retailer's perspective as where the customers are actually located. Telegeography has recently produced a '*Global Internet Map 2002*', which provides details of the Internet's global infrastructure mapped against a map of the real world (see Figure 10.1). The map provides details of the Internet backbone infrastructure, the density of hosts in particular geographical regions and ISP charge rates around the globe plus other statistical details. The map provides a clear indication of where are the major routes for data traffic around the globe. However, Coffman and Odlyzko (1998) point out that it is important to recognise that the backbone infrastructure connecting all the networks together is only a part of the Internet universe. A great deal of data traffic is local.

User distribution

The *Computer Industry Almanac* (2002) predicts that by 2005 there will be in excess of 1 billion Internet users around the globe; the current population is just under 500 million (see Table 10.1).

Table 10.1 Global Internet user populations

Continent[1]	Population[2]	Internet users
North America	422.60 million	159.56 million
Asia	2,919.91 million	104.46 million
Europe	651.57 million	133.66 million
South America	267.50 million	16.90 million
Australasia	23.20 million	6.30 million
Africa	195.56 million	2.04 million
Total	4.48 billion	422.92 million

1 North America includes the whole of Central America and the West Indies; Europe includes Russia.
2 Only includes countries which have data available on Internet users. Does not include all countries of the world.

Original data source: CyberAtlas, http://cyberatlas.internet.com

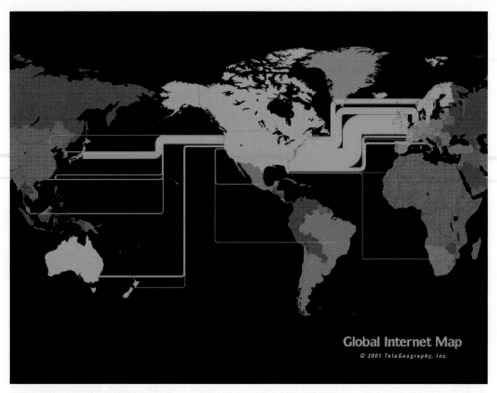

Figure 10.1 Global Internet map

Source: www.telegeography.com © TeleGeography, Inc. 2001

Statistics gathered and collated by CyberAtlas.com have been used to create Tables 10.1 and 10.2 and Figure 10.2. The CyberAtlas team have summarised findings from many surveys around the world, aiming at establishing the size of the global Internet user populations. Whilst these figures many not provide definitive results, they are very useful for showing general distributions of Internet user populations.

North America continues to have the largest number of Internet users, but interestingly the USA does not have the highest density of users per head of population

Table 10.2 A selection of countries and their levels of Internet adoption

Country	Internet users per head of population	Rank	Population	Internet users
Iceland	60.1%	1	278 000	167 000
United Kingdom	58.3%	2	56.6 million	33 million
Hong Kong	54.2%	3	7.2 million	3.9 million
USA	51.4%	4	278 million	143 million
Sweden	50.6%	5	8.9 million	4.5 million
Norway	48.9%	6	4.5 million	2.2 million
Switzerland	46.6%	7	7.3 million	3.4 million
Canada	44.9%	8	31.6 million	14.2 million
Australia	25.8%	24	19.4 million	5 million
Italy	19.1%	27	57.7 million	11 million
Japan	17.4%	31	126.8 million	22 million
Mexico	2.3%	52	101.8 million	2.3 million
China	2.6%	50	1.3 billion	33.7 million
India	0.5%	59	1 billion	5 million
Vietnam	0.03%	69	80 million	22 000

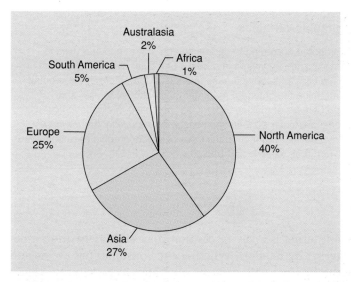

Figure 10.2 Number of Internet users per continent, as a percentage of all Internet users

(see Tables 10.1 and 10.2). In Iceland just over 60 per cent of the population are connected to the Internet whereas in the USA the figure is 51.4 per cent. The size and density of user populations vary considerably from country to country but the density of user populations tends to follow the Internet infrastructure shown on the Global Internet Map (see Figure 10.1). In general, northern European countries have a higher level of Internet penetration per head of population than southern European and former Eastern bloc countries. In Asia, very highly populated countries like India and China have very low levels of Internet penetration but it is important to note that the user population in China is growing rapidly. Since 1999 the number of Internet users in China has grown by approximately 2146.67 per cent, compared with the Scandinavian countries where the rate was around 36 per cent for a similar period.

In summary, mapping the features of the Internet is seemingly a rather imprecise *art*, but perhaps it is possible to identify potentially viable market segments by looking at the geography of the Internet in terms of the quality of the Internet infrastructures that support user access and the general distribution of Internet populations in terms of location and user numbers per head of population.

Internet consumer markets

The geographical location of a market is a useful factor insofar as the physical location will provide an insight into cultural factors likely to affect consumer purchasing behaviour. Moreover, the physical location of a particular market will have associated logistical issues that will need to be resolved (see later in this chapter and Chapter 11) prior to entry into a particular online market. However, there are other segmentation variables that should be considered when segmenting Internet markets: behavioural and psychographic variables.

It is important for businesses wishing to operate in Internet markets to recognise the differences between on- and offline target markets. Additionally, they should consider whether there is a difference in consumer behaviour between these two types of potential target markets.

> ### Behavioural and psychographic variables
>
> Traditionally, markets are segmented according to certain criteria that a marketer uses to divide a population. The criteria provide an insight into how a particular cluster of potential consumers might behave. In the case of behavioural segmentation the nature of the product and the purchase situation determine the criteria a marketer might choose to use, and include: what are the *expected benefits* of making a particular purchase, the *situation or reason* for making the purchase, particular *benefits the consumer is seeking*, the *frequency and quantity* of purchases of a particular product. In the case of psychographic segmentation the focus is on the individual, and their *lifestyle* and *personality*.

● Internet buyers

Consumer demand for the Internet is a key factor that may ultimately drive widespread adoption of the Internet by retailers. Whether the consumer has access and how they use or perceive the Internet will affect its ultimate success (Shirky, 1997). Internet retailing offers a retail experience that is totally different from that of fixed-location retailing (Westland and Au, 1997). Comparison and price shopping across a greater number of sites will be easier and could be achieved within minutes. Indeed, in the USA it is more common for consumers to use the Internet to find information about a product in the early part of the buying decision-making process than to buy directly on the Web. They will subsequently purchase the product through the fixed-location store or order by telephone or fax (Ernst and Young, 1999).

From a retailing perspective the use of the Internet is an elective activity whereby consumers require effort to access retail web sites and select products. As a consequence, carefully planned shopping online may dominate, rather than impulse shopping. Also, online consumers incur costs that they can directly attribute to their shopping behaviour. Payment for call charges could mean that a virtual shopping trip is a costly event. This suggests that web sites that are not well designed, and which require the potential customer to browse through many screens before locating their chosen products, could easily deter customers from ever returning to the site. Furthermore, the inability to allow consumers to touch the merchandise (purchased via the Internet) remains a problem for some consumers and particular types of products. The Internet also places demands on end-users, requiring them to understand the complexity of web site design. Additionally, the difficulties encountered in locating web sites and searching and sorting through the Internet may also deter some consumer segments from switching to the Internet to do their shopping and the cost of access. Consumer behaviour is also affected by gender, age and income.

- *Gender*: the previous imbalance between the genders amongst Internet users is showing signs of evening out. According to Nielsen NetRatings (2001), 51.7 per cent of active US Internet-users are women, but men do still tend to go online more often and spend more time online than women. Men are more likely to use the Internet at their place of work whereas women are increasingly using the Internet at home.
- *Age*: in general, with regard to the age, use of the Internet is on the increase across all age groups. In particular, Internet use among children in the USA and the UK is over 70 per cent and a large proportion of these take part in the shopping process by choosing colours and product specifications. Teenagers increasingly like to use the Internet to e-mail friends and relatives, although a high proportion use SMS services (see Chapter 3). In Europe, teenagers account for 12 per cent of the European online population and they are spending more and more time online

(Jupiter Media Metrix, 2001). University students represent a highly connected age group, as nearly all American and UK university students are online and using the Web, which is often the first place they go to search for information. Generally, older adult shoppers are increasing in numbers and in the amount they spend online. In particular, 35–54-year-olds are likely to spend more than the over-55s. However, over half of online of shoppers aged between 55 and 70 now shop more online than they did a year ago.

- *Income*: the average income of Internet users, previously well above average, is now falling significantly to around national average incomes in North America and northern European countries.

Regardless of particular characteristics, user populations are increasing and so is the volume of Internet sales. Retailers are quickly learning how to conduct themselves in the digital environment. However, online retailing still accounts for only a relatively small percentage of total retail sales.

● Business-to-consumer retail formats

Retail format

The general nature of the retail mix in terms of range of products and services, pricing policy, promotional programmes, operating style and store design and visual merchandising; examples include mail-order retailers (non-store-based) and department-store retailers.

According to Levy and Weitz (1995) retailers survive and prosper by satisfying customer needs more effectively than the competition, addressing customer needs through type of merchandise, variety and assortment of merchandise and levels of customer service. Traditionally, there are two main types of established retail companies: (1) those operating from fixed-location stores, such as department and convenience stores; and (2) non-store-based operations such as catalogue retailing and direct selling. The fine detail of these various operating styles has gradually evolved to accommodate current customer needs. Internet retailing has rapidly emerged, emulating non-store-based operations, and new entrants like Amazon demonstrate how the Internet can potentially completely redefine customer needs using the Internet and the Web to create a virtual retail environment with extensive global coverage. Currently there are several different formats that have been adopted by companies operating in business-to-consumer markets, which include:

- *Bricks and clicks* – established retailers operating from bricks-and-mortar stores integrate the Internet into their businesses either strategically or tactically as a marketing tool or channel to market. Currently, the most successful online retailer in the world is Tesco.com, where *personal shoppers* select the customers' goods in local stores. This is not the only approach a business might choose to fulfil customer orders – networks of strategically placed warehouses provide another option. This approach was initially chosen by J. Sainsbury's plc but they are currently re-planning the logistical side of their online shopping services.
- *Clicks and mortar* – virtual merchants designing their operating format to accommodate consumer demands by trading online supported by a physical distribution infrastructure. Virtual channels have distinct advantages over traditional marketing channels in that they potentially reduce barriers to entry. The location issue, considered to be the key determinant of retail patronage (Finn and Louviere, 1990), is in the physical sense reduced, along with the need for sizeable capital investment in stores. The best-known virtual merchant using this format is Amazon.com, the world's largest online bookstore.
- *Pureplays* – or 'clicks-only' are organisations that operate entirely online. In reality it is almost impossible for a business to operate online without a point of access to the Internet. Therefore, generally speaking, the term 'pureplay' refers to retailers that do not have fixed-location stores, e.g. www.jungle.com. The broader definition

Figure 10.3 Intermediary – Respond.com (www.respond.com)

creates confusion with the term 'clicks and mortar'. Perhaps the most feasible explanation for the lack of commonly understood e-terminology is the immaturity of Internet business in general.

- *Intermediaries* – who link Internet technology and the retail supplier with the consumer. Such organisations perform the mediating task in the world of e-commerce between producers, suppliers and consumers (Sarkar et al., 1996). Established businesses might lack the resources, in terms of both staff and technological infrastructure, to operate their Web activities internally. This creates an opportunity for the intermediary to step in and provide Web solutions and they could eventually replace established retail businesses. The growth in importance of intermediaries has led to the use of the term 'reintermediation' (see Chapter 7).

  A good example of an online retail format intermediary is Respond.com (www.respond.com), see Figure 10.3. This company uses the Internet and the Web to connect buyers and sellers by e-mail. The buyer fills in an online form giving details of the product he or she wants, together with its price. This form is then sent as an e-mail to the supplier who may be able to service the enquiry. Respond.com then sends e-mails to the consumer, providing him or her with the offer.

- *Manufacturers* of consumer goods also see the Internet as an opportunity to regain some of their power lost to the retailers in the past by the shortening of distribution channels. The process of disintermediation works by that manufacturer excluding the retailer altogether and marketing directly to the customer, thus shortening the value chain and/or the supply chain by trading electronically and shifting the balance of power closer to the end-consumer (see Mini Case Study 10.1). Early examples of disintermediation originated within the banking industry, when it was noticed that information technology and industry regulation had reduced the need for retail banks as intermediaries.

Mini Case Study 10.1

Dell.com

Dell developed a direct-to-market business model, which enabled it to remain at the forefront of e-commerce, serving businesses across the globe with computers and IT solutions. The company continually updates its direct approach to manufacturing and selling via the Internet and in doing so ensures that its business model is the most efficient and effective within the industry (www.dell.com, 2002). By supplying customers directly (whether in business-to-consumer or business-to-business markets), Dell is able through the use of the Internet to provide increased customer satisfaction by offering highly competitive pricing – achieved through directly selling to the customer supported by very efficient e-procurement and fulfilment systems. Additionally, Dell is able to offer customers a highly specialised service with each product being made to their particular specifications and supported by equally tailored service packages.

Activity 10.1

Mini Case Study 10.1 describes a company that is perhaps well-placed to trade online due to the nature of the products they sell and their target markets, but this is not always the case.

Task

Discuss questions 1 and 2 in small groups (of 3 or 4) and make a list of the key issues raised. You should then use this information to help you provide a solution for question 3.

1 Consider the likely advantages for a manufacturing organisation like Dell when serving individual retail customers via the Internet.

2 Now consider the likely disadvantages that a large manufacturing company producing breakfast cereals might face if they were to sell directly to individual retail customers via the Internet.

3 Suggest at least three different ways that the breakfast cereals manufacturer might effectively use the Internet to interact with potential retail customers.

For some hints visit www.warburtons.co.uk to see how this manufacturing company uses the Web to interact with their retail customers.

Any one of these types could become the archetypal *model Internet retailer* and could thus affect the future growth of the online retail market as a retail environment. Potentially, if virtual merchants (brick and clicks, pureplays, intermediaries) prove to be highly successful, established retailers operating from a fixed-location store could find themselves increasingly being replaced by new Internet-based retail formats (Van Tassel and Weitz, 1997). The implications are considerable, as ultimately the Internet could fundamentally alter the way that consumers shop and thus revolutionise the retail environment, transforming the local high street into a global *virtual high street*. New entrants may benefit from financial freedom to develop an organisation suited to supporting the logistical demands of the new format (thus addressing the 'last mile' problems faced by established retailers). Established retailers can create competitive advantages from brand equity and high levels of customer service – effectively preventing new entrants from establishing a foothold in highly competitive retail markets. However, if established retailers continue to dominate retail supply and develop their current integrated approach to retailing through the use of technologies such as EPOS (electronic point of sale), EFTPOS (electronic funds transfer at point of sale) and loyalty cards, bringing them closer to the customer, then the Internet could be used to support these operations. In this scenario, revolution is less likely to occur. Whichever type of retailer dominates may ultimately determine consumer demand for online shopping and thus the future development of the Internet.

According to Doherty et al. (1999), there are a number of characteristics of a business that are likely to determine the extent to which retailers have adopted the Internet and the online format they might choose. The characteristics include:

- **Size** – *small and medium-sized retailers* are, according to research, the category most likely to adopt the Internet owing to their greater flexibility (Auger and Gallaugher, 1997). The advantages include access to a wider market previously inaccessible and low-cost advertising, but the disadvantages include medium-term financial risk and scalability. Small-scale operations may be able to handle the picking and logistics due to the small numbers involved but problems will arise when expansion is considered and the need to sustain a larger operation becomes apparent. However, the comparatively high levels of uptake are not apparent. Indeed, it is *large retailers* (across Europe) that have been quick to incorporate the Internet into their retail offer. Examples are: in France, Carrefour (www.carrefour.fr), in Italy, Benetton (www.benetton.com), and in Austria, Magnet online (www.magnet.at). However, the Web offer varies considerably – increasingly some retailers offer their entire range of goods and services via the Internet while others present selected ranges of information content only. The cause of this uneven rate of adoption is not entirely clear. According to Fletcher Research (www.fletch.co.uk), grocery retailers are not maximising the potential of their offer: they are missing opportunities to interact with customers by offering limited product ranges and by not keeping their web sites up to date. A number of large UK retailers have begun to develop *portal web sites* (see Chapter 4) as an attempt to attract customers to use their web sites as a gateway to the Internet and encourage customers to spend the majority of their time in the retailer's own site in much the same way as they attempt to keep them in their retail stores.

- **Activity category** – the particular products and services offered to consumers can affect a business's usage of the Internet. Products and services may be in a digital or physical form, each of which has associated advantages and disadvantages. Delivery is an issue for sellers of physical goods as is the Internet's inability to let customers experience the tactile qualities of a product prior to making a purchasing decision. Indeed, product class has had a profound effect on the success rate of certain online businesses. For instance, books and wine are readily sold via the Internet as they do not require extensive product descriptions but high-fashion items present difficulties and often there is a high return rate for clothing sold online. Digital products do not encounter the logistical difficulties associated with physical goods but encounter problems with pricing and control of copyright as a digitised product can be copied, as can music products. Ticket and online booking services are enjoying comparative success online, e.g. e-bookers.com, expedia.com, as they offer secure online transaction facilities.

- **Logistics** – accommodating demands for new levels of service in global electronic marketplaces could reinforce the critical significance of logistical infrastructures in determining online success (see Chapter 11). Logistical infrastructure might even determine the next generation of market leaders as its effective management provides an opportunity to create competitive advantage (Fernie and Sparks, 1998). From a retail perspective it is important to consider how the Internet is incorporated into retail activities in order to determine the importance of logistics (see Activity 10.2). If the Internet's primary role is as a promotional tool rather than a retail channel to market there is obviously less emphasis on the logistical infrastructure. Morganosky (1997) says, 'The Internet is still a medium for communicating information rather than conducting sales transactions'. Establishing a new logistical infrastructure to service the needs of Internet customers is proving to be a barrier to its immediate development as a retail channel. Established mail-order and direct marketing operators are taking advantage of the Internet channel, due to their not being store-based and having established direct distribution systems (Shi and Salesky, 1994), e.g. Great Universal's www.shoppersuniverse.com.

- **Outsourcing** – if companies lack internal capacity they could decide to employ a third party to manage their online access, outsourcing some or all of their Internet operations (Clemons et al., 1993). From an operational perspective, fixed-location retailers might involve a third-party distribution company to bridge the gap between the customer order and delivery to the customer (Gourley, 1996; Parker, 1996).

Activity 10.2

The last mile problem

Consumers are becoming increasingly aware of the Internet as a channel to market. As established brand names move part or all of their offer online, customers are regularly turning to the Web to make their purchasing decisions. They are not only reviewing product information and reviews but also are now ready to buy online as a mainstream way of shopping rather than as just a novelty experience. As a result the home delivery market is growing. Paradoxically, this success is causing logistical problems, which threaten the future success of online business-to-consumer trade. The problem is how to get the goods the '*last mile*'. A UK government Foresight (2001) report gives estimates that by 2005 home delivery will be worth £34.5 billion. However, they also predict: 'As customer demand [for remote purchasing] increases, the likelihood of their being at home to receive their purchases decreases' (Foresight, 2001).

There have been a number of possible solutions to the delivery problem, including unattended delivery points in the form of secure purpose-built boxes or collection points at a local store where customers could collect their goods when convenient, but none have been particularly well received by the consumers. Whatever the solution at the customer end there are wider implications; at the company level they must resolve warehousing and distribution and the cost associated with providing a service which involves many deliveries of small quantities; at a societal level any increase in the number of small vans required to deliver online orders as in the case of online grocery retailer tesco.com is likely to cause further local traffic congestion.

Task

1 List five physical products that you or one of your neighbours might purchase via the Internet and require delivering to your home. Try to choose products from different categories, e.g. an item of clothing, fresh food, furniture, drink and computer equipment.

2 State the times of day you are available at home to receive delivery of these goods.

3 Describe the difficulties that an online retailer attempting to deliver the goods to you might encounter.

4 Suggest a solution for the *last mile* problem that will encourage consumers to increase the amount of goods they purchase via the Internet.

This section has discussed the choices a retailer wishing to operate online might consider and how some established characteristics of a business might affect decisions of which format to adopt for current and future online operations.

Online retail activities

As we have seen, businesses trading in consumer markets can choose to serve their customers via different combinations of physical and digital channels. Whatever online format a business chooses, decisions will also be taken about the actual function of any Internet- and Web-based activities; these will primarily fall into one of two categories: (1) information functions, (2) interactive functions.

● Information functions

Web sites provide retailers with an important opportunity to give customers information. Many companies see the Web as a means of expanding customer services through offering their customers wider ranges of information than is possible in-store. One of the greatest advantages of the Web according to UK retailers is its ability to facilitate the dispersion of low-cost information. Retailers have been proactive about providing information on their web sites, and offer a wider range of different types of information:

- *Product information* includes product descriptions and prices, promotional information and web advertisements, colour swatches and graphical images (see Figure 10.4), e.g. www.andsotobed.co.uk.

Figure 10.4 Product information at AndSoToBed (www.andsotobed.co.uk)

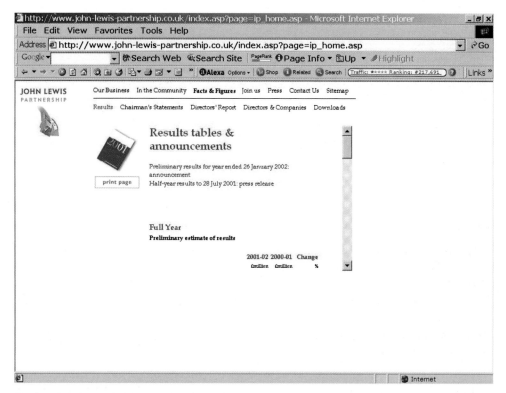

Figure 10.5 Financial information (www.john-lewis-partnership.co.uk)

- *Financial information* includes company reports, annual statements and investor information. The depth of coverage can vary considerably, as can the extent of accessibility. In some instances the consumer is required to provide address details so that reports can be mailed (see Figure 10.5).
- *Company information* includes such items as history of the company, store location information, details of employees and company incentive schemes (see Figure 10.6).
- *Press releases* appear in various forms. Some companies use press releases as part of their consumer promotions (see Figure 10.7), whereas others include such information in their corporate web sites aimed at enhancing the overall profile of the brand(s).
- *Recruitment information* – companies have recruitment features providing potential applicants with job details. Some companies provide the facility to request application forms or even apply for jobs online (see Figure 10.8).

● Interactive functions

Interactive use of the Internet involves more than simply the provision of promotional information. It includes activities such as ordering of catalogues, promotional literature and 'free gifts' and encouraging customers to provide market research data as well as sales ordering and payment transactions. Interactive ways of using the Internet and the Web include:

- *Marketing communications tool*: the Internet is frequently used as an advertising channel. Traditional advertising channels such as broadcasting and print media enable a one-to-many dialogue based on communications theory (Schramm,

Figure 10.6 Company information (www.thorntons.co.uk)

Figure 10.7 Press releases (www.richersounds.com)

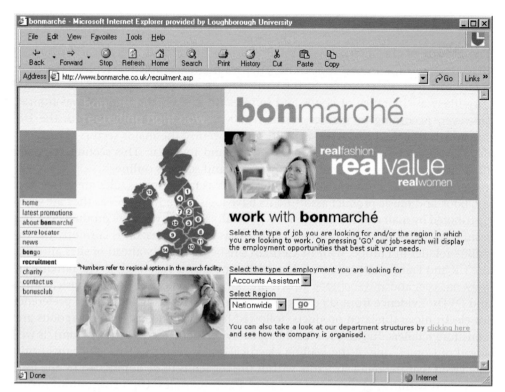

Figure 10.8 Recruitment information from Bonmarché (www.bonmarche.co.uk)

1955) between senders and receivers. The communication process is normally constrained by time, namely the speed of response of participants, but communication can become 'conversations at electronic speeds' if conducted via interactive services such as the Internet (Fill, 1999).

- *Direct communication* – as an interactive channel for direct communication and data exchange (Verity, 1995) the Internet enables focused targeting and segmentation opportunities for more closely monitoring consumer behaviour. E-mail provides a direct non-intrusive means of communication between firm and customer (Cassettari, 1995).

- *Marketing research tool* – the Internet's interactivity facilitates the collection of consumer data, providing the opportunity to gather personal information from online consumers while they browse through web sites, complete online questionnaires and respond to e-mails.

- *Sales channel* – the selling of goods and services online can take several different forms: the order is placed online while the delivery and payment are made through real-world channels; online ordering where the delivery of goods in required in the real world and the payment facility has options online or offline; the total process, namely the order, payment and delivery of the product occurs via the Internet, e.g. purchasing software and online bidding as on the eBay site (www.ebay.com).

In summary, businesses may choose to utilise the Internet in a number of different ways to communicate and interact with their domestic consumers. The particular methods that they adopt may vary, from just providing information to online transactions including ordering and payment for goods and services.

● What's in the e-store?

The growth of the Internet as a retail channel has caused speculators to suggest that at some time in the future the Internet might completely replace the more traditional high-street stores. In the early days of Internet commerce this was not very likely as the range of goods and services on sale via the Internet was limited. However, According to Verdict Research (2001), year-on-year growth (in the UK) has grown threefold to £3.3bn in 2001 and currently the major sectors driving the growth in online retailing are food, clothing and footwear. This section considers the extent of the current availability of goods and services online.

Certain product groups may have advantages as far as online sales are concerned, e.g. book and music product assortments have logistical advantages as they are easily distributed by mail and the consumer is generally familiar with the product class (see Mini Case Study 10.2). According to CyberAtlas (2002), Amazon is currently the top online retailer in Europe, with its German site being slightly ahead of sites aimed at the UK and France, in terms of unique visitor numbers. Also high in the ranking are www.fnac.com and www.bol.com, which are both also sellers of books, music, videos and DVDs. Evidence from US experience of Internet retailing indicates a preference for electronic and related products, followed by miscellaneous shopping goods and non-store retailers. In the UK a leading grocery retailer, Tesco plc (tesco.com), is well ahead of Comet, one of the leading electrical goods retailers. This is not unsurprising, given that the retail structure within the UK tends to be dominated by the food sector and within that sector, by the large food multiples. High concentration and competition combined with static food sales and possible saturation of the market, suggest that the major UK food multiples may perceive the Internet to provide additional growth via a new marketing channel.

It might also be expected that UK non-store or mail-order companies are likely to be early adopters seeking to extend their 'paper formats into the electronic world of cyber-commerce' (Jones and Biasiotto, 1999). Currently, the home shopping market struggles to maintain about five to six per cent of all European retail sales. Unless online retailers can overcome consumer resistance to non-store-based formats, the potential of the Internet, compared with traditional mail-order, may be limited: its key advantage will be the ability to directly target niche markets.

Mini Case Study 10.2 has shown that there is a wide range of retail activity sectors represented on the Web; however, the depth of product choice is likely to be rather limited as the majority of sectors have less than a third of the country's retailers offering goods for sale online.

In addition to the more traditional retail activity sectors discussed above, other parts of the service sector have begun to trade online in consumer markets. Retail banks in particular are seeing a significant increase in the number of online customers. According to Neilsen Net Rating (2001), finance and investment sites are the *'stickiest'* (Chapter 7) of all web sites in the USA, e.g. Schwab.com and etrade.com. However, it is not only in the USA where online banking is popular, as the same is true of Poland where there are now over half a million online bank accounts; other examples where online banking is popular include Hong Kong, Canada, China and the UK. Acceptance of online banking is a significant move forwards for online trade as it demonstrates that consumer acceptance of the notion of secure transactions is increasing. Insecurity of the Web has been regularly cited as an inhibiting factor for online consumers. Other service sectors that are benefiting from online trading include travel, and booking flights, accommodation and event tickets online increasingly satisfies tourism customers.

Online goods for sale in the UK

A four-year research study looking at the adoption of the Internet in the UK found that certain product activity sectors had increased their online sales capacity more rapidly than other activity sectors (Ellis-Chadwick et al., 2002). For instance, the number of alcohol retailers offering an online sales facility has increased by 38 percentage points, moving from 6% in 1997 to 44% in 2000. Similar rapid rates of growth have also been experienced for toys and books. The rapid rates of expansion in these sectors might in part be due to the suitability of their products for an Internet format, but also due to the competition many have experienced from Internet 'start-ups'. For example, the phenomenal growth of Amazon.com and Cdnow.com have put book and music retailers under great pressure, whilst the launch of sites such as Virginwines.com has put the alcohol retailer under pressure.

Table 10.3 shows the percentage of retailers offering goods online by the category of products they sell.

Table 10.3 Online product offers, 2000

Retail activity category	Percentage offering goods online, 2000
Clothing	16
Footwear	4
Jewellery	17
Alcohol retailers	44
Convenience stores	2
Grocers	30
Health & beauty	8
DIY	24
Electricals	37
Furnishings	12
Books	41
Sports	26
Toys	42
Mail order	32
Mixed	17
Speciality foods retailers	5

Discussion points

● To what extent do you believe that convenience and speciality food retailers (including confectioners, butchers and greengrocers) will offer their goods for sale online?

● Discuss which category you think will have 100% of the retailers in the activity sector online first, and why you think this will happen.

One of the most noticeable factors about the e-store is that it is now open for trade as an increasing number of businesses are offering products and services for sale via the Internet. However, there are still major limitations as choice is restricted, logistical support variable reliability and customer service of varying quality. Therefore at the present time the Internet does not offer a serious threat to established retailers. Notwithstanding the current limitations, there are examples of how established markets have been disrupted by Internet offers. Indeed, the success of low-cost airlines easyJet and Ryan Air has demonstrated that the Internet channel to market is presenting opportunities for businesses to rethink how they go to market and in doing so is signalling that there are likely to be major changes to the way people shop in the future.

Implications for Internet retail marketing strategy

In conclusion, it is now widely acknowledged that there is a need for a company to have a coherent Internet strategy underpinned by a clear vision of how it may take advantage of the Internet. An online retailer's strategy is likely to be affected by the type of online format it adopts, the type of products and services it sells and the market segments it chooses to serve.

Retailers will defend their existing market share through consideration of strategic and competitive forces. It is the actions of retailers and their on- and offline behaviour in response to peer actions and new entrants' behaviour and success rate that are likely to shape the future of the Internet as a retail environment. Retailers need to ensure that the value created by retailing via the Internet is additional rather than a redistribution of profitability from current retail channels to shopping via computers and interactive television.

It has been suggested that by removing the physical aspects of the retail offer the Internet may also provide the opportunity for increased competition (Alba et al., 1997). Pureplays can easily combine e-commerce software with scheduling and distribution to bypass traditional retail distributors. These virtual merchants could therefore threaten existing distribution channels for consumer products. The Internet is thus likely to appeal to new entrants who have not already invested in a fixed-location network. However, the boom and bust of the dot-com era has demonstrated that this opportunity must be supported with a sound business plan aimed at generating profits and not media attention *per se*.

Summary

A number of issues have been examined in this chapter, from the geography of the Internet to the difficulties of international fulfilment. During these discussions various evidence has been offered that suggests that retailers are more convinced about the importance of the Internet than they were three years ago despite the dramatic fall in the value of technology stocks during the last two years. The period of experimentation seems to be over and retailers are making significant and perhaps more importantly more focused efforts to make the Internet work for them.

Increasingly, superfluous information is being removed from web sites and being replaced with sites that have a real role to play within a retailer's portfolio. From the consumer's perspective, concerns over security still remain a significant reason why many will not shop online, and a major part of consumer use of the Internet is still associated with pre-purchase information searching. However, the infrastructure that forms the Internet continues to expand, and the content providers and the users continue to grow in numbers. Therefore it is reasonable to suggest that in the future an ever-increasing number of business-to-consumer transactions will be conducted via the Internet.

1 The Internet provides an innovative and interactive medium for communications and transactions between retail businesses and consumers.

2 There are several different online retail formats that a retailer may choose to follow, which may include a mix of Internet and physical-world offerings. Furthermore, bricks-and-mortar retailers and pureplay retailers use the Internet in

various ways and combinations including sales, ordering and payment, information provision and market research.

3 Web sites focusing on the consumer vary in their function. Some offer a whole suite of interactive services whereas others just provide information. The logistical problems associated with trading online are limiting the product assortment some retailers offer.

4 Retailers should pay close attention to the online markets they are wishing to serve and should also understand there are differences between the on- and offline customer experiences.

5 The extent to which the Internet is being used by retailers is increasing both in terms of the number of retail business that are online and the extent to which the Internet is being integrated into almost every aspect of retailing. Retailers must choose how they can best employ the Internet in order to serve their customers rather than whether to adopt the Internet at all.

6 The Internet has already become an important retail channel. Even so, it only accounts for a small percentage of total retail sales.

EXERCISES

Self-assessment exercises

1 Explain the effect of the 'dot-com' era on the growth of the Internet.

2 Describe the variables that a retailer might consider when trying to identify a target market.

3 Describe the different types of business models an online retailer might follow.

4 List the various activities a retailer might include in a customer-facing web site.

Essay and discussion questions

1 Evaluate the potential of the Internet as a 'retail channel'.

2 Discuss whether you consider that all products on sale in the high street can be sold just as easily via the Internet.

3 Australasia is home to approximately 2 per cent of the Internet users around the globe whereas the USA is home to 40 per cent. Describe how an online retailer might choose to target a market. Illustrate your answer with examples.

4 Select three web sites that demonstrate the different ways in which a retailer might use the Internet to interact with its customers. Compare the contents of the web sites and explain what the potential benefits are for the customers of each of the sites.

Examination questions

1 Does the Internet provide retailers with a means of access to a truly global market place? Discuss.

2 It was once predicted that the Internet would replace high-street stores and that within ten years the majority of retail purchases would be made online. Discuss the extent to which you think the goods and services available via the Internet can satisfy the needs of the average consumer.

3 Compare and contrast the operational difficulties that a bricks-and-mortar retailer faces with those of a pureplay retailer.

References

Alba, J., Lynch, J.C., Weitz, B., Janiszewski, C., Lutz, R., Sawyer, A. and Wood, S. (1997) Interactive home shopping. Consumer, retailer and manufacturer incentives to participate in electronic marketplaces, *Journal of Marketing*, 61(July), 38–53.

Auger, P. and Gallaugher, J.M. (1997) Factors affecting the adoption of the Internet-based sales presence for small businesses, *Information Society*, 13(1), 55–74.

BBC Business News (2000a) Online shopping set to boom. http://news.bbc.co.uk/hi/english/business/newsid_606.../606862.st, 17 January.

BBC Business News (2000b) Top web retailer collapses. http://news.bbc.co.uk/hi/english/business/newsid_752.../752293.st., 18 May.

Cassettari. S. (1995) Discovering the missing pieces in your business strategy, *Internet for Business Users Conference*, Madrid.

Clemons, G., Reddi, S. and Row, M.C. (1993) The impact of information technology on the organization of economic activity; the move to the middle hypothesis, *Journal of Management Information Systems*, 10(2).

Coffman, K.G. and Odlyzko, A. (1998) The size and growth rate of the Internet, *First Monday*, Issue 3, no. 10. www.firstmonday.dk/issues/issue3_10/coffman

Computer Industry Almanac (2002) Internet Users Will Top 1 Billion in 2005. Wireless Internet Users Will Reach 48% in 2005. http://www.c-i-a.com/Age

Doherty, N.F., Ellis-Chadwick, F.E. and Hart, C.A. (1999) Cyber retailing in the UK: the potential of the Internet as a retail channel, *International Journal of Retail and Distribution Management*, 27(1), 22–36.

Dunne, P. and Lusch, R.F. (1999) *Retailing*. Dryden Press, London.

Ellis-Chadwick, F.E., Doherty, N.F. and Hart, C. (2002) Signs of change? A longitudinal study of Internet adoption by UK retailers, *Journal of Retailing and Consumer Services*, 9(2).

Ernst and Young (1999) *The Second Annual Ernst and Young Internet Shopping Study*, New York.

Fernie, J. and Sparks, L. (1998) *Logistics and Retail Management*. Kogan Page, London.

Fill, C. (1999) *Marketing Communications: Contexts, Contents and Strategies*, 3rd edn. Prentice Hall, London.

Finn, A. and Louviere, J. (1990) Shopping centre patronage models; fashioning a consideration set segmentation solution, *Journal of Business Research*, 21, 277–88.

Foresight (2001) *@ Your Home: New Markets for Customer Service and Delivery*, Department of Trade and Industry, www.foresight.gov.uk.

Gourley, C. (1996) The emergence of online malls has shoppers putting up their feet and retailers scrambling to theirs. How will this shift the supply chain? *Distribution*, 95(13), 28.

Hagel, J. III and Armstrong, A.G. (1997) *Net Gain – Expanding Markets through Virtual Communities*. Harvard Business School Press, Boston.

Jones, K. and Biasiotto, M. (1999) Internet retailing: current hype or future reality? *The International Journal of Retail Distribution and Consumer Research*, 9(1), 69–79.

Jupiter Media Metrix (2001) Today's teenagers will shape tomorrow's Internet. www.jmm.com

Kahin, B. (1995) The Internet and the national information infrastructure. In *Public Access to the Internet*, Brian Kahin and James Keller (eds), publication of the Harvard Information Infrastructure Project, MIT Press, Cambridge, MA and London.

Kämäräinen, V., Småros, J., Holmström, J. and Jaakola, T. (2001) Cost-effectiveness in the e-grocery business, *International Journal of Retail and Distribution Management*, 29(1), 41–9.

Levy, M. and Weitz, B.A. (1995) *Retailing Management*, 2nd edn. Irwin, Chicago.

Morganosky, M.A. (1997) Retailing and the Internet: a perspective on the top 100 US retailers, Research Note, *International Journal of Retail and Distribution Management*, 25(11), 372–7.

Mulhern, F.J. (1997) Retail marketing: from distribution to integration, *International Journal of Research in Marketing*, 14, 103–24.

Parker, C. (1996) It's nothing personal, *Net*, 25, November, 56–62.

Raymond, E.S. (1996) *The New Hacker's Dictionary*, 3rd edn. MIT Press, Cambridge, MA.

Sarkar, M.B., Butler, B. and Steinfield, C. (1996) Intermediaries and cybermediaries: a continuing role for mediating players in the electronic marketplace, *Journal of Computer-Mediated Communication*, 1(3).

Schramm, W. (1955) How communication works, in W. Schramm (ed.) *The Process and Effects of Mass Communications*. University of Illinois Press, Urbana, IL.

Shi, C.S. and Salesky, A.M. (1994) Building a strategy for electronic home shopping, *The McKinsey Quarterly*, No. 4.

Shirky, C. (1997) Alternative strategy suggestion, *Communications of the ACM*, 40 (July), 24.

Teather, D. (2000) Clickmango rescue effort fails, *Guardian*, 6 September.

Van Tassel, S. and Weitz, B.A. (1997) Interactive home shopping: all the comforts of home, *Direct Marketing*, 59(10), 40–1.

Verdict Research (2001) *Electronic Shopping 2002*. Verdict Research, London.

Verity, J. (1995). The Internet, *Business Week*, 14 November, no. 3398, 80–8.

Wells, M. (2000) TV show asks entrepreneurs: who wants to net a million? *Guardian*, 17 April.

Westland, C.J. and Au, G. (1997) A comparison of shopping experiences across three competing digital retailing interfaces, *International Journal of Electronic Commerce*, 2(2), 57–69.

Further reading

Afuah, A., Arbor, A. and Tocci, C. (2001) *Internet Business Models and Strategies*. McGraw-Hill, New York.

Alexander, Nicholas (1997) *International Retailing*. Blackwell Business, Oxford.

Levy, M. and Weitz, B. (2001) *Retail Management*. McGraw-Hill, New York.

Oz, E. (2001) *Foundations of E-Commerce*. Prentice Hall, Upper Saddle River, NJ.

Rayport, J. and Jaworski, B. (2001) *E-Commerce*. McGraw-Hill, London.

Rayport, J. and Jaworski, B. (2001) *Cases in E-Commerce*. McGraw-Hill, London.

Turban, E., King, D., Lee, J., Merrill, W. and Ching, H. (2001) *Electronic Commerce*, 2nd edn. Prentice Hall, London.

Web links

- CyberAtlas Web User Populations (2002). http://cyberatlas.internet.com/big_picture/geographics/article/0,1323,5911_151151,00.html (03/03/02).

- Dell.com (2002) www.dell.com.

- Internet Software Consortium www.isc.org/ds/new-survey.html

- Nua.com (2001) www.nua.com/surveys/index.cgi?f=VS&art_id=905357512&rel=true.

- Yourable.com www.yourable.com/TwoShare/getPage/00Main/Site/Press.

- Nielsen NetRatings (2001) www.nielsennetratings.com.

Chapter 11

Business-to-business Internet marketing

Links to other chapters

This chapter should be read in conjunction with these chapters:

➤ Chapter 2, the macro-environment
➤ Chapter 4, Internet marketing strategy

Learning objectives

After reading this chapter, the reader should be able to:

● Identify the principal uses of the Internet in business-to-business markets
● Clarify the meaning of business-to-business use of the Internet
● Understand the impact of Internet technologies on buyer–supplier processes, relationships and markets
● Identify key business-to-business solutions facilitated by the use of Internet technologies

Questions for marketers

Key questions for marketing managers related to this chapter are:

● How is the traditional sales process changed online?
● What are the applications for B2B e-commerce?
● How is buying enhanced digitally?

Introduction

Michael Porter (1985), Bill Gates (1999), Don Tapscott (1997) and many other writers and researchers agree that technology, in particular digital technology, is changing the very nature of business. There is much evidence to support these views, which are becoming increasingly significant as the number of companies using the Internet increases. According to research, 93% of US and 86% of UK companies are using the Internet, and their online activities include sales, marketing, order fulfilment, supply chain management and a range of other business-to-business activities (Taylor Nelson Sofres, 2002).

In the past much of the media commentary on Internet technology and its commercial exploitation has covered the way in which the Internet will affect businesses operating in consumer markets. Arguably, it will be business-to-business sectors where Internet technologies will have the most far-reaching impact. This is not only due to the higher volume of trade but also because of how companies respond to the challenges created by the Internet and associated technology. It is possible that Internet adoption could completely alter competitive market structures and reshape business environments. Indeed, Andy Grove, the chairman of Intel, blatantly states: 'In five years time all companies will be Internet companies, or they won't be companies at all' (Flatt and Cooper, 2000).

This chapter includes: consideration of the circumstances in which business-to-business use of the Internet occurs; examination of organisational exchanges and buying and selling processes off- and online; the impact of Internet technology on organisational markets (industrial, reseller and government); and online marketing strategies. It concludes by offering suggestions of how online business-to-business trading might develop in the future. Throughout the chapter case examples are used to support and develop ideas and concepts.

Business-to-business context

Business-to-business markets are quite different from business-to-consumer markets. According to Jobber (2001), there are typically fewer customers that are likely to buy goods in bulk quantities. What are the implications of this? First, with fewer buyers, the existence of suppliers tends to be well known. This means that efforts to promote a web site using methods such as banner advertising or listing in search engines are less important than for consumer brands. Indeed, impulse purchases, and those based on emotional motives are rare in organisational buying situations. As a result many of the techniques used to promote goods and services in consumer markets are less effective in organisational markets. From an e-marketing perspective many promotional techniques have been developed with consumer markets in mind (see Mini Case Study 11.1). Of course, business-to-business suppliers with many potential customers will use promotion methods that correspond more closely to those of the retail market. Secondly, the existence of larger buyers is likely to mean that each is of great value to the supplier. The supplier therefore needs to understand the buyers' needs from the web site and will put effort into developing the Web-based content and services necessary to deliver these services. The types of services needed to support the customer relationship are summarised well by Patricia Seybold in her book *Customers.com* (1999) in which she suggests principles for an effective business strategy for the Internet.

Corporate Internet communications

According to Fill (2002), 'corporate communications are simply a part of the process that translates corporate identity into corporate image'. In general, organisations are attempting to present consistent and coherent messages about their brands, but this does not necessarily apply to the use of the Internet. Indeed, some financial-service-sector organisations have created online brands that have completely separate brand identities. Potentially, this approach provides protection for the parent brand from any negative values associated with the online brand. Examples include Smile (The Co-op Group), Marbles (HFC Bank Plc) and Cahoot (Abbey National).

Furthermore, some online advertising techniques are rarely used as part of a corporate communications campaign. For instance, the 'irritation factor' evoked by animated 'banner ads' and 'pop-ups', which have been proven to be an effective way to create awareness and interest among online consumers, is wholly inappropriate in business-to-business markets as they can be considered intrusive and disruptive.

Discussion points

- Are there any features of 'pop-up' adverts that could make the technique attractive to corporate advertisers?

- Suggest situations in business-to-business markets where the use of 'pop-ups' would be appropriate.

This introductory mini-case provides details of potential tactical problem from an e-marketing communications perspective. The next part of the section highlights other key themes, which will be used to structure the chapter's discussion of organisational markets and the impact of Internet technologies.

● Key themes and concepts

In traditional commercial situations (offline), there are some broad differences between organisational markets and consumer markets. These are:

- the behaviour of organisations during the buying and selling processes – organisational exchanges;
- the nature of the markets in which the buying and selling takes place – focusing on industrial, reseller and government markets;
- the strategies that define the aims and objectives of a company's buying and selling activities – marketing strategies.

These key themes will provide the structure for the content of this chapter; each one will be examined in turn and will include consideration of the actual processes that are involved (based on the experience of offline situations) and changes that are occurring as a result of the adoption of Internet technologies.

At this point it is important to remind ourselves that the concept of e-commerce is just as relevant in business markets as it is in consumer markets (see Chapter 1). Moreover, business-to-business activities include both buy- and supply-side transactions (see Chapter 1). The nature of organisational exchanges will now be discussed in more detail.

Interorganisational exchanges

Commerce, by definition (Chambers, 1991) is an interchange of merchandise on a large scale between nations, organisations or individuals. It is the trading of goods and services, which forms the basis of marketplace exchanges. Bagozzi (1978) described market exchanges as independent transactions that satisfy the short-term self-interests of individuals, while Dwyer et al. (1987) highlighted the importance of the length of relationship when defining the exchange concept. Their explanation of exchange focused on the longer-term relationships established between parties that wish to establish a continuing trading relationships. Relational exchanges have become increasingly important. In fact, there has been a general sense of willingness, on behalf of suppliers and customers alike, to develop increasingly close 'emotional' relationships based on trust (Vandermerwe, 1993). Whilst buyers reward suppliers with brand loyalty, suppliers in turn develop strategies to continually energise this 'connective' relationship. However, Ellis-Chadwick et al. (2002) question whether this trend will continue as customers and suppliers increasingly become physically connected to one another via computer networks. They suggest that relationships may revert to the more transaction-based relationships of thirty years ago.

● Traditional and reverse market exchanges

Traditionally, the exchange process is initiated by the seller, who will attempt to satisfy the demands of the buyer either by producing goods and services which explicitly meet the buyer's needs or by aggressive sales and communications campaigns designed to persuade the buyer to purchase a particular product or service. However, Blenkhorn and Banting (1991) discuss the concept of reverse marketing, first recognised in the mid-1980s. In this scenario, the buyer initiates the exchange process by making the seller aware of their purchasing requirements (see Figure 11.1) and in doing so changes the nature of the relationship into 'an aggressive kind of purchasing' (Leenders and Blenkhorn, 1988). Globally, current trends are towards reduction in the number of suppliers, increasing demands on the quality of goods supplied, closer cooperation between supplier and buyer, and, for perhaps the first time for many organisations, a strategic approach towards purchasing.

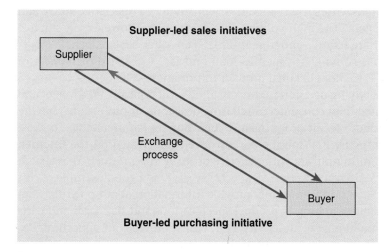

Figure 11.1 Market exchanges: traditional and reverse

The adoption of Internet technologies is enabling companies to further develop the reverse marketing model. General Electric not only provides producers with specifications for the corporation's purchasing requirements but also uses an auction mechanism to bid prices down. A further derivation of the same model has been adopted by priceline.com. In this case the buyer is encouraged to state the price they are prepared to pay for flights and accommodation. Priceline.com then acts as intermediary between buyer and seller in order to meet buyer demands with supplier availability and willingness to supply at said price. These are not isolated examples: many organisations are adopting online purchasing strategies focusing on cost reduction. Therefore it is reasonable to consider whether, as commercial organisations increasingly integrate Internet technologies into their buying and selling activities, the whole process is becoming ever more rational and focused on transactions as suggested by Ellis-Chadwick et al. (2002).

● The traditional buying process

In addition to market exchanges, organisational buying typically involves a decision making process, which is different from consumer purchasing behaviour. Organisational buying decisions are influenced by the following key factors: the power and number of individuals in the *buying group* involved in the purchasing decision, the *type and size of purchase* and *choice criteria*, which inform the purchase decision and the level of *risk* involved.

- *The buying group*. Webster and Wind (1996) identified different profiles for participants involved in an organisational *buying group*: users, influencers, buyers, deciders and gatekeepers. The composition of the buying group varies according to a company's requirements regarding financial control and authorisation procedures. The key question to consider is the extent to which Internet technologies are impacting on this traditional model of the organisational buying group. This point is discussed in some detail in the next section.
- *The size and type of purchase*. These will vary dramatically according to the scale of the purchase. Companies such as train makers will have low-volume, high-value orders; others selling items such as stationery will have high-volume, low-value orders. With the low-volume, high-value purchase the Internet is not likely to be involved in the transaction itself since this will involve a special contract and financing arrangement. The high-volume, low-value orders, however, are suitable for e-commerce transactions and the Internet can offer several benefits over traditional methods of purchase such as mail and fax, e.g. speed of transfer of information, access to more detailed product information.
- *Choice criteria*. The buying decision for organisations will typically take longer and be more complicated than consumer purchasing decisions, as professional buying groups assess product specifications against their buying requirements. To assist in this evaluation, many B2B-specific portals have been created on the Internet, with the aim of uniting buyers with sellers who have the products that match their requirements. TechSavvy.com (www.techsavvy.com) is a good example of this (see Figure 11.2). Such portals not only provide information about potential suppliers, but also enable searching of product specifications and standards and parts catalogues. You should now read Activity 11.1, which provides an opportunity to develop more in-depth understanding of the evaluation process and the roles of individuals in the buying group.

Figure 11.2 TechSavvy.com

● *The level of risk.* This varies depending on the type of product. In the case of routine-purchase, low-cost goods required say for maintenance or repair purposes the level of risk associated with a wrong purchase is low. However, in the case of a high-cost product, say either a capital equipment purchase or a bulk quantity of raw material used in a manufacturing process, then the associated risk of making a wrong purchase is high. The Internet affords buyers and sellers the opportunity to be well informed about a potential purchase, thereby reducing the risks associated with the functionality of a particular product or service. However, online fraud and forgery are increasing and global legal systems do not yet have laws to protect every aspect of commercial use of the Internet, especially online contracts (Sparrow, 2000). Therefore, the advantage of accessing a wide range of new trading partners across the Internet's global trading network is somewhat reduced by the threat of a previously unknown party entering into contract fraudulently. As a result, the risk of trading with new suppliers via the Internet is potentially higher than in a face-to-face situation.

In summary, the traditional buying process can be affected variously by the adoption of the Internet. Choice criteria are a factor where the Internet's capacity to store and distribute information can generally benefit all purchasing situations (except in cases involving situations of fraudulent use and misrepresentation). The size of the purchase will determine the suitability of the Internet as a channel on which to conduct a transaction. Finally, the effect of the Internet on levels of risk is variable. The remainder of this section briefly examines commercial Internet solutions that are pertinent to the buy-side of market exchanges.

Mini Case Study 11.2

Online signatures

Clicking 'OK' can be legally binding, but few people bother to read the small print.

(Herskind, 2002)

According to Kenn Herskind, in business-management roles individuals regularly sign documents that are legally binding. They do so (despite often not reading the small print), being fully aware that the contents of the document are legally binding. The same applies to virtual contracts and signatures. However, in the instance when a 'digital signature' is used instead of writing the signature you just click the 'OK' or 'I agree' button (usually situated at the end of the small print). Herskind argues that clicking a button is too simple and that 'people just don't feel bound by this as they did when they take out a pen and sign in ink'. The recommendations are that companies should create a signing process that engenders trust and has a feeling of 'gravitas'.

Discussion point

Suggest how organisations could make the digital signing of virtual contracts seem more important in order to reflect the legally binding nature of the contract.

Activity 11.1

Tailoring the content for appropriate members of the buying decision (Web)

This activity involves assessing an e-commerce investment proposal from a chief information officer (CIO). It uses a web site to evaluate the suitability of various consultants as potential partners.

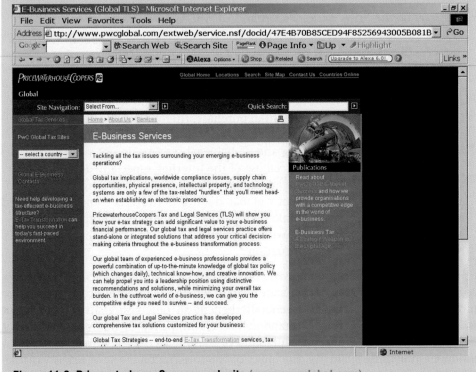

Figure 11.3 PricewaterhouseCoopers web site (www.pwcglobal.com)

Scenario

An engineering company that sells gas turbines to the global market is intending to use the Internet to enable e-commerce integration with both its suppliers and its customers. It is looking to work with one of the leading professional services firms to specify and possibly implement such a system. The engineering company is looking for a company that has experience with dealing with e-commerce projects. Different senior members of the company and some potential users of the system are planning to benchmark the different firms' web sites to assess their credibility and suitability for working on the project.

Task

In a group of three or more, identify different members of the buying decision team as follows:

- *users* (representatives of marketing and purchasing who will work with the chosen firm);
- *influencers* (chief information officer and chief financial officer);
- *deciders* (chief executive officer).

Each team member should visit one of the following firms' web sites:

1 Accenture (www.accenture.com)
2 PricewaterhouseCoopers (www.pwcglobal.com)
3 KPMG (www.kpmg.com)
4 IBM (www.ibm.com)
5 Ernst & Young (www.ey.com)

Each team should then prepare a one-page report or presentation summarising the suitability of the firm to work with the engineering company based on the information contained on the company web sites numbered 1–5 above.

A separate discussion group can be held to analyse which aspects of the web site design and content influenced the decision.

● Digitally enhanced buying

According to Croom (2001) the use of Internet-based technologies will affect procurement systems by making them 'leaner'. Buyers will become more informed with increased access to product information available on the Web. Changes may occur in the configuration of the buying group: the purchasing function will become more streamlined, and restructuring of the supply chain will also be possible.

- *More informed buyers*: The US-based BuyerZone.com is a leading online marketplace, which brings together premier internet-based 'Request for Quote' service with its original award-winning purchasing guides. This research facility serves the needs of small-business owners by providing access to relevant and timely information. Additionally, BuyerZone.com provides a guided buying experience that empowers customers to easily evaluate and quickly make the right purchases for all their business needs. It is also important to be aware that a major challenge for the Internet marketers is that access to information empowers the buyer in the purchasing decision-making process, as online information becomes available to assist purchasing from all of a company's competitors. Therefore, each business needs to make an effort to provide '*better*' information than its competitors if it wishes to retain customers. An example of a business that uses such a tool to help assist the buying decision is Marshall Industries, which provides an on-screen tool that helps show customers the range of products available that meet their needs. Regardless of such innovations, Croom (2001) suggests that in the future, especially in 'routine purchasing' situations, companies will be more inclined to completely outsource the purchasing function and in doing so will make the quality of the information and its search facilities largely irrelevant.

- *Streamlining of the purchasing function*: Another change to the buying process, which may occur as a result of adoption of Internet-based technology, is a change to the people involved in the buying decision. Internet solutions are in certain instances enabling organisations to streamline the purchasing function both in terms of the number of supplier contacts (electronic data interchange via the Internet facilitates access to increasing numbers of suppliers) and the empowerment of company individuals involved in the buying decision through access to consistent and coherent information.

- *Restructuring of the supply chain*: Internet technologies are increasingly being used to improve efficiency and reduce costs by focusing on the whole production process and coordinate all of an organisation's supply activities. The Just-In-Time (JIT) approach towards purchasing, popularised in the UK by Japanese car manufacturers (Nissan, Toyota) during the 1980s streamlined many logistical aspects associated with stock holding and manufacturing processes. However, the Internet has enabled further benefits to be introduced into almost every aspect of logistics associated with manufacturing. Ireland Freight Services Global Logistics, a freight company, is currently ranked in the top 10% of exporting freight companies in the UK. It has achieved this success by developing Vendorvillage.com, which is a virtual warehouse. The benefits are integrated supply chains and improved logistical flows in manufacturing facilities (see Case Study 11.1).

The next section considers the wider implications of adoption of Internet technologies into purchasing practices.

E-buy business models

The above discussion of how adoption of Internet technologies potentially reduces costs associated with the supply-side of organisational activities has encouraged writers and practitioners alike to suggest that online purchasing methods should be considered as business models.

- *E-procurement*: Timmers (2000) suggested that e-procurement, defined as 'tendering and procurement of goods and services', is a business model that has effectively been implemented by businesses around the globe. Kalakota and Robinson (2000) advocate that increasing an organisation's profitability through cost reduction makes online procurement an important strategic issue. However, while organisations like Marshall Industries (a large American electronic components company) and many others have undoubtedly made significant cost savings by shifting many previously manually processed paper-based tasks to the Web, it is important to consider whether this is a 'quick-fix solution' to satisfy shareholder aspirations in the light of the turbulent 'dot-com boom and bust era' showing that Internet

CASE STUDY 11.1

Vendorvillage.com – multifunctional Web-based supply chain solution

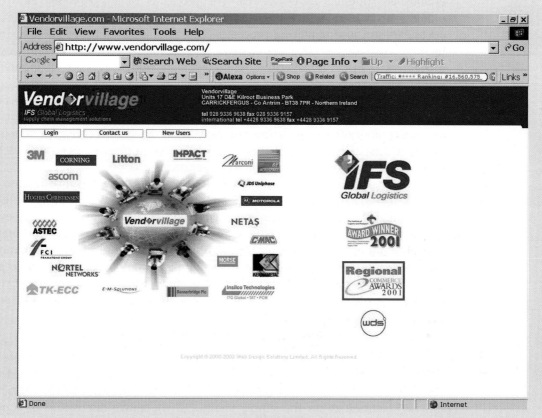

Figure 11.4 Vendorvillage web site (www.vendorvillage.com)

Vendorvillage.com is an award-winning Web-based company providing solutions in storage and handling, supply chain and manufacturing logistics. Ireland Freight Services (IFS) is a multi-modal transport solution provider company based in County Antrim. In 1999, in conjunction with Web Design Solutions, it developed an Internet software solution that could fully integrate all aspects of the supply chain tool. This solution then became based online. As a result, Vendorvillage became the first fully Web-based vendor-managed inventory hub in Northern Ireland, and provided e-commerce solutions throughout the supply chain (ecommerce-awards.co.uk, 2001). Emphasis was placed on ensuring a smooth flow of materials through manufacturing with enhanced inventory management practice, and the efficient use and control of stock within the supply chain.

Discussion point

To what extent do the solutions offered by Vendorvillage require a company to already be employing JIT purchasing solutions?

technologies can make a real difference to profitability or whether such models can produce long-term benefits.

- *Online purchasing auctions*: These again are referred to as a business model (Timmers, 2000). Real-time online purchasing auctions are used by buyers and suppliers globally. General Electric (GE) involves both established and non-established suppliers in e-auctions. The model is of a Web-based electronic bidding mechanism, which operates is a similar way to those held in traditional auction rooms and tendering processes. However, in the case of GE the aim is to drive costs down via a competitive, open bidding process. The downward movement of prices is sometimes referred to as a 'reverse auction' as opposed to a bidding situation where prices are driven upwards. GE purchasing managers, do not always select the lowest bid as they will assess the potential risks associated with the supplier: say, the ability to fulfil the order, quality and requirements for after-sales service issues, rejection rates, quality of goods. An emergent benefit of this model is that e-auctions allow companies to monitor competitive pricing, which helps the organisation reduce total costs.

- *E-fulfilment*: Although not currently referred by many as a business model, the delivery of goods in a timely and appropriate fashion is central to the re-engineering of the supply chain (see Case Study 11.1). According to a survey by Forester research, 'fulfilment' will be an area of significant growth for businesses operating online. However, over 80% of organisations cannot fulfil international orders because of the complexities of shipping, although there are some geographical locations that are better served by local warehouse support networks than others, e.g. parts of Europe and Asia. Further discussion of 'last mile' problems can be found in Chapter 10.

Time will inevitably establish the validity of the proposition that online purchasing practices are sustainable business models. Notwithstanding this point, there are some key benefits associated with online purchasing which should be noted (see Table 11.1). This table is based on Croom's (2001) investigation of the impact of Web-based technology on the supply chain and the above discussions of supply-side market exchanges. The next section examines the sell-side of organisational activities.

Table 11.1 Potential advantages of online purchasing systems

Advantage factor	Online purchasing situations
Quality of information	Ensures access to comparable information whereas incomplete knowledge can cause confusion in human-based systems as parties may not have access to the same information.
Uncertainty	Is potentially lower than for human systems. This means that in routine purchasing situations (at least) there is potential advantage in outsourcing the purchasing function. Potentially, removes some of the need for vertical integration.[1]
Risk	From a functional perspective risk can be reduced by improvement of buyer information. However, the risk of fraud is significantly increased when dealing with previously unknown buyers and suppliers.
Frequency	Allows better management of ordering (automated grouping of small orders is practicable).
Coordination	Rather than having networks only link existing trading partners in a tightly coupled arrangement, such new electronic markets could conceivably include larger numbers of buyers and sellers (Malone et al., 1987). Additionally, reduces the costs of searching for appropriate goods and services.

[1] Vertical integration refers to the practice of supply chain activities being controlled within an organisation.

● The traditional selling process

This discussion of the sales-side of organisational exchanges primarily focuses on marketing communication activities and the types of relationships that form between buyers and sellers. According to Fill (2002), the number of people involved in purchasing adds to the complexity of the decision making process. He goes on to say that because of this factor personal selling is the predominant method of marketing communications.

Personal selling

Typically, this involves analysis of the situation in which the selling will take place, which can be done by examining the type of customer for the purpose of this chapter.

The kinds of customers to be considered are those operating in industrial, reseller and government markets. This method of communication is the most expensive element of the communication mix and therefore should be very well targeted and objectives should be clearly stated from the outset of any sales initiative (Fill, 2002). Personal selling helps to build relationships between buyers and sellers, especially when there is a high level of complexity involved in the buyer's purchasing decision. The personal sales representative can interact with the buyer, providing (in some cases) immediate answers to queries about a particular product or service. Typically, personal selling will be used when there are a relatively small number of buyers in the market purchasing high-value goods; their information needs will be high due to product complexity and negotiations will form part of the pricing policy (Fill, 2002). The sales process can be considered as part of a relational market exchange whereby the seller seeks out the buyer, establishing their needs, expectations and requirements, delivers the sales messages, negotiates the terms of the sale and determines any after-sales support requirements.

● E-sales

Clearly, personal selling is not a mode of marketing communication that can easily be transposed on to the Web. Given the high levels of personal selling used in industrial markets it is unsurprising to discover that the spend on online advertising is comparatively low. Additionally, as discussed earlier (see Mini Case Study 11.1) many online advertising techniques are aimed at online consumer markets (see Table 11.2). However, Internet advertising does offer an opportunity to create highly

Table 11.2 Examples of online advertising spend

Category	Online advertising spend (first half of 2001), $m
USA (total spend)	7900
Retailers (USA)	299.404
Media and advertising firms (USA)	261.440
Financial companies (USA)	177.879
Computers and software (USA)	149.753
Public transport and hotel accommodation (USA)	68.016
UK (total spend)	90.028

Source: CyberAtlas http://cyberatlas.internet.com/markets/advertising/article/0,,5941_881631,00.html#table

tailored, fast communications, which can deliver high information content at comparatively low cost (Gattiker et al., 2000). Indeed, prior to the economic slowdown of 2001, especially in technology stocks, research (Jupiter Communications and Media Metrix, 2000) was indicating that B2B advertising was the fastest growing sector for online publishers even though the majority of online advertising spend continues to be aimed at consumer markets. The uptake of online advertising is low in Europe compared to the USA, but according to eMarketeers (2001) in Europe, the UK has the highest number of online adverts followed by Italy, Germany, France, Spain, the Netherlands, Sweden, Austria, Belgium and Denmark (top ten in order).

One part of the sales process where Internet technologies have great potential is customer feedback mechanisms.

Product evaluation and feedback

The Internet offers opportunities for businesses to improve the quality of customer service and at the same time reduce costs. Quality of service can be improved by providing buyers with access to the right answer to their queries in real-time. Using customer information and diagnostic tools Dell Computers (www.dell.com) analyses the buyer query, diagnoses the problem and then instantly recommends possible solutions. Through providing web-based support or buyer-driven question and answer sessions Dell have to employ fewer staff to provide the required level of after sales support (see Mini Case Study 11.3).

Mini Case Study 11.3

Cisco excels in pre-sales and after-sales service

Cisco is a leading e-commerce business with the majority of its business online. The success has been achieved through e-commerce activities. A particularly interesting part of its online operations is its customer service provision.

In the early 1990s Cisco was a relatively small company, but was growing rapidly. This success caused a problem – a backlog in the area of after-sales support. This problem developed since Cisco's electronic components such as routers and hubs need configuration after delivery. The queries that arise are of a highly technical nature and at the time there were many customer questions. The solution was to provide online support whereby if possible customers could resolve their own problems; however, highly specialised engineers were also available to deal with particularly troublesome problems. Susan Bostrom, head of Cisco's Internet Solutions Group, said the idea was 'almost an instant success': it became a 'self-inflating balloon of knowledge'. The expansion of knowledge occurred as customers not only gleaned information from Cisco's customer query web site but also shared their experiences with Cisco and other customers. The support system has continued to be a success and today almost 80 per cent of customer queries are answered online. Cisco's sales have increased tenfold while the number of customer support staff has only doubled.

Source: Cisco System web site www.cisco.com

E-sales innovations

Despite the potential limitations for use of Internet-based technologies in B2B environments some innovative and creative solutions have been developed.

Order management systems

SAP Portals and Hewlett-Packard have recently announced their intentions to provide open portal solutions, which offer fully integrated packages that provide companies with complete end-to-end solutions. In other words, their promise is to unify disparate applications, information and services. However, the availability of high-performance solutions does not necessarily equate to high levels of uptake of such solutions. Many organisations are currently taking a piecemeal approach towards the adoption of Internet technologies. There are examples where the inbound logistical and e-procurement systems are completely integrated with the outbound systems, e.g. POSCO, the world's largest steel manufacturer, which uses Oracle's E-Business Suite in order to reduce budgeting time (by as much as 80 days in some instances), reduce costing time and sales planning lead time, and simplify orders processing for tens of thousands of daily orders. However, in the main, this is not the case, especially in European industrial markets. Research by Ellis-Chadwick and Doherty (2001) into the uptake of Internet technologies in the UK brewery sector found that, in general, companies in this sector were only making limited use of the Internet and the Web. Similar results were also found in reseller markets where, whilst some companies are developing complex networks, aggregating players in the performance network through Web-based trading portals, the majority of retailers are merely establishing an online presence to provide customers with company information.

Avatars and 'smartbots'

These are software solutions that can be used to create 'virtual assistants'. They have automated features that can be integrated into a company's online sales and purchasing activities. Artificial Life Inc. have developed 'smartbots', which are user-friendly intelligent software programs that use artificial intelligence (AI) and natural language to automate tasks. Artificial Life Inc. have a suite of 'bots': a 'consultative salesbot' that converses with web site visitors in spoken language; 'self-help assistant' which acts as a web site tour guide. LifeFX partnered with eGain Communications Corp. provide similar virtual agent software that powers avatars (see Case Study 11.2). Their customers include Motorola, which has used the avatars to interact with customers who are can choose a virtual guide to help them purchase wireless handsets.

> **Avatar**
>
> A term used in computer-mediated environments to mean a 'virtual person'. Derived from the word's original meaning: '*n.* the descendant of a Hindu deity in a visible form; incarnation; supreme glorification of any principle' (Chambers, 1991).

E-CRM

Electronic customer relationship management is a key element of e-business in much the same way that building long-term relationships is important to an offline business. E-CRM techniques have been discussed in detail in Chapter 6. This issue will be returned to in the final section of the chapter.

This concludes the discussion of the buy- and sell-side of market exchanges and the impact of Internet technologies on organisations' behaviour during the process associated with market exchanges.

Virtual buying groups

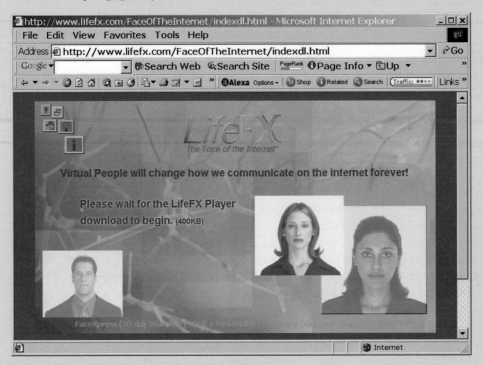

Figure 11.5 LifeFX – the face of the Internet web site

www.lifefx.com/FaceOfTheInternet/indexdl.html

Most of the current revenue opportunities for business avatars occur in customer relationship management (CRM) situations, where software avatars can lever advantage over conventional software by using powerful natural language conversational software to personalise the Web experience. The aim is to make customers feel more comfortable when asking questions.

LifeFX has created software (LifeFX facemail™) that adds a human face to standard e-mail communications. Companies can create virtual representatives for sales, service, guides and spokespeople. Motorola, Sprint, Kodak and IBM have recently entered negotiations with LifeFX to produce software agents (Mirror Image, 2001).

More companies use e-mail than any other form of communication via the Internet. Bill Clausen, Chief Marketing Officer of LifeFX, states, 'As we provide a growing number of consumers with a more human interface for personal communications over the Internet, it is important that we get our LifeFX facemail software to users without delay'. LifeFX facemail offers the opportunity to add a 'fun, entertaining and easy-to-use way for consumers to add expression to email communication'; additionally, the software allows users to input their own recorded voice (Mirror Image, 2001).

Questions

1 At which of the following points in the personal selling process could 'facemail' replace a human sales representative:
- prospective stage whereby the seller seeks out the buyer;
- evaluation of customer needs, expectations and requirements;
- delivery of the sales messages;
- negotiation of the terms of the sale;
- determining any after-sales support requirements?

2 For each stage of the sales process explain the potential advantages of using 'facemail' as part of an organisation's promotional strategy.

Organisational markets

The nature of the markets in which business-to-business commerce takes place was the second key theme highlighted at the beginning of the chapter as being important to consider. According to Jobber (2001) there are three main types of organisational markets:

1 industrial;
2 reseller;
3 government.

These different markets will now be examined to establish the nature of the markets in terms of the goods and services involved in market exchanges and the impact and uptake of Internet technologies.

● Industrial markets

The economic activities a company engages in allow it to be classified using Standard Industry Codes that facilitate statistical analysis (at a government level) and common activity structures (for non-governmental administrational purposes).

Standard Industry Codes, first introduced in 1948, are regularly updated to reflect changes over time to accommodate new products and new industries. SIC UK are integrated into European and international coding to ensure consistency in classification of organisations by activity (Central Statistical Office, 1992). All types of organisations, even wholesaling and retailing, are referred to by SICs.

Our discussion of industrial markets (from the marketing context) refers to organisations that come under the SIC headings:

● Agriculture and hunting and forestry;
● Fishing;
● Manufacturing: fuel processing and production, chemicals and man-made fibre, metal goods, engineering and vehicles industry and other manufacturing;
● Electricity and gas supply;
● Construction.

Some of the manufacturing sectors are dominated by a small number of very large companies, particularly those which require major capital funding and investment, e.g. ship building and the manufacture of chemicals. Additionally, in the case of extraction industries and those relying on specific raw materials, they can be aggregated together in geographical regions. However, other manufactures can be quite numerous, small in size and widely dispersed, e.g. specialist engineering companies, livestock farmers.

Impact and uptake of Internet technologies

Examples abound of how industrial organisations have utilised the Internet at different stages in the supply chain (see Figure 11.6). Doherty et al. (1999) suggest that there are key stages to Internet adoption. An organisation will begin by establishing its intention to use Internet technologies; then there will be an initial developmental period, prior to implementation. Implementation can involve adoption of a wide range of Internet technologies and Web-based applications (as discussed earlier in this chapter). The Web-based applications will be used to create either information-focused or interactive (including marketing-communication, two-way interaction and exchange transactions) web sites.

Figure 11.6 Solar Turbines – a Caterpillar company

Solar Turbines web site (http://esolar.cat.com/solar/main/1,1455,7_1003_10090-10140,00.html http)

In the case of industrial companies web sites can be used to provide buyers with a high level of specific product information (see Figure 11.6).

Another example is the case of the world's train manufacturers, where there are just five key companies. The fact that there are very few is significant from a market research point of view. To provide potential and existing clients with information, each manufacturer will publish information about new contracts, new products and testimonials from existing customers. This information will also be of great interest to competitors. The Web provides a means of finding such information more rapidly and tends to give greater depth of information than other sources. This has led companies to employ staff specifically to find and summarise information from competitors. Therefore it is important to strike a careful balance between disclosing too much information (for competitors) and not enough (for customers). This problem has largely been overcome by the use of password- and firewall-protected extranets (see Chapter 1 for further details).

Trading communities and specialist e-market portals have been developed that bring together many suppliers in a particular marketplace. Newview Technologies (formerly e-steel) allows buyers and sellers of steel to transact business with each other in a personalised and secure environment. These are not isolated examples as Internet uptake in industrial markets is quite high.

● Reseller markets

Organisations in these markets buy products and services in order to resell them. Under the SIC systems these types of organisations include:

Table 11.3 Levels of uptake of the Internet by country

Country	Online marketing rank	Online transactions (invoicing) rank	Online transactions (payments) rank
Canada	4 (55%)	1 (30%)	2 (21%)
France	7 (34%)	8 (8%)	7 (7%)
Germany	3 (57%)	6 (11%)	4 (20%)
Italy	6 (42%)	4 (11%)	6 (10%)
Japan	8 (22%)	6 (9%)	8 (6%)
Sweden	5 (52%)	4 (11%)	3 (23%)
UK	1 (61%)	3 (14%)	1 (28%)
USA	2 (58%)	2 (29%)	5 (19%)

Source: DTI (2000)

The study does not classify companies by industrial activities, but in this instance provides broad insight into online purchasing.

- Wholesale and retail trade;
- Repair of motor vehicles, motor cycles, household and personal goods, hotels and restaurants;
- Transport, storage and communications;
- Financial institutions;
- Estate agents and letting.

This covers a very diverse collection of organisations where company size and market-sector structures vary considerably. The UK Department of Trade and Industry commissioned a benchmarking study aimed at measuring the UK's performance against other benchmarked countries in order to establish the UK's progress in the information age (DTI, 2000) and investigate levels of Internet uptake across eight different countries. Table 11.3 shows the results of part of the study looking at supplier-facing Web-based activities. The results of this study help to show levels of Internet uptake in terms of stage of development.

It has been suggested (DTI, 2000; Doherty et al., 1999) that the use of the Web for online marketing (information-based only) signifies an early stage of Internet adoption; Table 11.3 suggests that companies in the UK, USA, Germany, Canada and Sweden are at the forefront of Internet adoption and that half the nations' businesses have developed an Internet presence. However, the percentages of companies that have developed more sophisticated Web operations involving actual transactions and by definition are involved in commerce online are much lower, e.g. evidence of both online invoicing and payment being around 30% of all companies surveyed. It should be noted that reseller markets are discussed in more detail in Chapter 9.

● Government markets

These consist of government agencies and bodies that buy goods and services that are required to carry out specific functions and provide particular services. Governments control vast funds of public money generated from direct and indirect taxation. In many instances, purchasing requirements exceed those of large private commercial organisations. Under the SIC system the types of organisations include:

- Public administration;
- Education;

- Health services;
- Other community, social and personal services activities.

The UK government is committed to modernising public services and is looking towards the Internet and the Web to achieve many of its aims. In broad terms, the government has set 'a target that 100% of government services should be capable of being delivered online by 2005. Government departments have developed e-business strategies (see e-envoy Web link) to ensure this target is met'. More specifically, the aims are to develop new service delivery channels and the 'elimination of paper trails'.

The focus on e-business permeates all aspects of UK government (see Mini Case Study 11.4). D. Court, Chief Executive of the Northern Ireland Purchasing Agency, reports that substantial changes to procurement in commercial markets have demonstrated how adoption of Internet technologies can improve communications

---

Mini Case Study 11.4

NHS Purchasing and Supply Agency

The National Health Service Purchasing Agency works with around 400 NHS trusts and health authorities and manages 3000 national purchasing contracts. The NHS spends approximately £11 billion per annum on purchasing goods and services for the health service.

The aim is for the Agency to develop and implement an e-commerce strategy that will:

- embrace and integrate all business processes from 'demand' through to payment;
- embrace all key players in the NHS supply environment;
- expect the NHS to 'act' on a once only basis in programme design and application;
- change the function of purchasing from transactional to strategic.

It is envisaged that on satisfaction of the above aims sourcing, display of products and prices and ordering of goods and transacting with suppliers will all be done electronically. Additional expectations are that when the e-commerce strategy is fully implemented there will be systems that can offer facilities for budgeting and planning, reporting and control, demand forecasting and more focused strategic analysis.

The scope of the e-commerce operation is to include all the NHS's primary, secondary and tertiary suppliers into a trading network. The size of the network will be extensive but will primarily focus on business-to-business trading relationships, not trading relationships with the general public (business-to-consumer).

The anticipated advantages of implementing this project are that it will:

- improve efficiency by streamlining transactional processes with suppliers. This will be achieved by automating manual processes, enhancing control mechanisms, optimising procurement practices, standardising and sharing procedures and information in a coherent and consistent manner;
- provide opportunities to obtain greater leverage over prices by aggregating demand for goods and services across the network;
- improve levels of transparency

It is also anticipated that both the NHS and their suppliers will benefit from successful implementation of the e-commerce strategy.

Source: NHS Purchasing and Supply E-Commerce Strategy for the NHS document.

and reduce process and transaction costs. Public-sector purchasing departments have been quick to respond. In Northern Ireland an e-procurement system for the public service has already been established. 'Much of the Agency's ability to advance its electronic commerce systems derives from its success in being awarded funds from the government's Invest to Save Budget for the specific purpose of developing a purchasing system to take forward the use of Internet technology' (Court, 2001).

The UK government is highly committed to being at the forefront of the information age. In the past, prior to the commercial exploitation of the Internet the French government made a significant commitment towards electronic trading in the form of the Télétel project, which created benefits for consumers and stimulated a new trading format for businesses. However, the long-term strategic advantage of this project is now being brought into question as a result of the expansion of the Internet (see Chapter 9). It is possible that in the future, current Internet procurement strategies will also be overtaken.

● E-markets

Currently the NHS is planning on developing a private trading network for itself and its suppliers. Whether that remains the model for the future is not currently relevant but it is important for a business to consider the type of trading network it will use to develop the transactional part of its e-commerce activities. There are already a number of specialist portals that have been created for particular industries (see techsavvy.com and Chapter 2). But there are still more business sectors that are debating whether they should join established global trading networks (GTN) such as the one created by CommerceOne. The main proposition for this e-marketplace is that it brings together many buyers and many suppliers and in doing so increases the value of the market as new suppliers and new buyers make new trading connections. CommerceOne is eager for e-markets to operate on a global scale, which is achieved by linking together e-marketplaces around the globe. For companies to benefit from access to a global system of e-markets they must be able to resolve any problems they may have with their international fulfilment systems. They will also need to have interoperable payment systems and product catalogues, if new trading links are to be successfully established. Interoperability and open trading will inhibit progress for some organisations because of the nature of the products they sell. The music business is currently experiencing tremendous difficulties associated with the pirating of music in the portable MP3 format. As a result they are unlikely to wish to trade on such an open platform. Indeed, it is likely that major music companies will create their own digital distribution networks, in order to protect the product and perhaps more importantly the price of the product.

In summary, Internet technologies have created a dynamic online trading environment and those organisations that are managed by far-sighted management teams have seized the opportunity to exploit the new business environment and have secured competitive advantage by being the first to offer a particular innovative online service. Other organisations have not reacted positively and could fall behind as their management teams lack the required experience or vision of the future to embrace the Internet fully. It has been said that Europe is significantly behind the USA in terms of Internet adoption and innovation. However, the majority of large organisations in Europe have at least established a marketing web site and smaller organisations are quickly catching up – except in the UK where the growth rate is comparatively slow even with a major government initiative aimed at encouraging e-commerce development amongst SMEs.

E-marketing strategies

The final key theme is the strategy of definition of the aims and objectives of a company's buying and selling activities. It is not the aim of this section to revisit the process of planning online marketing strategies (which has been discussed in Chapter 4), but to consider how practice in Internet adoption is affecting the focus of e-marketing strategies in business-to-business sectors.

It is perhaps reasonable to suggest that organisations are reconsidering the e-commerce proposition in the light of the boom-and-bust dot-com era. Indeed, there is a good deal of emphasis currently being placed on the supply-side of e-commerce strategies. Streamlining of procurement systems through the use of Internet technologies can make significant cost reductions, which can produce useful financial benefits. Furthermore, organisations operating in business-to-business sectors are better placed to implement such systems than the business-to-consumer organisations because they are:

- familiar with the use of the similar techniques of EDI (although this was beyond the reach of many SMEs);
- under pressure to trade using e-commerce as often major customers such as supermarkets may stipulate that their suppliers must use e-commerce for reasons of efficiency and cost. Alternatively, if a company's products are not available direct on the Internet then the company may lose sales to other companies whose products are available;
- usually involved in long-term relationships, making it more worthwhile to set up links between business partners;
- more likely to be involved in a greater volume of transactions, thereby justifying the initial outlay required to develop the Internet-based systems.

It is possible that in the next few years the focus of e-commerce development will be on (1) online purchasing strategies and (2) international fulfilment solutions, which is rather different from the focus at the end of the 1990s when online businesses were being established to drive the sell-side of online commerce (particularly in consumer markets).

One final consideration of the wider impact of the adoption of Internet technologies on e-marketing strategies is the extent to which relationships between buyers and suppliers will become much more transactionally focused.

Exploratory research into the uptake of Internet technologies in the financial-services sector in three European countries (Ellis-Chadwick et al., 2002) has found evidence to suggest that some financial organisations are focusing on high levels of human contact during the service encounter whereas others are not. Furthermore, the companies that do not offer high levels of human contact during the service encounter are those that are investing heavily in Internet-based systems. The key suggestion is that the extent to which an organisation moves its operations online will determine the extent to which the relationship becomes 'transactional' or 'relational'. This is shown in diagrammatic form in Figure 11.7. This matrix shows possible choices for an organisation trying to determine the extent to which it might integrate Internet technologies into its operations.

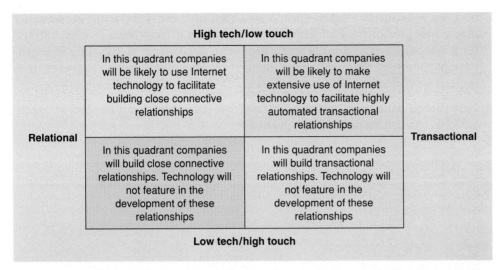

Figure 11.7 Company approaches towards use of Internet technology and human relationships

Summary

1 Business-to-business marketing via the Internet needs to be approached differently from business-to-consumer marketing. Some of the key differences are:
  - The buying decision is often complex and involves different groups of people, depending upon the type of purchase. Information providing the appropriate level of detail should be made available via the Internet and the Web. Features should be included that facilitate purchasing decisions, e.g. Cisco Systems customer service support mechanism.
  - The sales process in business-to-business markets is traditionally dominated by personal selling, which involves a high level of personal contact. However, in routine purchasing situations Internet technologies are increasingly being used to automate the process. Innovative solutions are also being developed that could provide 'digital sales agents', which could reduce the extent to which a human sales force is required.
  - The impact of increased integration of Internet technologies into the buying and selling sides of an organisation's activities could cause a shift in the orientation of the relationship away from the 'relational' towards the 'transactional'. Any such change of emphasis is likely to have an impact on marketing communication strategies.
  - Despite the fact that business-to-business market structures tend to have fewer customers placing larger orders (especially in industrial and government markets) adoption of Internet technologies represents opportunities to streamline purchasing and sales operations and in doing so enables an organisation to make significant cost savings. Furthermore, there are also opportunities to create additional value and competitive advantage through the redesign of established offline practices.

2 There is now a high level of basic Internet use in business-to-business markets. Organisations need to consider using the Internet beyond their marketing communication activities and investigate ways to integrate Internet technologies into the core of their business operations. Large organisations operating in

business-to-business markets should be ahead of those in business-to-consumer markets as previous use of technology such as EDI have been well established for a number of years. For the small and micro-sized business operating in organisational markets there are many barriers to be broken down. However, it is imperative that such issues be addressed.

3 Case studies have been used to illustrate how the Internet can be used in organisational markets to use valued advantages.

EXERCISES

Self-assessment exercises

1 Summarise how a business might employ the Internet and the World Wide Web to assist buyers at different stages of the procurement cycle.

2 How does business-to-business marketing on the Internet differ from business-to-consumer marketing?

3 What are the implications of wide-scale adoption of the Internet in organisational markets?

4 To what extent can Internet technologies replace a human sales representative?

5 Explain the meaning of the term 'e-commerce' and its role in organisational markets.

Essay and discussion questions

1 Discuss why a business operating in an industrial market might be cautious about putting new product specifications on the company web site.

2 Discuss the likelihood of organisations in government markets totally automating all of their agencies' buying and selling activities.

3 Consider the extent to which e-procurement is a valid business model.

4 Explain the difference between transactional and marketing information web sites.

Examination question

1 Jack and Harry run an organic farm in the Yorkshire Dales, which produces high-quality specialist lettuces. It is a small but very profitable business which does not make any use of the Internet or computer technology. As a Web consultant, suggest how Jack and Harry might benefit from investment in:
   a. a web site containing marketing information;
   b. a transactional web site.

References

Bagozzi, R. (1978) Marketing as exchange: a theory of transactions in the market place, *American Behavioral Science*, 21(4), 257–61.

Bicknell, C. (2000) Bankruptcy Lawyers Smell Blood, *Wired*. The Condé Nast Publications.

Blenkhorn, D.L. and Banting, P.M. (1991) How reverse marketing changes buyer–seller's roles, *Industrial Marketing Management*, 20(6), 185–91.

Central Statistical Office (1992) *Introduction to Standard Industrial Classification of Economic Activities SIC(92)*. CSO Publications, London.

Chambers (1991) *Chambers Concise Dictionary*. Chambers, Edinburgh.

Court, D. (2001) *The Fourth Annual Report and Accounts of the Government Purchasing Agency*. www.gpa-ni.gov.uk.

Croom, S. (2001) Restructuring supply chains through information channel innovation, *International Journal of Operations and Production Management*, 21(4), 504.

Doherty, N.F., Ellis-Chadwick, F.E. and Hart, C.A., (1999) Cyber retailing in the UK: the potential of the Internet as a retail channel, *International Journal of Retail and Distribution Management*, 27(1), 22–36.

DTI (2000) *Business in the Information Age: A Benchmarking Study*. Queen's Printer and Controller, HMSO.

Dwyer, R., Schurr, P. and Oh, S. (1987) Developing buyer–seller relationships, *Journal of Marketing*, 51 (April), 11–27.

Ellis-Chadwick, F.E. and Doherty, N.F. (2001) The uptake and application of e-commerce within the brewery sector: an empirical analysis, *Constructing IS Futures*, R. Hackney (ed.). Manchester Metropolitan University, 11th Annual Business Information Technology Conference, Manchester (CD-ROM).

Ellis-Chadwick, F.E., McHardy, P. and Wiesehofer, H. (2002) Online customer relationships in the European financial services sector: a cross-country investigation, *International Journal of Financial Services Marketing*, 6(4).

e-marketers (2001) UK leads European Online Ad Market (27 Aug). www.emarketer.com/estatnews.

Fill, C. (2002) *Marketing Communications: Context, Strategies and Applications*. Prentice Hall.

Flatt, S. and Cooper, D. (2000) Performance Excellence: Caught in the Web. www2.tntech.edu/mayberry/2000N-caught.htm#_edn1.

Gates, B. (1999) Speech to students at London Business School, March.

Gattiker, U.E., Perlusz, S. and Bohmann, K. (2000) Using the Internet for B2B activities: a review and further direction for research, *Internet Research Electronic Networking Application and Policy*, 10(2), 126–40.

Herskind, K. (2002) Online signatures need greater authority, *Revolution*, 16 January.

Jobber, D. (2001) *Principle of Marketing*, 3rd edn. McGraw-Hill.

Jupiter Communications and Media Metrix (2000) www.jup.com/company/pressrelease.jsp?doc=pr000817.

Kalakota, R. and Robinson, M. (2000) *E-Business Roadmap for Success*. Addison-Wesley, Reading, MA.

Leenders, M.R. and Blenkhorn, D.L. (1988) *Reverse Marketing: The New Buyer–Supplier Relationship*. Free Press, New York.

Malone, T.W., Yates, J. and Benjamin, R.I. (1987) Electronic markets and electronic hierarchies, *Communications of the ACM*, 30(6), 484–96.

Mirror Image (2001) www.mirror-image.com/news/pressrelease.cfm?news_item_id=326: LifeFX teams with Mirror Image to further enhance consumers' positive experience, *instaContent Global Distribution Service Optimizes Downloads of LifeFX's Revolutionary Software*. Woburn, MA, 10 July.

Porter, M. (1985) *Competitive Advantage*. Free Press, New York.

Seybold, P. (1999) *Customer.com*. Century Business Books, Random House, London.

Sparrow, A. (2000) *E-Commerce and the Law: The Legal Implications of Doing Business Online*. Financial Times/Prentice Hall, Harlow.

Symonds, M. (1999) The Net Imperative, *The Economist*, 26 July.

Tapscott, D. (1997) *Growing Up Digital*. McGraw-Hill, New York.

Taylor Nelson Sofres, www.nua.com/surveys/index.cgi?f=VS&art_id=905357707&rel=true (access date, February 2002).

Timmers, P. (2000) *Electronic Commerce Strategies and Business to Business Trading*. Wiley, Chichester.

Turnbull, P.W. (1999) Business-to-Business Marketing: Organizational Buying Behaviour, Relationships and Networks in Baker, M. (ed.) *The Marketing Book* (4th edn.). Butterworth-Heinemann.

Vandermerwe, S. (1993) *From Tin Soldiers to Russian Dolls: Creating Value through Services*, Butterworth Heinemann, Oxford.

Webster, F.E. and Wind, Y. (1992) *Organizational Buyer Behaviour*. Prentice Hall, Englewood Cliffs, NJ, 78–80.

Further reading

Baker, M. (ed.) (1999) *The Marketing Book*. Butterworth Heinemann, Oxford: Chapter 6, Business-to-business marketing: organisational buying behaviour, relationships and networks by Peter Turnbull, is recommended.

Jobber, D. (2001) *Principle of Marketing*, 3rd edn. McGraw-Hill.

Kotler, P., Armstrong, G., Saunders, J. and Wong, V. (1999) *Principles of Marketing*. Prentice Hall Europe, Hemel Hempstead. *See* companion Prentice Hall web site for 8th US edition (cw.prenhall.com/bookbind/pubbooks/kotler). *See* Chapter 7, Business markets and business buyer behaviour.

Leonidou, K. (1995) Export barriers: non-exporters' perceptions, *International Marketing Review*, 12(1), 4–25.

Web links

- Ecommerce Awards 2001 www.ecommerce-awards.co.uk/cases/2001/case12.php.
- Newview Technologies www.newview.com/home.shtml
- Modernising Government, 1999 www.cabinet-office.gov.uk/moderngov/whtpaper/summary.htm.
- E-envoy http://www.e-envoy.gov.uk/ egov/online_now/ebusiness_strategies/estrats.htm
- SIC http://qb.soc.surrey.ac.uk/resources/classification/sic92.pdf

Glossary

A

Above the fold A term, derived from printed media, which is used to indicate whether a **banner advertisement** or other content is displayed on a web page without the need to scroll. This is likely to give higher **clickthrough**, but note that the location of the 'fold' within the web browser is dependent on the screen resolution of a user's personal computer.

Access platform A method for customers to access digital media.

Access provider A company providing services to enable a company or individual to access the **Internet**. Access providers are divided into **Internet service providers (ISPs)** and **online service providers (OSPs)**.

Acquisition *See* **Customer acquisition**.

Active Server Page (ASP) A type of **HTML** page (denoted by an .asp file name) that includes **scripts** (small programs) that are processed on a **web server** before the web page is served to the user's **web browser**. ASP is a Microsoft technology that usually runs on a **Microsoft Internet Information Server** (usually on Windows NT). The main use of such pro-grams is to process information supplied by the user in an online **form**. A query may then be run to provide specific information to the customer such as delivery status on an order, or a personalised web page.

ActiveX A programming language standard developed by Microsoft, which permits complex and graphical customer applications to be written and then accessed from a **web browser**. ActiveX components are standard controls that can be incorporated into web sites and are then automatically **downloaded** for users. Examples are graphics and animation or a calculator form for calculating interest on a loan or a control for graphing stock prices. A competitor to **Java**.

Ad creative The design and content of an ad.

Ad impression Similar in concept to a **page impression**; describes one viewing of an advertisement by a single member of its audience. The same as **ad view**, a term that is less commonly used.

Ad inventory The total number of **ad impressions** that a **web site** can sell over time (usually specified per month).

Ad rotation When advertisements are changed on a **web site** for different user sessions. This may be in response to ad **targeting** or simply displaying different advertisements from those on a list.

Ad serving The term for displaying an advertisement on a **web site**. Often the advertisement will be served from a different **web server** from the site on which it is placed. For example, the URL for displaying the advertisement is http://ad.doubleclick.net.

Ad space The area of a web page that is set aside for **banner advertising**.

Ad view Similar in concept to a **page impression**; describes one viewing of an advertisement by a single member of its audience. The same as **ad impression**, the term that is more commonly used.

Advertisement Advertisements on **web sites** are usually **banner advertisements** positioned as a masthead on the page.

Advertising broker *See* **Media broker**.

Advertising networks A collection of independent **web sites** of different companies and media networks, each of which has an arrangement with a single advertising broker (*see* **Media broker**) to place **banner advertisements**.

Affiliate networks A reciprocal arrangement between a company and third-party sites where traffic is directed to the company from third-party sites through **banner advertisements** and links and incentives. In return for linking to the **destination site** the third-party site will typically receive a proportion of any resulting sale.

Agents Software programs that can assist people to perform tasks such as finding particular information such as the best price for a product.

Aggregated buying A form of customer union where buyers collectively purchase a number of items at the same price and receive a volume discount.

Analysis phase The identification of the requirements of a **web site**. Techniques to achieve this may include **focus groups**, questionnaires sent with existing customers or interviews with key accounts.

Animated banner advertisements (animated GIFs) Early **banner advertisements** featured only a single advertisement, but today they will typically involve several different images, which are displayed in sequence to help to attract attention to the banner and build up a theme, often ending with a call to action and the injunction to click on the banner. These advertisements are achieved through supplying the **ad creative** as an animated **GIF** file with different layers or frames, usually a rectangle of 468 by 60 **pixels**. Animated banner advertisements are an example of **rich media advertisements**.

Announcements *See* **Site announcements**.

Archie A database containing information on what documents and programs are located on **FTP** servers. It would not be used in a marketing context unless one were looking for a specific piece of software or document name.

Asymmetric encryption Both parties use a related but different key to encode and decode messages.

Attrition rate Percentage of site visitors that are lost at each stage in making a purchase.

Audit (external) Consideration of the business and economic environment in which the company operates. This includes the economic, political, fiscal, legal, social, cultural and technological factors (usually referred to by the acronym **STEP**).

Audit (internal) A review of **web site** effectiveness.

Auditors *See* **Site auditors**.

Authentication *See* **Security methods**.

Autoresponders Software tools or **agents** running on **web servers**, which automatically send a standard reply to the sender of an **e-mail** message. This may provide information to a standard request sent to, say, price_list@company_name.com, or it could simply state that the message or order has been forwarded to the relevant person and will be answered within two days. (Also known as mailbots.)

Availability *See* **Security methods**; **Site availability**.

Avatar A term used in computer-mediated environments to mean a 'virtual person'. Derived from the word's original meaning: '*n*. the descendant of a Hindu deity in a visible form; incarnation; supreme glorification of any principle'.

Backbones High-speed communications links used to enable Internet communications across a country and internationally.

Bandwidth Indicates the speed at which data are transferred using a particular network medium. It is measured in bits per second (bps).
kbps (one kilobit per second or 1000 bps; a modem operates at up to 56.6 kbps).

Mbps (one megabit per second or 1 000 000 bps; company networks operate at 10 or more Mbps). Gbps (one gigabit per second or 1 000 000 000 bps; fibre-optic or satellite links operate at Gbps).

Banner advertisement A typically rectangular graphic displayed on a web page for purposes of brand building or driving traffic to a site. It is normally possible to perform a **clickthrough** to access further information from another **web site**. Banners may be static or animated (*see* **Animated banner advertisements**).

Behavioural traits of web users Web users can be broadly divided into **directed** and **undirected information seekers**.

Bid A commitment by a trader to purchase under certain conditions.

Brand The sum of the characteristics of a product or service perceived by a user.

Brand equity The brand assets (or liabilities) linked to a brand's name and symbol that add to (or subtract from) a service.

Brand identity The totality of brand associations including name and symbols that must be communicated.

Branding The process of creating and evolving successful brands.

Bricks and mortar A traditional organisation with limited online presence.

Broadband technology A term referring to methods of delivering information across the **Internet** at a higher rate by increasing **bandwidth**.

Brochureware A **web site** in which a company has simply transferred ('migrated') its existing paper-based promotional literature on to the **Internet** without recognising the differences required by this medium.

Broker *See* **Media broker**.

Browser *See* **Web browser**.

Business model A summary of how a company will generate revenue, identifying its product offering, value-added services, revenue sources and target customers.

Business-to-business (B2B) Commercial transactions between an organisation and other organisations (inter-organisational marketing).

Business-to-business exchanges or marketplaces Virtual intermediaries with facilities to enable trading between buyers and sellers.

Business-to-consumer (B2C) Commercial transactions between an organisation and consumers.

Buy-side e-commerce E-commerce transactions between a purchasing organisation and its suppliers.

Call centre A location for **inbound** and **outbound telemarketing**.

Callback service A direct response facility available on a **web site** to enable a company to contact a customer by phone at a later time as specified by the customer.

Catalogue Catalogues provide a structured listing of registered **web sites** in different categories. They are similar to an electronic version of *Yellow Pages*. Yahoo! and Excite are the best known examples of catalogues. (Also known as **directories**.)

The distinction between **search engines** and catalogues has become blurred since many sites now include both facilities as part of a **portal** service.

Certificate A valid copy of a **public key** of an individual or organisation together with identification information. It is issued by a **trusted third party (TTP)** or **certification authority (CA)**.

Certification authority (CA) An organisation issuing and managing **certificates** or **public keys** and private keys to individuals or organisations together with identification information.

Channel behaviour Describes which content is visited and the time and duration.

Channel conflicts A significant threat arising from the introduction of an **Internet** channel is that while **disintermediation** gives the opportunity for a company to sell direct and increase the profitability of products it can also threaten existing distribution arrangements with existing partners.

Channel outcomes Records customer actions taken as a consequence of a visit to a site.

Channel profitability The profitability of the web site, taking into account revenue and cost and discounted cash flow.

Channel promotion Measures assess why customers visit a site – which adverts have they seen, which sites have they been referred from.

Channel satisfaction Evaluation of the customer's opinion of the service quality on the site and supporting services such as e-mail.

'Clicks and mortar' A business combining online and offline presence.

Clicks-only or Internet pureplay An organisation with principally an online presence.

Click-stream A record of the path a user takes through a **web site**. Click-streams enable **web site** designers to assess how their site is being used.

Clickthrough A clickthrough (ad click) occurs each time a user clicks on a **banner advertisement** with the mouse to direct them to a web page that contains further information.

Clickthrough rate Expressed as a percentage of total **ad impressions**, and refers to the proportion of users viewing an advertisement who click on it. It is calculated as the number of clickthroughs divided by the number of **ad impressions**.

Click-tracking **Java** technology can be used to track movements of individual users to a **web site**.

Client–server The client–server architecture consists of client computers such as PCs sharing resources such as a database stored on a more powerful server computer.

Co-branding An arrangement between two or more companies where they agree to jointly display content and perform joint promotion using brand logos or **banner advertisements**. The aim is that the brands are strengthened if they are seen as complementary. This is a reciprocal arrangement, which can occur without payment.

Collaborative filtering Profiling of customer interest coupled with delivery of specific information and offers, often based on the interests of similar customers.

Commoditisation The process whereby product selection becomes more dependent on price than differentiating features, benefits and value-added services.

Common Gateway Interface (CGI) A method of processing information on a **web server** in response to a customer's request. Typically a user will fill in a Web-based **form** and the results will be processed by a CGI script (application). **Active Server Pages (ASP)** are an alternative to a CGI script.

Competitive intelligence (CI) A process that transforms disaggregated information into relevant, accurate and usable strategic knowledge about competitors, position, performance, capabilities and intentions.

Competitor analysis Review of Internet marketing services offered by existing and new competitors and adoption by their customers.

Computer telephony integration The integration of telephony and computing to provide a platform for applications that streamline or enhance business processes.

Confidentiality *See* **Security methods**.

Consumer-to-business (C2B) Consumers approach the business with an offer.

Consumer-to-consumer (C2C) Informational or financial transactions between consumers, but usually mediated through a business site.

Content Content is the design, text and graphical information that forms a web page. Good content is the key to attracting customers to a **web site** and retaining their interest or achieving repeat visits.

Content management Software tools for managing additions and amendments to web site content.

Convergence A trend in which different hardware devices such as televisions, computers and telephones merge and have similar functions.

Conversion marketing Using marketing communications to maximise conversion of potential customers to actual customers.

Conversion rate Proportion of visitors to a site, or viewers of an advert, who take an action.

Cookies Cookies are small text files stored on an end-user's computer to enable **web sites** to identify the user. They enable a company to identify a previous visitor to a site, and build up a profile of that visitor's behaviour.

Core product The fundamental features of the product that meet the users' needs.

Core tenants A shopping centre or mall is usually a centrally owned managed facility. In the physical world, the management will aim to include in the mall stores that sell a different but complementary range of merchandise and include a variety of smaller and larger stores. The core tenants or 'anchor stores' as they are often called are the dominant large-scale store operators that are expected to draw customers to the centre.

Cost models for Internet advertising These include per-exposure, per-response and per-action costs.

Cost per mille (CPM) Cost per 1000 **ad impressions**.

Cost per targeted mille (CPTM) Cost per targeted thousand for an advertisement. (*See also* **Targeting**.)

Countermediation Creation of a new intermediary by an established company.

Customer acquisition Techniques used to gain new customers.

Customer extension Techniques to encourage customers to increase their involvement with an organisation.

Customer lifecycle The stages each customer will pass through in a long-term relationship through acquisition, retention and extension.

Customer orientation Providing content and services on a **web site** consistent with the different characteristics of the audience of the site.

Customer profiling Using the web site to find out customers' specific interests and characteristics.

Customer relationship management (CRM) A marketing-led approach to building and sustaining long-term business with customers.

Customer retention Techniques to maintain relationships with existing customers.

Customer selection Identifying key customer segments and targeting them for relationship building.

Cybermediaries **Intermediaries** who bring together buyers and sellers or those with particular information or service needs.

Cyberspace and cybermarketing These terms were preferred by science-fiction writers and tabloid writers to indicate the futuristic nature of using the Internet, the prefix 'cyber' indicating a blurring between humans, machines and communications. The terms are not frequently used today since the terms **Internet**, **intranet** and **World Wide Web** are more specific and widely used.

Data fusion The combining of data from different complementary sources (usually geodemographic and lifestyle or market research and lifestyle) to 'build a picture of someone's life' (M. Evans (1998) From 1086 to 1984: direct marketing into the millennium, *Marketing Intelligence and Planning*, 16(1), 56–67).

Data warehousing and data mining Extracting data from legacy systems and other resources; cleaning, scrubbing and preparing data for decision support; maintaining data in appropriate data stores; accessing and analysing data using a variety of end-user tools; and mining data for significant relationships. The primary purpose of these efforts is to provide easy access to specially prepared data that can be used with decision support applications such as management reports, queries, decision support systems, executive information systems and data mining.

Database marketing The process of systematically collecting, in electronic or optical form, data about past, current and/or potential customers, maintaining the integrity of the data by continually monitoring customer purchases, by enquiring about changing status, and by using the data to formulate marketing strategy and foster personalised relationships with customers.

Decryption The process of decoding (unscrambling) a message that has been encrypted using defined mathematical rules.

Deep linking Jakob Nielsen's term for a user arriving at a site deep within its structure or where search engines index a mirrored copy of content normally inaccessible by search engine **spiders**.

Demand analysis for e-commerce Assessment of the demand for e-commerce services amongst existing and potential customer segments using the ratio Access : Choose : Buy online.

Demographic characteristics Variations in attributes of the populations such as age, sex and social class.

Design phase (of site construction) The design phase defines how the site will work in the key areas of **web site** structure, **navigation** and **security**.

Destination site Frequently used to refer to the site that is visited following a **clickthrough** on a **banner advertisement**. Could also apply to any site visited following a click on a **hyperlink**.

Destination store A retail store in which the merchandise, selection, presentation, pricing or other unique features act as a magnet for the customer.

Development phase (of site construction) 'Development' is the term used to describe the creation of a **web site** by programmers. It involves writing the **HTML** content, creating graphics, writing any necessary software code such as **Java**Script or **ActiveX** (programming).

Differential advantage A desirable attribute of a product offering that is not currently matched by competitor offerings.

Differential pricing Identical products are priced differently for different types of customers, markets or buying situations.

Digital brand A digital brand is a brand identity used for a product or company online that differs from the traditional brand. (Also known as an online brand.)

Digital cash An electronic version of cash in which the buyer of an item is typically anonymous to the seller. (Also referred to as virtual or electronic cash or e-cash.)

Digital certificates (keys) A method of ensuring **privacy** on the **Internet**. **Certificates** consist of keys made up of large numbers that are used to uniquely identify individuals. *See also* **Public key**.

Digital signatures The electronic equivalent of written signatures which are used as an online method of identifying individuals or companies using **public-key encryption**.

Digital television Information is received and displayed on a digital television using binary information (0s and 1s), giving options for better picture and sound quality and providing additional information services based on interactivity. *See also* **Interactive digital TV**.

Direct marketing Marketing to customers using one or more advertising media aimed at achieving measurable response and/or transaction.

Direct response Usually achieved in an Internet marketing context by **callback services**.

Directed information seeker Someone who knows what information he or she is looking for.

Directories Directory **web sites** provide a structured listing of registered web sites in different categories. They are similar to an electronic version of *Yellow Pages*. Yahoo! and Excite are the best known examples of directories. (Also known as **catalogues**.)

Disintermediation The removal of **intermediaries** such as distributors or brokers that formerly linked a company to its customers. In particular, disintermediation enables a company to sell direct to the customer by cutting out the middleman.

Disruptive technologies New technologies that prompt businesses to reappraise their strategic approaches.

Domain name The **web address** that identifies a **web server**. *See* **Domain name system**.

Domain name registration The process of reserving a unique **web address** that can be used to refer to the company web site.

Domain name system The domain name system (DNS) provides a method of representing Internet Protocol (IP) addresses as text-based names. These are used as **web addresses**. For example, www.microsoft.com is the representation of site 207.68.156.58. Domain names are divided into the following categories:

● Top-level domain names such as *.com* or *.co.uk*. (Also known as **Global (or generic) top-level domain names (gLTD)**.)
● Second-level domain names. This refers to the company name and is sometimes referred to as the 'enterprise name', e.g. *novell.com*.

- Third-level or sub-enterprise domain names. This may be used to refer to an individual server within an organisation, such as *support.novell.com*.

Doorway pages Specially constructed pages which feature keywords for particular product searches. These often redirect visitors to a home page.

Download The process of retrieving electronic information such as a web page or **e-mail** from another remote location such as a **web server**.

Drip irrigation Collecting information about customer needs through their lifetime.

Dynamic pricing Prices can be updated in real time according to the type of customer or current market conditions.

Dynamic web page A page that is created in real time, often with reference to a database query, in response to a user request.

Early adopters Companies or departments that invest in new marketing techniques and technologies when they first become available in an attempt to gain a competitive advantage despite the higher risk entailed than that involved in a more cautious approach.

Early (first) mover advantage An early entrant into the marketplace has this advantage.

E-business *See* **Electronic business**.

E-cash *See* **Digital cash**.

E-commerce *See* **Electronic commerce**.

Effective frequency The number of exposures or **ad impressions** (frequency) required for an advertisement to become effective.

E-government The use of Internet technologies to provide government services to citizens.

Electronic business (e-business) All electronically mediated information exchanges, both within an organisation and with external stakeholders supporting the range of business processes.

Electronic cash *See* **Digital cash**.

Electronic commerce (e-commerce) All financial and informational electronically mediated exchanges between an organisation and its external stakeholders. (*See* **Buy-side e-commerce** and **Sell-side e-commerce**.)

Electronic commerce transactions Transactions in the trading of goods and services conducted using the Internet and other digital media.

Electronic data interchange (EDI) The exchange, using digital media, of standardised business documents such as purchase orders and invoices between buyers and sellers.

Electronic mail (e-mail) Sending messages or documents, such as news about a new product or sales promotion between individuals. A primitive form of **push** channel. E-mail may be **inbound** or **outbound**.

Electronic mail advertising Advertisements contained within e-mail such as newsletters.

Electronic mall *See* **Virtual mall**.

Electronic marketing Achieving marketing objectives through use of electronic communications technology.

Electronic marketspace A virtual marketplace such as the **Internet** in which no direct contact occurs between buyers and sellers.

Electronic Shopping or ES test This test was developed by de Kare-Silver to assess the extent to which consumers are likely to purchase a particular retail product using the **Internet**. (*See* **EShock**.)

Electronic tokens Units of digital currency that are in a standard electronic format.

E-marketing *See* **Electronic marketing**.

Emergent strategy Strategic analysis, strategic development and strategy implementation are interrelated and are developed together.

Encryption The scrambling of information into a form that cannot be interpreted. **Decryption** is used to make the information readable.

Enterprise application integration The middleware technology that is used to connect together different software applications and their underlying databases is now known as 'enterprise application integration (EAI)' (*Internet World*, 1999).

Entry page The page at which a visitor enters a **web site**. It is identified by a **log file analyser**. *See also* **Exit page** and **Referring site**.

Environmental scanning and analysis The process of continuously monitoring the environment and events and responding accordingly.

EShock Michael de Kare-Silver speculates in his 1998 book of this name (Basingstoke, UK: Macmillan) that by 2005–7 consumers using the **Internet** as their preferred method of making purchases will account for 15–20 per cent of total purchases. This will lead to ever-decreasing margins for retailers, who will be forced to close substantial parts of their retail networks.

Evaluating a web site *See* **Web site measurement**.

Exchange *See* **Business-to-business exchanges or marketplaces**.

Exit page The page from which a visitor exits a **web site**. It is identified by a **log file analyser**.

Exposure-based payment Advertisers pay according to the number of times the ad is viewed.

Extended product Additional features and benefits beyond the core product.

Extension *See* **Customer extension**.

Extranet An extranet is formed by extending the **intranet** beyond a company to customers, suppliers, collaborators or even competitors. This is password-protected to prevent access by general Internet users.

File Transfer Protocol (FTP) A standard method for moving files across the **Internet**. FTP is available as a feature of **web browsers** that is sometimes used for marketing applications such as **downloading** files such as product price lists or specifications. Standalone FTP packages such as WSFTP are commonly used to update **HTML** files on **web servers** when **uploading** revisions to the **web server**.

Firewall A specialised software application mounted on a server at the point where the company is connected to the Internet. Its purpose is to prevent unauthorised access into the company by outsiders. Firewalls are essential for all companies hosting their own **web server**.

Flow Describes a state in which users have a positive experience from readily controlling their **navigation** and interaction on a **web site**.

Focus groups Online focus groups have been conducted by w3focus.com. These follow a bulletin board or discussion group form where different members of the focus group respond to prompts from the focus group leaders.

Form A method on a web page of entering information such as order details.

Forward auctions Item purchased by highest bid made in bidding period.

Frame A technique used to divide a web page into different parts such as a menu and separate content.

Global (or generic) top-level domain names (gLTD) The part of the **domain name** that refers to the

category of site. The gLTD is usually the rightmost part of the domain name such as .co.uk or .com.

Globalisation The increase of international trading and shared social and cultural values.

Gopher Gopher is a directory-based structure containing information in certain categories.

Graphic design All factors that govern the physical appearance of a web page.

Graphics Interchange Format (GIF) GIF is a graphic format used to display images within web pages. An interlaced GIF is displayed gradually on the screen, building up an image in several passes.

Hit A hit is recorded for each graphic or block of text requested from a **web server**. It is not a reliable measure for the number of people viewing a page. A **page impression** is a more reliable measure denoting one person viewing one page.

Home page The index page of a **web site** with menu options or links to other resources on the site. Usually denoted by <web address>/index.html.

House list A list of prospect and customer names, e-mail addresses and profile information owned by an organisation.

HTML (Hypertext Markup Language) A standard format used to define the text and layout of web pages. HTML files usually have the extension .HTML or .HTM.

HTTP (Hypertext Transfer Protocol) A standard that defines the way information is transmitted across the **Internet**.

Hyperlink A method of moving between one web site page and another, indicated to the user by text highlighted by underlining and/or a different colour. Hyperlinks can also be achieved by clicking on a graphic image such as a **banner advertisement** that is linked to another **web site**.

Inbound e-mail **E-mail** arriving at a company.

Inbound customer contact strategies Approaches to managing the cost and quality of service related to management of customer enquiries.

Incidental offline advertising Driving traffic to the web site is not a primary objective of the advert.

Infomediary An **intermediary** business whose main source of revenue derives from capturing consumer information and developing detailed profiles of individual customers for use by third parties.

Information organisation schemes The structure chosen to group and categorise information.

Initiation of web site project This phase of the project should involve a structured review of the costs and benefits of developing a **web site** (or making a major revision to an existing web site). A successful outcome to initiation will be a decision to proceed with the site **development phase**, with an agreed budget and target completion date.

Insertion order A printed order to run an advertisement campaign. It defines the campaign name, the **web site** receiving the order and the planner or buyer giving the order, the individual advertisements to be run (or who will provide them), the sizes of the advertisements, the campaign beginning and end dates, the **CPM**, the total cost, discounts to be applied, and reporting requirements and possible penalties or stipulations relative to the failure to deliver the impressions.

Integrity *See* **Security methods**.

Interactive banner advertisement A **banner advertisement** that enables the user to enter information.

Interactive digital TV (iDTV) Television displayed using a digital signal delivered by a range of media – cable, satellite, terrestrial (aerial). Interactions can be provided through phone line or cable service.

Interactivity The medium enables a dialogue between company and customer.

Intermediaries Online sites that help bring together different parties such as buyers and sellers.

Interruption marketing Marketing communications that disrupt customers' activities.

Internet The physical network that links computers across the globe. It consists of the infrastructure of network servers and communication links between them, which are used to hold and transport the vast amount of information on the Internet. The Internet enables transfer of messages and transactions between connected computers worldwide.

Internet contribution An assessment of the extent to which the **Internet** contributes to sales is a key measure of the importance of the Internet to a company.

Internet EDI Use of electronic data interchange standards delivered across non-proprietary Internet Protocol networks.

Internet governance Control of the operation and use of the Internet.

Internet marketing The application of the Internet and related digital technologies to achieve marketing objectives.

Internet marketing metrics *See* **Metrics for Internet marketing**.

Internet marketing strategy Definition of the approach by which Internet marketing will support marketing and business objectives.

Internet pureplay An organisation with the majority of its customer-facing operations online, e.g. Egg.

Internet Relay Chat (IRC) A communications tool that allows a text-based 'chat' between different users who are logged on at the same time. Of limited use for marketing purposes except for special-interest or youth products.

Internet service providers (ISPs) Companies that provide home or business users with a connection to access the Internet. They can also host **web sites** or provide a link from **web servers** to enable other companies and consumers access to a corporate web site.

Interstitial ads Ads that appear between one page and the next.

Intranet A network within a single company that enables access to company information using the familiar tools of the **Internet** such as **web browsers** and **e-mail**. Only staff within a company can access the intranet, which will be password-protected.

Java A programming language standard supported by Sun Microsystems, which permits complex and graphical customer applications to be written and then accessed from a **web browser**. An example might be a form for calculating interest on a loan. A competitor to **ActiveX**.

Joint Photographic Experts Group (JPEG) A compressed graphics standard specified by the JPEG. Used for graphic images typically requiring use of many colours, such as product photographs where some loss of quality is acceptable. The format allows for some degradation in image quality to enable more rapid download.

Lead Details about a potential customer (prospect). (*See* **Qualified lead**.)

Lead generation offers Offered in return for customers providing their contact details and characteristics. Commonly used in B2B marketing where free information such as a report or a seminar will be offered.

List broker Will cource the appropriate e-mail list(s) from the list owner.

List owner Has collected e-mail addresses which are offered for sale.

Live web site Current site accessible to customers, as distinct from **test web site**.

Localisation Designing the content of the **web site** in such a way that it is appropriate to different audiences in different countries.

Log file A file stored on a **web server** that records every item **downloaded** by users.

Log file analysers Tools that are used to build a picture of the amount of usage of different parts of a **web site** based on the information contained in the **log file**.

Loyalty techniques Customers sign up to an incentive scheme where they receive points for repeat purchases, which can be converted into offers such as discounts, free products or cash. (Also known as online incentive schemes.)

Mailbots *See* **Autoresponders**.

Maintenance process The work involved in running a live **web site** such as updating pages and checking the performance of the site.

Marketing mix The series of seven key variables (Product, Price, Place, Promotion, People, Process and Physical evidence) that are varied by marketers as part of the customer offering.

Marketplace *See* **Business-to-business exchanges or marketplaces**.

Marketspace A virtual marketplace such as the Internet in which no direct contact occurs between buyers and sellers. (Also known as electronic marketspace.)

Markup language *See* **HTML, XML**.

Mass customisation The ability to create tailored marketing messages or products for individual customers or a group of similar customers (a bespoke service), yet retain the economies of scale and the capacity of mass marketing or production.

Mass marketing One-to-many communication between a company and potential customers with limited tailoring of the message.

Measurement *See* **Web site measurement**.

Media broker A company that places advertisements for companies wishing to advertise by contacting the **media owners**.

Media buyer The person within a company wishing to advertise who places the advertisement, usually via a **media broker**.

Media owners The owners of **web sites** (or other media such as newspapers) that accept advertisements.

Metadata Literally, data about data – a format describing the structure and content of data.

Meta search engines Meta search engines submit keywords typed by users to a range of **search engines** in order to increase the number of relevant pages since different search engines may have indexed different sites. An example is the metacrawler search engine or www.mamma.com.

Meta tags Text within an **HTML** file summarising the content of the site (content meta tag) and relevant keywords (keyword meta tag), which are matched against the keywords typed into **search engines**.

Metrics for Internet marketing Measures that indicate the effectiveness of **Internet marketing** activities in meeting customer, business and marketing objectives.

Micropayments (microtransactions) **Digital cash** systems that allow very small sums of money (fractions of 1p) to be transferred, but with lower security. Such small sums do not warrant a credit card payment, because processing is too costly.

Microsite Specialised content that is part of a **web site** that is not necessarily owned by the organisation. If owned by the company it may be as part of an **extranet**. (*See also* **Nested ad content**.)

Microsoft Internet Information Server (IIS) Microsoft IIS is a **web server** developed by Microsoft that runs on Windows NT.

Mixed-mode buying The process by which a customer changes between online and offline channels during the buying process.

Navigation The method of finding and moving between different information and pages on a **web site**. It is governed by menu arrangements, site structure and the layout of individual pages.

Nested ad content This refers to the situation when the person undertaking the **clickthrough** is not redirected to a corporate or brand site, but is instead taken to a related page on the same site as that on which the advertisement is placed. (Sometimes referred to as **microsite**.)

Non-repudiability *See* **Security methods**.

Offer An incentive in direct marketing or a product offering.

Offline promotion *See* **Promotion (online and offline)**.

Offline web metric Offline measures are those that are collated by marketing staff recording particular marketing outcomes such as an enquiry or a sale. They are usually collated manually, but could be collated automatically.

One-to-one marketing A unique dialogue that occurs directly between a company and individual customers (or less strictly with groups of customers with similar needs). The dialogue involves a company in listening to customer needs and responding with services to meet these needs.

Online brand *See* **Digital brand**.

Online incentive schemes *See* **Loyalty techniques**.

Online promotion *See* **Promotion (online and offline)**.

Online promotion contribution An assessment of the proportion of customers (new or retained) who are reached by online communications and are influenced as a result.

Online revenue contribution An assessment of the direct contribution of the Internet or other digital media to sales, usually expressed as a percentage of overall sales revenue.

Online service providers (OSPs) An OSP is sometimes used to distinguish large **Internet service providers (ISPs)** from other access providers. In the UK, AOL, Freeserve, VirginNet and LineOne can be considered OSPs since they have a large amount of specially developed content available to their subscribers. Note that this term is not used as frequently as ISP, and the distinction between ISPs and OSPs is a blurred one since all OSPs are also **ISPs** and the distinction only occurs according to the amount of premium content (only available to customers) offered as part of the service.

Online service quality gap The mismatch between what is expected and delivered by an online presence.

Online value proposition (OVP) A statement of the benefits of e-commerce services that ideally should not be available in competitor offerings or offline offerings.

Online web metrics Online measures are those that are collected automatically on the **web server**, often in a server **log file**.

Operational effectiveness Performing similar activities better than rivals. This includes efficiency of processes.

Opt-in e-mail The customer is only contacted when he or she has explicitly asked for information to be sent (usually when filling in an on-screen form).

Opt-out e-mail The customer is not contacted subsequently if he or she has explicitly stated that he or she does not want to be contacted in future. Opt-out or **unsubscribe** options are usually available within the e-mail itself.

Outbound e-mail E-mail sent from a company.

Outsourcing Contracting an outside company to undertake part of the **Internet marketing** activities.

Overt Typically an animated ad that moves around the page and is superimposed on the web site content.

Page impression One page impression occurs when a member of the audience views a web page. (*See also* **Ad impression** and **Reach**.)

Page request The process of a user selecting a **hyperlink** or typing in a **uniform resource locator (URL)** to retrieve information on a specific web page. Equivalent to **page impression**.

Page view *See* **Page impression**.

People variable The element of the marketing mix that involves the delivery of service to customers during interactions with those customers.

Perfect market An efficient market where there are an infinite number of suppliers and buyers and complete price transparency.

Performance drivers Critical success factors that determine whether business and marketing objectives are achieved.

Performance measurement system The process by which metrics are defined, collected, disseminated and actioned.

Performance of web site Performance or quality of service is dependent on its availability and speed of access.

Permission marketing Customers agree (opt in) to be involved in an organisation's marketing activities, usually as a result of an incentive.

Personalisation Web-based personalisation involves delivering customised content for the individual through web pages, e-mail or **push technology**.

Phone-me A **callback** facility available on the **web site** for a company to contact a customer by phone at a later time, as specified by the customer.

Physical evidence variable The element of the marketing mix that involves the tangible expression of a product and how it is purchased and used.

Pixel The small dots on a computer screen that are used to represent images and text. Short for 'picture element'. Used to indicate the size of **banner advertisements**.

Place The element of the marketing mix that involves distributing products to customers in line with demand and minimising cost of inventory, transport and storage.

Plug-in A program that must be **downloaded** to view particular content such as an animation.

Portal A **web site** that acts as a gateway to the information on the Internet by providing **search engines**, **directories** and other services such as personalised news or free e-mail.

Portfolio analysis Evaluation of value of current e-commerce services or applications.

Positioning Customers' perception of the product offer relative to competitors.

Prescriptive strategy The three core areas of strategic analysis, strategic development and strategy implementation are linked together sequentially.

Price transparency Customer knowledge about pricing increases due to increased availability of pricing information.

Price variable The element of the marketing mix that involves defining product prices and pricing models.

Pricing model Describes the form of payment such as outright purchase, auction, rental, volume purchases and credit terms.

Privacy A moral right of individuals to avoid intrusion into their personal affairs. (*See also* **Security methods**.)

Process variable The element of the marketing mix that involves the methods and procedures companies use to achieve all marketing functions.

Product variable The element of the marketing mix that involves researching customers' needs and developing appropriate products. (*See* **Core product** and **Extended product**.)

Profiling *See* **Customer profiling**.

Promotion (online and offline) Online promotion uses communication via the **Internet** itself to raise awareness about a site and drive traffic to it. This promotion may take the form of links from other sites, **banner advertisements** or targeted e-mail messages. Offline promotion uses traditional media such as television or newspaper advertising and word of mouth to promote a company's **web site**.

Promotion variable The element of the marketing mix that involves communication with customers and other stakeholders to inform them about the product and the organisation.

Prosumer 'Producer + consumer'. The customer is closely involved in specifying their requirements in a product.

Prototypes and prototyping A prototype is a preliminary version of part (or a framework of all) of a **web site** that can be reviewed by its target audience, or the marketing team. Prototyping is an iterative process where web site users suggest modifications before further prototypes are made and the final version of the site is developed.

Psychographic segmentation A breakdown of customers according to different characteristics.

Public key A unique identifier of a buyer or a seller that is available to other parties to enable secure e-commerce using **encryption** based on digital certificates.

Public-key encryption An asymmetric form of **encryption** in which the keys or **digital certificates** used by the sender and receiver of information are different. The two keys are related, so only the pair of keys can be used together to encrypt and decrypt information.

Public-key infrastructure (PKI) The organisations responsible for issuing and maintaining certificates for public-key security together form the PKI.

Pull media The consumer is proactive in selection of the message through actively seeking out a web site.

Push media Communications are broadcast from an advertiser to consumers of the message who are passive recipients.

Push technology The delivery of Web-based content to the user's desktop without the need for the user to visit a site to **download** information. E-mail can also be considered to be a push technology. A particular type of information is a push channel.

Qualified lead Contact and profile information for a customer with an indication of the level of their interest in product categories.

Reach The number of unique individuals who view an advertisement.

RealNames A service for matching company names and brands with **web addresses**.

Referrer The site that a visitor previously visited before following a link.

Referring sites A **log file** may indicate which site a user visited immediately before visiting yours. (*See also* **Clickthrough**, **Destination site** and **Exit page**.)

Registration (individuals) The process whereby an individual subscribes to a site or requests further information by filling in contact details and his or her needs using an electronic form.

Registration (of domain name) The process of reserving a unique **web address** that can be used to refer to the company **web site**.

Reintermediation The creation of new **intermediaries** between customers and suppliers providing services such as supplier search and product evaluation.

Relationship marketing Consistent application of up-to-date knowledge of individual customers to product and service design, which is communicated interactively in order to develop a continuous, mutually beneficial and long-term relationship.

Repeat visits If an organisation can encourage customers to return to the web site then the relationship can be maintained online.

Repurposing Developing for a new access platform, such as the Web, content which was previously used for a different platform.

Resource analysis Review of the technological, financial and human resources of an organisation and how they are utilised in business processes.

Results-based payment Advertisers pay according to the number of times the ad is clicked on.

Retail channel Retailers' use of the Internet as both a communication and a transactional channel concurrently in business-to-consumer markets.

Retail format This is the general nature of the retail mix in terms of range of products and services, pricing policy, promotional programmes, operating style or store design and visual merchandising; examples include mail-order retailers (non-store-based) and department-store retailers.

Retention *See* **Customer retention**.

Return on advertising spend (ROAS) This indicates amount of revenue generated from each referrer. ROAS = Total revenue generated from referrer / Amount spent on advertising with referrer.

Return on investment (ROI) This indicates the profitability of any investment, or in an advertising context, for each referring site.
ROI = Profit generated from investment / Cost of investment.
ROI = Profit generated from referrers / Amount spent on advertising with referrer.

Return path An interaction where the customer sends information to the iDTV provider using a phone line or cable.

Revenue models Describe methods of generating income for an organisation.

Reverse auctions Item purchased from lowest bidding supplier in bidding period.

Rich-media advertisements Advertisements that are not static, but provide animation, sound or interactivity. An example of this would be a **banner advertisement** for a loan in which a customer can type in the amount of loan required, and the cost of the loan is calculated immediately.

Robot A tool, also known as a **spider**, that is employed by **search engines** to index web pages of registered sites on a regular basis.

Run of site A situation where a company pays for **banner advertisements** to promote its services across a **web site**.

Sales generation offers These are offers that encourage product trial. A coupon redeemed against a purchase is a classic example.

Sales promotions The Internet offers tremendous potential for sales promotions of different types since it is more immediate than any other medium – it is always available for communication, and tactical variations in the details of the promotion can be made at short notice.

Saturation of the Internet Access to the **Internet** will reach saturation as home PC ownership reaches a limit, unless other access devices become popular.

Scenario-based analysis Models of the future environment are developed from different starting points.

Scenario of use A particular path or flow of events or activities performed by a visitor to a web site.

Scripts Scripts can run either on the user's browser (client-side scripts) (*see* **Web browser**) or on the **web server** (server-side scripts).

Search engines Specialised **web sites** that use automatic tools known as **spiders** or **robots** to index web pages of registered sites. Users can search the index by typing in keywords to specify their interest. Pages containing these keywords will be listed, and by clicking on a **hyperlink** the user will be taken to the site.

Search engine listing The list of sites and descriptions returned by a search engine after a user types in keywords.

Search engine ranking The position of a site on a particular search engine, e.g. 3rd.

Secure Electronic Transaction (SET) A standard for **public-key encryption** intended to enable secure **electronic commerce transactions** lead-developed by Mastercard and Visa.

Secure HTTP Encrypted **HTTP**.

Secure Sockets Layer (SSL) A commonly used **encryption** technique for scrambling data such as credit card numbers as they are passed across the Internet from a **web browser** to a **web server**.

Security methods When systems for **electronic commerce** are devised, or when existing solutions are selected, the following attributes must be present:

1 *Authentication* – are parties to the transaction who they claim to be? This is achieved through the use of digital certificates.
2 *Privacy and confidentiality* – are transaction data protected? The consumer may want to make an anonymous purchase. Are all non-essential traces of a transaction removed from the public network and all intermediary records eliminated?
3 *Integrity* – checks that the message sent is complete, i.e. that it is not corrupted.
4 *Non-repudiability* – ensures sender cannot deny sending message.
5 *Availability* – how can threats to the continuity and performance of the system be eliminated?

Seeding The viral campaign is started by sending an e-mail to a targeted group that are likely to propagate the virus.

Segmentation Identification of different groups within a target market in order to develop different offerings for each group.

Sell-side e-commerce E-commerce transactions between a supplier organisation and its customers.

Server log file *See* **Online web metrics**.

Service quality The level of service received on a **web site**. Dependent on reliability, responsiveness and availability of staff and the **web site** service.

Serving Used to describe the process of displaying an advertisement on a **web site** (**ad serving**) or delivering a web page to a user's **web browser**. (*See* **Web server**.)

Short Message Service (SMS) The formal name for text messaging.

Site *See* **Web site**.

Site announcements Usually used to describe the dissemination of information about a new or revised **web site**.

Site auditors Auditors accurately measure the usage for different sites as the number of ad impressions and clickthrough rates. Auditors include ABC (Audit Bureau of circulation) and BPA (Business Publication Auditor) International.

Site availability An indication of how easy it is to connect to a **web site** as a user. In theory this figure should be 100 per cent, but for technical reasons such as failures in the server hardware or upgrades to software, sometimes users cannot access the site and the figure falls below 90 per cent.

Site design template A standard page layout format which is applied to each page of a web site.

Site measurement *See* **Web site measurement**.

Site navigation scheme Tools provided to the user to move between different information on a web site.

Site re-launch Where a **web site** is replaced with a new version with a new 'look and feel'.

Site statistics Collected by **log file analysers**, these are used to monitor the effectiveness of a **web site**.

Site 'stickiness' An indication of how long a visitor stays on a site. **Log file analysers** can be used to assess average visit times.

Site visit One site visit records one customer visiting the site. Not equivalent to **User session**.

Site-visitor activity data Information on content and services accessed by e-commerce site visitors.

Sitemapping tools These tools diagram the layout of the **web site**, which is useful for site management, and can be used to assist users.

SMART metrics SMART metrics must be:
- Specific;
- Measurable;
- Actionable;
- Relevant;
- Timely.

Smartcards Physical cards containing a memory chip that can be inserted into a smartcard reader before items can be purchased.

Social exclusion Part of society is excluded from the facilities available to the remainder.

Soft lock-in Electronic linkages between supplier and customer increase switching costs.

Software agents *See* **Agents**.

Spam Unsolicited e-mail (usually bulk mailed and untargeted).

Spamming Bulk e-mailing of unsolicited mail.

Specific offline advertising Driving traffic to the web site or explaining the online proposition is a primary objective of the advert.

Spider A tool, also known as a **robot**, that is employed by **search engines** to index web pages of registered sites on a regular basis.

Splash page A preliminary page that precedes the normal **home page** of a **web site**. Site users can either wait to be redirected to the home page or can follow a link to do this. Splash pages are not now commonly used since they slow down the process whereby customers find the information they need.

Sponsorship Sponsorship involves a company paying money to advertise on a **web site**. The arrangement may involve more than advertising. Sponsorship is a similar arrangement to **co-branding**.

Stages in web site development The standard stages of creation of a **web site** are **initiation**, feasibility, **analysis**, **design**, **development** (**content** creation), **testing** and **maintenance**.

Static web page A page on the web server that is invariant.

STEP A framework for assessing the macro-environment, standing for Social, Technological, Economic and Political (including legal).

Storyboarding Using static drawings or screenshots of the different parts of a **web site** to review the design concept with customers or clients.

Strategic analysis Collection and review of information about an organisation's internal processes and resources and external marketplace factors in order to inform strategy definition.

Strategic positioning Performing different activities from rivals or performing similar activities in different ways.

Strategy formulation Generation, review and selection of strategies to achieve strategic objectives.

Strategy process model A framework for approaching strategy development.

Streaming media Sound and video that can be experienced within a web browser before the whole clip is downloaded.

Style guide A definition of site structure, page design, typography and copy defined within a company. (*See* **Graphic design**.)

Superstitials Pop-up adverts that require interaction to remove them.

Surfer An **undirected information seeker** who is often looking for an experience rather than information.

Symmetric encryption Both parties to a transaction use the same key to encode and decode messages.

Tagging Tracking of origin of customers and their spending patterns.

Target marketing strategy Evaluation and selection of appropriate segments and the development of appropriate offers.

Targeting (through banner advertisers) **Advertising networks** such as DoubleClick offer advertisers the ability to target advertisements dynamically on the World Wide Web through their 'DART' targeting technology. This gives advertisers a means of reaching specific audiences.

Telemarketing using the Internet Mainly used for inbound telemarketing, including sales lines, carelines for goods and services and response handling for direct response campaigns.

Telnet A program that allows remote access to data and text-based programs on other computer systems at different locations. For example, a retailer could check to see whether an item was in stock in a warehouse using a telnet application.

Template *See* **Site design template**.

Test web site A parallel version of the site to use before the site is made available to customers as a **live web site**.

Testing content Testing should be conducted for **plug-ins**; for interactive facilities and integration with company databases; for spelling and grammar; for adherence to corporate image standards; for implementation of **HTML** in different **web browsers**; and to ensure that links to external sites are valid.

Testing phase Testing involves different aspects of the **content** such as spelling, validity of links, formatting on different **web browsers** and dynamic features such as form filling or database queries.

Traffic-building campaign The use of **online** and **offline promotion** techniques such as **banner advertising**, **search engine** promotion and reciprocal linking to increase the audience of a site (both new and existing customers).

Transaction log file A web server file that records all page requests.

Transfer Control Protocol/Internet Protocol (TCP/IP) The passing of data packets around the Internet occurs via TCP/IP. For a PC to be able to receive web pages or for a server to host web pages it must be configured to support this protocol.

Trusted third parties (TTP) Companies with which an agreement has been reached to share information.

Undirected information seeker A person who does not know what information they are looking for – a **surfer**.

Uniform (universal) resource locator (URL) Text that indicates the **web address** of a site. A specific **domain name** is typed into a **web browser** window and the browser will then locate and load the **web site**. It is in the form of: http://www.domain-name.extension/filename.html.

Unsubscribe An option to **opt out** from an e-mail newsletter or discussion group.

Upload The transfer of files from a local computer to a server. Usually achieved using **FTP**. E-mail or web site pages can be uploaded to update a remote server.

Usenet newsgroup An electronic bulletin board used to discuss a particular topic such as a sport, hobby or business area. Traditionally accessed by special newsreader software, these can now be accessed via a **web browser** from www.deja.com.

User-centred design Design based on optimising the user experience according to all factors, including the user interface, which affect this.

User session Used to specify the frequency of visits to a site. Not equivalent to **site visit**.

Validation Validation services test for errors in **HTML** code which may cause a web page to be displayed incorrectly or for links to other pages that do not work.

Value chain A model that considers how supply chain activities can add value to products and services delivered to the customer.

Value network The links between an organisation and its strategic and non-strategic partners that form its external value chain.

Value proposition of site The benefits or value of a **web site** that are evident to its users.

Vertical portals These are generally business-to-business sites that will host **content** to help participants in an industry to get their work done by providing industry news, details of business techniques, and product and service reviews.

View *See* **Page impression**.

Viral marketing E-mail used to transmit a promotional message to another potential customer.

Viral referral An 'e-mail a friend or colleague' component to an e-mail campaign or part of web site design.

Virtual cash *See* **Digital cash**.

Virtual community An Internet-based forum for special-interest groups to communicate using a bulletin board to post messages.

Virtual mall A **web site** that brings together different electronic retailers at a single virtual (online) location. This contrasts with a fixed-location infrastructure – the traditional arrangement where retail organisations operate from retail stores situated in fixed locations such as real-world shopping malls. (Also known as 'electronic mall'.)

Virtual merchants Retailers such as Amazon that only operate online – they have no fixed-location infrastructure.

Virtual organisation An organisation that uses information and communications technology to allow it to operate without clearly defined physical boundaries between different functions. It provides customised services by outsourcing production and other functions to third parties.

Virtual private network Private network created using the public network infrastructure of the Internet.

Virtualisation The process whereby a company develops more of the characteristics of the virtual organisation.

Visit *See* **Site visit**.

Walled garden A limited range of e-commerce services on iDTV (compared to the Internet).

Web application protocol (WAP) A standard that enables mobile phones to access text from web sites.

Web addresses (universal resource locators – URLs) Web addresses refer to particular pages on a **web server**, which is hosted by a company or organisation. The technical name for web addresses is **uniform** or **universal resource locators (URLs)**.

Web analytics Reporting and analysis of data on web site visitor activity.

Web browsers Browsers such as Netscape Navigator and Microsoft Internet Explorer provide an easy method of accessing and viewing information stored as **HTML** web documents on different **web servers**.

Webmaster The webmaster is responsible for ensuring the quality of a **web site**. This means achieving suitable availability, speed, working links between pages and connections to company databases. In small companies the webmaster may be responsible for graphic design and content developerment.

Web servers Web servers are used to store the web pages accessed by **web browsers**. They may also contain databases of customer or product information, which can be queried and retrieved using a browser.

Web site **Content** accessible on the **World Wide Web** that is created by a particular organisation or individual. The location and identity of a web site is indicated by its **web address (URL)** or **domain name**. It may be stored on a single server in a single location, or a cluster of servers.

Web site measurement The process whereby metrics such as **page impressions** are collected and evaluated to assess the effectiveness of **Internet marketing** activities in meeting customers, business and marketing objectives.

Wide Area Information Service (WAIS) An Internet service that has been superseded by the World Wide Web.

Wireless Markup Language (WML) Standard for displaying mobile pages such as transferred by WAP.

World Wide Web A medium for publishing information on the Internet. It is accessed through **web browsers**, which display web pages and can now be used to run business applications. Company information is stored on **web servers**, which are usually referred to as **web sites**.

XML An advanced markup language giving better control than **HTML** over format for structured information on web pages.

Subject index

Most references are to **marketing**, **Internet** and **United Kingdom**, which are therefore generally omitted as entries or qualifiers.

Emboldened page numbers indicate **chapters** and terms that are **highlighted** in text. *Most* of these terms are also defined in the glossary on pages 451–66.

Name index